MANAGEMENT

FOURTH EDITION

MANAGEMENT

FOURTH EDITION

Stephen P. Robbins
San Diego State University

PRENTICE HALL
Englewood Cliffs, New Jersey 07632

Library of Congress Cataloging-in-Publication Data

Robbins, Stephen P.
    Management / Stephen P. Robbins. – 4th ed.
       p.   cm.
    Includes bibliographical references and index.
    ISBN 0-13-061797-0
    1. Management.   I. Title.
HD31.R5647   1994
658–dc20   93-19009
                                   CIP

Production Supervision: Lisa Kinne
Development Editor: David Cohen
Acquisition Editors: Valerie Ashton/Natalie Anderson
Assistant Editor: Lisamarie Brassini
Copy Editor: Joanne Palmer
Marketing Manager: Frank Lyman
Design Director: Patricia H. Wosczyk
Interior Design: Kenny Beck
Cover Design: Rosemarie Paccione
Prepress Buyer: Trudy Pisciotti
Manufacturing Buyer: Patrice Fraccio
Photo Research: Teri Stratford
Photo Editor: Lorinda Morris-Nantz
Production Assistant: Renee Pelletier
Editorial Assistants: Diane Peirano/Eileen Deguzman

© 1994, 1991, 1988, 1984 by Prentice-Hall, Inc.
A Simon & Schuster Company
Englewood Cliffs, New Jersey 07632

Printed in the United States of America

10 9 8 7 6 5 4 3 2 1

ISBN 0-13-061797-0

Prentice-Hall International (UK) Limited, *London*
Prentice-Hall of Australia Pty. Limited, *Sydney*
Prentice-Hall Canada Inc., *Toronto*
Prentice-Hall Hispanoamericana, S.A., *Mexico*
Prentice-Hall of India Private Limited, *New Delhi*
Prentice-Hall of Japan, Inc., *Tokyo*
Simon & Schuster Asia Pte., Ltd., *Singapore*
Editora Prentice-Hall do Brasil, Ltda., *Rio de Janeiro*

To
Fast Tracks,
Quick Starts,
Favorable Tail Winds,
And a Plentiful Supply of Ben-Gay

ABOUT THE AUTHOR

STEPHEN P. ROBBINS received his Ph.D. from the University of Arizona. He previously worked for the Shell Oil Company and Reynolds Metals Company. Since completing his graduate studies, Dr. Robbins has taught at the University of Nebraska at Omaha, Concordia University in Montreal, the University of Baltimore, Southern Illinois University at Edwardsville, and San Diego State University.

Dr. Robbins' research interests have focused on conflict, power, and politics in organizations, as well as the development of effective interpersonal skills. His articles on these and other topics have appeared in such journals as *Business Horizons,* the *California Management Review, Business and Economic Perspectives, International Management, Management Review, Canadian Personnel and Industrial Relations Journal,* and *The Journal of Management Education.* In recent years, Dr. Robbins has been spending most of his time writing textbooks. His books are currently used in more than 800 U.S. colleges and universities.

In Dr. Robbins' "other life," he participates actively in masters' track and field competition. In 1993, he broke or tied world indoor records at 55, 60, and 200 meters; and outdoor records at 100 and 200 meters. He is currently the age 50–54 reigning U.S. national sprint champion.

BRIEF CONTENTS

CONTENTS

PART TWO
DEFINING THE MANAGER'S TERRAIN

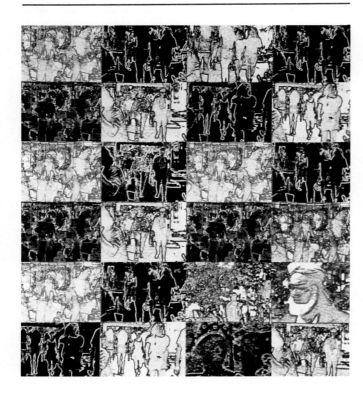

CHAPTER 3
Organizational Culture and Environment: The Constraints   67

CHAPTER 4
International Management: Responding to a Global Environment   93

CHAPTER 5
Social Responsibility and Managerial Ethics   117

CHAPTER 6
Decision Making; The Essence of the Manager's Job   149

PART THREE
PLANNING

CHAPTER 7
Foundations of Planning   185

PART FOUR
ORGANIZING

CHAPTER 10
Foundations of Organizing 279

CHAPTER 11
Organization and Job Design Options 307

PART FIVE
LEADING

CHAPTER 14
Foundations of Behavior   413

CHAPTER 15
Understanding Groups and Teamwork   439

CHAPTER 16
Motivating Employees   463

PART SIX
CONTROLLING

CHAPTER 21
Operations Management 625

PREFACE

A preface should provide answers to certain key questions. I have specifically identified five: (1) What assumptions have guided the development of this book? (2) What important features are continued from the previous edition? (3) What's new in this revision? (4) How does the book facilitate learning for the reader? (5) Who else, besides the person whose name is on the front cover, helped to create this book? Let me try now to answer each of these questions.

Assumptions

Every author who sits down to write a book has a set of assumptions—either explicit or implied—that guide what is included and what is excluded. I want to state mine upfront.

Management is an exciting field. The subject matter encompassed in an introductory management text is inherently exciting. We're talking about the real world. We're talking about why upstart Southwest Airlines is beating the pants off established carriers like American and United in dozens of markets; how Microsoft, a company that 15 years ago had annual sales of less than $10 million, can grow into an enterprise so valuable that it has made its co-founder and CEO the richest man in America; how to cut waste and control costs in hospitals; and techniques that can make your state motor vehicle department more efficient and responsive to clients.

A good management text should capture this excitement. Nowhere is it written that a textbook *has* to be dry and boring! If its subject matter is exciting, the text should reflect that fact. It should include lots of examples and photographs to make concepts come alive, capture the excitement of the field, and convey this excitement to the reader.

Management should not be studied solely from the perspective of "top management" or "billion-dollar corporations." The subject matter in management encompasses everyone from the lowest supervisor to the chief executive officer. The content should give as much attention to the challenges and opportunities in supervising fifteen clerical workers as those in directing a cadre of MBA-educated executive vice presidents. Similarly, not everyone wants to work for a *Fortune* 500 company. Readers who are interested in working in small businesses or not-for-profit organizations should find the descriptions of management concepts applicable to their needs.

Content should emphasize relevance. Before an author commits something to paper and includes it in his or her text, it should meet the "So what?" test. Why would someone need to know this fact or that? If the relevance isn't overtly clear, either the item should be omitted or its relevance should be directly explained.

Content should be timely. We live in dynamic times. Changes are taking place at an unprecedented pace. A textbook in a dynamic field like management must reflect this fact by including the latest concepts and practices.

Retained from the Previous Edition

The third edition contained a number of topics and features that adopters considered unique or particularly popular with students. Those have obviously been retained.

Organization of Part II. This section is unique among management textbooks. It defines the parameters of the manager's job. Chapter 3 demonstrates that there are constraints on managers from both inside and outside the organization. These are the organization's culture and external environment. Within these constraints, managers utilize their discretion through the decision making process. Chapter 6 demonstrates that decision making permeates all the major functions that managers perform. In between, Chapter 4 describes the global economy and how it is reshaping the manager's job, and Chapter 5 demonstrates the need for managers to consider social responsibility and ethical concerns when making decisions.

"Managing From a Global Perspective" boxes. In addition to the discussion of globalization in Chapter 4, there are boxes throughout the text that reinforce the need to rethink management issues in a global context.

"Ethical Dilemmas in Management" boxes. To increase student awareness of the broad range of ethical issues managers face, each chapter poses an ethical dilemma for students to address. A number of these dilemmas are new to this edition.

"Managers Who Made a Difference" boxes. These boxes present managers whose actions have had a significant impact on their organization's performance. Almost all of the managers described in these boxes are new to this edition.

Self-Assessment exercises. When I first introduced self-assessment exercises in the second edition (1988), they were truly novel for a management text. Now most books have them. While the idea is no longer unique, you will find that I've improved the focus and relevance of these exercises with each subsequent edition.

Relevant topics. This fourth edition continues to include relevant topics that many management texts ignore. For instance, students consistently praise the presentation of time management skills in Chapter 9. And the subject of interpersonal skills (Chapter 18) is clearly important to managerial effectiveness but is still overlooked by a number of management authors.

Writing style. This revision continues my commitment to present management concepts in a lively and conversational style. I carefully blend theories and examples. My goal is to present material in an interesting and relevant manner without oversimplifying the discussion. Of course, because writing style is a subjective interpretation, only you can accurately judge whether I've successfully achieved my goal.

New Content

The research base for this revision has been completely updated. New topics—such as work force diversity, electronic meetings, negotiation skills, and Kohlberg's stages of moral development—have been added to this edition. Current trends have been introduced into the history chapter so as to better integrate the past and future of management practice. And the material on individual and group behavior has been expanded from one chapter to two (Chapters 14 and 15) to meet the increased demand by faculty for more behavioral science material in the introductory management course. Additionally, there are several new features you'll find in this revision:

Total quality management. Discussion of TQM concepts and techniques is integrated throughout the text. For instance, in Chapter 8, TQM is presented as a strategic weapon. In Chapter 9, TQM's benchmarking techniques are described.

The changing face of management practice. Today's successful organizations are lean, flexible, and fast on their feet. They're empowering their employees, designing jobs around teams, and learning to embrace change. In boxes throughout the book, we'll describe the dynamic changes confronting today's managers and how they're responding.

For your immediate action. Each chapter in this book ends with a "For Your Immediate Action" memo. These exercises are a response to instructors' criticisms that many students have difficulty expressing themselves concisely in written form. FYIA provides an opportunity for instructors to assign short, problem-focused writing assignments that apply concepts from a chapter and for students to evaluate a problem and write up a concise analysis. These exercises are designed to complement the increasing popularity of writing-across-the-curriculum programs in colleges and universities.

Video cases. New to this edition are video cases at the end of each chapter. These are based on specific videos from the ABC News/Prentice Hall Video Library. This includes programming from ABC's World News Tonite, Nightline, Business World, On Business, 20/20, and This Week With David Brinkley. Videos to accompany each of the 21 cases are available to show in class either to start or extend class discussion of the cases.

In-Text Learning Aids

A good textbook should teach as well as present ideas. Toward that end, I've tried to make this book an effective learning tool. Let me specifically point out some pedagogical features that are designed to help readers better assimilate the material presented.

Chapter objectives. Before you start a trip, it's valuable to know where you're headed. That way, you can minimize detours. The same holds true in reading a text. To make your learning more efficient, each chapter of this book opens with a list of learning objectives that describe what you should be able to do after reading the chapter. These objectives are designed to focus your attention on the major issues within each chapter.

Chapter summaries. Just as objectives clarify where one is going, chapter summaries remind you where you've been. Each chapter of this book concludes with a concise summary organized around the opening learning objectives.

Key terms. Every chapter includes a number of key terms that you'll need to know. These terms are highlighted in bold print when they first appear and are defined at that time in the adjoining margin. These same terms are also grouped together at the end of the book in the Glossary.

Review questions. Every chapter in this book ends with a set of eight to ten review questions. If you have read and understood the contents of a chapter, you should be able to answer these questions. They are drawn directly from the material in the chapter.

Discussion questions. In addition to the review questions, each chapter also has four or five discussion questions that go beyond the content of the chapter. They require you to integrate, synthesize, or apply management concepts. The discussion questions allow you to demonstrate that you not only know the facts in the chapter but also can use those facts to deal with more complex issues.

ACKNOWLEDGMENTS

Every author relies on the comments of reviewers, and mine were particularly helpful. I want to thank the following people for their comments and suggestions:

W. L. Loh—Mohawk Valley Community College, Lavelle Mills—Tarleton State University, Elliot M. Ser—Barry University, Anne C. Cowden—California State University, Sacramento, Russell Kent—Georgia Southern University, Roy Cook—Fort Lewis College, Judson C. Faurer—Metro State College, Phyllis G. Holland—Valdosta State College, Diane L. Ferry—University of Delaware, Aline Arnold—Eastern Illinois University, Janice Feldbauer—Austin Community College, Donald Conlon—University of Delaware, Gary L. Whaley—Norfolk State University, James Spee—The Claremont Graduate School, Joseph F. Michlitsch—Southern Illinois University—Edwardsville, John L. Kmetz—University of Delaware, Suhail Abboushi—Duquesne University, Philip M. VanAuken—Baylor University, Augustus B. Colangelo—Penn State, Dale M. Feinauer—University of Wisconsin, Oshkosh.

In addition, I want to thank my colleague at San Diego State, Mark Butler, for his work on the Annotated Instructor's Edition of the text. His margin notes in the AIE provide instructors with a wealth of examples and teaching ideas to supplement lectures.

Of course a book is not a book without a publisher. Mine is Prentice Hall. With apologies ahead of time to anyone whom I may have overlooked, I want to thank the people at P-H who helped me create this revision and its supplement package (in alphabetical order): Natalie Anderson, Valerie Ashton, Kenny Beck, Lisamarie Brassini, David Cohen, Lori Cowen, Eileen Deguzman, Will Ethridge, Patrice Fraccio, Lisa Kinne, Frank Lyman, Lori Morris-Nantz, Rosemarie Paccione, Joanne Palmer, Diane Peirano, Trudy Pisciotti, Belen Poltorak, Alison Reeves, Sandra Steiner, Teri Stratford, and Pat Wosczyk.

Stephen P. Robbins

CHAPTER 1

Managers and Management

LEARNING OBJECTIVES

After Reading This Chapter, You Should Be Able To:

1. Differentiate managers from operatives.
2. Define management.
3. Distinguish between effectiveness and efficiency.
4. Identify the roles performed by managers.
5. Differentiate the activities of successful managers from effective ones.
6. Explain whether the manager's job is generic.
7. Explain the value of studying management.

Sister Irene Kraus presides at a meeting of the Daughters of Charity management council at their headquarters in St. Louis, Missouri.

Managers come in all sizes, shapes, and colors, and in both genders. They also perform their work in a wide variety of organiza-

tions. Take Sister Irene Kraus, for example.[1] As a sixty-six-year-old nun, running the largest chain of private, not-for-profit hospitals in the United States, she's not the stereotypical image that you are likely to envision when you hear about high-powered managers. But Sister Irene *is* a high-powered manager. She has a Masters degree in business administration, and she's chief executive of the Daughters of Charity National Health System, overseeing thirty-six acute-care hospitals and nineteen other health-care facilities. Her organization's revenues exceed $3 billion a year. More impressively, with most hospitals—profit and not-for-profit alike—losing money, the Daughters of Charity are profitable. Occupancy rates at their hospitals are significantly above the industry average, and in fiscal 1990, the Daughters realized a surplus of about $190 million.

As Sister Irene demonstrates, successful managers don't fit a mold. Managers can be found from under age eighteen to over eighty. They are nowadays as frequently women as they are men.[2] And they not only run large corporations, but small businesses, government agencies, hospitals, museums, schools, and such nontraditional organizations as cooperatives as well. Some hold positions at the top of their organizations, while others are near the bottom. These people also can be found doing their managerial work in every country on the globe.

This book is about the work activities that Sister Irene and the tens of millions of other managers like her do. In this chapter, we want to introduce you to managers and management by answering, or at least beginning to answer, these questions: *Who* are managers? *What* is management and *what* do managers do? And *why* should you spend your time studying management?

Who Are Managers?

organization
A systematic arrangement of people to accomplish some specific purpose.

Managers work in a place we call an organization. Therefore, before we can identify who managers are, it is important to clarify what we mean by the term *organization*.

An **organization** is a systematic arrangement of people to accomplish some specific purpose. Your college or university is an organization. So are fraternities, government agencies, churches, the Xerox Corporation, your neighborhood gas station, the American Medical Association, the New York Yankees baseball team, and the Salvation Army. These are all organizations because they all have three common characteristics.

First, each has a distinct purpose. This purpose is typically expressed in terms of a goal or set of goals. Second, each is composed of people. Third, all organizations develop a systematic structure that defines and limits the behavior of its members. This would include, for example, creating rules and regulations, identifying some members as "bosses" and giving them authority over other members, or writing up job descriptions so that members know what they are supposed to do. The term *organization* therefore refers to an entity that has a distinct purpose, includes people or members, and has a systematic structure.

operatives
People who work directly on a job or task and have no responsibility for overseeing the work of others.

managers
Individuals in an organization who direct the activities of others.

Managers work in organizations, but not everyone in an organization is a manager. For simplicity's sake, we can divide organizational members into two categories: operatives or managers. **Operatives** are people who work directly on a job or task and have *no* responsibility for overseeing the work of others. The people who attach fenders in an automobile assembly line, cook your hamburger at McDonald's, or process your license renewal application at the state motor vehicles office are all operatives. In contrast, **managers** direct the activities of other people. They are shown in the colored areas in Figure 1–1. Managers may also have some operative responsibilities; for example, an insurance claims' supervisor may also have basic responsibilities to process insurance claims in addition to overseeing the activities of the other claims clerks in the department. However, our definition presumes that a

Good management skills don't apply only to the running of large manufacturing corporations. Most management opportunities in the 1990s will be in small, mostly service businesses. Poor management is the chief cause of the current fiscal crisis in the hospital industry. The Salvation Army uses state-of-the-art management techniques to stretch its $1 billion annual budget across 20 million people in more than 10,000 facilities. New management took the Oakland Athletics professional baseball club and turned it into a winner. Bought for less than $13 million in 1980, the A's are now worth about $100 million.

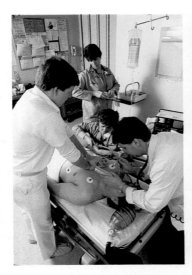

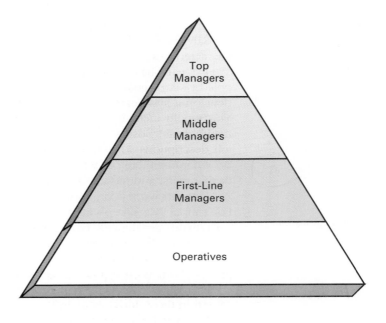

FIGURE 1-1
Organizational Levels

first-line managers
Supervisors; the lowest level of management.

manager has subordinates. Also, as shown in Figure 1–1, we typically classify managers as either first-line, middle, or top.

Identifying exactly who the managers are in an organization is not a difficult task, although you should be aware that managers come packaged in a variety of titles. **First-line managers** are usually called supervisors. In a manufacturing plant, the first-line (or lowest level) manager may be called a foreman. On an athletic team, this job carries the title of coach. Middle managers may have titles such as department or agency head, project leader, unit chief, district manager, dean, bishop, or division manager. At or near the top of an organization, managers typically have titles such as vice president, president, chancellor, managing director, chief operating officer, chief executive officer, or chairman of the board. In a manufacturing company, a twenty-five-year managerial career might include the following sequence of job titles: production foreman, shift foreman, scheduling manager, assistant plant superintendent, plant superintendent, plant manager, district operations manager, eastern regional manufacturing manager, and vice president of manufacturing. In a large metropolitan school district, a twenty-five-year journey up the managerial ladder might include titles such as department head, principal, assistant superintendent for administrative affairs, and district superintendent.

What Is Management and What Do Managers Do?

Just as organizations have common characteristics, so do managers. In spite of the fact that their titles vary widely, there are common characteristics to their jobs—regardless of whether the manager is a $25,000-a-year supervisor in the mailroom at Hershey Foods who oversees a staff of five or the $1.2 million-a-year chairman of the board of AT&T responsible for coordinating an organization with 300,000 employees and an annual sales total of $63 billion. In this section, we define management, present the classical functions of management, review recent research on managerial roles, and consider the universal applicability of managerial concepts.

Defining Management

management
The process of getting activities completed efficiently with and through other people.

efficiency
The relationship between inputs and outputs, seeks to minimize resource costs.

effectiveness
Goal attainment.

The term **management** refers to the process of getting activities completed efficiently with and through other people.

The *process* represents the functions or primary activities engaged in by managers. These functions are typically labeled planning, organizing, leading, and controlling. We elaborate on these functions in the next section.

Efficiency is a vital part of management. It refers to the relationship between inputs and outputs. If you get more output for a given input, you have increased efficiency. Similarly, if you can get the same output from less input, you again increase efficiency. Since managers deal with input resources that are scarce—money, people, equipment—they are concerned with the efficient use of these resources. Management, therefore, is concerned with minimizing resource costs.

It is not enough simply to be efficient. Management is also concerned with getting activities completed; that is, it seeks **effectiveness.** When managers achieve their organizations' goals, we say they are effective. So efficiency is concerned with means and effectiveness with ends. (See Figure 1–2.)

Efficiency and effectiveness are interrelated. For instance, it is easier to be effective if one ignores efficiency. Seiko could produce more accurate and attractive timepieces if it disregarded labor and material input costs. Some federal agencies have been regularly attacked on the grounds that they are reasonably effective but extremely inefficient; that is, they get their jobs done but at a very high cost.

FIGURE 1–2
Management Seeks Efficiency and Effectiveness

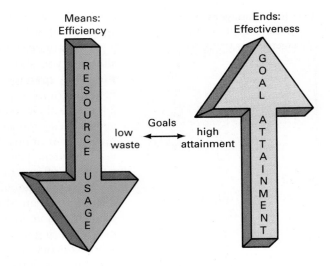

General Motors is less efficient than Ford. It takes GM about 50 percent more time than Ford—27 labor hours versus 18—to assemble a mid-size car, at a labor cost of $30 an hour. Including preassembly and parts, experts estimate it costs GM approximately $1000 more than it costs Ford to build a similar car.

Management is therefore concerned not only with getting activities completed (effectiveness), but also with doing so as efficiently as possible.

Can organizations be efficient and yet not be effective? Yes, by doing the wrong things well! A number of colleges have become highly efficient in processing students. Through the use of computer-assisted learning, large classes, and heavy reliance on part-time faculty, the administrators have significantly cut the cost of educating each student. Yet some of these colleges have been criticized by students, alumni, and accrediting agencies for failing to educate their students properly. Of course, high efficiency is associated more typically with high effectiveness. And poor management is most often due to both inefficiency and ineffectiveness or to effectiveness achieved through inefficiency.

Management Functions

In the early part of this century, a French industrialist by the name of Henri Fayol wrote that all managers perform five management functions: They plan, organize, command, coordinate, and control.[3] In the mid-1950s, two professors at UCLA used the functions of planning, organizing, staffing, directing, and controlling as the framework for a textbook on management that for twenty years was unquestionably the most widely sold text on the subject.[4] The most popular textbooks (and this one is no exception) still continue to be organized around **management functions,** though these have generally been condensed down to the basic four: planning, organizing, leading, and controlling. (See Figure 1–3.) Let's briefly define what each of these functions encompasses.

If you don't have any particular destination in mind, any road will get you there. Since organizations exist to achieve some purpose, someone has to define that purpose and the means for its achievement. Management is that someone. The **planning** function encompasses defining an organization's goals, establishing an overall strategy for achieving these goals, and developing a comprehensive hierarchy of plans to integrate and coordinate activities.

Managers are also responsible for designing an organization's structure. We call this function **organizing.** It includes the determination of what tasks are to be done, who is to do them, how the tasks are to be grouped, who reports to whom, and where decisions are to be made.

Every organization contains people, and it is management's job to direct and coordinate these people. This is the **leading** function. When managers motivate

management functions
Planning, organizing, leading, and controlling.

planning
Includes defining goals, establishing strategy, and developing plans to coordinate activities.

organizing
Determining what tasks are to be done, who is to do them, how the tasks are to be grouped, who reports to whom, and where decisions are to be made.

leading
Includes motivating subordinates, directing others, selecting the most effective communication channels, and resolving conflicts.

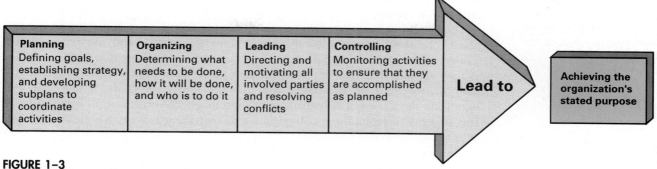

Planning	Organizing	Leading	Controlling
Defining goals, establishing strategy, and developing subplans to coordinate activities	Determining what needs to be done, how it will be done, and who is to do it	Directing and motivating all involved parties and resolving conflicts	Monitoring activities to ensure that they are accomplished as planned

Lead to

Achieving the organization's stated purpose

FIGURE 1–3
Management Functions

THE
CHANGING
FACE OF
MANAGEMENT
PRACTICE

Defense Contractors Finally Tackle Mismanagement and Waste

It's no more "business as usual" among the world's defense contractors.[6] Shrinking worldwide defense budgets, brought about by the fall of communism and changing national priorities, are forcing such companies as Lockheed, LTV, Grumman, General Dynamics, Northrop, Martin Marietta, and McDonnell Douglas to do something they should have done decades ago—improve their management.

The United States plans to reduce its armed forces by 25 percent between 1991 and 1995. Defense suppliers in countries such as Britain, France, and Brazil have expanded their international military sales efforts. And countries that have been longtime customers of U.S. arms manufacturers, including Pakistan, Egypt, and Taiwan, have begun building weapons of their own. As a result, there are now too many defense suppliers chasing too few programs.

Shrinking markets, competition, and efficiency have traditionally been alien concepts to defense contractors. Not anymore! To survive, management has been cutting waste and improving operations. It has become increasingly clear that only the most efficient and highest-quality defense contractors will make it through this shake-out. So these companies have begun laying off thousands of employees, closing underutilized plants, refusing to bid on unprofitable contracts, seeking new market niches, and pushing for increased productivity. For instance, McDonnell Douglas plans to layoff up to 17,000 workers. Lockheed is cutting 5,500 jobs, selling $200 million worth of excess plant and office space, and moving into civilian businesses such as building and running airports all over the world. LTV has begun painstakingly analyzing hundreds of the processes it uses in manufacturing rockets for the U.S. Army in order to find ways to make them cheaper, faster, and better.

Formerly, when there was an abundance of business and minimal competition, and excess costs were passed on to customers in higher prices with no questions asked, defense contractors had little motivation to practice good management. Those days are now history.

controlling

Monitoring activities to ensure that they are being accomplished as planned and correcting any significant deviations.

subordinates, direct the activities of others, select the most effective communication channel, or resolve conflicts among members, they are engaging in leading.

The final function managers perform is **controlling.** After the goals are set, the plans formulated, the structural arrangements delineated, and the people hired, trained, and motivated, something may still go amiss. To ensure that things are going as they should, management must monitor the organization's performance. Actual performance must be compared with the previously set goals. If there are any significant deviations, it is management's job to get the organization back on track. This process of monitoring, comparing, and correcting is what we mean when we refer to the controlling function.

The continued popularity of the functional approach is a tribute to its clarity and simplicity. But is it an accurate description of what managers actually do?[5] Following the functional approach, it is easy to answer the question, What do managers do? They plan, organize, lead, and control. But is this really true of all managers? Fayol's original functions were not derived from a careful survey of thousands of managers in hundreds of organizations. Rather, they merely represented observations based on his experience in the French mining industry.

Mintzberg found that managers engage in a large number of varied activities and face constant interruptions such as telephone calls.

Management Roles

In the late 1960s, Henry Mintzberg undertook a careful study of five chief executives at work.[7] What he discovered challenged several long-held notions about the manager's job. For instance, in contrast to the predominant views at the time that managers were reflective thinkers who carefully and systematically processed information before making decisions, Mintzberg found that his managers engaged in a large number of varied, unpatterned, and short-duration activities. There was little time for reflective thinking because the managers encountered constant interruptions. Half of these managers' activities lasted less than nine minutes. But in addition to these insights, Mintzberg provided a categorization scheme for defining what managers do based on actual managers on the job.

management roles

Specific categories of managerial behavior.

Mintzberg concluded that managers perform ten different but highly interrelated roles. The term **management roles** refers to specific categories of managerial behavior. As shown in Table 1–1, these ten roles can be grouped as those primarily concerned with interpersonal relationships, the transfer of information, and decision making.

interpersonal roles

Roles that include figurehead, leader, and liaison activities.

Interpersonal Roles All managers are required to perform duties that are ceremonial and symbolic in nature. When the president of a college hands out diplomas at commencement or a factory supervisor gives a group of high school students a tour of the plant, he or she is acting in a *figurehead* role. All managers have a role as a *leader*. This role includes hiring, training, motivating, and disciplining employees. The third role within the interpersonal grouping is the *liaison* role. Mintzberg described this activity as contacting external sources who provide the manager with information. These sources are individuals or groups outside the manager's unit, and may be inside or outside the organization. The sales manager who obtains information from the personnel manager in his or her same company has an internal liaison relationship. When that sales manager has contacts with other sales executives through a marketing trade association, he or she has an outside liaison relationship.

informational roles

Roles that include monitoring, disseminating, and spokesperson activities.

Informational Roles All managers will, to some degree, receive and collect information from organizations and institutions outside their own. Typically, this is done through reading magazines and talking with others to learn of changes in the public's tastes, what competitors may be planning, and the like. Mintzberg called this the *monitor* role. Managers also act as a conduit to transmit information to organiza-

TABLE 1-1
Mintzberg's Managerial Roles

Role	Description	Identifiable Activities
Interpersonal		
Figurehead	Symbolic head; obliged to perform a number of routine duties of a legal or social nature	Greeting visitors; signing legal documents
Leader	Responsible for the motivation and activation of subordinates; responsible for staffing, training, and associated duties	Performing virtually all activities that involve subordinates
Liaison	Maintains self-developed network of outside contacts and informers who provide favors and information	Acknowledging mail; doing external board work; performing other activities that involve outsiders
Informational		
Monitor	Seeks and receives wide variety of special information (much of it current) to develop thorough-understanding of organization and environment; emerges as nerve center of internal and external information about the organization	Reading periodicals and reports; maintaining personal contacts
Disseminator	Transmits information received from outsiders or from other subordinates to members of the organization—some information is factual, some involves interpretation and integration of diverse value positions of organizational influencers	Holding informational meetings; making phone calls to relay information
Spokesperson	Transmits information to outsiders on organization's plans, policies, actions, results, etc.; serves as expert on organization's industry	Holding board meetings; giving information to the media
Decisional		
Entrepreneur	Searches organization and its environment for opportunities and initiates "improvement projects" to bring about change; supervises design of certain projects as well	Organizing strategy and review sessions to develop new programs
Disturbance handler	Responsible for corrective action when organization faces important, unexpected disturbances	Organizing strategy and review sessions that involve disturbances and crises
Resource allocator	Responsible for the allocation of organizational resources of all kinds—in effect, the making or approval of all significant organizational decisions	Scheduling; requesting authorization; performing any activity that involves budgeting and the programming of subordinates' work
Negotiator	Responsible for representing the organization at major negotiations	Participating in union contract negotiations

Source: Henry Mintzberg, *The Nature of Managerial Work* (New York: Harper & Row, 1973), pp. 93–94. Copyright © 1973 by Henry Mintzberg. Reprinted by permission of Harper & Row, Publishers, Inc.

tional members. This is the *disseminator* role. When they represent the organization to outsiders, managers also perform a *spokesperson* role.

decisional roles
Roles that include those of entrepreneur, disturbance handler, resource allocator, and negotiator.

Decisional Roles   Finally, Mintzberg identified four roles that revolve around the making of choices. As *entrepreneurs,* managers initiate and oversee new projects that will improve their organization's performance. As *disturbance handlers,* managers take corrective action in response to previously unforeseen problems. As *resource allocators,* managers are responsible for allocating human, physical, and monetary resources. Last, managers perform as *negotiators* when they discuss and bargain with other groups to gain advantages for their own units.

An Evaluation   A number of follow-up studies have tested the validity of Mintzberg's role categories across different types of organizations and at different levels within given organizations.[8] The evidence generally supports the idea that managers—regardless of the type of organization or level in the organization—perform similar roles. However, the emphasis that managers give to the various roles seems to change with hierarchical level.[9] Specifically, the roles of disseminator, figurehead, negotiator, liaison, and spokesperson are more important at the higher levels than at the lower ones. Conversely, the leader role is more important for lower-level managers than it is for either middle- or top-level managers.

Have these ten roles, which are derived from actual observations of managerial work, invalidated the more traditional functions of planning, organizing, leading, and controlling? No!

First, the functional approach still represents the most useful way of conceptualizing the manager's job. "The classical functions provide clear and discrete methods of classifying the thousands of activities that managers carry out and the techniques they use in terms of the functions they perform for the achievement of organizational goals."[10] Second, although Mintzberg may offer a more detailed and elaborate classification scheme of what managers do, these roles are substantially reconcilable with the four functions.[11] Many of Mintzberg's roles align smoothly with one or more of the functions. Resource allocation is part of planning, as is the entrepreneurial role. All three of the interpersonal roles are part of the leading function. Most of the other roles fit into one or more of the four functions, but not all of them do. The difference is substantially explained by Mintzberg's intermixing management activities and pure managerial work.[12]

All managers do *some* work that is not purely managerial. The fact that Mintzberg's executives spent time in public relations or raising money attests to the precision of Mintzberg's observational methods, but shows that not everything a manager does is necessarily an essential part of the manager's job. This may have resulted in some activities being included in Mintzberg's schema that should not have been.

Do the comments above mean that Mintzberg's role categories are invalid? Not at all! Mintzberg has clearly offered new insights into what managers do. The attention his work has received is evidence of the importance attributed to defining management roles. But, as we will point out in the next chapter, management is a young discipline that is still evolving. Future research comparing and integrating Mintzberg's roles with the four functions will continue to expand our understanding of the manager's job.

Are Effective Managers Also Successful Managers?

Fred Luthans and his associates looked at the issue of what managers do from a somewhat different perspective.[13] They asked the question: Do managers who move up most quickly in an organization do the same activities and with the same emphasis as those managers who do the best job? You would tend to think that those managers

Is It Wrong to Tell a Lie?

An instructor might not be able to change moral standards in a college classroom, but he or she can teach students how to analyze questions so that they can bring to bear whatever moral standards they have when they make decisions.

If you haven't already done so, there is no better time than now to develop a rule or set of rules against which you can measure the "rightness" or "wrongness" of your decisions and actions. It may be nothing more provocative than "Do unto others as you would have them do unto you." Or it might also be a question or set of questions that you consistently ask: How would I feel about explaining what I did to my parents or children? How would I feel if the action I took was described, in detail, on the front page of my local newspaper? Have I avoided even the appearance of a conflict of interest in my decision? Would my action infringe on the liberty or constitutional rights of others?

Let's begin our look at ethical dilemmas in management by asking: Is it wrong to tell a lie?

Mintzberg found that managers play a number of roles, one of which is to act as a spokesperson. In this specific role, a manager transmits information to people outside the organization. Occasionally, the facts that the manager must transmit and explain aren't particularly flattering to the organization. This presents the dilemma of whether or not it is unethical to tell a lie.

For example, a senior manager is reviewing her company's financial performance for the previous year at the annual stockholders' meeting. The news is not good. Sales dropped 30 percent, and profits are down 50 percent. A stockholder asks the manager, "What caused this drastic decline and has it been corrected?" The manager knows that the primary cause of the decline was a series of poor top-management decisions made over the past several years, but she also knows that's not what her management colleagues want her to say. Further, she personally believes that the decline is far from over, but she recognizes that's not what the stockholders want to hear.

Should this manager lie? Is lying always wrong, or is it acceptable under certain circumstances? What, if any, would those circumstances be? What do *you* think?

who were the most effective in their jobs would also be the ones who were promoted the fastest. But that's not what appears to happen.

Luthans and his associates studied more than 450 managers. What they found was that these managers all engaged in four managerial activities.

1. *Traditional management:* Decision making, planning, and controlling
2. *Communication:* Exchanging routine information and processing paperwork
3. *Human resource management:* Motivating, disciplining, managing conflict, staffing, and training
4. *Networking:* Socializing, politicking, and interacting with outsiders

The "average" manager studied spent 32 percent of his or her time in traditional management activities, 29 percent communicating, 20 percent in human resource management activities, and 19 percent networking. However, the amount of time and effort that different managers spent on these four activities varied a great deal. Specifically, as shown in Figure 1–4, managers who were *successful* (defined in terms

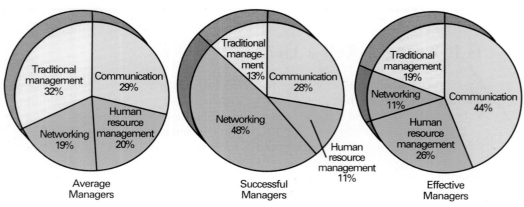

FIGURE 1–4

Distribution of Time per Activity by Average, Successful, and Effective Managers

Based on Fred Luthans, Richard M. Hodgetts, and Stuart A. Rosenkrantz, *Real Managers* (Cambridge, Mass.: Ballinger Publishing, 1988).

These middle-level managers at Mobil Oil spend a majority of their time in planning and organizing.

First-level managers at Mobil Oil spend the majority of their time in the leading function.

of the speed of promotion within their organization) had a very different emphasis than managers who were *effective* (defined in terms of the quantity and quality of their performances and the satisfaction and commitment of their subordinates). Networking makes the biggest relative contribution to manager success, while human resource management activities made the least relative contribution. Among effective managers, communication made the largest relative contribution and networking the least.

This study adds important insights to our knowledge of what managers do. On average, managers spend approximately 20 to 30 percent of their time on each of the four activities of traditional management, communication, human resource management, and networking. However, successful managers don't give the same emphasis to activities as do effective managers. In fact, they do almost the opposite. This challenges the historical assumption that promotions are based on performance, vividly illustrating the importance that social and political skills play in getting ahead in organizations.

Is the Manager's Job Universal?

We have previously mentioned the universal application of management. To this point, we have discussed management as if it were generic; that is, a manager is a manager regardless of where he or she manages. If management is truly a generic discipline, then what a manager does should be essentially the same regardless of whether he or she is a top-level executive or low-level supervisor; in a business firm or a government agency; in a large corporation or small business; or located in Paris, France, or Paris, Texas. Let's take a closer look at the generic issue.

Organizational Level   We have already acknowledged that the importance of managerial roles varies depending on the manager's level in the organization. But the fact that a supervisor in a research laboratory at Dow Chemical doesn't do exactly the same things that the president of Dow Chemical does should not be interpreted to mean that their jobs are inherently different. The differences are of degree and emphasis, but not of function.

In functional terms, as managers move up the organization, they do more planning and less direct supervising. This is visually depicted in Figure 1–5. All managers,

FIGURE 1–5 Distribution of Time per Function by Organizational Level

Source: Adapted from T. A. Mahoney, T. H. Jerdee, and S. J. Carroll, "The Job(s) of Management," *Industrial Relations,* vol. 4, no. 2 (1965), p. 103.

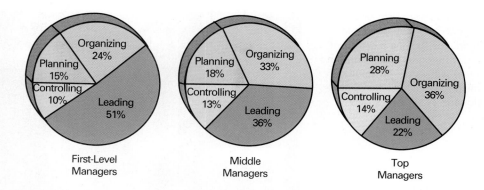

First-Level Managers

Middle Managers

Top Managers

regardless of level, make decisions. They perform planning, organizing, leading, and controlling functions. But the amount of time they give to each function is not necessarily constant. Additionally, the content of the managerial functions changes with the manager's level. For example, as we'll demonstrate in Chapter 11, top managers are concerned with designing the overall organization, while lower-level managers focus on designing the jobs of individuals and work groups.

Organizational Type   Does a manager who works for the Internal Revenue Service or a public library do the same things that a manager in a business firm does? Put another way, is the manager's job the same in both profit and not-for-profit organizations? The answer is: For the most part, yes.[14]

First, let's dispense with a few myths that surround the manager's job in public organizations.

Myth #1: Decisions in public organizations emphasize political priorities, while decisions in business organizations are rational and apolitical. *Truth:* Decisions in all organizations are influenced by political considerations. We'll discuss this fact in Chapter 6.

Myth #2: Public decision makers, in contrast to their business counterparts, are constrained by administrative procedures that limit managerial authority and autonomy. *Truth:* As we'll show in Chapter 3, almost all managers find that significant constraints have been placed on their managerial discretion.

Myth #3: It's hard to get high performance out of government employees because, compared to their business counterparts, they're lazy, more security oriented, and less motivated. *Truth:* The evidence indicates that there is no significant difference in the motivational needs between public and business employees.[15]

Regardless of the type of organization a manager works in, there are commonalities to his or her job. All make decisions, set objectives, create workable organization structures, hire and motivate employees, secure legitimacy for their organization's existence, and develop internal political support in order to implement programs.

Of course, there are some noteworthy differences. The most important is measuring performance. Profit, or "the bottom line," acts as an unambiguous measure of the effectiveness of a business organization. There is no such universal measure in not-for-profit organizations. Measuring the performance of schools, museums, government agencies, or charitable organizations, therefore, is made considerably more difficult. Managers in these organizations generally don't face the market test for performance.

Our conclusion is that, while there are distinctions between the management of profit and not-for-profit organizations, the two are far more alike than they are different. Both are similarly concerned with studying the role of decision makers as they plan, organize, lead, and control.

Giant firms such as IBM and General Motors may dominate the headlines, but the majority of business managers work—and in the future will work—in small organizations such as this vegetable stand in New York's Little Italy.

small business

An independently owned and operated profit-seeking enterprise having fewer than five hundred employees.

Organizational Size   Is the manager's job any different in a small organization than in a large one? This question is best answered by looking at the job of managers in small business firms and comparing them to our previous discussion of managerial roles. First, however, let's define small business and the part it plays in our society.

There is no commonly agreed-upon definition of a small business because of different criteria used to define "small"—for example, number of employees, annual sales, or total assets. For our purposes, we'll call a **small business** any independently owned and operated, profit-seeking enterprise that has fewer than five hundred employees.

Small businesses may be little in size, but they have a very large impact on our society. Statistics tell us that small businesses comprise about 97 percent of all nonfarm businesses in the United States; they employ over 60 percent of the private work force; they dominate such industries as retailing and construction; and they will generate half of all new jobs during the next decade. Moreover, small businesses are where the job growth has been in recent years. Between 1980 and 1990, *Fortune* 500 companies *cut* 3.4 million jobs. But companies with fewer than 500 employees *created* more than 13 million jobs during that same period.[16]

Now to the question at hand: Is the job of managing a small business different from that of managing a large one? A study comparing the two found that the importance of roles differed significantly.[17] As illustrated in Figure 1–6, the small-business manager's most important role is that of spokesperson. The small-business manager spends a large amount of time doing such outwardly directed things as meeting with customers, arranging financing with bankers, searching for new opportunities, and stimulating change. In contrast, the most important concerns of a manager in a large organization are directed internally—toward deciding which organizational units get what available resources and how much of them. According to this study, the entrepreneurial role—looking for business opportunities and planning activities for performance improvement—is least important to managers in large firms.

Compared to a manager in a large organization, a small-business manager is more likely to be a generalist. His or her job will combine the activities of a large corporation's chief executive with many of the day-to-day activities undertaken by a first-line supervisor. Moreover, the structure and formality that characterize a man-

FIGURE 1-6
Importance of Managerial Roles
in Small and Large Firms

Source: Adapted from Joseph G. P.
Paolillo, "The Manager's Self-Assessments
of Managerial Roles: Small vs. Large
Firms," *American Journal of Small Business,* January-March, 1984, pp. 61-62.

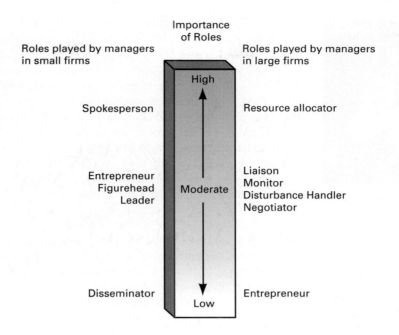

ager's job in a large organization tend to give way to informality in small firms. Planning is less likely to be a carefully orchestrated ritual. The organization's design will be less complex and structured. And control in the small business will rely more on direct observation than on sophisticated computerized monitoring systems.[18]

Again, as with organizational level, we see differences in degree and emphasis, but not in function. Managers in both small and large organizations perform essentially the same activities; only how they go about them and the proportion of time they spend on each are different.

Cross-national Transferability   The last generic management issue concerns whether management concepts are transferable across national borders. If managerial concepts were completely generic, they would apply universally, regardless of economic, social, political, or cultural differences. Studies that have compared preferred managerial practices between countries have not generally supported the universality of management concepts. In Chapter 4, we'll examine some specific differences between countries. At this point, it is sufficient to say that most of the concepts we'll be discussing in future chapters apply to the United States, Canada, Great Britain, Australia, and other English-speaking democracies. However, we would have to modify these concepts if we wanted to apply them in India, China, Chile, or any other country whose economic, political, social, or cultural environment differs greatly from that of the so-called free-market democracies.

The Value the Marketplace Puts on Managers

Good managers can turn straw to gold. Poor managers can do the reverse. This realization has not been lost on those who design compensation systems for organizations. Managers tend to be more highly paid than operatives. As a manager's

Stanley C. Gault built his reputation by turning around Rubbermaid Inc. from a small company into a highly regarded $1 billion global concern. He retired from Rubbermaid at age 65. In the fall of 1991, Goodyear lured him out of retirement with a three-year package to head up the tire and rubber company. He earned $1.1 million in his first year and $1.3 million for the next two. He also negotiated stock and stock options on over 600,000 shares of Goodyear, mostly below the market. In his first six months on the job, Goodyear showed its best quarterly earnings in nearly four years.

authority and responsibility expand, so typically does his or her pay. Moreover, many organizations willingly offer extremely lucrative compensation packages to get and keep good managers.

If you were privy to the compensation paid employees at such large public accounting firms as Price Waterhouse and Arthur Andersen, you would discover an interesting fact. Their best accounting specialists rarely earn more than $75,000 a year. In contrast, the annual income of their senior managing partners is rarely less than $125,000 and, in some cases, may exceed $750,000. The fact that these firms pay their managers considerably more than their nonmanagers is a measure of the importance placed on effective management skills. What is true at these accounting firms is true in most organizations. Good managerial skills are a scarce commodity, and compensation packages are one measure of the value that organizations place on them.

Do all managers make six-figure incomes? No! Such salaries are usually reserved for senior executives. What could you expect to make as a manager? The answer to this question depends on your level in the organization, your education and experience, the type of business the organization is in, comparable pay standards in the community, and how effective a manager you are. Most first-line supervisors earn between $25,000 and $45,000 a year. Middle managers start near $35,000 and top out at around $90,000. Senior managers in large corporations can earn $1 million a year or more. In 1990, for instance, the average cash compensation (salary plus annual bonus) for chief executives at the fifty largest publicly held U.S. corporations was $2.48 million.[19] In many cases, this was enhanced by stock options. In that same year, John Sculley earned $2.2 million as head of Apple Computer. But he made another $14.5 million from cashing in previously granted stock options.[20]

Management salaries reflect the market forces of supply and demand. Management superstars, like superstar athletes in professional sports, are wooed with signing bonuses, interest-free loans, performance incentive packages, and guaranteed contracts.

Why Study Management?

The first reason for studying management is that we all have a vested interest in improving the way organizations are managed. Why? Because we interact with them every day of our lives. Does it frustrate you when you have to spend three hours in a department of motor vehicles office to get your driver's license renewed? Are you perplexed when none of the salespeople in a department store seem interested in helping you? Are you angered when you call an airline three times and their representatives quote you three different prices for the same trip? As a taxpayer, doesn't it seem like something is wrong when you read about the Department of Defense spending $700 for a hammer or $1500 for a toilet seat? These are all examples of problems caused by poor management. Organizations that are well managed—including Wal-Mart, Toyota Motors, Motorola, Merck Pharmaceuticals, Siemens, and Toys 'R' Us—develop a loyal constituency, grow, and prosper. Those that are poorly managed—for example, Sears or Wang Laboratories—find themselves with a declining customer base and reduced revenues. Eventually, the survival of poorly managed organizations becomes threatened. Thirty years ago, Gimbels, W.T. Grant, and Eastern Airlines were thriving corporations. They employed tens of thousands of people and provided goods and services on a daily basis to hundreds of

Roger Penske at Detroit Diesel Corp.

Good managers *do* make a difference in an organization's performance! Take the case of Detroit Diesel Corp.[21]

In 1987, Detroit Diesel was owned by General Motors. The company held a paltry 3.2 percent of the market for heavy-truck engines. Between 1982 and 1987, the company had lost $600 million. Then, in 1988, former auto racer turned transportation tycoon Roger Penske bought control of the firm. Keeping the same senior management team and hourly workforce that floundered under GM, Penske immediately began instituting changes that would transform Detroit Diesel into a small, focused, market-driven organization.

Penske began meeting regularly with union leaders. He also initiated a marathon series of small-group meetings with the entire workforce. His goal? To get employees to understand what the business was about. Penske introduced profit sharing and economic incentives for attendance. He convinced workers that while the company had a superior product, the highest quality standards had to be achieved if the company was to beat the competition. Further, Penske made Detroit Diesel a leaner, more responsive firm by cutting nearly a quarter of the company's white-collar workforce and eliminating some departments. He also pushed authority down to lower levels in the organization, which allowed for much faster decision making.

Penske has succeeded in invigorating Detroit Diesel and making it a viable competitor in the truck-engine market. The company's market share has risen to an impressive 28 percent and is still climbing. The company is now profitable and hiring more workers. Absenteeism is down by almost half. And employee morale is high following three years of profit-sharing bonuses, the most recent averaging $600 per person.

thousands of customers. But weak management did them in. Today these companies no longer exist.

The second reason for studying management is the reality that once you graduate from college and begin your career, you will either *manage* or *be managed.* For those who plan on careers in management, an understanding of the management process forms the foundation upon which to build their management skills. But it would be naive to assume that everyone who studies management is planning a career in management. A course in management may only be a requirement for a degree you want, but that needn't make the study of management irrelevant. Assuming that you will have to work for a living and recognizing that you will almost certainly work in an organization, you will be a manager and/or work for a manager. If you plan on working for a manager, you can gain a great deal of insight into the way your boss behaves and the internal workings of organizations by studying management. The point is that you needn't aspire to be a manager to gain something valuable from a course in management.

Summary

This summary is organized by the chapter-opening learning objectives found on page 1.

1. Managers are individuals in an organization who direct the activities of others. They have such titles as supervisor, department head, dean, division manager, vice president, president, and chief executive officer. Operatives are nonmanagerial personnel. They work directly on a job or task and have no responsibility for overseeing the work of others.

2. Management refers to the process of getting activities completed efficiently with and through other people. The process represents the functions or primary activities of planning, organizing, leading, and controlling.

3. Effectiveness is concerned with getting activities completed—that is, goal attainment. Efficiency is concerned with minimizing resource costs in the completion of those activities.

4. Henry Mintzberg concluded from his study of five chief executives that managers perform ten different roles or behaviors. He classified them into three sets. One set is concerned with interpersonal relationships (figurehead, leader, liaison). The second set relates to the transfer of information (monitor, disseminator, spokesperson). The third set deals with decision making (entrepreneur, disturbance handler, resource allocator, negotiator).

5. Fred Luthans and his associates found that successful managers—those who got promoted most quickly—emphasized networking activities. In contrast, effective managers—those who performed best—emphasized communication. This suggests the importance of social and political skills in getting ahead in organizations.

6. Management has several generic properties. Regardless of level in an organization, all managers perform the same four functions; however, the emphasis given to each function varies with the manager's position in the hierarchy. Similarly, for the most part, the manager's job is the same regardless of the type of organization he or she is in. The generic properties of management are found mainly in the world's English-speaking democracies, and it is therefore dangerous to assume that they are universally transferable outside so-called free-market democracies.

7. People in all walks of life have come to recognize the important role that good management plays in our society. The study of management, for those who aspire to managerial positions, provides the body of knowledge that will help them to be more effective managers. For those who do not plan on careers in management, the study of management can give them a great deal of insight into the way their bosses behave and into the internal activities of organizations.

Review Questions

1. What is an organization? Why are managers important to an organization's success?

2. Are all effective organizations also efficient? Discuss.

3. What four common functions do all managers perform? Briefly describe them.

4. Contrast the four functions with Mintzberg's ten roles.

5. What are the four managerial activities identified by Luthans? Contrast the emphasis placed on these four activities by average, successful, and effective managers.

6. How does a manager's job change with his or her level in the organization?

7. In what ways would the mayor's job in a large city and the president's job in a large corporation be similar? In what ways would they be different?

8. How might the job of an owner-manager of a small business compare with the job of president of a large corporation?

9. How would a large corporation justify paying its senior executives high six-figure or even seven-figure annual compensation packages?

10. How might the study of management benefit an accounting major who plans on (a) working for a large accounting firm or (b) starting his or her own small accounting firm?

Discussion Questions

1. Would you describe management as a profession in the same way that law or accounting is a profession? Support your position.

2. Is your college instructor a manager? Discuss in terms of both Fayol's managerial functions and Mintzberg's managerial roles.

3. Ralph Larsen, the chairman of Johnson & Johnson, makes more than four times as much money each year as President Clinton. In fact, the most senior executive in almost every one of the 100 largest U.S. corporations makes more than the president. Discuss the ways in which Larsen's and the president's roles as managers are the same and different. Why do you think Larsen makes more money as a manager than does the president?

4. Some so-called managers oversee only assembly line robots or a roomful of computers. Can they really be managers if they have no subordinates?

5. Peter Berczi is a successful mid-level manager at Ford Motor Co. of Canada. However, Peter is a bit bored with his job and would like a change of pace. Peter, who was born in Hungary and raised in Canada, has an offer to manage the local school in a small village in northern Hungary. What factors might affect his switch from one managerial position to the other?

SELF-ASSESSMENT EXERCISE

How Strong Is Your Motivation to Manage in a Large Organization?

The following questions evaluate your motivation to manage in large and complex organizations. They are based on seven established role dimensions in the manager's job. For each question, circle the number that best describes the strength of your motivation.

	Weak						Strong
1. I have a desire to build positive relationships with my superiors.	1	2	3	4	5	6	7
2. I have a desire to compete with peers in games and sports.	1	2	3	4	5	6	7
3. I have a desire to compete with peers in work-related activities.	1	2	3	4	5	6	7
4. I have a desire to behave in an active and assertive manner.	1	2	3	4	5	6	7
5. I have a desire to tell others what to do and to impose sanctions in influencing others.	1	2	3	4	5	6	7
6. I have a desire to stand out from the group in a unique and highly visible fashion.	1	2	3	4	5	6	7
7. I have a desire to carry out the routine duties often associated with managerial work.	1	2	3	4	5	6	7

Turn to page SK-1 for scoring directions and key.

Source: Based on John B. Miner and Norman R. Smith, "Decline and Stabilization of Managerial Motivation Over a 20-Year Period," *Journal of Applied Psychology,* June 1982, p. 298.

COMPU*SPEED*SOFTWARE

To: Ken Capersan, Vice President
From: Michael Wong, President
Subject: Management Development

Who would have thought that we'd hit sales of $10 million in our second full year of operation? But we did it! That's the good news. The bad news is that our growth is far outpacing even our most ambitious projections. We hoped to add ten to fifteen new people this year. We ended up adding thirty-seven.

Per our discussion earlier this week, I agree with you that we simply are not finding enough good people from outside to fill the management slots we're creating. We need to begin growing our own managers from among our software programmers and other professionals.

Let's create our own in-house management training program. After we identify those on our staff with the interest and aptitude for managerial responsibilities, we can put them through our program. We might set aside a morning, once a week, for classes. And we can use the conference room that adjoins my office.

Write up a proposal, not to exceed two pages, describing what you think should be the content of our course. Assume the course runs four hours a week for ten weeks. Also, assume the trainees have neither prior experience nor any formal course work in the field. Finally, I think you should gear the program towards the activities and problems that supervisors or first-level managers are likely to face.

Assume you are Ken Capersan. Write a proposal, not to exceed 400 words, concisely stating the content you would include in this management training program.

This fictionalized memorandum was created for educational purposes only. It is not meant to reflect either positively or negatively on management practices at CompuSpeed Software.

CASE APPLICATION

Two Days In the Life of Jerre L. Stead

Jerre L. Stead is chairman and chief executive officer of Square D Co., an Illinois-based manufacturer of electrical products with annual sales of $1.6 billion. Stead has been in his job for two years. The following highlights two days in his executive life.

Day One

6:56 a.m.   Stead leaves home and drives himself to a small local airport where he boards the company jet for a day trip to the switch-gear division plant in Smyrna, Tennessee. Joining Stead in the car ride is Jodie Glore, a vice president who oversees the $500 million switch-gear division. They discuss ways to encourage people in the company to disagree with one another and their bosses. Stead feels that previous management encouraged taking orders and that people have forgotten how to challenge authority.

7:43 a.m.   The two buckle into the corporate jet for the 80-minute flight. Stead reminisces about his twenty-one-year career at Honeywell and his eventual decision to leave and join Square D. He discusses the sluggish and dispirited company he inherited at Square D. His major concern right now is that he has scores of managers who have no stomach for taking risks or assuming responsibility. To help change their feelings, he visits each of Square D's fifty-two facilities around the world at least once every eighteen months.

9:38 a.m.   Touching down in Smyrna, Stead and Glore are met by Jim Clark, who is switch-gear division manager. In Clark's car, the conversation turns immediately to efforts by the International Union of Electrical Workers to organize the plant. If the union stands a chance it is because of Smyrna's poor pension-benefit program. "That's got to be fixed," Stead says. It will become a refrain throughout the day.

9:46 a.m.   Clark pulls up to a red-brick building where a new product is being developed. Stead greets the project manager and chats with software designers and engineers. After a quick tour of the small building, the project manager briefs Stead on the new product, a computerized meter that monitors and analyzes power coming into a factory. Stead asks questions about the product's profitability and market potential, then instructs Glore to make sure that securities analysts see the new-product presentation.

10:27 a.m.   Stead hops into a van for a short ride to the Smyrna switch-gear division plant. In the conference room, he sits at the head of the table. Four presentations are made. Stead asks dozens of questions, interspersing his remarks with bits of advice or broader lessons. His style is Socratic—gentle prodding through deliberate but open-ended questions.

12:31 p.m.   In Clark's office, Stead mentions a letter he received from a plant accountant. The author accuses one of the plant controller's subordinates of having him cook the books. The controller tells Stead the letter is "false and slanderous." Revenge, he ventures, might be a motive—the accuser knows he's about to be dismissed. Stead agrees: "We don't want that kind of person here," he says. "End of story."

12:43 p.m. Stead makes a phone call to an annoyed customer. He apologizes for a delivery problem. Stead claims he spends 20 percent of his time with customers, often smoothing over complaints.

12:57 p.m. Clark and his assistants lead another round of presentations.

2:27 p.m. Stead arrives at the employee cafeteria to field questions from plant operating personnel. Questions come slowly and haltingly. But the questions that do come focus on the company's response to the union organizing drive and the inadequacy of the company's pension program.

3:44 p.m. More briefings with top Smyrna people. When the conversation turns to the union organizing effort, Stead urges Glore, "Fix the pension plan. As far as I'm concerned, you can do that tomorrow."

6:57 p.m. Back from Smyrna, Stead gets a call on his car phone as he drives home. It's from Walt Kurczewski, Square D's general counsel. The minutes from the last board meeting, Kurczewski says, will be going out by overnight mail in plenty of time for directors to review the material for next week's board meeting in Toronto.

Day Two

8:10 a.m. Stead arrives for work late because of a dental appointment. After checking with his secretary and making a quick call, he dashes to the boardroom. Around the sprawling mahogany conference table sit six members of Stead's executive staff. They've gathered for the annual human-resources review, a practice Stead introduced to discuss succession, training and development, and personnel issues.

11:19 a.m. Stead calls a unit manager into his office for a "skip-level" session. Stead explains the purpose of the skip-level meeting—to give the unit manager a chance to skip over his boss, an executive VP, and talk to Stead directly.

1:53 p.m. Stead phones the company's investment banker. A foreign competitor has offered to make a sizable—and unwelcome—investment in Square D. They discuss various strategies for responding to this competitor.

2:09 p.m. General counsel Kurczewski strolls into Stead's office to discuss a meeting of the Square D foundation, which Kurczewski directs. Stead wants to put more money into health-care issues.

2:36 p.m. Stead rushes down to his car and over to a local hotel. In a small meeting room, he joins 20 employees, all hearing-impaired. They are assembled for a graduation ceremony at the company's Vision College, an in-house institution that teaches a two-day course on customer service, quality, and personal accountability. With a sign-language translator at his side, Stead congratulates the graduates and acknowledges their critiques of the program.

4:03 p.m.   Back in his office, Stead has one of his biweekly meetings with Bob Carpenter, a young VP in charge of support services. They go over a presentation that Carpenter plans to give next week at the Toronto board meeting.

5:06 p.m.   Yuris Vikmanis, executive vice president of Square D's industrial-control group, stands outside Stead's office to schmooze. Their conversation contrasts markedly with an exchange between them at this morning's meeting. "Let me understand what you're saying, but I'm not questioning you . . ." Vikmanis had said. "You can question anything you like," Stead told him.

Questions

1. Analyze Stead's activities using Mintzberg's framework.
2. Do you think Stead uses his time well? Explain.
3. What, if anything, do you think he should do differently? Why?
4. Do you think Stead's efforts to encourage disagreement will undermine managerial authority at Square D? Discuss.

Source: Based on Patrick Houston, "48 Hours on the Job," *Business Month,* September 1990, pp. 42–49.

VIDEO CASE

Kay Graham of the Washington Post

When Kay Graham stepped down in 1991 as chief executive officer of the Washington Post, she left a lasting legacy. When she took over the Post in 1963, it was a solid but nondescript newspaper. On her retirement twenty-eight years later, the paper had become a powerful and influential newspaper of world class.

Ms. Graham was born into a wealthy banking family. Her father, Eugene Meyer, bought the Washington Post in 1933. The paper was bankrupt and virtually disintegrating. Pumping in cash, he upgraded the editorial pages but had little influence on improving the news pages. When Meyer died, he left the newspaper to Kay who, by this time, had married Phil Graham. Kay never spent a moment thinking she would be involved in the paper. Shy and unassuming, she let her husband run the Post. Phil Graham wanted to turn the Post into a powerful paper, but not necessarily a great one. He essentially used the paper to push his own liberal agenda and to further the interests of friends such as John F. Kennedy. Mentally unstable, Phil Graham committed suicide in 1963.

Key Graham thought she was ill prepared for her new responsibilities of running the Post. A graduate of Vassar and the University of Chicago, Kay describes herself as brought up to please. "It never occurred to me that I could run anything." She had no experience. But she listened and learned on the job. Most importantly, she hired first-rate people. Over her twenty-eight years at the helm of the Post, she turned out to be a gutsy publisher, who risked the company to print the Pentagon Papers and backed her reports through Watergate. For instance, publishing the Pentagon Papers, which described secret plans during the Vietnam War, was a major risk. Claiming freedom of speech, she resisted pressure from the Nixon White House and published the papers in full. Her determination to set high standards of excellence helped to turn the Washington Post into the' successful and powerful institution that it is today.

A role model for women from the mid-1960s through the early 1990s, Graham said about her retirement, "Organizations need young people. It's very dangerous to stay too long."

Questions

1. What factors, if any, in Ms. Graham's background might suggest success as a manager? What does this suggest for using personality-types to predict management success?

2. Kay Graham illustrates that you don't need to study management to be an effective manager. Discuss the advantages of management education over "on the job" learning.

3. Graham says, "Organizations need young people." But don't they also need experience? Discuss.

Source: "Kay Graham: Person of the Week," *ABC World News Tonight,* May 10, 1991.

CHAPTER 2

The Evolution of Management

LEARNING OBJECTIVES

After Reading This Chapter, You Should Be Able To:

1. Explain the value of studying management history.
2. Identify some major pre-twentieth-century contributions to management.
3. Explain why the first half of this century is described as a period of diversity.
4. Define Frederick Taylor's principles of scientific management.
5. Summarize scientific management's contribution to management.
6. Identify Henri Fayol's contributions to management.
7. Define Max Weber's ideal bureaucracy.
8. Explain the Hawthorne studies' contributions to management.
9. Contrast the approaches taken by human relations' advocates and the behavioral science theorists.
10. Distinguish between the process, systems, and contingency approaches.
11. Define work force diversity.
12. Describe why managers have become increasingly concerned with stimulating innovation and change.
13. Define the five primary components of TQM.

The detailed training that UPS drivers receive comes directly from scientific management techniques developed at the turn of the century.

United Parcel Service employs 150,000 people and delivers an average of nine million packages a day to locations throughout the United States and 180 countries. To achieve its claim of "running the tightest ship in the shipping business," UPS's management methodically trains its employees in how to do their jobs as efficiently as possible. For instance, consider the job of a delivery driver.[1]

Industrial engineers at UPS have time-studied each driver's route and set standards for each delivery, stop, and pickup. These engineers have recorded every second taken up by stoplights, traffic, detours, doorbells, walkways, stairways, and coffee breaks. Even bathroom stops are put into the standards. All of this is then fed into company computers to provide detailed time standards for every driver, every day.

To meet their objective of 130 deliveries and pickups each day, drivers must follow the engineers' procedures exactly. As they approach a delivery stop, drivers shed their seat belts, toot their horns, and cut their engines. In one seamless motion, they are required to yank up their emergency brakes and push their gearshifts into first. They're now ready for takeoff after their deliveries. The drivers slide to the ground with their clipboards under their right arms and their packages in their left hands. Their keys, teeth up, are in their right hands. They take one look at the package to fix the address in their minds. Then they walk to the customer's door at the prescribed 3-feet-per-second and knock first to avoid lost seconds searching for the doorbell. After making the delivery, they do the paperwork on the way back to the truck.

Does this rigid time scheduling seem obsessive? Maybe. Does it make for high efficiency? You bet! Productivity experts describe UPS as one of the most efficient companies anywhere. As a case in point, Federal Express averages only 80 stops a day versus the UPS average of 130. And all of this seems to positively influence UPS's bottom line. Although the company is privately held, it is widely recognized as being highly profitable.

The procedures used at United Parcel Service to achieve optimum efficiency were not invented by UPS. They came out of the work in scientific management undertaken nearly a hundred years ago. Yet, as UPS demonstrates, these procedures still apply today.

The purpose of this chapter is to demonstrate that a knowledge of management history can help you to understand theory and practice as they are today. This chapter will introduce you to the origins of many contemporary management concepts and demonstrate how they have evolved to reflect the changing needs of organizations and society as a whole. We'll also introduce a number of important trends and issues that management currently faces in order to link the past with the future and demonstrate that the field of management is still evolving.

Historical Background

Organized endeavors that are overseen by people responsible for planning, organizing, leading, and controlling activities have existed for thousands of years. The Egyptian Pyramids and the Great Wall of China are current evidence that projects of tremendous scope, employing tens of thousands of people, were undertaken well before modern times. The Pyramids are a particularly interesting example. The construction of a single Pyramid occupied over 100,000 people for twenty years.[2] Who told each worker what he or she was supposed to do? Who ensured that there would be enough stones at the site to keep workers busy? The answer to questions such as these is management. Regardless of what managers were called at the time, someone had to plan what was to be done, organize people and materials to do it, lead and direct the workers, and impose some controls to ensure that everything was done as planned.

Even the Bible refers to management concepts. For instance, the following quotation dramatizes the need for a manager to delegate authority in a large organization and to review only the unusual or exceptional cases that cannot be resolved by lower-level managers. Moses' father-in-law is speaking to Moses:

> The thing that thou doest is not good. Thou wilt surely wear away, both thou, and this people that is with thee; for this thing is too heavy for thee; thou art not able to perform it thyself alone. Hearken now unto my voice, I will give thee counsel. . . . Moreover thou shalt provide out of all the people able men . . . and place such over them, to be rulers of thousands, and rulers of hundreds, rulers of fifties, and rulers of tens. And let them judge the people at all seasons: and it shall be, that every great matter they shall bring unto thee, but every small matter they shall judge; so shall it be easier for thyself, and they shall bear the burden with thee. If thou shalt do this thing, and God command thee so, then thou shalt be able to endure, and all this people shall go to their place in peace.[3]

The Roman Catholic Church also represents an interesting example of the practice of management. The current structure of the Church was essentially established in the

The largest of the Pyramids contained more than two million stone blocks, each weighing several tons. The quarries from which the blocks came were many miles from the sites where the Pyramids were constructed. Someone had to design the structure, find a stone quarry, and arrange for the stones to be cut and moved—probably over land and by water—to the construction site.

second century A.D. At that time, its objectives and doctrines were more rigorously defined. Final authority was centralized in Rome. A simple authority hierarchy was created, which has remained basically unchanged for nearly 2,000 years.

These examples from the past demonstrate that organizations have been with us for thousands of years and that management has been practiced for an equivalent period. However, it has been only in the past several hundred years, particularly in the last century, that management has undergone systematic investigation, acquired a common body of knowledge, and become a formal discipline for study.

The Roman Catholic Church is a world-wide organization but is essentially composed of only five levels: Parish Priest, Bishop, Archbishop, Cardinal, and Pope. This simple, flat structure has proven effective for nearly 2,000 years.

division of labor
The breakdown of jobs into narrow, repetitive tasks.

Industrial Revolution
The advent of machine power, mass production, and efficient transportation.

Adam Smith's name is more typically cited in economics courses for his contributions to classical economic doctrine, but his discussion in *The Wealth of Nations,* published in 1776, included a brilliant argument on the economic advantages that organizations and society would reap from the **division of labor.** He used the pin-manufacturing industry for his examples. Smith noted that ten individuals, each doing a specialized task, could produce about 48,000 pins a day among them. However, if each were working separately and independently, those ten workers would be lucky to make 200—or even ten—pins in one day. If each worker had to draw the wire, straighten it, cut it, pound heads for each pin, sharpen the point, and solder the head and pin shaft, it would be quite a feat to produce ten pins a day!

Smith concluded that division of labor increased productivity by increasing each worker's skill and dexterity, by saving time that is commonly lost in changing tasks, and by the creation of labor-saving inventions and machinery. The wide popularity today of job specialization—in service jobs like teaching and medicine as well as on assembly lines in automobile plants—is undoubtedly due to the economic advantages cited over 200 years ago by Adam Smith.

Possibly the most important pre-twentieth-century influence on management was the **Industrial Revolution.** Begun in the eighteenth century in Great Britain, the Revolution had crossed the Atlantic to America by the end of the Civil War. Machine power was rapidly being substituted for human power. This, in turn, made it more economical to manufacture goods in factories. For instance, before the Industrial Revolution, an item such as a blanket was made by one person, typically at home. The worker would shear wool from his or her sheep, twist the wool into yarn, dye the yarn, weave the blanket manually on a home loom, and then sell the finished product to merchants who would travel to farms buying merchandise that then would be sold at regional fairs or markets. The introduction of machine power, combined with the division of labor, made it possible to have large, efficient factories using power-driven equipment. A blanket factory with 100 people doing specialized tasks—some making wool into yarn, some dyeing, others working on the looms—could manufacture large numbers of blankets at a fraction of their previous cost. But these factories required managerial skills. Managers were needed to forecast demand, ensure that enough wool was on hand to make the yarn, assign tasks to people, direct daily activities, coordinate the various tasks, ensure that the machines were kept in good working order and that output standards were maintained, find markets for the finished blankets, and so forth. When blankets were made individually at home, there was little concern with efficiency. Suddenly, however, when the factory owner had 100 people working for him or her and a regular payroll to meet, it became important to keep workers busy. Planning, organizing, leading, and controlling became necessary.

The advent of machine power, mass production, the reduced transportation costs that followed the rapid expansion of the railroads, and almost no governmental regulation also fostered the development of big corporations. John D. Rockefeller was putting together the Standard Oil monopoly, Andrew Carnegie was gaining control of two-thirds of the steel industry, and similar entrepreneurs were creating other large businesses that would require formalized management practices. The need for a formal theory to guide managers in running their organizations had arrived. However, it was not until the early 1900s that the first major step toward developing such a theory occurred.

The Period of Diversity

The first half of this century was a period of diversity in management thought. Scientific management looked at the field from the perspective of how to improve the productivity of operative personnel. The general administrative theorists were concerned with the overall organization and how to make it more effective. One group of writers and researchers emphasized the human resource or "people side" of management, while another group focused on developing and applying quantitative models.

In this section we present the contributions of these four approaches. Keep in mind that each is concerned with the same "animal"; the differences reflect the backgrounds and interests of the writers. A relevant analogy is the classic fable of the blind people and the elephant. The first person touches the side of the elephant and declares that an elephant is like a wall. The second touches the trunk and says the elephant is like a snake. The third feels one of the elephant's tusks and believes the elephant to be like a spear. The fourth grabs a leg and says that an elephant is like a tree. The fifth touches the elephant's tail and concludes that the animal is like a rope. Each of these blind people is encountering the same elephant, but what they "see" depends on where they stand. Similarly, each of the following perspectives is correct and makes an important contribution to our understanding of management. However, each is also a limited view of a larger "animal."

Scientific Management

If one had to pinpoint the year that modern management theory was born, one could make a strong case for 1911. This was the year that Frederick Winslow Taylor's *Principles of Scientific Management* was published. Its contents would become widely accepted by managers throughout the world. The book described the theory of **scientific management**—the use of the scientific method to define the "one best way" for a job to be done. The studies conducted before and after the book's publication would establish Taylor as the father of scientific management.

Frederick Taylor Frederick Taylor did most of his work at the Midvale and Bethlehem Steel companies in Pennsylvania. As a mechanical engineer with a Quaker-Puritan background, he was consistently appalled at the inefficiency of workers. Employees used vastly different techniques to do the same job. They were prone to "taking it easy" on the job. Taylor believed that worker output was only about one-third of what was possible. Therefore, he set out to correct the situation by applying the scientific method to jobs on the shop floor. He spent more than two decades pursuing with a passion the "one best way" for each job to be done.

It's important to understand what Taylor saw at Midvale Steel that aroused his determination to improve the way things were done in the plant. At the time, there were no clear concepts of worker and management responsibilities. Virtually no effective work standards existed. Workers purposely worked at a slow pace. Management decisions were of the "seat-of-the-pants" nature, based on hunch and intuition. Workers were placed on jobs with little or no concern for matching their abilities and aptitudes with the tasks they were required to do. Most important, management and workers considered themselves to be in continual conflict. Rather than cooperating to their mutual benefit, they perceived their relationship as a zero-sum game—any gain by one would be at the expense of the other.

Taylor sought to create a mental revolution among both the workers and management by defining clear guidelines for improving production efficiency. He defined four principles of management, listed in Table 2–1; he argued that following these principles would result in the prosperity of both management and workers. Workers would earn more pay, and management more profits. The current application of these principles at United Parcel Service continues to provide some support for Taylor's expectations. UPS delivery drivers earn over $18.00 an hour. With overtime, they average better than $50,000 a year.[4] At the same time, management is able to generate consistently high profits.

Probably the most widely cited example of scientific management has been

scientific management
The use of the scientific method to define the "one best way" for a job to be done.

Frederick Taylor (1856-1915) was the father of scientific management.

TABLE 2-1   Taylor's Four Principles of Management

1. Develop a science for each element of an individual's work, which replaces the old rule-of-thumb method.

2. Scientifically select and then train, teach, and develop the worker. (Previously, workers chose their own work and trained themselves as best they could.)

3. Heartily cooperate with the workers so as to ensure that all work is done in accordance with the principles of the science that has been developed.

4. Divide work and responsibility almost equally between management and workers. Management takes over all work for which it is better fitted than the workers. (Previously, almost all the work and the greater part of the responsibility were thrown upon the workers.)

Taylor's pig iron experiment. Workers loaded "pigs" of iron weighing 92 pounds onto rail cars. Their average daily output was 12.5 tons. Taylor believed that by scientifically analyzing the job to determine the one best way to load pig iron, the output could be increased to between forty-seven and forty-eight tons per day.

Taylor began his experiment by looking for a physically strong subject who placed a high value on the dollar. The individual Taylor chose was a big, strong Dutch immigrant, whom he called Schmidt. Schmidt, like the other loaders, earned $1.15 a day, which even at the turn of the century was barely enough for a person to survive on. As the following quotation from Taylor's book demonstrates, Taylor used money—the opportunity to make $1.85 a day—as the primary means to get workers like Schmidt to do exactly as they were told:

"Schmidt, are you a high-priced man?" "Vell, I don't know vat you mean." "Oh, yes you do. What I want to know is whether you are a high-priced man or not." "Vell, I don't know vat you mean." "Oh, come now, you answer my questions. What I want to find out is whether you are a high-priced man or one of these cheap fellows here. What I want to know is whether you want to earn $1.85 a day or whether you are satisfied with $1.15, just the same as all those cheap fellows are getting." "Did I vant $1.85 a day? Vas dot a high-priced man? Vell, yes, I vas a high-priced man."[5]

Using money to motivate Schmidt, Taylor went about having him load the pig irons, alternating various job factors to see what impact the changes had on Schmidt's daily output. For instance, on some days Schmidt would lift the pig irons by bending his knees, whereas on other days he would keep his legs straight and use his back. He experimented with rest periods, walking speed, carrying positions, and other variables. After a long period of scientifically trying various combinations of procedures, techniques, and tools, Taylor succeeded in obtaining the level of productivity he thought possible. By putting the right person on the job with the correct tools and equipment, by having the worker follow his instructions exactly, and by motivating the worker through the economic incentive of a significantly higher daily wage, Taylor was able to reach his 48-ton objective.

Another Taylor experiment dealt with shovel sizes. Taylor noticed that every worker in the plant used the same-sized shovel, regardless of the material he was moving. This made no sense to Taylor. If there was an optimum total shovel weight that would maximize a worker's shoveling output over an entire day, then Taylor thought the size of the shovel should vary depending on the weight of the material being moved. After extensive experimentation, Taylor found that twenty-one pounds was the optimum shovel capacity. To achieve this optimum weight, heavy material such as iron ore would be moved with a small-faced shovel and light material such as coke with a large-faced shovel. Based on Taylor's findings, supervisors would no longer merely tell a worker to "shovel that pile over there." Depending on the material to be moved, the supervisor would now have to determine the appropriate shovel size and assign that size to the worker. The result, of course, was again significant increases in worker output.

Using similar approaches to other jobs, Taylor was able to define the one best way for doing each job. He could then, after selecting the right people for the job, train them to do it precisely in this one best way. To motivate workers, he favored incentive wage plans. Overall, Taylor achieved consistent improvements in productivity in the range of 200 percent or more. He reaffirmed the role of managers to plan and control and that of workers to perform as they were instructed. The *Principles of Scientific Management,* as well as other papers that Taylor wrote and presented, spread his ideas not only in the United States, but also in France, Germany, Russia, and Japan. One of the biggest boosts in interest in scientific management in the United States came during a 1910 hearing on railroad rates before the Interstate Commerce Commission. Appearing before the commission, an efficiency expert claimed that railroads could save a million dollars a day (equivalent to about $14 million a day in 1994 dollars) through the application of scientific management! The early acceptance of scientific management techniques by U.S. manufacturing companies, in fact, gave them a comparative advantage over foreign firms that made U.S. manufacturing efficiency the envy of the world—at least for fifty years or so.

Frank and Lillian Gilbreth Taylor's ideas inspired others to study and develop methods of scientific management. His most prominent disciples were Frank and Lillian Gilbreth.

A construction contractor by background, Frank Gilbreth gave up his contracting career in 1912 to study scientific management after hearing Taylor speak at a professional meeting. Along with his wife Lillian, a psychologist, he studied work arrangements to eliminate wasteful hand-and-body motions. The Gilbreths also experimented in the design and use of the proper tools and equipment for optimizing work performance.[6] Frank Gilbreth is probably best known for his experiments in reducing the number of motions in bricklaying.

By carefully analyzing the bricklayer's job, he reduced the number of motions in the laying of exterior brick from eighteen to four and one-half. On interior brick, the eighteen motions were reduced to two. He developed a new way to stack bricks, utilized the scaffold to reduce bending, and even devised a different mortar consistency that reduced the need for the bricklayer to level the brick by tapping it with a trowel.

The Gilbreths were among the first to use motion picture films to study hand-and-body motions. They devised a microchronometer that recorded time to $\frac{1}{2000}$ second, placed it in the field of study being photographed, and thus determined how long a worker spent enacting each motion. Wasted motions missed by the naked eye could be identified and eliminated. The Gilbreths also devised a classification scheme to label seventeen basic hand motions—such as "search," "select," "grasp," "hold"— which they called **therbligs** ("Gilbreth" spelled backward with the "th" transposed). This allowed the Gilbreths a more precise way of analyzing the exact elements of any worker's hand movements.

Henry L. Gantt A close associate of Taylor at Midvale and Bethlehem Steel was a young engineer named Henry L. Gantt. Like Taylor and the Gilbreths, Gantt sought to increase worker efficiency through scientific investigation. But he extended some of Taylor's original ideas and added a few of his own. For instance, Gantt devised an incentive system that gave workers a bonus for completing their jobs in less time than the allowed standard. He also introduced a bonus for foremen to be paid for each

Frank and Lillian Gilbreth used scientific management techniques to reduce wasteful hand-and-body motions in jobs.

therbligs
A classification scheme for labeling seventeen basic hand motions.

Gantt chart
A graphic bar chart that shows the relationship between work planned and completed on one axis and time elapsed on the other.

worker who made the standard plus an extra bonus if all the workers under the foreman made it. In so doing, Gantt expanded the scope of scientific management to encompass the work of managers as well as that of operatives.

However, Gantt is probably most noted for creating a graphic bar chart that could be used by managers as a scheduling device for planning and controlling work. The **Gantt chart** showed the relationship between work planned and completed on one axis and time elapsed on the other. Revolutionary for its day, the Gantt chart allowed management to see how plans were progressing and to take the necessary action to keep projects on time. The Gantt chart and modern variations of it are still widely used in organizations as a method for scheduling work.

Putting Scientific Management into Perspective   Why did scientific management receive so much attention? Certainly, many of the guidelines Taylor and others devised for improving production efficiency appear to us today to be common sense. For instance, one can say that it should have been obvious to managers in those days that workers should be carefully screened, selected, and trained before being put into a job.

To understand the importance of scientific management, you have to consider the times in which Taylor, the Gilbreths, and Gantt lived. The standard of living was low. Production was highly labor intensive. Midvale Steel, at the turn of the century, may have employed twenty or thirty workers who did nothing but load pig iron onto rail cars. Today, their entire daily tonnage could probably be done in several hours by one person with a hydraulic lift truck. But they didn't have such mechanical devices. Similarly, the breakthroughs Frank Gilbreth achieved in bricklaying are meaningful only when you recognize that most quality buildings at that time were constructed of brick, that land was cheap, and that the major cost of a plant or home was the cost of the materials (bricks) and the labor cost to lay them.

To illustrate the point, if 30 percent of the cost of a $20,000 building represented the labor of bricklayers and if bricklayer productivity could be improved by 300 percent, the cost of that building would be reduced to $16,000. At the lower price, more buildings could be built because more people could afford them. Scientific management was important, therefore, because it could raise the standard of living of

Henry Ford used principles of scientific management in the creation of the automobile assembly line. Those principles allowed Ford to roll Model Ts off the assembly line at a rate of one every ten seconds. Ford proudly claimed that 90 percent of the jobs on his Model T assembly line could be learned in ten minutes.

entire countries. Additionally, spending six months or more studying one job—as Taylor did in the pig iron experiment—made sense only for labor-intensive procedures in which many workers performed the same tasks.

General Administrative Theorists

general administrative theorists

Writers who developed general theories of what managers do and what constitutes good management practice.

classical theorists

The term used to describe the scientific management theorists and general administrative theorists.

Another group of writers looked at the subject of management but focused on the entire organization. We call them the **general administrative theorists.** They are important for developing more general theories of what managers do and what constitutes good management practice. Because their writings set the framework for many of our contemporary ideas on management and organization, this group and the scientific management group are frequently referred to as the **classical theorists.** The most prominent of the general administrative theorists were Henri Fayol and Max Weber.

Henri Fayol   We mentioned Henri Fayol in the previous chapter for having designated management as a universal set of functions, specifically planning, organizing, commanding, coordinating, and controlling. Because his writings were important, let's take a more careful look at what he had to say.[7]

Fayol wrote during the same time as Taylor. However, whereas Taylor was concerned with management at the shop level (or what we today would describe as the job of a supervisor) and used the scientific method, Fayol's attention was directed at the activities of *all* managers, and he wrote from personal experience. Taylor was a scientist. Fayol, the managing director of a large French coal-mining firm, was a practitioner.

principles of management

Universal truths of management that can be taught in school.

Fayol described the practice of management as something distinct from accounting, finance, production, distribution, and other typical business functions. He argued that management was an activity common to all human undertakings in business, in government, and even in the home. He then proceeded to state fourteen **principles of management**—fundamental or universal truths—that could be taught in schools and universities. These principles are shown in Table 2–2.

bureaucracy

A form of organization marked by division of labor, hierarchy, rules and regulations, and impersonal relationships.

Max Weber   Max Weber (pronounced *Vay-ber*) was a German sociologist. Writing in the early part of this century, Weber developed a theory of authority structures and described organizational activity based on authority relations.[8] He described an ideal type of organization that he called a **bureaucracy.** It was a system characterized by division of labor, a clearly defined hierarchy, detailed rules and regulations, and impersonal relationships. Weber recognized that this "ideal bureaucracy" didn't exist in reality but, rather, represented a selective reconstruction of the real world. He meant it as a basis for theorizing about work and how work could be done in large groups. His theory became the design prototype for many of today's large organizations. The detailed features of Weber's ideal bureaucratic structure are outlined in Table 2–3.

Bureaucracy, as described by Weber, is not unlike scientific management in its ideology. Both emphasize rationality, predictability, impersonality, technical competence, and authoritarianism. While Weber's writings were less operational than Taylor's, the fact that his "ideal type" still describes many contemporary organizations attests to the importance of his work.

Putting the General Administrative Theorists into Perspective   A number of our current ideas and practices in management can be directly traced to the contributions of the general administrative theorists. For instance, the functional view of the manager's job owes its origin to Henri Fayol. Also, while many of his principles may not be universally applicable to the wide variety of organizations that exist today,

TABLE 2-2 Fayol's Fourteen Principles of Management

1. *Division of Work.* This principle is the same as Adam Smith's "division of labor." Specialization increases output by making employees more efficient.

2. *Authority.* Managers must be able to give orders. Authority gives them this right. Along with authority, however, goes responsibility. Wherever authority is exercised, responsibility arises.

3. *Discipline.* Employees must obey and respect the rules that govern the organization. Good discipline is the result of effective leadership, a clear understanding between management and workers regarding the organization's rules, and the judicious use of penalties for infractions of the rules.

4. *Unity of Command.* Every employee should receive orders from only *one* superior.

5. *Unity of Direction.* Each group of organizational activities that have the same objective should be directed by one manager using one plan.

6. *Subordination of Individual Interests to the General Interest.* The interests of any one employee or group of employees should not take precedence over the interests of the organization as a whole.

7. *Remuneration.* Workers must be paid a fair wage for their services.

8. *Centralization.* Centralization refers to the degree to which subordinates are involved in decision making. Whether decision making is centralized (to management) or decentralized (to subordinates) is a question of proper proportion. The task is to find the optimum degree of centralization for each situation.

9. *Scalar Chain.* The line of authority from top management to the lowest ranks represents the scalar chain. Communications should follow this chain. However, if following the chain creates delays, cross-communications can be allowed if agreed to by all parties and superiors are kept informed.

10. *Order.* People and materials should be in the right place at the right time.

11. *Equity.* Managers should be kind and fair to their subordinates.

12. *Stability of Tenure of Personnel.* High employee turnover is inefficient. Management should provide orderly personnel planning and ensure that replacements are available to fill vacancies.

13. *Initiative.* Employees who are allowed to originate and carry out plans will exert high levels of effort.

14. *Esprit de Corps.* Promoting team spirit will build harmony and unity within the organization.

TABLE 2-3 Weber's Ideal Bureaucracy

1. *Division of Labor.* Jobs are broken down into simple, routine, and well-defined tasks.

2. *Authority Hierarchy.* Offices or positions are organized in a hierarchy, each lower one being controlled and supervised by a higher one.

3. *Formal Selection.* All organizational members are to be selected on the basis of technical qualifications demonstrated by training, education, or formal examination.

4. *Formal Rules and Regulations.* To ensure uniformity and to regulate the actions of employees, managers must depend heavily on formal organizational rules.

5. *Impersonality.* Rules and controls are applied uniformly, avoiding involvement with personalities and personal preferences of employees.

6. *Career Orientation.* Managers are professional officials rather than owners of the units they manage. They work for fixed salaries and pursue their careers within the organization.

they became a frame of reference against which many current concepts have evolved.

Weber's bureaucracy was an attempt to formulate an ideal model around which organizations could be designed. It was a response to the abuses that Weber saw going on within organizations. Weber believed that his model could remove the ambiguity, inefficiencies, and patronage that characterized most organizations at that time. While not as popular as it was a decade ago, many of bureaucracy's components are still inherent in large organizations today.

The Human Resources Approach

Managers get things done by working with people. This explains why some writers and researchers have chosen to look at management by focusing on the organization's human resources. Much of what currently makes up the field of personnel management, as well as contemporary views on motivation and leadership, has come out of the work of those we have categorized as being part of the **human resources approach** to management.

human resources approach
The study of management that focuses on human behavior.

Early Advocates   While there were undoubtedly a number of people in the nineteenth and early part of the twentieth century who recognized the importance of the human factor to an organization's success, four individuals stand out as early advocates of the human resources approach. They were Robert Owen, Hugo Münsterberg, Mary Parker Follett, and Chester Barnard.

Robert Owen was a successful Scottish businessman who bought his first factory in 1789 when he was just eighteen. Repulsed by the harsh practices he saw in factories across Scotland—such as the employment of young children (many under the age of ten), thirteen-hour work days, and miserable working conditions—Owen became a reformer. He chided factory owners for treating their equipment better than their employees. He said that they would buy the best machines, but then buy the cheapest labor to run them. Owen argued that money spent on improving labor was one of the best investments that business executives could make. He claimed that showing

Robert Owen was an early critic of factory owners who hired child labor, worked them long hours, and provided inhuman working conditions.

concern for employees both was highly profitable for management and would relieve human misery.

Owen proposed a utopian workplace. As one author noted, Owen is not remembered in management history for his successes, but rather for his courage and commitment to reducing the suffering of the working class.[9] He was more than a hundred years ahead of his time when he argued, in 1825, for regulated hours of work for all, child labor laws, public education, company-furnished meals at work, and business involvement in community projects.[10]

Hugo Münsterberg created the field of industrial psychology—the scientific study of individuals at work to maximize their productivity and adjustment. His text, *Psychology and Industrial Efficiency*, was published in 1913. In it, he argued for the scientific study of human behavior to identify general patterns and to explain individual differences. Münsterberg suggested the use of psychological tests to improve employee selection, the value of learning theory in the development of training methods, and the study of human behavior in order to understand what techniques are most effective for motivating workers. Interestingly, he saw a link between scientific management and industrial psychology. Both sought increased efficiency through scientific work analyses and through better alignment of individual skills and abilities with the demands of various jobs. Much of our current knowledge of selection techniques, employee training, job design, and motivation is built on the work of Münsterberg.

One of the earliest writers to recognize that organizations could be viewed from the perspective of individual and group behavior was Mary Parker Follett.[11] A transitionalist writing in the time of scientific management but proposing more people-oriented ideas, Ms. Follett was a social philosopher. However, her ideas had clear implications for management practice. Follett thought that organizations should be based on a group ethic rather than individualism. Individual potential, she argued, remained only potential until released through group association. The manager's job was to harmonize and coordinate group efforts. Managers and workers should view themselves as partners—as part of a common group. As such, managers should rely more on their expertise and knowledge to lead subordinates than on the formal authority of their position. Her humanistic ideas influenced the way we look at motivation, leadership, power, and authority.

Also a transitionalist, Chester Barnard's ideas bridged classical and human resources viewpoints. Like Fayol, Barnard was a practitioner—he was president of New Jersey Bell Telephone Company. He had read Weber and was influenced by his writings. But unlike Weber, who had a mechanistic and impersonal view of organizations, Barnard saw organizations as social systems that require human cooperation. He expressed his views in his book, *The Functions of the Executive*,[12] published in 1938.

Barnard believed that organizations were made up of people who have interacting social relationships. The manager's major roles were to communicate and stimulate subordinates to high levels of effort. A major part of an organization's success, as Barnard saw it, depended on obtaining cooperation from its personnel. Barnard also argued that success depended on maintaining good relations with people and institutions outside the organization with whom the organization regularly interacted. By recognizing the organization's dependence on investors, suppliers, customers, and other external constituencies, Barnard introduced the idea that managers had to examine the environment and then adjust the organization to maintain a state of equilibrium. Regardless of how efficient an organization's production might be, if management failed either to ensure a continuous input of materials and supplies or to find markets for its outputs, then the organization's survival would be threatened.

Barnard is also important for his enlightened ideas on authority. The dominant or

traditional view of authority
The view that authority comes from above.

acceptance view of authority
The theory that authority comes from the willingness of subordinates to accept it.

Hawthorne studies
A series of studies during the 1920s and 1930s that provided new insights into group norms and behavior.

traditional view of authority at the time he wrote was that a superior's right to exact compliance from subordinates develops at the top and moves down through an organization. The ultimate source of a manager's authority, in the traditional view, was the society that allows the creation of social institutions. Barnard offered a contrasting position, arguing that authority comes from below. The **acceptance view of authority** proposed that authority comes from the willingness of subordinates to accept it. According to Barnard, there can be no such thing as persons of authority, but only persons to whom authority is addressed. Should an employee disobey a superior's directive, the disobedience is a denial of the directive's authority over the employee. Of course, superiors may be able to punish subordinates who don't comply; nevertheless, the superior's directive has not been complied with.

The Hawthorne Studies   Without question, the most important contribution to the human resources approach to management came out of the **Hawthorne studies** undertaken at the Western Electric Company's Hawthorne Works in Cicero, Illinois. These studies, originally begun in 1924 but eventually expanded and carried on through the early 1930s, were initially devised by Western Electric industrial engineers to examine the effect of various illumination levels on worker productivity. Control and experimental groups were established. The experimental group was presented with varying illumination intensities, while the control group worked under a constant intensity. The engineers had expected individual output to be directly related to the intensity of light. However, they found that as the light level was increased in the experimental group, output for both groups rose. To the surprise of the engineers, as the light level was dropped in the experimental group, productivity continued to increase in both groups. In fact, a productivity decrease was observed in the experimental group only when the light intensity had been reduced to that of moonlight. The engineers concluded that illumination intensity was not directly related to group productivity, but they could not explain the behavior they had witnessed.

In 1927, the Western Electric engineers asked Harvard professor Elton Mayo and his associates to join the study as consultants. Thus began a relationship that would last through 1932 and encompass numerous experiments covering the redesign of jobs, changes in the length of the workday and workweek, the introduction of rest periods, and individual versus group wage plans.[13] For example, one experiment

These six women were part of the experiments at the Hawthorne plant of Western Electric. The Hawthorne studies dramatized that a worker was not a machine, and scientific management's "one best way" approach had to be tempered to recognize the effects of group behavior.

was designed to evaluate the effect of a group piecework incentive pay system on group productivity. The results indicated that the incentive plan had less effect on a worker's output than did group pressure and acceptance and the concomitant security. Social norms or standards of the group, therefore, were concluded to be the key determinants of individual work behavior.

Scholars generally agree that the Hawthorne studies had a dramatic impact on the direction of management thought. Mayo's conclusions were that behavior and sentiments were closely related, that group influences significantly affected individual behavior, that group standards established individual worker output, and that money was less a factor in determining output than were group standards, group sentiments, and security. These conclusions led to a new emphasis on the human factor in the functioning of organizations and the attainment of their goals. They also led to increased paternalism by management.

The Hawthorne studies have not been without critics. Attacks have been made on procedures, analyses of the findings, and the conclusions drawn.[14] However, from an historical standpoint, it is of little importance whether the studies were academically sound or their conclusions justified. What is important is that they stimulated an interest in human factors. The Hawthorne studies went a long way in changing the dominant view at the time that people were no different than machines; that is, you put them on the shop floor, cranked in the inputs, and they produced a known quantity of outputs.

The Human Relations Movement   Another group within the human resources approach is important to management history for its unflinching commitment to making management practices more humane. Members of the **human relations movement** uniformly believed in the importance of employee satisfaction—a satisfied worker was believed to be a productive worker. For the most part, names associated with this movement—Dale Carnegie, Abraham Maslow, and Douglas McGregor—were individuals whose views were shaped more by their personal philosophies than by substantive research evidence.

Dale Carnegie is often overlooked by management scholars, but his ideas and teachings have had an enormous effect on management practice. His book, *How to Win Friends and Influence People,*[15] was read by millions in the 1930s, 1940s, and 1950s. In addition, during this same period, tens of thousands of managers and aspiring managers attended his management speeches and seminars.

What was the theme of Carnegie's book and lectures? Essentially, he said that the way to success was through winning the cooperation of others. Carnegie advised that the path to success resided in (1) making others feel important through a sincere appreciation of their efforts; (2) making a good first impression; (3) winning people to your way of thinking by letting others do the talking, being sympathetic, and "never telling a man he is wrong"; and (4) changing people by praising of good traits and giving the offender the opportunity to save face.[16]

Abraham Maslow, a humanistic psychologist, proposed a theoretical hierarchy of five needs: physiological, safety, social, esteem, and self-actualization.[17] In terms of motivation, Maslow argued that each step in the hierarchy must be satisfied before the next can be activated, and that once a need was substantially satisfied it no longer motivated behavior. Moreover, Maslow believed that self-actualization—that is, achieving one's full potential—was the summit of a human being's existence. Managers who accepted Maslow's hierarchy attempted to alter their organizations and management practices to reduce barriers that stood in the way of employees being able to self-actualize. In Chapter 16, we'll discuss and evaluate Maslow's need hierarchy in detail.

Douglas McGregor is best known for his formulation of two sets of assumptions—Theory X and Theory Y—about human nature.[18] We will also discuss these assump-

human relations movement
The belief, for the most part unsubstantiated by research, that a satisfied worker will be productive.

Abraham Maslow (1908-1970), a humanist psychologist, gave us one of our most widely recognized theories of motivation.

tions more fully in Chapter 16. Briefly, Theory X presents an essentially negative view of people. It assumes that they have little ambition, dislike work, want to avoid responsibility, and need to be closely directed to work effectively. On the other hand, Theory Y offers a positive view. It assumes that people can exercise self-direction, accept responsibility, and consider work to be as natural as rest or play. McGregor believed that Theory Y assumptions best captured the true nature of workers and should guide management practice.

The common thread that united human relations supporters, including Carnegie, Maslow, and McGregor, was an unshakeable optimism about people's capabilities. They believed strongly in their cause and were inflexible in their beliefs, even when faced with contradictory evidence. No amount of contrary experience or research evidence would alter their views. Of course, in spite of this lack of objectivity, advocates of the human relations movement had a definite influence on management theory and practice.

McGregor, for instance, taught for a dozen years at the Massachusetts Institute of Technology. Then he became the president of Antioch College. After six years at Antioch, he decided to return to his professorship at M.I.T. In his farewell address at Antioch, McGregor seemed to recognize that his philosophy had failed to cope with the realities of organizational life.

> I believed, for example, that a leader could operate successfully as a kind of adviser to his organization. I thought I could avoid being a "boss." Unconsciously, I suspect, I hoped to duck the unpleasant necessity of making difficult decisions, of taking the responsibility for one course of action, among many uncertain alternatives, of making mistakes and taking the consequences. I thought that maybe I could operate so that everyone would like me—that "good human relations" would eliminate all discord and disagreement. I couldn't have been more wrong. It took a couple of years, but I finally began to realize that a leader cannot avoid the exercise of authority any more than he can avoid responsibility for what happens to his organization.[19]

The irony in McGregor's case was that he went back to M.I.T. and began preaching his humanistic doctrine again. He continued doing so until his death.

Behavioral Science Theorists   One final category within the human resources approach encompasses a group of psychologists and sociologists who relied on the scientific method for the studying of organizational behavior. Unlike the theorists of the human relations movement, the **behavioral science theorists** engaged in *objective* research of human behavior in organizations. They carefully attempted to keep their personal beliefs out of their work. They sought to develop rigorous research designs that could be replicated by other behavioral scientists. In so doing, they hoped to build a science of organizational behavior.

behavioral science theorists
Psychologists and sociologists who relied on the scientific method for the study of organizational behavior.

Such psychologists as Fred Fiedler, Victor Vroom, Frederick Herzberg, Edwin Locke, David McClelland, and Richard Hackman have made important contributions to our current understanding of leadership, employee motivation, and the design of jobs. Researchers with a sociological perspective, too, have made significant advances toward our understanding of organizational behavior. For instance, Jeffrey Pfeffer, Kenneth Thomas, and Charles Perrow have added important insights to our understanding of power, conflict, and organization design. The contributions of each of these behavioral science theorists will be detailed in later chapters.

Putting the Human Resources Contributors into Perspective   Both scientific management and the general administrative theorists viewed organizations as machines. Managers were the engineers. They ensured that the inputs were available and that the machine was properly maintained. Any failure by the employee to generate the desired output was viewed as an engineering problem: It was time to redesign the job or grease the machine by offering the employee an incentive wage

ETHICAL
DILEMMAS IN
MANAGEMENT

Were Early Corporate Tycoons Benefactors or "Robber Barons"?

Management practices at the turn of the century were not always conducted with great integrity. People like Cornelius Vanderbilt and John D. Rockefeller built immensely successful railroads and oil companies by engaging in activities that some have described as unethical and irresponsible.

Vanderbilt gained control of the New York and Harlem railroad lines by bribing the New York state legislature and by stock manipulation. Rockefeller conspired with the railroads to extract rebates on his freight and obtained kickbacks on the oil that his rivals shipped. Rockefeller also engaged in ruthless competition, driving his competitors out of business and then buying their assets at a fraction of their value.

In spite of their unsavory practices, these early tycoons built companies that created tens of thousands of jobs and provided the industrial base for U.S. manufacturing preeminence during the first 60 years of this century. At one point, for instance, Vanderbilt employed more people than anyone in the United States. Some of these tycoons also returned a large portion of the profits they made back to society through their philanthropic efforts. Rockefeller, for instance, endowed the University of Chicago, gave millions to educate southern blacks, and established the Rockefeller Foundation, which continues to give away tens of millions of dollars each year.

Were business tycoons like Vanderbilt and Rockefeller benefactors or exploiters of society? Did they act unethically? What do *you* think?

plan. After all, who wouldn't work harder for a few more dollars? Apparently a lot of people! UPS, which we earlier described as being a modern-day proponent of scientific management principles, has pushed a number of its drivers so hard that they quit. As one driver put it, "They squeeze every ounce out of you. You're always in a hurry, and you can't work relaxed."[20] Contributors to the human resources approach forced managers in many organizations to reassess the simplistic machine-model view.

The Quantitative Approach

We close our discussion of the period of diversity with a review of quantitative contributions to the study of management. This approach has also been labeled as *operations research* or *management science.*

The quantitative approach to management evolved out of the development of mathematical and statistical solutions to military problems during World War II. For instance, when the British confronted the problem of how to get the maximum effectiveness from their limited aircraft capability against the massive forces of the Germans, they turned to their mathematicians to devise an optimum allocation model. Similarly, U.S. antisubmarine warfare teams used operations research techniques to improve the odds of survival for Allied convoys crossing the North Atlantic and for selecting the optimal depth-charge patterns for aircraft and surface vessel attacks on German U-boats.

After the war, many of the quantitative techniques that had been applied to military problems were moved into the business sector. One group of military

Today's managers regularly review quantitative data to improve their decision making.

officers, labeled the "Whiz Kids," joined Ford Motor Company in the mid-1940s and immediately began using statistical devices to improve decision making at Ford. Two of the most famous Whiz Kids were Robert McNamara and Charles "Tex" Thornton. McNamara rose to the presidency of Ford and then became U.S. Secretary of Defense. At the Department of Defense, he sought to quantify resource allocation decisions in the Pentagon through cost-benefit analyses. He concluded his career as head of the World Bank. Tex Thornton founded the billion-dollar conglomerate Litton Industries, again relying on quantitative techniques to make acquisition and allocation decisions.

What are these quantitative techniques, and how have they contributed to current management practice?

quantitative approach
The use of quantitative techniques to improve decision making.

The **quantitative approach** to management includes applications of statistics, optimization models, information models, and computer simulations. Linear programming, for instance, is a technique that managers can use to improve resource allocation choices. Work scheduling can be made more efficient as a result of critical-path scheduling analysis. Decisions on determining the optimum inventory levels a firm should maintain have been significantly influenced by the economic order quantity model.

The quantitative approach has contributed most directly to management decision making, particularly to planning and control decisions. Without denigrating the contribution of the quantitative approach it should be noted that it has never gained the influence on management practice that the human resources approach has. This is undoubtedly due to a number of factors: Many managers are unfamiliar with the quantitative tools; behavioral problems are more widespread and visible; and most students and managers can relate better to real, day-to-day people problems in organizations, such as motivating subordinates and reducing conflicts, than to the more abstract activity of constructing quantitative models.

Recent Years: Toward Integration

The previous discussion depicted four perspectives on management: the view of the foreman or supervisor, the whole organization, the manager as guiding and directing human resources, and the manager as developing quantitative models to make optimizing decisions. Each perspective has validity, but no single approach is a panacea. Occasional sporadic efforts were made during the period of diversity to synthesize the major writings of the time. For instance, in the early 1940s, Lyndall Urwick published *The Elements of Administration,* in which he noted numerous similarities in thought and terminology between scientific management and the general administrative theorists.[21] But these were exceptions. Concern with developing a unifying framework for management began in earnest only in the early 1960s. Like most fields of study, management, in its maturity, has moved toward integration.

The Process Approach

In December 1961, Professor Harold Koontz published an article in which he carefully detailed the diversity of approaches to the study of management and concluded that there existed a "management theory jungle."[22] Koontz conceded that each of the diverse approaches had something to offer management theory but then proceeded to demonstrate that (1) the human resources and quantitative approaches were not equivalent to the field of management, but rather were tools to be used by managers, and (2) a process approach could encompass and synthesize the diversity of the day. The **process approach,** originally introduced by Henri Fayol, is based on the management functions we discussed in the last chapter. The performance of these functions—planning, organizing, leading, and controlling—is seen as circular and continuous. (See Figure 1–3 on page 7).

Although Koontz' article stimulated considerable debate, most management teachers and practitioners held fast to their own individual perspectives.[22] But Koontz had made a mark. The fact that most current management textbooks follow the process approach is evidence that it continues to be a viable integrative framework.

The Systems Approach

The mid-1960s began a decade in which the idea that organizations could be analyzed in a systems framework gained a strong following. The **systems approach** defines a system as a set of interrelated and interdependent parts arranged in a manner that produces a unified whole. Societies are systems, and so too are automobiles, animals, and human bodies. The systems perspective, for instance, has been used by physiologists to explain how animals maintain an equilibrium state by taking in inputs and generating outputs.

There are two basic types of systems: closed systems and open systems. **Closed systems** are not influenced by and do not interact with their environment. Frederick Taylor's machine view of people and organizations was essentially a closed systems perspective. In contrast, an **open systems** approach recognizes the dynamic interaction of the system with its environment. While Barnard fostered the idea that organizations are open systems in the 1930s, widespread acceptance of the notion took another thirty years. Today, when we talk of organizations as systems, we mean open systems; that is, we acknowledge the organization's constant interaction with its environment.

Figure 2–1 shows a diagram of an organization from an open systems perspective. For a business firm, inputs would be material, labor, and capital. The transformation process would turn these inputs into finished products or services. The system's success depends on successful interactions with its environment; that is, those groups or institutions upon which it is dependent. These might include suppliers, labor unions, financial institutions, government agencies, and customers. The sale of outputs generates revenue, which can be used to pay wages and taxes, buy inputs, repay loans, and generate profits for stockholders. If revenues are not large enough to satisfy environmental demands, the organization shrinks or dies. As we discuss in the next chapter, management must understand its environment and the constraints that that environment imposes.

---

process approach
Management performs the functions of planning, organizing, leading, and controlling.

systems approach
A theory that sees an organization as a set of interrelated and interdependent parts.

closed systems
Systems that neither are influenced by nor interact with their environment.

open systems
Dynamic systems that interact with and respond to their environment.

FIGURE 2-1
The Systems Approach

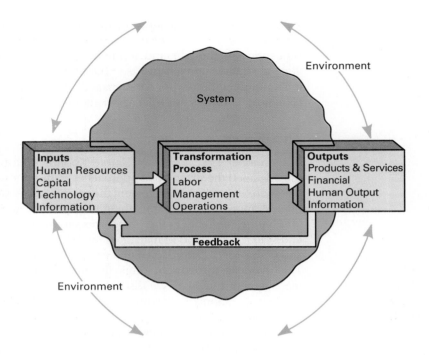

The contingency approach challenges the notion that "one size fits all." For the "best fit," management concepts need to be modified to reflect the situation.

How can the systems perspective be used to integrate the diverse approaches to management? Systems advocates envision the organization as being made up of "interdependent factors, including individuals, groups, attitudes, motives, formal structure, interactions, goals, status, and authority."[24] The job of a manager is to ensure that all parts of the organization are coordinated internally so that the organization's goals can be achieved. A systems view of management, for instance, would recognize that, regardless of how efficient the production department might be, if the marketing department does not anticipate changes in consumer tastes and work with the product development department in creating what consumers want, the organization's overall performance will be hampered. Similarly, if the purchasing department fails to acquire the right quantity and quality of inputs, the production department will not be able to do its job effectively. So the systems approach recognizes the interdependence of the various activities within the organization.

Additionally, the open systems approach recognizes that organizations are not self-contained. They rely on their environment for life-sustaining inputs and as sources to absorb their outputs. No organization can survive for long if it ignores government regulations, supplier relations, or the myriad of external constituencies upon which the organization depends.

The Contingency Approach

contingency approach
Recognizing and responding to situational variables as they arise.

Management, like life itself, is not based on simplistic principles. Insurance companies know that everyone doesn't have the same probability of being in an auto accident. Factors such as age, gender, past driving record, and number of miles driven per year are *contingencies* that influence accident rates. Similarly, you can't say that students always learn more in small classes than in large ones. An extensive body of research tells us that contingency factors such as course content and the teaching style of the instructor influence the relationship between class size and learning effectiveness. It's not just a coincidence that college courses in introductory psychology are often taught in mass lectures—the course content lends itself well to the straight lecture format. The **contingency approach** (sometimes called the

TABLE 2–4 Popular Contingency Variables

Organization Size. The number of people in an organization is a major influence on what managers do. As size increases, so do the problems of coordination. For instance, the type of organization structure appropriate for an organization of 50,000 employees is likely to be inefficient for an organization of fifty employees.

Routineness of Task Technology. In order for an organization to achieve its purpose, it uses technology; that is, it engages in the process of transforming inputs into outputs. Routine technologies require organizational structures, leadership styles, and control systems that differ from those required by customized or nonroutine technologies.

Environmental Uncertainty. The degree of uncertainty caused by political, technological, sociocultural, and economic changes influences the management process. What works best in a stable and predictable environment may be totally inappropriate in a rapidly changing and unpredictable environment.

Individual Differences. Individuals differ in terms of their desire for growth, autonomy, tolerance for ambiguity, and expectations. These and other individual differences are particularly important when managers select motivation techniques, leadership styles, and job designs.

---

situational approach) has been used in recent years to replace simplistic principles of management and to integrate much of management theory.[25]

Early management contributors, such as Taylor, Fayol, and Weber, gave us principles of management and organization that they generally assumed to be universally applicable. Later research, however, found exceptions to many of their principles. Division of labor, for example, is undoubtedly valuable in many situations, but jobs can also become *too* specialized. Insurance companies such as Travelers and Aid Association for Lutherans have found that they can successfully increase employee productivity by expanding rather than narrowing job tasks. Bureaucracy, as a structural form, is desirable in many situations, but there are places where other structural designs are *more* effective. Allowing employees to participate in decision making is sometimes a preferred leadership style, but not *all* the time. There are conditions under which leaders should autocratically make their decision and then tell their employees what it is.

A contingency approach to the study of management is intuitively logical. Since organizations are diverse—in size, objectives, tasks being done, and the like—it would be surprising to find that there would be universally applicable principles that would work in *all* situations. But, of course, it is one thing to say, *"It all depends"* and another to say *what* it depends upon. Management researchers, therefore, have been trying to identify these "what" variables. Table 2–4 describes four popular contingency variables. This list is not comprehensive—there are at least 100 different variables that have been identified—but it represents those most widely in use and gives you an idea of what we mean by the term *contingency variable*.

Current Trends and Issues: The Changing Face of Management Practice

Where are we today? What current management concepts and practices are shaping "tomorrow's history"? In this section, we'll answer these questions by introducing a number of trends and issues that are changing the way managers do their jobs. These issues will also be discussed in theme boxes, scattered throughout the book, entitled

"Managing From a Global Perspective," "Ethical Dilemmas in Management," and "The Changing Face of Management Practice."

Globalization

Management is no longer constrained by national borders. Burger King is owned by a British firm, and McDonald's sells hamburgers in Moscow. Exxon, a so-called American company, receives almost 75 percent of its revenues from sales outside the United States. Toyota makes cars in Kentucky, General Motors makes cars in Brazil, and Toyota and General Motors jointly own a plant that makes cars in California. Parts for Ford Motor Co.'s Crown Victoria come from all over the world: Mexico (seats, windshields, and fuel tanks); Japan (shock absorbers); Spain (electronic engine controls); Germany (antilock brake systems); and England (key axle parts). These examples illustrate that the world has become a global market and that effective managers need to adapt to cultures, systems, and techniques that are different from their own.

In the 1960s, Canada's prime minister described his country's proximity to the United States as analogous to sleeping with an elephant: "You feel every twitch the animal makes." In the 1990s, we can generalize this analogy to the entire world. A rise in interest rates in Germany instantly affects managers and organizations throughout the globe. The fall of Communism in Eastern Europe and the collapse of the Soviet Union create unlimited opportunities for business firms throughout the free world.

In Chapter 4, we'll explain the importance of viewing management globally and how this is changing the way managers do their job. We'll also reinforce this message with "Managing from a Global Perspective" boxes placed throughout the text.

Work Force Diversity

The bulk of the pre-1980s work force in North America consisted of male caucasians, working full-time to support a nonemployed wife and school-aged children. Such employees are now true minorities in organizations. At Levi Strauss, for instance, 56 percent of its 23,000 U.S. employees are minorities. Its top management level is 14 percent non-white and 30 percent female. Today's organizations are characterized by **work force diversity**—that is, workers are more heterogeneous in terms of gender,

work force diversity
Employees in organizations are heterogeneous in terms of gender, race, ethnicity or other characteristics.

When Jane Umanoff and Allen Parsons started their New York City bakery and catering firm, Umanoff and Parsons, they began hiring a diverse work force. 90 percent of their 35 current employees are foreign born—from Haiti, Trinidad, Jamaica, Grenada, the Dominican Republic, and Russia. Umanoff and Parsons have found out, after 15 years, that they are able to recruit excellent workers by expanding their search beyond the traditional white male candidates.

James Houghton at Corning

Some managers think that learning to understand and appreciate differences can be achieved merely by having people from diverse backgrounds work together. Others aggressively champion pluralism. One such champion is James Houghton, chairman of the board at Corning.[27]

Houghton found that between 1980 and 1987 turnover among women in professional jobs at Corning was double that of men and the rate for blacks was 2.5 times that for whites. This, incidentally, is not unusual. For example, one study reported that overall turnover rates for blacks in the U.S. work force are 40 percent higher than for whites.[28] Another study cited the turnover rate among women in management as being twice that among men.[29]

To find out why the turnover rate was so high among women and black professionals at Corning, Houghton appointed an internal task force. The task force concluded that peers didn't understand the special problems that blacks and women faced in the workplace. So Houghton created a diversity training program for managers and professionals. The company says that as a result of this program, the attrition rate for both blacks and women has declined.

race, and ethnicity. But diversity includes *anyone* who is different: the physically disabled, gays and lesbians, the elderly, and even those who are significantly overweight.

Until very recently, we took a "melting pot" approach to differences in organizations. We assumed that people who were different would somehow automatically want to assimilate. But we now recognize that employees don't set aside their cultural values and lifestyle preferences when they come to work. The challenge for management, therefore, is to make their organizations more accommodating to diverse groups of people by addressing different lifestyles, family needs, and work styles. The "melting pot" assumption is being replaced by the recognition and celebration of differences.[26]

As Figure 2–2 illustrates, new-worker growth in the United States through the rest of this decade will be occurring most rapidly among women and Hispanics. Almost two-thirds of all new entrants to the work force will be women. And by the year 2000, white non-Hispanic males will comprise only 39 percent of the total work force.[30]

Work force diversity has important implications for management practice. Managers will have to shift their philosophy from treating everyone alike to recognizing differences and responding to these differences in ways that will ensure employee retention and greater productivity, while at the same time not discriminating. Such organizations as Levi Strauss, Hewlett-Packard, Lotus Development, and U.S. West are providing sophisticated diversity training programs for their managers to help them better communicate, motivate, and lead.

Ethics

Many observers believe that we are currently suffering an ethics crisis. Behaviors that were once thought reprehensible—lying, cheating, misrepresenting, covering up

FIGURE 2-2
Composition of the New Worker Pool
(Percent increase in the number of new U.S. workers between 1987 and 2000)

Source: S. Pedigo, "Diversity in the Workforce: Riding the Tide of Change," *The Wyatt Communicator,* Winter 1991, p. 9.

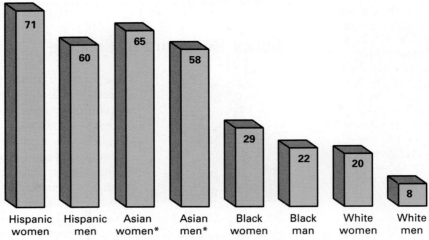

*Includes Native Americans and Pacific Islanders

mistakes—have become, in many people's eyes, acceptable or necessary practices. Managers profit from illegal use of insider information. Members of Congress write hundreds of bad checks. Even college students seem to have become caught up in this wave. A Rutgers University study of over 6000 students found that, among those anticipating careers in business, 76 percent admitted to having cheated on at least one test and 19 percent acknowledged having cheated on four or more tests.[31]

Concern over this perceived decline in ethical standards is being addressed at two levels. First, ethics education is being widely expanded in college curriculums. For instance, the primary accrediting agency for business schools now requires all its member programs to integrate ethical issues throughout their business curriculum. Second, organizations themselves are creating codes of ethics and introducing ethics training programs.

In Chapter 5, we'll discuss fundamental concepts relating to managerial ethics. In addition, we'll present a range of ethical dilemmas for you to consider in boxes placed throughout this book.

Stimulating Innovation and Change

The organizational world that existed when Taylor, Fayol, Weber, or even Koontz was writing no longer exists. Managers now confront an environment in which change is taking place at an unprecedented rate; new competitors spring up overnight and old ones disappear through mergers, acquisitions, or just failing to keep up with the changing marketplace. Constant innovations in computer and telecommunications technologies combined with the globalization of product and financial markets have created chaos. As a result, many of the past guidelines—created for a world that was far more stable and predictable—no longer apply. The successful organizations of the 1990s and beyond will be flexible, able to respond quickly, and led by managers who can effectively enact massive and revolutionary changes.

As you'll see in later chapters of this book, the need for innovation and change is requiring many organizations to reinvent themselves. Managers are restructuring their organizations by eliminating unnecessary levels of overhead, cutting redundant functions, and closing down low-performing units. And managers themselves are having to change their styles. They're transforming themselves from bosses into team leaders. Instead of telling people what to do, an increasing number of managers are finding that they become more effective when they focus on motivating, coaching, and cheerleading.

CEO Raymond Marlow, seen here with quality-assurance manager Julia Kendrick (left) and employee Theresa Waters, led Dallas-based Marlow Industries to a prestigious Malcolm Baldrige National Quality Award. With only 160 employees, this maker of thermoelectric coolers is the smallest business to ever win this award, which is given to recognize U.S. companies that excel in quality achievement and quality management.

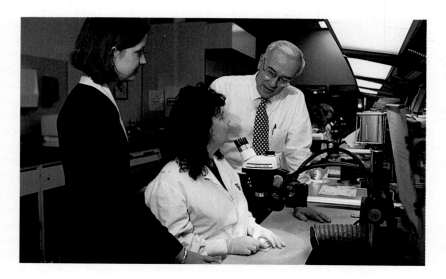

Total Quality Management

total quality management (TQM)

A philosophy of management that is driven by customer needs and expectations.

There is a quality revolution taking place in both business and the public sector.[32] The generic term that has evolved to describe this revolution is **total quality management,** or **TQM** for short. It was inspired by a small group of quality experts, the most prominent of them an American named W. Edwards Deming.

In 1950, Deming went to Japan and advised many top Japanese managers on how to improve their production effectiveness. Central to his management methods was the use of statistics to analyze variability in production processes. A well-managed organization, according to Deming, was one in which statistical control reduced variability and resulted in uniform quality and predictable quantity of output. Deming developed a fourteen-point program for transforming organizations. (We'll review this program in detail in Chapter 21 when we discuss operations management.)

Today, Deming's original program has been expanded into TQM—a philosophy of management that is driven by customer needs and expectations.[33] (See Table 2–5.)

TABLE 2-5   What is Total Quality Management?

1. Intense focus on the *customer*. The customer includes not only outsiders who buy the organization's products or services, but also internal customers (such as shipping or accounts payable personnel) who interact with and serve others in the organization.

2. Concern for *continual improvement*. TQM is a commitment to never being satisfied. "Very good" is not good enough. Quality can always be improved.

3. Improvement in the *quality of everything* the organization does. TQM uses a very broad definition of quality. It relates not only to the final product but how the organization handles deliveries, how rapidly it responds to complaints, how politely the phones are answered, and the like.

4. Accurate *measurement*. TQM uses statistical techniques to measure every critical variable in the organization's operations. These are compared against standards or benchmarks to identify problems, trace them to their roots, and eliminate their causes.

5. *Empowerment of employees*. TQM involves the people on the line in the improvement process. Teams are widely used in TQM programs as empowerment vehicles for finding and solving problems.

Importantly, however, the term "customer" in TQM is expanded beyond the traditional definition to include everyone who interacts with the organization's product or service either internally or externally. So TQM encompasses employees and suppliers, as well as the people who buy the organization's products or services. The objective is to create an organization committed to continuous improvement.

TQM represents a counterpoint to earlier management theorists who believed that low costs were the only road to increased productivity. The American automobile industry, in fact, represents a classic case of what can go wrong when attention is focused solely on trying to keep costs down. Companies like GM, Ford, and Chrysler ended up building products that a large part of the car-buying public rejected. Moreover, when the costs of rejects, repairing shoddy work, recalls, and expensive controls to identify quality problems were factored in, the American manufacturers actually were less productive than many foreign competitors. The Japanese demonstrated that it was possible for the highest quality manufacturers also to be among the lowest cost producers. Only recently have American auto manufacturers realized the importance of TQM and implemented many of its basic components, such as quality control groups, process improvement, teamwork, improved supplier relations, and listening to the needs and wants of customers.

TQM is important and we'll come back to it throughout the book. For example, we'll show the ways in which management can use TQM as a strategic weapon (Chapter 8) and for benchmarking competition (Chapter 9), the preferred structural design for TQM effectiveness (Chapter 11), the methods managers can use to implement TQM (Chapter 13), the role of teams in TQM (Chapter 15), and the quality improvement process in TQM (Chapter 21).

Empowerment

If you'll remember our discussion of scientific management, Frederick Taylor argued for the division of work and responsibility between management and workers. He wanted managers to do the planning and thinking. Workers were just to do what they were told. That prescription might have been good advice at the turn of the century, but today's workers are far better educated and trained than they were in Taylor's day. In fact, because of the complexity of many jobs, today's workers are often considerably more knowledgeable than their managers about how best to do their jobs. This fact has not been ignored by management. Managers recognize that they

In contrast to UPS, Federal Express empowers its people. It encourages and rewards them for efficiently managing their own time and for taking the initiative in quickly solving customer problems.

can often improve quality, productivity, and employee commitment by redesigning jobs and letting workers make job-related decisions. We call this process *empowering employees*.[34]

empowerment
Increasing the decision-making discretion of workers.

Empowerment builds on ideas originally made by human resources theorists. For many years, a lot of organizations stifled the capabilities of their work force. They overspecialized jobs and demotivated employees by treating them like unthinking machines. Recent successes at empowering employees in companies such as AT&T, Colgate-Palmolive, Delta Airlines, Federal Express, Motorola, and Wal-Mart suggest that the future lies in expanding the worker's role in his or her job rather than in practicing Taylor's segmentation of responsibilities.

The Bi-Modal Work Force

As recently as twenty years ago there were plenty of unskilled jobs in the steel, automobile, rubber, and similar manufacturing industries that paid solid middle-class wages. A young man in Pittsburgh, for example, could graduate from high school and immediately get a relatively high-paying and secure job in a local steel plant. That job would allow him to buy a home, finance a car or two, support a family, and enjoy other lifestyle choices that come with a middle-class income. But that's ancient history.[35] A good portion of those manufacturing jobs in first-world industrialized countries are gone—either replaced by automated equipment, reconstituted into jobs requiring considerably higher technical skills, or taken by workers in other countries who will do the same work for a fraction of the wages. What's left can best be described as a **bi-modal work force**—where employees tend to perform either low-skilled service jobs for near-minimum wages or high-skilled jobs that provide the means to maintain a middle-class or upper-class lifestyle.

bi-modal workforce
Employees tend to perform either low-skilled service jobs for near-minimum wage or high-skilled, well-paying jobs.

Figure 2–3 illustrates this bi-modal phenomenon, which has been created by the massive decline of blue-collar, manufacturing jobs that pay $25,000 to $35,000 a year in current dollars.

Most organizations' employee practices were designed to keep and motivate well-paid manufacturing employees and high-paid skilled workers. They don't, however, seem to be working very well with the low-skilled, low-paid service workers in the left curve of Figure 2–3.

At wages of $4.50 to $6.00 per hour, today's low-skilled workers can't come close to moving into the middle class. Moreover, their promotion opportunities are limited. This leads to a major challenge for managers: How do you motivate individuals who are making very low wages and have little opportunity to increase their pay signifi-

FIGURE 2–3
Wages for Low-Skilled and High-Skilled Labor

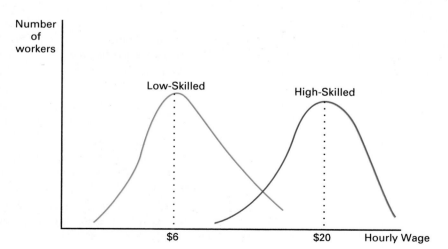

cantly either in their current jobs or through promotions? Can effective leadership make a difference? Can these employees' jobs be redesigned to make them more challenging? Does management have an ethical responsibility to raise these wages so they can provide employees with an adequate income? Should management target these jobs for elimination? These are questions that, until twenty years ago, managers didn't have to concern themselves with.

Summary

This summary is organized by the chapter-opening learning objectives found on page 27.

1. Studying management history helps you to understand theory and practice as they are today. It also helps you to see how current management concepts have evolved over time. Current management concepts are the result of continual development, testing, modification, retesting, and so on.

2. Important pre-twentieth-century contributions to management included the building of the Egyptian Pyramids, Adam Smith's writings on division of labor, and the Industrial Revolution. The building of the Pyramids was a monstrous project requiring the coordination of tens of thousands of workers. Clearly, this demanded management skills. Smith's writings on the manufacturing of pins vividly illustrated the dramatic economies that could be achieved through division of labor. The Industrial Revolution made it more economical to manufacture goods in factories, which, in turn, significantly increased the need for applying management techniques to production operations.

3. The first half of the twentieth century was a period of diversity in management thought. Scientific management sought production efficiencies by searching for "the one best way" to do each job. The general administrative theorists sought principles of management that applied to the entire organization. The human resources approach focused on the management of people. The quantitative approach used mathematical and statistical techniques to improve resource allocation decisions.

4. Frederick Taylor proposed four principles of management: (1) developing a science for each element of an individual's work, (2) scientifically selecting and training workers, (3) cooperating with workers, and (4) allocating responsibility to both management and workers.

5. Scientific management made possible dramatic increases—300 percent and more—in productivity. The application of its principles moved management from being a "seat-of-the-pants" practice to a serious, scientific discipline.

6. Henri Fayol was the first to define management as a universal set of functions: planning, organizing, commanding, coordinating, and controlling. He argued that management was an activity common to all human undertakings, and he identified fourteen principles of management that could be taught in schools and universities.

7. Max Weber defined the ideal bureaucracy as having division of labor, a clearly defined hierarchy, detailed rules and regulations, and impersonal relationships.

8. The Hawthorne studies led to a new emphasis on the human factor in the functioning of organizations and provided new insights into group norms and behavior. Management actively began to seek increased employee job satisfaction and higher morale.

9. Human relations advocates held strong personal convictions about people at work. They believed in the capability of people and argued for management practices that would increase employee satisfaction. In contrast, the behavioral

science theorists engaged in objective research on human behavior in organizations. They carefully attempted to keep their personal beliefs out of their scientific research.

10. A unifying framework for management began in earnest in the early 1960s. The process approach was proposed as a way to synthesize the diversity. Managers plan, organize, lead, and control according to the process approach. The systems approach recognizes the interdependency of internal activities in the organization and between the organization and its external environment. The contingency approach isolates situational variables that affect managerial actions and organizational performance.

11. Work force diversity refers to heterogeneity among workers in terms of gender, race, ethnicity, physical disabilities, sexual preference, age, or any other characteristic that makes people different.

12. Managers have become increasingly concerned with stimulating innovation and change because the environment in which organizations exist has become very dynamic. Successful organizations will be flexible, able to respond quickly, and led by managers who can effectively enact massive and revolutionary changes.

13. TQM focuses on the customer, seeks continual improvement, strives to improve the quality of everything, seeks accurate measurement, and empowers employees.

Review Questions

1. Explain the advantages of using division of labor in an organization.
2. How did the Industrial Revolution increase the need for a formal theory of management?
3. What relevance, if any, does scientific management have to current management practice? Explain.
4. How do Fayol's principles of management compare with Taylor's?
5. Describe the Hawthorne studies and their contribution to management practice.
6. How is the process approach integrative?
7. Explain how practicing managers can benefit by using the contingency approach.
8. What was W. Edwards Deming's contribution to management theory?
9. How can employee empowerment benefit organizations?
10. If the work force has truly become bi-modal, what are its implications for managers?

Discussion Questions

1. "The development of management thought has been determined by times and conditions." Do you agree or disagree with this statement? Discuss.
2. "Everyone wants a challenging job with opportunities for advancement." How does this statement reflect upon the human resources approach? How does it reflect upon empowerment and the bi-modal work force?
3. "Taylor and Fayol gave us some specific principles of management. The contingency approach says, 'it all depends.' We've gone backward in seventy-five

years—from a set of specific principles to a set of vague and ambiguous guidelines." Do you agree or disagree with this statement? Discuss.

4. It has been said that those who cannot remember the past are condemned to relive it. Analyze this statement by creating a scenario that demonstrates how the history of management thought could help you be a better manager today.

5. "TQM includes contributions from scientific management, the human resources approach, and the quantitative approach." Do you agree or disagree? Discuss.

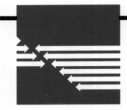

SELF-ASSESSMENT EXERCISE

Are You the Quantitative Type?

Instructions: Do numbers make you nervous? Do you suffer from math anxiety? To find out, score each of the following situations with the figure that corresponds to the intensity of your reaction.

Relaxed (1)
A little tense (2)
Tense (3)
Very tense (4)

How Do You Feel When You Are Called on to:				
1. Determine the amount of change you should get back from a purchase involving several items?	1	2	3	4
2. Calculate how much it will cost to buy a product on credit, figuring in the interest rate?	1	2	3	4
3. Total up a dinner bill for which you think you were over-charged?	1	2	3	4
4. Tell the waiter that you think the dinner bill is incorrect, then watch him total it up?	1	2	3	4
5. Estimate the number of words in an article or paper that you are trying to write to a specified length?	1	2	3	4
6. Figure out the number of pages left in a novel you are reading?	1	2	3	4
7. Compute the miles per gallon on your car?	1	2	3	4
8. Read your W-2 form?	1	2	3	4
9. Check over your monthly bank statement?	1	2	3	4
10. Listen to someone describe how to set the shutter speed, film speed, and *f*-stop readings on your new single-lens reflex camera?	1	2	3	4
11. Check someone else's figures in a simple calculation, such as addition or division?	1	2	3	4
12. Play card games, such as bridge or poker, that involve scoring?	1	2	3	4

13. Add 976 and 777 in your head?	1	2	3	4
14. Add 976 and 777 with a pencil and paper?	1	2	3	4
15. Listen to explanations about bank interest rates as you decide on a savings account?	1	2	3	4

Turn to page SK-1 of the Scoring Key for directions.

Source: Adapted from the *Mathematics Anxiety Rating Scale (MARS)*, copyright © 1972 by Richard M. Suinn. All rights reserved. Published by RMBSI, Inc., P.O. Box 1066, Ft. Collins, Colo. 80522.

The *Walt Disney* Company©

To: Staff Assistant
From: Director of Human Resources; Disney University; Orlando, Florida
Subject: New topics for our management training program

It's imperative that we keep the content of our management training program current. I read a wide variety of business and management periodicals to keep abreast of the latest findings and trends. But I'm always concerned that I may have overlooked some important new ideas.

To ensure that our program is current, I want you to do a literature search for me. Go to the library and review all the issues published in the last six months from one of the following periodicals: *Business Week, Fortune, Industry Week,* or *Nation's Business.*

Review the selected issues carefully to identify the latest management concept or technique that we might consider for inclusion in our training program. Give me a one-page memo in which you: (1) describe the concept or technique; (2) identify the positive effect on management according to its proponents; and (3) list what limitations might restrict its effectiveness in use by managers at Disney World.

This is a fictionalized account of a potentially real problem. It was written for academic purposes only and is not meant to reflect either positively or negatively on actual management practices at the Walt Disney Co.

Case Application

Reinventing Pro Fasteners Inc.

Steve Braccini started his San Jose, California company, Pro Fasteners Inc., in the early 1980s. Steve was president and head salesman. His wife, Cinde, ran the office. Their business? Distribution of industrial hardware and components to the electronics industry. After approximately a decade, Steve had built his company to annual sales of $5 million, and he had 25 employees.

Steve ran Pro by sheer force of will. His outgoing personality and perpetual restlessness acted as an energy force to drive the company. He got to work early and spent his days working the phones, giving orders, and ensuring that he was involved in every decision. At night he would unwind with a bottle.

Steve's strategy for Pro Fasteners was simple: Do tomorrow what you did today—only try to do a little more. He had little vision of where he wanted to go and certainly no plan for how to get there. But Steve had recently decided that it was time to get his drinking problem under control. He checked into the famed Betty Ford Clinic. He spent twenty-eight days learning to live without alcohol. When he got out, not only was he dry, he was a man with a mission.

"I began to realize a lot of things about myself," Steve said, "and the theories I had about myself for some reason corresponded to the business. The better I took care of myself, for example, the better I felt and the better I did. It was like this light went on. 'Oh—so the better I take care of the customers, the better they'll feel about me . . .' And it just went on from there." Cinde added, "The improvement he had chosen for himself he also imposed on Pro Fasteners. It was like, 'I've now realized something about myself—and *we* are going to change.'"

Steve wanted to soak up as much information on contemporary management concepts as he could. He read all the latest books on quality, empowerment, and team building. He began talking to other company presidents about what they were doing. He joined organizations made up of CEOs and entrepreneurs in order to tap others' ideas.

This was the beginning of Steve Braccini's attempt to reinvent his company. He was determined to reexamine every facet of Pro's operations. He wanted to transform its internal operations to ensure first-rate quality and service. He wanted to respond to the changing needs of his customers. He wanted to make sure that, at Pro Fasteners, the customer was king.

"Our customers weren't just saying, 'I want this part,'" said Steve. "It was 'I want it on my shelf all the time. And I want you to make sure it's there all the time.'" Implicit in each of these requests was both a promise and a threat. The promise was, "if you deliver the goods, there is a long term contract open," and the threat, "if you don't, we'll eliminate you as an approved vendor." Steve understood the implications. He was in a fiercely competitive business. His customers were slashing their supplier lists, and the distributors that survived would be the ones that best met their customers' needs.

Steve Braccini was determined that he was going to be one of the survivors. But he knew it would require turning his business upside down.

Questions

1. Drawing on contemporary management ideas introduced in this chapter, describe what Steve Braccini might do to reinvent his company.

2. Given that he takes the actions you suggested, what problems might he confront? What can he do to handle these problems?

Based on John Case, "Quality With Tears," *INC.*, June 1992, pp. 83–95.

VIDEO CASE
The U.S. Military as a Model in Race Relations

So far, the 1990s haven't been a particularly good decade for the U.S. Armed Forces. The end of the Cold War has resulted in plans for huge cuts in the military budget and major reductions in force. The Tailhook scandal exposed a long tradition of sexual harassment in the Navy. And President Clinton's attemjpt to eliminate discrimination against gays and lesbians in the military created a small furor among military brass and Congressional representatives. General Colin Powell, the military's highest ranking African-American, boldly challenged the President on the gay and lesbian issue, arguing that they undermine morale and discipline.

It might come somewhat as a surprise, then, to learn that the U.S. military represents a model of equal opportunity employment that business firms would do well to emulate. There is probably no other American institution that has as successfully eliminated discrimination toward blacks.

Following the Vietnam War, the Pentagon faced the reality that it could not staff the new all-volunteer military with whites alone. Blacks had to be actively recruited. Previous barriers in hiring, training, and promotion had to be removed. And they were.

Until the recent military cutbacks, the armed services had become one of the few institutions where blacks could feel confident that they would be judged on their job performance and not the color of their skin. In the early 1990s, while less than 20 percent of all white male high school graduates who were qualified for the service actually joined, more than 50 percent of comparably qualified black males did. The reason? The military had become the United States' largest equal opportunity employer. While Corporate America talks about the goal of equal opportunity, the military has succeeded in making it work. They've instilled the commitment to equality up and down the chain of command through extensive training and control of rewards. Young officers learn rapidly that prejudice and promotions don't coexist in the U.S. military.

Questions

1. The Civil Rights Act of 1964 outlawed racial discrimination. How successful do you think we've been in eliminating racial discrimination in Corporate America?

2. "The human resources approach to management opened the doors in organizations for women and people of color." Do you agree or disagree? Discuss.

3. What insights can corporate managers gain from this case for facilitating work force diversity?

4. Why is the military resisting the elimination of discrimination toward lesbians and gays? Aren't these arguments the same used to try to keep blacks out of the military fifty years ago?

Source: "Military as Model to Firms of Equal Opportunity Employer," *ABC World News Tonight*, June 23, 1992.

INTEGRATIVE EXERCISE FOR PART I

MANAGERIAL ROLES

PURPOSE

1. To examine the key components of a manager's job.
2. To contrast the job of a first-level supervisor with that of a top executive.
3. To apply the role concept to actual jobs.

REQUIRED KNOWLEDGE

1. The functions and roles of a manager's job.
2. The effect of organizational level on a manager's job.

TIME REQUIRED

Approximately 45 minutes.

INSTRUCTIONS

Consider the jobs of (a) supervisor of the painting department at the St. Louis assembly plant of Chrysler Corporation and (b) Chairman of the Board and Chief Executive Officer of Chrysler Corporation.

Table I–A presents a list of roles in which the supervisor and CEO might engage. For each of the above jobs:

1. List any of the roles that would *not* be relevant to the job and explain why.
2. For the remaining roles, give a specific example of something each might do as part of that job.
3. Rank in order the applicable roles for each job on the basis of the amount of time devoted to each role. (Give the role that demands the most time the number 1. No ties are allowed.)
4. Form into groups of three to five students. Discuss your individual analyses and, as a group, arrive at a rank order for each job, just as you did in the previous step individually.
5. Each group will appoint a spokesperson to present your group's conclusions and discuss the group decision with the class.

TABLE 1–A Allocation of Time for Chrysler Managers

Managerial Role	Specific Example*	Individual Ranking	Group Ranking
Job: Supervisor of Painting Department			
Figurehead			
Leader			
Liaison			
Monitor			
Disseminator			
Spokesperson			
Entrepreneur			
Disturbance handler			
Resource allocator			
Negotiator			
Job: Chairman of the Board and Chief Executive Officer			
Figurehead			
Leader			
Liaison			
Monitor			
Disseminator			
Spokesperson			
Entrepreneur			
Disturbance handler			
Resource allocator			
Negotiator			

*Write NA if not applicable, then explain why.

INTEGRATIVE CASE FOR PART I

A DAY IN THE LIFE OF CHUCK STONEMAN

Chuck Stoneman really believes in the old cliche "The early bird gets the worm." It's Tuesday morning, and Chuck has already been up for an hour. He spent twenty minutes on his stationary bike, showered, dressed, ate breakfast, and gave the morning newspaper a quick review. As Chuck pulls out of his driveway, he glances at his watch: 5:28 a.m.! It's only a 15 minute drive from Chuck's home to his office, where he's the Omaha plant manager for Lerner Bros. Foods. Lerner Bros. manufactures beef and pork products that are sold as private label brands at between sixty and seventy large supermarket chains.

As Chuck begins the drive, his thoughts float back to last night. He and his wife, Anne, had dinner out to celebrate their fifteenth wedding anniversary. They had talked about how they met—on a blind date arranged by mutual friends—and how they had both expected the worst. And they talked fondly of old friends that

they hadn't heard from in years. The talk last night made Chuck nostalgic. His mind begins to wander. He's thinking about how he ended up in Omaha, running a processing plant, with 650 people working for him.

Chuck graduated from the University of Illinois with a business degree in 1979. His first and only job was with Lerner Bros. He started as an assistant production scheduler in the Chicago plant. During the next dozen years, he moved through a series of jobs—senior production scheduler, production foreman, shift foreman, and assistant plant manager at the Kansas City operation. In 1991, he was promoted to his current job. An abbreviated organization chart shows where Chuck is on the "Lerner hierarchy" and the people who immediately report to him. (See Figure I–1.) Chuck and Anne like Omaha. It's a great place to raise their two kids, and Anne is finally getting the opportunity to use her degree in statistics as an actuary at Mutual of Omaha.

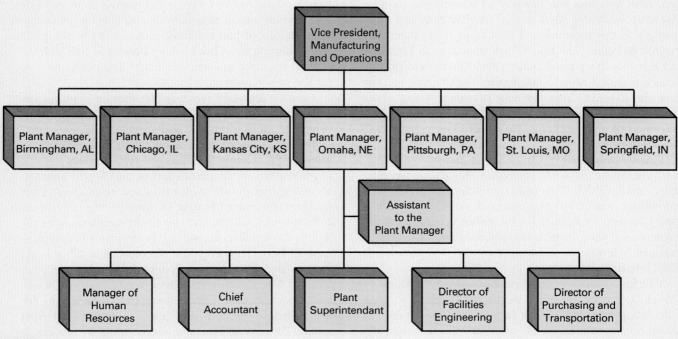

FIGURE I–1
Excerpt from Lerner Bros. Foods' Organization Chart

Chuck is in good spirits this morning. Recent productivity reports showed that Omaha had surpassed both the Kansas City and Birmingham plants and now has the highest per-employee labor productivity. For ten months running, Omaha has been the most profitable of the company's seven plants. Yesterday, in a phone call with his boss, Chuck learned that there was a $23,000 check on its way to him—his semi-annual performance bonus. In the past, the largest bonus Chuck had ever gotten has been for $8500.

Chuck is determined to get a lot accomplished today. As usual, he has kept his commitments to a minimum. Except for the 3:30 p.m. staff meeting, his day is open so he can get a number of important issues resolved. He's going to review the recent internal audit report carefully and rough out his response. He's going to go over the progress on the plant's TQM program. Chuck wants to begin planning next year's capital equipment budget. It's due in less than two weeks and he hasn't found time to get to it. Chuck also has a number of other important items on his "to do" list: Talk with the plant superintendent about several employee grievances; write the 10 minute speech he is expected to give at Friday's Chamber of Commerce meeting; and review his assistant's written response to OSHA, following their recent safety inspection.

Chuck arrives at the plant at 5:45. As he makes his way toward his office, he is intercepted by Beth, the general accounting supervisor. His first reaction: What is she doing here this early in the morning? He soon finds out. Beth tells him that her payroll coordinator didn't show up yesterday. Beth stayed until 10 p.m. last night and got in this morning at 4:30 a.m. to try to meet the payroll deadline. She tells Chuck that there is no way to get this month's payroll data to headquarters in on time. Chuck makes a note to talk to the plant's chief accountant and to let his boss, the vice president, know about the problem. Chuck prides himself on keeping his boss informed of any problems. He never likes to have his boss surprised.

Finally, in his office, Chuck notes that his computer is flashing. There are some messages. Reviewing his electronic mail, Chuck finds only one item that needs immediate action. His assistant had worked out next year's vacation schedule for the entire management and professional staff. It must be reviewed and approved. It takes only ten minutes, but it is another ten minutes that Chuck hadn't planned on.

The first priority is the capital equipment budget. Chuck uses his computer's worksheet program to begin calculating what equipment he needs and what the cost of each item will be. Barely one third through the pro-

ject, Chuck gets a call from the superintendent's office. During the night shift, one of the three main conveyor systems went out. Maintenance can overhaul it for a cost of about $45,000. The money isn't in the expense budget. To replace the system will cost about $120,000, and Chuck has already spent this year's capital budget. He arranges a meeting with the superintendent and plant accountant for 10 a.m.

Chuck is back working on the spreadsheet when the plant's transportation director pops into his office. He's having difficulty with rail car scheduling. After 20 minutes of discussion, the two work out a solution. Chuck makes a note to talk with the head of corporate transportation to complain about rail services to his plant. Are the other plants having similar problems? When does the company's rail contract come up again for bidding?

The interruptions on Chuck's day never seem to end. He gets a call from the legal staff at corporate headquarters. They need data to defend the company in a discrimination suit by a former Omaha employee. He transfers the call to his human resources department. Chuck's secretary has a number of letters that need his signature. Suddenly it's 10 o'clock. The accountant and superintendent are outside Chuck's office. The three review the conveyor system problem and rough out some options. They'll present them at this afternoon's staff meeting. It's now 11:15. No sooner does Chuck return to the capital budget than he gets a call from the head of corporate human resources. She spends half-an-hour updating Chuck on the company's strategy in the forthcoming union negotiations and getting his opinion about issues of particular concern to the Omaha plant. After hanging up, Chuck walks down the hall to his human resource manager's office. They compare notes on the negotiation strategy.

Chuck's secretary reminds him that he's late for his noon lunch with the local head of Omaha's Red Cross drive. He races to his car and arrives 10 minutes late.

By 1:45, Chuck's back at his office. The plant superintendent is waiting for him. The two go over modifications in the plant's layout and access areas to meet legal requirements for disabled employees. The meeting runs long because of three phone interruptions. Now it's 3:35. Chuck and the superintendent cross the hall to the conference room. The staff meeting typically runs an hour. However, the discussions of labor negotiations and the conveyor system problem prove lengthy. The meeting lasts over two hours. As Chuck walks back to his office, he realizes that he has to be getting home. He and Anne are hosting a dinner party tonight for several business and community leaders.

The drive home seems more like an hour than 15 minutes to Chuck. He's frustrated. Twelve hours earlier he was anxiously awaiting a productive day. With that day now gone, he wonders, "Did I accomplish *any-thing?*" He knows, of course, he has, but there was so much more he wanted to get done. Was today unique? Chuck has to admit it wasn't. He starts every day with good intentions and leaves frustrated. His days are a stream of fragmented activities, with constant unplanned interruptions. Did he plan his day poorly? He isn't sure. He purposely keeps his daily schedule open so he can communicate with people and be available when they need him. But he wonders if all managers' jobs are characterized by constant interruptions and putting out fires. Will he ever have time for planning and fire prevention?

Questions

1. How do you think Chuck's job compares with the typical manager's job?

2. Evaluate Chuck's activities in terms of Mintzberg's managerial roles.

3. Evaluate Chuck's activities in terms of the four functions of planning, organizing, leading, and controlling.

4. Evaluate Chuck's day in terms of the systems approach.

5. Is Chuck *efficient* at his job? *Effective?* Explain.

6. What, if anything, could Chuck do to be a better manager?

CHAPTER 3

Organizational Culture and Environment: The Constraints

LEARNING OBJECTIVES

After Reading This Chapter, You Should Be Able To:

1. Differentiate the symbolic from the omnipotent view of management.
2. Define organizational culture.
3. Identify the ten characteristics that make up an organization's culture.
4. Explain how culture constrains managers.
5. Distinguish between the general and specific environment.
6. Contrast certain and uncertain environments.
7. Explain how the environment constrains managers.

Johnson & Johnson no longer sells Tylenol in capsule form because of two apparently unrelated poisonings. Tylenol is now sold as solid caplets. These poisonings cost J&J a half-billion dollars and significantly hurt the company's financial performance, yet these incidents were something over which management had little control.

$\mathbf{I}$n the fall of 1982, eight Chicago-area residents died after taking Extra-Strength Tylenol capsules that had been laced with cyanide. In the winter of 1986, in a similar scenario, a New York woman died from a cyanide-laced Tylenol capsule. In both cases, the management at McNeil Consumer Products, the manufacturer and a division of Johnson & Johnson (J&J), claimed that it was blameless. Thorough investigations proved it right. Both poisonings were clearly the actions of deranged individuals. That fact, however, didn't reduce the devastating impact the poisonings had on Tylenol's sales and J&J's profits.[1]

After the 1982 incident, J&J recalled and destroyed 31 million bottles of Tylenol capsules, resulting in an after-tax write-off of $50 million. The company then spent nearly $300 million more to promote its repackaged "triple-sealed to resist tampering" capsules. It succeeded in restoring public trust in the product and reclaiming its market position. But after the 1986 poisoning, J&J's management decided to abandon the use of capsules in all its over-the-counter drugs and instead market them in the form of solid caplets. Again, the costs were high; approximately $150 million was spent to recall the capsules, reorganize the production process, and promote the new caplets.

Is the J&J case unique? It is if you focus on the tampering with the Tylenol product. But this case is not unique if you look at it as an instance where management is hit broadside by some action that it did not create and that it has little control over. A more recent incident confirms this point. In September 1992, a well-publicized Finnish study was released that showed a clear and strong relationship between a high level of iron in the body and heart attacks. Suddenly, iron supplement products were under siege. For the management of SmithKline Beecham PLC, which makes Geritol and other iron supplements, it was a devastating blow. With a sudden decline in sales, management was forced to redirect company resources to bolstering its iron supplement product lines.

J&J's and SmithKline's troubles were not of their own making. Incidents such as these raise the question of whether an organization's successes or failures are always directly attributable to management.

The Manager: Omnipotent or Symbolic?

omnipotent view
The view that managers are directly responsible for the success or failure of an organization.

symbolic view
The view that management has only a limited effect on substantive organizational outcomes because of the large number of factors outside of management's control.

The dominant view in management theory and in society is that managers are directly responsible for an organization's success or failure. We'll call this perspective the **omnipotent view of management.** In contrast, some observers have argued that managers have little influence on organizational outcomes. Instead, much of an organization's success or failure is said to be due to forces outside management's control. This perspective has been labeled the **symbolic view of management.**[2]

In this section, we want to review each of these positions. Our reason should be obvious. The analysis will go a long way in clarifying just how much credit or blame managers should receive for their organization's performance.

The Omnipotent View

In Chapter 1, we said, "Good managers can turn straw to gold. Poor managers can do the reverse." These statements reflect a dominant assumption in management theory: The quality of an organization's managers determines the quality of the organization itself. It's assumed that differences in an organization's effectiveness or efficiency are due to the decisions and actions of its managers. Good managers anticipate change, exploit opportunities, correct poor performance, and lead their organizations toward their objectives (and even change those objectives when necessary). When profits are up, management takes the credit and rewards itself with bonuses, stock options, and the like. When profits are down, the board of directors replaces top management in the belief that new management will bring improved results. As a case in point, the board at Prudential Securities replaced the firm's chief executive, George Ball, in early 1991.[3] Although he had held the job since 1982, big losses in 1990 brought about Ball's departure.

This view of managers as omnipotent is consistent with the stereotypical picture of the swashbuckling, take-charge executive who can overcome any obstacle in carrying out the organization's objectives. Chrysler's recently retired chairman Lee Iacocca, for example, became an American corporate folk hero in the mid-1980s as a result of his company's performance. When Iacocca took over Chrysler in the late 1970s, it was on the verge of bankruptcy. In 1980, the company lost $1.7 billion. But Iacocca cut costs and introduced new products, including the minivan. In 1984, Chrysler netted $2.4 billion in profits and Iacocca got most of the credit for the turn-around.[4] This omnipotent view, of course, is not limited to business organizations. It can, for instance, help to explain the high turnover among college coaches.

College coaches manage their teams. They decide which players to recruit and

Bobby Knight, the extremely successful basketball coach at Indiana University, earns high pay and is allowed his occasional instances of bizarre behavior. This reflects the omnipotent view—held by the IU administration, community, and alumni—that Knight is directly responsible for the success of the IU basketball program.

which players start, select assistant coaches, teach plays to their teams, and select every play during games. Coaches who lose more games than they win are seen as ineffective. They are fired and replaced by new coaches who, it is assumed, will correct the inadequate performance.

Regardless of extenuating circumstances, when organizations perform poorly, someone has to be held accountable. In our society, that role is played by management. Of course, when things go well, management gets the credit—even if it had little to do with causing the positive outcome.

The Symbolic View

A few years back, the board of directors of International Harvester (now called Navistar International) fired the company's chairman and chief executive officer, Archie McCardell. The company was losing tens of millions of dollars a month because farmers, suffering from depressed farm prices, couldn't afford to buy the farm machinery and heavy-duty trucks that International Harvester made. Of course, McCardell hadn't created the farm problem, nor was his firing likely to increase the demand for farm machinery and trucks. He was merely in the wrong place at the wrong time, and he lost his job because of it.

This example illustrates the symbolic view of managers. The symbolic view assumes that a manager's ability to affect outcomes is highly constrained. In this view, it is unreasonable to expect managers to have much of an effect on an organization's performance.

According to the symbolic view, an organization's results are influenced by a number of factors outside the control of management. These include the economy, government policies, competitors' actions, the state of the particular industry, the control of proprietary technology, and decisions made by previous managers in the organization. Referring back to our Chrysler example, it is interesting that by the late 1980s, Chrysler was again in financial trouble and suffering large losses. While some observers blamed Chrysler's problems on poor decisions made by Iacocca and his management team, a more plausible explanation lies outside Iacocca's control: Overcapacity in the industry created by new Japanese plants in the U.S.[5]

Following the symbolic view, management has, at best, only a limited effect on *substantive organizational outcomes.* What management does affect greatly are *symbolic* outcomes.[6] Management's role is seen as creating meaning out of randomness, confusion, and ambiguity. Management creates the illusion of control for the benefit of stockholders, customers, employees, and the public. When things go right, we need someone to praise. Management plays that role. Similarly, when things go wrong, we need a scapegoat. Management plays that role, too. However, according to the symbolic view, the *actual* part management plays in success or failure is minimal.

Reality Suggests a Synthesis

In reality, managers are neither impotent nor all-powerful. Internal constraints that restrict a manager's decision options exist within every organization. These internal constraints are derived from the organization's culture. In addition, external constraints impinge on the organization and restrict managerial freedom. These external constraints come from the organization's environment.

Figure 3–1 depicts the manager as operating within constraints. The organization's culture and environment press against the manager, restricting his or her options. Yet, in spite of these constraints, managers are not powerless. There still remains an area in which managers can exert a significant amount of influence on an organization's performance—an area in which good managers differentiate themselves from poor

Is the decline in sales of Rolls Royces and the company's recent losses due to poor management? A case can be made that Rolls Royce did well in the 1980s because of worldwide prosperity and a belief among consumers that "if you've got it, flaunt it." Rolls Royce was in the right place at the right time. In the early 1990s, a prolonged recession, the imposition of a luxury tax, and changing societal views that now frowned on conspicuous consumption all have ganged up to seriously hurt Rolls Royce sales. The declining sales are not management's fault. Rather, there are fewer people able to afford $100,000+ cars, and among those who can, it is no longer fashionable.

ones. In the remainder of this chapter, we'll discuss organizational culture and environment as constraints. But, as we'll also point out later in this book, these constraints need not be regarded as fixed in all situations. For some organizations, in certain circumstances, it may be possible to change and influence their culture and environment and thus expand their management's area of discretion.

The Organization's Culture

organizational culture
A system of shared meaning within an organization that determines, in large degree, how employees act.

We know that every individual has something that psychologists have termed "personality." An individual's personality is made up of a set of relatively permanent and stable traits. When we describe someone as warm, innovative, relaxed, or conservative, we are describing personality traits. An organization, too, has a personality, which we call the organization's *culture.*

What Is Organizational Culture?

What do we specifically mean by the term **organizational culture?** We use the term to refer to a system of *shared meaning.* Just as tribal cultures have totems and taboos that dictate how each member will act toward fellow members and outsiders, organizations have cultures that govern how its members should behave. In every organization, there are systems or patterns of values, symbols, rituals, myths, and practice that have evolved over time.[7] These shared values determine, in large degree, what employees see and how they respond to their world.[8] When confronted with a problem, the organizational culture restricts what employees can do by suggesting the correct way—"the way we do things here"—to conceptualize, define, analyze, and solve the problem.

Our definition of culture implies several things. First, culture is a perception. But this perception exists in the organization, not in the individual. As a result, individuals with different backgrounds or at different levels in the organization tend to describe

FIGURE 3–1
Parameters of Managerial
Discretion

the organization's culture in similar terms. That is the *shared* aspect of culture. Second, organizational culture is a descriptive term. It is concerned with how members perceive the organization, not with whether or not they like it. It describes rather than evaluates.

Though we currently have no definitive method for measuring an organization's culture, preliminary research suggests that cultures can be analyzed by assessing how an organization rates on ten characteristics.[9] They have been identified as follows:

1. *Member identity:* the degree to which employees identify with the organization as a whole rather than with their type of job or field of professional expertise.

2. *Group emphasis:* the degree to which work activities are organized around groups rather than individuals.

3. *People focus:* the degree to which management decisions take into consideration the effect of outcomes on people within the organization.

4. *Unit integration:* the degree to which units within the organization are encouraged to operate in a coordinated or interdependent manner.

5. *Control:* the degree to which rules, regulations, and direct supervision are used to oversee and control employee behavior.

6. *Risk tolerance:* the degree to which employees are encouraged to be aggressive, innovative, and risk-seeking.

ETHICAL DILEMMAS IN MANAGEMENT

Whistleblowing
Reporting unethical practices by your employer to outsiders such as the press, government agencies, or public interest groups.

Should Organizations Protect Whistleblowers?

What do you do when you discover that your boss or your entire organization is engaged in unethical practices? If you're an employee of the federal government, the 1989 Whistleblower's Protection Act provides you with means of redress and protection. If you are an employee of one of the nineteen state governments with similar legislation, you're also protected. But what if you're not among this select group?

Some organizations have created cultures that encourage free expression of controversial or dissenting views, protect employees with formal grievance procedures, and provide mechanisms whereby employees can anonymously report unethical practices to senior management. Others, however, regard **whistleblowing**—reporting unethical practices to outsiders such as the press, government agencies, or public interest groups—as the ultimate demonstration of disloyalty. Whistleblowing embarrasses managers and erodes their authority. In such organizations, whistleblowing can mean putting one's job or entire career on the line.

On the other hand, does loyalty to an organization require you to ignore unethical or illegal practices? Does an employee have to forgo his or her rights to free speech in order to keep a job? Many states have passed laws to protect whistleblowers. But even where there is legal protection, employees often still fear subtle forms of retaliation if they embarrass their boss, senior management, or the organization. What do *you* think about whistleblowing? Would *you* be willing to blow the whistle if it meant risking your job?

FIGURE 3–2
Characteristics of an
Organization's Culture

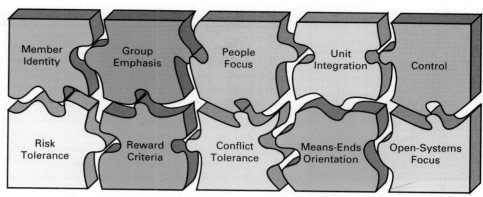

Organizational Culture

Elvis sighted in Vermont! To relieve the tension of work, Ben & Jerry's Homemade sponsors events like Elvis Day in which everyone—from top managers to production employees—is encouraged to participate. An essential part of Ben & Jerry's culture is a steadfast belief in fun. This culture affects the way the workers view the company and helps to keep the organization, and the ice cream, flowing smoothly.

7. *Reward criteria:* the degree to which rewards such as salary increases and promotions are allocated on employee performance criteria in contrast to seniority, favoritism, or other nonperformance factors.

8. *Conflict tolerance:* the degree to which employees are encouraged to air conflicts and criticisms openly.

9. *Means-ends orientation:* the degree to which management focuses on results or outcomes rather than the techniques and processes used to achieve those outcomes.

10. *Open-systems focus:* the degree to which the organization monitors and responds to changes in the external environment.

As illustrated in Figure 3–2, the organization's culture is a composite picture formed from these ten characteristics. Table 3–1 demonstrates how these characteristics can be mixed to create highly diverse organizations.

The characteristics listed above are relatively stable and permanent over time. Just as an individual's personality is stable and permanent—if you were outgoing last month, you're likely to be outgoing next month—so, too, is an organization's culture.

General Motors has been almost universally described as a cold, formal, risk-aversive firm. It was that way in the 1930s, and it is basically the same today. In contrast, Hewlett-Packard is an informal, loosely structured, and highly humanistic organization. Both General Motors and Hewlett-Packard have been essentially successful over the decades despite having completely different cultures.

The Source of Culture

An organization's culture usually reflects the vision or mission of the organization's founders. Because the founders have the original idea, they also have biases on how to carry out the idea. They are unconstrained by previous customs or ideologies. The founders establish the early culture by projecting an image of what the organization should be. The small size of most new organizations also helps the founders impose their vision on all organizational members. An organization's culture, then, results from the interaction between (1) the founders' biases and assumptions and (2) what the first employees learn subsequently from their own experiences.[10]

Thomas Watson at IBM and Frederick Smith at Federal Express are just two examples of individuals who have had an immeasurable influence on shaping their organizations' cultures. For instance, Watson's views on research and development,

Bill Gates is personally aggressive, competitive, and highly disciplined. These are the same characteristics often used to describe Microsoft, the software giant he cofounded and currently heads.

Table 3-1   Two Highly Diverse Organizational Cultures

Organization A

This organization is a manufacturing firm. Employees' loyalty is to the organization. There are extensive rules and regulations that employees are required to follow. Managers supervise employees closely to ensure that there are no deviations. Management is concerned with high productivity regardless of the impact on employee morale or turnover.

Work activities are designed around individuals. There are distinct departments and lines of authority, and employees are expected to minimize formal contact with other employees outside their functional area or line of command. Effort, loyalty, cooperation, and avoidance of errors are highly valued and rewarded. The company promotes only from within and believes that the best products are those developed inside the firm.

Organization B

This organization is also a manufacturing firm. Here, however, employees pride themselves on their technical skills, current expertise, and professional contacts outside the company. There are few rules and regulations, and supervision is loose because management believes that its employees are hardworking and trustworthy. Management is concerned with high productivity but believes that this comes from treating its people right. The company is proud of its reputation as being a good place to work.

Job activities are designed around work teams and team members are encouraged to interact with people across functions and authority levels. Managers are evaluated not only on their department's performance but on how well their department coordinates its activities with other departments in the organization. Promotions and other valuable rewards go to employees who make the greatest contributions to the organization, even when those employees have strange ideas, unusual personal mannerisms, or unconventional work habits. The company fills upper level positions with the best people available, which sometimes includes hiring people away from competitors. The company prides itself on being market-driven and rapidly responding to the changing needs of its customers.

product quality, employee attire, and compensation policies are still evident at IBM, although he died in 1956. Federal Express's aggressiveness, willingness to take risks, focus on innovation, and emphasis on service are central themes that founder Smith has articulated since the company's birth.

Strong Versus Weak Cultures

strong cultures
Organizations in which the key values are intensely held and widely shared.

While all organizations have cultures, not all cultures have an equal impact on employees. **Strong cultures**—organizations in which the key values are intensely held and widely shared—have a greater influence on employees than do weak cultures. The more that employees accept the organization's key values and the greater their commitment to those values, the stronger the culture is.

Whether an organization's culture is strong, weak, or somewhere in between depends on factors such as the size of the organization, how long it has been around, how much turnover there has been among employees, and the intensity with which the culture was originated. In some organizations, it's unclear what's important and what isn't—a characteristic of weak cultures. In such organizations, culture is less likely to affect managers. However, most organizations have moderate to strong cultures. There is relatively high agreement on what's important, what defines "good" employee behavior, what it takes to get ahead, and so forth. We should expect that a culture will have an increasing impact on what managers do as it becomes stronger.[11]

Mary Kay Ash of Mary Kay Cosmetics

Mary Kay Cosmetics is a highly successful company with a strong culture. The person who created this culture is the same person who founded the firm—Mary Kay Ash.[12]

The Mary Kay story is an inspiration to anyone with entrepreneurial aspirations. She was in her early 50s when she took her savings of $5,000 and started selling skin care products out of a small store in Dallas. Twenty years later, her firm had grown into an international corporation with annual sales of $300 million and a sales force of 200,000. Mary Kay Cosmetics today averages more than a 40 percent return on its equity—a percent which ranks among the highest in American industry.

Mary Kay attributes her success to developing a corporate culture that encourages and rewards its people—particularly the independent sales people that market her cosmetics. As she puts it, "We're only as good as our people." While she is committed to offering proven products of the highest quality, she has no monopoly on such products. What differentiates the Mary Kay firm from its competitors is the commitment to its sales people, training directors, and managers. Mary Kay selects the best people available and pays them top dollar. It makes every effort to encourage its people by reinforcing any and all positive sales efforts. Mary Kay has created a reward and incentive program that has allowed literally thousands of her sales representatives to earn in excess of $50,000 a year.

If there is one activity that best symbolizes the Mary Kay culture, it's the company's annual three-day meeting. It's a spectacular, "circus-like" event, combining inspiration, excitement, education, and employee recognition. One of its major purposes is to publicly recognize as many of Mary Kay's sales people as possible. Those with superior sales records are rewarded with money, jewelry, and the famous Mary Kay "pink Cadillacs." But more importantly, according to Mary Kay Ash, they receive public recognition before their peers. The result is a sales organization with unusual enthusiasm and team spirit.

Influence on Management Practice

Because it establishes constraints upon what they can and cannot do, an organization's culture is particularly relevant to managers. These constraints are rarely explicit. They are not written down. It even may be rare to hear them spoken. But they're there, and all managers quickly learn "the ropes to skip and the ropes to know" in their organizations. To illustrate, you won't find the following values written down anywhere, but each comes from a real organization:

Look busy even if you're not.

If you take risks and fail around here, you'll pay dearly for it.

Before you make a decision, run it by your boss so that he or she is never surprised.

We make our product only as good as the competition forces us to.

What made us successful in the past will make us successful in the future.

What made us successful in the past will make us successful in the future.

If you want to get to the top here, you have to be a team player.

The link between values such as these and managerial behavior is fairly straight-forward. If a business firm's culture supports the belief that profits can be increased by cost cutting and that the company's best interests are served by achieving slow but steady increases in quarterly earnings, managers down the line are unlikely to pursue programs that are innovative, risky, long term, or expansionary. In organizations whose culture conveys a basic distrust of employees, managers are much more likely to use an authoritarian leadership style than a democratic one. Why? The culture conveys to managers what is appropriate behavior. For example, the president of Honeywell Information Systems recognized the constraining role that culture was playing in his effort to get his managers to be less authoritarian.[13] He noted that his organization's culture would have to become more democratic if it was going to succeed in the marketplace. He explained that managers' shared beliefs in authoritarian management had to some extent predisposed them to keep information "very close to the vest," resulting in situations in which people didn't have all the data they needed to make descent decisions.

An organization's culture, especially a strong one, therefore constrains a manager's decision-making options concerning all management functions. As depicted in Table 3–2, the major areas of a manager's job are influenced by the culture in which he or she operates.

The Environment

The recognition that no organization is an island unto itself was a major contribution of the systems approach to management. Anyone who questions the impact of the external environment on managing should consider the following:

> One morning in January, 1993, Alaska Airlines' executives learned through a trade paper that United Airlines was cutting the price of a round-trip ticket between Los Angeles and Seattle from $399 to $289. As a competitor to United on this route and

Table 3–2   Examples of Managerial Decisions Affected by Culture

Planning

The degree of risk that plans should contain

Whether plans should be developed by individuals or teams

The degree of environmental scanning in which management will engage

Organizing

How much autonomy should be designed into employees' jobs

Whether tasks should be done by individuals or in groups

The degree to which department managers interact with each other

Leading

The degree to which managers are concerned with increasing employee job satisfaction

What leadership styles are appropriate

Whether all disagreements—even constructive ones—should be eliminated

Controlling

Whether to allow employees to control their own actions or to impose external controls

What criteria should be emphasized in employee performance evaluations

What repercussions will occur from exceeding one's budget

being determined not to lose market share, Alaska executives found themselves with no alternative other than to match United's cut-rate price.

Land's End mails hundreds of thousands of catalogs each year. When the U.S. Postal Service recently increased the cost of third-class mail by 23 percent, management promptly saw company profits plummet.

In order to respond to recent revisions in the Clean Air Act, management at Ford Motor Co. will have to spend billions of dollars during the 1990s to cut tail pipe emissions and to make vehicles that can run on alternative fuels.

As these examples show, there are forces in the environment that play a major role in shaping managers' actions. In this section, we will identify some of the critical environmental forces that affect management and demonstrate how they constrain managerial discretion.

Defining the Environment

environment
Outside institutions or forces that potentially affect an organization's performance.

The term **environment** refers to institutions or forces that are outside the organization and potentially affect the organization's performance. As one writer put it, "Just take the universe, subtract from it the subset that represents the organization, and the remainder is environment."[14] But it's really not that simple.

general environment
Everything outside the organization.

General Versus Specific Environment The **general environment** includes *everything* outside the organization, such as economic factors, political conditions, the social milieu, and technological factors. It encompasses conditions that *may* affect the organization but whose relevance is not clear. The development of the technology that permits the contents of an entire bookshelf to be placed on one small computer disk is an example of a condition in the general environment of publisher Simon & Schuster. Its effect on the book industry is unclear, yet its potential impact could be very great. Similarly, the strength of the U.S. dollar against the pound and franc is an environmental force for U.S. companies that operate in Great Britain and France, but its effect is best described as only potentially relevant.

specific environment
The part of the environment that is directly relevant to the achievement of an organization's goals.

The bulk of management's attention is usually given to the organization's specific environment. The **specific environment** is the part of the environment that is directly relevant to the achievement of an organization's goals. It consists of the critical constituencies or components that can positively or negatively influence an organization's effectiveness. The specific environment is unique to each organization and changes with conditions. Typically, it will include suppliers of inputs, clients or customers, competitors, government agencies, and public pressure groups. Lockheed Corporation depends heavily on defense contracts; therefore, the U.S. Department of Defense is in its specific environment. Of course, elements in an organization's specific environment can move into its general environment over time and vice versa. An appliance manufacturer that had previously never sold to Sears, Roebuck recently signed a three-year contract to sell Sears 40 percent of its output of washing machines, which are to be sold under the retailer's Kenmore brand. This action moved Sears from the manufacturer's general environment to its specific environment.

An organization's specific environment varies depending on the "niche" that the organization has made for itself with respect to the range of products or services it offers and the markets it serves. Timex and Rolex both make wristwatches, but their specific environments differ because they operate in distinctly different market niches. Miami-Dade Junior College and the University of Michigan are both institutions of higher education, but they do substantially different things and appeal to different segments of the higher-education market. The managers or administrators in these organizations face different constituencies in their specific environments.

A comparison of private colleges and state colleges may make this clearer. Tuition

Burger King is an example of an organization in McDonald's specific environment. Actions that Burger King's management takes regarding concerns such as menu offerings and pricing have a direct effect on McDonald's operations.

environmental uncertainty
The degree of change and complexity in an organization's environment.

environmental complexity
The number of components in an organization's environment and the extent of an organization's knowledge about its environmental components.

at private colleges is considerably higher than it is at public colleges. The survival of private colleges depends on a constant influx of new students who can pay the tuition, alumni donations, and a record of placing their graduates in good jobs and graduate schools. A public college's survival is most dependent on appropriations by the state legislature. The result is that private colleges expend more effort than state colleges on student recruitment, alumni relations, and placement services. State college administrators, on the other hand, spend a lot of their time lobbying in the state capital for increased appropriations. The importance of our point should not be lost: The environmental factors that one organization is dependent upon and that have a critical bearing on its performance may not be relevant to another organization at all, even though they may appear at first glance to be in the same type of business.

Assessing Environmental Uncertainty   The environment is important to managers because not all environments are the same. They differ by what we call their degree of **environmental uncertainty.** Environmental uncertainty, in turn, can be broken down into two dimensions: degree of change and degree of complexity.

If the components in an organization's environment change a lot, we call it a *dynamic* environment. If change is minimal, we call it a *stable* one. A stable environment might be one in which there are no new competitors, no new technological breakthroughs by current competitors, little activity by public pressure groups to influence the organization, and so forth. This might describe, for instance, Smith-Corona's environment in the 1960s.

Smith-Corona had few significant competitors in its market niche—portable typewriters. When kids went off to college in the 1960s or early 1970s, they typically took a new Smith-Corona manual or electric typewriter with them. With the exception of the introduction of the electric portable, the technology was unchanging. But beginning in the mid-to-late 1970s, major alterations began to occur in Smith-Corona's environment because of breakthroughs in technology. Low-cost personal computers could do word processing and other functions in addition to typing. Electronic typewriters could do everything an electric could do but more cheaply because they have far fewer moving parts. Firms such as Apple, IBM, and Canon had superior technical capabilities in this new technology. Smith-Corona saw its market for portable typewriters virtually collapse in less than six years. The degree of change in Smith-Corona's environment went from stable to dynamic.

Similarly, U.S. automakers since the mid-1970s have faced a dynamic environment. In the 1950s and 1960s, for instance, they could predict with extremely high accuracy each year's sales and profits. Then came increased government safety and emission regulations, foreign competition, and escalating gasoline prices. Suddenly, managers in the U.S. auto industry found themselves confronting a radically changed environment.

What about rapid change that is predictable? Retail department stores are a case in point. They typically make a quarter or a third of their sales in December. The drop-off from December to January is precipitous. Does this predictable change in consumer demand make department stores' environment dynamic? No. When we talk about degree of change, we mean change that is unpredictable. If change can be accurately anticipated, it is not an uncertainty with which managers have to deal.

The other dimension of uncertainty relates to the degree of **environmental complexity.** The degree of complexity refers to the number of components in an organization's environment and the extent of the knowledge that the organization has about those components. When the washing machine manufacturer signed a contract to sell 40 percent of its output to Sears, it lowered its number of customers. It thus reduced its environmental complexity. The fewer customers, suppliers, competitors, and government agencies that an organization is required to interact with, the less uncertainty there is in its environment.

Shaping Competitive Cultures

Some cultures help their organizations compete more effectively. Others actually hinder the organization. Whether an organization's culture is a positive or negative force essentially depends on how well the culture matches up with the organization's environment. The "right" culture for an organization facing a relatively stable environment is not likely to be effective when that environment turns dynamic.

Efforts to create a cultural revolution are taking place in many organizations today. Since their environments have become more dynamic, such companies as General Electric, IBM, Goodyear, Mobil, USX, and Xerox are trying to reshape their cultures to make themselves more competitive.

What kind of cultures are managers trying to create? While it's hard to generalize, it is usually true that dynamic environments match up best with cultures that encourage risk-taking and innovation, focus on ends rather than means, increase employee decision-making authority, facilitate inter-unit cooperation, and respond quickly and easily to their changing environment. IBM, as a case in point, is determined to shake up its bureaucratic culture and create a company that is more competitive and that has faster moving independent units. As part of this effort, it recently established a separate company—a wholly owned subsidiary of IBM—to develop, manufacture, distribute, and market personal computers.[15]

Of course, it's one thing for management to recognize the need to reshape its organizational culture and another to pull it off. The problem, as we've described, is that organizational cultures are relatively stable and enduring over time. That makes them very hard to change.

Complexity is also measured in terms of the knowledge an organization needs to have about its environment. Boeing managers must know a great deal about their suppliers' operations, for instance, if they are to ensure that the jet planes they build will perform without a flaw. Managers of retail grocery stores, in contrast, have a minimal need for sophisticated knowledge about their suppliers.

Environmental uncertainty is presented as a two-by-two matrix in Figure 3–3 on page 80. There are four cells, cell 1 being lowest in environmental uncertainty and cell 4 being highest. Management's influence on organizational outcomes is greatest in cell 1 and least in cell 4.

Since uncertainty is a threat to an organization's effectiveness, managers try to minimize it. Given a choice, managers would prefer to operate in environments like those in cell 1. But managers rarely have full control over that choice. For example, managers in firms that produced and marketed computer software in 1993 found themselves in cell 4. Because they chose this particular niche to operate in, they faced a highly dynamic and complex environment. Had they chosen to manufacture standard wire coat hangers, they would probably have found themselves in cell 1.

The Organization and Its Environment   Figure 3–4 on page 81 summarizes our position that an organization is a system that interacts with and depends upon its specific environment but remains ever mindful of the potential influences of its general environment.

In the following sections we elaborate on the components in both specific and general environments and demonstrate how environments can constrain the choices available to managers.

FIGURE 3-3
Environmental Uncertainty Matrix

		Degree of Change	
		Stable	**Dynamic**
Degree of Complexity	*Simple*	**CELL 1** Stable and predictable environment Few components in environment Components are somewhat similar and remain basically the same Minimal need for sophisticated knowledge of components	**CELL 2** Dynamic and unpredicatable environment Few components in environment Components are somewhat similar but are in continual process of change Minimal need for sophisticated knowledge of components
	Complex	**CELL 3** Stable and predictable environment Many components in environment Components are not similar to one another and remain basically the same High need for sophisticated knowledge of components	**CELL 4** Dynamic and unpredictable environment Many components in environment Components are not similar to one another and are in continual process of change High need for sophisticated knowledge of components

New York City comptroller Elizabeth Holtzman (seated) and Beverly Hamilton, deputy comptroller under Holtzman, were not pleased with management decisions at Lockheed. Hamilton, who oversees, $38 billion in New York pension funds that include a large block of Lockheed stock, recently met with Lockheed's CEO, Daniel Tellep. She told him both her own institution and others wanted a voice in the management of Lockheed. Seeing the institutions' power, Tellep offered them three representatives on an expanded board. Tellep was reacting to pressure from a group in Lockheed's environment, in this case an institutional stockholder.

The Specific Environment

As previously noted, different organizations face different specific environments. For most organizations, though, suppliers, customers, competitors, governmental agencies, and special-interest pressure groups are external factors that impose uncertainty.

Suppliers   When you think of an organization's suppliers, you typically think of firms that provide materials and equipment. For a building contractor, this includes firms that sell and rent bulldozers and trucks, office supply firms, lumber yards, hardware suppliers, and distributors of brick and concrete. But the term *suppliers* also includes providers of financial and labor inputs. Stockholders, banks, insurance companies, pension funds, and other similar institutions are needed to ensure a continuous supply of capital. Exxon can have rights to an oil field that can generate billions of dollars in profits, but the profits will remain only potential unless management can obtain the funds necessary to drill the wells. Labor unions, occupational associations, and local labor markets are sources of employees. A lack of qualified nurses, for instance, makes it difficult for a hospital to run efficiently.

Management seeks to ensure a steady flow of needed inputs at the lowest price possible. Because these inputs represent uncertainties—that is, their unavailability or delay can significantly reduce the organization's effectiveness—management typically goes to great efforts to ensure a steady flow. As you'll see later in this book, the reason most large organizations have departments of purchasing, finance, and personnel is the importance management places on the acquisition of machinery, equipment, capital, and labor inputs.

Customers   Organizations exist to meet the needs of customers. It is the customer or client who absorbs the organization's output. This is true even for government organizations. They exist to provide services, and we are reminded, especially at election time, that we indicate by the way we vote how satisfied we actually are as customers.

Customers obviously represent potential uncertainty to an organization. Customers' tastes can change. They can become dissatisfied with the organization's product or service. Of course, some organizations face considerably more uncertainty as a

FIGURE 3-4
The Organization and Its
Environment

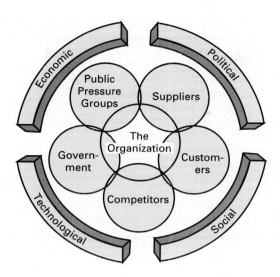

result of their customers than do others. In general, we would expect customers to represent greater uncertainty for a manager of an upscale restaurant, such as Spago in Los Angeles, than for a manager of a county hospital.

Competitors   All organizations, even monopolies, have one or more competitors. PepsiCo has Coca-Cola. General Motors has Toyota. New York University has Columbia, City University of New York, and a host of others. The U.S. Postal Service has a monopoly on mail service, but it competes against United Parcel, Federal Express, Western Union, and other forms of communication such as the telephone and fax machines.

No management can afford to ignore its competition. When they do, they pay a very serious price. Many problems incurred by the railroads, for instance, have been attributed to their failure to recognize who their competitors were. They believed they were in the railroad business when, in fact, they were in the transportation business. Trucking, shipping, aviation, and bus and private automobile transportation are all competitors of railroads. Fifteen years ago, the three major broadcasting networks—ABC, CBS, and NBC—virtually controlled what you watched on television. If your set was on, the probability was better than 90 percent that you were watching one of the major networks. Today, with the rapid expansion of cable, VCRs, and the syndicated programs sold to local stations, less than half of the average television viewer's time is spent watching programing from the major networks.

These examples illustrate that competitors—in terms of pricing, services offered, new products developed, and the like—represent an important environmental force that management must monitor and to which it must be prepared to respond.

Government   Federal, state, and local governments influence what organizations can and cannot do. Some federal legislation has tremendous impact. For example, consider the following: The Sherman Anti-Trust Act of 1890 sought to stop monopoly practices that resulted in restraint of trade. The National Labor Relations Act of 1935 stipulated that employers are required to recognize a union chosen by the majority of their employees; it also established procedures and rules governing collective bargaining. The Civil Rights Act of 1964 made it unlawful for an employer to discharge, refuse to hire, or discriminate in employment against an individual because of race, color, religion, sex, or national origin. To illustrate the impact that federal regulation has had on business firms, Table 3–3 lists thirteen pieces of legislation passed in the last twenty-five years.

Table 3-3 Significant Legislation Regulating Business Since 1970

Economic Stabilization Act of 1970
Fair Credit Reporting Act of 1970
Occupational Safety and Health Act of 1970
Consumer Product Safety Act of 1972
Equal Employment Opportunity Act of 1972
Employee Retirement Income Security Act of 1974
Toxic Substance Control Act of 1976
Pregnancy Discrimination Act of 1978
Airline Deregulation Act of 1978
Immigration Reform and Control Act of 1986
Tax Reform Act of 1986
Plant Closing Bill of 1989
Americans with Disabilities Act of 1990

Certain organizations, by virtue of their business, are scrutinized by specific government agencies. Organizations in the telecommunications industry—including telephone companies and radio and television stations—are regulated by the Federal Communications Commission. Publicly held companies must abide by the acceptable financial standards and practices as defined by the Securities and Exchange Commission. If your firm manufactures pharmaceuticals, what you can sell is determined by the Food and Drug Administration.

The federal government is not the only source of legal regulations that govern organizations. State and local governmental regulations extend and modify many federal standards. Los Angeles County, for instance, imposes considerably stiffer antipollution standards on business firms operating within its borders than do state or federal regulations.

Organizations spend a great deal of time and money to meet government regulations.[16] But the effects of these regulations go beyond time and money. They also reduce managerial discretion. They limit the choices available to managers.

Consider the decision to dismiss an employee.[17] Historically, employees were free to quit an organization at any time, and employers had the right to fire an employee any time with or without cause. Recent laws and court decisions, however, have put new limits on what employers may do. Employers are increasingly expected to deal with employees by following the principles of good faith and fair dealing. Employees who feel they have been wrongfully discharged can take their case to court. Juries are increasingly deciding what is or is not "fair." This has made it more difficult for managers to fire poor performers or dismiss employees for off-duty conduct. For example, IBM dismissed a female employee for dating someone who worked for a competitor. She sued IBM, arguing that her personal relationship wasn't expressly prohibited by IBM's policies and represented no conflict of interest. She won a $300,000 settlement from IBM.

Pressure Groups. Managers cannot fail to recognize the special-interest groups that attempt to influence the actions of organizations. Automobile manufacturers, toy makers, and airlines have all been visible targets of Ralph Nader's Center for Responsive Law. Conservative citizen-action groups have successfully pressured publishers of elementary and secondary American history textbooks to change content that their group members have found offensive. And it would be an unusual week if we didn't read that pro-life or pro-choice members were picketing, boycotting, or just threatening some organization in order to get its management to change its policies.

Eli Lilly reports that it fills out more than 27,000 federal forms annually, and Dow Chemical estimates that it spends more than $400 million a year to meet federal regulations.

As social and political movements change, so too does the power of pressure groups. For example, through its persistent efforts, Greenpeace has not only managed to make significant changes in the whaling, tuna fishing, and seal fur industries, but has also raised public awareness about those and other environmental concerns. Managers should be aware of the power that these groups can exert on their decisions.

The General Environment

In this section, we will discuss economic, political, social, and technological conditions that can affect the management of organizations. In contrast to the specific environment, these factors usually do not have as large an impact on an organization's operations. However, management must take them into account. For instance, recent research has uncovered a technology that might make it possible to produce an energy-efficient light bulb that would last at least twenty times as long as a standard bulb. Senior managers in the lighting divisions at General Electric and Philips recognize that this has the potential to have far-reaching effects on their units' growth and profitability, so they carefully follow progress on this research.

Economic Conditions Interest rates, inflation rates, changes in disposable income, stock market indexes, and the general business cycle are some of the economic factors in the general environment that can affect management practices in an organization.

For example, many of the world's largest financial institutions have recently learned how closely their fortunes are tied to the U.S. real estate industry. The collapse of the commercial real estate market, which began in 1989, reverberated through the banking and savings and loan industry. Many banks, including Citicorp and Chase Manhattan, that had lent heavily on commercial property absorbed huge losses and then had to lay off thousands of employees in order to reduce costs.

The British colony of Hong Kong reverts to Chinese control in 1997. The uncertainty surrounding this political changeover has significantly affected business investment in Hong Kong.

Similarly, the 1991–92 recession reminded many retailers of how dependent they are on consumer disposable income. That recession hit such firms as Macy's, Ames, and Zale Corp. particularly hard, requiring management to close stores and sell off assets.

Political Conditions   Political conditions include the general stability of the countries in which an organization operates and the specific attitudes that elected government officials hold toward the role of business in society.

In the United States, organizations have generally operated in a stable political environment. But management is a worldwide activity. Moreover, many U.S. firms have operations in countries whose record for stability is quite spotty—for example, El Salvador, Libya, Argentina, Chile, and Iran. The internal aspects of management require that organizations attempt to forecast major political changes in countries in which they operate. In this way, management can better anticipate political conditions, from the devaluation of a country's monetary unit to a dictator's decision to nationalize certain industries and expropriate their assets.

The recent collapse of the Soviet Union provides a vivid illustration. Many U.S., European, and Japanese companies had spent years engaged in tedious negotiations with Soviet officials to establish business relations in the Soviet Union. But in a few short months in 1991, all the rules changed. Communism died, capitalism suddenly became fashionable, and a united Soviet republic ceased to exist. What took its place was a commonwealth of fifteen independent states, each with a separate government. Almost overnight, companies around the world found potentially vast new markets had opened up, but they now had to deal with fifteen different governments and fifteen different political agendas.

Social Conditions   Management must adapt its practices to the changing expectations of the society in which it operates. As values, customs, and tastes change, so too must management. This applies to both their products and service offerings and their internal policies. Recent examples of social conditions that have had a significant impact on the management of certain organizations include the changing career expectations of women and the aging of the work force.

Inflation, the women's movement, and an increased divorce rate have all contributed to a dramatic increase in female labor-participation rates. Today, more than half of all adult women are gainfully employed outside the home. This change has hit particularly hard organizations like Avon Products and Tupperware that traditionally sold their products to housewives at home. Today's working woman tends to buy her cosmetics and housewares during her lunch hour or after work. Banks, automobile manufacturers, and women's apparel makers have also found their markets changing because of the career expectations of women. Women want expanded credit; they look for cars that are consistent with their new life-styles; and their wardrobe purchases increasingly are business suits rather than casual wear. Management has also had to adjust its internal organizational policies because of the increase in the number of working women. Organizations that fail to offer child care facilities, for instance, may lose in their efforts to hire competent women employees.

In 1970, the median age in the United States was under 28. It is now past 30 and will reach 35 by the end of this decade. Organizations that cater to the needs of seniors will have a larger market. This implies increased demand for health care and homes in the Sunbelt. It also means that organizations will have to redesign products and services for an aging market. Levi Strauss, for example, now produces fuller-cut jeans designed to fit the middle-aged person's body. Inside organizations, management can expect to have more employees in their fifties and sixties. This is likely to translate into more experienced workers with needs that differ from those of their younger counterparts. For instance, older workers tend to place greater value on such employee benefits as health insurance and pension plans and less value on college-tuition-reimbursement programs and generous moving allowances.

Technological Conditions   Our final consideration in the general environment is technology. We live in a technological age. In terms of the four components in the general environment, the most rapid change during the past quarter-century has probably occurred in technology. We now have automated offices, robots in manufacturing, lasers, integrated circuits, microdots, microprocessors, and synthetic fuels. Companies that make the most of technology, including Apple Computer, 3M, and General Electric, prosper. Similarly, hospitals, universities, airports, police departments, and even military organizations that adapt to major technological advances have a competitive edge over those that do not.

An example of how the technological environment affects management is in the design of offices. Offices have become communication centers. Management can now link its computers, telephones, word processors, photocopiers, fax machines, filing storage, and other office activities into an integrated system. For management of all organizations, this means faster and better decision-making capability. For firms that have historically sold products in only one part of the office market—those offering only typewriters or photocopying equipment, for instance—it means developing comprehensive office systems or being entirely excluded from the market. And for a company like Western Union, whose main cash generator as recently as 1987 was the Telex, the explosive growth of fax technology has brought the firm to the brink of bankruptcy.

Influence on Management Practice

As we have seen, organizations are not self-sufficient. They interact with, and are influenced by, their environment. Organizations depend on their environment as a source of inputs and as a recipient of its outputs. Organizations must also abide by the laws of the land and respond to groups that challenge the organization's actions. As such, suppliers, customers, government agencies, public pressure groups, and similar constituencies can exert power over an organization. This power, for instance, is unusually evident among publicly held corporations whose stock is controlled by such institutional investors as insurance companies, mutual funds, and pension plans. These institutions control 80 percent or more of the stock in CNA Financial, Capital Cities/ABC, Cigna, Lotus Development, Southwest Airlines, Bausch & Lomb, and Whirlpool.[18] As a result, the institutions' interests dictate management's interests. These institutions have the power to control boards of directors and indirectly to fire management. The result is that management's options are constrained to reflect the desires of these institutional investors.

A survey of 400 chief executives from among the 1000 largest U.S. companies indicates that environmental constituencies have increased their influence on management in recent years.[19] As shown in Table 3–4, except for labor unions, all of the listed forces in the environment generally expanded their influence between 1982 and 1987. Keep in mind that this survey addressed only *changes* since 1982. These forces were already powerful constraints on managerial decision making in the early 1980s!

Many of these environmental forces are dynamic and create considerable uncertainty for management. Customers' tastes and preferences change. New laws are passed. Suppliers can't meet contractual delivery dates. Competitors introduce new technologies, products, and services. To the degree that these environmental uncer-

TABLE 3-4   Influence of Forces in the Environment

In the late 1980s, 400 chief executives were asked, "Compared with five years ago, would you say that the following individuals or institutions have gained, lost, or kept their influence over decisions in companies such as yours?" They responded as follows:

Force in the Environment	Gained Influence	Lost Influence	Kept Influence	Not Sure
Institutions holding big stock blocks	47%	2%	42%	9%
Investment bankers	46	13	36	5
Stock analysts	48	4	43	5
Government regulators	41	20	34	5
Environmentalists	37	14	40	9
Consumer groups	28	14	49	9
Labor unions	2	54	34	10

Source: "Business Week/Harris Executive Poll," *Business Week,* October 23, 1987, p. 28.

tainties cannot be anticipated, they force management to respond in ways that it might not prefer. The greater the environmental uncertainty an organization faces, the more the environment limits management's options and its freedom to determine its own destiny.

Summary

This summary is organized by the chapter-opening learning objectives found on page 67.

1. The omnipotent view is dominant in management theory and in society. It argues that managers are directly responsible for the success or failure of an organization. In contrast, the symbolic view argues that management has only a limited effect on substantive organizational outcomes because of the large number of factors outside of management's control; however, management greatly influences symbolic outcomes.

2. Organizational culture is a system of shared meaning within an organization that determines, in large degree, how employees act.

3. An organization's culture is composed of ten characteristics: member identity, group emphasis, people-focus, unit integration, control, risk tolerance, reward criteria, conflict tolerance, means–end orientation, and open-systems focus.

4. Culture constrains managers because it acts as an automatic filter that biases the manager's perceptions, thoughts, and feelings. Strong cultures particularly constrain a manager's decision-making options by conveying which alternatives are acceptable and which are not.

5. The general environment encompasses forces that have the potential to affect the organization but whose relevance is not overtly clear. These typically include economic, political, social, and technological factors. The specific environment is that part of the environment that is directly relevant to the achievement of the organization's goals. Relevant elements in an organization's specific environment might include suppliers, customers, competitors, government agencies, and public pressure groups.

6. Environmental uncertainty is determined by the degree of *change* and *complexity* in the environment. Stable and simple environments are relatively certain. The more dynamic and complex the environment, the higher the uncertainty.

7. High environmental uncertainty limits management's options and its freedom to determine its own destiny.

Review Questions

1. Why does the omnipotent view of management dominate management theory?
2. According to the symbolic view, what is management's role in organizations?
3. Contrast strong and weak cultures. Which has the greatest impact on managers? Why?
4. Who typically have more influence on an organization's culture: a company's first managers or current managers? Explain.
5. How does culture affect a manager's execution of the four management functions?
6. Describe an effective culture for (a) a relatively stable environment and (b) a dynamic environment.
7. How can suppliers constrain managerial discretion?
8. How can federal government regulations constrain managerial discretion?
9. Why do managers try to minimize environmental uncertainty?
10. What effect, if any, does the general environment have on managerial practice?

Discussion Questions

1. Classrooms have cultures. Describe your class culture. Does it constrain your instructor? If so, how?
2. Define a local grocery store's specific environment. How does it constrain the store manager?
3. Refer to Table 3–1. How would a first-line supervisor's job differ in these two organizations?
4. Describe the general and specific environments for the President of the United States. In what ways do they constrain him? In what ways do they make him appear to be a symbolic manager and in what ways do they cast him as an omnipotent manager?
5. When a large corporation loses money for several years in a row, the board of directors almost always replaces the corporation's chief executive. Why?

SELF-ASSESSMENT EXERCISE

What Kind of Organizational Culture Fits You Best?

For each of the following statements, circle the level of agreement or disagreement that you personally feel:

SA = Strongly Agree
 A = Agree
 U = Uncertain
 D = Disagree
SD = Strongly Disagree

1. I like being part of a team and having my performance assessed in terms of my contribution to the team.   SA   A   U   D   SD

2. No person's needs should be compromised in order for a department to achieve its goals.   SA   A   U   D   SD

3. I prefer a job where my boss leaves me alone.   SA   A   U   D   SD

4. I like the thrill and excitement from taking risks.   SA   A   U   D   SD

5. People shouldn't break rules.   SA   A   U   D   SD

6. Seniority in an organization should be highly rewarded.   SA   A   U   D   SD

7. I respect authority.   SA   A   U   D   SD

8. If a person's job performance is inadequate, it's irrelevant how much effort he or she made.   SA   A   U   D   SD

9. I like things to be predictable.   SA   A   U   D   SD

10. I'd prefer my identity and status to come from my professional expertise than from the organization that employs me.   SA   A   U   D   SD

Turn to Scoring Keys for Self-Assessment Exercises.

WILLIAM STERN & COMPANY

To: Senior Research Associate
From: Dan Forrester; Director of Research
Subject: Relationship between company economic performance and top management turnover

Several of our clients have commented about the number of recent top-management shake-ups they've observed in companies in which they own stock. They asked me if I thought there was a direct relationship between declining profits in a firm and the departure of its chief executive. I had an opinion but I had to admit I was not up-to-date on the research.

Let me suggest four possible theories: (1) Consecutive quarterly declines in company profit lead to increased CEO turnover (2) It's not a decline in profits that leads to CEO departures, rather, it's several quarterly losses (3) The real issue is expectations. When a company's financial performance falls below the expectation of board members or security analysts, this creates pressure on the CEO, which leads to his departure (4) There is no relationship. CEO's are highly insulated. As long as they keep on good terms with their board of directors, their job security is assured.

Quite honestly, I don't know what the research indicates. I have identified two articles that you might want to look at as a point of departure. They are: J.R. Harrison, D.L. Torres, and S. Kukalis, "The Changing of the Guard: Turnover and Structural Change in Top-Management Positions," *Administrative Science Quarterly,* June 1988, pp. 211–32; and S.M. Puffer and J.B. Weintrop, "Corporate Performance and CEO Turnover; The Role of Performance Expectations," *Administrative Science Quarterly,* March 1991, pp. 1–19.

I want you to review the evidence and write up a one-page summary of what you find. Also, give me a bibliography of the sources you used.

This is a fictionalized account of a potentially real problem. It was written for academic purposes only and is not meant to reflect either positively or negatively on actual practices at William Stern & Co.

CASE APPLICATION

International Business Machines

College graduates in the 1960s considered it the "best of the best" when it came to job opportunities. International Business Machines (IBM) offered a wonderful balance of growth opportunities and job security. Here was a company that was leading the way in the computerization of business *and* had never laid off an employee.

Today, IBM is the fourth largest United States industrial corporation. It generates sales in excess of $64 *billion* a year from a product line that ranges from $800 typewriters to $100-million-plus data processing systems. But the current IBM offers employees nothing like the high growth–high security of thirty years ago. Today's IBM is burdened by a culture more appropriate to the time when IBM almost completely dominated the computer industry.

In recent years, IBM has fallen on tough times. The demand for its highly profitable mainframe computers has declined as more and more business firms have converted to personal computers that provide both high power and flexibility. And unfortunately for IBM, PCs have become essentially interchangeable, generic products and the focus of fierce price competition among several manufacturers. Profits in PCs are currently going to companies like Apple Computer that have developed innovative products for the increasingly demanding consumer. Currently, IBM holds about 25 percent of the PC market—a sharp contrast to the 50 percent it held a decade ago. In 1991, IBM suffered its first annual loss in its eighty-year history: A staggering $2.8 billion!

IBM's current problems can be understood better if we look at a couple of factors that were instrumental to the company's success: A conservative culture that was highly rule-bound and an undying commitment of service to the customer.

IBM's founder, Thomas Watson, had rules for almost everything. Dark business suits, white shirts, and striped ties were "the uniform." Drinking alcoholic beverages, even off the job, was prohibited. Employees were expected to accept frequent transfers—insiders liked to say that IBM stood for "I've Been Moved." Today, the rules are a bit less severe, but the conservative image is still alive. Ironically, this conservative culture, which served IBM well in times of growth and modest competition, has proven a major handicap in its current dynamic environment. Many of the same people that were attracted to IBM in the 1960s and 1970s because it provided predictable growth and security are now liabilities to the company because they are mismatched to a culture that now requires change and innovation.

IBM people are committed to customer service. The company's sales personnel continue to be the envy of the industry. They are thoroughly trained and highly knowledgeable. Most employees spent as long as their first six weeks with the company in training classes. Managers are still required to take at least forty hours of additional instruction each year. Despite its financial setbacks, IBM continues to spend hundreds of millions of dollars each year on education and training. Customers can feel confident that if they have a problem with IBM equipment, its sales and service personnel will be able to solve it. But this emphasis on service has come at the expense of product innovation. While many of its competitors have been offering new products literally on a monthly basis, IBM has "bet its chips" on service. Not that service isn't important. It's just that IBM's culture has focused on service while the market continues to demand and reward innovation.

IBM's response to its problems has included a massive reorganization. The company laid off 20,000 employees in 1991 and another 20,000 in 1992. Dramatic reassignments have become commonplace. In some cases, employees have been given jobs two or three levels lower in the hierarchy than they had previously held. You can imagine the effect of these changes on IBM employees. The company had a reputation for being a secure place to work, a place where no one ever got laid off. Suddenly that was no longer true. How would you feel if you had been a $60,000-a-year market researcher who, even though your pay had been unaffected, found yourself working in the mailroom? It happened at IBM in 1992!

Questions

1. How has IBM's specific environment changed in recent years?

2. How do the historical culture at IBM and recent changes in its environment act to constrain the company's top management?

3. In what ways might you use the symbolic view of management to describe IBM's previous success and current dilemma?

VIDEO CASE

Adapting to ADA

It became law effective in January 1992. The Americans with Disabilities Act (ADA) states that any business with twenty-five or more employees may not discriminate against the disabled in hiring. The law protects the estimated 14 million Americans of working age who are mentally or physically disabled.

The intention of ADA is to level the playing field by making it illegal for employers to discriminate against people with disabilities in hiring and promotion practices. It also requires that "reasonable accommodations be made, as long as they don't create an undue burden on the company involved." Some in the business community, especially small business owners, fear that compliance will be prohibitively expensive. A few suggest that the cost of meeting ADA regulations might drive them out of business. They cite the tens of thousands of dollars it will cost them to install wheelchair ramps, widen doors, make bathrooms wheelchair accessible, install special phones for the hearing impaired, and purchase optical scanners for the partially sighted.

A primary complaint of business executives is that the wording in the ADA legislation is ambiguous. For instance, what an employer considers "an undue burden," the courts might consider "reasonable." Fines of up to $50,000 for a small business could force them into bankruptcy.

ADA appears to be less of a burden for larger companies. The Meridian Bank of Philadelphia, for example, has begun training programs to help sensitize employees to the world of the disabled. Employees have their fingers taped and have to practice communicating their names in sign language; they stuff their ears with cotton and practice reading lips; and they have to undergo getting around a wheelchair obstacle course. The Hyatt hotel chain has also made extensive adjustments. They now offer handicapped rooms that are a bit larger than standard, closed caption television sets, and the like. Hyatt's management estimates the first-year cost at $15 million to $20 million in order to meet ADA requirements. But they see it as a way to increase business. "There are 42 million people out there who are disabled . . . this is a new market for us."

Questions

1. How does ADA constrain managerial discretion?
2. How can ADA be seen as a business opportunity?
3. Suppose you owned and managed a supermarket that employed seventy-five people. What would you do to comply with ADA? What effect, if any, do you think this would have on the price of goods in your store?

Source: "ADA and Cost to Business," *ABC News Business World,* January 26, 1992.

CHAPTER 4

International Management: Responding to a Global Environment

LEARNING OBJECTIVES

After Reading This Chapter, You Should Be Able To:

1. Explain the importance of viewing management from a global perspective.
2. Describe problems created by national parochialism.
3. Contrast multinational and transnational corporations.
4. Explain why many countries have become part of regional trading alliances.
5. Describe the typical stages by which organizations go international.
6. List the four dimensions of national culture.
7. Describe U.S. culture according to the four dimensions.

Hungary's Tungsram light bulb plant provides General Electric with an East European base.

General Electric is number two in the world, behind Philips, in the light bulb business. And if you didn't think light bulbs were big business, think again. In the United States alone, GE's lighting division employs 18,000 people and generates sales in excess of $2 billion a year. But GE can't become No. 1 in the world without a strong presence in Europe, where it holds a measly two percent of the market. So in January 1990, GE bought a controlling interest in Tungsram Co., a declining Hungarian light bulb maker that had been state owned. GE's strategy was simple. It needed greater access to Western European markets. It also wanted a foot in the door on the rebirth of Eastern Europe. So GE bought Tungsram to use as its vehicle to compete in Europe.[1]

What did GE get for its money? A company with twelve factories; a meager seven percent share of the Western European market; a low-cost but highly inefficient work force; and a product line that emphasized bulbs that were in the slow-growth, low-margin end of the lighting business.

Into this quagmire, GE sent George F. Vargas. Born and raised in Hungary, Vargas fled his homeland for the United States in 1956. A 28-year veteran of GE, Vargas has his work cut out for him as chief executive at Tungsram. Unlike his executive peers at GE's lighting division in the U.S., Vargas must consider the following:

- Both management and employees at Tungsram have only known how to do business under socialism. They have little or no understanding of modern management techniques or even market forces. For instance, workers at some Tungsram factories had regularly lined cartons of bulbs with rocks so they could collect bonuses for upping the volume they were shipping. Management encouraged this practice because their bonuses were based on pounds shipped.

- The most basic concepts of capitalism are completely alien to Tungsram's employees. This was illustrated when one of Vargas's U.S.-trained department heads lectured his Hungarian staff on the importance of keeping close track of inventory and receivables in order to measure their effect on profits. "What means profit?" asked one of his Hungarian engineers.

- Even though wages at Tungsram are about one-seventh of those paid by GE in the United States, the Hungarian firm is still grossly overstaffed. Experts say that Tungsram will need to lay off more than half its workers to become competitive. In the West, the solution would be easy: Make the cuts. But the Hungarians' deep fear of joblessness requires GE to take a much slower approach. During his first year, Vargas cut only 11 percent of the jobs at Tungsram, and these were all through normal attrition and early retirement.

The Tungsram example illustrates the new global environment of business. It's now a whole new ballgame for managers. With the world as a marketplace and national borders becoming meaningless, the potential for organizations to grow and expand becomes almost unlimited. However, new competitors can suddenly appear anytime, from anywhere. Managers who don't closely monitor changes in their global environment or fail to respond quickly to those changes are likely to find their organizations' survival in doubt.

Who Owns What?

One way to grasp the changing nature of the global environment is to consider the country of origin for ownership of some familiar companies. Take a look at the following list of companies. Which do you think are U.S.-owned? For the remaining, jot down the country in which you think the primary owners reside.

1. American Can Co. (packaging)
2. CBS Records (records and videos)
3. DuPont (chemicals)
4. Fireman's Fund (insurance)
5. Firestone Tire & Rubber (tires)
6. Jaguar (automobiles)
7. Miles Laboratories (pharmaceuticals)
8. Pillsbury (food processing)
9. Seagram (liquor and wines)
10. U.S. Borax and Chemical (mining)

You'll find the detailed answers in the notes at the end of the book.[2] The U.S.-owned firms on this list, incidentally, are DuPont and Jaguar. How well did you score? Were you aware of how many "name" companies that operate in the United States are actually foreign-owned?

To further dramatize the international aspects of business today, take a look at Table 4–1. This is a partial list of "U.S." companies that derive half or more of their income from foreign operations.

Attacking Parochialism

It is not unusual for Germans and Italians to speak three or four languages. Most Japanese schoolchildren begin studying English in the early elementary grades. On the other hand, most Americans study only English in school. Americans tend to think of English as the international business language. They don't see a need to study other languages.

TABLE 4-1 Selected Companies Deriving 50 Percent or More of Revenues from Non-U.S. Operations

Company	Non-U.S. Income as Percent of Total
Exxon	75.9
Gillette	68.1
Mobil	68.1
Coca-Cola	64.0
Colgate-Palmolive	63.8
Bankers Trust (NY)	63.6
IBM	62.3
Digital Equipment	59.8
Compaq Computer	57.6
Motorola	55.9
Hewlett-Packard	54.2
Citicorp	52.9
Dow Chemical	51.7

Source: "U.S. Corporations With the Biggest Foreign Revenues," *Forbes,* July 20, 1992, pp. 298–300. © Forbes Inc., 1992.

parochialism

A selfish, narrow view of the world; an inability to recognize differences between people.

Monolingualism is just one of the signs that Americans suffer from **parochialism.** That is, they view the world solely through their own eyes and perspective.[3] People with a parochial perspective do not recognize that other people have different ways of living and working. Parochialism has become an increasing obstacle for many U.S. managers. While their counterparts around the world have sought to better understand foreign customs and market differences, U.S. managers too frequently have been guilty of rigidly applying their values and customs to foreign cultures, often with adverse results.

A U.S. manager who was recently transferred to Saudi Arabia successfully obtained a million-dollar contract from a Saudi manufacturer. The manufacturer's representative had arrived at the meeting several hours late, but the U.S. executive considered this unimportant. The American was certainly surprised and frustrated to learn later that the Saudi had no intention of abiding by the contract. He had signed it only to be polite after showing up late for the appointment.

A U.S. executive operating in Peru was viewed by Peruvian managers as cold and unworthy of trust because, in face-to-face discussions, he kept backing up. He did not understand that, in Peru, the custom is to stand quite close to the person with whom you are speaking.

A U.S. manager in Japan offended a high-ranking Japanese executive by failing to give him the respect his position commanded. The manager was introduced to the Japanese executive in the latter's office. The American manager assumed that the executive was a low-level decision maker and paid him little attention because of the small and sparsely furnished office the executive occupied. He did not realize that the offices of top Japanese executives do not display the status accoutrements that their American counterparts do.

A manager raised in the Dominican Republic and working for a health products firm in the United States was perceived by colleagues as a "time waster." Back home, businesspeople would begin meetings with relaxed chitchat. In the United States, managers view such sociability as an unnecessary and time-consuming diversion.[4]

Successful global management requires enhanced sensitivity to differences in national customs and practices. Management practices that work in Chicago might

While few Americans have developed multilingual skills, most Japanese spend many years studying English in school. This gives them important insights into the cultures of English-speaking countries. Japanese managers are also far more likely to read books and periodicals written in English than their U.S. counterparts are to read Japanese publications.

not be appropriate in Shanghai. Later in this chapter and in theme boxes throughout the rest of this book, you will see how a global perspective on managing requires throwing off parochialism and carefully developing an understanding of cultural differences between countries.

The Changing Global Environment

A number of forces are reshaping the global environment. In this section, we'll discuss a few of the more important of these forces.

From Multinationals to Transnationals

multinational corporations
Companies that maintain significant operations in more than one country simultaneously but manage them all from one base in a home country.

transnational corporation
A company that maintains significant operations in more than one country simultaneously and decentralizes decision making in each operation to the local country.

International businesses have been with us for a long time. Siemens, Remington, and Singer, for instance, were selling their products in many countries in the nineteenth century. By the 1920s, some companies, including Fiat, Ford, Unilever, and Royal Dutch/Shell, had gone multinational. But it wasn't until the mid-1960s that **multinational corporations (MNCs)** became commonplace. These corporations—which maintain significant operations in two or more countries simultaneously, but are based in one home country—initiated the rapid growth in international trade. Most of the companies in Table 4–1 are MNCs, with subsidiaries and manufacturing facilities in countries throughout the world.

The global environment is extending the reach and goals of MNCs to create an even more generic organization—the **transnational corporation (TNC).** This type of organization doesn't seek to replicate its domestic successes by managing foreign operations from home. Rather, decision making in TNCs takes place at the local level. Nationals typically are hired to run operations in each country. And the products and marketing strategies for each country are uniquely tailored to that country's culture. Nestlé, for example, is a transnational. With operations in almost every country on the globe, it is the world's largest food company, yet its managers match their products to their consumers. Thus Nestlé sells products in parts of Europe, for instance, that aren't available in the United States or Latin America.

The Global Reach of Great Ideas

Colgate-Palmolive is a multinational corporation, selling its products around the globe.

We should point out that while managers of multinational and transnational organizations have become increasingly global in their perspectives and accept the reality that national borders no longer define corporations, politicians and the public have been slower to accept this fact. The 1992 recession, for instance, brought considerable backlash against Japanese products in the United States.[5] Many politicians and union leaders proposed that the sale of Japanese products was taking jobs from Americans.[6] The cry was "Buy American." The irony is that many of the so-called Japanese products that critics were attacking were made in the United States. As a case in point, Honda employs more than 10,000 Americans at four plants in Central Ohio and is now actually *exporting* Accords back to Japan. Moreover, a number of those so-called American cars sitting in Chrysler showrooms, cars with Dodge and Plymouth insignias, were made by Japanese workers employed by Mitsubishi Motors Corp. Similarly, most Sony televisions sold in the United States are made in California, while "American" manufacturer Zenith's TVs are made in Mexico. The message from these examples should be obvious: A company's national origin is no longer a very good gauge of where it does business or the national origin of its employees. Such companies as Siemens, Sony, and Samsung employ thousands of people in the United States. At the same time, such firms as Coca-Cola, Exxon, and Citicorp employ thousands in places like India, Hong Kong, and the United Kingdom. So phrases like "Buy American" represent old stereotypes that fail to reflect the changing global environment.

Regional Trading Alliances

Just a few years ago, international competition would be described in terms of country against country: the United States versus Japan, France versus Germany, Mexico versus Canada. In the 1990s, global competition is being reshaped by the creation of regional cooperation agreements. The most notable of these are the U.S.–Canadian alliance, the 12-nation European Community, the U.S.–Mexico border zones, and the U.S.–Mexico free-trade agreement.

U.S.–Canadian Alliance.   The trading barriers between the United States and Canada are coming down. These two countries were already the world's largest trading partners in 1989 when they created the U.S.-Canadian Free Trade Agreement. Its most

Coca-Cola, a multinational company with one of the world's best-known brand names, is a true global company. It has sales or bottling facilities in more than 150 countries.

MANAGERS
WHO MADE A
DIFFERENCE

Akiya Imura of Matsushita Electric Corp.

A global economy requires managers to be flexible. They must, for example, be ready to take an assignment some-place outside their home country. One such executive is Akiya Imura.[7] He is chief executive of Matsushita Electric Corporation of America (MECA), the American subsidiary of the largest consumer electronics firm in the world. You know MECA's products by brand names such as Panasonic, Technics, and Quasar.

Imura is a global manager. Born in Japan, he majored in English literature while in college in Osaka. Upon graduation, he spent twelve years with Panasonic in the United Kingdom. Since 1987, he's been at MECA's New Jersey headquarters. He is responsible for ten plants, scattered across the United States from Washington State to Tennessee, and for 10,000 employees, 9,600 of them Americans and 400 of them Japanese. In addition, he oversees a joint venture with Kodak, a high-tech laboratory in New Jersey, and the $661 million Panasonic Corporate Campus in Texas.

One of Imura's primary tasks at MECA is to bury the company's reputation for being too paternalistic and overly concerned with doing things the Japanese way. For instance, while Japanese workers enthusiastically work long hours and expect little in terms of immediate rewards, Imura finds American workers fixated on incentives and benefits. As a result of such observations, he is working toward blending Matsushita's historical Japanese roots with contemporary American values. "We're trying to create a second Matsushita in the United States," says Imura.

The primary means by which Imura hopes to achieve this end is through hiring and promoting more Americans. He recently promoted Richard Kraft, an American with fifteen years' experience at Matsushita, to the presidency of MECA. By sharing key decisions with Kraft, he hopes to bring the best from Japanese and American cultures to MECA.

immediate implications are increased competition for firms in each country and the movement of tens of thousands of Canadian jobs to the United States.

This Free Trade Agreement phases out tariffs on most goods traded between the two countries. It is also initiating a wave of consolidations as the typically smaller Canadian companies in relatively fragmented industries merge among themselves or with U.S. companies to form single giant firms. To prepare for the eventual battle for survival when U.S. and Canadian airlines are given unlimited access to the airports of both countries, Canadian Airlines International, which is Number 2 in market share, has bought Number 3, Wardair. To consolidate markets in the Canadian oil industry, Number 1 Imperial Oil has purchased Texaco Canada. Chicago-based packaging giant Stone Container bought Consolidated-Bathurst of Montreal to improve its pulp and paper position in Canada. The second and third largest Canadian breweries, Molson and Carling O'Keefe, have also merged. This allows them to better compete in Canada against U.S. heavyweights Anheuser-Busch and Miller Brewing and to prepare for a full-scale counterassault on the U.S. market.

This free trade agreement has not been without its critics, especially among

The U.S.-Canadian Free Trade Agreement has been an economic stimulant to many cities along each country's border. A number of U.S. firms, for instance, have located operations in Buffalo, New York, to gain easy access to Toronto and other Canadian markets.

Canadians. Their complaint: Hundreds of Canadian firms are relocating south of the border to reduce costs. Peraflex Hose, for instance, shifted much of its specialty-hose manufacturing to Buffalo, New York, from Toronto.[8] The company's president noted that his firm was able to find industrial property for $40,000 an acre compared to $430,000 for an equivalent Toronto property. He also said that shipping a 150-pound parcel to Detroit costs $18 from Buffalo and roughly $80 from Toronto, even though Toronto is seventeen miles closer.

European community

Currently, there are 330 million people living in the following 12 full-member countries: Belgium, Denmark, France, Greece, Ireland, Italy, Luxembourg, Netherlands, Portugal, Spain, the United Kingdom, and Germany.

The European Community.   The formation of the twelve-nation **European Community** in late 1992 united the 330 million people of Belgium, Denmark, France, Greece, Ireland, Italy, Luxembourg, the Netherlands, Portugal, Spain, the United Kingdom, and Germany. (See Figure 4–1.) Prior to the creation of the European Community, each of these twelve nations had border controls, border taxes, border subsidies, nationalistic policies, and protected industries. Now, as a single market, there are no national barriers to travel, employment, investment, and trade. A driver hauling cargo from Amsterdam to Lisbon can now clear four border crossings and five countries by showing a single piece of paper. Before the EC, that same driver needed two pounds of documents.

The primary motivation for the union of these twelve nations was to allow them to reassert their position against the industrial might of the United States and Japan. Working in separate countries that created barriers against one another, European industries were unable to develop the economies of scale enjoyed by the United

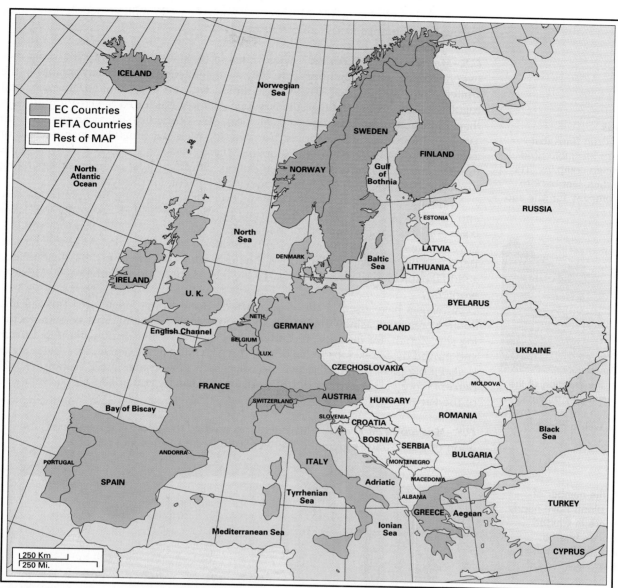

FIGURE 4–1
European Trade Alliances

States and Japan. The new EC, however, allows European firms to tap into what is now one of the world's single richest markets.

The European Community is furthering global competition. It is encouraging European multinationals and transnationals to consolidate and merge operations, as well as to form alliances with new partners. United States firms in such diverse industries as telecommunications equipment, pharmaceuticals, civilian aerospace, banking, automobiles, computers, electronics, food, and beverages now face vigorous challenges from their European counterparts. However, this consortium appears to be just the beginning—a host of other countries also want in.[9] First in line are the six countries of the European Free Trade Association: Austria, Finland, Iceland, Norway, Sweden, and Switzerland. EFTA has already approved a pact that virtually integrates its members into the Common Market. Next will be the countries of Czechoslovakia, Hungary, and Poland, which have agreed to open their markets to EC products by decade's end. So by the end of this decade, there is likely to be a

Greater European Economic Alliance encompassing 425 million people in at least twenty-one countries across all of Europe.

U.S.–Mexico Border Zones.   Wage rates in Mexico—which typically range between 55 cents and $1 an hour—are only a small fraction of the rates for labor in the United States and Canada. That fact, coupled with Mexico's limited governmental regulations and its proximity to the large U.S. market, has led to the creation of more than 2400 **maquiladoras** along the Mexican side of the U.S.–Mexican border from Texas to California. Maquiladoras are domestic Mexican firms that manufacture or assemble products for a foreign company. These products are then sent back to the foreign company for sale and distribution. Some of the companies operating maquiladoras include GE, Zenith, Honeywell, Hitachi, and Sanyo.[10]

Maquiladora operators don't pay taxes on capital equipment brought to Mexico, and they pay Mexican income taxes only on the value added—typically just labor costs—in Mexico. The concept of maquiladoras was devised by the Mexican and U.S. governments in 1965 to help develop both sides of the impoverished border region. But it was the massive devaluation of the peso, which occurred in 1982, that initiated a virtual explosion of maquiladoras. Today they employ more than 450,000 Mexican workers.

As wages have risen in the economies of Hong Kong, Singapore, Taiwan, and South Korea, increasingly firms have looked to Mexico as an alternative manufacturing site. Zenith, for instance, recently closed its television assembly plant in Taiwan and moved those 600 jobs to Mexico.[11] The proximity of Mexico to the United States is also a big plus. As an executive at Fisher-Price Toys commented, "Labor costs 25 percent more in Hong Kong and Taiwan, and we can be to market four weeks ahead of the Far East."[12]

U.S.–Mexico Free Trade.   Maquiladoras opened the door. The next step is the creation of a free-trade agreement between the United States and Mexico.

maquiladoras
Domestic Mexican firms that manufacture or assemble products for a foreign company. The products are then sent back to the foreign company for sale and distribution.

As a result of the creation of the European Community alliance, truck drivers can cross the France-Spain border with a minimum of paperwork.

Since 1982, the number of maquiladora plants have nearly tripled. They are in Ciudad Juárez, Nogales, Tijuana, Mexicali, and similar northern Mexican cities.

Do Maquiladoras Exploit Mexican Workers?

Do U.S., Japanese, and European corporations take advantage of Mexican workers by operating plants just south of the U.S. border? Are they exporting U.S. jobs?[13]

On one side are those who argue that maquiladoras exploit the large pool of unskilled Mexicans who have migrated north to these border cities to escape the poverty in inner Mexico. These people are desperate for work and are glad to take jobs at wages that are one-tenth those of employees just over the border. U.S. union officials further charge that maquiladoras have taken hundreds of thousands of U.S. jobs and will increasingly siphon off higher-paid jobs. Additionally, many Mexicans claim that the jobs and money come at too high a social cost; that is, northern Mexico is being Americanized. They are upset by the dilution of Mexican culture created by the spreading use of both English and the U.S. dollar.

The other side of the argument proposes that, far from feeling exploited, Mexican workers often find their clean, air-conditioned work surroundings a relief from their humble homes. While the pay is low by U.S. standards, these jobs are in high demand and provide an escape from poverty for hundreds of thousands of Mexicans. Moreover, proponents of maquiladoras stress that economics and global competition demand that production seek its lowest cost level. Firms north of the border that fail to transfer operations to gain cost benefits save jobs in the United States only in the short term. In the long term, competition will drive these firms out of business.

Are corporations that build plants south of the border profiting at the expense of exploited Mexican workers and taking jobs away from U.S workers? What do *you* think?

The United States has been pushing hard to negotiate a free-trade agreement with Mexico similar to that established with Canada. Supporters of such an agreement argue that it would create hundreds of thousands of jobs on both sides of the border and help stop the tidal wave of illegal immigration into the Southwestern states from Mexico. Critics, mostly from the United States, claim that such a pact will devastate many U.S. industries, increase U.S. joblessness, swamp the Southwest in a sea of Spanish, and hurt the environment.[14]

Separating truth from fiction on such an agreement is not easy. Two predictions, however, seem relatively certain if an agreement is put into place.[15] First, there will be different effects on different industries. As Mexico acquires all the markings and trappings of a developed society, U.S. producers of telecommunications equipment, computers, machinery, pharmaceuticals, financial services, and consumer goods are likely to benefit. The losers will likely be low tech, labor-intensive industries such as textiles, furniture, leather, and glass. Second, a lot of labor-intensive industries such as clothing manufacturing will move production from Asia to Mexico. This will create manufacturing jobs for Mexican workers and jobs in the United States in sales, warehousing, and management.

When, or if, a U.S.-Mexico trade agreement is negotiated, you should expect it to lead rapidly to a complete North American free-trade zone stretching from the Yukon to the Yucatán.[16] Encompassing Canada, the United States, and Mexico, it would consolidate 360 million consumers into a $6 trillion market—a market one-third larger than the European Community (see Figure 4–2).

FIGURE 4-2
North American Trade Areas

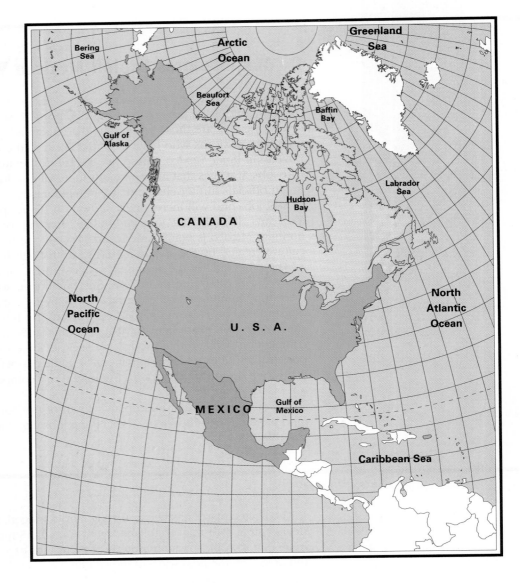

What's Next? A Pacific-Rim Block?   With the culmination of a European common market and the high likelihood of a North American free-trade zone, can a Pacific-Rim trading block be far away?

At this point, it is not much more than speculation.[17] But the creation of a Pacific-Rim block—which might include countries such as Japan, China, Australia, Taiwan, Thailand, and South Korea—would make a more self-reliant region, better able to provide both raw materials and markets within the region. Moreover, a unified Pacific Rim would have increased clout in trading with North America and Europe.

So Long Communism, Hello Capitalism!

The Cold War is over, communism is on the retreat, and capitalism is spreading throughout the world. In the last several years, Germany has been reunited; countries like Poland and Romania have introduced democratic governments; and the former Soviet Union has become a set of independent states trying to implement market-based reforms. With a few exceptions, such as Cuba, the world is opening up to free markets and profit-seeking enterprises.

In terms of the changing global environment, the spread of capitalism makes the world a smaller place. Business has new markets to conquer. Additionally, well-trained and reliable workers in such countries as Hungary, Slovakia, and the Czech Republic provide a rich source of low-cost labor. The implementation of free markets in Eastern Europe further underscores the growing interdependence between countries of the world and the potential for goods, labor, and capital to move easily across national borders.

How Organizations Go International

How does an organization evolve into a global organization? It typically proceeds through stages (see Figure 4–3).

In Stage I, management makes its first inroads toward going international merely by exporting its products to other countries. This is a passive step toward international involvement because management makes no serious efforts to tap foreign markets. Rather, the organization fills foreign orders only when—or if—they come in. For many firms in the mail-order business, this is the first and only stage in which they may engage.

In Stage II, management makes an overt commitment to sell its products in foreign countries or have them made in foreign factories. However, there is still no physical presence of company personnel outside the company's home country. On the sales side, Stage II typically is achieved either by sending domestic employees on regular business trips to meet foreign customers or by hiring foreign agents or brokers to represent the organization's product line. On the manufacturing side, management will contract with a foreign firm to make its products.

Stage III represents a commitment by management to pursue international markets aggressively. As shown in Figure 4–3, this can take a number of forms. Management can *license* or *franchise* the right to use its brand name, technology, or product specifications to another firm. This is a widely used practice among pharmaceutical companies and fast-food chains like Pizza Hut. *Joint ventures* are a larger commitment. They involve a domestic firm sharing the cost of developing new products or building production facilities in a foreign country. These are also sometimes referred to as *strategic alliances*. These partnerships provide a fast and less expensive way for companies to compete globally. Recent cross-border alliances include Corning and Ciba-Geigy, Volvo and Renault, Motorola and Toshiba, and Mitsubishi and Daimler-Benz. Management makes its greatest commitment to global operations when it sets up a *foreign subsidiary*. As noted earlier in the chapter, this is achieved either through domestic control (multinational operations) or by decentralized control wielded by foreign nationals (transnational operations).

FIGURE 4–3
How Organizations Go
International

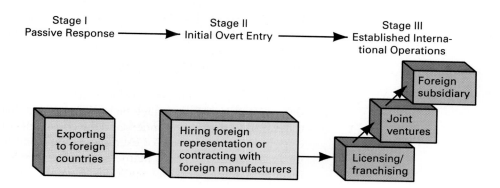

Pizza Hut has gone international by franchising its operation in locations such as Moscow.

Managing in a Foreign Environment

Assume for a moment that you're an American manager who is going to work for a branch of a U.S. multinational in a foreign country. You know that your environment will differ from the one at home, but how? What should you be on the lookout for?

Any manager who finds himself or herself in a strange country faces new challenges. In this section, we will look at these challenges and offer some guidelines for how to respond. Since most readers of this text were raised in the United States, we'll present our discussion through the eyes of an American manager. Of course, our analytical framework could be used by any manager, regardless of national origin, who has to manage in a foreign environment.

The Legal-Political Environment

U.S. managers are accustomed to stable legal and political systems. Changes are slow, and procedures are well established. Elections are held at regular intervals. Even changes in parties after a presidential election do not produce any quick, radical transformations. The stability of laws governing the actions of individuals and institutions allows for very accurate predictions. The same cannot be said for all nations.

Some countries have a history of unstable governments. Some South American and African countries have had six different governments in as many years. With each new government have come new rules. The goal of one government may be to nationalize the country's key industries; the goal of the next may be to stimulate free enterprise. Managers of business firms in these countries face dramatically greater uncertainty as a result of political instability.

The legal-political environment does not have to be unstable or revolutionary to be of concern to managers. Just the fact that a country's social and political system differs from that of the United States is important. Managers need to recognize these differences if they are to understand the constraints under which they operate and the opportunities that exist. For example, Hong Kong imposes few legal constraints on business. France imposes many. Laws differ between nations on industrial spying, restraint of trade, working conditions, the rights of privacy, the rights of workers, and so forth.

Political instability, such as the recent upheavals in Thailand, creates considerable uncertainty for managers.

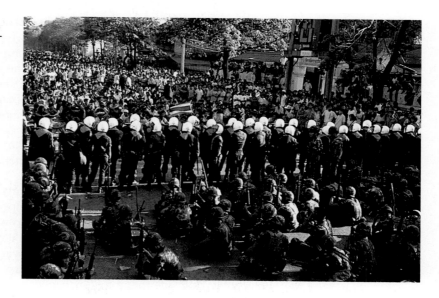

The Economic Environment

The global manager has economic concerns that the manager who operates in a single country doesn't have. Two of the most obvious are fluctuating currency rates and diverse tax policies.

A global firm's profits can alter dramatically, depending on the strength of its home currency and the currencies of the countries in which it operates. For instance, in the summer of 1993 the German mark stood at 1.57 to the U.S. dollar. In the mid-1980s, it took 2.85 marks to equal a dollar. A 50-million-mark profit in 1985 by a German subsidiary of a U.S. company converted to $17.5 million in U.S. dollars. The same profit eight years later resulted in $31.8 million in U.S. dollars. An investment by a U.S. firm in 1980 of 100 million Mexican pesos cost approximately $7 million in U.S. dollars. Between 1980 and 1993, the peso went from 114.5 to the dollar to a staggering 3400 to the dollar. Assuming for a moment that inflation had not raised the value of that original investment, the reconverted value of the $7 million dollars in 1993 would be less than $30,000! The point of these examples is to demonstrate that global organizations assume risks in production and marketing, but also have another risk (and a potential for profit) from fluctuating currency rates.

Similarly, diverse tax policies are a major worry for a global manager. Some host countries are more restrictive than the corporation's home country; others are far more lenient. About the only thing certain is that tax rules differ from country to country. Managers need precise knowledge of the various tax rules in the countries in which they operate to minimize their corporation's overall tax obligation.

The Cultural Environment

The final environmental force is the cultural differences between nations. As we know from Chapter 3, organizations have different internal cultures. Countries have cultures, too, as anthropologists have long been telling us. Like organizational culture, **national culture** is something that is shared by all, or most, inhabitants of a country and that shapes their behavior and the way they see the world.[18]

Does national culture override an organization's culture? For example, is an IBM facility in Germany more likely to reflect German ethnicity or IBM's corporate culture? Research indicates that national culture has a greater effect on employees than does their organization's culture.[19] German employees at an IBM facility in Munich will be influenced more by German culture than by IBM's culture. This means that as influen-

national culture
The attitudes and perspectives shared by individuals from a specific country that shape their behavior and the way they see the world.

tial as organizational culture is on managerial practice, national culture is even more so.

Legal, political, and economic differences among countries are fairly straightforward. The Japanese manager who works in the United States or his or her American counterpart in Japan can obtain information on their new country's laws or tax policies without too much difficulty. However, obtaining information about a new country's cultural differences is a lot more troublesome. The primary reason is that the "natives" are least capable of explaining their culture's unique characteristics to someone else. If you're an American raised in the United States, how would you characterize your culture? Think about it for a moment and then see how many of the points in Table 4–2 you correctly identified.

To date, the most valuable framework to help managers better understand differences between national cultures has been developed by Geert Hofstede.[20] He surveyed over 116,000 employees in 40 countries who worked for a single multinational corporation. What did he find? His huge data base indicated that national culture had a major impact on employees' work-related values and attitudes. In fact, it explained more of the differences than did age, sex, profession, or position in the organization. More important, Hofstede found that managers and employees vary on four dimensions of national culture: (1) individualism versus collectivism, (2) power distance, (3) uncertainty avoidance, and (4) quantity versus quality of life.[21]

individualism
A cultural dimension in which people are supposed to look after their own interests and those of their immediate family.

collectivism
A cultural dimension in which people expect others in their group to look after them and protect them when they are in trouble.

Individualism Versus Collectivism   **Individualism** refers to a loosely knit social framework in which people are supposed to look after their own interests and those of their immediate family. This is made possible because of the large amount of freedom that such a society allows individuals. Its opposite is **collectivism,** which is characterized by a tight social framework in which people expect others in groups of which they are a part (such as a family or an organization) to look after them and protect them when they are in trouble. In exchange for this, they feel they owe absolute loyalty to the group.

TABLE 4–2   What Are Americans Like?

Americans are very *informal*. They don't tend to treat people differently even when there are great differences in age or social standing.

Americans are *direct*. They don't talk around things. To some foreigners, this may appear as abrupt or even rude behavior.

Americans are *competitive*. Some foreigners may find Americans assertive or overbearing.

Americans are *achievers*. They like to keep score, whether at work or play. They emphasize accomplishments.

Americans are *independent and individualistic*. They place a high value on freedom and believe that individuals can shape and control their own destiny.

Americans are *questioners*. They ask a lot of questions, even of someone they have just met. Many of these questions may seem pointless ("How ya doing") or personal ("What kind of work do you do?").

Americans dislike *silence*. They would rather talk about the weather than deal with silence in a conversation.

Americans value *punctuality*. They keep appointment calendars and live according to schedules and clocks.

Americans value *cleanliness*. They often seem obsessed with bathing, eliminating body odors, and wearing clean clothes.

Source: Based on Margo Ernest, ed., *Predeparture Orientation Handbook: For Foreign Students and Scholars Planning to Study in the United States* (Washington, D.C.: U.S. Information Agency, Bureau of Cultural Affairs, 1984), pp. 103–5; Amanda Bennett, "American Culture Is Often a Puzzle for Foreign Managers in the U.S.," *Wall Street Journal*, February 12, 1986, p. 29; "Don't Think Our Way's the Only Way," *The Pryor Report*, February 1988, p. 9; and Ben J. Wattenberg, "The Attitudes Behind American Exceptionalism," *U.S. News & World Report*, August 7, 1989, p. 25.

Although it is a rich country, Japan scores high on collectivism. This helps to explain the popularity of teams in Japanese plants like this one at Mitsubishi.

power distance
A cultural measure of the extent to which a society accepts the unequal distribution of power in institutions and organizations.

uncertainty avoidance
A cultural measure of the degree to which people tolerate risk and unconventional behavior.

quantity of life
A national culture attribute describing the extent to which societal values are characterized by assertiveness and materialism.

quality of life
A national culture attribute that reflects the emphasis placed upon relationships and concern for others.

Hofstede found that the degree of individualism in a country is closely related to that country's wealth. Richer countries like the United States, Great Britain, and the Netherlands are very individualistic. Poorer countries like Colombia and Pakistan are very collectivist.

Power Distance   People naturally vary in terms of physical and intellectual abilities. This, in turn, creates differences in wealth and power. How does a society deal with these inequalities? Hofstede used the term **power distance** as a measure of the extent to which a society accepts the fact that power in institutions and organizations is distributed unequally. A high power distance society accepts wide differences in power in organizations. Employees show a great deal of respect for those in authority. Titles, rank, and status carry a lot of weight. When negotiating in high power distance countries, companies find it helps to send representatives with titles at least as high as those with whom they're bargaining. Countries high in power distance include the Philippines, Venezuela, and India. In contrast, a low power distance society plays down inequalities as much as possible. Superiors still have authority, but employees are not fearful or in awe of the boss. Denmark, Israel, and Austria are examples of countries with low power distance scores.

Uncertainty Avoidance   We live in a world of uncertainty. The future is largely unknown and always will be. Societies respond to this uncertainty in different ways. Some socialize their members into accepting it with equanimity. People in such societies are more or less comfortable with risks. They're also relatively tolerant of behavior and opinions that differ from their own because they don't feel threatened by them. Hofstede describes such societies as having low **uncertainty avoidance.** That is, people feel relatively secure. Countries that fall into this category include Singapore and Denmark.

A society that is high in uncertainty avoidance is characterized by an increased level of anxiety among its people, which manifests itself in greater nervousness, stress, and aggressiveness. Because people feel threatened by uncertainty and ambiguity in these societies, mechanisms are created to provide security and reduce risk. Their organizations are likely to have more formal rules, there will be less tolerance for deviant ideas and behaviors, and members will strive to believe in absolute truths. Not surprisingly, in organizations in countries with high uncertainty avoidance employees demonstrate relatively low job mobility, and lifetime employment is a widely practiced policy. Countries in this category include Japan, Portugal, and Greece.

Quantity versus Quality of Life   The fourth dimension, like individualism and collectivism, represents a dichotomy. Some cultures emphasize the **quantity of life** and value things like assertiveness and the acquisition of money and material goods. Other cultures emphasize the **quality of life,** the importance of relationships, and show sensitivity and concern for the welfare of others.

Hofstede found that Japan and Austria scored high on the quantity dimension. In contrast, Norway, Sweden, Denmark, and Finland scored high on the quality dimension.

We haven't the space to review the results Hofstede obtained for each of the 40 countries, although a dozen examples are presented in Table 4–3.

A Guide for U.S. Managers   Since we used the United States earlier as a point of reference, we'll conclude this section by (1) reviewing how the United States ranked on Hofstede's four dimensions and (2) considering how an American manager, working in another country, might be able to use Hofstede's research findings.

Comparing the forty countries on the four dimensions, Hofstede found the U.S.

TABLE 4-3 Examples of Hofstede's Cultural Dimensions

Country	Individualism/ Collectivism	Power Distance	Uncertainty Avoidance	Quantity of life*
Australia	Individual	Small	Moderate	Strong
Canada	Individual	Moderate	Low	Moderate
England	Individual	Small	Moderate	Strong
France	Individual	Large	High	Weak
Greece	Collective	Large	High	Moderate
Italy	Individual	Moderate	High	Strong
Japan	Collective	Moderate	High	Strong
Mexico	Collective	Large	High	Strong
Singapore	Collective	Large	Low	Moderate
Sweden	Individual	Small	Low	Weak
United States	Individual	Small	Low	Strong
Venezuela	Collective	Large	High	Strong

* A weak quantity score is equivalent to high quality of life.

Source: Based on G. Hofstede, "Motivation, Leadership, and Organization: Do American Theories Apply Abroad?" *Organizational Dynamics,* Summer 1980, pp. 42–63.

culture to be the highest among all countries on individualism, below average on power distance, well below average on uncertainty avoidance, and well above average on quantity of life. These conclusions are not inconsistent with the world image of the United States. That is, America is seen as fostering the individualistic ethic, having a representative government with democratic ideals, being relatively free from threats of uncertainty, and having a capitalistic economy that values aggressiveness and materialism.

Into which countries are U.S. managers likely to fit best? Which are likely to create the biggest adjustment problems? All we have to do is identify those countries that are most and least like the United States on the four dimensions.

The United States is strongly individualistic but low on power distance. This same pattern was exhibited by Great Britain, Australia, Canada, the Netherlands, and New Zealand. Those least similar to the United States on these dimensions were Venezuela, Colombia, Pakistan, Singapore, and the Philippines.

The United States scored low on uncertainty avoidance and high on quantity of life. This same pattern was shown by Ireland, Great Britain, the Philippines, Canada, New Zealand, Australia, India, and South Africa. Those least similar to the United States on these dimensions were Chile and Portugal.

These results empirically support part of what many of us suspected—that the American manager transferred to London, Toronto, Melbourne, or a similar Anglo city would have to make the fewest adjustments. In addition, the results further identify the countries in which "culture shock" is likely to be greatest and the need to modify one's managerial style most imperative.

Summary

This summary is organized by the chapter-opening learning objectives found on page 93.

1. Competitors are no longer defined within national borders. New competitors can suddenly appear anytime, from anywhere in the world. Managers must think globally if their organizations are to succeed over the long term.

2. National parochialism prevents people from recognizing that people in other countries have different ways of living and working. Parochial people rigidly

apply their own values and customs to foreign cultures. The result is that they fail to understand foreigners and reduce their ability to effectively work with such people.

3. Multinational corporations have significant operations functioning in two or more countries simultaneously, but primary decision making and control is based in the company's home country. Transnationals also have significant operations in multiple countries but decision making is decentralized to the local level.

4. Regional trading alliances create more powerful economic entities. Many countries have joined these alliances in order to compete more effectively. For instance, countries joined the European Community to compete more aggressively against such economically powerful countries as the United States and Japan.

5. The typical stages by which organizations go international are (1) exporting to foreign countries; (2) hiring foreign representation or contracting with foreign manufacturers; and (3) establishing international operations through licensing/franchising, joint ventures, and/or foreign subsidiaries.

6. The four primary dimensions in which nations differ are individualism versus collectivism, power distance, uncertainty avoidance, and quantity versus quality of life.

7. U.S. culture is characterized as being high on individualism, below average on power distance, well below average on uncertainty avoidance, and well above average on quantity of life.

Review Questions

1. How does a global economy create both opportunities and threats for managers?
2. Americans are more nationally parochial than Europeans. Why?
3. Describe the future for regional trading alliances.
4. What are the implications of a "United Europe" for managers of global organizations?
5. What are *maquiladoras*?
6. Based on the Ethical Dilemmas in Management box on p. 103, what response do you expect unions in the United States to give to a U.S.–Mexican free-trade zone?
7. What would motivate Pacific-Rim countries to form a cooperative trading block?
8. What is a *legal-political* environment? What is its relevance to understanding global management?
9. How do characteristics of a country's economic environment influence management practice?
10. How can an understanding of Hofstede's four dimensions help managers to be more effective in a global marketplace?

Discussion Questions

1. The politics of economic nationalism has no place in a borderless world. Do you agree or disagree? Discuss.
2. Can the Hofstede framework presented in this chapter be used to guide managers in a hospital in South Korea or a government agency in Peru? Discuss.

3. What political risks does the Ford Motor Company take in Mexico, Australia, Brazil, and Germany?

4. How might the U.S.–Canadian free-trade agreement effect an automobile manufacturer, like Chrysler, that has plants in both the U.S. and Canada?

5. In what ways do you think the global environment has changed or will change the way in which business firms select and train managers?

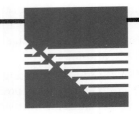

SELF-ASSESSMENT EXERCISE

The International Culture Quiz

How knowledgeable are you about customs, practices and facts regarding different countries? The following multiple-choice quiz will provide you with some feedback on this question.

1. In which country would *Ramadan* (a month of fasting) be celebrated by the majority of people?
   - a. Saudi Arabia
   - b. India
   - c. Singapore
   - d. Korea
   - e. All of the above

2. On first meeting your prospective Korean business partner, Lo Kim Chee, it would be best to address him as:
   - a. Mr. Kim
   - b. Mr. Lo
   - c. Mr. Chee
   - d. Bud
   - e. Any of the above are readily accepted

3. In Brazil, your promotional material should be translated into what language?
   - a. French
   - b. Italian
   - c. Spanish
   - d. No need to translate it
   - e. None of the above

4. In Japan it is important to:
   - a. Present your business card only after you have developed a relationship with your Japanese host
   - b. Present your business card with both hands
   - c. Put your company name on the card, but never your position or title
   - d. All of the above
   - e. None of the above

5. Which one of the following sports is the most popular worldwide?
   - a. Basketball
   - b. Baseball
   - c. Tennis
   - d. Futbol
   - e. Golf

6. For an American businessperson, touching a foreign businessperson would be least acceptable in which one of the following countries?
   - a. Japan
   - b. Italy
   - c. Slovenia
   - d. Venezuela
   - e. France

7. Which of the following would be an appropriate gift?
   a. A clock in China
   b. A bottle of liquor in Egypt
   c. A set of knives in Argentina
   d. A banquet in China
   e. None of the above would be appropriate

8. Which one of the following countries has the most rigid social hierarchy?
   a. United Kingdom   d. India
   b. United States   e. Germany
   c. Japan

9. Traditional western banking is difficult in which one of the following countries because their law forbids both the giving and taking of interest payments?
   a. Brazil   d. India
   b. Saudi Arabia   e. Greece
   c. Mongolia

10. The capital of Canada is:
    a. Toronto   d. Ontario
    b. Ottawa   e. Montreal
    c. Vancouver

Turn to page SK-1 for scoring directions and key.

Source: Prof. David Hopkins, University of Denver, 1991. With permission.

FOR YOUR IMMEDIATE ACTION

J. Pierre Nadeau's
CLUB 2000
Warehouse Shopping

To: André Filiatrault; Director of Operations
From: J.P. Nadeau, Managing Director

We need to begin thinking of our business in terms of a global strategy. We are now France's largest chain of warehouse shopping stores. When we open the new locations in Saint Etienne and Rennes later this year, we will have essentially saturated our major domestic markets. I want to begin pursuing the idea of entering the United Kingdom.

We don't know much about British culture, although there are several successful warehouse chains operating there. This tells me that there is a market for what we do. However, France is very different from the United Kingdom. We might encounter problems adjusting to Britain's system of free enterprise and to that country's unique geography. Also, we must consider the various options available to us for becoming an international company. André, I would like you to provide me with a brief analysis—not to exceed two pages—of what problems we should be prepared to face in moving into England, Wales, and Scotland. Specifically: (1) What cultural differences might we confront? (2) What would be the most cost-effective strategy for establishing operations in these countries?

This is a fictionalized account of a potentially real problem. It was written for academic purposes only and is not meant to reflect either positively or negatively on actual management practices at J. Pierre Nadeau's Club 2000 Warehouse Shopping.

CASE APPLICATION

Xerox of Mexico

Paul Hunt grew up in Houston and got his degree in business management from Texas A & M in 1986. Upon graduation, Paul took a job with the Xerox Corporation in Dallas as a personnel specialist. During his first two years, he split his time between recruiting on college campuses and establishing a training program for maintenance engineers. In 1988, Paul was promoted to Assistant Manager for Human Resources—Western Region. The company moved him to the western regional office in Denver.

Paul's annual performance appraisals were consistently high. The company believed that he had strong advancement potential. Though Paul was ambitious and made no attempt to hide his desire to move into higher management, even he was a bit surprised when he was called to Xerox's Connecticut headquarters in April 1992 and offered the position of Director of Human Resources for Xerox of Mexico. If he accepted the position, Paul would oversee a staff of twenty people in Mexico City and be responsible for all human resource activities—hiring, compensation, labor relations, and so on—for the company's Mexican operations. He was told that the combination of his outstanding job performance ratings and his ability to speak Spanish (Paul had taken four years of Spanish in high school and another twelve hours of advanced coursework in college) led the company to select him for the promotion.

Paul accepted the offer. Why not? It was an important promotion, meant a large increase in pay, and provided an opportunity to live in a foreign country.

Questions

1. Describe Mexico's national culture.
2. How does the culture in Mexico compare to the culture in which Paul grew up?
3. Based on the discussion in Chapter 1 of what managers do, what changes do you think Paul will need to make in his managerial style?

VIDEO CASE

Japanese-Owned Companies in America

Do Japanese-owned companies that operate in the United States practice racism? Do they discriminate? You be the judge.

Chet Mackentire got his "job of a lifetime." Based on his experience and contacts in the optical computer disk business, Ricoh Corp. hired Mackentire as sales manager at $75,000 a year. Under Mackentire's leadership, Ricoh, a Japanese-owned company, became number two in the optical disk industry, behind only Sony. But then Ricoh fired him. Mackentire has sued, claiming discrimination.

A number of American executives have recently begun to complain about the way Japanese-owned companies treat the American executives in their U.S. subsidiaries. These executives claim Japanese firms discriminate based on race and national origin. They suggest that American executives are hired just to start operations in the United States, then are let go to be replaced by Japanese managers. These critics go so far as to say that even when American managers have high-ranking titles in these companies, they are cut out of major meetings and decisions. They believe that there are no authentic upward career paths for non-Japanese in U.S. subsidiaries. In support of these claims, studies show that only 18 percent of top jobs in Japanese companies in the U.S. are held by Americans.

Spokespersons for the Japanese companies under attack admit that Japanese executives prefer to work with other Japanese executives. They say that Japanese people are not comfortable working with non-Japanese workers. They essentially argue that they are not discriminating against Americans, but they do acknowledge a clash of cultures and values. For instance, they point out that the Japanese view of a leader is a person who is quiet, strives for gaining consensus, and is a team player. In contrast, the Japanese see American leaders as assertive and individualistic. As such, they feel Americans don't fit into the way that Japanese managers make decisions. The Japanese claim that Americans can make it to the top in their U.S. operations, but they have to show patience.

Questions

1. Should it be illegal for Japanese-owned companies to impose their management style in their U.S. operations?

2. Women are routinely held back in Japan in favor of men for management positions. Would this be acceptable in the United States? Discuss.

3. Based on what you've read in this chapter, do you think the Japanese are stereotyping American executives, or are Americans actually more assertive, individualistic, and impatient than their Japanese counterparts?

4. What, if anything, could be done to make Japanese executives more sensitive to U.S. laws and customs?

Source: "No Room at the Top," *ABC 20/20,* September 27, 1991.

CHAPTER 5

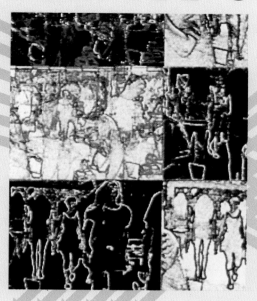

Social Responsibility and Managerial Ethics

LEARNING OBJECTIVES

After Reading This Chapter, You Should Be Able To:

1. Explain the classical and socioeconomic views of social responsibility.
2. List the arguments for and against business being socially responsible.
3. Differentiate social responsibility from social responsiveness.
4. Explain the relationship between corporate social responsibility and economic performance.
5. Define *stakeholders* and describe their role in social responsibility.
6. Define *ethics*.
7. Differentiate three views on ethics.
8. Identify the factors that affect ethical behavior.
9. Describe the stages of moral development.
10. Discuss various ways in which organizations can improve the ethical behavior of their employees.

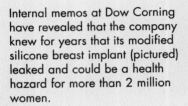

Internal memos at Dow Corning have revealed that the company knew for years that its modified silicone breast implant (pictured) leaked and could be a health hazard for more than 2 million women.

Thomas Talcott had been a materials engineer at Dow Corning for 24 years. His job had been to help develop silicone gel for the breast implant manufacturer (see photo). But in 1976 he resigned after the company switched to a more liquid gel designed to make the implants softer and more lifelike. Talcott feared that the thinner gel could rupture or leak and become a serious health hazard. His concerns were ignored by company executives for more than fifteen years. Dow Corning's official position, which it maintained until early 1992, was that their silicone gel implants had been thoroughly tested in animals and presented no health risk to the more than two million women who received them. It now appears that Talcott may have been right and that Dow Corning was not only aware of implant problems for decades but had tried to cover the problem up.[1]

Investigations by newspapers, the Federal Drug Administration, and Congressional subcommittees uncovered company memos indicating that Dow Corning was in such a rush to get its product on the market in 1975 that it either dismissed or short-circuited animal studies showing that silicone leaked from the implants. Internal memos revealed that Dow Corning misrepresented its research results to women, medical professionals, and FDA regulators. The memos showed that the company had long known that silicone could leak from its breast implants into some women's bodies. After decades of denials and stonewalling, Dow Corning finally admitted in early 1992 that it had not been completely honest. It rationalized not releasing the memos earlier for fear of panicking women. Yet, in an action certainly not likely to be very reassuring to those women with Dow Corning implants, the company stated in February 1992 that it would pay for implant removal for any woman who wanted it done but couldn't afford it. And at the same time, consistent with the omnipotent view of management that we presented in Chapter 3, the company announced that it had replaced its chief executive officer, thereby attempting to demonstrate to the public and critical constituencies that it was serious about responding to the implant problem. Shortly thereafter, Dow Corning announced that it would take a $94 million writeoff against potential litigation and get out of the implant business.

Is the Dow Corning cover-up a rare instance of corporate irresponsibility or is it just another example of a decline in business morality? That's not an easy question to answer. There is, however, a lot of evidence that suggests that ethics—or the lack of ethics—is a widespread problem. Consider the following:[2]

The selling of "pre-packaged" term papers for college students has become so blatant that firms advertise in publications such as *Rolling Stone*.

A poll of more than 6000 college students revealed that 76 percent of those planning business careers admitted to cheating on at least one test and 19 percent admitted to cheating on at least four tests.

In a scandal that shocked the world business community, Japanese investment firms admitted funneling illegal payments to cover the investment losses of favored corporate clients.

Monsanto recently paid a $1.2 million fine to the state of Massachusetts for trying to conceal the discharge of 200,000 gallons of acidic waste water.

A survey of 1400 executives found that 53 percent believed that most successful business people must sometimes fudge principles to get ahead.

In this chapter, we'll establish a foundation for understanding social responsibility and managerial ethics. The discussion of these topics is placed at this point in the text to link them to the preceding and following subjects. Specifically, we'll show that social responsibility is a response to a changing environment and that ethical considerations should be an important criterion in managerial decision making (the topic of Chapter 6).

What is Social Responsibility?

The issue of corporate social responsibility drew little attention before the 1960s. However, the activist movement at that time began to call into question the singular economic objective of business firms. Were large corporations irresponsible because they discriminated against women and minorities, as shown by the obvious absence of female and minority managers at that time? Did Kennecott Copper ignore its social responsibilities by allowing its smelters to pollute the air over hundreds of square miles of Arizona?

Before the 1960s, few people asked such questions. But times have changed. Managers are now regularly confronted with decisions that have a dimension of social responsibility—philanthropy, pricing, employee relations, resource conservation, product quality, and operations in countries with oppressive governments are some of the more obvious. To help managers make such decisions, let's begin by defining social responsibility.

Two Opposing Views

Few terms have been defined in as many different ways as *social responsibility.* Some of the more popular meanings include "profit making only," "going beyond profit making," "voluntary activities," "concern for the broader social system," and "social responsiveness."[3] Most of the debate has focused at the extremes. On one side, there is the classical—or purely economic—view that management's only social responsibility is to maximize profits. On the other side stands the socioeconomic position, which holds that management's responsibility goes well beyond making profits to include protecting and improving society's welfare.

classical view
The view that management's only social responsibility is to maximize profits.

The Classical View   The most outspoken advocate of the **classical view** is economist and Nobel laureate Milton Friedman.[4] He argues that most managers today are professional managers, which means that they don't own the businesses they run. They're employees, responsible to the stockholders. Their primary charge is therefore to conduct the business in the interests of the stockholders. And what are those interests? Friedman argues that the stockholders have a single concern: financial return.

According to Friedman, when managers take it upon themselves to spend their organization's resources for the "social good," they undermine the market mechanism. Someone has to pay for this redistribution of assets. If socially responsible actions reduce profits and dividends, stockholders are the losers. If wages and benefits have to be reduced to pay for social action, employees lose. If prices are raised to pay for social actions, consumers lose. If higher prices are rejected by the market and sales drop, the business might not survive—in which case, *all* the organization's constituencies lose. Moreover, Friedman contends that when professional managers pursue anything other than profit, they implicitly appoint themselves as nonelected policymakers. He questions whether managers of business firms have the expertise for deciding how society *should* be. That, Friedman would argue, is what we elect political representatives to decide.

Friedman's argument is probably best understood in terms of microeconomics. If socially responsible acts add to the cost of doing business, those costs have to be either passed on to consumers in higher prices or absorbed by stockholders through a smaller profit margin. In a competitive market, if management raises prices, it will lose sales. In a purely competitive market, given that the competition hasn't also assumed the costs of social responsibility, prices can't be raised without losing the entire market. Such a situation means that the costs have to be absorbed by the business, which results in lower profits.

The classical view would also argue that there are pressures in a competitive market for investment funds to go where they'll get the highest return. If the socially responsible firm can't pass on its higher social costs to consumers and has to absorb them internally, it will generate a lower rate of return. Over time, investment funds will gravitate away from socially responsible firms toward those that aren't, since the latter will provide the higher rate of return. That might even mean that if all the firms in a particular country—such as the United States—incurred additional social costs because management perceived this to be one of business's goals, the survival of entire domestic industries could be threatened by foreign competitors who chose not to incur such social costs.

The Socioeconomic View   The socioeconomic position counters that times have changed and with them society's expectations of business. This is best illustrated in the legal formation of corporations. Corporations are chartered by state governments. The same government that creates a charter can take it away. So corporations are not independent entities, responsible only to stockholders. They also have a responsibility to the larger society that creates and sustains them.

socioeconomic view
The view that management's social responsibility goes well beyond the making of profits to include protecting and improving society's welfare.

One author, in supporting the **socioeconomic view,** reminds us that "maximizing profits is a company's second priority, not its first. The first is ensuring its survival."[5]

Take the case of the Manville Corporation. Nearly fifty years ago, its senior management had evidence that one of its products, asbestos, caused fatal lung diseases. As a matter of policy, management decided to conceal the information from affected employees. The reason? Profits! In court testimony, a lawyer recalled how, in the mid-1940s, he had questioned Manville's corporate counsel about the company's policy of concealing chest X-ray results from employees. The lawyer had asked, "Do you mean to tell me you would let them work until they dropped dead?" The reply was, "Yes, we save a lot of money that way."[6] This might have been true in the short run, but certainly not in the long term. The company was forced to file for bankruptcy in 1982 to protect itself against tens of thousands of potential asbestos-related lawsuits. It emerged from bankruptcy in 1988, but with staggering asbestos-related liabilities. To compensate victims, Manville agreed to set up a personal injury settlement trust, funding it with $2.6 billion in cash and bonds and up to 20 percent of the company's annual profits through the year 2015.[7] Here is an example of what can happen when management takes a short-term perspective. Many workers died before their time, the stockholders lost a great deal of money, and a major corporation was forced into reorganization.

A major flaw in the classicists' view, as seen by socioeconomic proponents, is their time frame. Supporters of the socioeconomic view contend that managers should be concerned with maximizing financial returns over the *long run*. To do that, they must accept some social obligations and the costs that go with them. They must protect society's welfare by *not* polluting, *not* discriminating, *not* engaging in deceptive advertising, and the like. They must also play an affirmative role in improving society by involving themselves in their communities and contributing to charitable organizations.

A final point made by proponents of the socioeconomic position is that the classical view flies in the face of reality.[8] Modern business firms are no longer merely economic institutions. They lobby, form political action committees, and engage in other activities to influence the political process for their benefit. Society accepts and even encourages business to become involved in its social, political, and legal environment. That might not have been true thirty or forty years ago, but it is the reality of today.

Government health and safety inspections provide basic protection for employees. Many employers, however, consistent with the socioeconomic view, go beyond what the law requires.

Arguments For and Against Social Responsibility

What are the specific arguments for and against business assuming social responsibilities? In this section, we'll outline the major points that have been brought forward.[9]

Arguments For   The major arguments supporting the assumption of social responsibilities by business are:

1. *Public expectations.* Social expectations of business have increased dramatically since the 1960s. Public opinion in support of business pursuing social as well as economic goals is now well solidified.

2. *Long-run profits.* Socially responsible businesses tend to have more secure long-run profits. This is the normal result of the better community relations and improved business image that responsible behavior brings.

3. *Ethical obligation.* A business firm can and should have a conscience. Business should be socially responsible because responsible actions are *right* for their own sake.

4. *Public image.* Firms seek to enhance their public image to gain more customers, better employees, access to money markets, and other benefits. Since the public considers social goals to be important, business can create a favorable public image by pursuing social goals.

5. *Better environment.* Involvement by business can solve difficult social problems, thus creating a better quality of life and a more desirable community in which to attract and hold skilled employees.

6. *Discouragement of further government regulation.* Government regulation adds economic costs and restricts management's decision flexibility. By becoming socially responsible, business can expect less government regulation.

7. *Balance of responsibility and power.* Business has a large amount of power in society. An equally large amount of responsibility is required to balance it. When power is significantly greater than responsibility, the imbalance encourages irresponsible behavior that works against the public good.

8. *Stockholder interests.* Social responsibility will improve the price of a business's stock in the long run. The stock market will view the socially responsible company as less risky and open to public attack. Therefore, it will award its stock a higher price–earnings ratio.

9. *Possession of resources.* Business has the financial resources, technical experts, and managerial talent to provide support to public and charitable projects that need assistance.

10. *Superiority of prevention over cures.* Social problems must be dealt with at some time. Business should act on them before they become more serious and costly to correct and take management's energy away from accomplishing its goal of producing goods and services.

Arguments Against   The major arguments against business assuming social responsibility are:

1. *Violation of profit maximization.* This is the essence of the classical viewpoint. Business is most socially responsible when it attends strictly to its economic interests and leaves other activities to other institutions.

2. *Dilution of purpose.* The pursuit of social goals dilutes business's primary purpose: economic productivity. Society may suffer as both economic and social goals are poorly accomplished.

3. *Costs.* Many socially responsible activities don't pay their own way. Someone has to pay these costs. Business must absorb these costs or pass them on to consumers in higher prices.

4. *Too much power.* Business is already one of the most powerful institutions in our society. If it pursues social goals, it would have even more power. Society has given business enough power.

5. *Lack of skills.* The outlook and abilities of business leaders are oriented primarily toward economics. Businesspeople are poorly qualified to cope with social issues.

6. *Lack of accountability.* Political representatives pursue social goals and are held accountable for their actions. Such is not the case with business leaders. There are no direct lines of social accountability from the business sector to the public.

7. *Lack of broad public support.* There is no broad mandate from society for business to become involved in social issues. The public is divided on the issue. In fact, it is a topic that rarely fails to generate a heated debate. Actions taken under such divided support are likely to fail.

FIGURE 5–1
Levels of Social Involvement

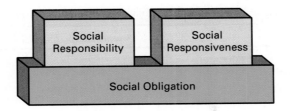

From Obligations to Responsiveness

social responsibility
An obligation, beyond that required by the law and economics, for a firm to pursue long-term goals that are good for society.

Now it's time to narrow in on precisely what *we* mean when we talk about **social responsibility.** It is a business firm's obligation, beyond that required by the law and economics, to pursue long-term goals that are good for society.[10] Note that this definition assumes that business obeys the law and pursues economic interests. We take as a given that all business firms—those that are socially responsible and those that aren't—will obey all laws that society imposes. Also note that this definition views business as a moral agent. In its effort to do *good* for society, it must differentiate between right and wrong.

We can understand social responsibility better if we compare it with two similar concepts: social obligation and social responsiveness.[11] As Figure 5–1 depicts, social obligation is the foundation of business's social involvement. A business has fulfilled its **social obligation** when it meets its economic and legal responsibilities and no more. It does the minimum that the law requires. A firm pursues social goals only to the extent that they contribute to its economic goals. In contrast to social obligation, both social responsibility and social responsiveness go beyond merely meeting basic economic and legal standards.

social obligation
The obligation of a business to meet its economic and legal responsibilities.

social responsiveness
The capacity of a firm to adapt to changing societal conditions.

Social responsibility adds an ethical imperative to do those things that make society better and *not* to do those that could make it worse. **Social responsiveness** refers to the capacity of a firm to adapt to changing societal conditions.[12]

Several years ago Best Western Hotels came out against a bill introduced in Congress that would require all sizable hotels (those over three stories) to install sprinklers in all rooms. Said the company's CEO, "We support public safety. But this is the sort of thing the local building codes should handle. The federal government shouldn't be policing this." In the five years preceding this comment, more than 400 people were killed in the United States in hotel fires. This is an example of an organization meeting its social obligation and nothing more.

The record industry shows its social responsiveness by repackaging compact discs. The 6-by-12 inch longbox cardboard packaging was designed to thwart shoplifters and to fit neatly into preexisting album bins. But the longbox consumed twice as much paper as it needed. In response to vocal environmentalists, the industry developed less wasteful packaging.

TABLE 5-1   Social Responsibility Versus Social Responsiveness

	Social Responsibility	**Social Responsiveness**
Major consideration	Ethical	Pragmatic
Focus	Ends	Means
Emphasis	Obligation	Responses
Decision framework	Long-term	Medium- and short-term

Source: Adapted from Steven L. Wartick and Philip L. Cochran, "The Evolution of the Corporate Social Performance Model," *Academy of Management Review,* October 1985, p. 766.

As Table 5–1 describes, social responsibility requires business to determine what is right or wrong and thus seek fundamental ethical truths. Social responsiveness is guided by social norms. The value of social norms is that they can provide managers with a more meaningful guide for decision making. The following makes the distinction clearer.

Suppose, for example, that a multiproduct firm's social responsibility is to produce reasonably safe products. Similarly, the same firm is responsive every time it produces an unsafe product: it withdraws the product from the market as soon as the product is found to be unsafe. After, say, ten recalls, will the firm be recognized as socially responsible? Will the firm be recognized as socially responsive? The likely answers to these questions are No to the first, but Yes to the second.[13]

When a company meets pollution control standards established by the federal government or doesn't discriminate against employees over the age of 40 in promotion decisions, it is meeting its social obligation and nothing more. The law says that the company may not pollute or practice age discrimination. In the 1990s, when Du Pont provides on-site child care facilities for employees, Procter & Gamble declares that Tide "is packaged in 100 percent recycled paper," and the head of the world's largest tuna canner says, "StarKist will not purchase, process or sell any tuna caught in association with dolphins," these firms are being socially responsive. Why? Pressure from working mothers and environmentalists make such practices pragmatic. Of course, if these same companies had provided child care, offered recycled packaging, or sought to protect dolphins back in the early 1970s, it probably would have been accurately characterized as a socially responsible action.

Advocates of social responsiveness believe that the concept replaces philosophical discourse with pragmatism. They see it as a more tangible and achievable objective than social responsibility.[14] Rather than assessing what is good for society in the long term, a socially responsive management identifies the prevailing social norms and then changes its social involvement to respond to changing societal conditions.

Social Responsibility and Economic Performance

In this section, we seek to answer the question, "do socially responsible activities lower a company's economic performance?"

More than a dozen studies have looked at this question.[15] All have some methodological limitations related to measures of "social responsibility" and "economic performance."[16] Most ascertain a firm's social performance by analyzing the content of annual reports, citations of social actions in articles on the company, or public perception "reputation" indexes. Such criteria certainly have flaws as objective, reliable measures of social responsibility. Whereas measures of economic performance (net income, return on equity, or per share stock prices) are more objective,

MANAGERS
WHO MADE A
DIFFERENCE

Faith Wohl at Du Pont Co.

Faith Wohl's official title is director of work-force partnering. Her actual job is to oversee and champion programs at Du Pont that address employees' personal and social concerns. A passionate advocate of pro-family policies, Wohl has been described as the company's "in-house conscience."[17]

Wohl joined Du Pont in 1973 and zipped through a number of assignments in public relations. In 1989, she was promoted to her current job, where she directs a nineteen-person staff that handles a variety of programs including job sharing, elder care, and workshops on work-force diversity and sexual harassment.

In the first three years on her current job, Wohl has turned once-staid Du Pont into a corporate ground-breaker that helps its employees balance family life and careers. For instance, Du Pont recently spent $1.5 million to build and renovate child-care centers near its major work sites; set up a day-care referral service that's used by Du Pont and 75 other companies; established "work-life" committees at more than 50 U.S. locations where employees can suggest new programs and changes in current ones; and introduced a pacesetting leave policy for birth, adoption, or a relative's illness—six months of unpaid time off, with full benefits, on top of six weeks' paid time off.

In spite of Wohl's successes, she sees room for Du Pont to do considerably more if the company is to become truly "family-friendly." For instance, one immediate project on her schedule is to provide buses to take employees' children from offices to summer camps. In the much longer term, Wohl would like to see Du Pont emulating French corporations by giving employees a month-long summer vacation.

they are generally used to indicate only short-term financial performance. It may well be that the impact of social responsibility on a firm's profits—either positive or negative—takes a number of years to work itself through. Assuming there is this time lag, studies that use short-term financial data aren't likely to show valid results. And there is also the issue of causation. If, for example, the evidence were to show that social involvement and economic performance were positively related, this wouldn't mean that social involvement *caused* higher economic performance. It might well be the reverse. That is, it might show that high profits permit firms the luxury of being socially involved.[18]

Given these cautions, what do the research studies find? The majority show a *positive* relationship between corporate social involvement and economic performance. Only one review of thirteen studies found a negative association—in this case, the price of socially responsible firms' stocks didn't do as well as national stock indices.[19] The logic underlying this positive relationship is that social involvement provides a number of benefits to a firm that more than offset their costs. These would include a positive consumer image, a more dedicated and motivated work force, and less interference from regulators.[20]

There is also another way to look at this issue. Let's examine a set of socially conscious mutual stock funds that have been developed in recent years and compare

Most socially conscious funds specifically exclude investments in companies like RJR Nabisco and Philip Morris because they're major manufacturers of tobacco products.

TABLE 5-2   Total Returns of Socially Conscious Funds, 1986-1990

Calvert Social Investment	74%
Dreyfus Third Century	59
Pax World	77
Pioneer Fund	68
Pioneer II	60
Pioneer III	47
All equity funds	69

Source: Lipper Analytical Services

their performance to the average of all mutual funds. Table 5–2 lists six of the largest and most popular funds in the United States that represent themselves as being responsible investors.[21] In recent years, these funds have not invested in companies that are connected with manufacturing defense weapons, that use nuclear power, that are involved in liquor, gambling, tobacco, price fixing, or criminal fraud. As you can see, between 1986 and 1990 these socially conscious funds performed very close to the same level as the average of equity funds as a group.

What can we draw from all this? In aggregate, the evidence suggests that the most meaningful conclusion we can make is that there is little substantive evidence to say that a company's socially responsible actions significantly reduce its long-term economic performance. Given the current political and social pressures on business to pursue social goals, this may have the greatest significance for managerial decision making. So, to answer our opening question, do socially responsible activities lower a company's economic performance? The answer seems to be "No!"

Is Social Responsibility Just Profit-Maximizing Behavior?

If social responsibility does not affect economic performance negatively, maybe the whole notion of social responsibility is just a fancy public relations concept that allows corporate management to appear socially conscious while it pursues its profit objectives. That is, socially responsible actions might be nothing more than profit-maximizing actions in disguise. While this line of questioning appears to be cynical, business students, the media, and other groups regularly challenge any implication that business's pursuit of social goals is altruistically motivated.

There is no question that some social actions taken by companies are motivated primarily by profits. In fact, the practice has acquired a name: **cause-related market-ing.**[22] Firms such as American Express, Coca-Cola, General Foods, and MasterCard make no apologies for capitalizing on the public's social conscience.[23] As an executive at American Express put it, "Social responsibility is a good marketing hook."[24]

The idea behind cause-related marketing is to find a social cause that fits well with a company's product or service, and then tie them together for mutual benefit. That, for instance, is what Razcal Corp., a small firm in Massachusetts that makes and sells a raspberry-lime soda for the teen market, recently did.[25] For years, Mothers Against Drunk Driving (MADD) had tried to get high schools to participate in a poster contest with an antidrinking theme. But few schools signed up. Razcal saw an opportunity. Both Razcal and MADD wanted to target teenagers, and both were interested in the issue of beverage consumption. So Razcal offered to pay for and execute a slick direct-mail campaign for the poster contest, which went to 4,000 high schools in New

cause-related marketing
Performing social actions that are motivated directly by profits.

Hurricane Andrew, which hit southern Florida and coastal Louisiana in August 1992, did tens of billions of dollars in damage and created a quarter-of-a-million homeless. Dozens of corporations responded. Building materials retailer Home Depot, for instance, *reduced* its prices for exterior plywood in its south Florida stores, foregoing millions in profits. Its competitors raised prices an average of 100 percent—from $8 to $16 per sheet. Says Jeff Barrington, manager of the Home Depot in Kendall, Florida, "This will pay us back—people will remember."

England. Three thousand students representing about 500 schools eventually participated in the contest. The total cost to Razcal—including mailings, promotions, and prizes—was $25,000. The result? Razcal's sales doubled in one year from 250,000 cases to 500,000. In addition, supermarkets waived shelf-space fees and even provided point-of-purchase displays to ally themselves with the MADD-Razcal antidrinking effort.

Research indicates that corporate philanthropy complements advertising and is motivated by profit considerations.[26] In fact, *Business Week* has described cause-related marketing as "the hottest thing going in philanthropy."[27]

So what's our conclusion? Is social responsibility just profit-maximizing behavior? While we obviously can't speak for the motivation of every "social" act by business firms, it is clear that at least some of these actions are profit motivated and consistent with the classical goal of economic maximization. Incidentally, this may explain why so many of the research studies cited in the previous section found a positive relationship between corporate social responsibility and economic performance.

A Guide Through the Maze

To this point, we've presented a number of issues related to social responsibility. Unfortunately, they don't lead us down a straight and clear path. In this section, we'll provide a modest guide through the maze and, in so doing, try to clarify the key issues.

The path will become easier to follow if we can identify the people to whom business managers are responsible. Classicists would say that stockholders or owners are their only legitimate concern. Progressives would respond that managers are responsible to any individual or group that is affected by the organization's decisions and policies.[28] These **stakeholders** are any constituency in an organization's environment: government agencies, unions, employees, customers, suppliers, host communities, and public interest groups.

Figure 5–2 illustrates a four-stage model of the expansion of an organization's

stakeholders
Any constituency in the environment that is affected by an organization's decisions and policies.

FIGURE 5-2
To Whom Is Management Responsible?

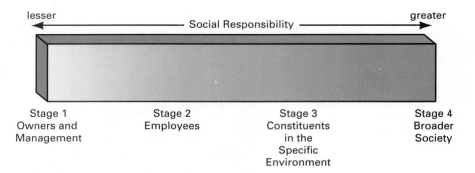

lesser ← Social Responsibility → greater

Stage 1	Stage 2	Stage 3	Stage 4
Owners and Management	Employees	Constituents in the Specific Environment	Broader Society

social responsibility.[29] What you do as a manager, in terms of pursuing social goals, depends on the person or persons to whom you believe you're responsible. A Stage 1 manager will promote the stockholders' interest by seeking to minimize costs and maximize profits. At Stage 2, managers will accept their responsibility to their employees and focus on human resource concerns. Because they'll want to get, keep, and motivate good employees, they'll improve working conditions, expand employee rights, increase job security, and the like.

At Stage 3, managers will expand their goals to include fair prices, high-quality products and services, safe products, good supplier relations, and similar practices. Stage 3 managers perceive that they can meet their responsibilities to stockholders only indirectly by meeting the needs of their other constituents.

Finally, Stage 4 aligns with the extreme socioeconomic definition of social responsibility. At this stage, managers are responsible to society as a whole. Their business is seen as a public property, and they are responsible for advancing the public good. The acceptance of such responsibility means that managers actively promote social justice, preserve the environment, and support social and cultural activities. They take these stances even if such actions negatively affect profits.

Each stage carries with it an increasing level of managerial discretion. As managers move to the right along the continuum in Figure 5–2, they have to make more judgment calls. At Stage 4, they are required to impose their values of right and wrong on society. When is a product, for example, dangerous to society? Is RJR Nabisco

These autoworkers are protesting layoffs at General Motors. Is GM acting socially irresponsible when it lays off employees? At what stage of Figure 5-2 would you say GM belongs?

doing "right" for society when it markets Oreo cookies but "wrong" when it sells cigarettes? Or perhaps producing cookies with a high sugar content is also wrong? Is a public utility that operates nuclear power plants behaving irresponsibly toward society? Is it wrong for a company to take advantage of all potential tax loopholes, even if this means paying little or no tax on billions of dollars of profits?

There is no simple right–wrong dichotomy that can help managers to make socially responsible decisions. Clearly, managers of business firms have a basic responsibility to obey the law and make a profit. Failure to achieve either of these goals threatens the organization's survival. Beyond that, managers need to identify the people to whom they believe they are responsible. We suggest that by focusing on their stakeholders and their expectations of the organization, managers reduce the likelihood that they will ignore their responsibilities to critical constituencies, or alienate them.

Managerial Ethics

Is it ethical for a salesperson to offer a bribe to a purchasing agent as an inducement to buy? What if the bribe comes out of the salesperson's commission? Does that make it any different? Is it ethical for someone to understate his or her educational qualifications in order to get a job during hard times if that person would ordinarily be considered overqualified for the job? Is it ethical for someone to use company gasoline for private use? How about using the company telephone for personal long-distance calls? Is it ethical to ask a company secretary to type personal letters?[30]

ethics
Rules and principles that define right and wrong conduct.

Ethics commonly refers to the rules or principles that define right and wrong conduct.[31] In this section, we want to look at the ethical dimension of managerial decisions. Many decisions that managers make require them to consider who may be affected—in terms of the result as well as the means.[32] We'll present three different views on ethics and look at the factors that influence a manager's ethics. We'll conclude by offering some suggestions for what organizations can do to improve the ethical behavior of employees.

Three Different Views on Ethics

utilitarian view of ethics
Decisions are made solely on the basis of their outcomes or consequences.

There are three different views on ethical standards.[33] The first is the **utilitarian view of ethics,** in which decisions are made solely on the basis of their outcomes or consequences. The goal of utilitarianism is to provide the greatest good for the greatest number. Following the utilitarian view, a manager might conclude that laying off 20 percent of the work force in her plant is justified because it will increase the plant's profitability, improve job security for the remaining 80 percent, and be in the best interest of stockholders. On one side, utilitarianism encourages efficiency and productivity and is consistent with the goal of profit maximization. On the other side, however, it can result in biased allocations of resources, especially when some of those affected lack representation or voice. Utilitarianism can also result in the rights of some stakeholders being ignored.

rights view of ethics
Decisions are concerned with respecting and protecting basic rights of individuals.

Another ethical perspective is the **rights view of ethics.** This position is concerned with respecting and protecting individual liberties and privileges, including the rights to privacy, freedom of conscience, free speech, and due process. This would include, for example, protecting the rights of employees to free speech when they report violations of laws by their employers. The positive side of the rights perspective is that it protects individuals' freedom and privacy. But it has a negative side in organizations: It can present obstacles to high productivity and efficiency by creating an overly legalistic work climate.

The culture that Sears, Roebuck created in its California auto centers encouraged employees to systematically recommend unneeded repairs to its customers. Sears settled the case by agreeing to pay California $3.5 million for legal costs, to contribute $1.5 million to auto repair training programs at community colleges, to distribute up to $46.6 million in free-merchandise coupons to disgruntled customers, and to make full refunds to consumers who believe they were overcharged on repairs.

theory of justice view of ethics

Decision makers seek to impose and enforce rules fairly and impartially.

The final view is the **theory of justice view of ethics.** This calls upon managers to impose and enforce rules fairly and impartially. A manager would be using a theory of justice perspective in deciding to pay a new entry-level employee $1.50 an hour over the minimum wage because that manager believes that the minimum wage is inadequate to allow employees to meet their basic financial commitments. Imposing standards of justice also comes with pluses and minuses. It protects the interests of those stakeholders who may be underrepresented or lack power; but it can encourage a sense of entitlement that reduces risk-taking, innovation, and productivity.

It has been found that most businesspeople continue to hold utilitarian attitudes toward ethical behavior.[34] This shouldn't be totally surprising, since this view is consistent with such goals as efficiency, productivity, and high profits. By maximizing profits, for instance, an executive can argue that he or she is securing the greatest good for the greatest number.

Because of the changing world of management, that perspective needs to change. Utilitarianism sacrifices the welfare of minorities in the interest of the majority. New trends toward individual rights and social justice mean that managers need ethical standards based on nonutilitarian criteria. This is a solid challenge to today's manager because making decisions using criteria such as individual rights and social justice involves far more ambiguities than using utilitarian criteria such as effects on efficiency and profits. The result, of course, is that managers increasingly find themselves facing ethical dilemmas.

Factors Affecting Managerial Ethics

Whether a manager acts ethically or unethically is the result of a complex interaction between the manager's stage of moral development and the moderating variables of individual characteristics, the organization's structural design, the organization's culture, and the intensity of the ethical issue.[35] (See Figure 5–3.) People who lack a strong moral sense are much less likely to do the wrong things if they are constrained by rules, policies, job descriptions, or strong cultural norms that frown on such behaviors. Conversely, very moral people can be corrupted by an organizational structure and culture that permit or encourage unethical practices. Moreover, managers are more likely to make ethical decisions on issues where high moral intensity is

MANAGING
FROM A
GLOBAL
PERSPECTIVE

Ethics in an International Context

Are ethical standards universal across national borders? Hardly! Social and cultural differences between countries are important environmental factors that define ethical and unethical behavior.

The manager of a Mexican firm bribes several high-ranking government officials in Mexico City to secure a profitable government contract for his firm. Such a practice would be seen as unethical, if not illegal, in the United States, but it's a standard business practice in Mexico.

Should IBM employees in Saudi Arabia adhere to U.S. ethical standards, or should the phrase "When in Rome do as the Romans do" guide them? If Airbus (a European firm) will pay a $10 million "broker's fee" to a middleman to get a major contract with a Middle Eastern airline, should Boeing be restricted from doing the same because such practices are considered improper in the United States?

In the case of payments to influence foreign officials or politicians, there is a law to guide U.S. managers. The Foreign Corrupt Practices Act, passed in 1977, makes it illegal for U.S. firms to knowingly corrupt a foreign official. Even this doesn't always reduce ethical problems to black or white. In some Latin American countries, for example, government bureaucrats are paid ridiculously low salaries because custom dictates that they receive small payments from those they serve. These payoffs grease the machinery of government and ensure that things get done. The Foreign Corrupt Practices Act does not expressly outlaw small payoffs to foreign government employees whose duties are primarily ministerial or clerical when such payoffs are an accepted part of a country's business practices.

Levi Strauss has decided to export its U.S. ethical standards.[36] After recently investigating its 400 foreign contractors, the company found that approximately 25 percent were overtly exploiting their workers. One contractor on the island of Saipan, for instance, worked its people 11 hours a day, seven days a week! Others routinely used child labor. To eliminate these abuses, Levi Strauss' management has adopted strict guidelines for its foreign contractors—including providing safe and healthy working conditions and requiring pay levels that are no lower than prevailing local wages. To insure that the guidelines are followed, inspectors from U.S. headquarters now make surprise visits.

involved. Let's look at the various factors that eventually influence whether managers behave ethically or unethically.

Stage of Moral Development   There is a substantial body of research that confirms the existence of three levels of moral development, each comprised of two stages.[37] At each successive stage, an individual's moral judgment grows less and less dependent on outside influences. The three levels and six stages are described in Table 5–3.

The first level is labeled *preconventional.* At this level, individuals respond to notions of right or wrong only when there are personal consequences involved, such as physical punishment, reward, or exchange of favors. Reasoning at the *conventional* level indicates that moral value resides in maintaining the conventional order

FIGURE 5-3
Factors Affecting Ethical/Unethical Behavior

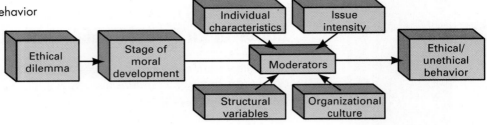

and the expectations of others. In the *principled* level, individuals make a clear effort to define moral principles apart from the authority of the groups to which they belong or society in general.

Research on these stages of moral development allows us to draw several conclusions.[38] First, people proceed through the six stages in a lock-step fashion. They gradually move up a ladder, stage by stage. They don't jump steps. Second, there is no guarantee of continued development. Development can terminate at any stage. Third, the majority of adults are at Stage 4. They are limited to obeying the rules and laws of society. Finally, the higher the stage a manager reaches, the more he or she will be predisposed to behave ethically. For instance, a Stage 3 manager is likely to make decisions that will receive approval by his or her peers; a Stage 4 manager will seek to be a "good corporate citizen" by making decisions that respect the organization's rules and procedures; and a Stage 5 manager is more likely to challenge organizational practices that he or she believes to be wrong. Many of the recent efforts by colleges to raise students' ethical awareness and standards are focused on helping them move to the principled level.

TABLE 5-3 Stages of Moral Development

Level	Stage description
Preconventional	
Influenced exclusively by personal interest. Decisions are made in terms of self-benefit as defined by the rewards and punishments that come from different types of behavior.	1. Sticking to rules to avoid physical punishment 2. Following rules only when it's in your immediate interest
Conventional	
Influenced by the expectations of others. Includes obedience to the law, response to the expectations of significant others, and a general sense of what is expected.	3. Living up to what is expected by people close to you 4. Maintaining conventional order by fulfilling obligations to which you have agreed
Principled	
Influenced by personal ethical principles of what is right. These may or may not be in accordance with rules or laws of society.	5. Valuing rights of others; and upholding nonrelative values and rights regardless of the majority's opinion 6. Following self-chosen ethical principles even if they violate the law

Source: Based on Lawrence Kohlberg, "Moral Stages and Moralization: The Cognitive-Developmental Approach," in T. Lickona, ed., *Moral Development and Behavior: Theory, Research, and Social Issues* (New York: Holt, Rinehart & Winston, 1976), pp. 34–35.

values

Basic convictions about what is right and wrong.

ego strength

A personality characteristic that measures the strength of a person's convictions.

locus of control

A personality attribute that measures the degree to which people believe they are masters of their own fate.

Individual Characteristics Every person enters an organization with a relatively entrenched set of **values.** Developed in an individual's early years—from parents, teachers, friends, and others—these values represent basic convictions about what is right and wrong. Thus managers in an organization often possess very different personal values.[39] Note that while *values* and *stage of moral development* may seem similar, they are not. The former are broad and cover a wide range of issues while the latter is specifically a measure of independence from outside influences.

Two personality variables have also been found to influence an individual's actions according to his or her beliefs about what is right or wrong. They are ego strength and locus of control.

Ego strength is a personality measure of the strength of a person's convictions. People who score high on ego strength are likely to resist impulses and follow their convictions more than those who are low on ego strength. That is, individuals high in ego strength are more likely to do what they think is right. We would expect managers with high ego strength to demonstrate more consistency between moral judgment and moral action than those with low ego strength.

Locus of control is a personality attribute that measures the degree to which people believe they are masters of their own fate. People with an internal locus of control believe that they control their own destinies, while those with an external locus believe that what befalls them in life is due to luck or chance. From an ethical perspective, externals are less likely to take personal responsibility for the consequences of their behavior and are more likely to rely on external forces. Internals, on the other hand, are more likely to take responsibility for consequences and rely on their own internal standards of right and wrong to guide their behavior.[40] Managers with an internal locus of control will probably demonstrate more consistency between their moral judgments and moral actions than will "external" managers.

Structural Variables An organization's structural design helps to shape the ethical behavior of managers. Some structures provide strong guidance, while others only create ambiguity for managers. Structural designs that minimize ambiguity and continuously remind managers of what is "ethical" are more likely to encourage ethical behavior.

Formal rules and regulations reduce ambiguity. Job descriptions and written codes of ethics are examples of formal guides that promote consistent behavior. Research continues to indicate, though, that the behavior of superiors is the strongest single influence on an individual's own ethical or unethical behavior.[41] People check to see what those in authority are doing and use that as a benchmark for acceptable practices and what is expected of them. Some performance appraisal systems focus exclusively on outcomes. Others evaluate means as well as ends. Where managers are appraised only on outcomes, there will be increased pressures to do "whatever is necessary" to look good on the outcome variables. Closely associated with the appraisal system is the way rewards are allocated. The more rewards or punishments depend on specific goal outcomes, the more pressure there is on managers to reach those goals and compromise their ethical standards. Structures also differ in the amount of time, competition, cost, and similar pressure they place on job incumbents. The greater the pressure, the more likely it is that managers will compromise their ethical standards.

Organization's Culture The content and strength of an organization's culture also influence ethical behavior.[42]

A culture that is likely to shape high ethical standards is one that is high in risk tolerance, high in control, and high in conflict tolerance. Managers in such a culture will be encouraged to be aggressive and innovative, aware that unethical practices will be found out, and will feel free to openly challenge demands or expectations they consider to be unrealistic or personally distasteful.

General Electric has made an impressive commitment to high ethical standards by its employees. For instance, GE employees can tap into specially designed interactive software on their personal computers to get answers to ethical questions. Additionally, the company has seminars and videos that encourage employees to report any wrongdoings. Nevertheless, GE recently pleaded guilty and paid $70 million to settle charges that it punished employees who reported wrongdoings. Employees claimed they were fired for following the company's compliance procedures.

A strong culture will exert more influence on managers than a weak one. If the culture is strong and supports high ethical standards, it should have a very powerful and positive influence on a manager's ethical behavior. Johnson & Johnson, for example, has a strong culture that has long stressed obligations to customers, employees, the community, and shareholders, in that order. When poisoned Tylenol was found on store shelves in 1982 and 1986, J&J employees across the United States independently pulled the product from these stores before J&J had even issued a statement concerning the poisonings. No one had to tell these people what was morally right; they knew what J&J would expect them to do. In a weak culture, however, managers are more likely to rely on subculture norms as a behavioral guide. Work groups and departmental standards will strongly influence ethical behavior in organizations that have weak overall cultures.

Issue Intensity   A student who would never consider breaking into an instructor's office in order to steal an introductory accounting exam doesn't think twice about asking a friend who took the same accounting course from the same instructor last term, what questions were on last term's exam. Similarly, an executive might think nothing about taking home a few office supplies yet be highly concerned about the possible embezzlement of company funds.

These examples illustrate the final factor that affects a manager's ethical behavior—the characteristics of the ethical issue itself.[43] As Figure 5–4 illustrates, six characteristics have been identified as relevant in determining issue intensity:[44]

1. How great a harm (or benefit) is done to victims (or beneficiaries) of the ethical act in question? *Example:* An act that puts 1000 people out of work is more harmful than one affecting only ten people.

2. How much consensus is there that the act is evil (or good)? *Example:* More Americans agree that it is evil to bribe a customs official in Texas than agree that it is evil to bribe a customs official in Mexico.

3. What is the probability that the act will actually take place and will actually cause the harm (or benefit) predicted? *Example:* Selling a gun to a known armed robber has greater probability of harm than selling a gun to a law-abiding citizen.

4. What's the length of time between the act in question and its expected consequences? *Example:* Reducing the retirement benefits of current retirees has greater

FIGURE 5–4
Characteristics Determining Issue Intensity

Greatness of Harm

Immediacy of Consequences

Consensus of Evil

Issue Intensity

Proximity to Victim

Probability of Harm

Concentration of Effect

immediate consequences than reducing the retirement benefits of current employees who are between the ages of 40 and 50.

5. How close do you feel (socially, psychologically, or physically) to the victims (or beneficiaries) of the evil (beneficial) act in question? *Example:* Layoffs in one's own work unit hit closer to home than do layoffs in a remote city.

6. How large is the concentrated effect of the ethical act on the people involved? *Example:* A change in the warranty policy denying coverage to ten people with claims of $10,000 has a more concentrated effect than a change denying coverage to 10,000 people with claims of $10.00.

Following these guidelines, the larger the number of people harmed, the greater the consensus that an act is evil, the higher the probability that an act will take place and actually cause harm, the shorter the length of time until the consequences of the act surface, and the closer the observer feels to the victims of the act, the greater the issue intensity. In aggregate, these six components determine how important an ethical issue is. And we should expect managers to behave more ethically when a moral issue is important to them than when it is not.

Toward Improving Ethical Behavior

A number of things can be done if top management seriously wants to reduce unethical practices in its organization. It can seek to select individuals with high ethical standards, establish codes of ethics and decision rules, lead by example, delineate job goals, and provide ethics training. Taken individually, these actions will probably not make much of an impact; but when all or most of them are implemented as part of a comprehensive program, they have the potential to improve an organization's ethical climate significantly. The key term here, however, is *potential*. There are no guarantees that a well-designed program will lead to the outcome desired. Dow Corning, for instance, has long been recognized as a pioneer in corporate ethics, and its ethics program has been cited as among the most elaborate in corporate America.[45] However, as we learned at the opening of this chapter, it didn't stop the cover-ups or misrepresentations of the result of studies on their silicone gel breast implants.

Selection Given that individuals are at different stages of moral development and possess different personal value systems and personalities, an organization's employee selection process—interviews, tests, background checks, and the like—should be used to weed out ethically undesirable applicants. This is no easy task. Even under the best of circumstances, individuals with questionable standards of right and wrong will be hired. That is to be expected and needn't be a problem if other controls are imposed. But the selection process should be viewed as an opportunity to learn about an individual's level of moral development, personal values, ego strength, and locus of control.[46]

Codes of Ethics and Decision Rules We have already seen how ambiguity about what is ethical can be a problem for employees. Codes of ethics are an increasingly popular response for reducing that ambiguity.[47] For instance, nearly 90 percent of Fortune 1000 companies have a stated code of ethics.[48]

A **code of ethics** is a formal document that states an organization's primary values and the ethical rules it expects its employees to follow. It has been suggested that codes should be specific enough to show employees the spirit in which they're supposed to do things, yet loose enough to allow for freedom of judgment.[49] These suggestions seem to have been applied at McDonnell Douglas, as shown in Figure 5–5.

code of ethics
A formal statement of an organization's primary values and the ethical rules it expects its employees to follow.

FIGURE 5-5
McDonnell Douglas' Code
of Ethics

Source: Courtesy of McDonnell
Douglas Corporation.

MCDONNELL DOUGLAS
Code of Ethics

Integrity and ethics exist in the individual or they do not exist at all. They must be upheld by individuals or they are not upheld at all. In order for integrity and ethics to be characteristics of McDonnell Douglas, we who make up the corporation must strive to be:

- Honest and trustworthy in all our relationships.
- Reliable in carrying out assignments and responsibilities.
- Truthful and accurate in what we say and write.
- Cooperative and constructive in all work undertaken.
- Fair and considerate in our treatment of fellow employees, customers, and all other persons.
- Law abiding in all our activities.
- Committed to accomplishing all tasks in a superior way.
- Economical in utilizing company resources.
- Dedicated in service to our company and to improvement of the quality of life in the world in which we live.

Integrity and high standards of ethics require hard work, courage, and difficult choices. Consultation among employees, top management, and the Board of Directors will sometimes be necessary to determine a proper course of action. Integrity and ethics may sometimes require us to forego business opportunities. In the long run, however, we will be better served by doing what is right than what is expedient.

Jack S. Llewellyn, President and CEO of Ocean Spray, believes that the CEO has to be the model for ethical standards. "It's like the Marine Corps: The leader has to be able to do everything the rest of the troops do, and he has to be able to do it better. I don't think written policy statements are worth anything. Managers will treat customers and workers fairly if the CEO does."

What do most codes of ethics look like? A survey of 83 codes of business ethics—including those of such varied firms as Exxon, Sara Lee, DuPont, Bank of Boston, and Wisconsin Electric Power—found that their content tended to fall into three clusters: (1) Be a dependable organizational citizen, (2) do not do anything unlawful or improper that will harm the organization, and (3) be good to customers.[50] Table 5–4 lists the variables included in each of these clusters in order of their frequency of mention. However, another study of 202 Fortune 500 corporations suggests that many codes of ethics are not as effective as they might be because they omit important issues.[51] Seventy-five percent, for example, fail to address personal character matters, product safety, product quality, environmental affairs, or civic and community affairs. In contrast, more than three-quarters mentioned issues such as relations with the U.S. government, customer/supplier relations, political contributions, and conflicts of interest. Authors of this study concluded that "codes are really dealing with infractions against the corporation, rather than illegalities on behalf of the corporation."[52] That is, codes tend to give most attention to areas of illegal or unethical conduct that are likely to decrease a company's profits.[53]

In isolation, ethical codes are not likely to be much more than public relations statements. Their effectiveness depends heavily on whether management supports them and how employees who break the codes are treated. When management considers them to be important, regularly reaffirms their content, and publicly reprimands rule breakers, codes can supply a strong foundation for an effective ethics program.

Another approach that uses formal written statements to guide behavior has been

TABLE 5–4 Clusters of Variables Found in 83 Corporate Codes of Business Ethics

Cluster 1. Be a Dependable Organizational Citizen.

1. Comply with safety, health, and security regulations.
2. Demonstrate courtesy, respect, honesty, and fairness.
3. Illegal drugs and alcohol at work are prohibited.
4. Manage personal finances well.
5. Exhibit good attendance and punctuality.
6. Follow directives of supervisors.
7. Do not use abusive language.
8. Dress in businesslike attire.
9. Firearms at work are prohibited.

Cluster 2. Do Not Do Anything Unlawful or Improper That Will Harm the Organization.

1. Conduct business in compliance with all laws.
2. Payments for unlawful purposes are prohibited.
3. Bribes are prohibited.
4. Avoid outside activities that impair duties.
5. Maintain confidentiality of records.
6. Comply with all antitrust and trade regulations.
7. Comply with accounting rules and controls.
8. Do not use company property for personal benefit.
9. Employees are personally accountable for company funds.
10. Do not propagate false or misleading information.
11. Make decisions without regard for personal gain.

Cluster 3. Be Good to Customers.

1. Convey true claims in product advertisements.
2. Perform assigned duties to the best of your ability.
3. Provide products and services of the highest quality.

Source: Fred R. David, "An Empirical Study of Codes of Business Ethics: A Strategic Perspective." Paper presented at the 48th Annual Academy of Management Conference, Anaheim, California; August 1988.

suggested by Laura Nash.[54] She proposes 12 questions that act as decision rules to guide managers in handling ethical dimensions in decision making. These questions are listed in Table 5–5.

Top Management's Leadership   Codes of ethics require a commitment from top management. Why? Because it's the top managers who set the cultural tone. They are role models in terms of both words and actions—though what they do is probably more important than what they say. If top managers, for example, use company resources for their personal use, inflate their expense accounts, give favored treatment to friends, or conduct similar practices, they imply that such behavior is acceptable for all employees.

Top management also sets the cultural tone by its reward and punishment practices. The choice of who and what are rewarded with pay increases and promotions sends a strong message to employees. The promotion of a manager for achieving impressive results in questionable ways indicates to everyone that those questionable ways are acceptable. When it uncovers wrongdoing, management must not only

TABLE 5–5   Twelve Questions for Examining the Ethics of a Business Decision

1. Have you defined the problem accurately?
2. How would you define the problem if you stood on the other side of the fence?
3. How did this situation occur in the first place?
4. To whom and to what do you give your loyalty as a person and as a member of the corporation?
5. What is your intention in making this decision?
6. How does this intention compare with the probable results?
7. Whom could your decision or action injure?
8. Can you discuss the problem with the affected parties before you make the decision?
9. Are you confident that your position will be as valid over a long period of time as it seems now?
10. Could you disclose without qualm your decision or action to your boss, your chief executive officer, the board of directors, your family, society as a whole?
11. What is the symbolic potential of your action if understood? If misunderstood?
12. Under what conditions would you allow exceptions to your stand?

Source: Reprinted by permission of *Harvard Business Review*. An exhibit from "Ethics Without the Sermon" by Laura L. Nash, November–December 1981, p. 81. Copyright © 1981 by the President and Fellows of Harvard College; all rights reserved.

punish the wrongdoer but publicize the fact and make the outcome visible for all to see. This sends another message: "Doing wrong has a price, and it's *not* in your best interest to act unethically!"

Job Goals   Employees should have tangible and realistic goals. Explicit goals can create ethical problems if they make unrealistic demands on employees. Under the stress of unrealistic goals, otherwise ethical employees will often take the attitude that "anything goes." On the other hand, when goals are clear and realistic, they reduce ambiguity for employees and motivate rather than punish.

Ethics Training   More and more organizations are setting up seminars, workshops, and similar training programs to try to improve ethical behaviors. Recent estimates indicate that 44 percent of companies provide some ethics training.[55] But these training programs are not without controversy. The primary debate surrounds whether you can actually teach ethics. Critics, for instance, stress that the effort is pointless since people establish their individual value systems when they are very young.[56] Proponents, on the other hand, note that several studies have found that values can be learned after early childhood.[57] In addition, they take heart from evidence that shows that teaching ethical problem solving can make an actual difference in ethical behavior;[58] that training has increased individuals' level of moral development;[59] and that, if it does nothing else, ethics training increases awareness of ethical issues in business.[60]

How do you teach ethics? Let's examine how it's done at Citicorp. There, as part of the company's comprehensive corporate-ethics training program, managers participate in a game that allows them to practice their understanding of the company's ethical standards.[61] Players move markers around a game board when they correctly answer multiple-choice questions presented on cards. Each card poses an ethical dilemma a bank employee might encounter. As the game progresses, players are "promoted" from entry-level employee to supervisor and eventually to senior manager.

As an example, one question asks: "After successfully completing a complex deal for a Japanese client, he presents you with a vase to express his appreciation. It's an expensive item, and accepting a gift of such value is clearly against Citicorp policy. Yet returning it would insult your client." Would you: (a) return the vase to the client and explain diplomatically that it's against Citicorp policy to accept gifts from clients; (b) accept the gift because you can't risk insulting an important client; (c) accept the gift on behalf of Citicorp, log it with premises management as a furnishing, and display it in a public area of the office; (d) accept the gift and use it as an award for an employee who displays service excellence? (Citicorp, by the way, likes answer "c.") Another question asks: "What if the manager of a competing bank calls to suggest colluding on interest rates?" If the player picks "ask to meet him and discuss it further," that player is "fired for cause" and is out of the game!

Ethical training sessions can provide a number of benefits.[62] They reinforce the organization's standards of conduct. They're a reminder that top management wants participants to consider ethical issues in their decisions. They clarify what practices are and are not permissible. Finally, when managers discuss common concerns among themselves, they become reassured that they aren't alone in facing ethical dilemmas. This can strengthen their confidence when they have to take unpopular but ethically correct stances.

Comprehensive Performance Appraisal   When performance appraisals focus only on economic outcomes, ends will begin to justify means. If an organization wants its managers to uphold high ethical standards, it *must* include this dimension in its appraisal process. For example, a manager's annual review might include a point-by-point evaluation of how his or her decisions stacked up against the organization's code of ethics as well as on the more traditional economic criteria. Needless to say, if the manager looks good on the economic criteria but scores poorly on ethical conduct, appropriate penalties need to be enacted.

Independent Social Audits   An important deterrent of unethical behavior is fear of being caught. Independent audits, which evaluate decisions and management practices in terms of the organization's code of ethics, increase the probability of detection. These audits can be routine evaluations, performed on a regular basis as are financial audits, or they can occur at random, with no prior announcement. An effective ethical program should probably include both. To maintain integrity, the auditors should be responsible to the organization's board of directors, and present their findings directly to the board. This not only gives the auditors clout but lessens the opportunity for retaliation from those being audited.

Formal Protective Mechanisms   Our last recommendation is for organizations to provide formal mechanisms so that employees who have ethical dilemmas can do something about them without fear of reprimand.

An organization might, for instance, designate ethical advisors. When employees face a dilemma, they could go to an advisor for guidance. The ethical advisor's role would first be as a sounding board, a channel to let employees openly verbalize their ethical problem, the problem's cause, and their own options. Then, after the options are clear, the advisor might take the role of an advocate who promotes the "right" alternatives. The organization might also create a special appeals process that employees could use without risk to themselves to raise ethical questions or blow the whistle on violators.

FIGURE 5-6
Social Responsibility and Ethics Over Time

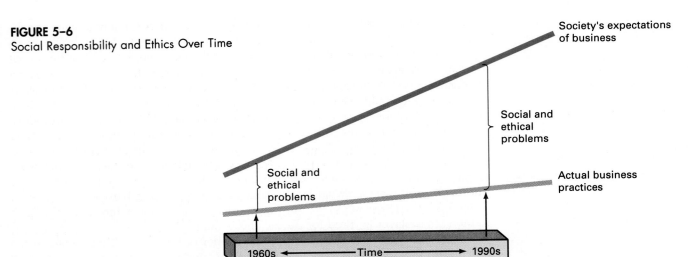

Source: Reprinted with permission of Macmillan Publishing Company from *Social Responsibility of Management* by Archie B. Carroll. (New York: Macmillan Publishing Company, 1984), p. 14.

A Final Thought

If you picked up a twenty-year-old management text, it's almost certain that you would not find a chapter on social responsibility and ethics. If you even found the terms in the text, they wouldn't receive more than a paragraph of attention. What has happened to bring about this evolution?

One line of thinking is that the recent focus on these topics is a response to a *decline* in business's willingness to accept its societal responsibilities and in the ethical standards of managers. For instance, a Gallup poll reported that 65 percent of Americans thought that the overall level of ethics in society declined between the mid-1970s and mid-1980s.[63] The widely publicized ethics scandals that rocked Wall Street in the late 1980s certainly didn't help that perception. However, experts on the role of business in society provide another explanation.[64] They contend that today's managers are *more* socially conscious and ethical than their counterparts of a generation ago. What has happened, as illustrated in Figure 5-6, is that the demands on business and the expectations of what is considered "proper conduct" have risen faster than the ability of business to raise its standards.

Society's expectations of business have changed. Cornelius Vanderbilt's famous phrase "the public be damned" was accepted by many in the 1890s. It certainly is not acceptable in the 1990s. It was acceptable for Cleveland steel plants to pollute Lake Erie in the 1950s, but it is not today.

This observation has implications for managers. Since society's expectations of its institutions are regularly undergoing change, managers must continually monitor these expectations. What is ethically acceptable today may be a poor guide for the future.

Summary

This summary is organized by the chapter-opening learning objectives found on page 117.

1. According to the classical view, business's social responsibility is only to maximize financial returns for stockholders. The opposing socioeconomic view holds that business has a responsibility to the larger society.

2. The arguments for business being socially responsible include public expectations, long-run profits, ethical obligation, public image, a better environment,

fewer government regulations, balancing of responsibility and power, stock-holder interests, possession of resources, and the superiority of prevention over cures. The arguments against hold that social responsibility violates the profit-maximization objective, dilutes the organization's purpose, costs too much, gives business too much power, requires skills that business doesn't have, lacks accountability, and lacks wide public support.

3. Social responsibility refers to business's pursuit of long-term goals that are good for society. Social responsiveness refers to the capacity of a firm to respond to social pressures. The former requires business to determine what is right or wrong and thus seek fundamental ethical truths, while the latter is guided by social norms.

4. Most research studies show a positive relationship between corporate social involvement and economic performance. The evidence does *not* find that acting in a socially responsible way significantly reduces a corporation's long-term economic performance.

5. A stakeholder is any constituency in an organization's environment that is affected by that organization's decisions and policies. By focusing on the organization's stakeholders and their expectations of the organization, management is less likely to ignore its responsibilities to critical constituencies.

6. Ethics refers to rules or principles that define right and wrong conduct.

7. The utilitarian view makes decisions based on their outcomes or consequences. The rights view seeks to respect and protect basic rights of individuals. The theory of justice view seeks to impose and enforce rules fairly and impartially.

8. Whether a manager acts ethically or unethically is the result of a complex interaction between the manager's stage of moral development, his or her individual characteristics, the organization's structural design, the organization's culture, and the intensity of the ethical issue.

9. There are three levels of moral development, each comprised of two stages. The first two stages are influenced exclusively by an individual's personal interests. Stages 3 and 4 are influenced by the expectations of others. Stages 5 and 6 are influenced by personal ethical principles of what is right.

10. A comprehensive ethical program would include selection to weed out ethically undesirable applicants, a code of ethics and decision rules, a commitment by top management, clear and realistic job goals, ethics training, comprehensive performance appraisals, independent social audits, and formal protective mechanisms.

Review Questions

1. Why is the social responsibility of business receiving so much more attention today than it did in the 1940s or 1950s?

2. According to the socioeconomic view of social responsibility, what are the flaws in the classical view?

3. Contrast *social responsibility* and *social responsiveness*. Which is more theoretical? Why?

4. What is *cause-related marketing?* Is it socially responsible in the classical view?

5. Which of the three views on ethics is most popular among businesspeople? Why?

6. What conditions are relevant in determining the degree of intensity a person is likely to hold on an ethical issue?

7. What behaviors are most likely to be mentioned as prohibited by an organization's code of ethics? Which are most likely not to be mentioned?

8. Over the past 20 years, has business become less willing to accept its societal responsibilities? Explain.

Discussion Questions

1. What does social responsibility mean to you? Do you think business firms should be socially responsible? Why?
2. Discuss this statement: "In the long run, those who do not use power in a way that society considers responsible will tend to lose it."
3. While Playboy Enterprises has a woman president, the magazine it publishes contains photographs and stories that may be regarded as exploitive. With this in mind, discuss the following: "Companies that promote women are acting ethically, but those that exploit women are acting unethically."
4. "The business of business is business." Review this statement from the (a) classical view and (b) socioeconomic view.

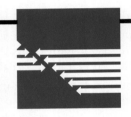

SELF-ASSESSMENT EXERCISE

What Are Your Personal Value Preferences?

Listed below are eighteen values. Indicate their importance to you by rank—ordering them from one to eighteen. Place a "1" next to the value that has the greatest importance as a guiding principle in your life, a "2" next to the one with the second highest importance, and so forth.

Values	Rank
AMBITIOUS (hard-working, aspiring)	_____
BROADMINDED (open-minded)	_____
CAPABLE (competent, effective)	_____
CHEERFUL (light-hearted, joyful)	_____
CLEAN (neat, tidy)	_____
COURAGEOUS (standing up for your beliefs)	_____
FORGIVING (willing to pardon others)	_____
HELPFUL (working for the welfare of others)	_____
HONEST (sincere, truthful)	_____
IMAGINATIVE (daring, creative)	_____
INDEPENDENT (self-reliant, self-sufficient)	_____
INTELLECTUAL (intelligent, reflective)	_____

LOGICAL (consistent, rational) _____

LOVING (affectionate, tender) _____

OBEDIENT (dutiful, respectful) _____

POLITE (courteous, well-mannered) _____

RESPONSIBLE (dependable, reliable) _____

SELF-CONTROLLED (restrained, self-disciplined) _____

Turn to page SK-2 for scoring directions and key.

Based on William C. Frederick and James Weber, "The Values of Corporate Managers and Their Critics: An Empirical Description and Normative Implications," in W. C. Frederick and L. E. Preston, eds., *Business Ethics: Research Issues and Empirical Studies* (Greenwich, Conn.: JAI Press, 1990), pp. 123–44.

To: L.W. Williamson; Director of Corporate Legal Affairs
From: David Childress; CEO
Subject: Protection of Whistleblowers

The Dawn Reddy "whistleblower" case has been a terrible embarrassment to this company. She argued in court that we would have ignored her claims that several executives in our Laboratory Division where she worked were taking payoffs from clients to falsify research findings in order to expedite the Federal Drug Administration's approval of those clients' drugs. She said she also feared reprisal from her direct superiors if she informed on them. This was her defense for going directly to the FDA with her allegations.

The loss of this case (and the $2.5 million settlement) makes it very clear that we have a serious problem. It is not enough that we fired the three managers involved in this scheme. We *must* do something immediately to change the ethical climate around here. No employee should need to go to outside authorities if he or she perceives wrongdoings. Employees must feel secure in knowing that we maintain high ethical standards and will protect any employee who reports unethical practices.

As a first step, I have spoken to Ms. Reddy and her attorneys. I told them that it is now evident that her superior's decision to fire her for "unsatisfactory performance" was a total fabrication. I told her that her superior had been terminated, as had his superior and another associate. I offered her her job back and told her I personally hoped she would return. She accepted my offer.

This case is now closed. But we must ensure that something like this *never* happens again! I want you to give me a written plan (not to exceed two pages in length) that describes specifically what we can do to (1) encourage employees to speak out if they see wrongdoings and (2) protect them when they do so.

---

* This organization has been disguised for obvious reasons.

CASE APPLICATION

Two Ethical Dilemmas in Starting Your Own Business

You've been involved with computers all your working life. Five years ago Rob Firman asked you to join his new data-processing company; today you're a sales manager in Firman's 20-person business. But you really want to own your own data-processing business, and for the past few months you've spent your evenings doing spreadsheets, developing customer lists, and otherwise mapping out the new venture. Firman knows nothing about your plans. You'll tell him as soon as you're ready to give notice.

In the meantime, you continue to put in a hard day's work. But now and then a difficult situation comes up. Here are two of them.

Ethical Dilemma One: The Key Employee

It's 5:30, and there's a knock on your office door. Quickly you rehearse your pitch one last time, even as you're calling for Lowrey to come in. The programmer enters and sits down, grinning.

"Did you hear?" he asks. "Seems the boss wants me to put on a tie and begin acting like an executive."

You congratulate him, but the doubt once more flickers across your mind. The start-up you're planning needs Lowrey. He's the quickest technical guy you've ever met. He has an incredible knack for making clients feel at ease. And more than once he's told you he'd like to be involved in a new venture someday.

If it weren't for Firman, you'd offer him a job right now.

Face it, you think, Firman put you where you are today. He not only hired you and trained you, he gave you more responsibility than you were ready for, confident that you'd grow into it. And you have—so quickly that now you're chafing under his sometimes-arrogant authority. When you leave, Firman may feel betrayed. But you steel yourself against the remorse. That's business. Firman is a big boy.

But what about Lowrey? Just last week Firman told you his hopes for the young man. He talked of broadening Lowrey's responsibilities, of eventually bringing him into management. Just the guy I need, he said, to help me take this company past $2 million.

You look again at Lowrey, sitting in your office, smiling to himself. You know he's essential to Firman's plans. But you also know where his long-term hopes lie, and that he'll take a job with your start-up if you offer one. You even think that Firman, if he weren't personally involved, would encourage you. "A man has to look out for himself," he likes to say.

Ethical Dilemma Two: The Customer

Lisa Meggett sips her coffee, leaving her words hanging. You bite off some bread, trying to chew slowly and think fast.

Meggett is managing partner of a consulting firm, one of Firman's customers, and you've been handling the account. Today you've asked her to lunch, ostensibly to discuss her longer-term data-processing needs. In fact, you want a chance to talk up your new company. You figure you can offer her the same services she's getting from Firman, only for 30 percent less. And now she has left an opening you could drive a minicomputer through.

"I'm afraid I have bad news," she had said. "I hope you won't take it personally, because I've always enjoyed working with you. But computers are so cheap now, we're planning on bringing our data processing in-house. We should save 20 percent over what we're paying you. Unless you can match that I'll have to close our account."

Give me a break, you think—not only can I beat it, I can show her exactly where her figures are wrong. She hasn't counted the cost of hiring, training, and keeping busy the new people she'll have to bring in. She hasn't counted overhead. The sales pitch is a no-brainer, and Meggett's firm could be a big customer for your planned new company. But that's not what's troubling you.

You were just leaving for lunch today when Firman came in. He was edgy. "Listen," he told you, "don't take any bull from these people. I play golf with one of the partners over there, and he's been going on about buying this new computer. I bet you hear all about their big in-house plans and how much money they'll save.

"My attitude is, let 'em go. They'll find out it's not so easy, and they'll come crawling back to us. This isn't tiddlywinks we're playing here. If that's their plan, say so long and wish them well."

Now, back at the restaurant, Meggett looks up, awaiting your response. You can take Firman's approach, even though (you can't help thinking) it amounts to shafting the customer. Or you can make your own pitch, offering Meggett the best deal she'll get and maybe landing your first account.

Questions

1. What do you do about dilemma one? Do you offer Lowrey a job, quit thinking about your start-up, or bite your tongue and not mention your plans until you've left?

2. What do you do about dilemma two? Do you do as Firman says, make your pitch to Ms. Meggett, or delay making your pitch until after you've left Firman?

3. How did your responses compare with others in your class? Class members should discuss the reasoning process by which they came to their decisions.

Source: John Case, "Honest Business," *INC.*, January 1990, pp. 65–66.

VIDEO CASE

General Electric's Automatic Coffee Maker

What did they know and when did they know it? These are the two questions that one has to ask regarding a malfunctioning automatic coffee maker manufactured by General Electric.

GE has sold more than 9 million of its model of coffee maker with an automatic timer. But the product had a basic design flaw. The thermostat in the coffee maker wears out after long use. Moreover, the 12 cent fuse that acts as a backup safety device occasionally fails. The result: the coffee maker gets uncontrollably hot and can potentially cause fires.

As many as 400 fires are reported to have been caused by defective GE coffee makers. When first identified as the cause of these fires, GE denied it. But they later admitted that about forty fires had been traced to problems with their product. Overall, GE's position has been that it has acted responsibly. It accurately notes that only a small fraction of the 9 million coffee makers were problems. Additionally, the company claims it reported the problem to the U.S. Consumer Product Safety Commission as it surfaced. Evidence suggests, however, that this second point is not true.

GE's own records show that, in 1981, the company estimated that the problems with the coffee maker's design would result in 168 claims. They also show that GE put the probability at only 42 percent that no one would be hurt as a result of this problem. In 1982, the company made some improvements in the product's design in response to hundreds of reported fire hazards. In 1984, GE sold its small appliance division (which included this coffee maker) to Black & Decker, which promptly added a second backup fuse for increased safety protection.

In March 1991, GE finally recalled these coffee makers. Yet, at that time, it was estimated that around 1 million were still in use, and some were being sold in second-hand thrift stores. Critics claim that GE knew it had a serious problem with this product as early as 1980 and that it dragged its feet—denying responsibility—for a dozen years. Meanwhile, homes were burning down and lives lost as a result of a defective product.

Questions

1. Was GE meeting its basic social obligation with its coffee maker problem? Explain.

2. Why do you think GE's management ignored the danger associated with this product?

3. Was GE's response consistent with a utilitarian view of ethics? Discuss.

4. If GE is guilty of denying and covering up a defective product, should its management be punished? What do you think an appropriate punishment would be?

Source: "Danger Brewing," *ABC's Primetime Live,* October 17, 1991.

CHAPTER 6

Decision Making: The Essence of the Manager's Job

After Reading This Chapter, You Should Be Able To:

1. Outline the steps in the decision-making process.
2. Define the rational decision maker.
3. Explain the limits to rationality.
4. Describe the perfectly rational decision-making process.
5. Describe the boundedly rational decision-making process.
6. Identify the two types of decision problems and the two types of decisions that are used to solve them.
7. Differentiate certainty, risk, and uncertainty decision conditions.
8. Identify the advantages and disadvantages of group decisions.
9. Describe four techniques for improving group decision making.

Since its birth as a tiny Texas commuter airline in 1971, Herb Kelleher has built Southwest Airlines into the eighth largest airline by devoting enormous attention to thousands of small decisions.

Herb Kelleher, chairman of Southwest Airlines, made the decision to remove the closets at the front of his firm's planes.[1] He didn't do it to gain more seats. Rather, he did it to improve the speed with which passengers can board and depart. Since all Southwest planes operate with open seating, the first people on the plane typically went to the closets first and then grabbed the nearest seats. Upon landing, departing passengers were held up while the people in the front rows rummaged through the closets for their bags.

As Kelleher put it, the removal of the closets was just one of "1,000 small decisions, all designed to achieve simplicity." Some of the other decisions he made to achieve this goal of simplicity included no meals, no reserved or first-class seats, no computerized reservation systems, no baggage transfers to other airlines, standardized aircraft (they're all Boeing 737s), and reusable boarding passes. Additionally, while other smaller airlines decided to fly to Europe or go head-to-head against their larger competitors, Kelleher has stayed with his niche strategy. "You have to exercise a certain amount of judgment with respect to what you're capable of and what you're not," says Kelleher. He decided early on to attack fewer markets, but with greater intensity. Southwest bombards a city with lots of flights. "We won't go in with just one or two flights. We'll go in with ten or twelve."

Kelleher seems to know what he's doing. Since its birth as a tiny commuter airline in 1971, he has built Southwest into the eighth-largest airline in the United States with revenues of $1.2 billion a year. Customers like Southwest's low fares and on-time schedules. The airline turns around nearly 85 percent of its flights in 15 minutes or less—other major airlines typically spend an hour at the gate—and it is one of the few profitable U.S. airlines. On a typical day, Southwest planes are in the air for 11 hours, versus an industry average of eight hours. And Southwest's cost per available-seat-mile of 6.5¢ blows away such competitors as American and USAir, whose costs are 9¢ and 15¢, respectively.

Herb Kelleher, like all managers, makes a lot of decisions—some small and some large. And the overall quality of these decisions goes a long way in determining their organization's success or failure. In this chapter, we examine the concept of "decision making."

The Decision-Making Process

decision-making process
A set of eight steps that include identifying a problem, selecting an alternative, and evaluating the decision's effectiveness.

Decision making is typically described as "choosing among alternatives." But this view is overly simplistic. Why? Because decision making is a *process* rather than the simple act of choosing among alternatives.

Figure 6–1 illustrates the **decision-making process** as a set of eight steps that begins with identifying a problem, moves to selecting an alternative that can alleviate the problem, and concludes with evaluating the decision's effectiveness. This process is as applicable to your personal decision about where you're going to take your summer vacation as it is to a corporate action such as Hershey Foods' decision to introduce a new candy bar. The process can also be used to describe both individual and group decisions. Let's take a closer look at the process in order to understand what each step encompasses.

Step 1: Identifying a Problem

problem
A discrepancy between an existing and a desired state of affairs.

The decision-making process begins with the existence of a **problem** or, more specifically, a discrepancy between an existing and a desired state of affairs.[2] Let's develop an example that illustrates this point and that we can use throughout this section. For the sake of simplicity, let's make the example something to which most of us can relate: the decision to buy a new car. Take the case of the manager of a manufacturing plant whose company car just blew its engine. Again, for simplicity's sake, assume that it's uneconomic to repair the car and that corporate headquarters requires plant managers to buy new cars rather than to lease them. So now we have a

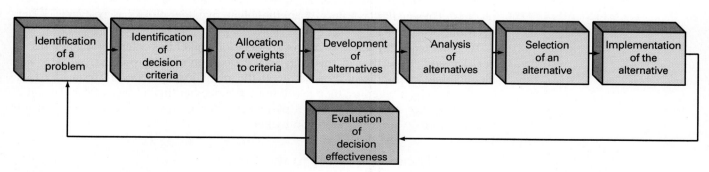

FIGURE 6–1
The Decision-Making Process

problem. There is a disparity between the manager's need to have a car that runs and the fact that her current one doesn't.

Unfortunately, this example doesn't tell us much about how managers identify problems. In the real world, most problems don't come with neon signs identifying them as such. While a blown engine might be a clear signal to the plant manager that she needs a new car, few problems are so obvious. Is a five percent decline in sales a *problem?* Or are declining sales merely a *symptom* of another problem, such as product obsolescence or an inadequate advertising budget? Also, keep in mind that one manager's "problem" is another manager's "satisfactory state of affairs." Problem identification is subjective. Furthermore, the manager who mistakenly solves the *wrong* problem perfectly is likely to perform just as poorly as the manager who fails to identify the *right* problem and does nothing. Problem identification is neither a simple nor an unimportant part of the decision-making process.[3]

Before something can be characterized as a problem, managers have to be aware of the discrepancy, they have to be under pressure to take action, and they must have the resources necessary to take action.[4]

How do managers become aware that they have a discrepancy? They obviously have to make a comparison between their current state of affairs and some standard. What is that standard? It can be past performance, previously set goals, or the performance of some other unit within the organization or in other organizations. In our car-buying example, the standard is a previously set goal—having a car that runs.

But a discrepancy without pressure becomes a problem that can be put off to some future time. To initiate the decision process, then, the problem must be such that it exerts some type of pressure on the manager to act. Pressure might include organizational policies, deadlines, financial crises, expectations from the boss, or an upcoming performance evaluation.

Finally, managers aren't likely to characterize something as a problem if they perceive that they don't have the authority, money, information, or other resources necessary to act on it. When managers perceive a problem and are under pressure to act, but they feel they have inadequate resources, they usually describe the situation as one in which unrealistic expectations are being placed upon them.

Step 2: Identifying Decision Criteria

decision criteria
Criteria that define what is relevant in a decision.

Once a manager has identified a problem that needs attention, the **decision criteria** that will be important in solving the problem must be identified. That is, managers must determine what is relevant in making a decision.

In our car-buying example, the plant manager has to assess what factors are relevant in her decision. These might include criteria such as price, model (two-door or four-door), size (compact or intermediate), manufacturer (foreign or domestic), optional equipment (automatic transmission, air conditioning, and so on), and repair records. These criteria reflect what the plant manager thinks is relevant in her decision.

Whether explicitly stated or not, every decision maker has criteria that guide his or her decision. Note that in this step in the decision-making process, what is *not* identified is as important as what *is*. If the plant manager doesn't consider fuel economy to be a criterion, then it will not influence her final choice of car. Thus if a decision maker does not identify a particular criterion in this second step, then it's treated as irrelevant to the decision maker.

Step 3: Allocating Weights to the Criteria

The criteria listed in the previous step are not all equally important. It's necessary, therefore, to weight the items listed in Step 2 in order to give them the correct priority in the decision.

TABLE 6-1 Criteria and Weight in Car-Replacement Decision

Criteria	Weight
Initial price	10[a]
Interior comfort	8
Durability	5
Repair record	5
Performance	3
Handling	1

[a] In this example, the highest rating for a criterion is 10 points.

How does the decision maker weigh criteria? A simple approach is merely to give *the* most important criterion a weight of ten and then assign weights to the rest against this standard. Thus, in contrast to a criterion that you gave a five, the highest-rated factor would be twice as important. Of course, you could begin by assigning 100 or 1,000 as the highest weight. Nevertheless, the idea is to use your personal preferences to assign a priority to the relevant criteria in your decision as well as to indicate their degree of importance by assigning a weight to each.

Table 6–1 lists the criteria and weights that our plant manager developed for her car-replacement decision. Price is the most important criterion in her decision, with such factors as performance and handling having low weights.

Step 4: Developing Alternatives

The fourth step requires the decision maker to list the viable alternatives that could succeed in resolving the problem. No attempt is made in this step to appraise these alternatives, only to list them. Let's assume that our plant manager has identified 13 cars as viable choices. They are: Acura Integra RS, Chevrolet Lumina, Eagle Premier LX, Ford Taurus L, Honda Accord LX, Hyundai Sonata GLS, Mazda 626 LX, Nissan Altima, Plymouth Acclaim, Pontiac Bonneville SE, Toyota Camry DLX, Volkswagen Passat, and Volvo 240.

Step 5: Analyzing Alternatives

Once the alternatives have been identified, the decision maker must critically analyze each one. The strengths and weaknesses of each alternative become evident as they are compared with the criteria and weights established in Steps 2 and 3.

Each alternative is evaluated by appraising it against the criteria. Table 6–2 shows the assessed values that the plant manager put on each of her thirteen alternatives after she had test-driven each car.

Keep in mind that the ratings given the thirteen cars shown in Table 6–2 are based on the assessment made by the plant manager. Again, we are using a 1 to 10 scale. Some assessments can be achieved in a relatively objective fashion. For instance, the purchase price represents the best price the manager can get from local dealers, and

TABLE 6-2 Assessment of the 13 Alternatives Against the Decision Criteria

Alternatives	Criteria					
	Initial Price	Interior Comfort	Durability	Repair Record	Perform-ance	Hand-ling
Acura Integra RS	5	6	10	10	7	10
Chevrolet Lumina	7	8	5	6	4	7
Eagle Premier LX	5	8	4	5	8	7
Ford Taurus L	6	8	6	7	7	7
Honda Accord LX	5	8	10	10	7	7
Hyundai Sonata GLS	7	7	5	4	7	7
Mazda 626 LX	7	5	7	7	4	7
Nissan Altima	8	5	7	9	7	7
Plymouth Acclaim	10	7	3	3	3	5
Pontiac Bonneville SE	4	10	5	5	10	10
Toyota Camry DLX	6	7	10	10	7	7
Volkswagen Passat	4	7	5	4	10	8
Volvo 240	2	7	10	9	4	5

When you made your decision on what college to attend, you might have considered factors such as location, size of the school, admission requirements, cost, availability of financial assistance, required courses, male-female ratio, prestige, where your best friend was applying, and the like. But these criteria were not all equally important in your final decision. That is, they might all have been relevant, but some were more relevant than others. For instance, some high school seniors consider cost and availability of financial assistance to be the crucial factors in their decision. They might prefer to go to school away from home, but cost considerations are more compelling.

consumer magazines report data from owners on frequency of repairs. But the assessment of handling is clearly a personal judgment. The point is that most decisions contain judgments. They are reflected in the criteria chosen in Step 2, the weights given to the criteria, and the evaluation of alternatives. This explains why two car buyers with the same amount of money may look at two totally different sets of alternatives or even look at the same alternatives and rate them so dissimilarly.

Table 6–2 represents only an assessment of the thirteen alternatives against the decision criteria. It does not reflect the weighting done in Step 3. If one choice had scored 10 on every criterion, you wouldn't need to consider the weights. Similarly, if the weights were all equal, you could evaluate each alternative merely by summing up the appropriate lines in Table 6–2. For instance, the Acura Integra would have a score of 48 and the Ford Taurus a score of 41. If you multiply each alternative assessment against its weight, you get Table 6–3. To illustrate, the Honda Accord scored 50 on durability, which was determined by multiplying the weight given to durability (5) by the manager's appraisal of the Honda on this criterion (10). The

TABLE 6–3   Assessment of Car Alternatives

Alternatives	Criteria						
	Initial Price	Interior Comfort	Durability	Repair Record	Performance	Handling	Totals
Acura Integra RS	50	48	50	50	21	10	229
Chevrolet Lumina	70	64	25	30	12	7	208
Eagle Premier LX	50	64	20	25	24	7	190
Ford Taurus L	60	64	30	35	21	7	217
Honda Accord LX	50	64	50	50	21	7	242
Hyundai Sonata GLS	70	56	25	20	21	7	199
Mazda 626 LX	70	40	35	35	12	7	199
Nissan Altima	80	40	35	35	21	7	218
Plymouth Acclaim	100	56	15	15	9	5	200
Pontiac Bonneville SE	40	80	25	25	30	10	210
Toyota Camry DLX	60	56	50	50	21	7	244
Volkswagen Passat	40	56	25	20	30	8	179
Volvo 240	20	56	50	45	12	5	188

summation of these scores represents an evaluation of each alternative against the previously established criteria and weights. Notice that the weighting of the criteria has significantly changed the ranking of alternatives in our example. The Acura, for instance, has gone from first to third. Both the Acura and the Pontiac Bonneville were first on three of the six criteria, but the Acura didn't do well on interior comfort and the Pontiac didn't score high on durability. And the high initial price for both the Acura and Pontiac worked against them.

Step 6: Selecting an Alternative

The sixth step is the critical act of choosing the best alternative from among those enumerated and assessed. Since we have determined all the pertinent factors in the decision, weighted them appropriately, and identified the viable alternatives, we merely have to choose the alternative that generated the highest score in Step 5. In our car purchase example (Table 6–3), the decision maker would choose the Toyota Camry. On the basis of the criteria identified, the weights given to the criteria, and the decision maker's assessment of each car's achievement on the criteria, the Toyota scored highest (244 points) and thus became the "best" alternative.

Step 7: Implementing the Alternative

While the choice process is completed in the previous step, the decision may still fail if it is not implemented properly. Therefore, Step 7 is concerned with putting the decision into action.

MANAGERS WHO MADE A DIFFERENCE

Geneva Overholser at the *Des Moines Register*

Geneva Overholser thinks newspapers have to do a better job of serving women, minorities, and the young.[5] Since leaving the *New York Times* in late 1988 to become editor of the *Des Moines Register,* she has made a series of decisions designed to make those goals reality. She's encouraged her staff to develop stories on battered farm wives, sexual abuse by fathers, child care, sexual harassment, gay Iowans, and rape. But Overholser's most controversial decision was to print Nancy Ziegenmeyer's story of how she was raped and the subsequent battle to have her assailant convicted. What was controversial about this story was that Ziegenmeyer allowed the paper to use her full name and no attempt was made to cover up the personal details in Ziegenmeyer's life.

Overholser has become a national figure largely as a result of urging sex-crime victims to speak out and her arguing that the common newspaper practice of keeping rape victims' names out of print stigmatizes women rather than protecting them: "If I seek a world in which newspapers routinely print rape victims' names, it is also a world in which rape victims are treated compassionately, the stigma eradicated."

Geneva Overholser's decisions have put her newspaper in the headlines. But they have also been recognized as making a difference. In the spring of 1991, she collected a Pulitzer Prize honoring her paper's articles on Nancy Ziegenmeyer.

implementation
Conveying a decision to those affected and getting their commitment to it.

Implementation includes conveying the decision to those affected and getting their commitment to it. As we'll demonstrate later in this chapter, groups or committees can help a manager achieve commitment. If the people who must carry out a decision participate in the process, they are more likely to endorse enthusiastically the outcome. (Parts III through V of this book detail how decisions are implemented by effective planning, organizing, and leading.)

Step 8: Evaluating Decision Effectiveness

The last step in the decision-making process appraises the result of the decision to see whether it has corrected the problem. Did the alternative chosen in Step 6 and implemented in Step 7 accomplish the desired result? The evaluation of such results is detailed in Part VI of this book, where we look at the control function.

What happens if, as a result of this evaluation, the problem is found to still exist? The manager then needs to dissect carefully what went wrong. Was the problem incorrectly defined? Were errors made in the evaluation of the various alternatives? Was the right alternative selected but improperly implemented? Answers to questions like these might send the manager back to one of the earlier steps. It might even require starting the whole decision process anew.

The Pervasiveness of Decision Making

The importance of decision making to every facet of a manager's job cannot be overstated. As Table 6–4 illustrates, decision making permeates all four managerial functions. In fact, this explains why managers—when they plan, organize, lead, and

TABLE 6–4   Examples of Decisions in the Management Functions

Planning

What are the organization's long-term objectives?
What strategies will best achieve these objectives?
What should the organization's short-term objectives be?
How difficult should individual goals be?

Organizing

How many subordinates should I have report directly to me?
How much centralization should there be in the organization?
How should jobs be designed?
When should the organization implement a different structure?

Leading

How do I handle employees who appear to be low in motivation?
What is the most effective leadership style in a given situation?
How will a specific change affect worker productivity?
When is the right time to stimulate conflict?

Controlling

What activities in the organization need to be controlled?
How should these activities be controlled?
When is a performance deviation significant?
What type of management information system should the organization have?

control—are frequently called *decision makers*. So it is not incorrect to say that decision making is synonymous with managing.[6]

The fact that almost everything a manager does involves decision making does not mean that decisions are always long, involved, or clearly evident to an outside observer. Much of a manager's decision-making activity is of a routine nature. Every day of the year you make a decision to deal with the problem of when to eat lunch. It's no big deal. You've made the decision thousands of times before. It offers few problems and can usually be handled quickly. It's the type of decision you almost forget *is* a decision. Managers make dozens of these routine decisions every day. Keep in mind that even though a decision seems easy to make or has been faced by a manager a number of times before, it is a decision nonetheless.

The Rational Decision Maker

rational
Describes choices that are consistent and value-maximizing within specified constraints.

Managerial decision making is assumed to be **rational.** By that we mean that managers make consistent, value-maximizing choices within specified constraints.[7] In this section, we want to take a close look at the underlying assumptions of rationality and then determine how valid these assumptions actually are.

Assumptions of Rationality

A decision maker who was perfectly rational would be fully objective and logical. He or she would define a problem carefully and would have a clear and specific goal. Moreover, the steps in the decision-making process would consistently lead toward selecting the alternative that maximizes that goal. Figure 6–2 summarizes the assumptions of rationality.

Problem clarity. In rational decision making, the problem is clear and unambiguous. The decision maker is assumed to have complete information regarding the decision situation.

Goal orientation. In rational decision making there is no conflict over the goal. Whether the decision involves purchasing a new car, selecting a college to attend, choosing the proper price for a new product, or picking the right applicant to fill a

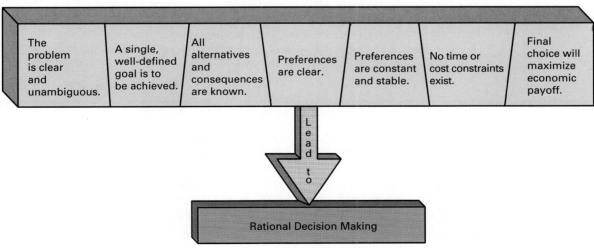

FIGURE 6–2
Assumptions of Rationality

ETHICAL DILEMMAS IN MANAGEMENT

Should Social Responsibility Play a Factor in the Decision to Relocate a Plant or Headquarters' Office?

In 1979, U.S. Steel (now USX Corp.) employed more than 26,000 people in the Monongahela Valley of Western Pennsylvania. After closing three mills, the number of employees is now under 4,000. R.J. Reynolds Tobacco was the dominant employer in Winston-Salem, North Carolina, for much of this century. When the tobacco firm absorbed Nabisco Brands in 1987, the thousands of company headquarters personnel were uprooted from Winston-Salem and moved to Atlanta. In 1989, RJR Nabisco again relocated its corporate headquarters, this time from Atlanta to New York City. In 1992, General Motors announced the closing of its Willow Run plant in Ypsilanti, Michigan, dealing another major blow to a community already suffering from long-term cutbacks in the auto industry.

Relocating plants and corporate headquarters can be devastating to small towns and even to large cities if the organization is a major employer.[8] For instance, Homestead, Pennsylvania, is one of the small towns in the Monongahela Valley that has been permanently altered as a result of USX's 1986 decision to close its mammoth Homestead Works plant, which once employed 15,000 steelworkers. Most of the former USX workers in their mid-40s or older who have found work are underemployed in part-time, low-paying jobs. Mental and physical problems are extremely common in the community. Police and other services have been drastically cut as the tax base has disappeared. Most of the stores in town are now closed and boarded up.

Many communities incur very high expenditures to entice and appease large employers. They build roads, schools, and hospitals for corporations and their personnel. They provide police and fire protection. Other businesses, of course, open up to service the needs of the corporation, its workers, and their families. The decision by management to relocate out of such communities—as experienced by places like Ypsilanti, Homestead, and Winston-Salem—can cause economic collapse in towns and whole regions.

Management can respond by arguing that it brought more to the relationship than the community gave back—specifically, high-paying jobs that allowed the community to grow and prosper—and that, in today's global economy, hometown loyalties cannot override economic considerations.

Should social responsibility play a factor in management's decision to relocate a plant or headquarters office? What do *you* think?

---

job vacancy, the decision maker has a single, well-defined goal that he or she is trying to reach.

Known options. It is assumed that the decision maker is creative, can identify all the relevant criteria, and can list all the viable alternatives. Further, the decision maker is aware of all the possible consequences of each alternative.

Clear preferences. Rationality assumes that the criteria and alternatives can be ranked according to their importance.

Constant preferences. In addition to a clear goal and preferences, it is assumed that the specific decision criteria are constant and that the weights assigned to them are stable over time.

No time or cost constraints. The rational decision maker can obtain full information about criteria and alternatives because it is assumed that there are no time or cost constraints.

Maximum payoff. The rational decision maker always chooses the alternative that will yield the maximum economic payoff.

These assumptions of rationality apply to any decision. However, since we're concerned with managerial decision making in an organization, we need to add one further assumption. Rational managerial decision making assumes that decisions are made in the economic best interests of the organization. That is, the decision maker is assumed to be maximizing the *organization's* interests, not his or her own interests.

Limits to Rationality

Managerial decision making *can* follow rational assumptions. If a manager is faced with a simple problem in which the goals are clear and the alternatives few, in which the time pressures are minimal and the cost of seeking out and evaluating alternatives is low, for which the organizational culture supports innovation and risk taking, and in which the outcomes are relatively concrete and measurable, the decision process is likely to follow the assumptions of rationality.[9] But most decisions that managers face don't meet all these tests.

Hundreds of studies have sought to improve our understanding of managerial decision making.[10] Individually, these studies often challenge one or more of the assumptions of rationality. Taken together, they suggest that decision making often veers from the logical, consistent, and systematic process that rationality implies. Let us examine some important insights that researchers have uncovered about the decision-making process:

1. There are limits to an individual's information-processing capacity.[11] Most people are able to hold only about seven pieces of information in short-term memory. When decisions become complex, individuals tend to create simple models that allow them to reduce the problem to understandable dimensions.

2. Decision makers tend to intermix solutions with problems.[12] The definition of a problem often includes a rough description of an acceptable solution. This clouds the objectivity of both the alternative-generation stage and the alternative-evaluation stage of the decision process.

3. Perceptual biases can distort problem identification.[13] We know that "except in detective stories, the facts don't speak for themselves; they must be interpreted."[14] The decision maker's background, position in the organization, interests, and past experiences focus his or her attention on certain problems and not others. The organization's culture can also distort a manager's perceptions: "Managers sometimes don't see what they believe can't be there."[15]

4. Many decision makers select information more for its accessibility than for its quality.[16] Important information, therefore, may carry less weight in a decision than information that is easy to get.

5. Decision makers tend to commit themselves prematurely to a specific alternative early in the decision process, thus biasing the process toward choosing that alternative.[17]

6. Evidence that a previous solution is not working does not always generate a search for new alternatives. Instead, it frequently initiates an **escalation of commitment** whereby the decision maker further increases the commitment of

escalation of commitment
An increased commitment to a previous decision despite evidence that it may have been wrong.

One of the most frequently cited examples of escalation of commitment is President Lyndon Johnson's decision regarding the Vietnam War. Despite continued information that bombing North Vietnam was not bringing the war any closer to conclusion, his solution was to increase the tonnage of bombs dropped.

resources to the previous course of action in an effort to demonstrate that the initial decision was not wrong.[18]

7. Prior decision precedents constrain current choices.[19] Decisions are rarely simple, discrete events. They are more aptly described as points in a stream of choices. Most decisions are really an accumulation of subdecisions made over long periods of time.

8. Organizations are made up of divergent interests that make it difficult, even impossible, to create a common effort toward a single goal. Decisions are therefore rarely directed toward achieving an overall organizational goal. Instead, there is a constant bargaining among managers, who perceive problems differently and prefer different alternatives.[20] The existence of divergent interests ensures that there will be differences in goals, alternatives, and consequences. Bargaining is needed to achieve compromise and support for implementing the final solution. Consequently, "where you stand depends on where you sit."[21] In ambiguous and contradictory situations, decisions are largely the outcome of power and political influences.[22]

9. Organizations place time and cost constraints on decision makers, which, in turn, limit the amount of search that a manager can undertake.[23] Thus, new alternatives tend to be sought in the neighborhood of old ones.[24]

10. In spite of the potential for diversity, a strong conservative bias exists in most organizational cultures.[25] Most organizational cultures reinforce the status quo, which discourages risk taking and innovation. In such cultures, employees are frequently rewarded for being "team players" and for not "making waves," and wrong choices have more of an impact on a decision maker's career than does the development of new ideas. So decision makers spend more effort trying to avoid mistakes than in developing innovative ideas.

Bounded Rationality

Do these limits to rationality mean that managers ignore the eight-step decision process we described at the beginning of this chapter? Not necessarily. Why? Because in spite of the limits to perfect rationality, managers are expected to appear to follow the rational process.[26] Managers know that "good" decision makers are *supposed* to do certain things: identify problems, consider alternatives, gather information, and act decisively but prudently. Managers can thus be expected to exhibit the correct decision-making behaviors. By doing so, managers signal to their superiors, peers, and subordinates that they are competent and that their decisions are the result of intelligent and rational deliberation.

Table 6–5 summarizes how the perfectly rational manager should proceed through the eight-step decision process. It also describes an alternative model—one followed by a manager operating under assumptions of **bounded rationality.**[27] In bounded rationality, managers construct simplified models that extract the essential features from problems without capturing all their complexity. Then, given information processing limitations and constraints imposed by the organization, managers attempt to behave rationally within the parameters of the simple model. The result is a **satisficing** decision rather than a maximizing one; that is, a decision in which the solution is "good enough."

The implications of bounded rationality on the manager's job cannot be overlooked. In situations in which the assumptions of perfect rationality do not apply (including many of the most important and far-reaching decisions that a manager makes), the details of the decision-making process are strongly influenced by the

bounded rationality

Behavior that is rational within the parameters of a simplified model that captures the essential features of a problem.

satisficing

Acceptance of solutions that are "good enough."

TABLE 6–5   Two Views of the Decision-Making Process

Decision-Making Step	Perfect Rationality	Bounded Rationality
1. Problem formulation	An important and relevant organizational problem is identified.	A visible problem that reflects the manager's interests and background is identified.
2. Identification of decision criteria	All criteria are identified.	A limited set of criteria are identified.
3. Allocation of weights to criteria	All criteria are evaluated and rated in terms of their importance to the organization's goal.	A simple model is constructed to evaluate and rate the criteria; the decision maker's self-interest strongly influences the ratings.
4. Development of alternatives	A comprehensive list of all alternatives is developed creatively.	A limited set of similar alternatives is identified.
5. Analysis of alternatives	All alternatives are assessed against the decision criteria and weights; the consequences for each alternative are known.	Beginning with a favored solution, alternatives are assessed, one at a time, against the decision criteria.
6. Selection of an alternative	*Maximizing decision:* the one with the highest economic outcome (in terms of the organization's goal) is chosen.	*Satisficing decision:* the search continues until a solution is found that is satisfactory and sufficient, at which time the search stops.
7. Implementation of alternative	Since the decision maximizes the single, well-defined goal, all organizational members will embrace the solution.	Politics and power considerations will influence the acceptance of, and commitment to, the decision.
8. Evaluation	The decision's outcome is objectively evaluated against the original problem.	Measurement of the decision's results are rarely so objective as to eliminate self-interests of the evaluator; possible escalation of resources to prior commitments in spite of both previous failures and strong evidence that allocation of additional resources is not warranted.

decision maker's self-interest, the organization's culture, internal politics, and power considerations. As you'll see in future chapters, the disparity between the perfectly rational view of how managers *should* make decisions and the bounded rationality description of how managers *actually* make them often explains the instances when management practice deviates from management theory.

The Growing Popularity of Intuitive Decision Making

A professor of quantitative methods once commented to me, "Decision making is easy. Just identify the appropriate model, specify the variables, plug in the numbers, and crank out the answer." This approach to managerial decision making reached its peak in the mid-1980s, when the focus of almost every major M.B.A. program had become teaching students quantitative decision models. The guiding principle that seemed to drive this approach was "if you can't quantify it, it doesn't exist!"

The flaws in this rational decision approach were far from minuscule. Quaker Oats, for instance, used state-of-the-art rational decision-making models in its effort to gain an upper hand in the pet food market.[28] However, Quaker's models didn't factor in the harsh, almost irrational way that competitors would throw amounts of money at low-profit markets. The result contributed to a sharp drop in Quaker Oats' earnings in the early 1990s.

The essence of the rational model is to replace intuition with systematic logic. But, as a result of experiences like that of Quaker Oats, intuitive decision making is gaining new followers in both business schools and executive suites. Experts no longer automatically assume that the use of intuition is an irrational or ineffective means for making decisions.[29] There is growing recognition that rational analysis can be over-emphasized and that, in certain instances, decision making can be improved by relying on the decision maker's intuition. So intuition doesn't replace rational analysis—rather, the two work to complement each other.

When are managers most likely to use intuitive decision making? Eight conditions have been identified: (1) When a high level of uncertainty exists; (2) when little previous precedent exists; (3) when variables are less scientifically predictable; (4) when "facts" are limited; (5) when facts don't clearly point the way to go; (6) when analytical data are of little use; (7) when several plausible alternative solutions exist to choose from, with good arguments for each; and (8) when time is limited and there is pressure to come up with the right decision.[30]

Is there a standard model that managers follow when using intuition? They seem to follow one of two approaches. They apply intuition to either the front or the back end of the decision-making process.[31]

When intuition is used at the front end, the decision maker tries to avoid analyzing the problem systematically. He or she gives intuition a free rein, trying to generate unusual possibilities and new options that might not normally emerge from an analysis of past data or traditional ways of doing things. A back end approach to using intuition relies on rational analysis in identifying and allocating weights to decision criteria, as well as in developing and evaluating alternatives. But after this is done, the decision maker stops the process in order to sift through and digest the information. This is best characterized by the action of "sleeping on the decision" for a day or two before making the final choice.

Problems and Decisions: A Contingency Approach

The *type* of problem a manager faces in a decision-making situation often determines how that problem is treated. In this section we present a categorization scheme for problems and for types of decisions. Then we show how the type of decision a manager uses should reflect the characteristics of the problem.

Types of Problems

Some problems are straightforward. The goal of the decision maker is clear, the problem familiar, and information about the problem easily defined and complete. Examples might include a customer wanting to return a purchase to a retail store, a supplier being late with an important delivery, a newspaper having to respond to an unexpected and fast-breaking news event, or a college's handling of a student who seeks to drop a class. Such situations are called **well-structured problems.** They align closely with the assumptions underlying perfect rationality.

Many situations faced by managers, however, are **ill-structured problems.** They are new or unusual. Information about such problems is ambiguous or incomplete. The selection of an architect to design a new corporate headquarters building is one example. So too is the decision to invest in a new, unproven technology.

Types of Decisions

Just as problems can be divided into two categories, so too can decisions. As we will see, *programmed,* or routine, decision making is the most efficient way to handle well-structured problems. However, when problems are ill-structured, managers must rely on *nonprogrammed* decision making in order to develop unique solutions.

Programmed decisions A waitress in a restaurant spills a drink on a customer's coat. The restaurant manager has an upset customer. What does the manager do? Since such occurrences are not infrequent, there is probably some standardized routine for handling the problem. For example, if it is the waitress's fault, if the damage is significant, and if the customer has asked for a remedy, the manager offers to have the coat cleaned at the restaurant's expense. This is a **programmed decision.**

Decisions are programmed to the extent that they are repetitive and routine and to the extent that a definite approach has been worked out for handling them. Because the problem is well-structured, the manager does not have to go to the trouble and expense of working up an involved decision process. Programmed decision making is relatively simple and tends to rely heavily on previous solutions. The "develop-the-alternatives" stage in the decision-making process is either nonexistent or given little attention. Why? Because once the structured problem is defined, its solution is usually self-evident or at least reduced to very few alternatives that are familiar and that have proven successful in the past. In many cases, programmed decision making becomes decision making by precedent. Managers simply do what they and others have done in the same situation. The spilled drink on the customer's coat does not require the restaurant manager to identify and weigh decision criteria nor develop a long list of possible solutions. Rather, the manager falls back on a systematic procedure, rule, or policy.

A **procedure** is a series of interrelated sequential steps that a manager can use for responding to a structured problem. The only real difficulty is in identifying the problem. Once the problem is clear, so is the procedure. For instance, a purchasing manager receives a request from accounting for five desktop printing calculators that

well-structured problems
Straightforward, familiar, easily defined problems.

ill-structured problems
New problems in which information is ambiguous or incomplete.

programmed decision
A repetitive decision that can be handled by a routine approach.

procedure
A series of interrelated sequential steps that can be used to respond to a structured problem.

can perform a certain set of functions. The purchasing manager knows that there is a definite procedure for handling this decision. Has the requisition been properly filled out and approved? If not, send the requisition back with a note explaining what is deficient. If the request is complete, the approximate costs are estimated. If the total exceeds $5,000, three bids must be obtained. If the total is $5,000 or less, only one vendor need be identified and the order placed. The decision-making process in this case is merely the executing of a simple series of sequential steps.

rule
An explicit statement that tells managers what they ought or ought not to do.

A **rule** is an explicit statement that tells a manager what he or she ought or ought not to do. Rules are frequently used by managers when they confront a well-structured problem because they are simple to follow and ensure consistency. In the illustration above, the $5,000 cutoff rule simplifies the purchasing manager's decision about when to use multiple bids. Similarly, rules about lateness and absenteeism permit supervisors to make discipline decisions rapidly and with a relatively high degree of fairness.

policy
A guide that establishes parameters for making decisions.

A third guide for making programmed decisions is a **policy.** It provides guidelines to channel a manager's thinking in a specific direction. In contrast to a rule, a policy establishes parameters for the decision maker rather than specifically stating what should or should not be done. As an analogy, think of the Ten Commandments as rules, and the U.S. Constitution as policy. The latter requires judgment and interpretation; the former do not.

Policies typically contain an ambiguous term that leaves interpretation to the decision maker. For instance, each of the following is a policy statement: "The customer shall always be *satisfied.*" "We promote from within, *whenever possible.*" "Employee wages shall be *competitive* for the community in which our plants are located." Notice that *satisfied, whenever possible,* and *competitive* are terms that require interpretation. The policy to pay competitive wages does not tell a given plant's personnel manager what he or she should pay, but it does give direction to the decision he or she will make. If other firms in the community are paying between $6.70 and $8.50 an hour for unskilled labor, the decision to set hourly rates at $6.40 or $9.00 clearly would not be within the guidelines set by company policy.

nonprogrammed decisions
Unique decisions that require a custom-made solution.

Nonprogrammed Decisions   Deciding whether or not to merge with another organization, how to restructure an organization to improve efficiency, or whether to close a money-losing division are examples of **nonprogrammed decisions.** Such decisions are unique and nonrecurring. When a manager confronts an ill-structured problem, or one that is novel, there is no cut-and-dried solution. It requires a custom-made response.

The creation of a marketing strategy for a new product represents an example of a nonprogrammed decision. It will be different from previous marketing decisions because the product is new, a different set of competitors exists, and other conditions that may have existed when previous products were introduced years earlier have changed. IBM's introduction of a personal computer in the early 1980s was unlike any other marketing decision the company had previously made. Certainly, IBM had a wealth of experience selling computers. It also had previously sold to small businesses and general consumers through its typewriter division. But it had no substantive experience in mass-marketing relatively low-cost personal computers. It faced such aggressive competitors as Apple, Hewlett-Packard, and Digital Equipment. The needs and sophistication of personal computer customers differed from those of buyers who purchased multimillion-dollar systems for their corporate headquarters. The hundreds of decisions that went into IBM's marketing strategy for personal computers had never been made before and thus were clearly of the nonprogrammed variety.

FIGURE 6–3
Types of Problems, Types of
Decisions, and Level in the
Organization

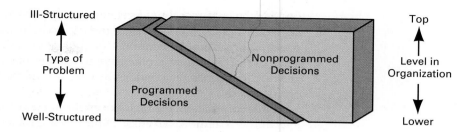

Integration

Figure 6–3 describes the relationship between the types of problems, the types of decisions, and level in the organization. Well-structured problems are responded to with programmed decision making. Ill-structured problems require nonprogrammed decision making. Lower-level managers essentially confront familiar and repetitive problems; therefore, they most typically rely on programmed decisions such as standard operating procedures. However, the problems confronting managers are more likely to become ill-structured as the managers move up the organizational hierarchy. Why? Because lower-level managers handle the routine decisions themselves and pass upward only decisions that they find unique or difficult. Similarly, managers pass down routine decisions to their subordinates in order to spend their time on more problematic issues.

Few managerial decisions in the real world are either fully programmed or nonprogrammed. These are extremes, and most decisions fall somewhere in between. Few programmed decisions are designed to eliminate individual judgment completely. At the other extreme, even the most unique situation requiring a nonprogrammed decision can be helped by programmed routines. It is best to think of decisions as *mainly* programmed or *mainly* nonprogrammed, rather than as fully one or the other.

A last point on this topic is that organizational efficiency is facilitated by the use of programmed decision making, which may explain its wide popularity. Wherever possible, management decisions are likely to be programmed. Obviously, this is not too realistic at the top of the organization, since most of the problems that top management confronts are of a nonrecurring nature. But there are strong economic incentives for top management to create standard operating procedures (SOPs), rules, and policies to guide other managers.

Programmed decisions minimize the need for managers to exercise discretion. This is relevant because discretion costs money. The more nonprogrammed decision making a manager is required to do, the greater the judgment needed. Since sound judgment is an uncommon quality, it costs more to acquire the services of managers who possess this ability.

Consider the following: One multibillion-dollar corporation has controllers (chief accounting managers) at each of its more than three dozen plants throughout the United States. The controllers typically have three to six supervisors reporting to them and are responsible for staffs of twenty-five to fifty. How much do you think those controllers earn? Would it surprise you to learn that, in 1994, most were earning within a thousand dollars of $38,000 a year? This seems extremely low compensation for such responsibilities, but the company has succeeded in making almost all of the controller's decisions highly programmed. Most of the controllers have only a high school education. They are not exceedingly talented. However, they can follow directions. The company has produced a 4,000-page accounting manual, which is continually updated. The manual tells each controller specifically how almost any problem he or she encounters should be handled. If the problem and the procedure for handling it cannot be found, the controller is instructed to call the head office, which will instruct the controller in what to do. Not surprisingly, calls to the head office concerning new problems are typically followed a month or so later by an addition to the manual to guide other plant controllers who might confront this same problem.

In this corporation, the high-priced talent makes all the nonprogrammed accounting decisions at the head office. When these problems become recurring ones, they write up SOPs and distribute them to all plant controllers. In this way, the company is able to get consistent and competent decision making without having to hire experienced individuals with a college education, possibly a master's degree, and a C.P.A. certificate, who would command annual salaries of $65,000 or more.

It should be mentioned that other areas in this company—purchasing, personnel, quality control—also have plant manuals that are regularly updated by their respective staffs at the head office.

Of course, some organizations try to economize by hiring less-skilled managers without developing programmed decision guides for them to follow. Take, for example, a small women's clothing store chain whose owner, because he chooses to pay low salaries, hires store managers with little experience and limited ability to make good judgments. This, in itself, needn't be a problem. The trouble is that the owner provides neither training nor explicit rules and procedures to guide the decisions of his store managers. The result has been continuous complaints by customers about things like promotional discounts, processing credit sales, and the handling of returns.

Analyzing Decision Alternatives

One of the more challenging tasks facing a manager is analyzing decision alternatives (Step 5 in the decision-making process). This section discusses approaches for analyzing alternatives under three different conditions: certainty, risk, and uncertainty.

Certainty

certainty
A situation in which a manager can make accurate decisions because the outcome of every alternative is known.

The ideal situation for making decisions is one of **certainty;** that is, the manager is able to make perfectly accurate decisions because the outcome from every alternative is known. As you might expect, this is *not* the situation in which most decisions are made. It is more idealistic than pragmatic.

Risk

risk
Those conditions in which the decision maker is able to estimate the likelihood of certain outcomes.

A far more relevant situation is one of **risk.** By risk, we mean those conditions in which the decision maker is able to estimate the likelihood of certain alternatives or outcomes. This ability to assign probabilities to outcomes may be the result of personal experience or secondary information. However, under the conditions of risk, the manager has historical data that allow him or her to assign probabilities to different alternatives. Let's look at an example.

Suppose that you manage a ski resort in the Colorado Rockies. You are contemplating whether to add another lift to your current facility. Obviously, your decision will be significantly influenced by the amount of additional revenue that the new lift would generate, and this will depend on the level of snowfall. The decision is made somewhat clearer when you are reminded that you have reasonably reliable past data on snowfall levels in your area. The data indicate that during the past ten years, you received three years of heavy snowfall, five years of normal snow, and two years of light snow. Can you use this information to determine the expected future annual revenue if the new lift is added? If you have good information on the amount of revenues for each level of snow, the answer is yes.

You can create an expected value formulation; that is, you can compute the conditional return from each possible outcome by multiplying expected revenues by probabilities. The result is the average revenue that can be expected over time if the given probabilities hold. As Table 6–6 shows, the expected revenue from adding a new ski lift is $687,500. Of course, whether that justifies a positive or negative decision would depend on the costs involved in generating this revenue—factors such as the cost of erecting the lift, the additional annual expenses for another lift, the interest rate for borrowing money, and so forth.

Uncertainty

uncertainty

A situation in which a decision maker has neither certainty nor reasonable probability estimates available.

What happens if we have to make a decision when neither certainty nor reasonable probability estimates are available? We call such a condition **uncertainty,** and choice will be influenced by the psychological orientation of the decision maker. The optimistic manager will follow a *maximax* choice (maximizing of the maximum possible payoff), the pessimist will pursue a *maximin* choice (maximizing the minimum possible payoff), while the manager who desires to minimize his maximum "regret" will opt for a *minimax* choice.

Consider the case of the marketing manager at Citibank in New York. He has determined four possible strategies for promoting Citibank's MasterCard throughout the Northeast. But the marketing manager is also aware that his major competitor, Chase Manhattan, has three competitive actions of its own for promoting its Visa card in the same region. In this case, we will assume that the Citibank executive has no previous knowledge that would allow him to place probabilities on the success of any of his four strategies. With these facts, the Citibank manager has formulated the matrix in Table 6–7 to show the various Citibank strategies and the resulting profit to Citibank depending on the competitive action chosen by Chase Manhattan.

In this example, if our Citibank manager is an optimist he will choose S_4, because that could produce the largest possible gain: $28 million. Note that this choice maximizes the maximum possible gain.

If our manager is a pessimist, though, he will assume that only the worst can occur. The worst outcome for each strategy is as follows: $S_1 = 11$; $S_2 = 9$; $S_3 = 15$; $S_4 = 14$. These are the most pessimistic outcomes from each strategy. Following the maximin choice, he would maximize the minimum payoff; that is, he would select S_3.

In the third approach, managers recognize that once a decision is made it will not necessarily result in the most profitable payoff. This suggests that there may be a

TABLE 6–6   Expected Value for Revenues from the Addition of One Ski Lift

Event	Expected Revenues	×	Probability	=	Expected Value of Each Alternative
Heavy snowfall	$850,000		0.3		$255,000
Normal snowfall	725,000		0.5		362,500
Light snowfall	350,000		0.2		70,000
					$687,500

TABLE 6-7   Payoff Matrix (in millions of dollars)

Citibank Marketing Strategies	Chase Manhattan's Response		
	CA_1	CA_2	CA_3
S_1	13	14	11
S_2	9	15	18
S_3	24	21	15
S_4	18	14	28

TABLE 6-8   Regret Matrix (in millions of dollars)

Citibank Marketing Strategies	Chase Manhattan's Response		
	CA_1	CA_2	CA_3
S_1	11	7	17
S_2	15	6	10
S_3	0	0	13
S_4	6	7	0

regret of profits forgone, regret referring to the amount of money that *could* have been made had a different strategy been used. Managers calculate regret by subtracting all possible payoffs in each category from the maximum possible payoff for each given event, in this case for each competitive action. For our Citibank manager, the highest payoff, given that Chase engages in CA_1, CA_2, CA_3, is $24 million, $21 million, and $28 million, respectively (the highest number in each column). Subtracting the payoffs in Table 6–7 from these figures produces the results shown in Table 6–8.

The maximum regrets are: S_1 = 17; S_2 = 15; S_3 = 13; and S_4 = 7. Since the minimax choice minimizes the maximum regret, our Citibank manager would choose S_4. By making this choice, he will never have a regret of profits forgone of more than $7 million. This contrasts, for example, with a regret of $15 million had he chosen S_2 and Chase Manhattan taken CA_1.

Group Decision Making

Many decisions in organizations, especially important decisions that have a far-reaching impact on organizational activities and personnel, are made in groups. It's a rare organization that doesn't at some time use committees, task forces, review panels, study teams, or similar groups as vehicles for making decisions. Studies tell us that managers spend up to 40 percent or more of their time in meetings.[32] Undoubtedly, a large portion of that time is involved with formulating problems, arriving at solutions to those problems, and determining the means for implementing the solutions. It's possible, in fact, for groups to be assigned any of the eight steps in the decision-making process.

In this section, we'll look at the advantages and disadvantages of both group and individual decision making, identify when groups should be preferred, and review the more popular techniques for improving group decision making.

Managers at Compaq Computer rely on groups as their central decision making approach.

Advantages and Disadvantages

Individual and group decisions each have their own set of strengths. Neither is ideal for all situations. Let's begin by reviewing the *advantages* that group decisions have over individual decisions.

1. *Provides more complete information.* There is often truth to the axiom that two heads are better than one. A group will bring a diversity of experience and perspectives to the decision process that an individual, acting alone, cannot.

2. *Generates more alternatives.* Because groups have a greater quantity and diversity of information, they can identify more alternatives than can an individual. This is most evident when group members represent different specialties. For instance, a group made up of representatives from engineering, accounting, production, marketing, and personnel will generate alternatives that reflect their diverse backgrounds. Such a multiplicity of "world views" often yields a greater array of alternatives.

3. *Increases acceptance of a solution.* Many decisions fail after the final choice has been made because people do not accept the solution. However, if the people who will be affected by a certain solution and who will help implement it get to participate in the decision making itself, they will be more likely to accept the decision and to encourage others to accept it. Group members are reluctant to fight or undermine a decision they have helped develop.

4. *Increases legitimacy.* The group decision-making process is consistent with democratic ideals and therefore decisions made by groups may be perceived as more legitimate than decisions made by a single person. The fact that the individual decision maker has complete power and has not consulted others can create a perception that a decision was made autocratically and arbitrarily.

If groups are so good, how did the phrase "A camel is a racehorse put together by a committee" become so popular? The answer, of course, is that group decisions are not without their drawbacks. The major *disadvantages* of group decision making are as follows.

1. *Time consuming.* It takes time to assemble a group. Additionally, the interaction that takes place once the group is in place is frequently inefficient. The result is

that groups almost always take more time to reach a solution than it would take an individual making the decision alone.

2. *Minority domination.* Members of a group are never perfectly equal. They may differ in rank in the organization, experience, knowledge about the problem, influence with other members, verbal skills, assertiveness, and the like. This creates the opportunity for one or more members to use their advantages to dominate others in the group. A minority that dominates a group frequently has an undue influence on the final decision.

groupthink
The withholding by group members of different views in order to appear in agreement.

3. *Pressures to conform.* There are social pressures to conform in groups. They can lead to what has been called **groupthink.**[33] This is a form of conformity in which group members withhold deviant, minority, or unpopular views in order to give the appearance of agreement. Groupthink undermines critical thinking in the group and eventually harms the quality of the final decision.

4. *Ambiguous responsibility.* Group members share responsibility, but who is actually responsible for the final outcome? In an individual decision, it is clear who is responsible. In a group decision, the responsibility of any single member is watered down.

Effectiveness and Efficiency

Whether groups are more effective than individuals depends on the criteria you use for defining effectiveness. Group decisions tend to be more *accurate.* The evidence indicates that, on the average, groups make better decisions than individuals.[34] This doesn't mean, of course, that *all* groups outperform *every* individual. Rather, group decisions have been found to be better than those that would have been reached by the average individual in the group. However, they are seldom better than the performance of the best individual.

If decision effectiveness is defined in terms of *speed,* individuals are superior. Group decision processes are characterized by give and take, which consumes time.

Effectiveness may mean the degree to which a solution demonstrates *creativity.* If creativity is important, groups tend to be more effective than individuals.[35] This requires, however, that the forces that foster groupthink be constrained. In the next section, we'll review several remedies for the groupthink ailment.

The final criterion for effectiveness is the degree of *acceptance* that the final decision achieves. As was previously noted, because group decisions have input from more people, they are likely to result in solutions that will be more widely accepted.

The effectiveness of group decision making is also influenced by the size of the group. The larger the group, the greater the opportunity for heterogeneous representation. On the other hand, a larger group requires more coordination and more time to allow all members to contribute. What this means is that groups probably should not be too large: a minimum of five to a maximum of about 15. Evidence indicates, in fact, that groups of five and, to a lesser extent, seven are the most effective.[36] Because five and seven are odd numbers, strict deadlocks are avoided. These groups are large enough for members to shift roles and withdraw from embarrassing positions but still small enough for quieter members to participate actively in discussions.

Effectiveness should not be considered without also assessing efficiency. Groups almost always stack up a poor second in efficiency to the individual decision maker. With few exceptions, group decision making consumes more work hours than does individual decision making. Exceptions occur when, to achieve comparable quantities of diverse input, the individual decision maker must spend a great deal of time reviewing files and talking to people. Because groups can include members from diverse areas, they can spend less time searching for information. However, as we noted, such decisions tend to be the exception. Generally, groups are less efficient

The Effect of National Culture on Decision-Making Styles

The way decisions are made—whether by group, participatively, or autocratically by an individual manager—and the degree of risk a decision maker is willing to take are just two examples of decision variables that reflect a country's cultural environment. Decision making in Japan, for instance, is much more group-oriented than in the United States, and characteristics of the Japanese national culture can explain why.[37]

The Japanese value conformity and cooperation. One can see this in their schools as well as in their business organizations. Before making decisions, Japanese CEOs collect a large amount of information, which is then used in consensus-forming group decisions. Since employees in Japanese organizations have high job security, managerial decisions take a long-term perspective rather than focusing on short-term profits, as is often the practice in the United States.

Senior managers in other nations—including France, Germany, and Sweden—also adapt their decision styles to their country's culture. In France, for instance, autocratic decision making is widely practiced, and managers avoid risks. Managerial styles in Germany reflect the German culture's concern for structure and order. There are extensive rules and regulations in German organizations. Managers have well-defined responsibilities and accept that decisions must go through channels. Decision styles of Swedish managers differ considerably from those of their French and German counterparts. Managers in Sweden are more aggressive; they take the initiative with problems and are not afraid to take risks. Senior managers in Sweden also push decisions down in the ranks. They encourage lower-level managers and employees to take part in decisions that affect them.

These examples are meant to remind you that managers need to modify their decision styles to reflect the national culture of the country in which they live as well as to reflect the organizational culture of the firm in which they work.

---

than individuals. In deciding whether to use groups, then, primary consideration must be given to assessing whether increases in effectiveness are more than enough to offset the losses in efficiency.

Techniques for Improving Group Decision Making

When members of a group meet face-to-face and interact with one another, they create the potential for groupthink. They can censor themselves and pressure other group members into agreement. Four ways of making group decision making more creative have been suggested: brainstorming, the nominal group and Delphi techniques, and electronic meetings.

Brainstorming   **Brainstorming** is a relatively simple technique for overcoming pressures for conformity that retard the development of creative alternatives.[38] It does this by utilizing an idea-generating process that specifically encourages any and all alternatives while withholding any criticism of those alternatives.

In a typical brainstorming session, a half-dozen to a dozen people sit around a table. The group leader states the problem in a clear manner that is understood by all participants. Members then "free-wheel" as many alternatives as they can in a given

brainstorming
An idea-generating process that encourages alternatives while withholding criticism.

time. No criticism is allowed, and all the alternatives are recorded for later discussion and analysis.

Brainstorming, however, is merely a process for generating ideas. The next two techniques go further by offering ways to arrive at a preferred solution.[39]

nominal group technique
A decision-making technique in which group members are physically present but operate independently.

Nominal Group Technique   The nominal group restricts discussion during the decision-making process, hence the term **nominal group technique.** Group members must be present, as in a traditional committee meeting, but they are required to operate independently. Specifically, the following steps take place:

1. Members meet as a group; but before any discussion takes place, each member independently writes down his or her ideas on the problem.

2. This silent period is followed by each member presenting one idea to the group. Each member takes his or her turn, going around the table, presenting one idea at a time until all ideas have been presented and recorded (typically on a flip chart or chalkboard). No discussion takes place until all ideas have been recorded.

3. The group now discusses the ideas for clarity and evaluates them.

4. Each group member silently and independently assigns a rank to the ideas. The final decision is determined by the idea with the highest aggregate ranking.

The chief advantage of this technique is that it permits the group to meet formally but does not restrict independent thinking as so often happens in the traditional interacting group.

Delphi technique
A group decision-making technique in which members never meet face to face.

Delphi Technique   A more complex and time-consuming alternative is the **Delphi technique,** which is similar to the nominal group technique except that it does not require the physical presence of the group members. This is because the Delphi technique never allows the group members to meet face to face. The following steps characterize the Delphi technique:

1. The problem is identified, and members are asked to provide potential solutions through a series of carefully designed questionnaires.

2. Each member anonymously and independently completes the first questionnaire.

3. Results of the first questionnaire are compiled at a central location, transcribed, and reproduced.

4. Each member receives a copy of the results.

5. After viewing the results, members are again asked for their solutions. The results typically trigger new solutions or cause changes in the original position.

6. Steps 4 and 5 are repeated as often as necessary until consensus is reached.

Like the nominal group technique, the Delphi technique insulates group members from the undue influence of others. It also does not require the physical presence of the participants. So, for instance, Minolta could use the technique to query its sales managers in Tokyo, Hong Kong, Paris, London, New York, Toronto, Mexico City, and Melbourne as to the best worldwide price for one of the company's new cameras. The cost of bringing the executives together at a central location is avoided, yet input from Minolta's major markets is obtained. Of course, the Delphi technique has its drawbacks. The method is extremely time-consuming. It is frequently not applicable when a speedy decision is necessary. Further, the method might not develop the rich array of alternatives that the interacting or nominal groups do. The ideas that might surface from the heat of face-to-face interaction might never arise.

electronic meetings
Decision making groups that interact by way of linked computers.

Electronic meetings   The most recent approach to group decision making blends the nominal group technique with sophisticated computer technology.[40] It's called the **electronic meeting.**

IBM uses electronic meetings to bring people from diverse backgrounds in the company together. More than 7000 IBMers have taken part in these meetings.

Once the technology for the meeting is in place, the concept is simple. Up to fifty people sit around a horseshoe-shaped table that is empty except for a series of computer terminals. Issues are presented to participants and they type their responses onto their computer screens. Individual comments, as well as aggregate votes, are displayed on a projection screen in the room.

The major advantages to electronic meetings are anonymity, honesty, and speed. Participants can anonymously type any message they want, and it will flash on the screen for all to see at the push of a board key. It also allows people to be brutally honest with no penalty. And it's fast—chitchat is eliminated, discussions don't digress, and many participants can "talk" at once without stepping on others' toes.

Experts claim that electronic meetings are as much as 55 percent faster than traditional face-to-face meetings.[41] Phelps Dodge Mining, for instance used the approach to cut its annual planning meeting from several days down to 12 hours. However, there are drawbacks. Those who can type quickly can outshine those who may be verbally eloquent but are lousy typists; those with the best ideas don't get credit for them; and the process lacks the informational richness of face-to-face oral communication. But because this technology is currently only in its infancy, the future of group decision making is very likely to include extensive usage of electronic meetings.

Summary

This summary is organized by the chapter-opening learning objectives found on page 149.

1. Decision making is an eight-step process: (1) formulation of a problem, (2) identification of decision criteria, (3) allocation of weights to the criteria, (4) development of alternatives, (5) analysis of alternatives, (6) selection of an alternative, (7) implementation of the alternative, and (8) evaluation of decision effectiveness.

2. The rational decision maker is assumed to have a clear problem, have no goal conflict, know all options, have a clear preference ordering, keep all preferences constant, have no time or cost constraints, and select a final choice that maximizes his or her economic payoff.

3. Rationality assumptions don't apply in many situations because (1) an individual's information-processing capacity is limited; (2) decision makers tend to intermix solutions with problems; (3) perceptual biases distort problem identification; (4) information may be selected more for its accessibility than for its quality; (5) decision makers often have favorite alternatives that bias their assessment; (6) decision makers sometimes increase commitment to a previous choice to confirm its original correctness; (7) prior decision precedents constrain current choices; (8) there is rarely agreement on a single goal; (9) decision makers must face time and cost constraints; and (10) most organizational cultures discourage taking risks and searching for innovative alternatives.

4. In the perfectly rational decision-making process: (1) the problem identified is important and relevant; (2) all criteria are identified; (3) all criteria are evaluated; (4) a comprehensive list of alternatives is generated; (5) all alternatives are assessed against the decision criteria and weights; (6) the decision with the highest economic outcome is chosen; (7) all organizational members embrace the solution chosen; and (8) the decision's outcome is objectively evaluated against the original problem.

5. In the boundedly rational decision-making process: (1) the problem chosen is visible and reflects the manager's interests and background; (2) a limited set of criteria is identified; (3) a simple model is constructed to evaluate criteria; (4) a limited set of similar alternatives is identified; (5) alternatives are assessed one

at a time; (6) the search continues until a satisficing solution is found; (7) politics and power influence decision acceptance; and (8) the decision's outcome is evaluated against the self-interests of the evaluator.

6. Managers face well- and ill-structured problems. Well-structured problems are straightforward, familiar, easily defined, and solved using programmed decisions. Ill-structured problems are new or unusual, involve ambiguous or incomplete information, and are solved using non-programmed decisions.

7. The ideal situation for making decisions occurs when the manager can make accurate decisions because he or she knows the outcome from every alternative. Such certainty, however, rarely occurs. A far more relevant situation is one of risk, when the decision maker can estimate the likelihood of certain alternatives or outcomes. If neither certainty nor reasonable probability estimates are available, uncertainty exists, and the decision maker's choice will be influenced by his or her psychological orientation.

8. Groups offer certain advantages: more complete information, more alternatives, increased acceptance of a solution, and greater legitimacy. On the other hand, groups are time-consuming, can be dominated by a minority, create pressures to conform, and cloud responsibility.

9. Four ways of improving group decision making are brainstorming, the nominal group technique, the Delphi technique, and electronic meetings.

Review Questions

1. How is implementation important to the decision-making process?
2. What is a *satisficing* decision?
3. What's the difference between a *rule* and a *policy?*
4. Why would an organization's senior executives favor developing a wide range of programmed decisions for middle- and lower-level managers?
5. Why might a manager use a simplified decision model?
6. Is the order in which alternatives are considered more critical under assumptions of perfect rationality or bounded rationality? Why?
7. What is *groupthink?* What are its implications for decision making?
8. Is group decision making effective? Efficient?

Discussion Questions

1. Why would decision making be described as "the essence of a manager's job"?
2. How might an organization's culture influence the way in which managers make decisions?
3. Describe a decision you have made that closely aligns with the assumptions of perfect rationality. Compare this with the process you used to select your college. Is there a deviation? Explain.
4. Why do you think organizations have increased the use of groups for making decisions during the past 20 years? When would you recommend using groups to make decisions?

5. Which step in the decision making process do you consider to be most important? Support your position.

SELF-ASSESSMENT EXERCISE

What's Your Intuitive Ability?

For each of the following questions, select the response that first appeals to you by circling the letter of that response. Be honest with yourself.

1. When working on a project, do you prefer to:
   a. be told what the problem is, but left free to decide how to solve it?
   b. get very clear instructions about how to go about solving the problem before you start?

2. When working on a project, do you prefer to work with colleagues who are:
   a. realistic?
   b. imaginative?

3. Do you admire people most who are:
   a. creative?
   b. careful?

4. Do the friends you choose tend to be:
   a. serious and hard working?
   b. exciting and often emotional?

5. When you ask a colleague for advice on a problem you have, do you:
   a. seldom or never get upset if he/she questions your basic assumptions?
   b. often get upset if he/she questions your basic assumptions?

6. When you start your day, do you usually:
   a. seldom make or follow a specific plan?
   b. make a plan first to follow?

7. When working with numbers, do you find that you:
   a. seldom or never make factual errors?
   b. often make factual errors?

8. Do you find that you:
   a. seldom daydream during the day and really don't enjoy doing so when you do it?
   b. frequently daydream during the day and enjoy doing so?

9. When working on a problem do you:
   a. prefer to follow the instructions or rules when they are given to you?
   b. often enjoy circumventing the instructions or rules when they are given to you?

10. When you are trying to put something together, do you prefer to have:
    a. step-by-step written instructions on how to assemble the item?
    b. a picture of how the item is supposed to look once assembled?

11. Do you find that the person who irritates you *the most* is the one who appears to be:
    a. disorganized?
    b. organized?

12. When an unexpected crisis comes up that you have to deal with, do you:
    a. feel anxious about the situation?
    b. feel excited by the challenge of the situation?

Turn to page SK-2 for scoring directions and key.

Source: Weston H. Agor, *AIM Survey* (El Paso, TX: ENP Enterprises, 1989), Part I. With permission.

For Your Immediate Action

Stephens Auto Parts

To: Pat Carlson; Senior Consultant; Toronto Consulting Group
From: Jan Stephens; President and Chief Executive Officer
Subject: Restructuring our decision-making process

Pat, I need some advice. I'm coming to you because you provided considerable advice to my father during the years when he built our company, and because you were his friend. Let me briefly bring you up to speed.

I graduated from college four years ago with a degree in business and immediately I took a job as an assistant manager in the home furnishings department of a large Toronto department store. But when Dad died suddenly of a heart attack four months ago, I responded to my mother's request that I come back and run the family business.

This job is very demanding but I think I can handle it. It's surprising how much I learned working summers for Dad and by just listening to the talk around the dinner table.

Stephens Auto Parts now has eleven stores, each with a very competent and experienced manager. Here in the main office, I have a staff of four; Rick Morse (director of store operations); Lynn Kibbey (head of purchasing); Dawn Baker (our accountant); and Lesley Del Corso (my administrative assistant). My dilemma is this. Rick and Lesley worked for my father for more than 15 years. They know this business backwards and forwards, while my experience is obviously very limited. I am currently running the business the way Dad did—consulting with others but making all the final decisions myself. However, I have been thinking of restructuring Rick's and Lesley's jobs in order to make them equal decision makers with me. If I do, we'll essentially have an "Office of the President" and make all key decisions as a group of three.

Could you give me your professional assessment of the pros and cons involved in my changing our current practices and your recommendation on what I should do in a two-page letter? I appreciate your assistance.

This is a fictionalized account of a potentially real problem. It was written for academic purposes only and is not meant to reflect either positively or negatively on actual management practices at Stephens Auto Parts.

CASE APPLICATION

Adidas vs. Nike

If you were a serious runner in the 1960s or early 1970s, there was only one real shoe choice: Adidas. A German company, Adidas pioneered lightweight running shoes for competitive athletes. As recently as the 1976 Olympics in Montreal, Adidas-equipped athletes accounted for more than 82 percent of all individual medal winners in track and field.

Adidas' strength was experimentation. It tried new materials and techniques to develop stronger and lighter shoes. It introduced kangaroo leather to toughen the sides of shoes, four-spiked running shoes, and track shoes with nylon soles and interchangeable spikes. Its high quality, innovation, and variety of products resulted in Adidas dominating international competition through the mid-1970s.

The physical fitness boom in the 1970s, though, caught Adidas by surprise. Suddenly millions of previously unathletic people became interested in exercise. And the fastest growing segment of the physical fitness market was jogging. It was estimated that by 1980, 25 to 30 million Americans were jogging and another 10 million wore running shoes for leisure wear. Secure in its market dominance, Adidas didn't pursue the jogging market very aggressively.

A host of competitors surfaced in the 1970s, including Puma, Brooks, New Balance, and Tiger. But one was to become more aggressive and innovative than the rest. That was Nike. Begun in Oregon by a former University of Oregon runner, Nike debuted its shoes in competition during the 1972 Olympic trials in Eugene, Oregon. Marathon runners who had been persuaded to wear the new shoes placed fourth through seventh. Competitors wearing Adidas, however, finished first, second, and third in those trials.

Nike's big breakthrough came in 1975 with the development of the "waffle sole," whose tiny rubber studs made it more springy than those of other shoes on the market. The popularity of the waffle sole, along with the rapidly expanding market for running shoes, resulted in sales of $14 million in 1976. This was against only $2 million in 1972. From that point on, sales skyrocketed. Today, Nike has sales in excess of $3.5 billion a year and is the industry leader with a 26 percent market share in athletic shoes.

Nike's success could be traced to its emphasis on (1) research and technological improvement and (2) its variety of styles and models. The company has nearly 100 employees working in research and development. Some of its R&D activities include high-speed photographic analyses of the human body in motion, the use of athletes on force plates and treadmills, wear testing with over 300 athletes in an organized program, and continual testing and study of new and modified shoes and materials.

On the marketing side, Nike offered the most comprehensive choice of styles for consumers. It appealed to all kinds of runners and conveyed the image of the most complete running-shoe manufacturer of them all.

By the time the running boom peaked in the early 1980s, Adidas had become an "also-ran" in the market. The competition had more innovative products, greater variety, and had successfully expanded into other sport markets. Nike, for instance, came to dominate the basketball and teen markets with its Air Jordan line. Others, such as L.A. Gear and Reebok, turned sport shoes into fashion-wear. By the early 1990s, Adidas' market share had fallen to a dismal 4 percent.

Questions

1. How did poor decision making lead to Adidas' significantly reduced market share by the early 1990s? Did uncertainty play any part in its troubles?

2. In the 1970s, decision making at Adidas was not structured around groups. How might a committee structure have resulted in a different outcome at Adidas?

3. What decisions did Nike's management make that helped lead to its success?

4. What, if anything, do you think Adidas' management can do today to correct past mistakes?

Source: This case is based on data included in Robert F. Hartley, *Management Mistakes and Successes* (New York: John Wiley & Sons, 1991), pp. 46–66.

VIDEO CASE

Explaining the Absence of Black College Football Coaches

For big-time Division 1-A football schools, it's a major decision. Who will be the head coach? Responsibility for the decision usually falls on the athletic director, but a lot of other people get involved—the college's president, the faculty representative to the NCAA, and prominent alumni and boosters. At a time when colleges and universities are actively promoting their efforts at increasing diversity, it's ironic that the head football coaches at the major universities are all white. It's particularly ironic because 30 percent or more of the players on these teams are black.

Here's some facts: In 1992, seventeen Division 1-A schools changed head coaches, but not one of them hired a black. There are many black assistants in football who are unquestionably qualified to assume a head coaching job, yet they rarely get interviews. Even when they do, they never get chosen. The appearance of prejudice is not only in football but in basketball and in women's sports. Sixty percent of basketball players at the NCAA's top 300 schools are black, while only 10 percent of their head coaches are black. And there's a male bias on women's teams, where men get most of the good coaching jobs. What's going on here?

One common conclusion is that the people who make the decision as to who coaches in big-time football are racists. A head football coach is the most visible member of the university community, and some decision makers may not be ready to have that person be black. Another explanation is "the old boys network." Athletic directors, who are predominantly white males, call their friends and acquaintances for recommendations. They want people who they're comfortable with—people who are like them. That, again, strongly favors white males.

Black assistant coaches and others in college sports have become highly critical of the dearth of blacks in head football coaching jobs at the major schools. Some claim that black assistants are hired only to recruit black players and that these assistants are hitting up against a glass ceiling. To further aggravate the problem is the fact that the NCAA seems to be doing little about it. While the NCAA, for instance, has a huge task force on gender equity, the same attention is not being paid to minorities.

Questions

1. What defines *a problem?* Why has gender-equity become a problem for the NCAA but not the absence of black head coaches?

2. What criteria do athletic directors appear to be using in their decisions and how does this affect their decision outcomes?

3. Is this an example of groupthink? Are athletic directors, presidents, and others who participate in the decisions to hire coaches risk-aversive? Discuss.

Source: "Where Are the Black College Football Coaches?" *ABC News Nightline,* September 7, 1992.

INTEGRATIVE EXERCISE FOR PART II

CRIME-SEVERITY DECISION

PURPOSE

To compare individual and group decision making.

REQUIRED KNOWLEDGE

1. The steps in the decision-making process.
2. Advantages of group decisions over individual decisions.

TIME REQUIRED

Approximately 45 minutes.

INSTRUCTIONS

1. Set up groups of five to ten participants.
2. Each class member will use column 1 in Table II-A to order the following 15 crimes by rank in terms of their severity. Give the most severe a rank of 1, the next severe a 2, and so on. The least severe is ranked 15. Do not talk to others in your group while doing your individual ranking. You have five minutes to complete this step.
3. After the individual rankings are complete, the groups are to arrive at a group ranking by use of consensus. (Use column 2.) This step is not to exceed 20 minutes in duration.
4. Your instructor will give you the actual rankings. Put these in column 3.
5. Calculate your individual and group error scores (columns 4 and 5) by scoring differences (ignore minus signs).
6. Group members are to compare their group error scores against their individual error scores. Did the performance of the group, as a whole, improve? Group members should then review the quality of discussion during the group decision making. Was there any difference in the quality of discussion in groups that had low group error scores compared to those that had high scores?

Source: Christopher Taylor, "Crimes, Death, and Stress: Three New Consensus Tasks," *Organizational Behavior Teaching Review,* Vol. XII, No. 2, 1987–1988, pp. 115–17.

TABLE II-A

Crime	Your Ranks	Group Ranks	Actual Ranks	Your Error	Group Error
Person kills victim by driving a car recklessly					
Person runs a narcotic ring					
Parent beats young child to death with fists					
Person plants bomb in public building; explosion kills one person					
Wife stabs husband to death					
Man forcibly rapes woman, who dies from injuries					
Legislator takes $10,000 company bribe to support favoring firm					
Man tries to entice minor into car for immoral purposes					
Person runs prostitution ring					
Husband stabs wife to death					
Person smuggles marijuana into country for resale					
Person shoots victim fatally during robbery					
Person commits arson; $500,000 damage					
Person breaks into home and steals $1,000					
Person kidnaps a victim					

Source: Christopher Taylor, "Crimes, Death, and Stress: Three New Consensus Tasks," *Organizational Behavior Teaching Review,* Vol. XII, No. 2, 1987–1988, pp. 115–17.

INTEGRATIVE CASE FOR PART II

GENERAL ELECTRIC

One day in 1983, a General Electric employee named John Gravitt complained to his division head about time-card cheating among supervisors and workers. He was dismissed that very day. Gravitt sued GE in 1984, and the company settled after acknowledging time-card alterations.

That cheating scandal and other cases prompted GE chairman Jack Welch to declare war on fraud inside his company. The result is what many experts claim to be one of the most elaborate and comprehensive ethics programs in corporate America. GE provides extensive training for employees. There are seminars and videos. There are mandatory compliance courses. There are toll-free numbers for reporting wrongdoings and even avenues for sending anonymous notes to Mr. Welch. The company goes so far as to spring pop quizzes on workers in hallways, asking, for instance, "What are the three ways to report wrongdoing?" Correct answers win a coffee mug. The primary message GE executives claim the company wants to convey to employees is that wrongdoings will not be tolerated and that employees needn't wait for a preponderance of evidence to report them.

In spite of GE's efforts, apparently a number of employees fear being fired for reporting wrongdoings. They cite a number of instances to support this fear:

Edward Russell, a former vice president of GE's Superabrasive division, claims he was fired because he alleged that a meeting between certain GE officials and a South African cartel was for the purpose of fixing industrial diamond prices. GE denies the charge and says Mr. Russell was fired for poor performance.

Patricia Della Croce, a government property administrator in one of GE's engine plants and a twenty-five-year GE veteran, says that in 1990 she told her supervisors that some co-workers in her unit were unfairly billing the government for parts in an engine development program. "I was told I wasn't a team player and was ostracized," she says. GE investigated her claim and found no wrongdoing. In early 1992, Ms. Della Croce was abruptly told her job had been eliminated.

Salvatore Cimorelli, who worked in the parts department at the same plant as Ms. Della Croce, tells a similar story. In spite of working at GE for twenty-nine years, he says he was dismissed in 1989 after complaining to his boss and to GE's legal department about employees altering time vouchers and overcharging the government on a test engine being developed at the plant.

David McDonald, manager of GE's international engine support operation in Cincinnati, Ohio, reported to his bosses in 1989 suspicions of payments in full on projects that hadn't even been started. This violated GE's compliance policies. Mr. McDonald, a twenty-nine-year veteran of GE, was fired in 1992 for what the company called "shortfall in compliance culture."

The most recent and most publicized case is that of Chester Walsh. A GE employee, Mr. Walsh uncovered a scheme by a high GE official and an Israeli general to divert U.S. aid for Israel into their personal accounts. With phony bills for projects that were never started by GE, the scheme defrauded the United States of about $42 million. But distrustful of GE's internal compliance system, Mr. Walsh kept his suspicions to himself for years. All the time, though, he continued to gather evidence. Then, instead of reporting this scheme to GE authorities, he filed suit against the company and alerted government authorities. Even though GE pleaded guilty to their offense and paid $70 million in fines, Mr. Walsh was fired for not using internal reporting channels. GE claims that Mr. Walsh's motivations were purely financial and that he allowed the fraud to spread for four years for personal gain. The U.S. False Claims Act, which seeks to protect whistleblowers, permits employees whose tips result in federal fines or assessments against U.S. contractors to receive up to 25 percent of the sums. Mr. Walsh's claim against GE made him a multi-millionaire. Mr. Walsh, however, argues differently. "I did a lot of research to see what happened to people who went up the chain of command and reported wrongdoings. All I found was they lost their jobs, their security; they lost everything."

Chester Walsh and these other GE employees may

not be paranoid. In 1990, the U.S. Defense Department formed a special unit solely to investigate allegations of wrongdoings at GE. Between 1990 and 1992, the unit referred sixty cases to various criminal investigative agencies. And only eleven of those sixty cases were voluntarily disclosed by GE. The rest came from government auditors or inside whistleblowers.

Some might consider it ironic that GE would have *any* whistleblowers, given the company's commitment to open communication. This is illustrated in its famous Work-Out program. Work-Out is a series of New England-style town meetings made up of 40 to 100 people from all ranks and functions. The three-day sessions begin with a talk by the boss, who roughs out an agenda—typically, to eliminate unnecessary meetings, forms, or other bureaucratic hurdles. Then the boss leaves. Aided by an outside facilitator, the group breaks into five or six teams, each tackling part of the agenda. For a day and a half they go at it, listing complaints, debating solutions, and preparing presentations for the final day. On the third day, the boss comes back and listens to team spokespersons make their proposals. By the rules of the game, the boss can make only three responses: He can agree on the spot; he can say no; or he can ask for more information and set a later decision date. In a typical year, 40,000 of GE's employees will take part in at least one Work-Out. GE boasts that Work-Out builds trust and empowers employees. As such, it should help create a culture that makes the reporting of wrongdoings easy and nonthreatening.

But it doesn't seem to work that way at GE. It is a huge and highly successful company. It employs 284,000 people, has sales in excess of $60 billion a year, and prides itself on its competitive culture. Some say that Chairman Welch's demands for ever-rising earnings put too much pressure on managers and employees—encouraging them to engage in shady practices in order to achieve their profit objectives. GE counters, saying that competitiveness and integrity are completely compatible.

Questions

1. How does GE's culture and environment influence the ethical decisions its managers make?
2. Do you think competitiveness and integrity are completely compatible?
3. Where do ethics fall in the decision-making process?
4. Is GE's firing of people who have identified wrongdoings consistent with rational decision-making? Discuss.
5. Several of GE's ethical problems concern the company's dealings with foreign countries such as South Africa and Israel. What special problems does the globalization of the marketplace cause in terms of ethics?
6. Jack Welch is genuinely concerned with eliminating wrongdoings at GE. What can he do now to regain employees' trust in the company's internal compliance system?

Based on Amal Kumar Naj, "GE's Drive to Purge Fraud is Hampered by Workers' Mistrust," *Wall Street Journal*, July 22, 1992, p. A1.

CHAPTER 7

Foundations of Planning

LEARNING OBJECTIVES

After Reading This Chapter, You Should Be Able To:

1. Define planning.
2. Explain the potential benefits of planning.
3. Distinguish between strategic and operational plans.
4. State when directional plans are preferred over specific plans.
5. Identify four contingency factors in planning.
6. Explain the commitment concept.
7. Explain why an organization's stated objectives might not be its real objectives.
8. Describes a typical MBO program.
9. Explain how MBO uses goals as motivators.

Matsushita has driven its U.S. competitors out of the American market for television sets. Part of its success is due to the company founder's establishment, in the early 1950s, of a long-term plan to dominate the U.S. market for TVs.

T hirty years ago, companies such as RCA, GE, and Zenith dominated the U.S. market for television sets.[1] Not anymore. Using brand names that include Panasonic and Quasar, the largest manufacturer of television sets in the world is a Japanese company called Matsushita. Similarly, if you go out today shopping for a video recorder, you'll see a lot of names that look familiar—Sylvania, Magnavox, Montgomery Ward—but they're all Matsushita-made. Now the largest consumer electronics firm on the globe—its product line runs from cathode ray tubes to inflight communication systems—Matsushita has grown to become the twelfth largest company in the world. In November 1990, the company paid more than $6 billion to buy MCA, the parent company of Universal Studios.

The Matsushita story is a saga of how extensive planning can facilitate the creation of a corporate giant. The company was founded at the end of World War II by Konosuke Matsushita. He committed himself to rebuilding Japan's power among nations by making Japan a leader in the emerging field of electronics. In the early 1950s, Matsushita set his sights on dominating the U.S. TV market. He formed a cartel with other Japanese TV manufacturers and proceeded aggressively to focus his efforts on the U.S. market. In twenty years, he whittled his U.S. competitors down from twenty-five to six. All his U.S. competitors eventually went bankrupt or were acquired by foreign interests.

Through thoughtful, long-term planning, Matsushita has become *the* major player in the consumer electronics industry. Matsushita's management views their company as a very long-term operation. As an illustrative point, the company actually has a 250-year plan! Obviously, Matsushita is a company that is attempting to leave nothing to chance.

This chapter presents the basics of planning. In the following pages, you'll learn the difference between formal and informal planning, why managers plan, the various types of plans that managers use, the key contingency factors that influence the types of plans that managers use in different situations, and the important role that objectives play in planning.

The Definition of Planning

What do we mean by the term *planning*? As we stated in Chapter 1, planning encompasses defining the organization's objectives or goals, establishing an overall strategy for achieving these goals, and developing a comprehensive hierarchy of plans to integrate and coordinate activities. It is concerned, then, with *ends* (what is to be done) as well as with *means* (how it is to be done).

Planning can be further defined in terms of whether it is informal or formal. All managers engage in planning, but it might be only the informal variety. In informal planning, nothing is written down, and there is little or no sharing of objectives with others in the organization. This describes planning in many small businesses; the owner-manager has a vision of where he or she wants to go and how he or she expects to get there. The planning is general and lacks continuity. Of course, informal planning exists in some large organizations, and some small businesses have very sophisticated formal plans.

When we use the term planning in this book, we are implying *formal* planning. Specific objectives are formulated covering a period of years. These objectives are committed to writing and made available to organization members. Finally, specific action programs exist for the achievement of these objectives; that is, management clearly defines the path it wants to take to get from where it is to where it wants to be.

The Purpose of Planning

Why should managers engage in planning? It gives direction, reduces the impact of change, minimizes waste and redundancy, and sets the standards to facilitate control.

Planning establishes coordinated effort. It gives direction to managers and non-managers alike. When all concerned know where the organization is going and what they must contribute to reach the objective, they can begin to coordinate their activities, cooperate with each other, and work in teams. A lack of planning can foster "zigzagging" and thus prevent an organization from moving efficiently toward its objectives.

By forcing managers to look ahead, anticipate change, consider the impact of change, and develop appropriate responses, planning reduces uncertainty. It also clarifies the consequences of the actions managers might take in response to change.

Planning also reduces overlapping and wasteful activities. Coordination before the fact is likely to uncover waste and redundancy. Further, when means and ends are clear, inefficiencies become obvious.

Finally, planning establishes objectives or standards that facilitate control. If we are unsure of what we are trying to achieve, how can we determine whether we have achieved it? In planning, we develop the objectives. In the controlling function, we compare actual performance against the objectives, identify any significant deviations, and take the necessary corrective action. Without planning, there can be no control.

Planning and Performance

Do managers and organizations that plan outperform those that don't? Intuitively, you would expect the answer to be a resounding "yes." Reviews of the evidence are generally affirmative, but that shouldn't be interpreted as a blanket endorsement of formal planning. We cannot say that organizations that formally plan *always* outperform those that don't.

Dozens of studies have been undertaken to test the relationship between planning and performance.[2] They allow us to draw the following conclusions. First, generally speaking, formal planning is associated with higher profits, higher return on assets, and other positive financial results. Second, the *quality* of the planning process and the appropriate *implementation* of the plans probably contribute more to high performance than does the *extent* of planning. Finally, in those studies in which formal planning hasn't led to higher performance, the environment is typically the culprit. When government regulations, powerful labor unions, and similar environmental forces constrain management's options, planning will have less of an impact on an organization's performance. Why? Because management will have fewer choices for which planning can propose viable alternatives. For example, planning might suggest that a manufacturing firm produce a number of its key parts in Asia in order to compete effectively against low-cost foreign competitors. But if the firm's contract with its labor union specifically forbids transferring work overseas, the value of the firm's planning effort is significantly reduced. Dramatic shocks from the environment can also undermine the best-laid plans. The stock market crash in October 1987 undermined most of the formal plans previously developed by brokerage firms. In conditions of such environmental uncertainty, there is no reason to expect that planners will necessarily outperform nonplanners.

Myths About Planning

There is no shortage of myths and misconceptions about planning. The following identifies a few common myths and seeks to clarify the misunderstanding behind them.

1. *Planning that proves inaccurate is a waste of management's time.* The end result of planning is only one of its purposes. The process itself can be valuable even if the results miss the target. Planning requires management to think through what it wants to do and how it is going to do it. This clarification can have significant value in and of itself. Management that does a good job of planning will have direction and purpose, and planning is likely to minimize the misdirection of energy. All this is in spite of missing the objectives being sought.

MANAGERS WHO MADE A DIFFERENCE

Christie Hefner at Playboy Enterprises

Christie Hefner may be the founder's daughter, but she's proving that she's executive material as she guides Playboy Enterprises through changing times.[3]

Hugh Hefner started *Playboy* magazine in the 1950s. It grew and prospered by promoting a lifestyle for males of guiltless sex and fast living. Christie, a highly intelligent graduate of Brandeis University, became president of Playboy Enterprises in 1982 and CEO in 1988. Her job has been to reshape the company in response to more conservative sexual attitudes and changing views of male and female roles. Her goal? To create an adult Disney.

Christie Hefner's strategy for the company has been focusing on three areas: the magazine, product licensing, and overseas markets. She's remaking *Playboy* into a men's magazine for the 1990s. It is taking a more reflective view of men's lives. For instance, Hefner says the magazine is addressing the widespread interest in how men are handling workplace problems and how they are coping with women. The company's previous strategy of licensing its rabbit head logo to almost any manufacturer willing to pay the licensing fee has been replaced with a new emphasis on quality. Playboy is revoking some licenses and letting others lapse on such products as tacky air fresheners, cheap underwear, and shoddy shoes. Instead, the company is creating its own designs for licensees and trying to get into swankier settings with an upscale clientele. Finally, Hefner is aggressively pursuing opportunities outside North America. Recognizing that the fall of repressive political regimes is invariably followed by a significantly increased interest in sex, Hefner has introduced foreign-licensed editions of *Playboy* into such places as Czechoslovakia, Hungary, and Poland. A Playboy licensee is opening twenty sportswear boutiques in mainland China to be run by the government.

So far, Christie Hefner's planning has paid off. Between 1988 and 1992, Playboy's earnings more than doubled.

2. *Planning can eliminate change.* Planning cannot eliminate change. Changes will happen regardless of what management does. Management engages in planning in order to *anticipate* changes and to develop the most effective response to them.

3. *Planning reduces flexibility.* Planning implies commitments, but it is a constraint only if management stops planning after doing it once. Planning is an ongoing activity. The fact that formal plans have been reasoned out and clearly articulated can make them easier to revise than an ambiguous set of assumptions carried around in some senior executive's head. Some plans, furthermore, can be made to be more flexible than others.

Types of Plans

The most popular ways to describe plans are by their breadth (strategic versus operational), time frame (short- versus long-term), and specificity (specific versus directional). However, these planning classifications are not independent of one

TABLE 7-1 Types of Plans

Categorized by	Types
Breadth	• Strategic
	• Operational
Time Frame	• Short-term
	• Long-term
Specificity	• Specific
	• Directional

strategic plans
Plans that are organizationwide, establish overall objectives, and position an organization in terms of its environment.

operational plans
Plans that specify details on how overall objectives are to be achieved.

short-term plans
Plans that cover less than one year.

long-term plans
Plans that extend beyond five years.

specific plans
Plans that are clearly defined and leave no room for interpretation.

directional plans
Flexible plans that set out general guidelines.

another. For instance, there is a close relationship between the short- and long-term categories and the strategic and operational categories. Table 7–1 lists all these types of plans according to category.

Strategic Versus Operational Plans

Plans that apply to the entire organization, that establish the organization's overall objectives, and that seek to position the organization in terms of its environment are called **strategic plans**. Plans that specify the details of how the overall objectives are to be achieved are called **operational plans**. Strategic and operational plans differ in their time frame, their scope, and whether or not they include a known set of organizational objectives.[4] Operational plans tend to cover shorter periods of time. For instance, an organization's monthly, weekly, and day-to-day plans are almost all operational. Strategic plans tend to include an extended time period—usually five years or more. They also cover a broader area and deal less with specifics. Finally, strategic plans include the formulation of objectives, whereas operational plans assume the existence of objectives. Operational plans offer ways of attaining these objectives.

Short-Term Versus Long-Term plans

Financial analysts traditionally describe investment returns as *short-, intermediate-,* and *long-term*. The short term covers less than one year. Any time frame beyond five years is classified as long-term. The intermediate term covers the period in between. Managers have adopted the same terminology to describe plans. For clarity, we'll emphasize **short-term** plans and **long-term** plans in future discussions.

Specific Versus Directional Plans

It seems intuitively correct that specific plans are always preferable to directional, or loosely guided, plans. **Specific plans** have clearly defined objectives. There is no ambiguity, no problem with misunderstandings. For example, a manager who seeks to increase his or her firm's sales by 20 percent over a given twelve-month period might establish specific procedures, budget allocations, and schedules of activities to reach that objective. These represent specific plans.

However, specific plans are not without drawbacks. They require clarity and a sense of predictability that often does not exist. When uncertainty is high, which requires management to maintain flexibility in order to respond to unexpected changes, then it is preferable to use directional plans.[5] (See Figure 7–1.)

Directional plans identify general guidelines. They provide focus but do not lock management into specific objectives or specific courses of action. Instead of a manager following a specific plan to cut costs by 4 percent and increase revenues by 6 percent in the next six months, a directional plan might aim at improving corporate profits by 5 to 10 percent during the next six months. The flexibility inherent in directional plans is obvious. This advantage must be weighed against the loss in clarity provided by specific plans.

Contingency Factors in Planning

In some cases, long-term plans make sense, in others they do not. Similarly, in some situations, directional plans are more effective than specific ones. What are these situations? In this section, we identify several contingency factors that affect planning.[6]

Level in the Organization

Figure 7–2 illustrates the general relationship between managerial level in an organization and the type of planning that is done. For the most part, operational planning dominates the planning activities of lower-level managers. As managers rise in the hierarchy, their planning role becomes more strategy-oriented. The planning effort by the top executives in large organizations is essentially strategic. In a small business, of course, the owner-manager needs to do both.

Life Cycle of the Organization

Organizations go through a **life cycle**. Beginning with the formative stage, organizations then grow, mature, and eventually decline. Planning is not homogeneous across these stages. As Figure 7–3 on page 193 depicts, the length and specificity of plans should be adjusted at each stage.

If all things were equal, management would undoubtedly benefit most by developing and using specific plans. Not only would this provide the clearest direction, it would also establish the most detailed bench marks against which to compare actual performance. However, all things aren't equal.

When an organization is mature, predictability is greatest. It is at this stage in the life cycle, therefore, when specific plans are most appropriate. Managers should rely more heavily on directional plans in an organization's infancy. It is at precisely this time that high flexibility is desired. Objectives are tentative, resource availability is more uncertain, and the identification of clients or customers is more in doubt. Directional plans, at this stage, allow managers to make changes as necessary. During the growth stage, plans become more specific as objectives become more definite, resources more committed, and loyalty of clients or customers more developed. The pattern reverses itself on the downward swing of the cycle. From maturity to decline, plans need to move from the specific to directional as objectives are reconsidered, resources reallocated, and other adjustments made.

The length of planning should also be related to the life cycle. Short-term plans

Developer Olympia & York's multi-billion dollar Canary Wharf project in London stands only partially finished. O&Y's management failed in their long-range planning to anticipate the dramatic collapse of the commercial real estate market in the early 1990s.

life cycle of the organization
Four stages that organizations go through: formation, growth, maturity, and decline.

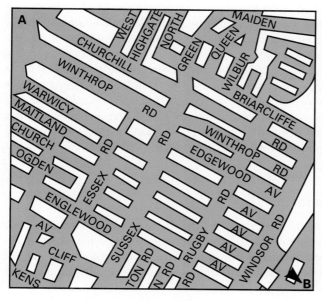

Directional Plans

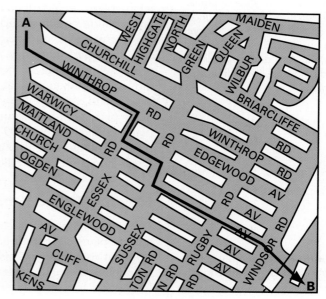

Specific Plans

FIGURE 7–1
Specific Versus Directional Plans

FIGURE 7-2
Planning in the Hierarchy of
Organizations

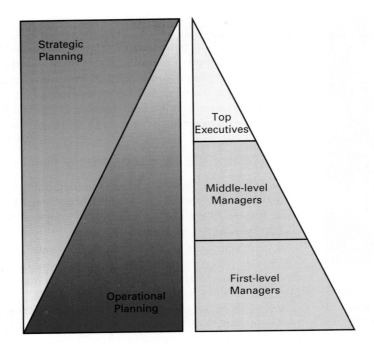

offer the greatest flexibility and therefore should be more prevalent during the formative and decline stages. Maturity is the time when stability is greatest and long-term plans can pay the biggest dividends.

Degree of Environmental Uncertainty

The greater the environmental uncertainty, the more plans should be directional and emphasis placed on the short term.

If rapid or important technological, social, economic, legal, or other changes are taking place, well-defined and precisely chartered routes are more likely to hinder an organization's performance than aid it. When environmental uncertainty is high, specific plans have to be altered to accommodate the changes—often at high cost and decreased efficiency. For example, in the late-1980s, when intense rate wars were raging among airlines on major cross-country routes, the airlines should have moved to more directional plans concerning price setting, number and size of aircraft allocated to routes, and operating budgets. Moreover, the greater the change, the less likely plans are to be accurate. For example, one study found that one-year revenue plans tended to achieve 99 percent accuracy in comparison to 84 percent for five-year plans.[7] Therefore, if an organization faces rapidly changing environments, management should seek flexibility.

Length of Future Commitments

The final contingency factor again relates to the time frame of plans. The more that current plans affect future commitments, the longer the time frame for which management should plan. This **commitment concept** means that plans should extend far enough to see through those commitments that are made today. Planning for too long or for too short a period is inefficient.

Managers are not planning for future decisions. Rather, they are planning for the

Managers of new businesses should rely on directional plans. Why? Because of the high uncertainty at this point in the life cycle of the business, flexibility is most important. And directional plans provide more flexibility than specific plans.

commitment concept
Plans should extend far enough to see through current commitments.

FIGURE 7–3
Plans and the Organization's Life
Cycle

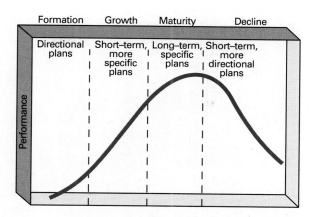

THE
CHANGING
FACE OF
MANAGEMENT
PRACTICE

In a Volatile World, Plans Must Be Flexible

Twenty years ago, the "best managed" corporations had large planning departments.[8] They generated countless five- and ten-year plans, which were updated
annually. General Electric, for example, once had a 350-member planning staff
that churned out hundreds of meticulously detailed reports. Nowadays, however,
planning is increasingly being done by divisional or unit managers as part of their
middle management responsibilities, and the plans themselves cover shorter
periods of time and are likely to consider a range of options. GE's formal planning
group is down to about twenty members and their only role is to advise operating
managers. The heads of GE's thirteen businesses now develop five one-page
reports each year that identify possible opportunities and obstacles in their industries over the forthcoming two years.

In a volatile world, only the foolish are cocky enough to believe that they can
accurately forecast the future. But that doesn't lessen the importance of plans.
Thus well-managed organizations are putting less time into highly detailed, quantitative plans and instead are developing multiple scenarios of the future. Southern
California Edison, an electric utility serving 3.9 million customers in California, has
created twelve possible versions of the future based on an economic boom, a Middle East oil crisis, expanded environmentalism, and other developments. This
approach to flexible planning came about after Southern California Edison's management realized that every long-range plan they had painstakingly constructed
during the 1970s and 1980s had been rendered virtually useless by unexpected
events—from OPEC price-fixing to new restrictions on sulfur emissions to nuclear
accidents like Chernobyl. And, of course, Southern California Edison is not unique
in facing an increasingly uncertain world. Most businesses are finding that their
environment has become more dynamic and uncertain. Moreover, not-for-profit
organizations are also experiencing similar changes. For instance, talk with managers in hospitals and colleges. Changing demographics, rising competitiveness,
shrinking government support, and skyrocketing costs are examples of forces that
are requiring managers in these organizations also to develop more flexible plans.

Weyerhaeuser Co. is planting trees today that won't reach maturity until about the year 2025. The commitment concept indicates that Weyerhaeuser's plans should extend far enough to cover business operations thirty to thirty-five years from now.

future impact of the decisions that they are currently making. Decisions made today become a commitment to some future action or expenditure. Tenure decisions in colleges and universities provide an excellent illustration of how the commitment concept should work.

When a college gives tenure to a faculty member, it is making a commitment to provide life-long employment for that individual. The tenure decision must therefore reflect an assessment by the college's administration that there will be a need for that faculty member's teaching expertise through his or her lifetime. If a college awards tenure to a thirty-year-old sociology instructor, it should have a plan that covers at least the thirty to forty or more years this instructor could be teaching in that institution. Most important, the plan should demonstrate the need for a permanent sociology instructor through that time period.

Interestingly, the commitment concept was ignored by many college administrators in the late 1960s and early 1970s. They tenured a number of instructors in disciplines that were then popular with students, such as philosophy and religion, without considering whether that popularity would continue throughout the period of commitment. As the demand for courses in these areas has declined, many college administrators have found themselves locked in with tenured faculty in low-demand areas. It will be interesting to see whether college administrators have learned from past mistakes.

Objectives: The Foundation of Planning

objectives
Desired outcomes for individuals, groups, or entire organizations.

Objectives are goals. We use the two terms interchangeably. What do these terms mean? They refer to desired outcomes for individuals, groups, or entire organizations.[9] They provide the direction for all management decisions and form the criterion against which actual accomplishments can be measured. It is for these reasons that they are the foundation of planning.

Multiplicity of Objectives

At first glance, it might appear that organizations have a singular objective—for business firms, to make a profit; for nonprofit organizations, to provide a service efficiently. But closer analysis demonstrates that all organizations have multiple

MANAGING FROM A GLOBAL PERSPECTIVE

Planning Under Extreme Uncertainty

In the early 1990s, Serbia was in the midst of a civil war. In Brazil, inflation was running at the rate of more than 1000 percent a year. In Peru, the country's president suspended the constitution and decided to rule by decree. If you were a manager in Serbia, Brazil, or Peru, would war, hyperinflation, changes in governmental control, or similar political or economic instabilities affect your planning practices? You bet they would!

In contrast to many parts of the world, managers in North America operate in an incredibly stable environment. While there may be uncertainty, it is relatively low. Elections are predictable and regular, economic policies are reasonably well managed by the federal government, social unrest is minimal, and when changes come, they tend to be evolutionary rather than revolutionary. This stability allows managers to make forecasts and plans that are far more predictable and concise than those of managers in countries such as Serbia, Brazil, Peru, Iran, Iraq, and Nicaragua.

Our point is not that managers in North America operate in a stable environment, because most don't. Rather the point is that, relative to many parts of the world, managers in North America face a comparatively predictable environment. This, in turn, allows them to develop more comprehensive plans because such plans are likely to be accurate and provide valuable guides for future action. In contrast, in a country like Brazil, which has been struggling with economic instability for years, managers in business firms would tend to minimize long-term planning and maintain flexibility by relying on directional plans.

objectives. Businesses also seek to increase market share and satisfy employee welfare. A church provides a "road to heaven through absolution," but it also assists the underprivileged in its community and acts as a gathering place for church members to congregate socially. No one measure can evaluate effectively whether an organization is performing successfully. Emphasis on one goal, such as profit, ignores other goals that must also be reached if long-term profits are to be achieved. Moreover, as we mentioned in Chapter 5, the use of a single objective almost certainly will result in undesirable practices, because managers will ignore important parts of their jobs in order to look good on the single measure.

Table 7–2 lists the ten most highly rated goals from a study of over eighty of the largest corporations in the United States.[10] The number of goals per company ranged from one to eighteen, the average being five to six. Except for profitability, the goals are applicable to nonprofit as well as business organizations. Notice, too, that although survival is not specifically mentioned by the firms, it is paramount to all organizations. Some of the criteria listed in Table 7–2 contribute directly to profits, but it is obvious that all organizations must survive if other objectives are to be achieved.

Real Versus Stated Objectives

stated objectives
Official statements of what an organization says—and what it wants various publics to believe—are its objectives.

Table 7–2 is a list of stated objectives. **Stated objectives** are official statements of what an organization says—and what it wants various publics to believe—are its objectives. However, stated objectives—which can be found in the organization's charter, annual report, public-relations announcements, or in public statements made by managers—are often conflicting and excessively influenced by what society believes organizations *should* do.

There is no single objective that characterizes an elementary school. Among its many objectives are transmitting basic reading, writing, and mathematics skills; teaching discipline; fostering the value of achievement; and developing good citizenship behaviors.

The conflict in stated goals exists because organizations respond to a vast array of constituencies. Unfortunately, these constituencies frequently evaluate the organization by different criteria. As a result, management is forced to say different things to different audiences. For example, a few years back, TWA was negotiating to get wage concessions from its flight attendants' union.[11] The union, not wanting to give up anything, was threatening to strike. To the union's representatives, TWA's management was saying, "If you strike, we'll dismantle the airline. By selling off aircraft and air routes, the company is worth more dead than alive." At the same time, the management was trying to calm the nerves of travel agents and potential passengers by saying the company was determined to fly and survive, even if its flight attendants struck. To support its intention, management said that it was training 1,500 people to step in if its attendants walked out. TWA's management had explicitly presented itself in one way to the union and in another way to the public. Was one true and the other false? No. Both were true, but they were in conflict.

Did you ever read an organization's objectives as they are stated in its brochures? Allstate says, "Our goal is to be known by consumers as the best insurer in America."[12] Bell Atlantic states that it is "responding to the imperative of global competition with greater personal accountability and the power of teamwork."[13] Southern Illinois University "emphasizes a commitment to quality education."[14] These types of statements are, at best, vague and are more likely representative of management's public relations skills than they are meaningful guides to what the organization is actually seeking to accomplish.

It shouldn't be surprising, then, to find that an organization's stated objectives are often quite irrelevant to what actually goes on in that organization.[15] In a corporation, for instance, one statement of objectives is issued to stockholders, another to customers, and still others to employees and to the public.[16]

The overall objectives stated by top management should be treated for what they are: "fiction produced by an organization to account for, explain, or rationalize to particular audiences rather than as valid and reliable indications of purpose."[17] The content of objectives is substantially determined by what those audiences want to hear. Moreover, it is simpler for management to state a set of consistent, understandable objectives than to explain a multiplicity of objectives. If you want to know what an organization's **real objectives** are, closely observe what members of the organization actually do. Actions define priorities. The university that proclaims the objectives of limiting class size, facilitating close student–faculty relations, and actively involving students in the learning process, and then puts its students into lecture halls of 300 or

real objectives
Objectives that an organization actually pursues, as defined by the actions of its members.

TABLE 7-2 Stated Objectives from a Survey of Large Corporations

Objective	Percent Acknowledging the Objective
Profitability Absolute dollars of profit or percentage return on invested capital	89
Growth Increase in total revenues, number of employees, and the like	82
Market Share An organization's percentage share of total industry sales	66
Social Responsibility Recognition of the organization's responsibility to the greater society in which it functions to help solve pollution, discrimination, urban, and similar problems	65
Employee Welfare Concern for the satisfaction of employees and the quality of their working life	62
Product Quality and Service Excellence of the product or service that the organization produces	60
Research and Development Success in generating new and innovative products and processes	54
Diversification Ability to identify and move into new markets	51
Efficiency Ability to convert inputs into outputs at the lowest cost	50
Financial Stability Performance on financial criteria void of erratic movements	49

Source: Adapted from Y. K. Shetty, "New Look at Corporate Goals," *California Management Review*, Vol. XVI, No. 2, p. 73. Reprinted by permission of the Regents. © 1978 by the Regents of the University of California.

The Seagram Co. Ltd., is a $6 billion a year company that produces and markets distilled spirits, wines, fruit juices, coolers, and mixers. The above is a statement of the company's mission and goals.

more, is not unusual. Nor is the automobile service center that promotes fast, low-cost repairs and then gives mediocre service at high prices. An awareness that real and stated objectives can deviate is important, if for no other reason than because it can help you to explain what might otherwise seem to be management inconsistencies.

Traditional Objective Setting

The traditional role of objectives is one of control imposed by an organization's top management. The president of a manufacturing firm *tells* the production vice president what he or she expects manufacturing costs to be for the coming year. The president *tells* the marketing vice president what level he or she expects sales to reach for the coming year. The city mayor *tells* his or her chief of police how much the departmental budget will be. Then, at some later point, performance is evaluated to determine whether the assigned objectives have been achieved.

The central theme in **traditional objective setting** is that objectives are set at the

traditional objective setting
Objectives are set at the top and then broken down into subgoals for each level in an organization. The top imposes its standards on everyone below.

top and then broken down into subgoals for each level of an organization. It is a one-way process: The top imposes its standards on everyone below. This traditional perspective assumes that top management knows what's best because only it can see the "big picture."

In addition to being imposed from above, traditional objective setting is often largely nonoperational.[18] If top management defines the organization's objectives in broad terms such as achieving "sufficient profits" or "market leadership," these ambiguities have to be turned into specifics as the objectives filter down through the organization. At each level, managers supply operational meaning to the goals. Specificity is achieved by each manager applying his or her own set of interpretations and biases. The result is that objectives lose clarity and unity as they make their way down from the top. (See Figure 7–4.)

Management By Objectives

L. Perrigo is a Michigan manufacturer of over-the-counter drugs and beauty aids.[19] When William Swaney took over as president, he found that the company relied on traditional objective setting. Managers had vague objectives, including "maintaining client communications" and "reviewing performance periodically." He wanted an objective-setting program that would specify exactly what his managers and employees were expected to accomplish and that would motivate rather than intimidate. What he installed was a system of participatory objective-setting. Each employee identified no more than ten critical changes that would make a difference in his or her job performance. Then each set specific, quantitative objectives for which he or she would be personally responsible. Examples included "submit budgets within two weeks of contract ratification" and "deliver the project within 3 percent of the budgeted cost."

William Swaney is using **management by objectives (MBO)**. It is a system in which specific performance objectives are jointly determined by subordinates and their superiors, progress toward objectives is periodically reviewed, and rewards are allocated on the basis of this progress. Rather than using goals to control, MBO uses them to motivate.

management by objectives (MBO)

A system in which specific performance objectives are jointly determined by subordinates and their superiors, progress toward objectives is periodically reviewed, and rewards are allocated on the basis of this progress.

FIGURE 7–4
Traditional Objective Setting

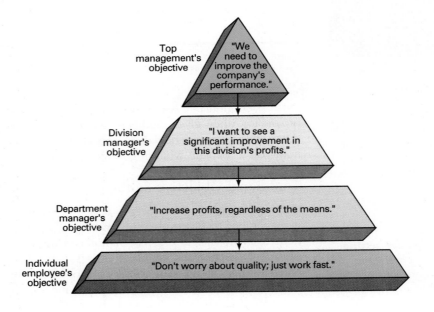

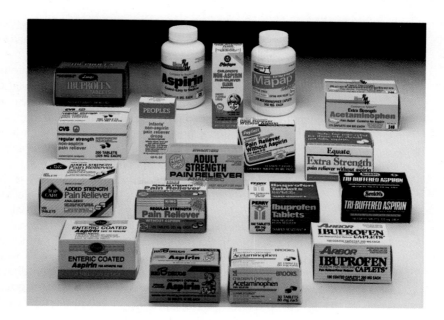

L. Perrigo, a manufacturer of over-the-counter drugs and beauty aids, uses management by objectives (MBO).

What Is MBO?   Management by objectives is not new. The concept goes back forty years.[20] Its appeal lies in its emphasis on converting overall objectives into specific objectives for organizational units and individual members.

MBO makes objectives operational by devising a process by which they cascade down through the organization. As depicted in Figure 7–5, the organization's overall objectives are translated into specific objectives for each succeeding level—divisional, departmental, individual—in the organization. Because lower unit managers jointly participate in setting their own goals, MBO works from the "bottom up" as well as from the "top down." The result is a hierarchy that links objectives at one level to those at the next level, For the individual employee, MBO provides specific personal performance objectives. Each person therefore has an identified specific contribution to make to his or her unit's performance. If all the individuals achieve their goals, then their unit's goals will be attained, and the organization's overall objectives will become a reality.

FIGURE 7–5
Cascading of Objectives

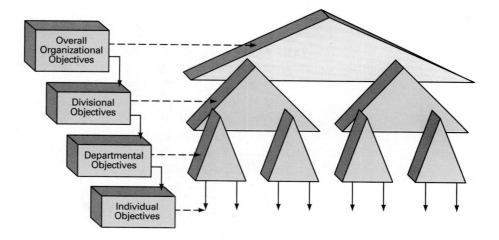

MBO's Common Elements There are four ingredients common to MBO programs. These are goal specificity, participative decision making, an explicit time period, and performance feedback.

The objectives in MBO should be concise statements of expected accomplishments. It's not adequate, for example, merely to state a desire to cut costs, improve service, or increase quality. Such desires have to be converted into tangible objectives that can be measured and evaluated. To cut departmental costs *by 7 percent*, to improve service by ensuring that all telephone orders are processed *within twenty-four hours of receipt*, or to increase quality by keeping returns to *less than 1 percent of sales* are examples of specific objectives.

In MBO the objectives are not unilaterally set by the boss and assigned to subordinates, as is characteristic of traditional objective setting. MBO replaces these imposed goals with participatively determined goals. The superior and subordinate jointly choose the goals and agree on how they will be achieved.

Each objective has a concise time period in which it is to be completed. Typically, the time period is three months, six months, or a year.

The final ingredient in an MBO program is feedback on performance. MBO seeks to give continuous feedback on progress toward goals. Ideally, this is accomplished by giving ongoing feedback to individuals so they can monitor and correct their own actions. This is supplemented by periodic formal appraisal meetings in which superiors and subordinates can review progress toward goals and further feedback can be provided.

Table 7–3 summarizes the typical steps in an MBO program.

Does MBO Work? Assessing the effectiveness of MBO is a complex task. Let's begin by briefly reviewing a growing body of literature on the relationship between goals and performance.[21]

If factors such as a person's ability and acceptance of goals are held constant, evidence demonstrates that more *difficult* goals lead to higher performance. Although individuals with very difficult goals achieve them far less often than those with very easy goals, they nevertheless perform at a consistently higher level. Of course, goals can be too hard. If individuals perceive a goal to be impossible instead of challenging, their desire to achieve it decreases, and the likelihood that they will abandon it increases.

Moreover, studies consistently support the finding that *specific* hard goals produce a higher level of output than do no goals or generalized goals such as "do your best." *Feedback* also favorably affects performance. Feedback lets a person know whether his or her level of effort is sufficient or needs to be increased. It can induce a person to

---

TABLE 7–3 Steps in a Typical MBO Program

---

1. The organization's overall objectives and strategies are formulated.
2. Major objectives are allocated among divisional and departmental units.
3. Unit managers collaboratively set specific objectives for their units with their superiors.
4. Specific objectives are collaboratively set for all department members.
5. Action plans, defining how objectives are to be achieved, are specified and agreed upon by managers and subordinates.
6. The action plans are implemented.
7. Progress toward objectives is periodically reviewed, and feedback is provided.
8. Successful achievement of objectives is reinforced by performance-based rewards.

Does MBO Require Manipulation?

A colleague once facetiously suggested that MBO stood for *manipulating by objectives*. He made his argument as follows:

1. Managers frequently have a specific set of goals in mind for an employee before the manager and employee ever sit down to begin the MBO process. These preconceived standards define the minimum goals that the manager is willing to accept.
2. Authentic employee participation therefore does not always take place. What takes place should more appropriately be called "pseudo-participation." That is, there is only the appearance of participation.
3. Nothing in the MBO process clarifies how to arrive at goals if the manager and subordinate are unable to reach agreement.
4. When conflicts exist, managers tend to use the power of their position to impose their goals on the subordinate.
5. This scenario suggests that MBO can be a device that allows managers to appear to be setting goals participatively when, in fact, the goals are really being assigned.

Proponents of MBO would counter that, although the preceding scenario undoubtedly happens, it is not really management by objectives. Moreover, managers must understand that anything less than complete participation by subordinates will undermine any MBO program's credibility and effectiveness. When differences occur, mature individuals can resolve them in a way that meets the needs of both the employee and the organization.

Is it unethical for a manager to enter a participative goal-setting session with a preestablished set of goals that the manager wants the employee to accept? Is it unethical for a manager to use his or her formal position to impose specific goals on an employee? What do *you* think?

raise his or her goal level after attaining a previous goal and can inform a person of ways in which to improve his or her performance.

The results cited above are all consistent with MBO's stress on specific goals and feedback. MBO implies, rather than explicitly states, that goals must be perceived as feasible. Research on goal setting indicates that MBO is most effective if the goals are difficult enough to require the person to do some stretching.

But what about participation? MBO strongly advocates that goals be set participatively. Does the research demonstrate that participatively set goals lead to higher performance than those assigned by a superior? Interestingly, the research comparing participatively set and assigned goals on performance has not shown any strong or consistent relationships.[22] When goal difficulty has been held constant, assigned goals frequently do as well as participatively determined goals, contrary to MBO ideology. Therefore it is not possible to argue for the superiority of participation as MBO proponents advocate. One major benefit from participation, however, is that it appears to induce individuals to establish more difficult goals.[23] Thus participation may have a positive impact on performance by increasing one's goal aspiration level.

Studies of actual MBO programs confirm that MBO effectively increases employee performance and organizational productivity. A review of seventy programs, for example, found organizational productivity gains in sixty-eight out of seventy of them.[24] This same review also identified top management commitment and involvement as important conditions for MBO to reach its potential. When top management had a high commitment to MBO and was personally involved in its implementation, the average gain in productivity was found to be 56 percent. When commitment and involvement were low, the average gain in productivity dropped to only 6 percent.

Summary

This summary is organized by the chapter-opening learning objectives found on page 185.

1. Planning is the process of determining objectives and assessing the way these objectives can best be achieved.

2. Planning gives direction, reduces the impact of change, minimizes waste and redundancy, and sets the standards to facilitate controlling.

3. Strategic plans cover an extensive time period (usually five or more years), cover broad issues, and include the formulation of objectives. Operational plans cover shorter periods of time, focus on specifics, and assume that objectives are already known.

4. Directional plans are preferred over specific plans when uncertainty is high and when the organization is in the formative and decline stages of its life cycle.

5. Four contingency factors in planning include a manager's level in the organization, the life stage of the organization, the degree of environmental uncertainty, and the length of future commitments.

6. A manager should plan just far enough ahead to see through those commitments he or she makes today.

7. An organization's stated objectives might not be its real objectives because management might want to tell people what they want to hear and because it is simpler to state a set of consistent, understandable objectives than to explain a multiplicity of objectives.

8. A typical MBO program includes eight steps: (1) The organization's overall objectives and strategies are formulated; (2) major objectives are allocated among divisions and departmental units; (3) unit managers collaboratively set specific objectives for their units with their superiors; (4) specific objectives are collaboratively set for all department members; (5) action plans are specified and agreed upon by managers and subordinates; (6) the action plans are implemented; (7) progress toward objectives is periodically reviewed, and feedback is provided; and (8) successful achievement of objectives is reinforced by performance-based rewards.

9. MBO establishes goals as motivators by letting people know exactly what is expected of them, getting them to participate in setting their goals, giving them continuous feedback on how well they're progressing toward their goals, and making their rewards contingent upon achieving their goals. Such factors increase motivation.

Review Questions

1. Contrast *formal* with *informal* planning.

2. How does planning affect an organization in terms of performance? In terms of eliminating change? Are these effects altered if the planning proves to be inaccurate?

3. Describe the six different types of plans discussed in this chapter.

4. How does the planning done by a top executive differ from that performed by a supervisor?

5. How does environmental uncertainty affect planning?

6. Do business organizations have only one real goal—to make a profit? How does this affect their stated goals?

7. How would you identify an organization's stated objectives? Its real objectives?

8. Contrast traditional objective setting and MBO.

9. What factors influence MBO's effectiveness?

Discussion Questions

1. What relationship do you see between planning and traditional objective setting? Between planning and controlling?

2. What effect do you think decision making (discussed in Chapter 6) has on planning? Discuss.

3. What relationships and overlaps do you see between the six types of plans? How do you think these types of plans can best be integrated?

4. What basic factors in MBO make it a logical technique for setting objectives? Would you expect it to work better in large or small organizations? Why?

5. Management guru W. Edwards Deming argues that management should eliminate numerical goals. He believes that programs like MBO are inconsistent with TQM's concern for continual improvement. According to Deming, MBO-type goals act as ceilings, rather than targets, and therefore limit productivity. Do you think specific, numerical goals can undermine the search for continual improvement? Discuss.

SELF-ASSESSMENT EXERCISE

Are You a Good Planner?

Instructions: Answer either Yes or No to each of the following eight questions:

	Yes	No
1. My personal objectives are clearly spelled out in writing.	_____	_____
2. Most of my days are hectic and disorderly.	_____	_____
3. I seldom make any snap decisions and usually study a problem carefully before acting.	_____	_____
4. I keep a desk calendar or appointment book as an aid.	_____	_____
5. I make use of "action" and "deferred action" files.	_____	_____
6. I generally establish starting dates and deadlines for all my projects.	_____	_____

	Yes	No
7. I often ask others for advice.	————	————
8. I believe that all problems have to be solved immediately.	————	————

Now turn to page SK-2 for scoring directions and key.

Sources: Ted Pollack, "Are You a Good Planner?," *Supervision*, January 1980, pp. 26–27. "How Good a Planner Are You?." *Supervision*, July 1983, p. 24; and "How to Be a Good Planner," *Supervision*, April 1984, pp. 25–26. Reprinted by permission of *Supervision*. Copyright © 1984 by The National Research Bureau, Inc., 424 North Third Street, Burlington, Iowa 52601.

BANK OF VANCOUVER

To: Jan Flatley, Head Loan Officer
Third Street Office

From: Michael Chong, Branch Manager
Third Street Office

Subject: Implementation of MBO program

This is to follow up yesterday's staff meeting and confirm my commitment to implement an MBO program in our branch.

Last year, your staff of four approved 582 loans totaling $14,650,000. This was down 4.3 percent from the previous year. Twenty-seven percent of your loans were commercial and 73 percent personal. Bad debts represented 1.65 percent of your portfolio (versus 1.88 percent in the previous year). Profits from your department last year were down more than 8 percent to $434,000.

Please give me a detailed outline of the steps you plan to take in the next 60 days that will lead to successful implementation of our MBO program in your area. In addition, I'd like you to provide me with a tentative list of your department's goals for the coming year. After reviewing your submission, I will arrange a meeting with you to discuss and finalize your department's goals.

This is a fictionalized account of a potentially real problem. It was written for academic purposes only and is not meant to reflect either positively or negatively on actual management practices at the Bank of Vancouver.

CASE APPLICATION

Schwinn Bicycle Co.

Ignaz Schwinn founded the bicycle company bearing his name in Chicago in 1895. It grew to become the world's largest bicycle manufacturer. In the 1960s, for instance, Schwinn held a 25 percent share of the United States bicycle market. But that was then and this is now.

Edward Schwinn Jr., the great-grandson of the founder, took over the company in 1979. By that time, problems had set in, and poor planning and decision making compounded those problems.

In the 1970s, Schwinn capitalized on its powerful retail distribution network and brand name to dominate the ten-speed business. But in the 1980s, the market shifted. Mountain bikes replaced ten-speeds as the largest sellers. And lightweight, high-tech exotic bikes grew in popularity among adult enthusiasts. Schwinn missed both market shifts. It responded slowly to these changes. Management focused on cost cutting rather than innovation. As a result, it began losing market share rapidly to more far-sighted manufacturers selling under the brand names Trek, Cannondale, Giant, and Diamond Back.

Maybe Schwinn's biggest mistake was failing to grasp that bicycles are a global product. The company was late in developing overseas markets and linking into foreign production facilities. Schwinn belatedly began, in the late 1970s, its foreign campaign by having many of its bicycles built in Japan. But by then, the expanding Taiwanese bike industry was already beating the Japanese producers on price. Again reacting after the competition, Schwinn began importing a small quantity of Taiwanese-made Giant bikes on which Schwinn placed its nameplate.

In what may have proven to be the company's dumbest move, management panicked when workers went on strike in 1981 at Schwinn's main factory in Chicago. Instead of negotiating a settlement, management closed the plant and sent its engineers and equipment to Giant's factory in Taiwan. As part of its new partnership with Giant, Schwinn handed over everything—technology, engineering, volume—that Giant needed to become a dominant bikemaker. In return, Schwinn imported the bikes and marketed them in the United States under the Schwinn name. Said one U.S. competitor, "Schwinn gave the franchise to Giant on a silver platter."

By 1984, the Taiwanese tail was wagging the American dog. Giant was shipping 700,000 bicycles a year to Schwinn under the Schwinn nameplate, fully 70 percent of Schwinn's sales. A few years later, Giant was using the knowledge it got from Schwinn to launch its own brand name in the United States.

By 1992, Giant and the China Bicycle Co. had become the world's dominant players in the global bike market. Giant, for instance, was selling seven out of every ten bikes it made under its own brand name. And what about Schwinn? When its market share dropped to 5 percent in October 1992, the company filed for bankruptcy.

Questions

1. How could more effective long-term planning have helped save Schwinn?
2. Using the contingency variables described in this chapter, explain what Schwinn's planning should have looked like in 1965, 1975, and 1985.

Source: Based on Andrew Tanzer, "Bury Thy Teacher," *Forbes,* December 21, 1992, pp. 90–95.

VIDEO CASE

Airlines and Planning in a Dynamic Environment

Oh how the game has changed. Prior to deregulation in 1978, prices in the airline industry were straightforward and expensive. All airlines charged the same fare for the same trip. There was no competition on price. Then came deregulation and all hell broke loose. Seventeen new airlines sprung up but few survived. Eastern, Pan Am, and Midway went out of business. Continental, America West, and TWA continued to fly but under Chapter 11 bankruptcy protection. The management at carriers such as American, Delta, and United take exception to bankruptcy laws that allow TWA and others to continue to fly while excused from paying interest and other debts. This allows the bankrupt carriers to unfairly undercut the healthy carriers and, in an odd sort of way, precipitate the demise of the few airlines that can pay their bills.

Just when things seem to be sorting themselves out, one of the airlines will start a price war or restructure prices. That's what happened in the spring of 1992. American Airlines announced that it was revolutionizing air fares by restoring simplicity and fairness to a system gone out of control. In place of a structure that had hundreds of different prices with all kinds of restrictions, American offered four simple prices: Regular coach, first class, and two discount fares—seven-day and twenty-one-day advance bookings. Within hours of American's announcement, TWA responded with massive discounts—30 to 40 percent below American's fares.

What's going on here? Are airlines being run by lunatics? What's going on is that the industry suffers from overcapacity. To fill seats, airlines are continually dreaming up schemes that they hope will encourage people to give up driving for flying and result in fliers choosing their airline over their competitors. Add in the cost of purchasing new planes and maintaining old ones, the escalation in fuel prices over the past twenty years, and the potential for new competition from foreign carriers and you have an industry in chaos. The only winners seem to be consumers, especially those who fly between major metropolitan cities. And their victory may be only in the short run. Should this chaos continue, there may be just three or four survivors, and they will be in a position to charge the maximum that the market will bear.

As an update to American's spring 1992 action, it should be noted that the simple four-category price structure was discontinued in February 1993. American's management said it was losing too much money and was forced to go back to its previous patch-quilt of prices.

Questions

1. Is it possible for airline managers to engage in long-term planning in this environment? Discuss.

2. What kind of plans would be most effective for an airline operating in 1974? 1994? Explain.

3. How might a contingency approach to planning be used for managers in the airline industry?

Source: "Future of U.S. Airlines," *ABC's This Week With David Brinkley,*" April 19, 1992.

CHAPTER 8

Strategic Management and Entrepreneurship

LEARNING OBJECTIVES

After Reading This Chapter, You Should Be Able To:

1. Explain the importance of strategic planning.
2. Differentiate corporate-, business-, and functional-level strategies.
3. Outline the steps in the strategic management process.
4. Explain SWOT analysis.
5. Describe the four business groups in the BCG matrix.
6. Identify and contrast the four adaptive business-level strategies.
7. Describe how to assess an organization's competitive advantage.
8. Explain what entrepreneurship is.
9. Compare how entrepreneurs and bureaucratic managers approach strategy.

While Alamo doesn't have a lot of locations, the ones they have tend to be big. This office in Orlando, Florida, which services customers coming to Disney World, is the largest car-rental office in the United States.

If you're in the airport rental car business, how do you successfully compete against the big four—Hertz, Avis, National, and Budget?

Michael Egan has an answer.[1] As chairman of Alamo Rent-A-Car, Egan has implemented a strategy that has propelled Alamo in less than twenty years into a $500 million company with profit margins second only to Avis. His strategy differentiates Alamo from its major competitors by focusing on low prices and low cost–high volume locations, and by renting to the budget-minded customer.

To gain position in the airport car rental market, Alamo has staked itself out as the low-priced alternative. It advertises daily rental prices as much as 20 percent below its bigger competitors, and with no extra charge for mileage. For example, Alamo will rent a Chevrolet Beretta in Los Angeles on a weekday for $38 a day with free mileage. Hertz charges $51.93 a day for that same car, and unless the customer reserves at least three days in advance, Hertz adds 32 cents for every mile driven over one hundred miles.

It's one thing to offer low prices, but how do you do that and remain profitable? Egan's answer: Locate in high-volume markets and cheaper locations. Alamo has only 105 locations in the United States and the United Kingdom, while Hertz has 5400 locations. But Alamo has carefully chosen to locate only in the most highly trafficked airports. So while Hertz has fifty times as many locations as Alamo, it rents only four times as many cars. Thus Alamo can keep its costs low by keeping its volume high. Additionally, Egan keeps his overhead low by locating most of Alamo's rental counters outside of airport terminals where rents are sky-high. Instead, Alamo's rental counters tend to be in nearby, less expensive locations.

The final component in Egan's strategy is his target market. Egan lets Hertz and Avis fight over the *Fortune* 100 executive with the big expense account. Alamo has chosen to go after the vacation traveler, although it has recently expanded its niche to seek out the budget-minded business traveler.

The Alamo case illustrates the value of strategic planning: By selecting a strategy that differentiates it from other car rental firms, Alamo has been able to compete profitably against larger and deeper-pocketed foes. An underlying theme in this chapter is that better strategies result in better organizational performance. Yet the fact that strategic planning plays a critical role in an organization's success has been widely recognized for only about twenty-five years.

The Increasing Importance of Strategic Planning

Before the early 1970s, managers who made long-range plans generally assumed that better times lay ahead. Plans for the future were merely extensions of where the organization had been in the past. However, the energy crisis, deregulation, accelerating technological change, and increasing global competition, as well as the other environmental shocks of the 1970s and 1980s, undermined this approach to long-range planning.[2] These changes in the rules of the game forced managers to develop a systematic means of analyzing the environment, assessing their organization's strengths and weaknesses, and identifying opportunities where the organization could have a competitive advantage. The value of strategic planning began to be recognized.

A recent survey of business owners found that 69 percent had strategic plans, and, among those owners, 89 percent responded that they had found their plans to be effective.[3] They cited, for example, that strategic planning gave them specific goals and provided their staffs with a unified vision. Today, strategic planning has moved beyond the private sector to include government agencies, hospitals, and educational institutions. For example, the skyrocketing costs of a college education, cutbacks in federal aid for students and research, and the decline in the absolute number of high school graduates have led many university administrators to assess their colleges' aspirations and identify a market niche in which they can survive and prosper.[4]

Levels of Strategy

If all organizations produced only a single product or service, the management of any organization could develop a single strategic plan that encompassed everything it did. But many organizations are in diverse lines of business. General Electric is in a variety of businesses—everything from the manufacture of aircraft engines and light bulbs to ownership of the NBC television network. American Brands is in tobacco, distilled spirits, life insurance, office products, hardware products, golf equipment, and optical goods. Each of these different businesses typically demands a separate strategy. Moreover, these multibusiness companies also have diverse functional departments such as finance and marketing that support each of their businesses. As a

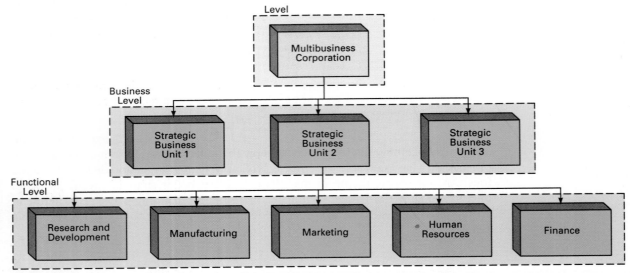

FIGURE 8-1
Levels of Strategy

result, we need to differentiate between corporate-level, business-level, and functional-level strategies (see Figure 8–1).

Corporate-Level Strategy

corporate-level strategy
Seeks to determine what businesses a corporation should be in.

If an organization is in more than one line of business, it will need a **corporate-level strategy.** This strategy seeks to answer the question: In what set of businesses should we be? Corporate-level strategy determines the roles that each business in the organization will play. At a company like Eastman Kodak, top management's corporate-level strategy integrates the business-level strategies for its film, pharmaceutical, chemical, computer-disk, battery, and other divisions.

Business-Level Strategy

business-level strategy
Seeks to determine how a corporation should compete in each of its businesses.

Business-level strategy seeks to answer the question: How should we compete in each of our businesses? For the small organization in only one line of business, or the large organization that has avoided diversification, the business-level strategy is typically the same as the organization's strategy. For organizations in multiple businesses, each division will have its own strategy that will define the products or services that it will offer, the customers it wants to reach, and the like. For example, Paramount Communications Corp. owns and operates entertainment businesses such as Paramount Pictures and Madison Square Garden as well as the publishing giant Simon & Schuster. Paramount's publishing division has its own unique business strategy that encompasses its trade, educational, and other publication products.

strategic business unit (SBU)
A single business or collection of businesses that is independent and formulates its own strategy.

When an organization is in a number of different businesses, planning can be facilitated by creating strategic business units. A **strategic business unit (SBU)** represents a single business or collection of related businesses. Each SBU will have its own distinct mission and competitors. This allows an SBU to have a strategy independent from the other businesses of the larger organization. In a company like General Electric, which is in many diverse lines of business, management may create a dozen or more SBUs.

The SBU concept of planning breaks business units up based on the following principles:

The organization is managed as a "portfolio" of businesses, each business unit serving a clearly defined product-market segment with a clearly defined strategy.

Each business unit in the portfolio develops a strategy tailored to its capabilities and competitive needs but consistent with the overall organization's capabilities and needs.

The total portfolio is managed to serve the interests of the organization as a whole—to achieve balanced growth in sales, earnings, and asset mix at an acceptable and controlled level of risk.[5]

Functional-Level Strategy

functional-level strategy
Seeks to determine how to support the business-level strategy.

Functional-level strategy seeks to answer the question: How do we support the business-level strategy? Functional departments such as research and development, manufacturing, marketing, human resources, and finance need to conform to the business-level strategy. If the development group in the Biscuit and Bakery division at Campbell Soup Co. creates a new Pepperidge Farm product, then the division's marketing department will need to develop a functional-level strategy to ensure that the new product is properly promoted when it's introduced.

In the remainder of this chapter, we'll focus our attention on corporate-level and business-level strategies. This is not to demean the importance of functional-level managers developing strategies for their units. Rather, it reflects the emphasis that researchers and practitioners have placed on developing strategic frameworks.

The Strategic Management Process

strategic management process
A nine-step process encompassing strategic planning, implementation, and evaluation.

The **strategic management process,** as illustrated in Figure 8–2, is a nine-step process that involves strategic planning, implementation, and evaluation. While strategic planning encompasses the first seven steps—through the formulation of corporate-, business-, and functional-level strategies—even the best strategies can go awry if management fails either to implement them properly or to evaluate their results. In this section we will examine in detail the various steps in the strategic management process.

Step 1: Identifying the Organization's Current Mission, Objectives, and Strategies

mission
The purpose of an organization.

Every organization has a **mission** that defines its purpose and answers the question: What business or businesses are we in? Defining the organization's mission forces

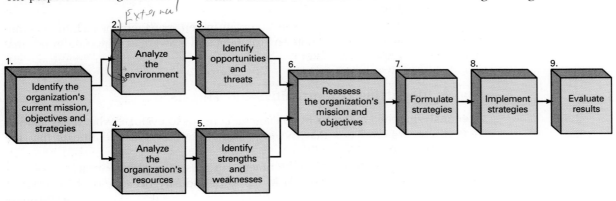

FIGURE 8–2
The Strategic Management Process

Objectives and strategies translate the mission into concrete terms. Black & Decker defines its mission as manufacturing and marketing tools and electrical equipment. One of the objectives of its power tools group is to increase sales by 20 percent a year for the next three years. A current strategy to achieve this objective is to modify the product line so that it can be sold worldwide.

management to identify the scope of its products or services carefully. It has been argued, for instance, that the decline of the railroads was due to their misdefining the business they were in. During the 1930s and 1940s, if the railroads had considered themselves to be in the transportation business instead of the railroad business, their fate might have been quite different.

What do you think the mission of Domino's Pizza is? If you said Domino's was in the pizza business, you'd be wrong. According to its founder and CEO, Tom Monaghan, Domino's is in the delivery business. The company's expertise lies in being able to deliver a product to millions of homes in thirty minutes or less. It just so happens that there is substantial demand for the speedy delivery of pizza. While specifying Domino's mission may seem like a small point, it isn't. It provides guidance for management. For instance, if Domino's was going to expand its product line, given its mission, management would be more likely to consider offering speedy home deliveries of pharmacy items to the bedridden than providing an extended menu of Italian food.

Determining the nature of one's business is as important for not-for-profit organizations as it is for business firms. Hospitals, government agencies, and colleges must also identify their missions. For example, is a college training students for the professions, training students for particular jobs, or educating students through a well-rounded, liberal education? Is it seeking students from the top 5 percent of high school graduates, students with low academic grades but high aptitude test scores, or students in the vast middle ground? Answers to questions such as these clarify the organization's current purpose.

Step 2: Analyzing the Environment

In Chapter 3, we presented the environment as a primary constraint on management action. Analyzing that environment is a critical component of the strategy process. Why? Because an organization's environment, to a large degree, defines management's options. A successful strategy will be one that aligns well with the environment.[6]

As a case in point, Panasonic is a major producer of home entertainment systems. But beginning in the mid-1980s, technological breakthroughs in miniaturization and the social trend toward living in smaller homes dramatically increased the demand for powerful, but highly compact, sound systems. The success of Panasonic's home-audio strategy depends on understanding the technological and social changes that are taking place in its environment.

Management of every organization needs to analyze its environment. It needs to know, for instance, what its competition is up to, what pending legislation might affect the organization, and what the supply of labor in locations where the organization operates is like.

Step 2 of the strategy process is complete when management has an accurate grasp of what is taking place in its environment and is aware of important trends that might affect its operations.

Step 3: Identifying Opportunities and Threats

After analyzing the environment, management needs to evaluate what it has learned in terms of opportunities that the organization can exploit and threats that the organization faces.[7]

Keep in mind that the same environment can present opportunities to one organization and pose threats to another in the same industry because of their different resources. In 1992, the long recession had created a weak U.S. economy. Business bankruptcies were at postdepression highs. Especially hurt were businesses—like home-furnishing retailers—that sold large ticket items whose purchase could be easily postponed. However, several large, prosperous, and well-managed chains of home-furnishing retailers saw this situation as an opportunity. They were able to buy up inventories of former competitors at bargain prices and to selectively take over these competitors' better locations. The result—a consolidation among the larger and more prosperous furniture retailers. So what an organization considers an opportunity or a threat depends on the resources that it controls.

Step 4: Analyzing the Organization's Resources

Now we move from looking outside the organization to looking inside. What skills and abilities do the organization's employees have? What is the organization's cash position? Has it been successful at developing new and innovative products? How does the public perceive the organization and the quality of its products or services?

This step forces management to recognize that every organization, no matter how large and powerful, is constrained in some way by the resources and skills it has available. A smaller automobile manufacturer, like Alfa Romeo, isn't able to move into making minivans simply because management sees opportunities there. Alfa Romeo doesn't have the resources to successfully enter the minivan market against the likes of Chrysler, Ford, Toyota, and Nissan.

Step 5: Identifying Strengths and Weaknesses

distinctive competence
The unique skills and resources that determine the organization's competitive weapons.

The analysis in Step 4 should lead to a clear assessment of the organization's strengths and weaknesses. Management can then identify the organization's **distinctive competence,** or the unique skills and resources that determine the organization's competitive weapons. Black & Decker, for instance, bought General Electric's small appliances division—which made coffeemakers, toasters, irons, and the like— renamed them, and capitalized on Black & Decker's reputation for quality and durability to make these appliances far more profitable than they had been under the GE name.

An understanding of the organization's culture and the strengths and liabilities it offers management is a crucial part of Step 5 that has only recently been getting the attention it deserves.[8] Specifically, managers should be aware that strong and weak cultures have different effects on strategy and that the content of a culture has a major effect on the content of the strategy.

In a strong culture, for instance, almost all employees will have a clear understanding of what the organization is about. This should make it easier for management to convey to new employees the organization's distinctive competence. A department store chain like Nordstrom, which has a very strong culture that embraces service and customer satisfaction, should be able to instill its cultural values in new employees in a much shorter time than can a competitor with a weak culture. The negative side of a strong culture, of course, is that it is more difficult to change. A strong culture may act as a significant barrier to acceptance of a change in the organization's strategies. In fact, the strong culture at Wang Labs undoubtedly kept top management from perceiving the need to adopt a new corporate strategy in the 1980s in response to changes in the computer industry. Successful organizations with strong cultures can become prisoners of their own past successes.

Cultures differ in the degree to which they encourage risk taking, exploit innovation, and reward performance. Since strategic choices encompass such factors, cultural values influence managerial preference for certain strategies. In a risk-aversive culture, for instance, management is more likely to favor strategies that are defensive, that minimize financial exposure, and that react to changes in the environment rather than try to anticipate those changes. Where risk is shunned, you shouldn't be surprised to find management emphasizing cost cutting and improving established product lines. Conversely, where innovation is highly valued, management is likely to favor new technology and product development instead of more service locations or a superior sales force.

Step 6: Reassessing the Organization's Mission and Objectives

SWOT analysis

Analysis of an organization's strengths and weaknesses, and its environmental opportunities and threats.

A merging of Steps 3 and 5 results in an assessment of the organization's opportunities (see Figure 8–3). This is frequently called **SWOT analysis** because it brings together the organization's *S*trengths, *W*eaknesses, *O*pportunities, and *T*hreats in order to identify a niche that the organization can exploit.

In light of the SWOT analysis and identification of the organization's opportunities, management needs to reevaluate its mission and objectives. Are they realistic? Do they need modification? If changes are needed in the organization's overall direction, this is where they are likely to originate. On the other hand, if no changes are necessary, management is ready to begin the actual formulation of strategies.

Step 7: Formulating Strategies

Strategies need to be set at the corporate, business, and functional levels. The formulation of these strategies follows the decision-making process described in Chapter 6. Specifically, management needs to develop and evaluate alternative strategies and then select a set that is compatible at each level and will allow the organization to best capitalize on its resources and the opportunities available in the environment.

Step 7 is complete when management has developed a set of strategies that will give the organization a competitive advantage. That is, management will seek to position the organization so that it can gain a relative advantage over its rivals. As you'll see later in this chapter, this requires a careful evaluation of the competitive forces that dictate the rules of competition within the industry in which the organization operates. Successful managers will choose strategies that give their organization the most favorable competitive advantage; then they will try to sustain that advantage over time.

Step 8: Implementing Strategies

The next-to-last step in the strategic management process is implementation. No matter how effective strategic planning has been, it cannot succeed if it is not

FIGURE 8–3
Identifying the Organization's Opportunities

Organization's resources

Opportunities in the Environment

Organization's Opportunities

When You Don't Want to Go It Alone: Strategic Alliances

SWOT analysis may identify an excellent opportunity in the environment to which management feels somehow inadequate to respond. The organization may, for instance, have inadequate resources or be unwilling to take on the full burden of risk. In such cases, managers are increasingly turning to strategic alliances as the means to exploit such opportunities. These alliances are joint partnerships between two or more firms that are created to gain a competitive advantage in a market. They are a strategic option that allow members to pool resources between two or more companies in the same country as well as across national boundaries (If you'll remember, we introduced strategic alliances in Chapter 4 when we discussed how organizations go international.) A few examples will illustrate how some companies are using strategic alliances to exploit opportunities both abroad and at home.

Designing a new commercial aircraft is expensive. It can require outlays of $3 to $4 billion before the first plane comes off the assembly line. This makes developing new aircraft a risky business even for the two biggest players in the commercial aviation industry—Boeing and Europe's Airbus. That's why these two rival companies are currently doing research jointly in developing the next generation of commercial aircraft. Their strategic alliance allows them to spread development costs and risk.

AT&T and NEC Corp. recently entered into a joint venture. AT&T has big ambitions in the semiconductor industry. It wants to sell a broad range of microchips head-to-head with some of the world's largest chip makers. The problem is that AT&T doesn't have the products to compete in the big leagues. So it joined up with NEC Corp., the big Japanese chip maker. AT&T is sharing its computer-aided-design technology, which NEC wants, for some of NEC's advanced logic chips. As an AT&T executive noted, "These days it's just too expensive to go it alone."[9]

Apple Computer has developed alliances with a number of other companies, including Sony and IBM. Apple didn't have enough engineers to handle the large number of new products it wanted to bring to market, so it turned to Sony for help. Sony's crack design team, with expertise in miniaturization, helped Apple develop a notebook-sized Macintosh computer called the PowerBook 100. In an effort to better compete for big-corporation business, Apple has joined up with IBM to create what both companies hope will be the next generation of portable computers for corporate use.

Managers are recognizing the positive synergy created by cooperative partnerships between organizations in sharing technology, financial resources, marketing channels, and the like. We should expect to see this trend toward strategic alliances expand throughout this decade.

---

implemented properly. Later chapters in this book will address a number of issues related to strategy implementation. A preview of some "coming attractions" will highlight these.

In Chapter 10, we'll discuss the strategy-structure relationship. We'll show how successful strategies require an organization structure that is properly matched. If an organization significantly changes its corporate-level strategy, it will need to make appropriate changes in its overall structural design.

Top management leadership is a necessary ingredient in a successful strategy. So,

Is "Going Bankrupt" an Unethical Strategy?

What do such companies as Texaco, Continental Airlines, and Southland Corp. have in common? Their managements have all used Chapter 11 of the U.S. Bankruptcy Code as a corporate strategy.[10]

The 1978 Bankruptcy Reform Act and its amendments were intended to make it easier for corporations to reorganize. The logic was that the use of Chapter 11 would allow declining companies to nurse themselves back to financial health. In the interim, managers and employees would keep their jobs, companies would be saved, and the economy would benefit. But the law no longer required that a company be insolvent before it could file for reorganization. Therefore, it gave management considerable leeway in determining the circumstances and timing of a bankruptcy filing. While Congress didn't intend for the new law to turn the Chapter 11 decision into a strategic option, that is essentially what it did. The discretionary nature of the act allowed organizations, almost at will, to escape from most any undesirable financial obligations. And some companies did just that.

Texaco, for instance, was found to have interfered in Pennzoil's attempt to buy Getty Oil. The courts gave Pennzoil a $10.5 billion judgment against Texaco. Texaco's management responded by filing for bankruptcy even though the company was enormously profitable. The strategy allowed Texaco to cut its obligation to Pennzoil down to $3 billion.

Continental Airlines' management used bankruptcy as a means to break the company's union agreements and other contractual obligations. In and out of bankruptcy several times in the past decade, Continental has been able to continue to operate and aggressively compete for airline customers. Many of Continental's passengers are completely unaware that they're flying on a "bankrupt" airline.

Southland Corp., which owns the 7–11 convenience-store chain, "prepackaged" its bankruptcy. It negotiated a deal with its creditors *before* filing its bankruptcy petition. The result: Creditors took a reduced payment and Southland reemerged out of bankruptcy in just four months.

Is it wrong for managers to use bankruptcy as a strategy? It does allow the company to continue to operate and thus save employees' jobs. It can, in the longer term, even create enhanced value for stockholders. But it can place an undue hardship on creditors and other claimants. Creditors may have to settle claims for just a few cents on the dollar. Landlords may be left with broken leases, and unions may be left with unenforceable labor agreements. And innocent customers who endured pain, suffering, or even death as a result of a company's negligence may be unable to achieve anything near an equitable financial settlement. When bankruptcy is used to evade responsibility and liability, is management acting unethically? What do *you* think?

too, is a motivated group of middle- and lower-level managers to carry out senior management's specific plans. Chapters 16 and 17 will discuss ways to motivate people and offer suggestions for improving leadership effectiveness.

Management might need to recruit, select, train, discipline, transfer, promote, and possibly even lay off employees to achieve the organization's strategic objectives. In Chapter 12, we'll show that if new strategies are to succeed, they often will require hiring new people with different skills, transferring some current employees to new positions, and laying off some employees.

Step 9: Evaluating Results

The final step in the strategic management process is evaluating results. How effective have our strategies been? What adjustments, if any, are necessary?

In Chapter 18, we'll review the control process. The concepts and techniques that we introduce in that chapter can be used to assess the results of strategies and to correct significant deviations.

Corporate-Level Strategic Frameworks

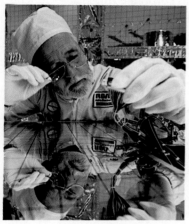

General Electric's new corporate-level strategy focuses solely on technology, service, and core manufacturing. Any of GE's 100 or more businesses that don't fit into one of these three categories are being sold off. This new strategy has resulted in the elimination of more than 100,000 jobs at GE including the sale of RCA.

stability strategy

A corporate-level strategy characterized by an absence of significant change.

growth strategy

A corporate-level strategy that seeks to increase the level of the organization's operations. This typically includes increasing revenues, employees, and/or market share.

We defined corporate-level strategy as asking the question: In what set of businesses should we be? Two popular approaches for answering this question are the grand strategies framework and the corporate portfolio matrix.

Grand Strategies

The WD-40 Co., Wal-Mart, and General Dynamics are successful, profitable companies. However, in recent years, each seems to be going in a different direction. WD-40's management seems content essentially to maintain the status quo. Wal-Mart is rapidly expanding its operations and developing new businesses. Meanwhile, General Dynamics is cutting back and selling off some of its businesses. These different directions can be explained in terms of grand or all-encompassing strategies.[11]

Stability A **stability strategy** is characterized by an absence of significant change. Examples of this strategy include continuing to serve the same clients by offering the same product or service, maintaining market share, and sustaining the organization's past return-on-investment record.

When should management pursue stability? When it views the organization's performance as satisfactory and the environment appears stable and unchanging.

It's not easy to identify organizations that are pursuing a stability strategy, if for no other reason than that few top executives are willing to admit it. In North America, growth tends to have universal appeal, and retrenchment is often accepted as a necessary evil. Moreover, the active pursuit of stability can result in management's being considered complacent or even smug.

We mentioned the WD-40 Co. as an example of a firm using this strategy. The company's highly profitable single product, a petroleum-based lubricant, has had its own unique niche and little competition since the 1950s, so management has little interest in changing the status quo.[12] Management seems happy to keep its good thing going.

Growth The pursuit of growth traditionally has had a magical appeal for North Americans. Supposedly bigger is better, and biggest is best. In our terms, a **growth strategy** means increasing the level of the organization's operations. This includes such popular measures as more revenues, more employees, and more of the market share. Growth can be achieved through direct expansion, a merger with similar firms, or diversification.

Such firms as Wal-Mart and McDonald's have pursued a growth strategy by way of direct expansion. When Chemical Bank absorbed Manufacturers Hanover Trust, it

WD-40 is found in 75 percent of U.S. homes and encounters little competition. The company only has seventy employees, but it recently earned an impressive $15.8 million on sales of $81.7 million.

retrenchment strategy
A corporate-level strategy that seeks to reduce the size or diversity of an organization's operations.

combination strategy
A corporate-level strategy that pursues two or more of the following strategies—stability, growth, or retrenchment—simultaneously.

BCG matrix
Strategy tool to guide resource allocation decisions based on market share and growth of SBUs.

cash cows
Products that demonstrate low growth but have a high market share.

stars
Products that demonstrate high growth and high market share.

question marks
Products that demonstrate high growth but low market share.

dogs
Products that demonstrate low growth and low market share.

cumulative learning curve
Assumes that when a business increases the amount of product manufactured, the per-unit cost of the product will decrease.

chose the merger route to growth. When General Cinema bought Harcourt Brace Jovanovich publishers, it was using diversification to achieve growth.

Retrenchment   Until the 1980s, *retrenchment* was a dirty word in North American management circles. No one wanted to admit that they were pursuing a **retrenchment strategy**—reducing the size or diversity of their operations. However, in the last decade, managing decline has become one of the most actively investigated issues in the field of management.[13] The reasons for this are numerous. Aggressive foreign competition, deregulation, mergers and acquisitions, and major technological breakthroughs are some of the more obvious. For instance, within months after Grand Metropolitan International bought Pillsbury, they laid off several thousand employees in Pillsbury's Minneapolis headquarters. Most of these jobs could be absorbed by Grand Met's staff.

There is no shortage of firms that have recently pursued a retrenchment strategy. A partial list would include some of the biggest names in corporate America—General Dynamics, Mobil Oil, Eastman Kodak, Chase Manhattan Bank, and Union Carbide. Recent changes in Eastern Europe and reductions in world tensions have led American military defense organizations, like the U.S. Army and Air Force, as well as major defense contractors such as Lockheed and Northrop, to pursue retrenchment strategies.

Combination   A **combination strategy** is the simultaneous pursuit of two or more of the previous strategies. For example, one business in the company may be pursuing growth while another in the same company is contracting. In the spring of 1992, for instance, General Motors was rapidly expanding its Electronic Data Systems unit. But it was cutting back heavily in its U.S. automobile manufacturing operations.

Corporate Portfolio Matrix

One of the most popular approaches to corporate-level strategy has been the corporate portfolio matrix.[14] Developed by the Boston Consulting Group in the early 1970s, this approach introduced the idea that each of an organization's SBUs could be plotted on a two-by-two matrix to identify which SBUs offer high potential and which are a drain on the organization's resources.[15] Their **BCG matrix** is shown in Figure 8–4. The horizontal axis represents market share, and the vertical axis indicates anticipated market growth. For definitional purposes, high market share means that a business is the leader in its industry; high market growth is defined as at least 10 percent annual growth in sales (after adjusting for inflation). The matrix identifies four business groups:

Cash cows (low growth, high market share). Products in this category generate large amounts of cash, but their prospects for future growth are limited.

Stars (high growth, high market share). These products are in a fast-growing market and hold a dominant share of that market but might or might not produce a positive cash flow, depending on the need for investment in new plant and equipment or product development.

Question marks (high growth, low market share). These are speculative products that entail high risks. They may be profitable but they hold a small percent of market share.

Dogs (low growth, low market share). This residual category doesn't produce much cash, nor does it require much. These products hold no promise for improved performance.

It is important to understand that the BCG matrix assumes the existence of a **cumulative learning curve**. This is the assumption that if a company is producing a

FIGURE 8-4
The BCG Matrix

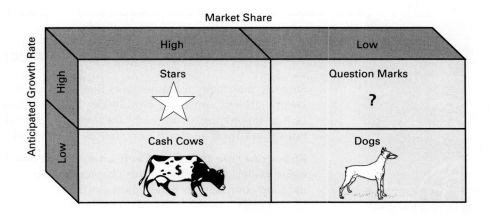

product and managing its production process properly, every significant increase in the cumulative amount of product manufactured will bring a predictable decrease in the per-unit cost of the product. Specifically, the Boston Consulting Group argues that doubling volume typically leads to a 20 to 30 percent reduction in unit cost. The obvious conclusion is therefore that businesses that hold the largest market share will have the lowest costs.

Now let's turn specifically to the implications of the BCG matrix for strategy. What strategy should management pursue with each group?

BCG's research finds that organizations that sacrifice short-run profits to gain market share yield the highest long-run profits. So management should "milk" the cows for as much as they can, limit any new investment in cows to the minimal maintenance level, and use the large amounts of cash the cows generate to invest in stars. Heavy investment in the stars pays high dividends. The stars, of course, will eventually develop into cash cows as their markets mature and growth declines. The hardest decision relates to the question marks. Some should be sold off and others turned into stars. But question marks are risky, and management wants to have only a limited number of these speculative ventures. The dogs propose no strategic problems—they should be sold off or liquidated at the earliest opportunity. There is little to recommend their retention or further investment by the company. Money obtained from selling off dogs can be used to buy or finance question marks. For example, the BCG matrix might advise McGraw-Hill management to sell off its trade book business because it's a dog, "milk" a cash cow like its college textbook business, and invest in a star like *Business Week* or a question mark like database information products.

Currently, light bulbs would be a cash cow for GE. Because of cutbacks in worldwide defense spending, GE's aerospace business has become a question mark. Aircraft engines and plastics are businesses that are currently stars at GE. With major network revenues falling and NBC facing a falling market share and minimal growth, GE might consider its television network a dog.

In recent years, the corporate portfolio concept (and the BCG matrix in particular) has lost much of its luster. Why? There are at least four reasons.[16] First, every organization has not found that increased market share leads to lower costs. To successfully proceed down the learning curve, management must tightly control costs. Unfortunately, not all managements have been able to do this. Second, the portfolio concept assumes that an organization's businesses can be divided into a reasonable number of independent units. For large, complex organizations, this has been a lot easier in theory than in practice. Third, contrary to predictions, many so-called dogs have shown consistently higher levels of profitability than their growing competitors with dominant market shares. Finally, given the rate at which the economy has been growing in recent years and the fact that a market can have only one leader, well over half of all businesses fall by definition into the dog category. Following the corporate portfolio concept, most organizations' businesses are cash cows and dogs, and there are few stars and question marks in which to invest.

In spite of these problems, the corporate portfolio matrix is a useful concept. It provides a framework for understanding disparate businesses and establishes priori-

The Limits to Strategic Management Frameworks

Strategic management frameworks that are popular in North America and Western Europe are not applicable worldwide. This was made blatantly clear in an analysis of four underlying assumptions for these strategic models and why these assumptions don't apply in Brazil or countries with similar environments.[17]

Firms operate within a freely competitive market   The strategic management models we discuss in this chapter assume competition. This is not the case in many countries. In Brazil, most prices are determined either by government decree or by industry councils composed of representatives of industry and government. In this climate, profit margins are not a result of competition between firms, but of negotiation with the government. Also restricting competition is the higher industry concentration. While in the United States there might be ten major players in the pharmaceutical industry, in Brazil there may only be two or three firms.

Firms operate under conditions of some predictability   Business strategies in Western industrialized nations assume that the environment is sufficiently predictable for making medium- and long-range plans that are reliable enough to serve as guides for action over time. However, this isn't true in Brazil. During a recent four-year period, *monthly* inflation rates in Brazil varied from −2 percent to +30 percent. Best forecasts miss the mark by 50 percent or more. During the last half of the 1980s, Brazil suffered through three general strikes that brought the entire country to a halt, two postal strikes (one lasting over a month), and several transportation strikes. Almost every year, the government introduces a new economic plan that totally revamps exchange rates, wages, prices, tax rates, interest rates, and the like. In this turbulent environment, accurate predictions are limited to the next few hours rather than months or years.

Innovation can be a competitive advantage   Companies headquartered in North America, such as 3M, Federal Express, and Microsoft, gain their competitive advantages through successful innovation. A number of strategic frameworks rely on differentiation through innovation as a major strategic option. But innovation provides no competitive advantage in Brazil. Why? The Brazilian culture does not encourage innovation, so any new advances need to come from more developed countries. However, since the state regulates every step in the transfer of technology process, innovative technologies are either forbidden outright or languish awaiting governmental approval. Innovations come to Brazil only after they have been widely accepted in more industrialized countries.

Market share is a critical factor in assessing performance   Finally, several of the strategic frameworks are built on high market share. This emphasis is probably well placed in North America and Europe, where studies repeatedly demonstrate a close relationship between high market share and high profits. In Brazil, however, market share is rarely open to manipulation by the firm. Lack of national integration and the preponderance of regional markets for many products lessen opportunities to enjoy economies of the scale typically associated with high market share.

This analysis should caution us against enthusiastically adopting popular strategic management models in many South American countries, African nations, or other countries where the models' assumptions don't apply.

ties for making strategic resource allocation decisions. However, it has clear limitations as a device for guiding management in setting corporate-level strategy.

Stop

Business-Level Strategic Frameworks

Now we move to the business level. The most popular frameworks to guide SBU managers are the adaptive strategy and competitive strategy approaches.

Adaptive Strategies

The adaptive strategy framework was developed from the study of business strategies by Raymond Miles and Charles Snow.[18] First, Miles and Snow identified four strategic types: defenders, prospectors, analyzers, and reactors. Then they demonstrated that success can be achieved with any of the first three strategies if there is a good fit between the strategy and the business unit's environment, internal structure, and managerial processes. However, Miles and Snow found that the reactor strategy often led to failure (see Table 8–1). Let's take a look at each of these four strategic types and explore how organizations have used them to their advantage.

Defenders   McDonald's has followed a defender strategy in the fast-food business. **Defenders** seek stability by producing only a limited set of products directed at a narrow segment of the total potential market. Within this limited niche, defenders strive aggressively to prevent competitors from entering their "turf." This strategy tends to be achieved through standard economic actions such as competitive pricing or creation of high-quality products or services. Defenders tend to ignore developments and trends outside their narrow niche, choosing instead to grow through market penetration and some limited product development. Over time, true defenders are able to carve out and maintain small niches within their industries that are difficult for competitors to penetrate.

Prospectors   Federal Express has followed a prospector strategy with its overnight parcel business. In direct contrast to defenders, **prospectors** seek innovation. Their strength is finding and exploiting new product and market opportunities. Prospectors depend on developing and maintaining the capacity to survey a wide range of environmental conditions, trends, and events. As a result, flexibility is critical to the success of prospectors.

Analyzers   Kellogg follows an analyzer strategy. It tries to minimize risk and maximize the opportunity for profit. **Analyzers** live by imitation. They copy the

defender
A business-level strategy that seeks stability by producing only a limited set of products directed at a narrow segment of the total potential market.

prospector
A business-level strategy that seeks innovation by finding and exploiting new product and market opportunities.

analyzer
A business-level strategy that seeks to minimize risk by following competitors' innovations but only after they have proven successful.

TABLE 8–1   Miles and Snow's Adaptive Strategies

Strategy Types	Goal(s)	Appropriate Environment	Appropriate Structure and Processes
Defenders	Stability and efficiency	Stable	Tight control, efficient operations, low overhead
Prospectors	Flexibility	Dynamic	Loose structure, innovative
Analyzers	Stability and flexibility	Moderate change	Tight control and flexibility, efficient operations, innovative
Reactors	Not clear	Any condition	Not clear

successful ideas of prospectors. Kellogg essentially follows its smaller and more innovative competitors with superior products, but only after the competitors have demonstrated that the market is there.

Analyzers must have the ability to respond to the lead of key prospectors, yet at the same time maintain operating efficiency in their stable product and market areas. Prospectors must have high profit margins to justify the risks that they take and to compensate for their productive inefficiencies. Analyzers tend to have smaller profit margins than do prospectors, but analyzers are more efficient.

reactor
A business-level strategy that characterizes inconsistent and unstable decision patterns.

Reactors   **Reactors** represent a residual strategy. The label is meant to describe the inconsistent and unstable patterns that arise when one of the other three strategies is pursued improperly. In general, reactors respond inappropriately, perform poorly, and are reluctant to commit themselves aggressively to a specific strategy for the future. In recent years, Wang Laboratories' management reluctantly found itself pursuing a reactor strategy. After its original strategy—manufacturing dedicated word processing and main-frame data processing equipment—faltered as personal computers skyrocketed in popularity, Wang's management struggled to find a new focus. In 1991 alone, Wang posted a loss of over $385 million.

Competitive Strategies

The most important recent ideas in strategic planning have come from the work of Michael Porter at Harvard's Graduate School of Business.[19] His competitive strategies framework demonstrates that managers can choose from among three generic strategies. Success depends on selecting the right strategy—one that fits the competitive posture of the organization and the industry of which it is a part. Porter's major contribution has been to detail carefully how management can create and sustain a competitive advantage that will achieve profitability above the industry average.

Industry Analysis   Porter begins by acknowledging that some industries are inherently more profitable than others. Pharmaceuticals, for instance, is an industry in which all competitors can achieve extremely high markups. However, this doesn't mean that a company can't make a lot of money in a "lean" industry. The key is gaining a competitive advantage. Consistent with this logic, we should expect that

Cooper Tire & Rubber is proof that you can make money in an industry even if you're a small player. It is only the ninth largest tire maker, but consistently generates the highest return to investors of all tire makers It does not sell through retail chains. Half of its production is private-label merchandise; the other half goes to independent dealers. Cooper refuses to compete for low-profit original-equipment sales to automakers. Instead, it concentrates on the replacement market, which is three times larger and growing faster.

There are substantial barriers to entry into the airline industry, an industry in which seven carriers control 90 percent of U.S. air traffic. Delta Airlines, for instance, flies 84 percent of the passengers to and from Atlanta's Hartsfield airport. This allows Delta to charge higher prices than if there were numerous competitors in the Atlanta market.

firms can lose money in so-called glamour industries like personal computers and cable television and make bundles in mundane industries like manufacturing fire trucks and selling junk auto parts. Porter would argue that success can be achieved in most industries—the trick is to find the right strategy.

In any industry, five competitive forces dictate the rules of competition:

1. *Barriers to entry:* Factors such as economies of scale, brand identity, and capital requirements determine how easy or hard it is for new competitors to enter an industry.

2. *Threats of substitutes:* Factors such as switching costs and buyer loyalty determine the degree to which customers are likely to switch their business to a competitor.

3. *Bargaining power of buyers:* Factors such as a buyer's volume, buyer information, and the availability of substitute products determine the amount of influence that buyers will have in an industry.

4. *Bargaining power of suppliers:* Factors such as the degree of supplier concentration and the availability of substitute inputs determine the power that suppliers will have over firms in the industry.

5. *Rivalry among existing competitors:* Factors such as industry growth and product differences determine how intense rivalry will be among firms in the industry.

These five forces, in aggregate (see Figure 8–5), determine industry profitability because they directly influence the prices that a firm can charge, its cost structure, and its investment requirements. Management should assess its industry's attractiveness by evaluating it in terms of these five factors. According to this framework, in 1993 the aluminum-window manufacturing business tended to be unattractive, while the

FIGURE 8–5
Forces in the Industry Analysis

Based on Michael E. Porter, *Competitive Strategy: Techniques for Analyzing Industries and Competitors* (New York: Free Press, 1980).

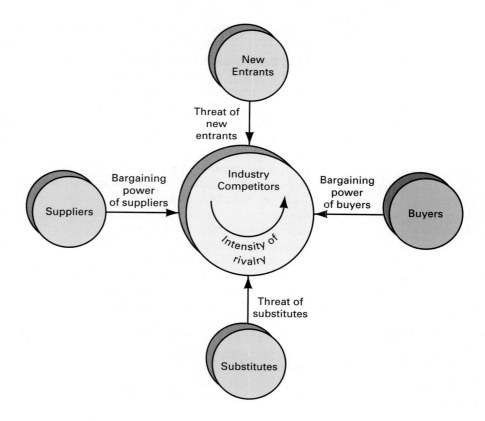

pharmaceuticals industry looked enormously attractive. Of course, industry dynamics are always changing. An industry that is favorable one day can become unfavorable the next. Managers need to reevaluate the status of their industry regularly.

Selecting a Competitive Advantage According to Porter, no firm can successfully perform at an above-average level by trying to be all things to all people. He proposes that management must select a strategy that will give its organization a competitive advantage. Management can choose from among three strategies: cost-leadership, differentiation, and focus. Which one management chooses depends on the organization's strengths and its competitor's weaknesses. Management should avoid a position in which it has to slug it out with everybody in the industry. Rather, the organization should put its strength where the competition isn't.

When an organization sets out to be the low-cost producer in its industry, it is following a **cost-leadership strategy.** Success with this strategy requires that the organization be *the* cost leader and not merely one of the contenders for that position. Additionally, the product or service being offered must be perceived as comparable to that offered by rivals, or at least acceptable to buyers.

How does a firm gain such a cost advantage? Typical means include efficiency of operations, economies of scale, technological innovation, low-cost labor, or preferential access to raw materials. Examples of firms that have used this strategy include Wal-Mart, Gallo wines, and Southwest Airlines.

The firm that seeks to be unique in its industry in ways that are widely valued by buyers is following a **differentiation strategy.** It might emphasize high quality, extraordinary service, innovative design, technological capability, or an unusually positive brand image. The key is that the attribute chosen must be different from those offered by rivals and significant enough to justify a price premium that exceeds the cost of differentiating.

There is no shortage of firms that have found at least one attribute that allows them to differentiate themselves from competitors. Intel (technology), Maytag (reliability), Mary Kay cosmetics (distribution), and L.L. Bean (service) are a few.

The first two strategies sought a competitive advantage in a broad range of industry segments. The **focus strategy** aims at a cost advantage (cost focus) or differentiation advantage (differentiation focus) in a narrow segment. That is, management will select a segment or group of segments in an industry (such as product variety, type of end buyer, distribution channel, or geographic location of buyers) and tailor the strategy to serve them to the exclusion of others. The goal is to exploit a narrow segment of a market. Of course, whether a focus strategy is feasible or not depends on the size of a segment and whether it can support the additional cost of focusing. Stouffer's used a cost-focus strategy in its Lean Cuisine line to reach calorie-conscious consumers seeking both high-quality products and convenience. Similarly, colleges that appeal to working students by offering only night classes hope to gain a competitive advantage over their rivals by following a differentiation-focus strategy. Recent research suggests that the focus strategy may be the most potent for small business firms.[20] This is because they typically don't have the economies of scale or internal resources to successfully pursue one of the other two strategies.

Porter uses the term **stuck in the middle** to describe organizations that are unable to gain a competitive advantage by one of these strategies. Such organizations find it very difficult to achieve long-term success. When they do, it is usually a result of competing in a highly favorable industry or having all their rivals similarly stuck in the middle.

Porter notes that successful organizations frequently get into trouble by reaching beyond their competitive advantage and ending up stuck in the middle. Laker Airways provides such a case. It began in 1977 by offering no-frills flights between

cost-leadership strategy
The strategy an organization follows when it wants to be the lowest-cost producer in its industry.

differentiation strategy
The strategy a firm follows when it wants to be unique in its industry along dimensions widely valued by buyers.

focus strategy
The strategy a company follows when it pursues a cost or differentiation advantage in a narrow industry segment.

stuck in the middle
Descriptive of organizations that cannot compete through cost-leadership, differentiation, or focus strategies.

London and New York at rock-bottom prices. This cost-leadership strategy resulted in a resounding success. In 1979, however, the firm began to add new routes and offer upscale services. This blurred the public's image of Laker, allowed the competition to make significant inroads, and led to Laker's declaration of bankruptcy in 1982.

Sustaining a Competitive Advantage   Long-term success with any one of the three strategies requires that the advantage be sustainable. That is, it must resist erosion by the actions of competitors or by evolutionary changes in the industry. This is no simple task. Technology changes, as do the tastes of customers. Most important, some advantages can be imitated by competitors. Management needs to create barriers that make imitation difficult or that reduce competitive opportunities. The use of patents and copyrights reduces opportunities for imitation. When there are strong economies of scale, reducing price to gain volume is a useful tactic. Tying up suppliers with exclusive contracts limits their ability to supply rivals. Encouraging government policies that impose import tariffs can limit foreign competition. Yet whatever actions it takes to sustain a competitive advantage, management cannot become complacent. Sustaining a competitive advantage requires constant action by management in order to keep one step ahead of the competition.

TQM as a Strategic Weapon

An increasing number of organizations are applying Total Quality Management as a way to build a competitive advantage. As we first discussed in Chapter 2, TQM focuses on quality and continuous improvement. To the degree that an organization can satisfy a customer's need for quality, it can differentiate itself from the competition and attract and hold a loyal customer base. Moreover, constant improvement in the quality and reliability of an organization's products or services can result in a competitive advantage others can't steal.[21] Product innovations, for example, offer little opportunity for sustained competitive advantage. Why? Because usually they can be quickly copied by rivals. But incremental improvement, which is an essential element of TQM, is something that becomes an integrated part of an organization's operations and can develop into a considerable cumulative advantage. To illustrate how TQM can be used as a strategic tool, let's look at General Motors' Buick City plant and the Polymer Products Division at DuPont.

When Herman Maass took over as manager of General Motors' Buick City plant in Flint, Michigan, in 1986, he thought his job was hopeless.[22] Buick's Le Sabre was almost dead last in every quality survey. Maass had to do something—and fast. He introduced a team-based manufacturing process that allowed workers to control production and to take responsibility for paying attention to every detail. Maass argued that the secret to improving quality at Buick City would be in giving employees—particularly hourly workers—the encouragement to share ideas and to act on those suggestions. The results Maass has achieved have been startling. Buick is now consistently ranked as the No. 1 domestic nameplate in J.D. Power's annual customer-satisfaction survey, and sales of cars produced at Buick City have held up remarkably well in a declining auto market.

When the Polymer Products Division at DuPont conducted a cost of quality survey in the mid-1980s, it found that internal and external failure costs amounted to approximately $400 million, which was about twice the earnings of the $3.5 billion business. In response, the division launched a strategic TQM effort.[23] It encouraged an outward focus on markets and customers; developed an organizational culture based on openness and trust; sought to satisfy the needs of customers, suppliers, employees, and stockholders; and established the practice of continuous improvement on a project-by-project basis. The program has made the division far more responsive to its various constituencies. Moreover, 90 percent of the division's products now meet quality standards versus 75 percent before the TQM program. And each year, management is finding the cost of quality dropping by about 10 percent, which equates to an annual savings of 3 percent of sales revenue.

Using TQM for competitive advantage does not apply only to manufacturing organizations. Oregon State University, for instance, introduced TQM in order to be more responsive to customers (students, faculty members, and groups that use university services) in an environment of budget cuts and increased competition among universities for top students. In only one year, employee teams came up with suggestions that reduced paperwork, increased efficiency, improved morale, and resulted in simplified procedures in many areas of the university. The ultimate goal, says OSU's president, is "a university free of complaints."[24]

Entrepreneurship: A Special Case of Strategic Planning

You've heard the story dozens of times. With only an idea, a few hundred dollars, and use of the family garage, someone starts what eventually becomes a multimillion-dollar corporation. In the case of Dell Computer, the only deviation is that Michael Dell began his business in his dorm room at the University of Texas.[25]

Michael Dell had been fascinated by computers since junior high. As an eighteen-year-old freshman at UT in 1983, he started selling disk drives and other components that he bought from dealers who had surplus inventory. His first customers were friends and fellow students at the university. Then Dell found that he could buy

Michael Dell is a successful entrepreneur. His company, Dell Computer, began in a college dorm room. In only ten years, company sales reached nearly $2 billion.

stripped-down versions of IBM PCs and add components that would significantly increase their power. By early 1984, Dell was selling $50,000 to $60,000 worth of customized computers and computer parts each month. That summer, he decided to quit school and devote his full attention to his computer business. He specialized in building complete PC systems for doctors, lawyers, and small businesses. In his first month out as a full-time business, he sold $180,000 worth of equipment. Each month thereafter, sales grew exponentially. After nine months, he had sales of $6 million and thirty-nine employees working for him.

What differentiates Dell Computer Corp. from its competitors? High-quality hardware, comprehensive service and technical support, and low prices. Dell sells to customers through the mail and other direct-marketing techniques, bypassing dealers. Also, Dell can custom design a personal computer system precisely to a customer's needs, build it, and ship it within three days. In 1992, Dell's 800 number was handling over 8,000 sales and service phone calls a day. Annual sales were close to $2 billion in fiscal 1992. And Michael Dell is a wealthy man, holding more than $150 million worth of stock in his company.

Strategic planning carries a "big business" bias. It implies a formalization and structure that fits well with large, established organizations that have abundant resources. But the primary interest of many students is not in managing large and established organizations. Like Michael Dell, Dave Thomas of Wendy's, or Fred Smith of Federal Express, they're excited about the idea of starting their own businesses from scratch. In this section, we'll demonstrate that many strategic planning concepts can be applied directly to those who wish to pursue the entrepreneurial route in management, but with a different emphasis.

What is Entrepreneurship?

entrepreneurship
A process by which individuals pursue opportunities, fulfilling needs and wants through innovation, without regard to the resources they currently control.

There is no shortage of definitions of entrepreneurship.[26] Some, for example, apply it to the creation of any new business. Others focus on intentions, claiming that entrepreneurs seek to create wealth, which is different from starting businesses merely as a means of income substitution (that is, working for yourself rather than working for someone else). When most people describe entrepreneurs, they use adjectives such as bold, innovative, venturesome, and risk-taking. They also tend to associate entrepreneurs with small businesses. We'll define **entrepreneurship** as a process by which individuals pursue opportunities, fulfilling needs and wants through innovation, without regard to the resources they currently control.[27]

It's important not to confuse managing a small business with entrepreneurship. Why? Because not all small-business managers are entrepreneurs.[28] Many don't innovate. A great many managers of small businesses are merely scaled-down versions of the conservative, conforming bureaucrats who staff many large corporations and public agencies.

Can entrepreneurs exist in large, established organizations? The answer to that question depends on one's definition of entrepreneur. The noted management guru, Peter Drucker, for instance, argues that they can.[29] He describes an entrepreneurial manager as someone who is confident of his or her ability, who seizes opportunities for innovation, and who not only expects surprises but capitalizes on them. He contrasts that with the trustee type of manager who feels threatened by change, is bothered by uncertainty, prefers predictability, and is inclined to maintain the status quo.

intrapreneurship
Creating the entrepreneurial spirit in a large organization.

Drucker's use of the term entrepreneurial, however, is misleading. By almost any definition of good management, his entrepreneurial type would be preferred over the trustee type. Moreover, the term **intrapreneurship** is now widely used to describe the effort to create the entrepreneurial spirit in a large organization.[30] Yet intrapreneurship can never capture the autonomy and riskiness inherent in true entrepre-

Anita Roddick, founder and CEO of the Body Shop International retail store chain, is another successful entrepreneur. She has capitalized on the idea of using social responsibility to sell skin care and bath products. For instance, her stores' products are made only from all-natural ingredients and nothing is tested on animals. Her chain of more than 700 stores has annual sales in excess of $400 million.

neurship. This is because intrapreneurship takes place within a larger organization; all financial risks are carried by the parent company; rules, policies, and other constraints are imposed by the parent; intrapreneurs have bosses or superiors to report to; and the payoff for success is not financial independence but rather career advancement.[31]

Characteristics of Entrepreneurs

One of the most researched topics in entrepreneurship has been the search to determine what, if any, psychological characteristics entrepreneurs have in common. A number of these characteristics have been found. These include hard work, self-confidence, optimism, determination, and a high energy level.[32] But three factors regularly sit on the top of most lists that profile the entrepreneurial personality. Entrepreneurs have a high need for achievement, believe strongly that they can control their own destinies, and take only moderate risks.[33]

The research allows us to draw a general description of entrepreneurs. They tend to be independent types who prefer to be personally responsible for solving problems, for setting goals, and for reaching these goals by their own efforts. They value independence and particularly don't like being controlled by others. While they're not afraid of taking chances, they're not wild risk takers. They prefer to take calculated risks where they feel that they can control the outcome.

The evidence on entrepreneurial personalities leads us to two obvious conclusions. First, people with this personality makeup are not likely to be contented, productive employees in the typical large corporation or government agency. The rules, regulations, and controls that these bureaucracies impose on their members frustrate entrepreneurs. Second, the challenges and conditions inherent in starting one's own business mesh well with the entrepreneurial personality. Starting a new venture, which they control, appeals to their willingness to take risks and determine their own destinies. But because entrepreneurs believe that their future is fully in their own hands, the risk they perceive as moderate is often seen as high by non-entrepreneurs.

Impetus for Entrepreneurship

What forces contribute to stimulating a person to become an entrepreneur? Let's look at some research findings.[34]

MANAGERS
WHO MADE A
DIFFERENCE

H. Wayne Huizenga at Blockbuster Entertainment Corp.

H. Wayne Huizenga made his first fortune leading Waste Management Inc. to the position of America's biggest trash hauler. When, at the age of 46, he left Waste Management, he began looking into the video business. What he saw was approximately 20,000 small video shops. What he also saw was an opportunity. Huizenga wanted to capitalize on the growing popularity of videos by creating a chain of video "superstores"—big, well-lighted outlets with at least twice the number of titles as most stores. His competitive advantage would be his knowledge of the rental business that he learned at Waste Management.[35] In 1987, this entrepreneur bought a fledgling Dallas chain of twenty video stores called Blockbuster as his base.

Within a year, Huizenga had expanded Blockbuster to 130 stores. Three years later, he had 1200 outlets and was adding a new one every day. Huizenga has turned his Blockbuster Entertainment into the dominant player in an industry with revenues of $10 billion a year, almost twice that of Hollywood's box office receipts. Today his company's sales exceed $1 billion a year and Wayne Huizenga is one of the richest men in America.

Bill Mow (left), Bugle Boy's founder and owner seen here with Vincent Nesi, Bugle Boy's president, is a prime example of how entrepreneurship fosters more entrepreneurship. In 1969, Mow founded Macrodata, a computer-based company that developed techniques for testing semiconductors. After being forced out in 1976, he began looking for a new business. The opportunity Mow saw wasn't in computers, though; it was in clothing. Capitalizing on his contacts with Asian suppliers and a need by American apparel wholesalers for low-cost, quality casual attire, but with no previous experience in garments, Mow created Bugle Boy, now a $500 million clothing company.

Entrepreneurship tends to flourish in supportive environments. American culture, for instance, places a high value on being your own boss and achieving personal success. In contrast, in other countries, including Ireland and Norway, failure is often seen as a disgrace. This helps to explain the wide popularity of entrepreneurial activities in the United States. Additionally, some areas of a country often become pockets of entrepreneurial subcultures. In the United States, the Route 128 area surrounding Boston, Silicon Valley and northern San Diego county in California, and the Research Triangle area in North Carolina are examples of communities that encourage and support entrepreneurs.

Supportive parents seem to play an important part in influencing the entrepreneurial tendencies of their offspring. Entrepreneurs typically have parents who encouraged them to achieve, be independent, and take responsibility for their actions.

Entrepreneurs usually have role models whom they have attempted to emulate. When you've seen someone else do something innovative and succeed, it makes innovation and success seem more realistically achievable. Not surprisingly, given this evidence, entrepreneurs tend to have self-employed or entrepreneurial fathers.

A final variable related to entrepreneurial activity is previous entrepreneurship. Past behavior is the best predictor of future behavior. Since it's generally easier to start a second, third, or fourth venture than it is to start the first one, beginning an entrepreneurial business tends to be a reoccurring activity for certain individuals.

Comparing Entrepreneurs and Traditional Managers

Table 8–2 summarizes some key differences between entrepreneurs and traditional bureaucratic managers. While the latter tend to be more custodial, entrepreneurs actively seek change by exploiting opportunities. When searching for these opportunities, entrepreneurs often put their personal financial security at risk. The hier-

TABLE 8-2   Comparing Entrepreneurs and Traditional Managers

	Traditional Managers	Entrepreneurs
Primary motivation	Promotion and other traditional corporate rewards such as office, staff, and power	Independence, opportunity to create, financial gain
Time orientation	Achievement of short-term goals	Achievement of five- to ten-year growth of business
Activity	Delegation and supervision	Direct involvement
Risk propensity	Low	Moderate
View toward failures and mistakes	Avoidance	Acceptance

Source: Based on Robert D. Hisrich, "Entrepreneurship/Intrapreneurship," *American Psychologist*, February 1990, p. 218.

archy in large organizations typically insulates traditional managers from these financial wagers and rewards them for minimizing risks and avoiding failures.

Strategy and the Entrepreneur

Entrepreneurs approach strategy differently than typical bureaucratic managers do. This can be seen in the order in which they address key strategic questions (see Table 8–3).

The entrepreneur's strategic emphasis is driven by perception of opportunity rather than by availability of resources.[36] The entrepreneur's inclination is to monitor the environment closely in search of opportunities. The resources at his or her disposal take a back seat to identifying an idea that can be capitalized upon.

Once an opportunity is spotted, the entrepreneur begins to look for ways to take advantage of it. Because of his or her personality makeup, the entrepreneur is confident that the opportunity can be exploited. Moreover, the entrepreneur is not afraid to risk financial security, career opportunities, family relations, or psychic well-being to get the new venture off the ground. Entrepreneurs tend to ignore the hard statistics against success: New businesses with fewer than ten employees have little more than a 75 percent chance of surviving a year and only about one chance in three

TABLE 8-3   The Order of Strategic Questions

Typical Bureaucratic Manager	Typical Entrepreneur
What resources do I control?	Where is the opportunity?
What structure determines our organization's relationship to its market?	How do I capitalize on it?
How can I minimize the impact of others on my ability to perform?	What resources do I need?
What opportunity is appropriate?	How do I gain control over them?
	What structure is best?

Source: Reprinted by permission of *Harvard Business Review*. An excerpt from "The Heart of Entrepreneurship" by Howard H. Stevenson and David E. Gumpert, March–April 1985, pp. 86–87. Copyright © 1985 by the President and Fellows of Harvard College; all rights reserved.

of lasting four years or more.[37] Nevertheless, the entrepreneur who sees an opportunity has the confidence and determination to believe that he or she will be on the winning side of those statistics.

Only after the entrepreneur has identified an opportunity and a way to exploit it does he or she begin to feel concerned about resources. But the entrepreneur's priorities are first to find out what resources are needed and then determine how they can be obtained. This is in contrast to typical bureaucratic managers who focus on the resources that are at their disposal. Entrepreneurs are often able to make imaginative and highly efficient use of very limited resources. Further, as entrepreneurship has grown in popularity, the availability of financial resources to support new ventures has increased. The rise of venture capital firms makes it more true than ever that if a new idea is promising enough, the capital to get it underway can be found.

Finally, when the resource obstacles have been overcome, the entrepreneur will put together the organizational structure, people, marketing plan, and other components necessary to implement the overall strategy.

Summary

This summary is organized by the chapter-opening learning objectives found on page 209.

1. In a dynamic and uncertain environment, strategic planning is important because it can provide managers with a systematic and comprehensive means for analyzing the environment, assessing their organization's strengths and weaknesses, and identifying opportunities in which their organization could have a competitive advantage.

2. Corporate-level strategy seeks to determine what set of businesses the organization should be in. Business-level strategy is concerned with how the organization should compete in each of its businesses. Functional-level strategy is concerned with how functional departments can support the business-level strategy.

3. The strategic management process is made up of nine steps: (1) Identifying the organization's current mission, objectives, and strategies; (2) Analyzing the environment; (3) Identifying opportunities and threats in the environment; (4) Analyzing the organization's resources; (5) Identifying the organization's strengths and weaknesses; (6) Reassessing the organization's mission and objectives based on its strengths, weaknesses, opportunities, and threats; (7) Formulating strategies; (8) Implementing its strategies; and (9) Evaluating results.

4. SWOT analysis refers to analyzing the organization's internal strengths and weaknesses as well as external opportunities and threats in order to identify a niche that the organization can exploit.

5. The BCG matrix identifies four business groups: stars, cash cows, question marks, and dogs.

6. At the business level, there are four adaptive strategies. Defenders operate in stable environments and produce a limited set of products for a narrow market segment. Prospectors operate in a dynamic environment, innovate, and seek flexibility. Analyzers minimize risk and maximize profit opportunities by seeking both flexibility and stability at the same time. Reactors are inconsistent and reluctant to commit themselves to any specific situation.

7. Management assesses its organization's competitive advantage by analyzing the forces that dictate the rules of competition within its industry (barriers to entry, substitutes, bargaining power of buyers and suppliers, and rivalry among competitors) and then selecting a strategy (cost-leadership, differentiation, or focus) that can best exploit its competitive posture.

8. Entrepreneurship refers to a process by which individuals pursue opportunities, fulfilling needs and wants through innovation, without regard to the resources they currently control.

9. Entrepreneurs approach strategy by first seeking out opportunities that they can exploit. Bureaucratic managers approach strategy by first determining the availability of their resources.

Review Questions

1. What level of strategies would be relevant to a large firm that produced only a single product?
2. Define an SBU.
3. Compare an organization's *mission* with its *objectives*.
4. What relevance does an organization's culture have to its strategy?
5. Is growth always the best strategy for an organization to pursue? Explain.
6. How should managers allocate resources among the four business groups in the BCG matrix?
7. What are the forces that dictate the rules of competition within an industry?
8. How can TQM provide a competitive advantage?
9. Are all small business managers entrepreneurs? Explain your answer.

Discussion Questions

1. What is McDonald's competitive advantage in its industry?
2. As we have seen in previous chapters, high-, mid-, and low-level managers make different types of decisions. How do you think this hierarchy applies to the three levels of strategic planning?
3. Perform a SWOT analysis on a local business you feel you know well. What, if any, competitive advantage has this business staked out?
4. Contrast the BCG matrix and the grand strategies framework. Which do you think is a more useful tool? Why?
5. More than 200 colleges now offer courses in entrepreneurship. Do you think entrepreneurship can be taught? Explain your answer. How might a major in entrepreneurship differ from a traditional major in management or marketing?

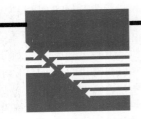

SELF-ASSESSMENT EXERCISE

Are You an Entrepreneur?

Instructions: This quiz is designed to see if you have traits associated with highly successful entrepreneurs. Rate yourself on each of the characteristics using a −2 to +2 scale as described at the top of the next page:

−2   I don't really have this characteristic
−1   I don't have very much of this
 0   Neutral or don't know
+1   I have this characteristic a little bit
+2   This characteristic is very strong in me

Characteristic	**−2**	**−1**	**0**	**+1**	**+2**
Self-confidence	____	____	____	____	____
Energy, diligence	____	____	____	____	____
Ability to take calculated risks	____	____	____	____	____
Creativity	____	____	____	____	____
Flexibility	____	____	____	____	____
Positive response to challenges	____	____	____	____	____
Dynamism, leadership	____	____	____	____	____
Ability to get along with people	____	____	____	____	____
Responsiveness to suggestions	____	____	____	____	____
Responsiveness to criticism	____	____	____	____	____
Knowledge of market	____	____	____	____	____
Perseverance, determination	____	____	____	____	____
Resourcefulness	____	____	____	____	____
Need to achieve	____	____	____	____	____
Initiative	____	____	____	____	____
Independence	____	____	____	____	____
Foresight	____	____	____	____	____
Profit orientation	____	____	____	____	____
Perceptiveness	____	____	____	____	____
Optimism	____	____	____	____	____
Versatility	____	____	____	____	____
Knowledge of product and technology	____	____	____	____	____

Turn to page SK-2 for scoring directions and key.

Source: Robert Marx, Todd Jick, and Peter Frost, *Management Live! The Video Book* (Englewood Cliffs, NJ: Prentice Hall, 1991), p. 291.

FOR YOUR IMMEDIATE ACTION

THE PRINCETON REVIEW

To: Members of the Executive Team
From: John Katzman, President
Subject: Reassessing our Strategy

While we are still riding a huge wave of success, I think we need to evaluate our strategy for the future. As you all know, in only a dozen years, we've become the dominant force in the test preparation business. Each year, we're putting tens of thousands of people through our preparation courses for SAT, GRE, GMAT, LSAT, and MCAT exams. We now blanket the U.S.A. and Canada with offices in 38 cities, and we're opening more offices all the time. Needless to say, we're providing stiff competition for our primary rival, Stanley Kaplan Educational Centers. But I don't want us to become complacent. We need to be concerned with what lies ahead for our business and what, if anything, we should do in terms of changing our strategy.

Of course, we want to maintain our rapid growth, but we've saturated most of the major North American markets. Does it make sense for us to expand overseas? What other areas could we expand into that would take advantage of our knowledge of learning processes, training, test taking, and the college experience?

I'd like each of you to prepare a brief working paper describing your perspective on the dynamics of our industry and providing a brief review of the strengths and weaknesses of the various options you think we might pursue.

This is a fictionalized account of a potentially real problem. It was written for academic purposes only and is not meant to reflect either positively or negatively on actual management practices at The Princeton Review.

CASE APPLICATION

The National: What Went Wrong With Their Strategy?

It had all the markings of a success: Just as *USA Today* became the first nation-wide general-interest newspaper, *The National* would become the first and only daily paper exclusively devoted to sports.

The planning began in November 1988. Emilo Azcarraga, a Mexican billionaire who controls 90 percent of Mexico's television programming, was convinced that there was a need for a daily sports paper. After all, interest in sports had mush-roomed in the 1980s. Attendance records were being broken almost yearly. The airwaves were becoming saturated with sporting events and sports information. And advertisers saw sports as a great vehicle for reaching affluent males between twenty-five and fifty-four.

What was Azcarraga's plan? Management would invest heavily in talent and technology to add as much value as it could to a commodity product—sports information. The product would include local as well as national coverage. Man-agement put together a star-studded cast of writers. Frank Deford, a writer for *Sports Illustrated* for twenty-seven years and a six-time Sportswriter of the Year, became editor-in-chief. He hired prize-winning columnists from *The Los Angeles Times, The Washington Post, The Boston Globe,* and *The New York Daily News* at salaries as high as $300,000 a year. Then they put together a state-of-the-art elec-tronic publishing system. They could beam copy via satellite to the paper's hub in New York, where stories would be edited and pages made up. That information would then be beamed back to print sites around the country.

The paper's first edition hit the streets of New York City, Chicago, and Los Angeles on January 31, 1990. It cost 50 cents and came out six times a week—Sunday through Friday. It had intensive, up-to-date reportage of local heroes in these three markets. It also had columns and cartoons, plus editorial and gossip pages. Each issue was thirty-two to forty-eight pages long, and about one-third of the pages were in color.

Azcarraga committed $100 million to the project. He figured that's how much he'd have to invest before the paper broke even in three to five years out. The plan was to add as many as a dozen bureaus to its initial three by the end of the first year and then expand into the fifteen largest U.S. markets. By the end of the second year, coverage and availability would peak at twenty-five markets, com-prising approximately 85 percent of the national market. However, initially 75 percent of the paper's income would come from single-copy sales, with the rest coming from advertising.

Projections of daily circulation were 200,000 for the three initial markets. By the time the paper reached its fifteen-market goal, circulation would be up to 1.3 mil-lion. Breakeven was estimated at about 740,000. For comparative purposes, it took *USA Today* eight years and about $500 million in losses to get to its 1.7 million cir-culation. At that level, *USA Today* is only breaking even. Projections for *The National,* for year one, if met, would generate sales of $46.8 million and a loss of $16.3 million. After four years, management expected to break even with sales of about $165 million.

There was no shortage of critics of this new concept. In some markets, includ-ing Los Angeles, people don't buy many newspapers on the street. This might have required *The National* to invest in home delivery for some markets. There are 3,000 magazine titles vying for space on the nation's newsstands. Only forty circulate more than one million copies. The $10 million allocated for first year promotion and advertising might have been too low. Some thought it should have been at least twice that. Still others questioned whether there were enough die-hard sports fanatics to justify a sports-only daily. Wasn't the sports section of *USA Today* enough?

Unfortunately for Azcarraga and the hundreds of people involved in *The National,* the paper ended up with sales far below projections and losses that even a billionaire couldn't accept gracefully. *The National* folded in December 1991.

Questions

1. Analyze the industry and management's strategy using the Porter framework.

2. Was this business destined to fail? What, if anything, could have been done differently to have increased the likelihood of success?

Source: Based on Edward O. Welles, "A Whole New Game," *INC.,* April 1990, pp. 58–69.

VIDEO CASE

Disney's Long-Term Strategy

The Walt Disney Co. was one of the major business success stories of the last decade. Under the guidance of Michael Eisner, Disney's management turned a host of underperforming assets into a money machine. They gave the animation group new life and the result was such monster hits as *Who Framed Roger Rabbit?, Beauty and the Beast,* and *Aladdin.* They created Touchstone Pictures, which generated a long list of money-making films such as *Ruthless People, Three Men and a Baby,* and *Good Morning, Vietnam.* They developed the concept of Disney Stores for shopping malls. And they expanded their theme parks to include the recent EuroDisney.

EuroDisney may be one of the few projects that the company developed in recent years that is not a runaway hit. When it opened in the spring of 1992, just outside of Paris, many expected it to be more successful that DisneyWorld. First year attendance projections were set at 11 million people. Six hotels with 5000 rooms stood ready to handle the overflowing crowds. But EuroDisney's first-year performance was a major disappointment. Some blame it on the economy. Others say that Disney's attempt to merely clone its U.S. theme parks was the problem. Some elaboration should be made on this latter point.

- The French reserve only one day a week—Sunday—for family outings. Going out with the family on a Saturday or a weekday isn't something they're used to doing.

- The French have long been adverse to strangers. The idea of being welcomed by strangers with bouyant smiles and a lighthearted greeting is not appreciated.

- In the United States, 50 percent of Disney visitors eat fast food at the parks. Most French people, however, don't snack.

- The French insist on eating lunch at exactly 12:30. They will not eat at 11 a.m. or 3 p.m.

- The French are very impatient. They are not comfortable waiting in long lines.
- French workers don't like to obey orders. They are not likely to take kindly to management's demands that they not smoke, chew gum, or converse with their co-workers.

For instance, the squeaky-clean image and strict dress code mandated by the company stirred up a controversy when EuroDisney recruited in London. Applicants complained about the clothing and appearance requirements. While long hair, beards, mustaches, and large earings are a "no-no" to Disney, many European applicants consider such image issues as overly restrictive.

Questions

1. What kind of strategy is the Walt Disney Co. pursuing?
2. What is Disney's competitive advantage?
3. What suggestions would you make to increase the likelihood that EuroDisney would be a major success?

Source: "Disney's Long-Term Strategy," *ABC's Business World,* March 29, 1992.

CHAPTER 9

Planning Tools and Techniques

LEARNING OBJECTIVES

After Reading This Chapter, You Should Be Able To:

1. Describe techniques for scanning the environment.
2. Contrast quantitative and qualitative forecasting.
3. Explain why budgets are popular.
4. List two approaches to budgeting.
5. Differentiate Gantt and load charts.
6. Identify the steps in a PERT network.
7. State the factors that determine a product's break-even point.
8. Describe the requirements for using linear programming.
9. Discuss how simulation can be a planning tool.
10. List five steps toward better time management.

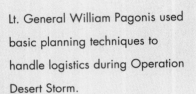

Lt. General William Pagonis used basic planning techniques to handle logistics during Operation Desert Storm.

I t was the late fall of 1990. Iraq had invaded Kuwait. The United States, along with a number of its allies, responded with Operation Desert Storm—a military action that involved sending in troops to free Kuwait. In what is now called the Persian Gulf War, several U.S. military men—particularly Generals Colin Powell and H. Norman Schwarzkopf—became national heroes. One officer, Lieutenant General William Pagonis, didn't get much media attention during the war, but he was, nevertheless, a major contributor. As commander of logistics, he was responsible for seeing that the 350,000 U.S. soldiers in the gulf during Operation Desert Storm had sufficient ammunition, food, fuel, and other critical supplies.[1]

The job Pagonis and his staff faced was staggering by almost any standard. Starting from scratch in August 1990, they built a distribution network of 50,000 workers, 100,000 trucks, and numerous massive, temporary warehouses in less than five months. They built a system that provided 1.5 million meals a day, supplied each division with 5,000 tons of ammunition and 500,000 gallons of fuel per day, and that could support the combat troops in the heart of battle for up to 60 days if necessary.

Along the way, Pagonis had to make critical adjustments. For instance, several foreign-flag crews refused to sail into the war zone, forcing Pagonis to order up replacement crews or to get supplies trucked deep into Saudi Arabia from Jedda on the Red Sea. And many of the U.S. ships were brought out of mothballs for the war. They were old. Pagonis had to find crews who could operate their old-fashioned steam turbines. In one case, Pagonis found an eighty-year-old seaman and brought him out of retirement to help. Then there was the trouble with chocolate. The heat made it melt in soldiers' hands, not in their mouths. Pagonis arranged for the Army to buy 12 million heat-resistant chocolate bars.

What kind of planning did Pagonis and his staff do? While some of it was strategic, most of their planning during Operation Desert Storm emphasized more day-to-day planning issues such as budgeting resources, scheduling the flow of supplies, and forecasting the need for trucks and ammunition.

In this chapter, we'll discuss a number of basic planning tools and techniques. We'll begin by looking at three planning techniques to assist managers in assessing their environment—environmental scanning, forecasting, and benchmarking. We'll review the most popular planning tool used by managers: budgets. We'll then discuss scheduling, break-even analysis, and other operational planning tools. Finally, we'll conclude this chapter by offering some ideas to help you in your personal, day-to-day planning. We'll present the key things you need to know about time management.

Techniques for Assessing the Environment

In Chapter 8, we detailed the strategic management process. In this section, we want to review several techniques that have been developed to help managers with one of the most challenging aspects of this process: assessing their organization's environment. Twenty years ago, environmental analysis was an informal endeavor based on intuitive judgments. Today, using structured techniques such as environmental scanning, forecasting, and benchmarking, a manager's ability to accurately analyze an organization's environment has improved measurably.

Environmental Scanning

Maria Iriti, who runs a glass company in Massachusetts, put in a bid of $18,000 to repair stained glass windows in a church. She won the bid but lost her shirt. She later found out that the next lowest bid had come in at $76,000. Iriti learned a valuable lesson from her mistake. She now keeps a folder on each competitor, socializes with them at trade shows, and has friends write to competitors for price lists and brochures.[2]

environmental scanning
The screening of much information to detect emerging trends and create scenarios.

Managers in both small and large organizations are increasingly turning to **environmental scanning** to anticipate and interpret changes in their environment.[3] The term, as we'll use it, refers to screening large amounts of information to detect emerging trends and create a set of scenarios.

The importance of environmental scanning was first recognized (outside of the national security establishment) by firms in the life insurance industry in the late 1970s.[4] Life insurance companies found that the demand for their product was declining. Yet all the key environmental signals they were receiving strongly favored the sale of life insurance. The economy and population were growing. Baby boomers were finishing school, entering the labor force, and taking on family responsibilities. The market for life insurance should have been expanding, but it wasn't. What the insurance companies had failed to recognize was a fundamental change in family structure in the United States.

Young families, who represented the primary group of buyers of new insurance policies, tended to be dual-career couples who were increasingly choosing to remain childless. The life insurance needs of a family with one income, a dependent spouse,

How do managers go about scanning the environment? How do they ascertain trends? The most effective method is to follow a formal search process. This includes reading mainstream publications such as newspapers, magazines, popular books, and trade journals; fringe literature such as politically extreme publications; and periodicals directed at particular groups such as *Working Woman* and *Ebony*. The objective is to tap into social, technological, economic, and political trends when they're in their infancy.

competitor intelligence

Environmental scanning activity that seeks to identify who competitors are, what they're doing, and how their actions will affect the focus organization.

and a houseful of kids are much greater than those of a two-income family with few, if any, children. That a multibillion-dollar industry could overlook such a fundamental social trend underscored the need to develop techniques for monitoring important environmental developments.

One of the fastest-growing areas of environmental scanning is **competitor intelligence.**[5] It seeks basic information about competitors: Who are they? What are they doing? How will what they're doing affect us? As Maria Iriti learned the hard way, accurate information on the competition can allow managers to *anticipate* competitor actions rather than merely *react* to them.

One expert on competitive intelligence emphasizes that 95 percent of the competitor-related information an organization needs to make crucial strategic decisions is available and accessible to the public.[6] In other words, competitive intelligence isn't organizational espionage. Advertisements, promotional materials, press releases, reports filed with government agencies, annual reports, want ads, newspaper reports, and industry studies are examples of readily accessible sources of information. Trade shows and the debriefing of your own sales force can be other good sources of information on competitors. Many firms even regularly buy competitors' products and have their own engineers break them down to learn about new technical innovations.

Extensive environmental scanning is likely to reveal a number of issues and concerns that could affect your organization's current or planned operations. Not all of these are likely to be equally important, so it's usually necessary to focus in on a limited set—say, three or four—that are most important and to develop scenarios based on each of these.

A **scenario** is a consistent view of what the future is likely to be. If, for instance, scanning uncovers increasing interest in Congress for raising the national minimum wage, McDonald's could create a multiple set of scenarios to assess the possible consequences of such an action. What would be the implications for its labor supply if the minimum were raised to $5.00 an hour? How about $5.50 an hour? What effect would these changes have on labor costs? How might competitors respond? Different assumptions would lead to different outcomes. The intention of this exercise is not to try to predict the future, but to reduce uncertainty by playing out potential situations under different specified conditions.[7] McDonald's could, for example, develop a set

scenario

A consistent view of what the future is likely to be.

of scenarios ranging from optimistic to pessimistic in terms of the minimum-wage issue. It would then be better prepared to initiate changes in its strategy to gain and hold a competitive advantage.

Forecasting

Environmental scanning creates the foundation for forecasts. Information obtained through scanning is used to form scenarios. These, in turn, establish premises for **forecasts,** which are predictions of future outcomes.

Types of Forecasts   Probably the two most popular outcomes for which management is likely to seek forecasts are future revenues and new technological breakthroughs. However, virtually any component in the organization's general and specific environment can receive forecasting attention.

Sara Lee's sales level drives purchasing requirements, production goals, employment needs, inventories, and numerous other decisions. Similarly, the University of Arizona's income from tuition and state appropriations will determine course offerings, staffing needs, salary increases for faculty, and the like. Both of these examples illustrate that predicting future revenues—**revenue forecasting**—is a critical element of planning for both profit and not-for-profit organizations.

Where does management get the data for developing revenue forecasts? Typically, it begins with historical revenue figures. For example, what were last year's revenues? This figure can then be adjusted for trends. What revenue patterns have evolved over recent years? What changes in social, economic, or other factors in the general

Bell Canada's management has developed a set of scenarios to reflect alternative political futures for Quebec. They range from Quebec continuing as a bilingual province within a unified Canada to it becoming a separate and independent country with its own government, currency, and military.

forecasts
Predictions of future outcomes.

revenue forecasting
Predicting future revenues.

MANAGING FROM A GLOBAL PERSPECTIVE

The Role of Global Scanning

Increasingly dynamic world markets mean that managers must expand the scope of their scanning efforts in order to gain vital information on those global forces that might impact their organization.[8] As one extreme example, Mitsubishi Trading Company employs over 60,000 market analysts around the world. Those analysts' principal job is to identify and feed market information to the parent company.

The sources that managers typically have used to scan the domestic environment are too limited. Managers need to internationalize their perspectives and information sources. For instance, they can subscribe to clipping services that review newspapers and business periodicals throughout the world and provide summaries. An increasing array of electronic services can provide topic searches and automatic updates in areas of special interest to managers.

The value of global scanning to management is, of course, largely dependent on the extent of the organization's global activity. But in an industry such as telephone communications, where the fastest growth is outside the highly developed countries, global scanning has become a virtual necessity. Some companies, including AT&T and U.S. West, are actively pursuing opportunities in less-developed countries such as Mexico, Brazil, and the Philippines. In such markets, where economic growth is substantial and only a small percentage of the population has telephones, the potential for products and services such as cellular telephones is enormous.

environment might alter the pattern in the future? In the specific environment, what actions can we expect from our competitors? Answers to questions like these provide the basis for revenue forecasts.

Between 1986 and 1990, some firms including Columbia and MCA, saw one of their basic products—vinyl long-playing records—almost disappear. Consumers still wanted to listen to music, but they preferred a new technology: compact discs. The record companies that successfully forecasted this technology and foresaw its impact on their business were able to convert their production facilities, adopt the technology, and beat their competition to the record store racks. Ironically, CDs are already under attack from digital tape technology. Again, those in the music business who accurately forecast when, or if, this technology will become the preferred music medium are likely to score big in the market.

technological forecasting
Predicting changes in technology and when new technologies are likely to be economically feasible.

Technological forecasting attempts to predict changes in technology and the time frame in which new technologies are likely to be economically feasible. The rapid pace of technological change has seen innovations in lasers, biotechnology, robotics, and data communications dramatically change surgery practices, pharmaceutical offerings, the processes used for manufacturing almost every mass-produced product, and the practicality of cellular telephones. Few organizations are exempt from the possibility that technological innovation might dramatically change the demand for their current products or services. The environmental scanning techniques discussed in the previous section can provide data on potential technological innovations.

quantitative forecasting
Applies a set of mathematical rules to a series of past data to predict future outcomes.

qualitative forecasting
Uses the judgment and opinions of knowledgeable individuals to predict future outcomes.

Forecasting Techniques   Forecasting techniques fall into two categories: quantitative and qualitative. **Quantitative forecasting** applies a set of mathematical rules to a series of past data to predict future outcomes. These techniques are preferred when management has sufficient "hard" data from which to work. **Qualitative forecasting,** on the other hand, uses the judgment and opinions of knowledgeable individuals. Qualitative techniques typically are used when precise data is scarce or difficult to obtain.

Table 9–1 lists some of the better-known quantitative and qualitative forecasting techniques.

Forecasting effectiveness   In spite of the importance of forecasting to strategic planning, managers have mixed success in forecasting events and outcomes accurately.[9]

Forecasting techniques are most accurate when the environment is static. The more dynamic the environment, the more likely management is to develop inaccurate forecasts. Forecasting has a relatively unimpressive record in predicting non-seasonal turning points such as recessions, unusual events, discontinuities, and the actions or reactions of competitors.

Although forecasting has a mixed record, research offers some suggestions for improving forecasting effectiveness.[10] First, use simple forecasting techniques. They tend to do as well as, and often better than, complex methods that tend to mistake random data for meaningful information. Second, compare every forecast with "no change." A no-change forecast is very accurate approximately half the time. Third, don't rely on a single forecasting method. Make forecasts with several models and average them, especially when you make longer-range forecasts. Fourth, don't assume that you can accurately identify turning points in a trend. What is typically perceived as a significant turning point is most often an unusual random event. And fifth, accuracy declines with expanding time frames. By shortening the length of forecasts you improve their accuracy.

TABLE 9-1   Forecasting Techniques

Techniques	Description	Application
Quantitative		
Time-series analysis	Fits a trend line to a mathematical equation and projects into the future by means of this equation	Predicting next quarter's sales based on four years of previous sales data
Regression models	Predicts one variable on the basis of known or assumed other variables	Seeking factors that will predict a certain level of sales (for example, price, advertising expenditures)
Econometric models	Uses a set of regression equations to simulate segments of the economy	Predicting change in car sales as a result of changes in tax laws
Economic indicators	Uses one or more economic indicators to predict a future state of the economy	Using change in GNP to predict discretionary income
Substitution effect	Uses a mathematical formulation to predict how, when, and under what circumstances a new product or technology will replace an existing one	Predicting the effect of microwave ovens on the sale of conventional ovens
Qualitative		
Jury of opinion	Combines and averages the opinions of experts	Polling all the company's personnel managers to predict next year's college recruitment needs
Sales-force composition	Combines estimates from field sales personnel of customers' expected purchases	Predicting next year's sales of industrial lasers
Customer evaluation	Combines estimates from established customers of expected purchases	Surveying of major dealers by a car manufacturer to determine types and quantities of products desired

Benchmarking for TQM

benchmarking
The search for the best practice among competitors or noncompetitors that lead to their superior performance.

A third strategic planning tool is **benchmarking.** This is the search for the best practices among competitors or noncompetitors that lead to their superior performance.[11] The basic idea underlying benchmarking is that management can improve quality by analyzing and then copying the methods of the leaders in various fields. As such, benchmarking is a very specific form of environmental scanning.

Xerox undertook what is widely regarded as the first benchmarking effort in the United States in 1979. Up to then, the Japanese had been aggressively copying the successes of others by traveling around, watching what others were doing, then

ETHICAL
DILEMMAS IN
MANAGEMENT

When Does Competitive Intelligence Become Espionage?

Texas Instruments hires a senior engineering executive from Motorola. While the new executive is certainly well qualified for his new position, so were a dozen or so other candidates. However, they didn't work for Motorola and have up-to-date knowledge of what new microchip products Motorola was developing. Is it unethical for Texas Instruments, one of Motorola's primary microchip competitors, to hire this executive? Is it acceptable to hire this executive but unacceptable to question him about Motorola's plans?

The vice president at a major book publishing company encourages one of her editors to interview for an editorial vacancy at a competing book publisher. The editor isn't interested in the position. The sole purpose of the interview will be to gain as much information as possible on the competitor's near-term publishing list and relay that information back to the vice president. Is going to such an interview unethical? Is asking a subordinate to engage in this intelligence mission unethical?

Neither of these situations involves obtaining publicly available information. Yet tactics like these are practiced by organizations in a number of highly competitive businesses.[12] When does competitive intelligence become espionage? Does any effort to conceal one's real motives when attempting to gather information automatically brand that action as unethical? What do *you* think?

---

applying their new knowledge to improve their products and processes. Xerox's management couldn't figure out how Japanese manufacturers could sell mid-size copiers in the United States for considerably less than Xerox's production costs. So the company's head of manufacturing took a team to Japan to make a detailed study of their competition's costs and processes. They got most of their information from Xerox's own joint venture, Fuji-Xerox, which knew its competition well. What the team found was shocking. Their Japanese rivals were light-years ahead of Xerox in efficiency. Benchmarking those efficiencies marked the beginning of Xerox's recovery in the copier field. Today, in addition to Xerox, companies such as AT&T, Du Pont, Ford, Eastman Kodak, and Motorola use benchmarking as a standard tool in their quest for quality improvement.

What does the benchmarking process look like? It typically follows four steps:

1. The organization forms a benchmarking planning team. The team's initial task is to identify what is to be benchmarked, identify comparative organizations, and determine data collection methods.

2. The team collects data internally on its own operations and externally from other organizations.

3. The data is analyzed to identify performance gaps and to determine the cause of differences.

4. An action plan is prepared and implemented that will result in meeting or exceeding the standards of others.

To illustrate its use in practice, let's look at its application at Ford Motor Co. Ford used benchmarking in the early 1980s in developing their highly successful Taurus. The company compiled a list of some 400 features its customers said were the most important, and then set about finding the car with the best of each. Then it tried to

Ford Motor Co. used benchmarking in the early 1980s in developing their highly successful Taurus.

match or top the best of the competition. When the Taurus was updated in 1992, Ford benchmarked all over again. For instance, the door handles on the latest Taurus were benchmarked against the Chevrolet Lumina, the easy-to-change taillight bulbs against the Nissan Maxima, and the tilt steering wheel against the Honda Accord.

Budgets

budget
A numerical plan for allocating resources to specific activities.

Few of us are unfamiliar with budgets. Most of us learned about them at an early age, when we discovered that unless we allocated our "revenues" carefully, we would consume our weekly allowance before half the week was out.

A **budget** is a numerical plan for allocating resources to specific activities. Managers typically prepare budgets for revenues, expenses, and such capital expenditures as machinery and equipment. It's not unusual, though, for budgets to be used for improving time, space, and the use of material resources. These latter types of budgets substitute nondollar numbers for dollar terms. Such items as person-hours, capacity utilization, or units of production can be budgeted for daily, weekly, or monthly activities. However, we'll emphasize dollar-based budgets in this section.

Why are budgets so popular? Probably because they are applicable to a wide variety of organizations and units within an organization. We live in a world in which almost everything is expressed in monetary units. Dollars, pesos, francs, yen, and the like are used as a common denominator within a country. Even human life has a monetary value. Insurance actuaries regularly compute the value of a lost eye, arm, or leg. While most people argue that life is priceless, American insurance companies and juries regularly convert the loss of human body parts or life itself into dollars and cents. It seems logical, then, that monetary budgets make a useful common denominator for directing activities in such diverse departments as production and marketing research, or at various levels in an organization. Budgets are one planning device that most managers, regardless of level in the organization, help to formulate.

Budgets can be used for control as well as for planning. When a budget is established, it becomes a planning tool because it gives direction. It tells what activities are important and how many resources should be allocated to each activity. A budget becomes a control mechanism when it provides standards against which resource consumption can be measured and compared. Keep in mind that a budget is not only a numerical plan, but also a control device for assessing how well activities are going.

Department Expense Budget
Calendar Year 1993

Item	Quarter			
	1st	*2nd*	*3rd*	*4th*
Salaries/Fixed	$ 93,600	$ 93,600	$ 93,600	$ 93,600
Salaries/Variable	10,000	15,000	10,000	30,000
Performance Bonuses				35,000
Office Supplies	2,500	2,500	2,500	2,500
Photocopying	3,000	3,000	3,000	3,000
Telephone	8,000	8,000	8,000	8,000
Mail	2,500	2,500	2,500	2,500
Travel	8,000	3,000	3,000	3,000
Library Development	1,500	1,500	1,500	1,500
Outside Consultants	0	12,000	0	0
Recruitment/Entertainment	5,000	2,000	2,000	3,000
Corporate Overhead	23,500	23,500	23,500	23,500
Total Quarterly Expenses	$157,600	$166,600	$149,600	$205,600

Types of Budgets

There is no shortage of items or areas for which budgets can be used. The following represent the ones managers are most likely to use.

revenue budget
A budget that projects future sales.

Revenue Budgets The **revenue budget** is a specific type of revenue forecast. It is a budget that projects future sales. If the organization could be sure of selling everything it produced, revenue budgets would undoubtedly be quite accurate. Managers would need only to multiply the sales price of each product by the quantity it could produce. But such situations rarely exist. Managers must take into consideration their competitors, advertising budget, sales force effectiveness, and other relevant factors, and they must make an estimate of sales volume. Then, on the basis of estimates of demand at various prices, managers must select an appropriate sales price. The result is the revenue budget.

expense budget
A budget that lists the primary activities undertaken by a unit and allocates a dollar amount to each.

Expense Budgets While revenue budgets are essentially a planning device for marketing and sales activities, expense budgets are found in all units within a firm and in not-for-profit and profit-making organizations alike. **Expense budgets** list the primary activities undertaken by a unit to achieve its goals and allocate a dollar amount to each. Lower expenses, when accompanied by stable quantity and quality of output, translate into greater efficiency. In times of severe competition, recession, or the like, managers typically look first at the expense budget as a place to make cuts and improve economic efficiencies. Because all expenses do not correspond with volume, they do not decline at the same rate when the demand for products or services drops. Managers therefore give particular attention to so-called fixed expenses—that is, those that remain relatively unchanged regardless of volume. As production drops, the variable expenses tend to control themselves because they fall with volume.

profit budget
A budget used by separate units of an organization that combines revenue and expense budgets to determine the unit's profit contribution.

Profit Budgets The units in an organization that have easily determined revenues are often designated as profit centers and use profit budgets for planning and control. **Profit budgets** combine revenue and expense budgets into one. They are typically used in large organizations with multiple plants and divisions. Each manufacturing plant in a corporation, for instance, might charge its monthly expenses plus a charge for corporate overhead against its monthly billing revenues. Some organizations create artificial profit centers by developing transfer prices for interorganizational transactions. As a case in point, the exploration division of Texaco produces oil only for Texaco's refining division, and so the exploration unit has no real sales. However, Texaco has made the exploration unit a profit center by establishing prices for each barrel of oil the division drills and then "sells" to the refining division. The internal transfers create revenue for the exploration division and allow managers in that division to formulate and be evaluated against their profit budget.

cash budget
A budget that forecasts how much cash an organization will have on hand and how much it will need to meet expenses.

Cash Budgets **Cash budgets** are forecasts of how much cash the organization will have on hand and how much it will need to meet expenses. This budget can reveal potential shortages or the availability of surplus cash for short-term investments.

capital expenditure budget
A budget that forecasts investments in property, buildings, and major equipment.

Capital Expenditure Budgets Investments in property, buildings, and major equipment are called *capital expenditures*. These are typically substantial expenditures both in terms of magnitude and duration. For example, Chrysler's decision to build a new production plant would represent a commitment of more than $700 million. It would require an outlay of funds over several years, and it would require many years for management to recoup its investment. The magnitude and duration of these investments can justify the development of separate budgets for these expenditures. Such **capital expenditure budgets** allow management to forecast future

THE CHANGING FACE OF MANAGEMENT PRACTICE

Loosening the Powerful Grip of Budgets

Budgets have long been *the* most popular planning tool of management. But the traditional view of budgets is being rethought. A number of well-managed organizations, including 3M, Emerson Electric, and Franco-British CMB Packaging, are loosening the grip of budgets on their organizational units.[13]

The complaints about budgets tend to center on their limited focus, their inflexibility, their tendency to discourage interunit cooperation, and, too often, their encouragement of idiotic actions in order to "look good" on the numbers.

Budgets assume that everything important can be quantified and translated into this quarter's or this year's dollars. But a lot of important activities don't show up in budgets. For example, a budget can show what a firm spent on customer service, but not what value customers put on it. And organizations have historically made "coming in on budget" a major managerial goal. Yet just because a budget was not overspent doesn't mean it was well spent.

Quarterly and annual budgets often block managers from shifting resources quickly. Instead of becoming guidelines, budgets become rigid restraints that limit flexibility. Someone has a great idea that justifies immediate action but nothing happens because "it's not in the budget." Once formalized, budgets can become ends in themselves.

Because all key units in an organization typically have their own budgets, managers in each unit tend to maximize only their own unit's self-interest, even at the expense of the overall organization. In the 1990s, when organizations are trying to foster interunit cooperation and seeking to break down structural barriers, budgets tend only to increase turf battles. Manufacturing units, for example, become more concerned with minimizing costs through long and stable production runs than with quickly responding to customers' needs for a small quantity of a specific item.

Finally, stories of bizarre behaviors created by budgets are legendary. For example, the use-it-or-lose-it mentality explains why managers can become obsessed with spending everything left in their budgets at the end of a given period, because next year's allocations are based on last year's expenditures. Or a desire to meet a budget explains why a manager would impose a fourth-quarter spending freeze that eventually costs more than it saves.

Acknowledging the downside of budgets doesn't mean that organizations are throwing them out. For the most part, the benefits of budgets exceed their costs. But progressive managements are recognizing that an obsessive emphasis on meeting budgets can discourage new ideas, risk-taking, and flexibility. So managements are downplaying the importance of budgets, making them less binding, and linking unit budgets in order to encourage cooperation.

---

fixed budget
A budget that assumes a fixed level of sales or production.

variable budget
A budget that takes into account those costs that vary with volume.

capital requirements, to keep on top of important capital projects, and to ensure that adequate cash is available to meet these expenditures as they come due.

Variable Budgets   The budgets previously described are based on the assumption of a single specified volume—that is, they are **fixed budgets.** They assume a fixed level of sales or production volume. Most organizations, however, are not able to predict volume accurately. Moreover, a number of costs—such as labor, material, and some administrative expenses—vary with volume. **Variable budgets** are designed to deal with these facts. Since plans can change, standards need to be flexible to adjust to these changes. Variable budgets represent flexible standards. They can help managers to better plan costs by specifying cost schedules for varying levels of volume.

Approaches to Budgeting

There are essentially two approaches managers can take to budgeting. By far the most popular approach is the traditional or *incremental budget*. But in recent years, managers in some organizations have been trying to make budgets more effective by experimenting with the *zero-base budget*. Let's look at each of these approaches.

incremental budget
A budget that allocates funds to departments according to allocations in the previous period.

Incremental Budgets The **incremental** (or traditional) **budget** has two identifying characteristics. First, funds are allocated to departments or organizational units. The managers of these units then allocate funds to activities as they see fit. Second, an incremental budget develops out of the previous budget. Each period's budget begins by using the last period as a reference point. Only incremental changes in the budget request are reviewed. Each of these characteristics, however, creates a problem.

When funds are allocated to organizational units, it becomes difficult to differentiate activities within units. Why? Because organizational units typically have a multiple set of goals and hence engage in a number of activities. Incremental budgets don't take this diversity of activities into consideration. They focus on providing funds for units rather than for activities within the units. Given that units have multiple goals, it seems reasonable to conclude that (1) some goals are more important than others, and (2) unit managers have varying degrees of success in achieving these multiple goals. Incremental budgets throw everything into the same pot. Thus, as planning devices, they lack sufficient focus and specificity.

The incremental budget is particularly troublesome when top management seeks to identify inefficiencies and waste. In fact, inefficiencies tend to grow in the incremental budget because they tend to get hidden. In the typical incremental budget, nothing ever gets cut. Each budget begins with the funds allocated for the last period—to which unit managers add a percentage for inflation and requests for those new or expanded activities they seek to pursue. Top management looks only at the requests for incremental changes. The result is that money can be provided for activities long after their need is gone.

zero-base budgeting (ZBB)
A system in which budget requests start from scratch, regardless of previous appropriations.

Zero-Base Budgets **Zero-base budgeting (ZBB),** originally developed by Texas Instruments, requires managers to justify their budget requests in detail from scratch, regardless of previous appropriations.[14] It's designed to attack the second drawback we mentioned in incremental budgets: activities that have a way of becoming immortal. Once established, organizational activities can take on lives of their own. This is especially true in public organizations. For instance, one researcher noted that the State of New York's *Temporary* Commission of Investigation had issued its *sixteenth* annual report and that the Federal Metal and Nonmetallic Mine Safety Board of Review was abolished only after its executive secretary admitted in a front-page newspaper interview that he had no work to perform.[15]

ZBB shifts the burden of proof to the manager to justify why his or her unit should get any budget at all. The ZBB process reevaluates all organizational activities to see which should be eliminated, funded at a reduced level, funded at the current level, or increased. As illustrated in Figure 9–1, the process consists of three steps:

1. Each discrete departmental activity is broken down into a decision package.
2. The individual decision packages are ranked according to their benefit to the organization during the budget period.

3. Budget resources are allocated to the individual packages according to preferential rank in the organization.[16]

The *decision package* is a document that identifies and describes a specific activity. Usually prepared by operating managers, it includes a statement of the expected result or purpose of the activity, its costs, personnel requirements, measures of performance, alternative courses of action, and an evaluation of the benefits from performance and consequences of nonperformance from an organizationwide perspective. In more specific terms, each package lists a number of alternative methods of performing the activity, recommends one of these alternatives, and delineates effort levels. These *effort levels* identify spending targets—for instance, how the activity would be completed at 70, 90, and 110 percent of the current budget level. Any large organization that adopts ZBB will have literally thousands of these packages.

Once department managers have completed the decision packages, the packages are forwarded to the top executive group, which determines how much to spend and where to spend it. This is done by ascertaining the total amount to be spent by the organization and then by ranking all packages in order of decreasing benefits to the organization. Packages are accepted down to the spending level. When properly executed, the ZBB process carefully evaluates every organizational activity, assigns it a priority, and results in either the continuation, modification, or termination of the activity.

ZBB is no panacea. Like incremental budgeting, it has its own set of drawbacks.[17] It increases paperwork and requires time to prepare; the important activities that managers want funded tend to have their benefits inflated; and the eventual outcome rarely differs much from what would occur through an incremental budget.

The difficulty and expense of implementing ZBB suggest that it is not for every organization. The politics of large organizations often undermine any potential gain

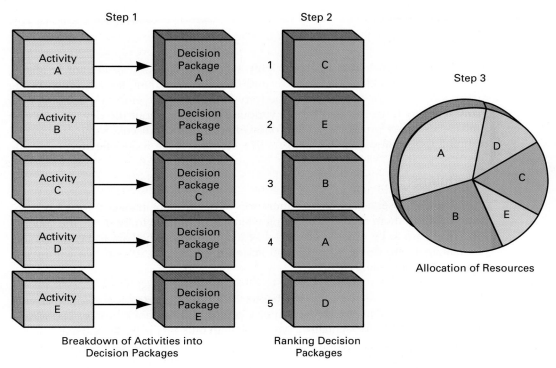

FIGURE 9-1
The Zero-Base Budget Process

Texas Instruments introduced zero-base budgeting as a means of prioritizing projects and improving efficiency.

that ZBB might produce. It is possibly most effective in smaller public organizations, in supporting staff units in business firms, or in declining organizations. For example, because the resource requirements of staff units in business firms, which include areas like market research and personnel, are rarely related directly to the firm's output, it's difficult to determine whether their budgets are realistic or denote efficient operation. Thus for this type of unit, ZBB may be a valuable planning and control device. Also, ZBB is compatible with managing declining resources.[18] When organizations face cutbacks and financial restraints, their managers particularly look for devices that allocate limited resources effectively. ZBB can be just such a device.

Operational Planning Tools

Flo's Take-Out Chicken is a large, highly successful fast-food restaurant in Miami, Florida. Florence Jackson, who owns and runs the restaurant, spends much of her time setting up work schedules for the forty-five people she employs, deciding how many registers to keep open during various times throughout the day, and solving similar day-to-day problems. In the following pages, we'll discuss some operational planning tools that can help managers like Florence to be more effective.

Scheduling

If you were to observe a group of supervisors or department managers for a few days, you would see them regularly detailing what activities have to be done, the order in which they are to be done, who is to do each, and when they are to be completed. The managers are doing what we call **scheduling.** In this section, we will review some useful scheduling devices.

scheduling
A listing of necessary activities, their order of accomplishment, who is to do each, and time needed to complete them.

The Gantt Chart As we noted in Chapter 2, the Gantt chart was developed around the turn of the century by Henry Gantt, a protégé of Frederick Taylor. The idea is inherently simple. It is essentially a bar graph with time on the horizontal axis and the activities to be scheduled on the vertical axis. The bars show output, both planned and actual, over a period of time. The Gantt chart visually shows when tasks are supposed to be done and compares that to the actual progress on each. It is a simple but important device that allows managers to detail easily what has yet to be done to complete a job or project and to assess whether it is ahead of, behind, or on schedule.

FIGURE 9-2
A Gantt Chart

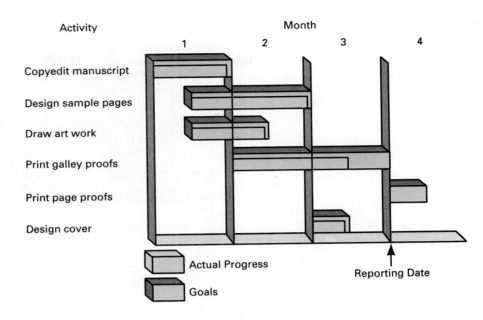

Figure 9–2 depicts a simplified Gantt chart that was developed for book production by a manager in a publishing firm. Time is expressed in months across the top of the chart. The major activities are listed down the left side. The planning comes in deciding what activities need to be done to get the book finished, the order in which they need to be done, and the time that should be allocated to each activity. Where a box sits within a time frame reflects its planned sequence. The shading represents actual progress. The chart becomes a control device when the manager looks for deviations from the plan. In this case, everything has been accomplished on schedule except the printing of galley proofs. This is two weeks behind schedule. Given this information, the manager of this project might want to take some corrective action either to pick up the two lost weeks or to ensure that no further delays will occur. At this point, the manager can expect that the book will be published at least two weeks later than planned if no corrective action is taken.

load chart
A modified Gantt chart that schedules capacity by work stations.

The Load Chart   A **load chart** is a modified Gantt chart. Instead of listing activities on the vertical axis, load charts list either whole departments or specific resources. This allows managers to plan and control for capacity utilization. In other words, load charts schedule capacity by work stations.

For example, Figure 9–3 shows a load chart for six production editors at the same publishing firm. Each editor supervises the production and design of a number of books. By reviewing a load chart like the one shown in Figure 9–3, the executive editor, who supervises the six production editors, can see who is free to take on a new book. If everyone is fully scheduled, the executive editor might decide not to accept any new projects, to accept new projects and delay others, to make the editors work overtime, or to employ more production editors. In Figure 9–3, only Lisa and Maurice are completely booked for the next six months. Since the other editors have some unassigned time, they might be able to accept one or more new projects.

PERT Network Analysis   Gantt and load charts are helpful as long as the activities or projects being scheduled are few in number and independent of each other. But, what if a manager had to plan a large project such as a reorganization, the launching of a cost-reduction campaign, or the development of a new product that required coordinating inputs from marketing, production, and product design personnel? Such projects require coordinating hundreds or thousands of activities, some of which must be done simultaneously and some of which cannot begin until earlier activities

FIGURE 9–3
A Load Chart

= Work Scheduled

Program Evaluation and Review Technique (PERT)
A technique for scheduling complicated projects comprising many activities, some of which are interdependent.

have been completed. If you're constructing a building, you obviously can't start erecting walls until the foundation is laid. How, then, can you schedule such a complex project? You could use the Program Evaluation and Review Technique.

The **Program Evaluation and Review Technique**—usually just called PERT or PERT network analysis—was originally developed in the late 1950s for coordinating the more than 3,000 contractors and agencies working on the Polaris submarine weapon system.[19] This project was incredibly complicated, with hundreds of thousands of activities that had to be coordinated. PERT is reported to have cut two years off the completion date for the Polaris project.

A PERT network is a flowchartlike diagram that depicts the sequence of activities needed to complete a project and the time or costs associated with each activity. With a PERT network, a project manager must think through what has to be done, determine which events depend on one another, and identify potential trouble spots. PERT also makes it easy to compare the effects alternative actions will have on scheduling and costs. Thus PERT allows managers to monitor a project's progress, identify possible bottlenecks, and shift resources as necessary to keep the project on schedule.

To understand how to construct a PERT network, you need to know three terms: *events, activities,* and *critical path.* Let's define these terms, outline the steps in the PERT process, and then develop an example.

events
End points that represent the completion of major activities in a PERT network.

Events are end points that represent the completion of major activities. **Activities** represent the time or resources required to progress from one event to another. The **critical path** is the longest or most time-consuming sequence of events and activities in a PERT network.

activities
The time or resources needed to progress from one event to another in a PERT network.

Developing a PERT network requires the manager to identify all key activities needed to complete a project, rank them in order of dependence, and estimate each activity's completion time. This can be translated into five specific steps:

critical path
The longest sequence of activities in a PERT network.

1. Identify every significant activity that must be achieved for a project to be completed. The accomplishment of each activity results in a set of events or outcomes.

2. Ascertain the order in which these events must be completed.

PERT network
A flowchartlike diagram showing the sequence of activities needed to complete a project and the time or cost associated with each.

3. Diagram the flow of activities from start to finish, identifying each activity and its relationship to all other activities. Use circles to indicate events and arrows to represent activities. This results in a flowchart diagram that we call the **PERT network.**

4. Compute a time estimate for completing each activity. This is done with a weighted average that employs an *optimistic* time estimate (t_o) of how long the

Aerospace and construction firms like General Dynamics and Bechtel regularly use PERT schedules to manage complex projects.

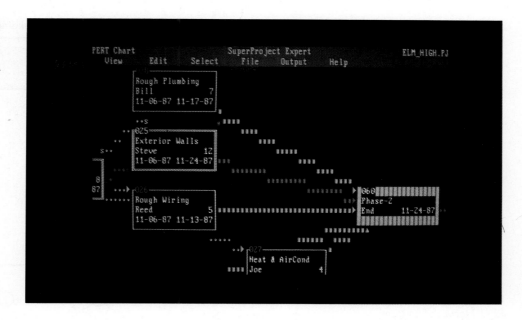

activity would take under ideal conditions, a *most-likely* estimate (t_m) of the time the activity normally should take, and a *pessimistic* estimate (t_p) that represents the time that an activity should take under the worst possible conditions. The formula for calculating the expected time (t_e) is then

$$t_e = \frac{t_o + 4t_m + t_p}{6}$$

5. Finally, using a network diagram that contains time estimates for each activity, the manager can determine a schedule for the start and finish dates of each activity and for the entire project. Any delays that occur along the critical path require the most attention because they delay the entire project. That is, the critical path has no slack in it; therefore, any delay along that path immediately translates into a delay in the final deadline for the completed project.

As was noted at the beginning of this section, most PERT projects are quite complicated and may be composed of hundreds or thousands of events. Such complicated computations are best done with a computer using specialized PERT software.[20] But for our purposes, let's work through a simplified example. Assume that you are the superintendent of a construction company. You have been assigned to oversee the construction of an office building. Because time really is money in your business, you must determine how long it will take to put up the building. You have carefully dissected the entire project into activities and events. Table 9–2 outlines the major events in the construction project and your estimate of the expected time required to complete each activity. Figure 9–4 depicts the PERT network based on the data in Table 9–2.

Your PERT network tells you that if everything goes as planned, it will take fifty weeks to complete the building. This is calculated by tracing the network's critical path: A–B–C–D–G–H–J–K. Any delay in completing the events along this path will delay the completion of the entire project. For example, if it took six weeks instead of four to put in the floor covering and paneling (event I), this would have no effect on the final completion date. Why? Because C–D + D–I + I–J equals only thirteen weeks, while C–E + E–G + G–H + H–J equals sixteen weeks. However, if you wanted to cut

TABLE 9-2 A PERT Network for Erecting an Office Building

Event	Description	Expected Time (in weeks)	Preceding Event
A	Approve design and get permits	10	None
B	Dig subterranean garage	6	A
C	Erect frame and siding	14	B
D	Construct floors	6	C
E	Install windows	3	C
F	Put on roof	3	C
G	Install internal wiring	5	D,E,F
H	Install elevators	5	G
I	Put in floor covering and paneling	4	D
J	Put in doors and interior decorative trim	3	I,H
K	Turn over to building management group	1	J

FIGURE 9-4
PERT Network Diagram

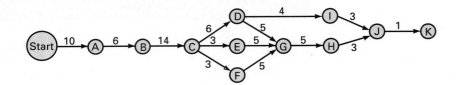

the fifty-week time frame, you would give attention to those activities along the critical path that could be speeded up.

Break-Even Analysis

How many units of a product must an organization sell in order to break even—that is, to have neither profit nor loss? A manager might want to know the minimum number of units that must be sold to achieve her profit objective or whether a current product should continue to be sold or be dropped from the organization's product line. **Break-even analysis** is a widely used technique for helping managers to make profit projections.[21]

Break-even analysis is a simplistic formulation, yet it is valuable to managers because it points out the relationship between revenues, costs, and profits. To compute the break-even point (*BE*), the manager needs to know the unit price of the product being sold (*P*), the variable cost per unit (*VC*), and total fixed costs (*TFC*).

An organization breaks even when its total revenue is just enough to equal its total costs. But total cost has two parts: a fixed component and a variable component. *Fixed costs* are expenses that do not change, regardless of volume. Examples include insurance premiums and property taxes. Fixed costs, of course, are fixed only in the short term because, in the long run, commitments terminate and are thus subject to variation. *Variable costs* change in proportion to output and include raw materials, labor costs, and energy costs.

The break-even point can be computed graphically or by using the following formula:

$$BE = \frac{TFC}{P - VC}$$

This formula tells us that (1) total revenue will equal total cost when we sell enough units at a price that covers all variable unit costs and (2) the difference between price and variable costs, when multiplied by the number of units sold, equals the fixed costs.

break-even analysis
A technique for identifying the point at which total revenue is just sufficient to cover total costs.

FIGURE 9–5
Break-Even Analysis

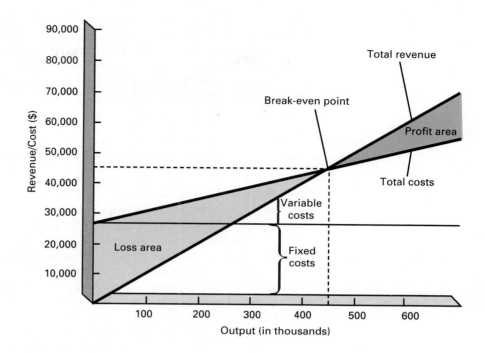

For example, assume that Dave's Photocopying Service charges $0.10 per photo-copy. If fixed costs are $27,000 a year and variable costs are $0.04 per copy, Dave can compute his break-even point as follows: $27,000/($0.10 − $0.04) = 450,000 copies, or when annual revenues are $45,000. This same relationship is shown graphically in Figure 9–5.

As a planning tool, break-even analysis could help Dave to set his sales objective. For example, he could establish the profit he wants and then work backward to determine what sales level is needed to reach that profit. Break-even analysis could also tell Dave how much volume has to increase to break even if he's currently running at a loss or how much volume he can afford to lose and still break even if he's currently operating profitably. In some cases, such as the management of profession-al sports franchises, break-even analysis has shown the projected volume of ticket sales required to cover all costs to be so unrealistically high that the best action for management to take is to get out of the business.

Linear Programming

Dan Collier has a manufacturing plant that produces two kinds of firearms, a .38 revolver and a 9-mm semiautomatic pistol. Business is good. He can sell all of the firearms he can produce. This is his dilemma: Given that both pistols go through the same production departments, how many of each type should he make to maximize his profits?

A closer look at Dan's operation tells us that he can use a mathematical technique called **linear programming** to solve his resource allocation dilemma. As we'll show, linear programming is applicable to Dan's problem, but it can't be applied to all resource allocation situations. Besides requiring limited resources and the objective of optimization, it requires that there be alternative ways of combining resources to produce a number of output mixes. There must also be a linear relationship between variables.[22] This means that a change in one variable will be accompanied by an exactly proportional change in the other. For Dan's business, this condition would be met if it took exactly twice the amount of raw materials and hours of labor to produce two of a given firearm as it took to produce one.

linear programming
A mathematical technique that solves resource allocation prob-lems.

TABLE 9–3 Production Data for Pistols

| Department | Number of Hours Required (per unit) | | Monthly Production Capacity (in hours) |
	.38 Revolvers	Semiautomatics	
Manufacturing	2	4	1,200
Assembly	2	2	900
Profit per unit	$100	$180	

What kinds of problems lend themselves to linear programming? Selecting transportation routes that minimize shipping costs, allocating a limited advertising budget among various product brands, making the optimum assignment of personnel among projects, and determining how much of each product to make with a limited number of resources are a few. Let's return to Dan's problem and see how linear programming could help him to solve it. Fortunately, Dan's problem is relatively simple, so we can solve it rather quickly. For complex linear programming problems, there is computer software that has been designed specifically to help develop solutions.

First, we need to establish some facts about Dan's business. Dan has computed the profit margins on the pistols at $100 for the revolver and $180 for the semiautomatic. He can therefore express his *objective function* as: maximum profit = $100R + $180S, where R is the number of revolvers produced and S is the number of semiautomatics produced. Additionally, Dan knows the time each pistol must spend in each department and the monthly production capacity (1,200 hours in manufacturing and 900 hours in assembly) for the two departments (see Table 9–3). The production capacity numbers act as *constraints* on his overall capacity. Now Dan can establish his constraint equations:

$$2R + 4S \leq 1,200$$
$$2R + 2S \leq 900$$

Of course, since neither pistol can be produced in a volume less than zero, Dan can also state that $R \geq 0$ and $S \geq 0$.

Dan has graphed his solution as shown in Figure 9–6. The shaded area represents the options that don't exceed the capacity of either department. This area represents his *feasibility region*. Dan's optimal resource allocation will be defined at one of the corners within this feasibility region. Point C is the farthest from the origin and provides the maximum profits within the constraints stated. At point A, profits would be 0. At points B and D, profits would be $54,000 and $45,000, respectively. At point C, however, profits would be $57,000.

Queuing Theory

You are a supervisor for the San Francisco Bay Bridge Toll Authority. One of the decisions you have to make is how many of the thirty-six toll booths you should keep open at any given time. Queuing theory, or what is frequently referred to as *waiting-line theory*, could assist you with this problem.

Whenever a decision involves balancing the cost of having a waiting line against the cost of service to maintain that line, it can be made easier with **queuing theory.** This includes such common situations as determining how many gas pumps are needed at gas stations, tellers at bank windows, or check-in lines at airline ticket counters. In each situation, management wants to minimize cost by having as few stations open as possible, yet not so few as to test the patience of customers. Referring back to our toll-booth example, during rush hours you could open all thirty-six and

queuing theory
A technique that balances the cost of having a waiting line against the cost of service to maintain that line.

FIGURE 9-6
Graphical Solution to Dan
Collier's Linear Programming
Problem

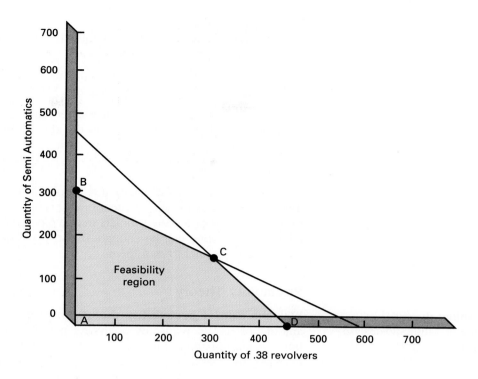

keep waiting time to a minimum, or you could open only one, minimize staffing costs, and risk a riot.

The mathematics underlying queuing theory is beyond the scope of this book. But you can see how the theory works in a simple example. Assume that you're a bank supervisor. One of your responsibilities is assigning tellers. You have five teller windows, but you want to know whether you can get by with only one window open during an average morning. You consider twelve minutes to be the longest you would expect any customer to wait patiently in line. If it takes four minutes, on average, to serve each customer, the line should not be permitted to get longer than three deep (12 minutes ÷ 4 minutes per customer = 3 customers). If you know from

Queuing theory can help managers balance the costs of a waiting line against the cost of maintaining that line.

past experience that during the morning people arrive at the average rate of two per minute, you can calculate the probability that the line will become longer than any number (n) customers as follows:

$$P_n = \left(1 - \frac{arrival\ rate}{service\ rate}\right) \times \left(\frac{arrival\ rate}{service\ rate}\right)^n$$

where n = 3 customers, *arrival rate* = 2 per minute, and *service rate* = 4 minutes per customer. Putting these numbers into the above formula generates the following:

$$P_3 = \left(1 - \frac{2}{4}\right) \times \left(\frac{2}{4}\right)^3 = \left(\frac{1}{2}\right)\left(\frac{8}{64}\right) = \frac{8}{128} = .0625$$

What does a P_3 of .0625 mean? It tells you that the likelihood of having more than three customers in line during the morning is one chance in sixteen. Are you willing to live with four or more customers in line 6 percent of the time? If so, keeping one teller window open will be enough. If not, you'll need to add windows and assign additional personnel to staff them.

Probability Theory

With the help of **probability theory,** managers can use statistics to reduce the amount of risk in plans. By analyzing past predictable patterns, a manager can improve current and future decisions. It makes for more effective planning when, for example, the marketing manager at Porsche/North America, who is responsible for the 968 line, knows that the mean age of his customers is 35.5 years, with a standard deviation of 3.5. If he assumes a normal distribution of ages, the manager can use probability theory to calculate that 95 of every 100 customers are between 28.6 and 42.4 years of age. If he were developing a new marketing program, he could use this information to target his marketing dollars more effectively.

Marginal Analysis

The concept of marginal, or incremental, analysis helps decision makers to optimize returns or minimize costs. **Marginal analysis** deals with the additional cost in a particular decision, rather than the average cost. For example, the commercial dry cleaner who wonders whether she should take on a new customer would consider not the total revenue and the total cost that would result after the order was taken, but rather what additional revenue would be generated by this particular order and what additional costs. If the incremental revenues exceeded the incremental costs, total profits would be increased by accepting the order.

Simulation

Boeing Co. is designing its 777 airplane on a huge computer system. Engineers iron out bugs on video screens, where changes are easy and cheap to make. By simulating the plane's design on a computer, rather than building a full-size mock-up, Boeing's management hopes to save as much as 20 percent of the estimated $4 billion to $5 billion development costs.[23]

Managers are increasingly turning to simulation as a means for trying out various planning options. They are using **simulation** to create a model of a real-world phenomenon and then manipulating one or more variables in the model to assess their impact. Simulation can deal with problems addressed by linear programming, but it can also deal with more complex situations.

How might a manager use simulation? Let's see how it was used by a library director at a large university. She was planning the interior design and layout for a

Computer simulations of assemblies in the Boeing 777, such as the cockpit and forward fuselage, allow engineers to spot problems and try various changes with minimal cost.

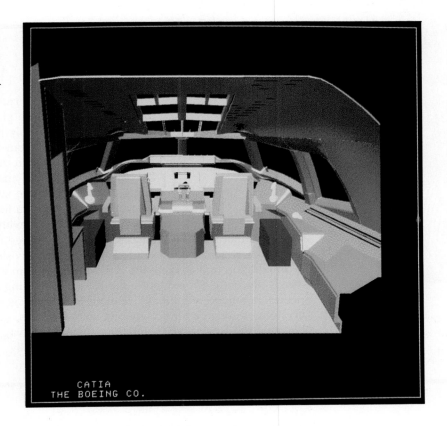

CATIA
THE BOEING CO.

new library building. The proper location of certain collections, study areas, offices, and information desks was crucial for the effective operation of the new facility. The director gathered information on the various collections, their usage rates, the demand pattern for periodicals, and the like. Then, with the assistance of a simulation expert, she developed a computer simulation model of the facility. The model expressed, in mathematical terms, the key variables in the library's design and layout. By altering these variables, the simulation model described the possible effects on library operations and cost. Most important, because the entire exercise was simulated on a computer, thousands of options could be plugged in and their probable results evaluated. This allowed for the identification of an optimum design, while minimizing any disruption in the ongoing operations of the library.

Do any of the following describe you?

> You do interesting things before the uninteresting things?
>
> You do things that are easy before things that are difficult?
>
> You do things that are urgent before things that are important?
>
> You work on things in the order of their arrival?
>
> You wait until a deadline approaches before really moving on a project.[24]

time management
A personal form of scheduling time effectively.

If you answered yes to one or more of these questions, you could benefit from time management. In this section, we'll present some suggestions to help you manage your time better. We'll show you that **time management** is actually a

Willa Martin at General Motors

Willa Martin began her career at General Motors in the mid-1970s as a buyer in purchasing. Today, she is manager of competitive analysis at GM's AC Rochester division in Flint, Michigan.[25]

Martin's job is to scan the environment for the Rochester division. She analyzes what the competition is doing through extensive investigative research and then she interprets these data for division executives. She is particularly concerned with identifying practices and processes that have been successfully implemented by competitors and determining which, if any, might be integrated into her division's operations.

In addition to analyzing the competition, Martin also closely follows industry trends. Recently, for example, she has been looking at the creation of the European Economic Community, clean air legislation, government-mandated fuel economy standards for automobile manufacturers, the proposed free-trade act between the United States and Mexico, and the ways in which these issues might affect products the Rochester division sells globally.

personal form of scheduling. Managers who use their time effectively know what activities they want to accomplish, the best order in which to take the activities, and when they want to complete those activities.

Time as a Scarce Resource

Time is a unique resource in that, if it's wasted, it can *never* be replaced. While people talk about *saving time,* the fact is that time can never actually be saved. It can't be stockpiled for use in some future period. If lost, it can't be retrieved. When a minute is gone, it is gone forever.

The positive side of this resource is that all managers have it in equal abundance. While money, labor, and other resources are distributed unequally in this world, thus putting some managers at a disadvantage, every manager is allotted twenty-four hours every day and seven days every week. Some just use their allotments better than others.

Focusing on Discretionary Time

Managers can't control all of their time. They are routinely interrupted and have to respond to unexpected crises. It's necessary, therefore, to differentiate between response time and discretionary time.[26]

The majority of a manager's time is spent responding to requests, demands, and problems initiated by others. We call this **response time** and treat it as uncontrollable. The portion that *is* under a manager's control is called **discretionary time.** Most of the suggestions offered to improve time management apply to its discretionary component. Why? Because only this part is manageable!

Unfortunately for most managers, particularly those in the lower and middle ranks of the organization, discretionary time makes up only about 25 percent of their work

response time
Uncontrollable time spent responding to requests, demands, and problems initiated by others.

discretionary time
The part of a manager's time that is controllable.

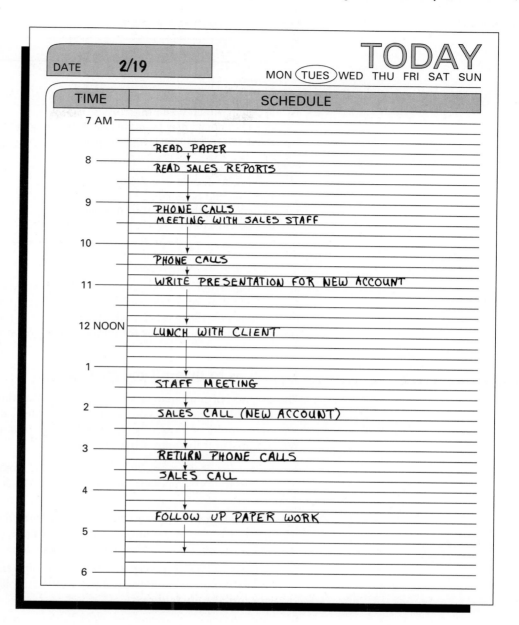

The best log is a daily diary or calendar broken into fifteen-minute intervals. To get enough information from which to generalize, you need about two weeks' worth of entries. During this two-week period, enter everything you do in the diary in fifteen-minute segments. To minimize memory loss, post the entries as you do them. Keep in mind that honesty is important. You want to record how you *actually* spent your time, not how you *wished* you had spent your time!

hours.[27] Moreover, discretionary time tends to become available in small pieces—five minutes here, five minutes there. Thus it is very difficult to use effectively. The challenge, then, is to know what time is discretionary and then to organize activities so as to accumulate discretionary time in blocks large enough to be useful. Managers who are good at identifying and organizing their discretionary time accomplish significantly more, and the things they accomplish are more likely to be high-priority activities.

How Do You Use Your Time?

How do managers, or any individuals for that matter, determine how well they use their time? The answer is that they should keep a log or diary of daily activities for a short period of time, then evaluate the data they gather.

Try keeping such a diary. When it is complete, you will have a detailed time and

TABLE 9–4 Analyzing Activities for Importance and Urgency

Rate Each Activity for

Importance

A. Very important: must be done
B. Important: should be done
C. Not so important: may be useful, but is not necessary
D. Unimportant: doesn't accomplish anything

Urgency

A. Very urgent: must be done now
B. Urgent: should be done now
C. Not urgent: can be done sometime later
D. Time not a factor

activity log. Then you can analyze how effectively you use your time. Rate each activity in terms of its importance and urgency. (See Table 9–4.) If you find that many activities received C's or D's, you'll find the next sections valuable. They provide detailed guidelines for better time management.[28]

Five Steps to Better Time Management

The essence of time management is to use your time effectively. This requires that you know the objectives you want to accomplish, the activities that will lead to the accomplishment of those objectives, and the importance and urgency of each activity. We've translated this into a five-step process.

1. *Make a list of your objectives.* What specific objectives have you set for yourself and the unit you manage? If you're using MBO, these objectives are already in place.

2. *Rank the objectives according to their importance.* Not all objectives are of equal importance. Given the limitations on your time, you want to make sure you give highest priority to the most important objectives.

3. *List the activities necessary to achieve your objectives.* What specific actions do you need to take to achieve your objectives? Again, if you're using MBO, these action plans are already laid out.

4. *For each objective, assign priorities to the various activities required to reach the objective.* This step imposes a second set of priorities. Here, you need to emphasize both importance and urgency. If the activity is not important, you should consider delegating it to someone below you. If it's not urgent, it can usually wait. This step will identify activities that you *must* do, those you *should* do, those you'll get to *when you can,* and those that can be *delegated to others.*

5. *Schedule your activities according to the priorities you've set.* The final step is to prepare a daily plan. Every morning, or at the end of the previous work day, make a list of the five or so most important things you want to do for the day. If the list grows to ten or more activities, it becomes cumbersome and ineffective. Then set priorities for the activities listed on the basis of importance and urgency.

Some Additional Points to Ponder

Follow the 10–90 Principle Most managers produce 90 percent of their results in only 10 percent of their time. It's easy for managers to get caught up in the activity

William Berrios, of Berrios Construction Co. in San Francisco, conducts a time management workshop for his office staff.

trap and confuse actions with accomplishments. Those who use their time well make sure that the critical 10 percent gets highest priority.

Know Your Productivity Cycle   Each of us has a daily cycle. Some of us are morning people, while others are late-afternoon or evening people. Managers who know their cycle and schedule their work accordingly, can significantly increase their effectiveness. They handle their most demanding problems during the high part of their cycle, when they are most alert and productive. They relegate their routine and undemanding tasks to their low periods.

Remember Parkinson's Law   Parkinson's Law says that work expands to fill the time available. The implication for time management is that you can schedule *too* much time for a task. If you give yourself an excess amount of time to perform an activity, you're likely to pace yourself so that you use up the entire time allocation.

Group Less Important Activities Together   Set aside a regular time period each day to make phone calls, do follow-ups, and perform other kinds of busywork. Ideally, this should be during your low cycle. This avoids duplication, waste, and redundancy; it also prevents trivia from intruding on high-priority tasks.

Minimize Disruptions   When possible, try to minimize disruptions by setting aside that part of the day when you are most productive as a block of discretionary time. Then, try to insulate yourself. During this time you should limit access to your work area and avoid interruptions. Refuse phone calls or visits during these hours. You can set aside other blocks of time each day when your door is open for unexpected visits and when you can initiate or return all your calls. The ability to insulate yourself depends on your organization's culture, your boss, and how much faith you have in your subordinates. But most critical is your level in the organization. Generally, the higher up you are in an organization, the less crucial it is that you be available for every emergency. In contrast, most supervisors can be out of touch with the work areas they oversee for only short periods of time.

Beware of Wasting Time in Poorly Run Meetings   Meetings take up a large proportion of a manager's time. They also tend to run on at length. If you're running a meeting, you should set a time limit at the outset. You should prepare a written agenda for the meeting and stick to it. Another suggestion, which is a bit bizarre but works wonders for keeping meetings brief, is to require all members to remain standing. As soon as people sit down and get comfortable, they lose any motivation to keep a discussion tightly focused on the issues. Some managers have no chairs in their office other than the one they occupy. Visitors are subtly encouraged to avoid wasting the manager's time. Managers usually move important meetings that demand a long and thoughtful discussion to an adjoining conference room that has an ample supply of chairs.

Summary

This summary is organized by the chapter-opening learning objectives found on page 241.

1. Techniques for scanning the environment include reading newspapers, magazines, books, and trade journals; reading competitors' ads, promotional materials, and press releases; attending trade shows; debriefing sales personnel; and reverse engineering of competitor's products.

2. Quantitative forecasting applies a set of mathematical rules to a set of past data in order to predict future outcomes. Qualitative forecasting uses judgments and the opinions of knowledgeable individuals to predict future outcomes.

3. Budgets are popular planning devices because money is a universal common denominator that can be used in all types of organizations and by managers at all levels.

4. The most popular approach to budgeting is the traditional, or incremental, budget, which is based on past allocations. However, its drawbacks have led to increased interest in zero-base budgets, which make no reference to past allocations.

5. Gantt and load charts are scheduling devices. Both are bar graphs. Gantt charts monitor planned and actual activities over time; load charts focus on capacity utilization by monitoring whole departments or specific resources.

6. The five steps in developing a PERT network are: (1) identifying every significant activity that must be achieved for a project to be completed; (2) determining the order in which these activities must be completed; (3) diagramming the flow of activities in a project from start to finish; (4) estimating the time needed to complete each activity; and (5) using the network diagram to determine a schedule for the start and finish dates of each activity and for the entire project.

7. A product's break-even point is determined by the unit price of the product, its variable cost per unit, and its total fixed costs.

8. For linear programming to be applicable, a problem must have limited resources, constraints, an objective function to optimize, alternative ways of combining resources, and a linear relationship between variables.

9. Simulation is an effective planning tool because it allows managers to simulate, on a computer, thousands of potential options at very little cost. By simulating a complex situation, managers can see how changes in variables will affect outcomes.

10. Five steps toward better time management include: (1) making a list of objectives, (2) ranking the objectives in order of importance, (3) listing the activities necessary to achieve the objectives, (4) assigning priorities to each activity, and (5) scheduling activities according to the priorities set.

Review Questions

1. How is scanning the environment related to forecasting?
2. What is a scenario and how does competitor intelligence help managers to formulate one?
3. How can benchmarking improve the quality of an organization's products or processes?
4. What is a budget? Must it always be based on monetary units?
5. What is the significance of the critical path in a PERT network?
6. What is the value of break-even analysis as a planning tool?
7. Explain probability theory and marginal analysis.
8. How can managers assess how well they currently manage their time?
9. How might a manager use his or her discretionary time more effectively?

Discussion Questions

1. Assume that you manage a large fast food restaurant in downtown Philadelphia, and you want to know the amount of each type of sandwich to make and the number of cashiers to have on each shift. What type of planning tool(s) do you

think will be useful to you? What type of environmental scanning, if any, would you likely do in this management job?

2. "Budgets are both a planning and a control tool." Explain this statement.

3. Develop a Gantt chart for writing a college term paper.

4. "You can't teach time management. People who are good at it tend to be structured and compulsive individuals by nature." Do you agree or disagree? Discuss.

5. "Forecasting is a waste of a manager's time because no one can accurately predict the future." Do you agree or disagree with this statement? Discuss.

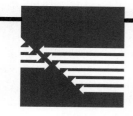

SELF-ASSESSMENT EXERCISE

Do You Know Your Daily Productivity Cycle?

Directions: Please check the response for each item that best describes you.

1. Considering only your own "feeling best" rhythm, at what time would you get up if you were entirely free to plan your day?

5:00–6:30 a.m.	_____(a)
6:30–7:45 a.m.	_____(b)
7:45–9:45 a.m.	_____(c)
9:45–11:00 a.m.	_____(d)
11:00 a.m.–12:00 (noon)	_____(e)

2. Considering only your "feeling best" rhythm, at what time would you go to bed if you were entirely free to plan your evening?

8:00–9:00 p.m.	_____(a)
9:00–10:15 p.m.	_____(b)
10:15 p.m.–12:30 a.m.	_____(c)
12:30–1:45 a.m.	_____(d)
1:45–3:00 a.m.	_____(e)

3. Assuming normal circumstances, how easy do you find getting up in the morning? (Check one.)

Not at all easy	_____(a)
Slightly easy	_____(b)
Fairly easy	_____(c)
Very easy	_____(d)

4. How alert do you feel during the first half hour after you wake up in the morning? (Check one.)

Not at all alert	_____(a)
Slightly alert	_____(b)
Fairly alert	_____(c)
Very alert	_____(d)

5. During the first half hour after awakening in the morning, how tired do you feel? (Check one.)

Very tired	_____(a)
Fairly tired	_____(b)
Fairly refreshed	_____(c)
Very refreshed	_____(d)

6. You have decided to engage in some physical exercise. A friend suggests that you do this one hour twice a week and the best time for him is 7:00–8:00 a.m. Bearing in mind nothing else but your own "feeling best" rhythm, how do you think you would perform?

   Would be in good form _____(a)
   Would be in reasonable form _____(b)
   Would find it difficult _____(c)
   Would find it very difficult _____(d)

7. At what time in the evening do you feel tired and, as a result, in need of sleep?

   8:00–9:00 p.m. _____(a)
   9:00–10:15 p.m. _____(b)
   10:15 p.m.–12:30 a.m. _____(c)
   12:30–1:45 a.m. _____(d)
   1:45–3:00 a.m. _____(e)

8. You wish to be at your peak performance for a test which you know is going to be mentally exhausting and will last for two hours. You are entirely free to plan your day, and considering only your own "feeling best" rhythm, which ONE of the four testing times would you choose?

   8:00–10:00 a.m. _____(a)
   11:00 a.m.–1:00 p.m. _____(b)
   3:00–5:00 p.m. _____(c)
   7:00–9:00 p.m. _____(d)

9. One hears about "morning" and "evening" types of people. Which ONE of these types do you consider yourself to be?

   Definitely a morning type _____(a)
   More a morning than an evening type _____(b)
   More an evening than a morning type _____(c)
   Definitely an evening type _____(d)

10. When would you prefer to rise (provided you have a full day's work—8 hours) if you were totally free to arrange your time?

    Before 6:30 a.m. _____(a)
    6:30–7:30 a.m. _____(b)
    7:30–8:30 a.m. _____(c)
    8:30 a.m. or later _____(d)

11. If you always had to rise at 6:00 a.m., what do you think it would be like?

    Very difficult and unpleasant _____(a)
    Rather difficult and unpleasant _____(b)
    A little unpleasant but no great problem _____(c)
    Easy and not unpleasant _____(d)

12. How long a time does it usually take before you "recover your senses" in the morning after rising from a night's sleep?

    0–10 minutes _____(a)
    11–20 minutes _____(b)
    21–40 minutes _____(c)
    More than 40 minutes _____(d)

13. Please indicate to what extent you are a morning or evening *active* individual.

Pronounced morning active (morning alert and evening tired)	_____(a)
To some extent, morning active	_____(b)
To some extent, evening active	_____(c)
Pronounced evening active (morning tired and evening alert)	_____(d)

Please turn to page SK-2 for scoring directions and key.

Source: Carlla S. Smith, Christopher Reilly, and Karen Midkiff, "Evaluation of Three Circadian Rhythm Questionnaires With Suggestions for an Improved Measure of Morningness," *Journal of Applied Psychology,* October 1989, p. 734. With permission.

READ IT AGAIN, SAM!

The Source for Pre-Read Books

To: Dana Murray, Director of Marketing
From: Bob Stratford, President
Subject: Benchmarking the competition

As we make the move to expand our used-book superstore business beyond our current Arizona market—to go from three stores to forty or more by decade's end—we should benchmark the best practices of other bookstores and used-merchandise retailers. I'd like you to take responsibility for this benchmarking project.

We can start with an intelligence collection plan. Specifically, I'd like you first to identify a set of firms who might have creative and effective ideas that we could clone. These might be general retailers, small booksellers, large book chains such as B. Dalton, or anybody else you think we could learn from. Then I'd like you to visit these stores, talk with their managers and/or employees, draw up a list of best-practices that seem to help these firms achieve superior performance and get some ideas that we might benefit from. Finally, I'd like you to write up a brief report summarizing your findings.

CASE APPLICATION

Transport Systems

Transport Systems, a regional trucking company operating out of Denver, Colorado, is having profitability problems as a result of deregulation in the trucking industry. Management wants to decrease driver turnover and reduce the use of its own trucks by hiring more independent owner-operators to haul products and materials. Top management has therefore instructed the director of operations to launch a program to recruit owner-operators. The director has identified the following activities that will be required for such a program.

Activities to decrease turnover of all drivers (company and owner-operator):

A. Establish terminal facilities for drivers (food, showers, parking, and so on).

B. Implement terminal facility standards.

C. Design a diesel fuel purchase program.

D. Implement the diesel fuel purchase program.

Activities to recruit the desired number of owner-operators:

E. Advertise for owner-operators.

F. Establish a bonus system for employees who recommend new owner-operators who are placed under contract.

G. Revise procedures, train staff to sign up new owner-operators, and begin sign-ups.

After careful thought, the director of operations has concluded that some activities must be completed before others can begin. The sequencing requirements among all activities are shown in Table CA9–1.

The director has also computed estimates of the activity times for the driver program. They are shown in Table CA9–2.

TABLE CA9–1   Sequencing of Activities

Activity	Preceding Activity
A. Establish terminal facility standards	None
C. Design fuel program	None
B. Implement terminal facility standards	A
D. Implement fuel program	C
F. Establish bonus system	B,D
E. Advertise	B,D
G. Sign up owner-operators	F,E

Source: Adapted from Charles N. Greene, Everett E. Adam, Jr., and Ronald J. Ebert, Management for Effective Performance (Englewood Cliffs, N.J.: Prentice-Hall, 1985), pp. 736–37. With permission.

TABLE CA9–2   Activity Time Estimates for Driver Program (in weeks)

Activity	Optimistic Time t_o	Most Likely Time t_m	Pessimistic Time t_p
A	2½	6½	7½
B	15	20	37
C	2	4	6
D	5	6½	11
E	3	5	7
F	½	2	3½
G	5	6	7

Questions

1. Draw a PERT network of this program.
2. Calculate the expected time for each activity and include it in the PERT network.
3. How long should this program take?
4. What's the critical path in this program? What are the implications of delays in activities along this path?

VIDEO CASE

MVP Athletic Shoes

MVP Athletic Shoes is certainly no immediate threat to Nike or Reebok. This Michigan company employs only thirty-five people and sells 150,000 pairs of shoes a year—a drop in the bucket considering that the U.S. athletic shoe market is 388 *million* pairs a year.

So what is MVP Athletic Shoes? MVP is the brainchild of Harold Martin. He decided that there was a niche market that others had missed. Focusing on the Michigan area, he saw a market of 634,000 students who, on average, bought four pairs of athletic shoes per year. Why not sell leather athletic shoes, in the $50 to $60 range, with personalized high school and college colors and logos? This was the perfect vehicle for students to show pride in their schools. And Martin also came up with an innovative marketing approach—he arranged for student clubs to sell the shoes by giving them $19 for each pair they sell. Thus Martin not only has a unique product, he has a sales force motivated to earn money to support their club and school activities.

In 1992, MVP expected to sell 150,000 pairs of shoes, which was up from 50,000 pairs in 1991. The company believes it can continue at this 300 percent growth rate for some time because they represent less than .01 percent of the total market. Yet, MVP is not resting on its recent successes. The company has taken its concept to corporations with the intent of selling them on the spirit of "belongingness" that MVP shoes represent. MVP has also approached retail sporting outlets about distributing college lines and contracted with national retailers to sell Star Trek shoes to Trekkies and a new "X" line developed to capitalize on the renewed interest in slain civil rights leader Malcolm X. Martin envisions expanding into other areas besides shoes: for instance, caps, jackets, and other sports-related clothing. As Martin puts it, "We have more business opportunities than the dollars to match the opportunity."

Questions

1. How would environmental scanning help MVP to identify market opportunities?
2. Where would MVP go to gain information on its key competitors?
3. How might MVP use break-even analysis and marginal analysis?
4. What potential problems do you think MVP will face in the next couple of years? How can they be addressed?

Source: "MVP Athletic Shoes," *ABC's Business World,* March 8, 1992.

GOAL SETTING

PURPOSE

1. To practice goal setting.
2. To compare performance among groups.

REQUIRED KNOWLEDGE

1. The value of goals on performance.

TIME REQUIRED

Approximately 30 minutes.

INSTRUCTIONS

Your instructor will divide the class into approximately three equal groups. The first group is to remain in the class. Students in the other two groups are to wait outside the classroom.

   Your instructor will now start the exercise. Follow his or her directions carefully.

Source: This exercise is based on Jiing-Lih Farh and Arthur G. Bedeian, "Understanding Goal Setting: An In-Class Experiment," *Organizational Behavior Teaching Review,* Vol. 12, Issue 3, 1987–88, pp. 75–79.

INTEGRATIVE CASE FOR PART III

SOUTHWEST AIRLINES: THE LOW-COST OPERATOR

We introduced Southwest Airlines and its CEO, Herb Kelleher, at the beginning of Chapter 6. We return to this company, and present it as an integrative case, because of its remarkable success record against much larger and wealthier competitors.

MEASURES OF SUCCESS

By almost any measure you use, Southwest Airlines has to be considered a highly effective and successful company. Starting in 1971 with four airplanes, Southwest had become the seventh largest U.S. carrier, with 141 planes, sales of $1.2 billion, and profits of nearly $75 million by 1993. This last statistic is particularly impressive because companies like Delta, American, and United were reporting huge losses during this period. In its twenty-two years of business, Southwest has been profitable every year except for its first two. As other airlines struggle in bankruptcy, laying off flight crews and mechanics, and cutting routes, Southwest merrily goes about pursuing its growth plans by buying more planes, expanding into new cities, and hiring personnel.

As noted in Chapter 6, Southwest is the low-cost operator in its industry. Its cost per available-seat-mile is 6.5 cents versus 9 cents at American and 15 cents at USAir. But perhaps Southwest's most impressive measure of success is the fact that its efficiency has won the U.S. Department of Transportation's "triple crown"—monthly citations for the best on-time performance, fewest lost bags, and fewest overall complaints—eleven times. No other airline has won it even once.

WHAT'S UNIQUE ABOUT SOUTHWEST AIR?

Southwest's mission is straightforward: airline service that is cheap, simple, and focused. The company is determined to be the lowest-cost operator in the airline

business. It achieves this by offering a no-frills approach to service. Southwest's low fares result in filled planes, loyal customers, and competitors who are increasingly choosing to withdraw from markets rather than fight Southwest's dirt-cheap prices.

No frills

While other major carriers subscribe to expensive computerized reservation systems, Southwest doesn't. There are no first-class seats on Southwest flights. Like on a bus, no seat is assigned. Gate agents issue reusable numbered plastic cards on a first-come, first-aboard basis. And there are no meals served on flights. This "no frills" approach allows Southwest to load and unload passengers quickly—in about 15 minutes—and average eleven trips a day on every plane. Watching gate agents, mechanics, and ground crew work a plane turnaround reminds you of a precision pit-crew during a refilling stop at the Indianapolis 500. The end result is a level of efficiency and operating costs that absolutely overwhelms the competition.

Standardization of planes

Southwest flies only one type of aircraft, the fuel-efficient Boeing 737. This standardization of equipment cuts inventory costs for spare parts and minimizes training of flight and maintenance crews.

Market selection

Southwest essentially has no hubs. It is a short-haul, point-to-point carrier. Its average flight time is fifty-five minutes. As such, it doesn't make connections with other carriers and doesn't have to transfer baggage.

Southwest's market is thirty-four cities in fifteen states. It focuses on serving cities in the Sunbelt and the Midwest. It flies only as far east as Cleveland. But while Southwest may be limited in the cities it covers, it bombards those cities with a large number of flights. For example, each day the company flies seventy-eight times between Dallas and Houston, forty-six times

Source: Based on Edward O. Welles, "Captain Marvel," *INC.*, January 1992, pp. 44–47; Bridget O'Brian, "Southwest Airlines Is a Rare Air Carrier: It Still Makes Money," *Wall Street Journal,* October 26, 1992, p. A1; and Richard Woodbury, "Prince of Midair," *Time,* January 25, 1993, p. 55.

between Phoenix and Los Angeles, and thirty-four times between Las Vegas and Phoenix. This makes it very tough on the competition to come anywhere close to Southwest's frequency of service.

Low fares

Southwest isn't kidding when it says it offers low fares. Its average fare is $58. After Southwest began St. Louis–Kansas City, Missouri service in 1991 and Cleveland–Chicago in 1992, the average fare for these routes dropped from about $300 to $59. In most of its markets, Southwest is cheaper than comparable inter-city bus prices. Says CEO Kelleher, "We've created a solid niche—our main competition is the automobile. We're taking people away from Toyota and Ford."

Low operating costs and debt

Southwest spends an average of $43,707 a year on salary and benefits for each unionized worker. That compares with $58,816 at Delta and an industry average of $45,692. Additionally, most airlines today are burdened with debt. Southwest's debt, at 49 percent of equity, is the lowest among any U.S. carrier. The company also has the highest Standard & Poor's credit rating in the airline industry.

Loyal employees

From the airline's inception, founder and CEO Kelleher has sought to make Southwest a fun place to work. He schmoozes with employees, who know him as "Uncle Herb." He stages weekly parties at corporate headquarters in Dallas and encourages such zany antics by his flight attendants as organizing trivia contests, delivering instructions in rap, and awarding prizes for the passengers with the largest holes in their socks. Flight attendants wear bunny costumes for Easter, turkey outfits on Thanksgiving, and reindeer antlers at Christmas. Kelleher, himself, frequently dresses in clown suits or Elvis costumes. The purpose of all this is to generate a gung-ho spirit that will boost productivity.

Kelleher's approach seems to work. Employees work hard without complaints. They comment favorably about feeling appreciated and enjoying their jobs. And turnover, at 7 percent, is the industry's lowest. In what other company have you ever heard of employees needling management about having too little to do? Maintenance supervisors in Kansas City felt so under-

worked in 1985 that four of them formed the "Boredom Club," petitioning management to increase flights from three a day. "We had two to three hours between flights, and you can only clean so much," said one member. The "club" has disbanded now that Southwest has thirty-seven flights a day into Kansas City.

Management isn't taking its fun-loving culture for granted. The company recently formed a team of forty-four employees from various locations to devise ways of keeping Southwest intimate and preserving its less-serious culture as the airline grows and prospers.

Satisfying the customer

Southwest's past and future are eventually defined by meeting the needs of customers. Low costs, coupled with lots of flights and dependable service, have translated into a growing set of highly loyal customers. In California, where Southwest has become a dominant player, some San Jose residents drive an hour north to board Southwest's Oakland flights, skipping the local airport where American has a hub. Similarly, so many Atlantans were forgoing Delta's huge base there and driving 150 miles to Birmingham, Alabama, to fly Southwest that an entrepreneur started a van service between the two airports.

"Sure you get herded on the plane, and sure you only get peanuts and a drink," says Richard Spears, vice president of a Tulsa, Oklahoma, oil research firm, "but Southwest does everything they can to get you to the right place on time, and that's most important."

Questions

1. Describe Southwest's strategy. Why does it work? Do you think this strategy would work if Southwest were to become one of the Big 3 airlines?

2. Would you describe Southwest as a defender, a prospector, or an analyzer? Explain your answer.

3. Is Herb Kelleher an entrepreneur? Defend your position.

4. Do you think MBO would be successful at Southwest Airlines? Why or why not?

5. Against whom might Southwest benchmark its practices? What might those practices be? What companies outside the airlines do you think might benefit by benchmarking against Southwest Airlines? Why?

CHAPTER 10

Foundations of Organizing

LEARNING OBJECTIVES

After Reading This Chapter, You Should Be Able To:

1. Define organization structure.
2. Identify the advantages and disadvantages of division of labor.
3. Contrast power with authority.
4. Explain why wider spans of control are related to increased efficiency.
5. Identify the five different ways by which management can departmentalize.
6. Contrast mechanistic and organic organizations.
7. Explain the strategy-determines-structure thesis.
8. Summarize the effect of size on structure.
9. Explain the effect of technology on structure.
10. Describe how environmental uncertainty affects structure.

Gerry and Lilo Leeds found that their company, CMP Publications, had outgrown its highly centralized organization structure. They reorganized around semi-autonomous publishing groups.

The best laid plans often fail because managers don't have the right structure in place. And what's the *right* structure at one time may be inappropriate a year or two later. Gerry and Lilo Leeds, the husband and wife team that run CMP Publications, recognize these facts.[1]

The Leedses founded CMP in 1971. By 1987, their firm produced ten business newspapers and magazines that were leaders in their respective markets. Even more encouraging, their markets—computers, communications technology, business travel, and health care—provided plenty of opportunities for growth. But this growth potential might never have been realized had the Leedses continued using the organization structure they had in place.

The organization they had originally created for CMP centralized all key decision making in their hands. While this worked fine in the early years, by 1987 it was no longer effective. The Leedses became harder to see. People wanting to meet with Gerry, for instance, would begin lining up outside his office at eight in the morning. The answers to day-to-day questions were harder and harder for employees to get. And important decisions that required rapid responses were regularly delayed. CMP had grown too big for its original structure.

The Leedses recognized the problem and reorganized. First, they broke the company into manageable units—essentially creating semiautonomous companies within the company—and put a separate manager in charge of each. Then they gave each of these managers the authority to run and grow his or her own division. Second, the Leedses created a publications committee to oversee the various divisions. Each of the division managers sits on this committee, as do the Leedses. The division managers report to the publications committee, which in turn ensures that all the divisions operate within CMP's overall strategy.

These structural changes have proved effective. CMP now puts out a total of fourteen publications, sales are nearing $200 million a year, and revenue growth continues to reach management's goal of 30 percent annually.

The CMP Publications' example illustrates the importance that selecting the right structure plays in an organization's evolution. In this chapter, we'll present the foundations of organization structure. We'll define the concept and its key components, introduce basic organization design options, and consider contingency variables that determine when certain design options work better than others.

Defining Organization Structure and Design

organization structure
An organization's framework as expressed by its degree of complexity, formalization, and centralization.

complexity
The amount of differentiation in an organization.

formalization
The degree to which an organization relies on rules and procedures to direct the behavior of employees.

centralization
The concentration of decision-making authority in upper management.

decentralization
The handing down of decision-making authority to lower levels in an organization.

organization design
The construction or changing of an organization's structure.

Organization structure describes the organization's framework. Just as human beings have skeletons that define their shapes, organizations have structures that define theirs. An organization's structure can be dissected into three parts: complexity, formalization, and centralization.[2]

Complexity considers the amount of differentiation in an organization. The more division of labor there is in an organization, the more vertical levels in the hierarchy, and the more geographically dispersed the organization's units, the more difficult it is to coordinate people and their activities. Hence we use the term *complexity*.

The degree to which an organization relies on rules and procedures to direct the behavior of employees is **formalization.** Some organizations operate with a minimum of such standardized guidelines, whereas others, some of them quite small, have all kinds of regulations instructing employees in what they can and cannot do. The more rules and regulations in an organization, the more formalized the organization's structure.

Centralization considers where the decision-making authority lies. In some organizations, decision making is highly centralized. Problems flow up to senior executives who choose the appropriate action. In other organizations, decision-making authority is passed down to lower levels. This is known as **decentralization.**

When managers construct or change an organization's structure, they are engaged in **organization design.** When we discuss managers making structural decisions—for example, determining the level at which decisions should be made or the number of standardized rules for employees to follow—we are referring to organization design. In the next chapter, we'll show how the three parts of organization structure can be mixed and matched to create various organization designs.

Basic Organization Design Concepts

The classical concepts of organization design were formulated by the general administrative theorists we discussed in Chapter 2. They offered a set of principles for managers to follow in organization design. More than sixty years have passed since most of these principles were originally proposed. Given the passing of that much time and all the changes that have taken place in our society, you might think that

Division of labor produces efficiencies. Could Cessna produce one Citation jet a year if one person had to build the entire plane? One's skills at performing a task successfully increase through repetition. Less time is spent in changing tasks, in putting away one's tools and equipment from a prior step in the work process, and in getting ready for another. It is easier and less costly to find and train workers to do specific and repetitive tasks, especially for highly sophisticated and complex operations.

these principles would be pretty worthless today. Surprisingly, they're not! For the most part, they still provide valuable insights into designing effective and efficient organizations. Of course, we have also gained a great deal of knowledge over the years as to the limitations of these principles.

In this section, we'll discuss the five basic classical principles that have guided organization design decisions over the years. We'll also present an updated analysis of how each has had to be modified to reflect the increasing sophistication and changing nature of organizational activities.

Division of Labor

The Classical View We mentioned division of labor in our discussion of Adam Smith and the evolution of management thought. Division of labor means that, rather than an entire job being done by one individual, it is broken down into a number of steps, each step being completed by a separate individual. In essence, individuals specialize in doing part of an activity rather than the entire activity. Assembly-line production, in which each worker does the same standardized task over and over again, is an example of division of labor.

Division of labor makes efficient use of the diversity of skills that workers hold. In most organizations, some tasks require highly developed skills; others can be performed by the untrained. If all workers were engaged in each step of, say, an organization's manufacturing process, all would have to have the skills necessary to perform both the most demanding and the least demanding jobs. The result would be that, except when performing the most highly skilled or highly sophisticated tasks, employees would be working below their skill level. Because skilled workers are paid more than unskilled workers and their wages tend to reflect their highest level of skill, it represents an inefficient usage of resources to pay highly skilled workers to do easy tasks.

The Contemporary View Classical writers viewed division of labor as an unending source of increased productivity. At the turn of the twentieth century and earlier, this generalization was undoubtedly accurate. Because specialization was not widely

FIGURE 10-1
Economies and Diseconomies of
Division of Labor

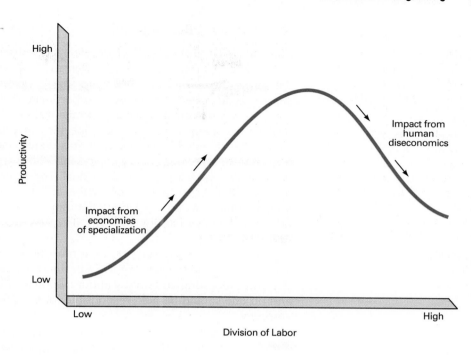

practiced, its introduction almost always generated higher productivity. But a good thing can be carried too far. There is a point at which the human diseconomies from division of labor—which surface as boredom, fatigue, stress, low productivity, poor quality, increased absenteeism, and high turnover—exceed the economic advantages (see Figure 10-1).

By the 1960s, that point had been reached in a number of jobs. In such cases, productivity could be increased by enlarging, rather than narrowing, the scope of job activities.[3] For instance, in the next chapter, we'll discuss successful efforts to increase productivity by giving employees a variety of activities to do, allowing them to do a whole and complete piece of work, and putting them together into teams. Each of these ideas, of course, runs counter to the division of labor concept. Yet, overall, the division of labor concept is alive and well in most organizations today. We have to recognize the economies it provides in certain types of jobs, but we also have to recognize its limitations.

Unity of Command

unity of command
The principle that a subordinate should have one and only one superior to whom he or she is directly responsible.

The Classical View   Classical writers professing the **unity of command** principle argued that a subordinate should have one and only one superior to whom he or she is directly responsible. No person should report to two or more bosses. Otherwise, a subordinate might have to cope with conflicting demands or priorities from several superiors. In those rare instances when the unity of command principle had to be violated, the classical viewpoint always explicitly designated that there be a clear separation of activities and a supervisor responsible for each.

The Contemporary View   The unity of command concept was logical when organizations were comparatively simple. Under most circumstances it is still sound advice, and most organizations today closely adhere to this principle. Yet there are instances, which we'll introduce in the next chapter, when strict adherence to the unity of command creates a degree of inflexibility that hinders an organization's performance.[4]

Authority and Responsibility

authority
The rights inherent in a managerial position to give orders and expect them to be obeyed.

The Classical View   **Authority** refers to the rights inherent in a managerial position to give orders and expect the orders to be obeyed. Authority was a major tenet of the classical writers; it was viewed as the glue that held the organization together. It was to be delegated downward to subordinate managers, giving them certain rights while providing certain prescribed limits within which to operate.

Each management position has specific inherent rights that incumbents acquire from the position's rank or title. Authority therefore relates to one's position within an organization and ignores the personal characteristics of the individual manager. It has nothing directly to do with the individual. The expression "The king is dead; long live the king" illustrates the concept. Whoever is king acquires the rights inherent in the king's position. When a position of authority is vacated, the person who has left the position no longer has any authority. The authority remains with the position and its new incumbent.

responsibility
An obligation to perform assigned activities.

When we delegate authority, we must allocate commensurate **responsibility.** That is, when one is given "rights," one also assumes a corresponding "obligation" to perform. Allocating authority without responsibility creates opportunities for abuse, and no one should be held responsible for something over which he or she has no authority.

Classical writers recognized the importance of equating authority and responsibility. Additionally, they stated that responsibility cannot be delegated. They supported this contention by noting that the delegator was held responsible for the actions of his delegates. But how is it possible to equate authority and responsibility, if responsibility cannot be delegated?

The classicists' answer was to recognize two forms of responsibility: *operating* responsibility and *ultimate* responsibility. Managers pass on operating responsibility, which may then be passed on further. But there is an aspect of responsibility—its ultimate component—that must be retained. A manager is ultimately responsible for the actions of his or her subordinates to whom the operating responsibility has been

Johnson & Johnson takes decentralizing authority seriously. The presidents of its 166 separate companies are not only encouraged to act independently, they're expected to. Some presidents see their bosses at company headquarters only four times a year. Top management believes that creating smaller, self-governing units makes those units more manageable, quicker to react to their markets, and more accountable.

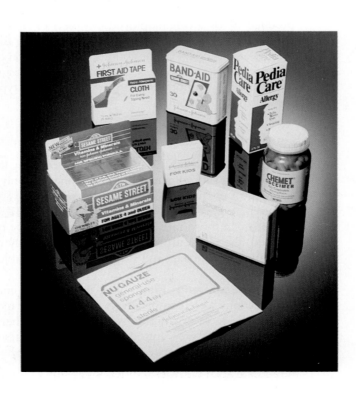

FIGURE 10-2
The Chain of Command

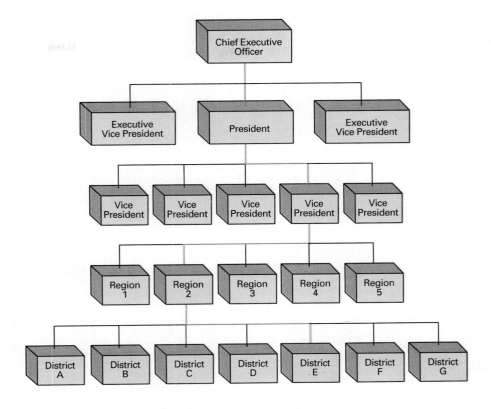

line authority
The authority that entitles a manager to direct the work of a subordinate.

chain of command
The flow of authority from the top to the bottom of an organization.

staff authority
Authority that supports, assists, and advises holders of line authority.

passed. Therefore managers should delegate operating responsibility equal to the delegated authority; however, ultimate responsibility can never be delegated.

The classical writers also distinguished between two forms of authority relations: line authority and staff authority. **Line authority** is the authority that entitles a manager to direct the work of a subordinate. It is the superior–subordinate authority relationship that extends from the top of the organization to the lowest echelon, following what is called the **chain of command.** This is shown in Figure 10–2. As a link in the chain of command, a manager with line authority has the right to direct the work of subordinates and to make certain decisions without consulting others. Of course, in the chain of command, every manager is also subject to the direction of his or her superior.

Sometimes the term *line* is used to differentiate *line* managers from *staff* managers. In this context, line emphasizes managers whose organizational function contributes directly to the achievement of organizational objectives. In a manufacturing firm, line managers are typically in the production and sales functions, whereas executives in personnel and accounting are considered staff managers. But whether a manager's function is classified as line or staff depends on the organization's objectives. For example, at Snelling and Snelling, a personnel placement organization, personnel interviewers have a line function. Similarly, at the accounting firm of Price Waterhouse, accounting is a line function.

The definitions given above are not contradictory but, rather, represent two ways of looking at the term *line*. Every manager has line authority over his or her subordinates, but not every manager is in a line function or position. This latter determination depends on whether or not a function directly contributes to the organization's objectives.

As organizations get larger and more complex, line managers find that they do not have the time, expertise, or resources to get their jobs done effectively. In response, they create **staff authority** functions to support, assist, advise, and generally reduce

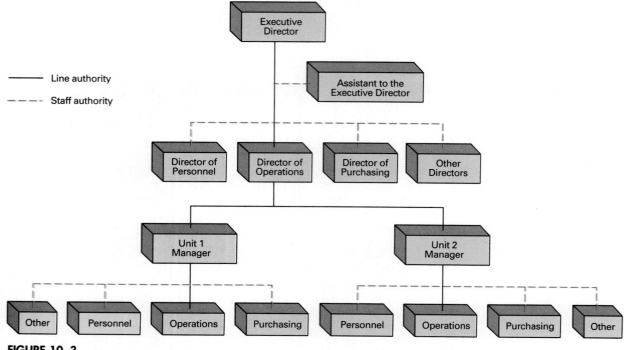

Line authority

Staff authority

FIGURE 10–3
Line and Staff Authority

some of the informational burdens they have. The hospital administrator can't effectively handle all the purchasing of supplies that the hospital needs, so she creates a purchasing department. The purchasing department is a staff department. Of course, the head of the purchasing department has line authority over her subordinate purchasing agents. The hospital administrator might also find that she is overburdened and needs an assistant. In creating the position of assistant to the hospital administrator, she has created a staff position.

Figure 10–3 illustrates line and staff authority.

The Contemporary View The classical writers were enamored with authority. They actively assumed that the rights inherent in one's formal position in an organization were the sole source of influence. They believed that managers were all-powerful.

This might have been true sixty or more years ago. Organizations were simpler. Staff was less important. Managers were only minimally dependent on technical specialists. Under such conditions, influence is the same as authority; and the higher a manager's position in the organization, the more influence he or she had. However, those conditions no longer hold. Researchers and practitioners of management now recognize that you don't have to be a manager to have power, nor is power perfectly correlated to one's level in the organization. Authority is an important concept in organizations, but an exclusive focus on authority produces a narrow, unrealistic view of influence in organizations. Today, we recognize that authority is but one element in the larger concept of power.[5]

The terms *authority* and *power* are frequently confused. Authority is a right, the legitimacy of which is based on the authority figure's position in the organization. Authority goes with the job. **Power,** on the other hand, refers to an individual's capacity to influence decisions. Authority is part of the larger concept of power. That is, the formal rights that come with an individual's position in the organization are just one means by which an individual can affect the decision process.

power
The capacity to influence decisions.

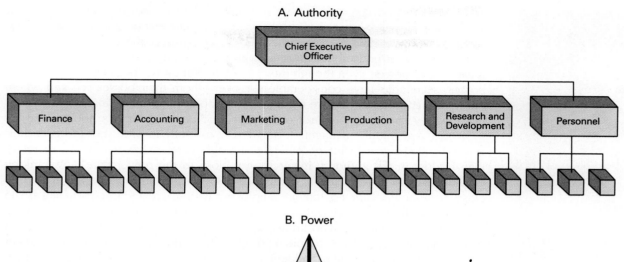

A. Authority

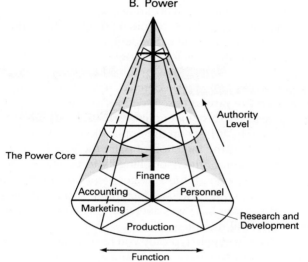

B. Power

FIGURE 10–4
Authority Versus Power

Figure 10–4 visually depicts the difference between authority and power. The two-dimensional arrangement of boxes in part A portrays authority. The area in which the authority applies is defined by the horizontal dimension. Each horizontal grouping represents a functional area. The influence one holds in the organization is defined by the vertical dimension in the structure. The higher one is in the organization, the greater one's authority.

Power, on the other hand, is a three-dimensional concept (see the cone in part B of Figure 10–4). It includes not only the functional and hierarchical dimensions, but also a third dimension called *centrality*. While authority is defined by one's vertical position in the hierarchy, power is made up of both one's vertical position and one's distance from the organization's *power core,* or center.

Think of the cone in Figure 10–4 as being an organization. The center of the cone is the power core. The closer you are to the power core, the more influence you have on decisions. The existence of a power core is, in fact, the only difference between A and B in Figure 10–4. The vertical hierarchy dimension in A is merely one's level on the outer edge of the cone. The top of the cone corresponds to the top of the hierarchy, the middle of the cone to the middle of the hierarchy, and so on. Similarly, the functional groups in A become wedges in the cone. Each wedge represents a functional area.

The cone analogy explicitly acknowledges two facts: (1) the higher one moves in an organization (an increase in authority), the closer one moves to the power core; and (2) it is not necessary to have authority in order to wield power because one can move horizontally inward toward the power core without moving up.

Have you ever noticed that secretaries of high-ranking executives usually have a great deal of power, even though they have little authority? As gatekeepers for their bosses, secretaries have considerable say over whom their bosses see and when. Furthermore, because they are regularly relied upon to pass information on to their bosses, they have some control over what their bosses hear. It's not unusual for $75,000-a-year middle managers to tread very carefully in order not to upset their boss's $25,000-a-year secretary. Why? Because the secretary has power! The secretary may be low in the authority hierarchy but close to the power core. Low-ranking employees who have relatives, friends, or associates in high places might also be close to the power core. So, too, are employees with scarce and important skills. The lowly production-engineer with twenty years of experience in a company might be the only one in the firm who knows the inner workings of all the old production machinery. When pieces of this old equipment break down, no one but this engineer understands how to fix them. Suddenly, the engineer's influence is much greater than it would appear from his level in the vertical hierarchy.

How does one acquire power? John French and Bertram Raven have identified five sources or bases of power: coercive, reward, legitimate, expert, and referent.[6]

The **coercive power** base is defined by French and Raven as being dependent on fear. One reacts to this power out of fear of the negative results that might occur if one failed to comply. It rests on the application, or the threat of application, of physical sanctions such as the infliction of pain; the generation of frustration through restriction of movement; or the controlling by force of basic physiological or safety needs.

In the 1930s, when John Dillinger went into a bank, held a gun to a teller's head, and asked for money, he was incredibly successful at getting compliance with his request. His power base was coercive. A loaded gun gives its holder power because others are fearful that they will lose something that they hold dear: their lives.

If you are a manager, typically you have some coercive power. You may be able to suspend or demote employees. You may be able to assign them work activities they find unpleasant. You may even have the option of dismissing employees. These all represent coercive actions. But you don't have to be a manager to hold coercive power. For instance, a subordinate who is in a position to embarrass his or her boss in public and who successfully uses this power to gain advantage is using coercion.

The opposite of coercive power is **reward power.** People comply with the wishes or directives of another because it produces positive benefits; therefore, one who can distribute rewards that others view as valuable will have power over them. These rewards can be anything that another person values. In an organizational context, we think of money, favorable performance appraisals, promotions, interesting work assignments, friendly colleagues, and preferred work shifts or sales territories.

Coercive and reward power are actually counterparts of each other. If you can remove something of positive value from another or inflict something of negative value upon him or her, you have coercive power over that person. If you can give someone something of positive value or remove something of negative value, you have reward power over that person. Again, as with coercive power, you don't need to be a manager to be able to exert influence through rewards. Rewards such as friendliness, acceptance, and praise are available to everyone in the organization. To the degree that an individual seeks such rewards, your ability to give or withhold them gives you power over that individual.

Legitimate power and authority are one and the same. Legitimate power represents the power a person receives as a result of his or her position in the formal hierarchy.

Positions of authority include coercive and reward powers. Legitimate power,

A two-year power struggle at Time-Warner culminated in four days of maneuvering in February 1992. Gerald Levin (pictured), vice-chairman of T-W, used his close ties with the company's ailing CEO and intricate knowledge of the company's diverse businesses to oust Nicholas J. Nicholas, Jr., Time-Warner's president and contractually-defined CEO-designate. Attaining the support of the Board of Directors, Levin engineered Nicholas' "resignation" and his own appointment as president and new heir to the throne at Time-Warner.

coercive power
Power that is dependent on fear.

reward power
Power based on the ability to distribute anything that others may value.

legitimate power
Power based on one's position in the formal hierarchy.

however, is broader than the power to coerce and reward. Specifically, it includes acceptance by members of an organization of the authority of a position. When school principals, bank presidents, or army captains speak (assuming that their directives are viewed to be within the authority of their positions), teachers, tellers, and first lieutenants listen and usually comply.

expert power
Power based on one's expertise, special skill, or knowledge.

Expert power is influence wielded as a result of expertise, special skill, or knowledge. In recent years, as a result of the explosion in technical knowledge, expert power has become an increasingly potent power source in organizations. As jobs have become more specialized, management has increasingly become dependent on staff "experts" to achieve the organization's goals. As an employee increases his or her knowledge of information that is critical to the operation of a work group, and to the degree that that knowledge is not possessed by others, expert power is enhanced. To illustrate the point, if a computer system is critical to a unit's work, and if one employee, say Chris, knows how to repair it and no one else within 200 miles does, then the unit is dependent on Chris. If the system breaks down, Chris can use her expertise to obtain ends that she could never achieve by her position's authority alone. In such a situation, you should expect the unit's manager to try to have others trained in the workings of the computer system or to hire someone with this knowledge in order to reduce Chris's power. As others become capable of duplicating Chris's specialized activities, her expert power diminishes.

The last category of influence that French and Raven identified was **referent power.** Its base is identification with a person who has desirable resources or personal traits. If I admire and identify with you, you can exercise power over me because I want to please you.

referent power
Power based on identification with a person who has desirable resources or personal traits.

Referent power develops out of admiration of another and a desire to be like that person. You might consider the person you identify with as having *charisma*. If you admire someone to the point of modeling your behavior and attitudes after him or her, this person possesses referent power over you. Referent power explains why celebrities are paid millions of dollars to endorse products in commercials. Marketing research shows that people like Bill Cosby, Elizabeth Taylor, and Michael Jordan have the power to influence your choice of photo processors, perfume, and athletic shoes. With a little practice, you or I could probably deliver as smooth a sales pitch as these celebrities, but the buying public does not identify with you and me. In organizations, the charismatic individual—manager or otherwise—can influence superiors, peers, and subordinates.

Span of Control

span of control
The number of subordinates a manager can direct efficiently and effectively.

The Classical View How many subordinates can a manager efficiently and effectively direct? This question of **span of control** received a great deal of attention from early writers. While there was no consensus on a specific number, the classical writers favored small spans—typically no more than six—in order to maintain close control.[7] However, several writers did acknowledge level in the organization as a contingency variable. They argued that as a manager rises in an organization, he or she has to deal with a greater number of ill-structured problems, so top executives need a smaller span than do middle managers, and middle managers require a smaller span than do supervisors.

Why is the span of control concept important? To a large degree, it determines the number of levels and managers an organization has. All things being equal, the wider or larger the span, the more efficient the organization design. An example can illustrate the validity of this statement.

Assume that we have two organizations, each of which has approximately 4,100 operative employees. As Figure 10–5 illustrates, if one has a uniform span of four and the other a span of eight, the wider span would have two fewer levels and approx-

FIGURE 10-5
Contrasting Spans of Control

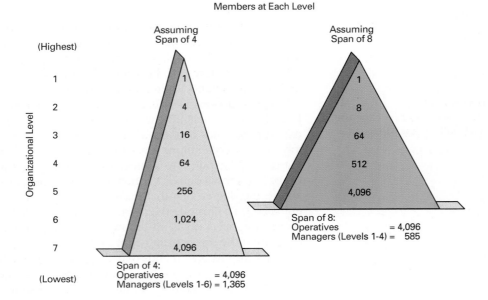

service being offered, the target customer or client, the geographic territory being covered, or the process being used to turn inputs into outputs. No single method of imately 800 fewer managers. If the average manager made $35,000 a year, the wider spans would save $28 million a year in management salaries! Obviously, wider spans are more *efficient* in terms of cost. But at some point, wider spans reduce *effectiveness*.

The Contemporary View   In 1992, Wal-Mart surpassed Sears as the number one retailer in the United States. Management guru Tom Peters predicted this result a few years earlier: "Sears doesn't have a chance," he said. "A twelve-layer company can't compete with a three-layer company."[10] Peters might have exaggerated the point a bit, but it clearly reflects the fact that in recent years the pendulum has swung toward designing flat structures with wide spans of control.

More and more organizations are increasing their spans of control. For example, the span for managers at such companies as General Electric and Reynolds Metals has expanded to ten or twelve subordinates—twice the number of fifteen years ago.[11] The span of control is increasingly being determined by looking at contingency variables. For instance, it's obvious that the more training and experience subordinates have, the less direct supervision they need. Therefore managers who have well-trained and experienced employees can function with a wider span. Other contingency variables that will determine the appropriate span include similarity of subordinate tasks, the complexity of those tasks, the physical proximity of subordinates, the degree to which standardized procedures are in place, the sophistication of the organization's management information system, the strength of the organization's culture, and the preferred style of the manager.[12]

Departmentalization

The Classical View   The classical writers argued that activities in the organization should be specialized and grouped into departments. Division of labor creates specialists who need coordination. This coordination is facilitated by putting specialists together in departments under the direction of a manager. Creation of these departments is typically based on the work functions being performed, the product or

Should You Follow Orders With Which You Don't Agree?

A few years back, a study of business executives revealed that most had obeyed orders that they had found personally objectionable or unethical.[8] Far more thought-provoking was a survey taken among the general public near the end of the Vietnam War. In spite of public dismay over the actions of some military personnel during that war, about half the respondents said that they would have shot civilian men, women, and children in cold blood if they had been ordered to do so by their commanding officer.[9]

If you were asked to follow orders that you believed were unconscionable, would you comply? For example, what if your boss asked you to destroy evidence that he or she had been stealing a great deal of money from the organization?

What if you merely disagreed with the orders? For instance, what if your boss asked you to bring him or her coffee each morning even though no such task is included in your job description? What would *you* do?

Chairman Paul H. O'Neill recently wiped out two layers of top management at Alcoa. He now has the twenty-five presidents of the company's different businesses report directly to him. By widening his *span of control,* O'Neill hopes to make Alcoa— especially its upper management —more responsive to change.

**functional
departmentalization**
Grouping activities by functions performed.

product departmentalization
Grouping activities by product line.

customer departmentalization
Grouping activities on the basis of common customers.

departmentalization was advocated by the classical writers. The method or methods used should reflect the grouping that would best contribute to the attainment of the organization's objectives and the goals of individual units.

One of the most popular ways to group activities is by functions performed, or **functional departmentalization.** A manufacturing manager might organize his or her plant by separating engineering, accounting, manufacturing, personnel, and purchasing specialists into common departments. (See Figure 10–6.) Functional departmentalization can be used in all types of organizations. Only the functions change to reflect the organization's objectives and activities. A hospital might have departments devoted to research, patient care, accounting, and so forth. A professional football franchise might have departments entitled Player Personnel, Ticket Sales, and Travel and Accommodations.

Figure 10–7 illustrates the **product departmentalization** method used at Sun Petroleum Products. Each major product area in the corporation is placed under the authority of a vice president who is a specialist in, and is responsible for, everything having to do with his or her product line. Notice, for example, in contrast to functional departmentalization, that manufacturing and other major activities have been divided up to give the product managers (vice presidents, in this case) considerable autonomy and control.

If an organization's activities are service-related rather than product-related, each service would be autonomously grouped. For instance, an accounting firm would have departments for tax, management consulting, auditing, and the like. Each offers a common array of services under the direction of a product or service manager.

The particular type of customer the organization seeks to reach can also be used to group employees. The sales activities in an office supply firm, for instance, can be broken down into three departments to serve retail, wholesale, and government customers. (See Figure 10–8.) A large law office can segment its staff on the basis of whether they serve corporate or individual clients. The assumption underlying **customer departmentalization** is that customers in each department have a common set of problems and needs that can best be met by having specialists for each.

Another way to departmentalize is on the basis of geography or territory—

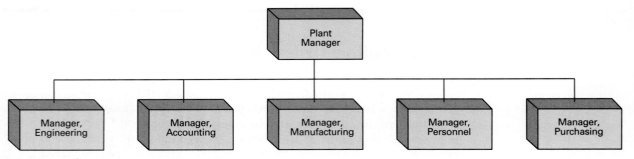

FIGURE 10-6
Functional Departmentalization

geographic departmentalization
Grouping activities on the basis of territory.

process departmentalization
Grouping activities on the basis of product or customer flow.

Another way to departmentalize is on the basis of geography or territory—**geographic departmentalization.** The sales function might have western, southern, midwestern, and eastern regions. (See Figure 10–9.) A large school district might have six high schools to provide for each of the major geographical territories within the district. If an organization's customers are scattered over a large geographic area, this form of departmentalization can be valuable.

Figure 10–10 depicts the various production departments in an aluminum plant. Each department specializes in one specific phase in the production of aluminum tubing. The metal is cast in huge furnaces; sent to the press department, where it is extruded into aluminum pipe; transferred to the tube mill, where it is stretched into various sizes and shapes of tubing; moved to finishing, where it is cut and cleaned; and finally arrives in the inspect, pack, and ship department. Since each process requires different skills, this method offers a basis for the homogeneous categorizing of activities.

Process departmentalization can be used for processing customers as well as products. If you have ever been to a state motor vehicle office to get a driver's license, you probably went through several departments before receiving your license. In some states, applicants must go through three steps, each handled by a separate department: (1) validation, by the motor vehicles division; (2) processing, by the licensing department; and (3) payment collection, by the treasury department.

The Contemporary View   Most large organizations continue to use most or all of the departmental groups suggested by the classical writers. Black & Decker, for instance, organizes each of its divisions along functional lines, organizes its manufacturing units around processes, departmentalizes sales around geographic regions, and divides each sales region into customer groupings. But two recent trends need to be mentioned. First, customer departmentalization has become increasingly emphasized. Second, rigid departmentalization is being complemented by the use of teams that cross over traditional departmental lines.

Today's competitive environment has refocused the attention of management to its customers. To better monitor the needs of customers and to be able to respond to changes in those needs, many organizations have given greater emphasis to customer departmentalization. Xerox, for example, has eliminated its corporate marketing staff and placed marketing specialists out in the field.[13] This allows the company to better identify its customers and to respond faster to their requirements.

We are also seeing a great deal more use of teams today as a device for accomplishing organizational objectives. A list of some of the companies using cross-departmental teams include Ford, Digital Equipment, Boeing, Rubbermaid, and Polaroid. As tasks have become more complex and diverse skills are needed to accomplish these tasks, management has increasingly introduced the use of teams and task forces.

FIGURE 10–7
Product Departmentalization

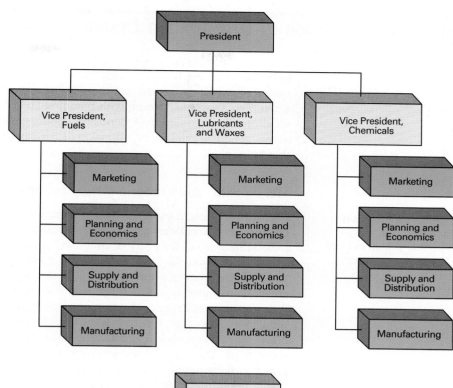

FIGURE 10–8
Customer Departmentalization

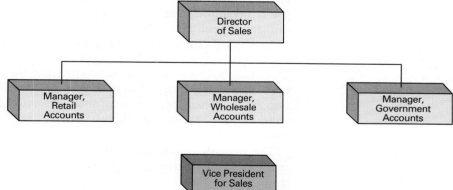

FIGURE 10–9
Geographic Departmentalization

FIGURE 10–10
Process Departmentalization

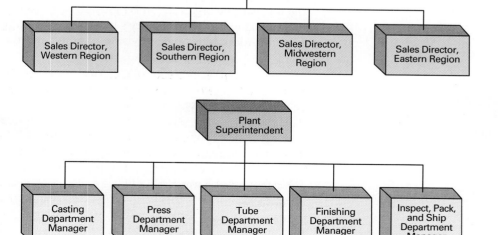

A Contingency Approach to Organization Design

If we combine the classical principles, we arrive at what most of the early writers believed to be the ideal structural design: the mechanistic or bureaucratic organization. Today, we recognize that there is no single "ideal" organization design for all situations. As we discovered with planning and so many management concepts, the ideal organization design depends on contingency factors. In this section, we'll look at two generic models of organization design and then look at the contingency factors that favor each.

Mechanistic and Organic Organizations

mechanistic organization (bureaucracy)
A structure that is high in complexity, formalization, and centralization.

Figure 10–11 describes two diverse organizational forms.[14] The **mechanistic organization** (or **bureaucracy**) was the natural result of combining the classical principles. Adherence to the unity of command principle ensured the existence of a formal hierarchy of authority, with each person controlled and supervised by one superior. Keeping the span of control small at increasingly higher levels in the organization created tall, impersonal structures. As the distance between the top and the bottom of the organization expanded, top management would increasingly impose rules and regulations. Because top managers couldn't control lower-level activities through direct observation and ensure the use of standard practices, they substituted rules and regulations. The classical writers' belief in a high degree of division of labor created jobs that were simple, routine, and standardized. Further specialization through the use of departmentalization increased impersonality and the need for multiple layers of management to coordinate the specialized departments.

In terms of our definition of organization structure, we find the classicists advocating that *all* organizations be high in complexity, high in formalization, and high in centralization. Structures would be efficiency machines, well oiled by rules, regulations, and routinization. The impact of personalities and human judgments, which impose inefficiencies and inconsistencies, would be minimized. Standardization would lead to stability and predictability. Confusion and ambiguity would be eliminated.

organic organization (adhocracy)
A structure that is low in complexity, formalization, and centralization.

The **organic organization** (also referred to as an **adhocracy**) is a direct contrast to the mechanistic form. It is low in complexity, low in formalization, and decentralized.

The organic organization is a highly adaptive form that is as loose and flexible as the mechanistic organization is rigid and stable. Rather than having standardized jobs and regulations, the adhocracy's loose structure allows it to change rapidly as needs require. Adhocracies have division of labor, but the jobs people do are not stand-

FIGURE 10–11
Mechanistic Versus Organic Organizations

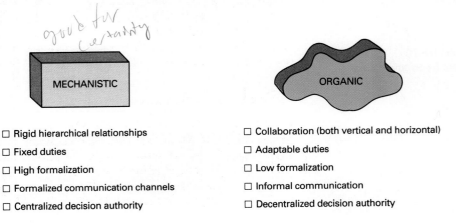

MECHANISTIC

☐ Rigid hierarchical relationships
☐ Fixed duties
☐ High formalization
☐ Formalized communication channels
☐ Centralized decision authority

ORGANIC

☐ Collaboration (both vertical and horizontal)
☐ Adaptable duties
☐ Low formalization
☐ Informal communication
☐ Decentralized decision authority

John A. Young at Hewlett-Packard

Successfully reducing the level of bureaucracy in a company is frequently compared, in difficulty, to teaching an elephant to dance. Yet John A. Young, the recently retired chief executive at Hewlett-Packard, can take credit for pulling off the trick.[15]

In early 1990, Young became aware of how HP's bureaucracy was slowing up decision making when he learned that endless meetings about technical decisions had delayed the company's development of a series of high-speed workstations by more than a year. Originally introduced to foster communication between HP's various operating groups and to evaluate all decisions, the thirty-eight in-house committees were pushing up costs, restricting innovation, and slowing down decision making. For example, it took nearly one hundred people on nine committees seven months just to come up with a name for HP's NewWave Computing software.

Young immediately attacked the problem by revamping HP's corporate structure. He wiped out the company's committee structure and flattened the organization. He divided the computer business into two largely autonomous groups, one handling personal computers, printers, and other products sold through dealers, and the second overseeing sales of workstations and minicomputers to big customers. He also broke up the single corporate sales force so that each computer group got its own sales and marketing team.

The results have been impressive. One general manager, who now has to deal with only three committees rather than thirty-eight, commented: "We are doing more business and getting product out quicker with fewer people." The numbers also support the success of Young's reorganization. Quarterly profits shot up 49 percent between 1991 and 1992.

ardized. Employees tend to be professionals who are technically proficient and trained to handle diverse problems. They need very few formal rules and little direct supervision because their training has instilled in them standards of professional conduct. For instance, a computer engineer is given an assignment. He doesn't need to be given procedures on how to do it. Most problems he can solve himself or resolve after conferring with colleagues. Professional standards guide his behavior. The organic organization is low in centralization in order for the professional to respond quickly to problems and because top management cannot be expected to possess the expertise to make necessary decisions.

Strategy and Structure

An organization's structure is a means to help management achieve its objectives. Since objectives are derived from the organization's overall strategy, it is only logical that strategy and structure should be closely linked. More specifically, structure should follow strategy. If management makes a significant change in its organization's strategy, it will need to modify structure to accommodate and support this change.

The first important research on the strategy-structure relationship was a study of close to 100 large U.S. companies conducted by Alfred Chandler.[16] After tracing the development of these organizations over a period of fifty years and compiling extensive case histories of companies such as DuPont, General Motors, Standard Oil of New Jersey, and Sears, Chandler concluded that changes in corporate strategy precede and lead to changes in an organization's structure. Specifically, he found that organizations usually begin with a single product or line. The simplicity of the strategy requires only a simple or loose form of structure to execute it. Decisions can be centralized in the hands of a single senior manager, while complexity and formalization will be low. As organizations grow, their strategies become more ambitious and elaborate.

From the single product line, companies often expand their activities within their industry by acquiring suppliers or selling their products directly to customers. For example, General Motors not only assembles automobiles but also owns companies that make air conditioners, electrical equipment, and other car components. This vertical integration strategy makes for increased interdependence between organizational units and creates the need for a more complex coordination device. This is achieved by redesigning the structure to form specialized units based on functions performed. Finally, if growth proceeds further into product diversification, structure needs to be adjusted again to gain efficiency. A product diversification strategy demands a structural form that allows for the efficient allocation of resources, accountability for performance, and coordination between units. This can be achieved best by creating many independent divisions, each responsible for a specified product line. In summary, Chandler proposed that as strategies move from single product to vertical integration to product diversification, management will move from an organic to a more mechanistic organization.

Recent research has generally confirmed the strategy-structure relationship but has used the strategy terminology presented in Chapter 8.[17] For instance, organizations pursuing a prospector strategy must innovate to survive. An organic organization matches best with this strategy because it is flexible and maximizes adaptability. In contrast, a defender strategy seeks stability and efficiency. This can best be achieved with a mechanistic organization.

Size and Structure

There is considerable historical evidence that an organization's size significantly affects its structure.[18] For instance, large organizations—those typically employing 2,000 or more employees—tend to have more specialization, horizontal and vertical differentiation, and rules and regulations than do small organizations. However, the relationship isn't linear. Rather, size affects structure at a decreasing rate. The impact of size becomes less important as an organization expands. Why is this? Essentially, once an organization has around 2,000 employees, it is already fairly mechanistic. An additional 500 employees will not have much impact. On the other hand, adding 500 employees to an organization that has only 300 members is likely to result in a shift toward a more mechanistic structure.

Technology and Structure

Every organization uses some form of technology to convert its inputs into outputs. To attain its objectives, the organization uses equipment, materials, knowledge, and/ or experienced individuals, and puts them together into certain types and patterns of activities. For instance, college instructors teach students by a variety of methods:

3M makes a conscious effort to keep its work units as small as possible. The 52,000 U.S. employees of 3M are divided among thirty-seven divisions and nine subsidiaries. Among the company's ninety-one manufacturing plants, only five employ 1,000 people or more, and the average company installation has 270 employees.

Today's Successful Organizations are Increasingly Lean, Fast, and Flexible

A generation ago, successful managers valued stability, predictability, and efficiency through economies of scale. But many of yesterday's "stars" have faded. The following list contrasts the strong performing organizations in various industries in the 1960s and 1990s:

Industry	1960s Star	1990s Star
Airlines	Pan Am	Southwest Airlines
Automobiles	General Motors	Toyota
Broadcasting	CBS	CNN
Computers	IBM	Dell Computers
Financial services	Merrill Lynch	Charles Schwab
General retailing	Sears	Wal-Mart
Specialty retailing	Macy's	The Limited
Medical services	Massachusetts General Hospital	Quik Care
Steel	USX (U.S. Steel)	Nucor
Telecommunications	AT&T	MCI

What common structural factors characterize the 1990s stars? They're lean, fast, and flexible. More specifically, they are often considerably smaller than their counterparts of the 1960s, are flat rather than tall, have replaced hierarchy with teams, and organize around processes or customers instead of functions.[19]

Big isn't necessarily inefficient. Companies such as 3M, Johnson & Johnson, GE, Wal-Mart, Hewlett-Packard, The Limited, and Microsoft have managed to blend large size with agility. But they still typically break up their organizations into smaller, more flexible units. Few managers today accept the notion that large organizations should automatically produce at lower cost because of economies of scale. In the steel industry, for example, many of Nucor's minimills are 20 to 60 percent more efficient than the larger plants of USX and Bethlehem.

As noted earlier in the chapter, management is cutting layers out of their organizations and widening the span of control. Toyota, for instance, has seven layers between its chief executive and workers versus twenty-one at GM and seventeen at Ford. The twenty-one people who make up the staff of Nucor's headquarters, including the chairman and secretaries, look after twenty-two steel plants across the United States.

In place of rigid departments, managers are using teams that cut across functions. And the guiding organizational concept is focusing on the needs of the customer or work processes. The 1500 employees at Eastman Kodak who make black and white film are now organized horizontally. These employees don't work in departments, but in what they call "the flow." A twenty-five-member leadership team watches the flow. Within the flow are "streams" defined by customers (Kodak business units). In the streams, most employees work in semiautonomous teams.

formal lectures, group discussions, case analyses, programmed learning, and so forth. Each of these methods is a type of technology.

In the early 1960s, British scholar Joan Woodward demonstrated that organization structures adapt to their technology. While few researchers in organization design would argue today that technology is the *sole* determinant of structure, clearly it is an important contributor.[20] Let's look at Woodward's research and update the work on classifying different types of technology.

Joan Woodward   The initial interest in technology as a determinant of structure can be traced to the work of Joan Woodward.[21] She studied nearly one hundred small manufacturing firms in the south of England to determine the extent to which classical principles such as unity of command and span of control were related to firm success. She was unable to derive any consistent pattern from her data until she segmented her firms into three categories based on the size of their production runs. The three categories, representing three distinct technologies, had increasing levels of complexity and sophistication. The first category, **unit production,** was comprised of unit or small-batch producers that manufactured custom products such as tailor-made suits and turbines for hydroelectric dams. The second category, **mass production,** included large-batch or mass-production manufacturers that made items like refrigerators and automobiles. The third and most technically complex group, **process production,** included continuous-process producers like oil and chemical refiners.

Woodward found that (1) distinct relationships existed between these technology classifications and the subsequent structure of the firms and (2) the effectiveness of the organizations was related to the "fit" between technology and structure.

For example, the number of vertical levels increased with technical complexity. The median number of vertical levels for firms in the unit, mass, and process categories were three, four, and six, respectively. More important, from an effectiveness standpoint, the more successful firms in each category clustered around the median for their production group. But not all the relationships were linear. As a case in point, the mass-production firms scored high in terms of overall complexity and formalization, whereas the unit and process firms rated low on these structural dimensions. Imposing rules and regulations, for instance, was impossible with the nonroutine technology of unit production and unnecessary in the highly standardized process technology. A summary of her findings is shown in Table 10–1.

After carefully analyzing her findings, Woodward concluded that specific structures were associated with each of the three categories and that successful firms met the requirements of their technology by adopting the proper structural arrangements. Within each category, the firms that most nearly conformed to the median figure for

unit production
The production of items in units or small batches.

mass production
Large-batch manufacturing.

process production
Continuous-process production.

TABLE 10–1   Woodward's Findings on Technology, Structure, and Effectiveness

	Unit Production	**Mass Production**	**Process Production**
Structural characteristics	Low vertical differentiation	Moderate vertical differentiation	High vertical differentiation
	Low horizontal differentiation	High horizontal differentiation	Low horizontal differentiation
	Low formalization	High formalization	Low formalization
Most effective structure	Organic	Mechanistic	Organic

each structural component were the most effective. She found that there was no one best way to organize a manufacturing firm. Unit and process production are most effective when matched with an organic structure; mass production is most effective when matched with a mechanistic structure.

Charles Perrow   One of the major limitations of Woodward's technological classification scheme was that it applied only to manufacturing organizations. Since manufacturing firms represent fewer than half of all organizations, technology needed to be operationalized in a more generic way if the concept was to have meaning across all organizations. Charles Perrow suggested such an alternative.[22]

Perrow directed his attention to knowledge technology rather than production technology. He proposed that technology be viewed in terms of two dimensions: (1) the number of exceptions individuals encounter in their work and (2) the type of search procedures followed to find successful methods for responding adequately to these exceptions. The first dimension he termed **task variability;** the second he called **problem analyzability.**

The exceptions in task variability are few when the job is high in routineness. Examples of jobs that normally have few exceptions in their day-to-day practice include those of a worker on a manufacturing assembly line and a fry cook at McDonald's. At the other end of the spectrum, if a job has a great deal of variety, it will have a large number of exceptions. This would characterize top management positions, consulting jobs, and jobs such as putting out fires on off-shore oil platforms.

The second dimension, problem analyzability, assesses search procedures. The search can, at one extreme, be described as well defined. An individual can use logical and analytical reasoning in the search for a solution. If you're basically a high B student and you suddenly fail the first exam in a course, you logically analyze the problem and find a solution. Did you spend enough time studying for the exam? Did you study the right material? Was the exam fair? How did other good students do? Using this kind of logic, you can find the source of the problem and rectify it. At the other extreme are ill-defined problems. If you're an architect given an assignment to design a building to conform to standards and constraints that you've never encountered before or read about, you won't have any formal search technique to use. You will have to rely on your prior experience, judgment, and intuition to find a solution. Through guesswork and trial and error you might find an acceptable choice.

Perrow used these two dimensions, task variability and problem analyzability, to construct the two-by-two matrix shown in Figure 10–12. The four cells in this matrix represent four types of technology: routine, engineering, craft, and nonroutine.

Routine technologies (cell 1) have few exceptions and have easy-to-analyze problems. The mass-production processes used to make steel and automobiles or to

---

task variability
The number of exceptions individuals encounter in their work.

problem analyzability
The type of search procedures employees follow in responding to exceptions.

FIGURE 10–12
Perrow's Technology Classification

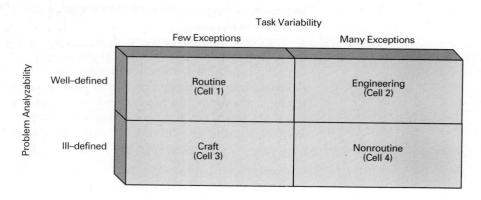

refine petroleum belong in this category. Engineering technologies (cell 2) have a large number of exceptions, but they can be handled in a rational and systemized manner. The construction of bridges falls in this category. Craft technologies (cell 3) deal with relatively difficult problems but with a limited set of exceptions. Shoemaking and furniture restoring fit in this category. Finally, nonroutine technologies (cell 4) are characterized by many exceptions and difficult-to-analyze problems. This technology describes many aerospace operations, such as Rockwell International's development of the space shuttle.

In summary, Perrow argued that if problems can be systematically analyzed, the technologies of cells 1 and 2 are appropriate. Problems that can be handled only by intuition, guesswork, or unanalyzed experience require the technology of cell 3 or 4. Similarly, if new, unusual, or unfamiliar problems appear regularly, they would be in either cell 2 or 4. If problems are familiar, then cell 1 or 3 is appropriate.

What do these conclusions mean for the technology–structure relationship? Perrow argued that control and coordination methods should vary with technology type. The more routine the technology, the more highly structured the organization should be. Conversely, nonroutine technologies require greater structural flexibility. Thus, according to Perrow, the most routine technology (cell 1) can be best accomplished through standardized coordination and control. These technologies should be aligned with structures that are high in both formalization and centralization. At the other extreme, nonroutine technologies (cell 4) demand flexibility. Basically, they would be decentralized, have high interaction among all members, and be characterized as having a minimum degree of formalization. In between, craft technology (cell 3) requires the problem solving be done by those with the greatest knowledge and experience. That means decentralization. And engineering technology (cell 2), because it has many exceptions but analyzable search processes, should have decision-making centralized but should maintain flexibility through low formalization.

What Does It Mean?   The common theme in studies of technology is that the processes or methods that transform inputs into outputs differ by their degree of routineness. In general, the more routine the technology, the more standardized the structure can be. We should expect management to meet routine technologies with a mechanistic organization. The more nonroutine the technology, the more organic the structure.[23]

Environment and Structure

In Chapter 3 we introduced the organization's environment as a constraint on managerial discretion. Research has demonstrated that environment is also a major influence on structure.[24] Essentially, mechanistic organizations are most effective in stable environments. Organic organizations are best matched with dynamic and uncertain environments.

The evidence on the environment–structure relationship helps to explain why so many managers have restructured their organizations to be lean, fast, and flexible. Global competition, accelerated product innovation by all competitors, and increased demands from customers for higher quality and faster deliveries are examples of dynamic environmental forces. Mechanistic organizations tend to be ill-equipped to respond to rapid environmental change. As a result, we're seeing managers redesigning their organizations in order to make them more organic.

Organization Structures Reflect Cultural Values

An organization's structure must adapt to its environment. Included in that environment is the national culture of the country in which the organization is located. Research confirms that organizations mirror, to a considerable degree, the cultural values of their host country.[25]

In a country with a high power distance rating, people prefer that decisions be centralized. Similarly, uncertainty avoidance relates to formalization. High uncertainty avoidance relates to high formalization. Based on these relationships, we find certain patterns. French and Italian managers tend to create rigid bureaucracies that are high in both centralization and formalization. Managers in India prefer centralization and low formalization. Germans prefer formalization with decentralization.

The extensive use of work teams in a country like Japan can also be explained in terms of national culture. Japan scores high on collectivism. In such a culture, employees prefer more organic organizations built around work teams. In contrast, employees in India—where power distance values are high—are likely to perform poorly in teams. They feel more comfortable working in mechanistic, authority-dominated structures.

A recent study of managers' perceptions of the "ideal" organization in the People's Republic of China (PRC) found preferences for structures that fit with their culture.[26] Executives in the PRC favored high participation in their organizations. The researchers noted that this reflected the cultural value placed on allowing workers formal participation in the planning process as well as retaining some worker authority over the appointment and retention of managers. Managers in the PRC also have an aversion to conflict and a need to "save face," which fosters a mechanistic structure with clear lines of authority and unambiguous standard operating procedures. In addition, managers in the PRC were found to shun internal competition and individual risk-taking initiatives. This is consistent with traditional Chinese values of collective responsibility.

Summary

This summary is organized by the chapter-opening learning objectives found on page 279.

1. An organization's structure is a measure of its degree of complexity, formalization, and centralization.

2. The advantages of division of labor relate to economic efficiencies. It makes efficient use of the diversity of skills that workers hold. Skills are developed through repetition. Less time is wasted. Training is also easier and less costly. The disadvantage of division of labor is that it can result in human diseconomies. Excessive division of labor can cause boredom, fatigue, stress, low productivity, poor quality, increased absence, and high turnover.

3. Authority relates to rights inherent in a position. Power describes all means by which an individual can influence decisions, including formal authority. Authority is synonymous with legitimate power. However, a person can have coercive,

reward, expert, or referent power without holding a position of authority. Thus authority is actually a subset of power.

4. Wider spans of control mean that a manager has more subordinates reporting to him or her. The more subordinates that a manager can effectively supervise, the lower the cost of administrative overhead, and the more efficient the manager becomes.

5. Managers can departmentalize on the basis of function, product, customer, geography, or process. In practice, most large organizations use all five.

6. The mechanistic organization or bureaucracy rates high in complexity, formalization, and centralization. The organic organization or adhocracy scores low on these same three structural dimensions.

7. The "strategy-determines-structure" thesis argues that structure should follow strategy. As strategies move from single-product, to vertical integration, to product diversification, structure must move from organic to mechanistic.

8. Size affects structure at a decreasing rate. As size increases, so too do specialization, formalization, vertical differentiation, and decentralization. But it has less of an impact on large organizations than on small ones because once an organization has around 2000 employees it tends to be fairly mechanistic.

9. All other things equal, the more routine the technology, the more mechanistic the organization should be. The more nonroutine the technology, the more organic the structure should be.

10. All other things equal, stable environments are better matched with mechanistic organizations, while dynamic environments fit better with organic organizations.

Review Questions

1. Which is more efficient—a wide or a narrow span of control? Why?
2. Why did the classical writers argue that authority should equal responsibility?
3. Can the manager of a staff department have line authority? Explain.
4. What are the five sources of power?
5. In what ways can management departmentalize?
6. Explain Perrow's technology framework and discuss its implications for organization design.
7. Why did the classical authors favor a mechanistic organization?
8. Under what conditions is the mechanistic organization most effective? When is the organic organization most effective?

Discussion Questions

1. Can you reconcile the following two statements: (a) an organization should have as few levels as possible to foster coordination; and (b) an organization should have narrow spans of control to facilitate control.
2. How are authority and organization structure interlocked?
3. Why is an understanding of power important?
4. Is your college organized as a mechanistic or an organic organization? Is this the type of structure you would ideally choose for it? Explain.

SELF-ASSESSMENT EXERCISE

How Power-Oriented Are You?

Statement	Disagree		Neutral	Agree	
	A Lot	A Little		A Little	A Lot
1. The best way to handle people is to tell them what they want to hear.	1	2	3	4	5
2. When you ask someone to do something for you, it is best to give the real reason for wanting it rather than giving reasons that might carry more weight.	1	2	3	4	5
3. Anyone who completely trusts anyone else is asking for trouble.	1	2	3	4	5
4. It is hard to get ahead without cutting corners here and there.	1	2	3	4	5
5. It is safest to assume that all people have a vicious streak, and it will come out when they are given a chance.	1	2	3	4	5
6. One should take action only when it is morally right.	1	2	3	4	5
7. Most people are basically good and kind.	1	2	3	4	5
8. There is no excuse for lying to someone else.		2	3	4	5
9. Most people forget the death of their father more easily than the loss of their property.	1	2	3	4	5
10. Generally speaking, people won't work hard unless they're forced to do so.	1	2	3	4	5

Turn to page SK-3 for scoring directions and key.

Source: R. Christie and F. L. Geis, Studies in Machiavellianism. © *Academic Press* 1970. *Reprinted by permission.*

ONTARIO ELECTRONICS LTD.

To: Claude Fortier, Special Assistant to the President
From: Ian Campbell, President
Subject: Organizing for Growth

I cannot help but be impressed with marketing's projected sales for 1995 through 1997. Unfortunately, our current production facilities are totally inadequate to meet these sales objectives. We are going to have to expand our operations.

There are two alternatives we can consider. We can expand our plant here in Scarborough. We have the land to build a large addition. We could probably build a facility that would allow us to go from our current 1400 employees to around 3000. On the other hand, we could build a completely new and separate plant on property on which we currently hold an option north of Toronto. If we build there, it could handle another 1400 to 1500 people.

I want to present these two options to the board, with a recommendation, at our next meeting. I would like you to look at each option, and then give me a brief report describing the pluses and minuses of each. Please give special attention to the structural implications of having two plants versus one.

This is a fictionalized account of a potentially real problem. It was written for academic purposes only and is not meant to reflect either positively or negatively on actual management practices at Ontario Electronics Ltd.

CASE APPLICATION

Barnes Hospital

The following episode took place on a cool October day at Barnes Hospital in St. Louis.

Diane Polanski called Dr. Davis, the hospital's administrative director, and asked for an immediate appointment. Davis could sense by the anxiousness in Diane's voice that something was up. He told her to come right up. About five minutes later, Polanski walked into Diane's office and handed him her letter of resignation.

"I can't take it any longer here, Dr. Davis," she began. "I've been a nursing supervisor in the maternity wing for four months, but I can't get the job done. How can I do a job when I've got two or three bosses, each one with different demands and priorities? Listen, I'm only human. I've tried my darndest to adapt to this job but I don't think it's possible. Let me give you an example, but believe me, this is not an unusual case. Things like this are happening every day.

"When I came into my office yesterday morning at about 7:45, I found a message on my desk from Dana Jackson [the hospital's head nurse]. She told me that she needed the bed-utilization report by 10:00 A.M. that day, so that she could make her presentation to the board in the afternoon. I knew the report would take at least an hour and a half to prepare. Thirty minutes later, Joyce [the nursing floor supervisor and Diane's immediate supervisor] came in and asked me why two of my nurses were not on duty. I told her that Dr. Reynolds [head of surgery] had taken them off my floor and was using them to handle an overload in the emergency surgical wing. I told her I had objected, but Reynolds said there were no other options. So what did Joyce say? She told me to get those nurses back in the maternity section immediately. What's more, she would be back in an hour to ensure that I got things straightened out! I'm telling you, Dr. Davis, things like this happen a couple of times a day. Is this any way to run a hospital?"

Questions

1. What is the formal chain of command?
2. Has anyone acted outside his or her authority?
3. What can Dr. Davis do to improve conditions?
4. "There's nothing wrong with the structure at Barnes Hospital. The problem is that Diane Polanski is an ineffective supervisor." Do you agree or disagree? Support your position.
5. Could Ms. Polanski have developed any power bases that might have allowed her to deal better with the competing demands on her?

VIDEO CASE

Kathleen Betts: Bureaucracy's Hero

Andy Warhol said that the day will come when "Everyone will be famous for fifteen minutes." Kathleen Betts, a part-time worker for the State of Massachusetts, got her fifteen minutes in 1991.

First a bit of background on Kathy: She's a young mother of two. She has a bachelor's degree in psychology from Boston College and a Masters in Public Health from Boston University. In order to devote time to her children, she works only three days a week as co-director of Acute Hospital Reimbursement for the Massachusetts Department of Public Welfare. Her job is to wade through reams of federal regulations to find ways to save the state money.

Kathy's job is not the kind that typically leads to fame and notoriety. But Kathy noticed a federal regulation that others in Massachusetts hadn't. She noticed a loophole that would allow Massachusetts to transfer the payment of uncompensated hospital care from the state to Medicaid. In simple terms, she found a way to get the federal government to pay 50 percent of these hospital charges.

You're probably thinking, "Big deal." It was! In June 1991, Massachusetts received $489 million that the law said was due the state. In essence, Kathy Betts had found the state nearly a half-a-billion dollars! The governor rewarded her with a bonus of $10,000.

Questions

1. What does this case imply about division of labor?
2. What type of authority, if any, does Kathy Betts have?
3. Using Perrow's classification, describe the technology of Kathy's job.
4. What does this case say regarding the effectiveness of the mechanistic organization?

Source: "Person of the Week: Kathleen Betts," *ABC World News Tonight,* June 7, 1991.

CHAPTER 11

Organization and Job Design Options

LEARNING OBJECTIVES

After Reading This Chapter, You Should Be Able To:

1. Describe the strengths of the functional structure.
2. Contrast the divisional and functional structures.
3. Define the simple structure.
4. Explain the strengths of the matrix structure.
5. Explain the recent popularity of the network structure.
6. Identify the advantages of using organic appendages.
7. Contrast job specialization, job enlargement, and job enrichment.
8. Identify the core dimensions in the job characteristics model.
9. Describe the advantages and disadvantages of flexible work hours.
10. Explain the preferred structural design for TQM programs.

ABB uses a dual chain of command—with country managers and segment managers—to coordinate its various businesses, which include the manufacturing of high-speed trains.

Have you ever heard of ABB? Most people haven't. Yet this global equipment giant has sales of $29 billion a year and is bigger than Westinghouse. It is, for instance, the world leader in high-speed trains, robotics, and environmental control.[1]

ABB was created in 1988 through the merger of ASEA, a Swedish engineering group, with Brown Boveri, a Swiss competitor. Management then added seventy more companies to create the current ABB giant.

We introduce ABB here because its management faced an interesting challenge: How do you organize a corporation that has 210,000 employees in locations around the world, that frequently shifts whole businesses from one country to another, and that tries to get its various businesses to share technology and products? Percy Barnevik, ABB's chairman, believes that he has an answer. He has drastically cut the staff at the corporation's headquarters and introduced a dual chain of command structure that gives all employees a country manager and a business sector manager.

Before the merger, Brown Boveri had 4000 people in its Baden, Switzerland, headquarters. ASEA had 2000 in its Swedish headquarters. Barnevik cleaned house at these head offices. Today, 150 people occupy ABB's modest headquarters in west Zurich. The rest were either fired or sent to subsidiaries. Barnevik is restructuring ABB so it can be competitive in all major world markets. A lean headquarters staff means that top management must decentralize decision making down to the operating units.

Perhaps the most innovative organizational idea that Barnevik has introduced is the dual chain of command. ABB has about one hundred country managers who run traditional, national companies with local boards of directors. Most of these managers are citizens of the country in which they work. In addition, there are sixty-five global managers who are organized into eight segments: transportation; process automation and engineering; environmental devices; financial services; electrical equipment; and three electric power businesses, generation, transmission, and distribution. This structure, according to Barnevik, makes it easier for managers such as Gerhard Schulmeyer, a German who heads ABB's U.S. businesses as well as the automation segment, to make use of technology from other countries. For instance, Schulmeyer used techniques developed by ABB in Switzerland to service U.S. steam turbines and ABB's European technology to convert a Michigan nuclear reactor into a natural–gas-fired plant.

In this chapter, we'll show that there are a number of structural options at management's disposal. While the previous chapter provided the foundations of organization theory, it oversimplified structural designs. In the real world, there are few purely mechanistic or organic organizations. Rather, there are a variety of structural options that tend *toward* either the mechanistic or the organic. This chapter presents a number of these options, loosely categorized as either mechanistic or organic.

However, this chapter is concerned with more than just organization design. It is also concerned with job design. Managerial decisions on how employees' day-to-day jobs should be designed and arranged—which include considerations such as the amount of freedom and discretion an employee should have, whether individuals should work alone or as part of a team, the most effective arrangement of work hours, and the like—are an essential part of the organizing function. Moreover, making organizational design decisions is not a universal activity for all managers. Most supervisors and other low-level managers have little or no say about the number or kind of rules and regulations their unit will contain or how many levels of hierarchy will exist between the top and the bottom of the organization. For the most part, decisions concerning an organization's overall structure are made by senior-level executives, possibly with some consultation with subordinate managers. In performing the organizing function, lower-level managers are usually far more concerned with designing tasks or jobs than with making major decisions about the organization's structure. Therefore, in this chapter we'll also consider the job design options that managers need to consider as part of their organizing responsibilities.

Mechanistic Design Options

When contingency factors favor a mechanistic design, one of two options is most likely to be considered. The *functional* structure's primary focus is on achieving the efficiencies of division of labor by grouping like specialists together. The *divisional* structure creates self-contained, autonomous units that are usually organized along mechanistic lines.

One point needs reiterating before we describe these structures. While both generally fall into the mechanistic category (they are clearly more mechanistic than organic), in practice few take on all the properties of a purely mechanistic structure.

The Functional Structure

"Listen, nothing happens in this place until we *produce* something," stated the production executive. "Wrong," interrupted the research and development manager. "Nothing happens until we *design* something!" "What are you talking about?" asked the marketing executive. "Nothing happens here until we *sell* something!" Finally, the exasperated accountant responded, "It doesn't matter what you produce, design, or sell. No one knows what's happening until we *tally up the results!*"

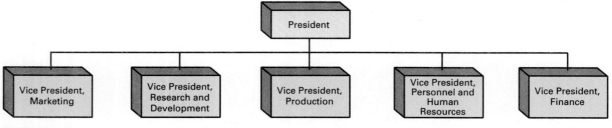

FIGURE 11-1
Functional Structure in a Manufacturing Organization

functional structure
A design that groups similar or related occupational specialties together.

This dialogue is an undesirable result of the functional structure. We introduced departmentalization in the previous chapter, so the idea of organizing around functions is already familiar to you. The **functional structure** merely expands the functional orientation to make it the dominant form for the entire organization. As depicted in Figure 11–1, management can choose to organize its structure by grouping similar and related occupational specialties together. When it does this, management has chosen a functional structure.

The strength of the functional structure lies in the advantages that accrue from specialization. Putting like specialties together results in economies of scale, minimizes duplication of personnel and equipment, and makes employees comfortable and satisfied because it gives them the opportunity to "talk the same language" as their peers.

The obvious weakness of the functional structure was illustrated at the opening of this section: The organization frequently loses sight of its best interests in the pursuit of functional goals. No one function is totally responsible for end results, so members within individual functions become insulated and have little understanding of what people in other functions are doing. Because only top management can see the whole picture it must assume the coordination role. The diversity of interests and perspectives that exists between functions can result in continual conflict between functions as each tries to assert its importance. An additional weakness of the functional structure is that it provides little or no training for future chief executives. The functional executives only see one narrow segment of the organization: the one dealing with their function. Exposure to other functions is limited. As a result, the structure does not give managers a broad perspective on the organization's activities.

The Divisional Structure

General Motors, Hershey Foods, Burlington Industries, and Xerox are examples of organizations that have adopted the divisional structure. An illustration of what this structural form looks like at Hershey Foods Corp. can be seen from the organization chart in Figure 11–2.

divisional structure
An organization structure made up of autonomous, self-contained units.

The **divisional structure,** which was pioneered in the 1920s by General Motors and DuPont, is designed to foster self-contained units. Each unit or division is generally autonomous, with a division manager responsible for performance and holding complete strategic and operational decision-making authority. At Hershey Foods, each of the groups is a separate division headed by a president who is totally responsible for results. As in most divisional structures, a central headquarters provides support services to the divisions. This typically includes financial and legal services. Of course, the headquarters also acts as an external overseer to coordinate and control the various divisions. Divisions are, therefore, autonomous within given parameters. Division managers are usually free to direct their division as they see fit, as long as it is within the overall guidelines set down by headquarters.

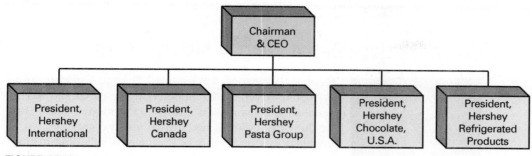

FIGURE 11–2
Divisional Structure at Hershey Foods Corp.

A closer look at divisional structures reveals that their "innards" contain functional structures. The divisional framework creates a set of autonomous "little companies." Within each of these companies lies another organizational form, and it is almost always of the functional variety.

What advantages does the divisional structure offer? It focuses on results. Division managers have full responsibility for a product or service. The divisional structure also frees headquarters staff from being concerned with day-to-day operating details so that they can pay attention to long-term and strategic planning.

In contrast to functional structures, the divisional form is also an excellent vehicle for developing senior executives. Division managers gain a broad range of experience in running their autonomous units. The individual responsibility and independence give them an opportunity to run an entire company with its frustrations and satisfactions. So a large organization with fifteen divisions has fifteen division managers who are developing the kind of generalist perspective that is needed in the organization's top spots.

The major disadvantage of the divisional structure is duplication of activities and resources. Each division, for instance, may have a marketing research department. In the absence of autonomous divisions, all of the organization's marketing research might be centralized and done for a fraction of the cost that divisionalization requires. Thus the divisional form's duplication of functions increases the organization's costs and reduces efficiency.

Organic Design Options

In this section, we present a selection of organic design options. These include the simple, matrix, network, task force, and committee structures.

Most organizations in North America are small. To be specific, 94 percent of all businesses in the United States have fewer than fifty employees.[2] Small organizations don't require a highly complex, formal structural design. What they need is a *simple* structure—that is, one that minimizes structural complexity. The *matrix* structure is an organic device that provides management with both high accountability for results and economies of specialization. It's popular in aerospace industries, high-tech companies, and professional organizations that operate in dynamic environments. The organic design of the future may be the *network* structure. The network design is a small central organization that contracts with other companies and suppliers to perform its manufacturing, distribution, marketing, or other crucial business functions. Its flexibility lies in the fact that management can move quickly to exploit new markets or new technologies because it "rents" the people, manufacturing facilities,

George Hatsopoulos at Thermo Electron Corp.

George N. Hatsopoulos founded Thermo Electron Corp. in 1956 as a vehicle for undertaking research and development projects related mostly to thermodynamics.[3] But by the early 1980s, it had grown into a company engaged in a broad mix of businesses, including instrument manufacturing, industrial heat treating, and specialty metal machining. Moreover, the company continued to develop new products, often in unrelated fields.

To manage his company better, Hatsopoulos came up with an innovative derivation of the divisional structure. He divided his firm into bite-sized chunks, each unit being an independent public company with its own CEO and board of directors. In 1992, there were eight of these independent companies. Hatsopoulos predicts there will be twenty by 2000. The majority shareholder in each company, however, is Thermo Electron Corp.

By turning operating divisions into public companies, entrepreneurial managers attain greater independence while leaving the parent company with a measure of control. For instance, because of its strong financial position, Thermo Electron can borrow money at low rates and relend it to its publicly traded divisions at rates lower than banks would charge. Additionally, this structure lowers overhead costs for each division. Division managers can treat their divisions as independent units and share in the appreciation of their unit's stock. At the same time, they can draw on Thermo Electron's resources for administrative and financial-management services, technical assistance, public relations, accounting, and legal services.

and services it needs instead of "owning" them. We wrap up our discussion of organic design options by considering the *task force* and *committee* structures. Each can be used as an organic appendage to a mechanistic organization. Each adds flexibility to the typically inflexible mechanistic structure.

The Simple Structure

If "bureaucracy" is the term that best describes most large organizations, "simple structure" is the one that best characterizes most small ones.

simple structure
An organization that is low in complexity and formalization but high in centralization.

A **simple structure** is defined more by what it is not than by what it is. It is not an elaborate structure.[4] If you see an organization that appears to have almost no structure, it is probably of the simple variety. By that we mean that it is low in complexity, has little formalization, and has its authority centralized in a single person. The simple structure is a "flat" organization; it usually has only two or three vertical levels, a loose body of employees, and one individual in whom the decision-making authority is centralized.

The simple structure is most widely practiced in small businesses in which the manager and the owner are one and the same. This, for example, is illustrated in Figure 11–3—an organization chart for a retail men's store. Jack Gold owns and manages this store. Although Jack Gold employs five full-time salespeople, a cashier, and extra personnel for weekends and holidays, he "runs the show."

Jack Gold's Men's Store has a simple structure. Decision making in the simple structure is basically informal. All important decisions are centralized in the senior executive, who, because of the organization's low complexity, can obtain key information readily and act rapidly when required. In addition, since complexity is low and decision making is centralized, the senior executive in the simple structure frequently has a wide span of control.

The strengths of the simple structure are obvious. It is fast, flexible, and inexpensive to maintain, and accountability is clear. One major weakness is that it is effective only in small organizations. It becomes increasingly inadequate as an organization grows because its low formalization and high centralization result in information overload at the top. As size increases, decision making becomes slower and can eventually come to a standstill as the single executive tries to continue making all the decisions. This often proves to be the undoing of many small businesses. When a company's sales begin to exceed about $5 million a year, it's very difficult for the owner-manager to make all the choices. If the structure isn't changed and made more elaborate, the firm is likely to lose momentum and eventually fail. The simple structure's other weakness is that it is risky: everything depends on one person. One heart attack can literally destroy the organization's information and decision-making center.

The Matrix Structure

The functional structure offers the advantages that accrue from specialization. The divisional structure has a greater focus on results but suffers from duplication of

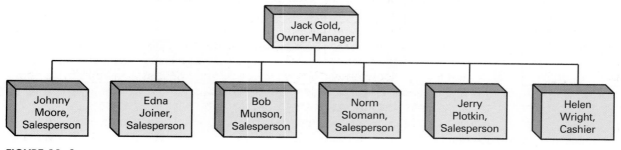

FIGURE 11–3
Organization Chart for a Simple Structure (Jack Gold's Men's Store)

matrix structure

A structural design that assigns specialists from functional departments to work on one or more projects that are led by a project manager.

activities and resources. If the organization were to be completely organized around products—that is, if each product the company produced had its own supporting functional structure—the focus on results would again be high. Each product could have a product manager responsible for all activities related to that product. This, too, would result in redundancy, however, since each product would require its own set of functional specialists. Does any structure combine the advantages of functional specialization with the focus and accountability that product departmentalization provides? The answer is Yes, and it's called the **matrix structure.**

The matrix structure creates a *dual chain of command.* It explicitly breaks the classical principle of unity of command. Functional departmentalization is used to gain the economies from specialization. But overlaying the functional departments is a set of managers who are responsible for specific products, projects, or programs within the organization. (We will use these terms—products, projects, programs—interchangeably, since matrix structures can use any of the three.) Figure 11–4 illustrates the matrix structure of an aerospace firm. Notice that along the top of the figure are the familiar functions of engineering, accounting, personnel, and so forth. Along the vertical dimension, however, the various projects that the aerospace firm is currently working on have been added. Each project is directed by a manager who staffs his or her project with people from the functional departments. The addition of this vertical dimension to the traditional horizontal functional departments, in effect, weaves together elements of functional and product departmentalization—hence the term *matrix.*

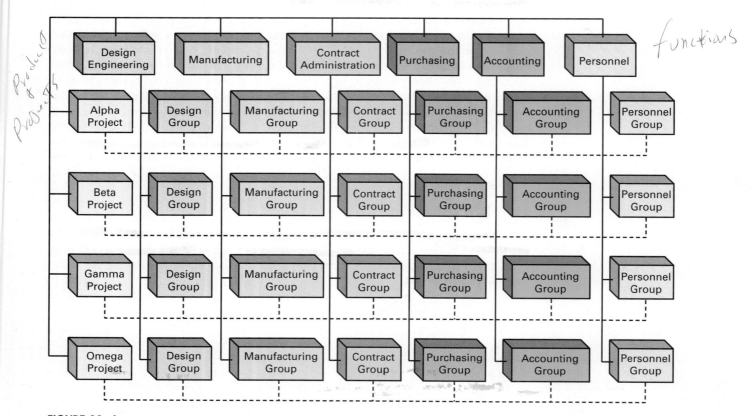

FIGURE 11–4

A Matrix Organization in an Aerospace Firm

How does the matrix work? Employees in the matrix have two bosses: their functional departmental manager and their product or project manager. The project managers have authority over the functional members who are part of that manager's project team. The purchasing specialists, for instance, who are responsible for procurement activities on the Gamma project are responsible to both the manager of Purchasing and the Gamma project manager. Authority is shared between the two managers. Typically, this is done by giving the project manager authority over project employees relative to the project's goals. However, decisions such as promotions, salary recommendations, and annual reviews remain the functional manager's responsibility. To work effectively, project and functional managers must communicate regularly and coordinate the demands upon their common employees.

The matrix creates an overall structure that possesses the strengths of both functional and product departmentalization while avoiding their weaknesses.[5] That is, the functional form's strength lies in putting like specialists together, which minimizes the number necessary, and it allows for the pooling and sharing of specialized resources across products. Its primary drawback is the difficulty in coordinating the tasks of the specialists so that their activities are completed on time and within the budget. The product form, on the other hand, has exactly the opposite benefits and disadvantages. It facilitates the coordination among specialties to achieve on-time completion and meet budget targets. Furthermore, it provides clear responsibility for all activities related to a product or project. But no one is responsible for the long-run technical development of the specialties, and this results in duplication of costs.

If management chooses to implement a matrix structure, it can opt for either the temporary or the permanent variety. The aerospace structure shown in Figure 11–4 illustrates a temporary matrix. Because the projects the organization undertakes change over time, the structure at any given time is temporary. When new contracts are secured in the aerospace firm, project teams are created by drawing members from functional departments. A team exists only for the life of the project it is working on. This might be a few months or a half-dozen years. In an organization that has a number of projects, at any given time some are just starting up, others are well along, and still others are winding down.

The product dimension of the permanent matrix stays relatively intact over time. Large business schools use the permanent matrix when they superimpose product structures—undergraduate programs, graduate programs, executive programs, and so forth—over functional departments of management, marketing, and accounting. (See Figure 11–5.) Directors of product groups utilize faculty from the departments in order to achieve their goals. For example, the director of the master's program staffs his or her courses from members of the various departments. Notice that the matrix provides clear lines of responsibility for each product line. The responsibility for success or failure of the executive development program, for instance, lies directly with its director. Without the matrix, it would be difficult to coordinate faculty among the development program's various course offerings. Furthermore, if there are any problems with the program, the matrix avoids the passing of responsibility among the functional department chairpersons.

Our examples should make the matrix's strengths evident: it can facilitate coordination of a multiple set of complex and interdependent projects while still retaining the economies that result from keeping functional specialists grouped together.

The major disadvantages of the matrix lie in the confusion it creates and its propensity to foster power struggles. When you dispense with the unity of command principle, you significantly increase ambiguity. Confusion can exist over who reports to whom. This confusion and ambiguity, in turn, plant the seeds for power struggles. Because the relationships between functional and project managers typically are not

Departments

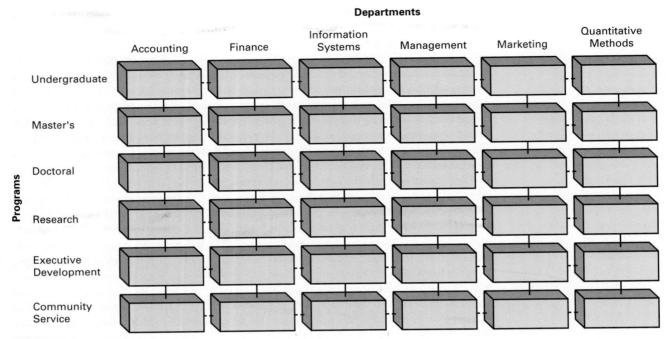

FIGURE 11–5
Matrix Structure in a School of Business

specified by rules and procedures, they need to be negotiated, and this gives rise to power struggles. Deciding whether to implement the matrix requires managers to weigh these disadvantages against the advantages.

The Network Structure

network structure
A small centralized organization that relies on other organizations to perform its basic business functions on a contract basis.

A new form of organization design is currently gaining popularity. It allows management great flexibility in responding to new technology, fashion, or low-cost foreign competition. It is the **network structure**—a small central organization that relies on other organizations to perform manufacturing, distribution, marketing, or other crucial business functions on a contract basis.[6]

The network structure is a viable option for the small organization. Magicorp, for example, runs a small shop that makes graphics transparencies. It relies on other companies for the rest of its operations. People who use graphics software on their personal computers send data by phone lines to Magicorp's office in Wilmington, Ohio. Why is Magicorp in Wilmington? Because the Airborne Express hub is there, making fast turnarounds possible. Rather than do its own marketing, Magicorp relies on graphics software vendors to promote its services, paying these vendors on a royalty basis.

The network structure is also applicable to large organizations. Nike, Esprit, Emerson Radio, and Liz Claiborne are large companies that have found that they can sell hundreds of millions of dollars of products every year and earn a very competitive return with few or no manufacturing facilities of their own and only a few hundred employees. What these firms have done is to create an organization of relationships. They connect with independent designers, manufacturers, commissioned sales representatives, or the like to perform the functions they need on a contract basis.

Other large companies have developed variants of the network structure by farming out just a limited set of functions. National Steel Corp. contracts out its mail room operations. AT&T farms out its credit-card processing. Mobil Corp. has turned over maintenance of its refineries to another firm. And most book publishing companies—the large ones as well as the small ones—rely on outside contractors for editing, designing, printing, and binding.

The network stands in sharp contrast to those divisional structures that have many vertical levels of management and those in which organizations seek to control their destiny through ownership. In such organizations, research and development are done in-house, production occurs in company-owned manufacturing plants, and sales and marketing are performed by their own employees. To support all this, management has to employ extra personnel including accountants, human resource specialists, and lawyers. In the network structure, most of these functions are bought outside the organization. This gives management a high degree of flexibility and allows the organization to concentrate on what it does best. For most U.S. firms, that means focusing on design or marketing. Emerson Radio Corporation, for example, designs and engineers its TVs, stereos, and other consumer electronic products, but it contracts out their manufacture to Asian suppliers.

Figure 11–6 shows a network structure in which management contracts out all of the primary functions of the business. The core of the network organization is a small group of executives. Their job is to oversee directly any activities that are done in-house and to coordinate relationships with the other organizations that manufacture, distribute, and perform other crucial functions for the network organization. The dotted lines in Figure 11–6 represent those contractual relationships. In essence, managers in network structures spend most of their time coordinating and controlling external relations.

The network organization is not appropriate for all endeavors. It fits industrial companies such as toy and apparel firms, which require very high flexibility in order to respond quickly to fashion changes. It also fits firms whose manufacturing operations require low-cost labor that is available only outside the United States and can best be utilized by contracting with foreign suppliers. On the negative side, management in network structures lacks the close control of manufacturing operations that exists in more traditional organizations. Reliability of supply is also less predictable. Finally, any innovation in design that a network organization acquires is susceptible to being "ripped off." It is very difficult, if not impossible, to guard closely innovations that are under the direction of management in another organization. Yet with

FIGURE 11–6
A Network Structure

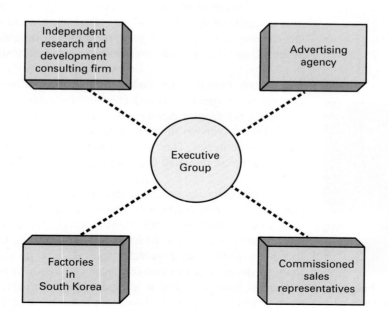

**MANAGING
FROM A
GLOBAL
PERSPECTIVE**

The Structure of Multinationals

The challenge in managing a multinational corporation (MNC) is greater than in the traditional domestic firm.[7] For instance, in addition to the normal risks inherent in a business enterprise, the MNC is more vulnerable to political instability, changes in laws, and exchange-rate fluctuations. Therefore MNCs must have a structure that provides greater environmental scanning capability to allow managers to monitor, and quickly respond to, changes in their environment. Moreover, the high complexity created by geographically dispersed units requires superior structural mechanisms to allow for communicating over distances, often in different languages, and to facilitate rapid responses to diverse market demands.

When organizations move into global markets, they typically begin by adding an international division. However, this is rarely adequate for the true multinational. To attain the goal of becoming a fully integrated global organization, many move to a multinational matrix structure. This simultaneously blends product and geographic departmentalization. For instance, a multinational might have a product manager for each of its major marketing areas in North America, Latin America, Europe, and Asia. The major advantage of the multinational matrix is to allow an organization to respond more quickly and appropriately to the unique requirements of these various geographic markets for a company's products.

computers in one organization now interfacing and communicating directly with computers in other organizations, the network structure is becoming an increasingly viable alternative.

Organic Appendages

The design options previously described are intended for organizationwide application. Sometimes, however, management might want to maintain an overall mechanistic structure but gain the flexibility of an organic structure. An alternative is to append an organic structural unit to a mechanistic organization. Two examples of such appendages are the task force and the committee structure.

task force structure
A temporary structure created to accomplish a specific, well-defined, complex task that requires the involvement of personnel from a number of organizational subunits.

The Task Force The **task force structure** is temporary structure created to accomplish a specific, well-defined, and complex task that requires the involvement of personnel from a number of organizational subunits. It can be thought of as a scaled-down version of the temporary matrix. Members serve on the task force until its goal is achieved. Then the task force is disbanded, and its members move on to a new task force, return to their permanent functional department, or leave the organization.[8]

The task force is a common tool of consumer product firms. For instance, when the Kellogg Co. decides to create a new breakfast cereal, it brings together people with expertise in product design, food research, marketing, manufacturing, finance, and other relevant functions to formulate the product, design its package, determine its market, compute its manufacturing costs, and project its profits. Once the problems have been worked out and the product is ready to be mass produced, the task force disbands, and the cereal is integrated into the permanent structure. At Kellogg, the new cereal is then assigned its own product manager and becomes a part of Kellogg's matrix structure.

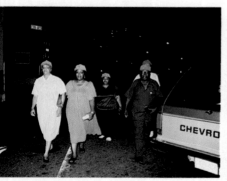

This Washington, D.C. Neighborhood Crime Watch patrol is an example of a task force.

committee structure

A structure that brings together a range of individuals from across functional lines to deal with problems.

The Committee Structure Another option that combines a range of individual experiences and backgrounds for dealing with problems and cuts across functional lines is the **committee structure.**

Committees may be temporary or permanent in nature. A temporary committee is typically the same as the task force. Permanent committees facilitate the unity of diverse inputs as does the task force, but they offer the stability and consistency of the matrix. However, committees are appendages. Members of the committee are permanently attached to a functional department. They can meet at regular or irregular intervals to analyze problems, make recommendations or final decisions, coordinate activities, or oversee projects. As a result, they are mechanisms for bringing together the input of diverse departments. Colleges frequently use permanent committees for everything from student admissions to faculty promotions and alumni relations. Large business firms use committees as coordinating and control mechanisms. For instance, many firms have a compensation committee to review salary and bonuses provided to management personnel and an audit committee to objectively evaluate the organization's operations. A few firms even use the committee as the central coordinating device in their structure. J.C. Penney has a management committee that consists of the firm's top fourteen executives. They debate and pass on decisions to such disparate areas as strategic planning, public affairs, personnel, and merchandising. Permanent subcommittees are used to focus on key parts of the business, while temporary committees are formed for specific issues, such as what to do with the company's troubled Treasury discount store operation.

A Buyer's Guide to Organization Design Options

What conditions make one organization design preferable to another? Table 11–1 summarizes the options we have discussed and notes the conditions that favor each.

Certain structures are designed to work well in large organizations that are specialized. These include the functional and divisional structures. Both are essentially bureaucracies or mechanistic structures.

The simple structure is effective when the number of employees is few, when the organization is new, and when the environment is simple and dynamic.[9] Small size usually means less repetitive work, so standardization is less attractive. Small size also makes informal communication both convenient and effective. All new organizations tend to adopt the simple structure because management has not had the time to elaborate the structure. A simple environment is easily comprehended by a single individual, yet the structure's flexibility allows it to respond rapidly to unpredictable contingencies.

The matrix attempts to obtain the advantages of specialization without its disadvantages. When the organization has multiple programs or products and functional departmentalization, it can create program or product managers who direct activities across functional lines.

The network structure is a product of the computer revolution. By being linked to other organizations, an industrial firm can be in the manufacturing business without having to build and operate its own plants. The network is an excellent vehicle for the manufacturing firm that is just getting started because it minimizes risks and commitments. Because it requires few fixed assets, it also lessens financial demands on the organization. To succeed, however, management must be skilled in developing and maintaining relationships with suppliers. If any one of the firms that the network organization has contracted with fails to meet its commitments, the network organization ends up the loser.

The task force and committee structures were offered as appendages to mechanistic structures. Both are meant to be used when it is necessary to bring together

TABLE 11–1 Organization Design Options

Design	Strengths	When and Where to Use
Functional	Economies through specialization	In single-product or -service organizations
Divisional	High accountability for results	In large organizations; in multiple-product or multiple-market organizations
Simple	Speed, flexibility, economy	In small organizations; during formative years of development; in simple and dynamic environments
Matrix	Economies through specialization and accountability for product results	In organizations with multiple products or programs that rely on functional expertise
Network	Speed, flexibility, economy	In industrial firms; during formative years of development; when many reliable suppliers are available; when low-cost foreign labor is available
Task force	Flexibility	In organizations with important tasks that have specific time and performance standards, that are unique and unfamiliar, that require expertise that crosses functional lines
Committee	Flexibility	In organizations with tasks that require expertise that crosses functional lines

personnel from across functional lines. Because the task force is a temporary design, it is also an ideal vehicle for tackling important tasks that have specific time and performance standards and that are unique and unfamiliar. Once a task is familiar and needs to be repeated, a mechanistic design can handle it in a more standardized and efficient manner.

Job Design Options

If you put an organization under a microscope, you would find that it is composed of thousands, maybe even millions, of tasks. These tasks, in turn, are aggregated into jobs.[10] The jobs that people do in any organization should not evolve by chance. Management should design jobs thoughtfully to reflect the organization's technology, as well as the skills, abilities, and preferences of its employees. When this is done, employees can reach their full productive capabilities.

We use the term **job design** to refer to the way in which tasks are combined to form complete jobs. Some jobs are routine because the tasks are standardized and repetitive; others are nonroutine. Some require a large number of varied and diverse skills; others are narrow in scope. Some jobs constrain employees by requiring them to follow very precise procedures; others allow employees substantial freedom in how they do their work. Some jobs are most effectively accomplished by groups of employees working as a team, whereas other jobs are best done by individuals acting independently. Our point is that jobs differ in the way their tasks are combined, and these different combinations create a variety of job designs.

job design
The way in which tasks are combined to form complete jobs.

Job Specialization

For the first half of this century, job design was synonymous with division of labor or job specialization. Using guidelines laid down by the likes of Adam Smith and Frederick Taylor, managers sought to make jobs in organizations as simple as possible. This meant dividing them into minute, specialized tasks (see Figure 11–7 for specialized jobs required to construct an office building). However, as we noted earlier, jobs can become too specialized. When this happens, employees often begin to rebel. They express their frustrations and boredom by taking "mental health days" off, socializing around the workplace instead of being productive, ignoring the quality of their work, or abusing alcohol and drugs. Efficiency then declines.

The principles of job specialization continue to guide the design of many jobs. Manufacturing workers still perform simple, repetitive jobs on assembly lines. Office clerks sit at computer terminals and perform standardized tasks. Even nurses, accountants, and other professionals find that many of their tasks require performing narrow, specialized activities.

Job Rotation

job rotation
Periodic lateral transfers of workers among jobs involving different tasks.

One of the earliest efforts at moving away from job specialization and its drawbacks was the introduction of **job rotation.** This approach to job design allows workers to diversify their activities and avoid boredom.

There are actually two types of rotation: vertical and horizontal. *Vertical* rotation refers to promotions and demotions. When we talk about job rotation, however, we mean the *horizontal* variety.

Horizontal job transfers can be instituted on a planned basis—that is, by means of a training program whereby the employee spends two or three months in an activity and is then moved on. (See Figure 11–8 on page 323). This approach, for example, is common among large Wall Street law firms, in which new associates work for many different partners before choosing an area of specialization. Horizontal transfers can also be made on a situational basis by moving the person to another activity when the previous one is no longer challenging or when the needs of work scheduling require it. In other words, people may be put in a continual transfer mode. Rotation, as employed by many large organizations in their programs to develop managerial talent, may include moving people between line and staff positions, often allowing a worker to understudy a more experienced employee.

The advantages of job rotation are clear. It broadens employees and gives them a range of experiences. Boredom and monotony, which develop after a person has acquired the skills to perform his or her task effectively, are reduced when transfers are made frequently. Finally, since a broader experience permits a greater understanding of other activities within the organization, people are more rapidly prepared to assume greater responsibility, especially at the upper echelons. In other words, as one moves up in the organization, it becomes increasingly necessary to understand the intricacies and interrelationships of activities; and these skills can be more quickly acquired by moving about within the organization.

On the other hand, job rotation is not without its drawbacks. Training costs are increased, and productivity is reduced by moving a worker into a new position just when his or her efficiency at the prior job was creating organizational economies. An extensive rotation program can result in a vast number of employees being situated in positions for which their experience is very limited. Even though there might be significant long-term benefits from the program, the organization must be equipped to deal with the day-to-day problems that arise when inexperienced personnel perform new tasks and when rotated managers make decisions based on little experience with the activity at hand. Job rotation can also demotivate intelligent and

FIGURE 11-7
Job Specialization

FIGURE 11–8
Job Rotation

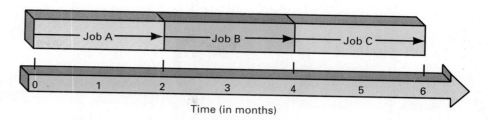

Time (in months)

aggressive trainees who seek specific responsibility in their chosen specialty. Finally, there is some evidence that rotation that is involuntarily imposed on employees increases absenteeism and accidents.[11]

Job Enlargement

job enlargement
The horizontal expansion of a job; an increase in job scope.

job scope
The number of different tasks required in a job and the frequency with which the job cycle is repeated.

Another early effort at increasing the horizontal diversity in a worker's tasks was **job enlargement.** This option increases **job scope;** that is, it increases the number of different tasks required in a job and decreases the frequency with which the job cycle is repeated. (See Figure 11–9.) By increasing the number of tasks an individual performs, job enlargement increases job diversity. Instead of only sorting the incoming mail by department, for instance, a mail sorter's job could be enlarged to include physically delivering the mail to the various departments or running outgoing letters through the postage meter.

Efforts at job enlargement have met with less-than-enthusiastic results. As one employee who experienced such a redesign on his job remarked, "Before I had one lousy job. Now, through enlargement, I have three lousy jobs!" Job enlargement attacked the lack of diversity in overspecialized jobs, but it provided few challenges and little meaning to a worker's activities.

Job Enrichment

job enrichment
Vertical expansion of a job by adding planning and evaluating responsibilities.

job depth
The degree of control employees have over their work.

More than seven thousand sales clerks at a number of Montgomery Ward stores are taking on responsibilities—including approving checks and handling merchandise-return problems—that historically had been reserved for store managers.[12] These Ward's employees have had their jobs enriched. Job enrichment has proven effective in dealing with some of the shortcomings of job enlargement.

Job enrichment increases **job depth** (see Figure 11–10). What this means is that

FIGURE 11–9
Job Enlargement

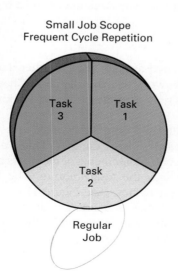

Small Job Scope
Frequent Cycle Repetition

Regular Job

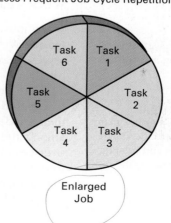

Large Job Scope
Less Frequent Job Cycle Repetition

Enlarged Job

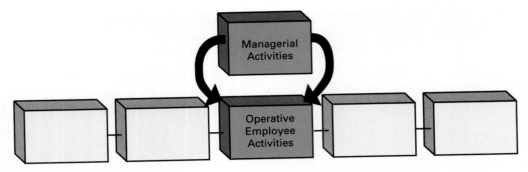

FIGURE 11-10
Job Enrichment

This wood room operator at Superior Paper Co. is required to master up to 14 area skills before she is eligible for promotion. The reason? Superior's management finds that flexibility boosts productivity.

job enrichment allows employees greater control over their work. They're allowed to assume some of the tasks typically done by their supervisors—particularly planning and evaluating their own work. The tasks in an enriched job should allow workers to do a complete activity with increased freedom, independence, and responsibility; these tasks should also provide feedback so that individuals can assess and correct their own performances.

How does management enrich jobs? Citibank found that its back office, where personnel processed all the firm's financial transactions, was suffering severe backlogs and unacceptably high error rates.[13] The source of the problem was believed to be the design of jobs in this area. Jobs were split up so each person performed a single, routine task over and over again. Citibank's management enriched these jobs by redesigning the work around customer types. Tasks were combined, and individual employees were given complete processing and customer-service responsibility for a small group of customers in a defined product area. In the newly designed jobs, employees dealt directly with customers and handled entire transactions from start to finish. And when a problem occurred, the employee responsible received the complaint directly and was accountable for solving it. The result? This enrichment program improved the quality of work as well as employee motivation and satisfaction.

The Citibank example shouldn't be taken as a blanket endorsement of job enrichment. The evidence generally shows that job enrichment reduces absenteeism and turnover costs; but on the critical issue of productivity, the evidence is inconclusive.[14] In some situations, job enrichment has increased productivity; in others, it has decreased it. However, when productivity decreases, there does appear to be consistently more conscientious use of resources and a higher quality of product or service.

Work Teams

work teams
Groups of individuals that cooperate in completing a set of tasks.

When jobs are designed around groups rather than individuals, the result is **work teams.** We'll discuss work teams in detail in Chapter 14. However, because teams represent an increasingly popular job design option, we need to consider them here briefly.

integrated work team
A group that accomplishes many tasks by making specific assignments to members and rotating jobs among members as the tasks require.

There are basically two types of work teams: integrated and self-managed. In **integrated work teams,** a large number of tasks are assigned to a group. The group then decides the specific assignments of members and is responsible for rotating jobs among the members as the tasks require. The team still has a supervisor who oversees the group's activities. (See Figure 11-11.) Integrated work teams are used frequently in such activities as building maintenance and construction. In the cleaning of a large office building, for example, the foreman will identify the tasks to be completed and then let the maintenance workers, as a group, choose how the tasks

FIGURE 11-11
Integrated Work Teams

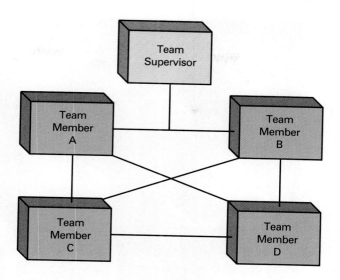

self-managed work team
A vertically integrated team that is given almost complete autonomy in determining how a task will be done.

are to be allocated. Similarly, a road construction crew frequently decides, as a group, how its various tasks are to be completed.

Self-managed work teams are more vertically integrated and have a wider range of discretion than their integrated counterparts. The self-managed work team is given a goal to achieve and then is free to determine work assignments, rest breaks, inspection procedures, and so forth.[15] These teams often even select their own members and have the members evaluate one another's performances. As a result, supervisory positions become less important and may sometimes be eliminated. (See Figure 11–12.)

Thousands of organizations have redesigned their employees' work tasks around self-managed teams. Maybe the most visible examples are in the auto industry. Chrysler used these teams to develop their elite new Viper sports car and their LH line of mid-sized cars. General Motors uses teams to build its Saturn cars. And Volvo has been using self-managed teams for years to build its automobiles. But self-managed teams have wide applications beyond automobile manufacturing. AT&T, for instance, implemented them in 1990 at the company's submarine systems plant in New Jersey.

FIGURE 11-12
Self-Managed Work Teams

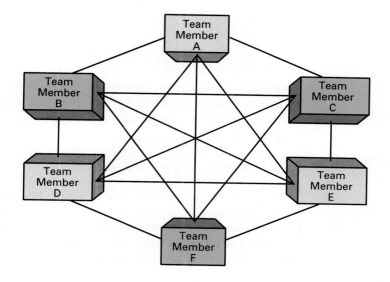

The use of self-managed teams at Picker International, a manufacturer of high-tech x-ray equipment, has resulted in a doubling of productivity over the past five years.

job characteristics model
A framework for analyzing and designing jobs; identifies five primary job characteristics, their interrelationships, and impact on outcome variables.

skill variety
The degree to which a job includes a variety of activities that call for a number of different skills and talents.

task identity
The degree to which a job requires completion of a whole and identifiable piece of work.

task significance
The degree to which a job has a substantial impact on the lives or work of other people.

autonomy
The degree to which a job provides substantial freedom, independence, and discretion to an individual in scheduling and carrying out his or her work.

feedback
The degree to which carrying out the work activities required by a job results in an individual's obtaining direct and clear information about the effectiveness of his or her performance.

In two years, the teams successfully reduced costs by more than 30 percent and saved the plant from being closed.[16]

The Job Characteristics Model

None of the prior approaches provided a conceptual framework for analyzing jobs or for guiding managers in designing jobs. The **job characteristics model** (JCM) offers such a framework.[17] It identifies five primary job characteristics, their interrelationships, and their impact on employee productivity, motivation, and satisfaction.

Core Dimensions   According to the JCM, any job can be described in terms of five core dimensions, defined as follows:

Skill variety, the degree to which a job requires a variety of activities so that an employee can use a number of different skills and talents.

Task identity, the degree to which a job requires completion of a whole and identifiable piece of work.

Task significance, the degree to which a job has a substantial impact on the lives or work of other people.

Autonomy, the degree to which a job provides substantial freedom, independence, and discretion to the individual in scheduling the work and determining the procedures to be used in carrying it out.

Feedback, the degree to which carrying out the work activities required by a job results in the individual's obtaining direct and clear information about the effectiveness of his or her performance.

Figure 11–13 presents the model. Notice how the first three dimensions—skill variety, task identity, and task significance—combine to create meaningful work. That is, if these three characteristics exist in a job, we can predict that the person will view his or her job as being important, valuable, and worthwhile. Notice, too, that jobs that possess autonomy give the job incumbent a feeling of personal respon-

FIGURE 11-13
Job Characteristics Model

Source: J. Richard Hackman and J. Lloyd Shuttle, eds., *Improving Life at work* (Glenview, IL: Scott, Foresman and Co., 1977). With permission of authors.

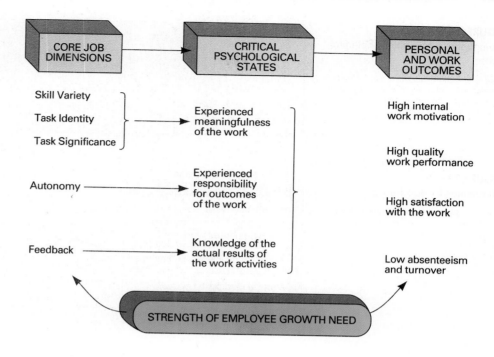

sibility for the results and that, if a job provides feedback, the employee will know how effectively he or she is performing.

From a motivational standpoint, the model says that internal rewards are obtained when one *learns* (knowledge of results) that one *personally* (experienced responsibility) has performed well on a task that one *cares about* (experienced meaningfulness).[18] The more these three conditions are present, the greater will be the employee's motivation, performance, and satisfaction, and the lower his or her absenteeism and likelihood of resigning. As the model shows, the links between the job dimensions and the outcomes are moderated or adjusted for by the strength of the individual's growth need—that is, the employee's desire for self-esteem and self-actualization. This means that individuals with a high growth need are more likely to experience the psychological states when their jobs score high on the core dimensions than are their low-growth-need counterparts. High-growth-need individuals will respond more positively to the psychological states, when they are present, than will low-growth-need individuals.

Predictions from the Model   The core dimensions can be combined into a single index as shown in Figure 11–14. To score high on motivating potential, jobs must be high on at least one of the three factors that lead to experiencing meaningfulness; they must also be high on both autonomy and feedback. If jobs score high on motivating potential, the model predicts that motivation, performance, and satisfaction will be positively affected, while the likelihood of absence and turnover will be lessened.[19]

Guides for Managers   The JCM provides specific guidance to managers in the designing of jobs. (See Figure 11–15.) The following suggestions, which derive from the JCM, specify the types of changes in jobs that are most likely to lead to improvements in each of the five core dimensions:

1. *Combine tasks.* Managers should put existing fractionalized tasks back together to form a new, larger module of work. This increases skill variety and task identity.

FIGURE 11-14
Computing a Motivating Potential
Score

Source: J. Richard Hackman and J. Lloyd
Shuttle, eds., *Improving Life at Work* (Glen-
view, IL: Scott, Foresman and Co., 1977).
With permission of authors.

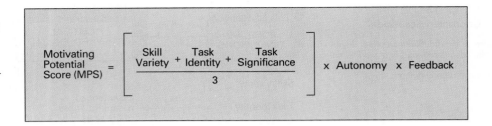

$$\text{Motivating Potential Score (MPS)} = \left[\frac{\text{Skill Variety} + \text{Task Identity} + \text{Task Significance}}{3} \right] \times \text{Autonomy} \times \text{Feedback}$$

FIGURE 11-15
Guidelines for Job Redesign

Source: J. Richard Hackman and J. Lloyd
Shuttle, eds., *Improving Life at Work* (Glen-
view, IL: Scott, Foresman and Co., 1977).
With permission of authors.

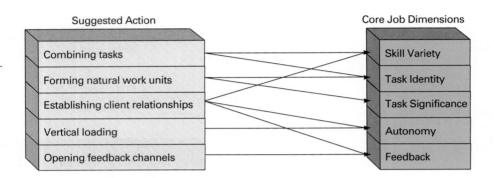

Suggested Action

| Combining tasks |
| Forming natural work units |
| Establishing client relationships |
| Vertical loading |
| Opening feedback channels |

Core Job Dimensions

| Skill Variety |
| Task Identity |
| Task Significance |
| Autonomy |
| Feedback |

The jobs of many crafts people,
such as this stained glass artist,
score high on the job characteristics model.

compressed workweek
A workweek comprised of four
ten-hour days.

2. *Create natural work units.* Managers should design tasks that form an identifiable and meaningful whole. This increases employee "ownership" of the work and encourages employees to view their work as meaningful and important rather than as irrelevant and boring.

3. *Establish client relationships.* The client is the user of the product or service that the employee works on. Wherever possible, managers should establish direct relationships between workers and their clients. This increases skill variety, autonomy, and feedback for the employee.

4. *Expand jobs vertically.* Vertical expansion gives employees responsibilities and controls that were formerly reserved for management. It partially closes the gap between the "doing" and "controlling" aspects of the job, and it increases employee autonomy.

5. *Open feedback channels.* By increasing feedback, employees not only learn how well they are performing their jobs but also whether their performances are improving, deteriorating, or remaining at a constant level. Ideally, employees should receive performance feedback directly as they do their jobs rather than from management on an occasional basis.[20]

Scheduling Options

A final set of job design options deals with the scheduling of work. For instance, a job for most people in North America means leaving home and going to a place of work, arriving at 8:00 or 9:00 in the morning, putting in a fixed set of approximately eight hours, and doing this routine five days a week. However, it doesn't have to be this way. Depending on labor-market conditions, the type of work that has to be done, and employee preferences, management might consider implementing a compressed workweek of four days, flexible work hours, or job sharing. Management also might consider using contingent or temporary workers or allowing employees to work at home through telecommuting.

The Compressed Workweek We define the **compressed workweek** as comprised of four ten-hour days. While there have been experiments with three-day weeks and other compressed workweek variants, we will limit our attention to four-day, forty-hour (4–40) programs.

Their proponents claim that 4–40 programs have a favorable effect on employee absenteeism, job satisfaction, and productivity.[21] Some argue that a four-day work-week provides employees with more leisure time, decreases commuting time, decreases requests for time off for personal matters, makes it easier for an organization to recruit employees, and decreases time spent on tasks such as setting up equipment. However, some potential disadvantages have been noted. Among these are a decrease in workers' productivity near the end of the longer workday, a decrease in service to customers and clients, unwillingness to work longer days when needed to meet deadlines, and underutilization of equipment.[22]

Maybe the most telling characteristic of the four-day workweek, from management's perspective, is that it appears to have different short-term and long-term effects.[23] When first implemented, the compressed workweek achieves many of the results claimed by its advocates: higher morale, less dissatisfaction, and less absenteeism and turnover. However, after approximately one year many of these advantages disappear. Employees then begin to complain about increased fatigue and the difficulty of coordinating their jobs with their personal lives (the latter is a particular problem for working mothers). Managers also find drawbacks. More scheduling of work is involved, overtime rates frequently must be paid for hours worked in excess of eight during the workday, and general difficulties arise in coordinating work. Moreover, since managers still tell employees when to arrive and when to leave, the compressed workweek does little to increase the worker's freedom, specifically in the selecting of work hours that suit him or her best.

As a result, the compressed workweek is no panacea for dealing with the problems of standardized jobs. It has been suggested, however, that the desire for increased worker freedom can be achieved through flexible work hours.

flexible work hours (flextime)
A scheduling system in which employees are required to work a number of hours a week, but are free, within limits, to vary the hours of work.

Flexible Work Hours   **Flexible work hours** (also popularly known as **flextime**) is a scheduling system in which employees are required to work a specific number of hours a week, but are free to vary those hours within certain limits. As shown in Figure 11–16, each day consists of a common core, usually five or six hours, with a flexibility band surrounding it. For example, not counting a one-hour lunch break, the core may be 9:00 A.M. to 3:00 P.M., with the office actually opening at 6:00 A.M. and closing at 6:00 P.M. All employees are required to be at their jobs during the common-core periods, but they are allowed to accumulate their remaining hours from before and/or after the core time. Some flextime programs allow extra hours to be accumulated and turned into a free day off each month.

How widespread is flextime? In the early 1970s, few organizations offered this scheduling option. By the early 1990s, about 40 percent of major companies offered the flextime option.[24] These include such companies as Aetna Life & Casualty, Avon Products, Du Pont, and Hewlett-Packard.

And what is flextime's record? Most of the evidence stacks up favorably. It tends to reduce absenteeism, improve morale, and improve worker productivity.[25] For example, one study found that flextime reduced tardiness in 42 percent of the companies

FIGURE 11–16
A Flexible Work Schedule

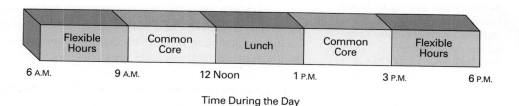

Time During the Day

surveyed, improved morale in 39 percent, and improved productivity in 33 percent.[26] The explanation for these findings is that flextime allows employees to schedule their work hours to better align with personal demands, and employees are able to exercise discretion over their work hours. The result is that employees are more likely to adjust their work activities to the hours during which they are individually more productive and that better align with their off-work commitments.

Of course, flextime does have drawbacks, especially in its effect on the manager's job.[27] It produces problems for managers in directing subordinates outside the common-core period, causes confusion in shift work, increases difficulties when someone with a particular skill or knowledge is not available, and makes planning and controlling more cumbersome and costly for managers. Also, keep in mind that many jobs can't be converted to flextime: salesperson in a department store, office receptionist, and assembly-line operator are examples of jobs in which the jobholder must depend on others inside or outside the organization—and vice versa. Where such interdependence exists, flextime is usually not a viable alternative.

job sharing
The practice of having two or more people split a forty-hour-a-week job.

Job sharing **Job sharing** is a recent work-scheduling innovation. It allows two or more employees to split a traditional forty-hour-a-week job. So, for example, one person might perform the job from 8 A.M. to 12 P.M., while another performs the same job from 1 P.M. to 5 P.M.

Because job sharing is a newer idea than flextime, its use is less common, but it is gaining an increasing following. About 16 percent of U.S. business firms allow job sharing; 11 percent have actually set up job-sharing programs.[28]

Why would management opt for job sharing? It allows the organization to draw upon the talents of more than one individual in a given job and to acquire skilled workers who might not be available on a full-time basis. For instance, retirees and individuals with school-age children may not be responsive to the demands of a full-time position but would work in a job in which those demands could be shared with others. In addition, job sharing can enhance productivity. Job sharers typically have better attendance records than regular, full-time employees.[29] And as an executive at Northeast Utilities Service Co. observed, while full-time employees seldom work to their maximum all day, two job sharers often give four hours of "full-bore production."[30]

contingent workers
Temporary and part-time workers who supplement an organization's permanent work force.

Contingent workers Organizations that face dynamic environments need staffing flexibility. That explains why more and more organizations are using **contingent workers**—temporaries and part-timers who supplement an organization's permanent work force.[31] For instance, 8 percent of Delta Air Lines' work force is made up of employees who understand that their jobs are temporary.[32] At Apple Computer, it's almost 17 percent.[33] Through contingent workers, companies like Delta and Apple can boost productivity in busy times and avoid painful layoffs and bad publicity in slack periods by keeping their stable core of permanent employees small. Thus the use of contingent workers allows management a great deal of increased flexibility. Contingent jobs, in turn, satisfy workers' needs for autonomy and job diversity. On the negative side, for people who want the stability of permanent jobs, contingent-worker status can be demoralizing and even perceived as a second-class status in the labor force.[34]

Joan Girardi (left) and Stephanie Kahn are job sharing at American Express. They enroll college students as cardholders. Kahn covers the job Monday, Tuesday, and Thursday, while Girardi works on Tuesday, Wednesday, and Friday. Each supervises two of their team's four professionals.

Contingent workers now represent 25 percent of the work force, and their number is growing at a rate of 20 percent annually.[35] Contingent workers include low-skilled part-time employees and office temporaries, but the contingent work force also includes a growing pool of such professionals as computer designers, accountants, and lawyers. As management seeks devices to increase organizational flexibility, we can expect to see more organizations creating two-tier labor systems—a small core of permanent employees supplemented by a continually expanding and shrinking pool of contingent workers.

Are Organizations Exploiting Contingent Workers?

Contingent workers provide management with increased flexibility—but at what price to the workers themselves?

For some workers, the rapid growth in demand for contingent workers is a blessing. For example, it is a great opportunity for people who want to work only on a part-time basis. Being a disposable employee, however, is not necessarily a status everyone seeks willingly. Data from the Bureau of Labor Statistics indicate that 3.8 million part-timers would prefer full-time work but can't find it.[36]

Contingent workers often suffer in terms of pay and benefits. On average, they earn 40 percent less than permanent employees. Some 70 percent of part-timers have no employee-provided retirement plan, and 42 percent receive no health insurance coverage.[37]

Are organizations that use contingent workers cutting costs by exploiting these people? Are these organizations shirking their responsibilities to these workers and to society as a whole? Should federal legislation be passed that would mandate minimum fringe benefits for part-time workers? What do *you* think?

---

telecommuting
The linking by computer and modem of workers at home with co-workers and management at an office.

Telecommuting   Computer technology is opening still another alternative for managers in the way they arrange jobs. That alternative is to allow employees to perform their work at home by **telecommuting**.[38] Many white-collar occupations can now be carried out at home—at least technically. A computer in an employee's home can be linked to those of co-workers and managers by modems.

In the United States, approximately 5.5 million people now telecommute, doing such things as taking orders over the phone, filling out reports and other forms, and processing or analyzing information.[39] Among employers who offer telecommuting as an option are major companies such as Levi Strauss, Pacific Bell, AT&T, IBM, Johnson & Johnson, American Express, and J.C. Penney.

For employees, the two biggest pluses of telecommuting are the decrease in the time and stress of commuting in urban areas and the increase in flexibility in coping with family demands. But it also introduces potentially new problems for employees. For example, will they miss the regular social contact that a formal office provides? Might they be less likely to be considered for salary increases and promotions? Is being out of sight equivalent to being out of mind? Answers to questions such as these are central to determining whether telecommuting will continue to expand in the future.

TQM and Structural Design

Several concepts introduced in this and the prior chapter have become important components in the Total Quality Management movement. These include vertical differentiation, division of labor, and centralization.

One common characteristic of TQM programs is an effort to reduce vertical differentiation. By widening spans of control and flattening organizations, management cuts overhead and improves vertical communication.

A second common TQM characteristic is reduced division of labor. High division of labor emphasizes specialization, promotes an "us versus them" mentality, and

One of the advantages of tele-commuting is that it allows employees to better balance their work and family responsibilities.

retards collaboration and horizontal communication. As a result, TQM encourages enrichment of jobs and the use of teams that cut across functional specializations.

Finally, TQM emphasizes decentralized decision making. Authority and responsibility are pushed as far down, and as close to the customer, as is possible. The reason, of course, is that TQM's success depends on quickly and continually responding to the changing needs of customers.

Amoco Production Co. illustrates the effectiveness of these structural changes.[40] The company, a subsidiary of the Chicago oil giant, realized that its matrix structure— six tiers of management cross-laden with a multitude of functional units—had become too cumbersome. Geologists, for instance, were spending nearly 40 percent of their time in committee meetings trying to get approvals to search for oil when they actually could have been searching for oil. So Amoco's management reorganized. They eliminated three layers of management and dismantled the functional hierarchies. Workers were grouped into units of approximately 500, organized around multidisciplinary teams, and given considerable authority to make decisions. Noted one unit leader, "We're finding more oil and getting better financial results with the same number of professionals and fewer managers."[41]

Summary

This summary is organized by the chapter-opening learning objectives found on page 307.

1. The functional structure groups similar or related occupational specialties together. It takes advantage of specialization and provides economies of scale by allowing people with common skills to work together.

2. The divisional structure is composed of autonomous units, with managers having full responsibility for a product or service. However, these units are frequently organized as functional structures inside their divisional framework. So divisional structures typically contain functional structures within them.

3. The simple structure is low in complexity, has little formalization, and has authority centralized in a single person. It is widely used in small businesses.

4. By assigning specialists from functional departments to work on one or more projects led by project managers, the matrix structure combines functional and product departmentalization. It thus has the advantage of both specialization and high accountability.

5. The recent popularity of the network structure is due to its high flexibility. It allows management to perform manufacturing, distribution, marketing, or other crucial business functions with a minimal commitment of resources.

6. Organic appendages allow organizations to be responsive and flexible while, at the same time, maintaining an overall mechanistic structure.

7. Job specialization is concerned with breaking jobs down into ever-smaller tasks. Job enlargement is the reverse. It expands jobs horizontally by increasing their scope. Like enlargement, job enrichment expands jobs, but vertically rather than horizontally. Enriched jobs increase depth by allowing employees greater control over their work.

8. The core job dimensions in the job characteristics model are skill variety, task identity, task significance, autonomy, and feedback.

9. The main advantage of flexible work hours is greater freedom for employees. It allows them to complete nonwork commitments without incurring absences. Additionally, it allows employees to better align their work schedule with their personal productivity cycle. The major drawback of flexible work hours is that it creates coordination problems for managers.

10. TQM encourages low vertical differentiation, minimal division of labor, and decentralized decision making.

Review Questions

1. Show how both the functional and matrix structures might create conflict within an organization.

2. Why is the simple structure inadequate in large organizations?

3. When should management use
   a. the matrix structure?
   b. the network structure?
   c. a task force?

4. Contrast *job enlargement* with *job enrichment* in terms of the job characteristics model.

5. Describe how a job can be enriched.

6. Why would managers choose to have job sharing programs?

7. Compare the compressed work week to flextime. What advantages and disadvantages do they each have?

8. If you were a manager, why might you resist offering flexible work hours to your employees?

9. Why might professionals who could find permanent jobs seek employment as contingent workers?

10. Why might telecommuting prove to be better in theory than in practice?

Discussion Questions

1. Can an organization have *no* structure?

2. Which structural design—divisional, simple, or matrix—would you most prefer to work in? Least prefer? Why?

3. Do you study in groups or alone? Which do you feel is more effective? Relate your answer to designing jobs in the 1990s.

4. Identify two jobs that you're familiar with: one that you think you would like to do continuously and one that you would never want to do. Compare them in terms of the JCM. Compare them also in terms of compensation and prestige in the community. Do you think compensation and prestige are positively correlated with a high MPS?

5. "What a manager does in terms of the *organizing function* depends on what level he or she occupies in the organizational hierarchy." Discuss.

SELF-ASSESSMENT EXERCISE

Is an Enriched Job for You?

Instructions: People differ in what they like and dislike in their jobs. Listed below are twelve pairs of jobs. For each pair, indicate which job you would prefer. Assume that everything else about the jobs is the same—pay attention only to the characteristics actually listed for each pair of jobs. If you would prefer the job in the left-hand column (Column A), indicate how much you prefer it by putting a check mark in a blank to the left of the Neutral point. If you prefer the job in the right-hand column (Column B), check one of the blanks to the right of Neutral. Check the Neutral blank only if you find the two jobs equally attractive or unattractive. Try to use the Neutral blank rarely.

Column A		Column B
1. A job that offers little or no challenge.	Strongly prefer A — Neutral — Strongly prefer B	A job that requires you to be completely isolated from co-workers.
2. A job that pays very well.	Strongly prefer A — Neutral — Strongly prefer B	A job that allows considerable opportunity to be creative and innovative.
3. A job that often requires you to make important decisions.	Strongly prefer A — Neutral — Strongly prefer B	A job in which there are many pleasant people to work with.
4. A job with little security in a somewhat unstable organization.	Strongly prefer A — Neutral — Strongly prefer B	A job in which you have little or no opportunity to participate in decisions that affect your work.

Column A		Column B
5. A job in which greater responsibility is given to those who do the best work.	Strongly prefer A — Neutral — Strongly prefer B	A job in which greater responsibility is given to loyal employees who have the most *seniority*.
6. A job with a supervisor who sometimes is highly critical.	Strongly prefer A — Neutral — Strongly prefer B	A job that does not require you to use much of your talent.
7. A very routine job.	Strongly prefer A — Neutral — Strongly prefer B	A job in which your co-workers are not very friendly.
8. A job with a supervisor who respects you and treats you fairly.	Strongly prefer A — Neutral — Strongly prefer B	A job that provides constant opportunities for you to learn new and interesting things.
9. A job that gives you a real chance to develop yourself personally.	Strongly prefer A — Neutral — Strongly prefer B	A job with excellent vacations and fringe benefits.
10. A job in which there is a real chance you could be laid off.	Strongly prefer A — Neutral — Strongly prefer B	A job with very little chance to do challenging work.
11. A job with little freedom and independence to do your work in the way you think best.	Strongly prefer A — Neutral — Strongly prefer B	A job with poor working conditions.
12. A job with very satisfying teamwork.	Strongly prefer A — Neutral — Strongly prefer B	A job that allows you to use your skills and abilities to the fullest extent.

Turn to page SK-3 for scoring directions and key.

Source: J. R. Hackman and G. R. Oldham (1974), *The Job Diagnostic Survey: An Instrument for the Diagnosis of Jobs and the Evaluation of Job Redesign Projects.* Technical Report No. 4. New Haven, Conn.: Yale University, Department of Administrative Sciences. With permission.

CAPARELLI SHIPPING CO.

To: Mac Wilkins, Director of Human Resources
From: Ricco Caparelli, President
Subject: High turnover among truck drivers

I just got finished reviewing the results from our annual employee attitude survey. It occurs to me that the information in this report goes a long way toward helping us understand why turnover is so high among our drivers.

As we've discussed a number of times, our annual turnover rate of 30 to 35 percent is too high. Only seventeen of our current ninety drivers have been here more than two years. It costs us a lot to find and train replacements. Customers comment on how they're always meeting new drivers from our company. Meanwhile, our competitors have turnover rates in the 10 to 15 percent range.

We know our pay is competitive. In fact, there were few complaints about money in the survey results. The major complaint our drivers have is that they find their jobs boring and repetitive. They come to work, pick up their daily schedules, find their pre-loaded trucks, then follow the specific instructions outlined by the route dispatcher for making their deliveries.

I think we need to consider redesigning the jobs of our drivers. I'd like you to prepare a short report describing how we might restructure their jobs. We want to make their jobs less boring but not less efficient. What ideas do you have?

This is a fictionalized account of a potentially real problem. It was written for academic purposes only and is not meant to reflect either positively or negatively on actual management practices at Caparelli Shipping Co.

CASE APPLICATION

Magna International

Magna International is one of the top ten auto parts makers in North America. This Canadian firm produces 4,000 components—from flywheels to fenders—for nearly every major auto manufacturer with a U.S. factory. For instance, it is Chrysler's biggest component supplier.

Magna's top management has long been committed to keeping the company's structure loose and giving a great deal of freedom to its unit managers. In the mid-1980s, the company had more than 10,000 employees and almost $1 billion (Canadian) in annual sales. These employees were organized into 120 separate enterprises. Each enterprise operated under its own name and had exactly one factory. Magna's philosophy was to keep units small—no more than 200 people—to encourage entrepreneurship and focus responsibility squarely with the plant manager. When a plant got more work than it could handle, rather than add to the plant's size, Magna would "clone" the facility and start a new company.

This structure worked fine during the 1980s. Overall sales grew thirteen-fold during that decade. Plant managers, acting with almost complete autonomy, aggressively expanded their businesses. Their motivation? They shared not only in their plant's profits, but all spin-offs that their business created. Thus, free from corporate interference, plant managers built factories, took on debt, and signed supply contracts with Detroit auto makers.

The bubble burst in 1990. Auto sales had slowed and the expansion-driven managers had burdened the company with $1 billion (U.S.) in new debt. In 1990, Magna lost $191 million on sales of $1.6 billion and seemed headed for bankruptcy. In January 1991, Magna stock fell to $2 a share.

But Magna didn't go bankrupt. Top management interceded and has turned the company's fortunes around. The company sold or shut nearly half of its factories and used the proceeds to pay off its debt. The remaining plants are small, new, efficient, and flexible. And management succeeded in getting increased use of Magna parts in popular cars such as the Ford Taurus and Toyota Camry. By 1992, Magna's sales had risen to $2 billion, earnings were $81 million, and the company's stock had rebounded to more than $26 a share. Top management claims that the company is more focused now than in the 1980s, with firmer controls and a ban on new debt.

Questions

1. Using structural concepts developed in the previous chapter, describe Magna International's structure in 1985. In 1992.

2. Magna isn't alone in changing its structure. Many companies, even large ones like IBM, are scorning bureaucracy and creating loosely-structured, independent businesses. Why?

3. What does the Magna case imply about creating a structure made up of a federation of independent businesses?

This case is based on John Case, "How to Grow Without Getting Big," *INC.*, December 1986, pp. 108–12; and Brian O'Reilly, "The Perils of Too Much Freedom," *Fortune*, January 11, 1993, p. 79.

CHAPTER 12

Human Resource Management

LEARNING OBJECTIVES

After Reading This Chapter, You Should Be Able To:

1. Describe the human resource management process.
2. Discuss the influence of government regulations on human resource decisions.
3. Differentiate between job descriptions and job specifications.
4. Contrast recruitment and decruitment options.
5. Explain the importance of validity and reliability in selection.
6. Describe the selection devices that work best with various kinds of jobs.
7. Identify the various training methods.
8. Describe six performance appraisal methods.
9. Outline the five stages in a career.
10. Explain the collective bargaining process.
11. Describe how HRM practices can facilitate work force diversity.
12. Explain why sexual harassment is a growing concern of management.

Microsoft is growing fast. It is adding approximately 150 new employees every month. Its continued success depends on its recruiters finding and hiring the best people available.

$\mathbf{M}$icrosoft Corp. is on its way to becoming *the* business success story of the late 20th century.[1] Established in 1975, this maker of personal computer software has experienced unprecedented growth. For instance, in 1990, sales hit $1.2 billion; in 1991, they shot up to $1.8 billion; and despite an economic recession sales grew to $2.7 billion in 1992. The stock market now values Microsoft at more than General Motors or IBM. Microsoft's success has made its co-founder, Bill Gates, the richest man in America.

But Microsoft is a knowledge-based business. Its continued growth depends on a steady stream of bright and motivated employees. As one senior vice president recently put it, "You can't hire bad programmers and get great software." In 1989, the company had 4,000 people on its payroll. By 1992, that number had passed 10,000. The task of filling Microsoft's staffing needs is truly overwhelming. To illustrate, in one recent year, Microsoft recruiters reviewed more than 120,000 résumés and conducted 7,400 face-to-face interviews in order to hire 2,000 new people.

Finding and hiring the best is top priority at Microsoft. When Bill Gates was asked about the most important thing he had done for the company in the previous year, he answered, "I hired a lot of smart people."

How does Microsoft find and select its people? Recruiters visit over 130 college campuses a year. Job candidates may be looked over several times on campus before they are flown to the company's headquarters outside Seattle. There, they spend a day being interviewed by at least four staffers from different parts of the organization. And interviewers' questions emphasize creativity and problem-solving skills rather than specific programming knowledge. Moreover, Microsoft's salaries tend to be on the low side, and sixty- to eighty-hour workweeks are common. So the company looks for individuals who value winning more than rewards. Of course, any interviewees who've done their homework know that stock options given to high-performing employees have made more than 2,000 of them millionaires.

Microsoft's selection process is obviously working. The firm has earned a reputation for hiring much of America's best young technical, marketing, and management talent. If the proof of the pudding is in the eating, Microsoft's growth record validates the effectiveness of its selection process.

As Microsoft illustrates, the quality of an organization is, to a large degree, merely the summation of the quality of people it hires and holds. Getting and keeping competent personnel is critical to the success of every organization, whether the organization is just starting or well established. Therefore, part of every manager's job in the organizing function is filling positions— that is, putting the right person into the right job.

Managers and Personnel Departments

Some readers may be thinking, "Sure, personnel decisions are important, but aren't they made by people in personnel departments? These aren't decisions that *all* managers are involved in."

It's true that, in large organizations, a number of the activities grouped under the label *human resource management* (HRM) often are done by specialists in personnel or human resource development. However, not all managers work in organizations that have formal personnel departments; and even those who do still have to be engaged in some human resource activities.

Small-business managers are an obvious example of individuals who frequently must do their hiring without the assistance of a personnel department. But even managers in billion-dollar corporations are involved in recruiting candidates, reviewing application forms, interviewing applicants, inducting new employees, appraising employee performance, making decisions about employee training, and providing career advice to subordinates. Whether or not an organization has a personnel department, *every* manager is involved with human resource decisions in his or her unit.

The Human Resource Management Process

human resource management process

Activities necessary for staffing the organization and sustaining high employee performance.

Figure 12–1 introduces the key components of an organization's **human resource management process.** It represents nine activities, or steps (the beige-shaded boxes), that, if properly executed, will staff an organization with competent, high-performing employees who are capable of sustaining their performance level over the long term.

The first four steps represent *human resource planning,* the adding of staff through *recruitment,* the reduction in staff through *decruitment,* and *selection,* resulting in the identification and selection of competent employees. Once you've got competent people, you need to help them adapt to the organization and ensure that their job skills and knowledge are kept current. You do this through *orientation* and *training.* The last steps in the HRM process are designed to identify performance problems, correct them, and help employees to sustain a high level of performance over their entire career. The activities included here include *performance appraisal, career development,* and, where employees are unionized, *labor–management relations.*

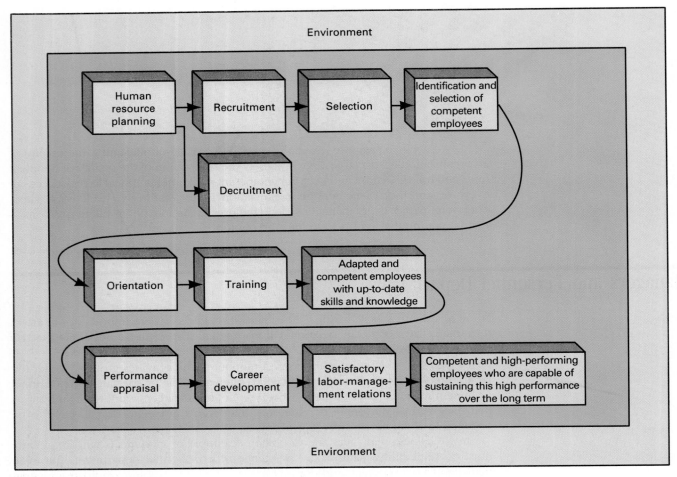

FIGURE 12–1
The Human Resource Management Process

Notice in Figure 12–1 that the entire HRM process is influenced by the external environment. In Chapter 3 we elaborated on the constraints that the environment places on management. Those constraints are probably most severe in the management of human resources. Before we review the nine steps in the process, therefore, we will briefly examine how environmental forces influence the process.

Important Environmental Considerations

Numerous environmental forces impinge on human resource management activities. For instance, approximately 16 percent of the U.S. work force is unionized. In unionized organizations, many key personnel decisions are regulated by the terms of collective bargaining agreements. These agreements usually define such things as recruitment sources; criteria for hiring, promotions, and layoffs; training eligibility; and disciplinary practices. But no environmental constraint can match the influence of government laws and regulations.

Since the mid-1960s, the federal government has greatly expanded its influence over HRM decisions by enacting new laws and regulations. (See Table 12–1.) As a result of this legislation, employers today must ensure that equal employment opportunities exist for job applicants and current employees. Decisions regarding who will

TABLE 12-1   Major U.S. Federal Laws and Regulations Related to Human Resource Management

Year	Law or Regulation	Description
1963	Equal Pay Act	Prohibits pay differences based on sex for equal work
1964 (amended in 1972)	Civil Rights Act, Title VII	Prohibits discrimination based on race, color, religion, national origin, or sex
1967 (amended in 1975)	Age Discrimination in Employment Act	Prohibits age discrimination against employees between 40 and 65 years of age
1973	Vocational Rehabilitation Act	Prohibits discrimination on the basis of physical or mental disabilities
1974	Privacy Act	Gives employees the legal right to examine letters of reference concerning them
1978	Pregnancy Discrimination Act, Title VII	Prohibits dismissal of women because of pregnancy alone and protects job security during maternity leaves
1978	Mandatory Retirement Act	Prohibits the forced retirement of most employees before the age of 70
1986	Immigration Reform and Control Act	Prohibits unlawful employment of aliens and unfair immigration-related employment practices
1988	Polygraph Protection Act	Limits an employer's ability to use lie detectors
1988	Worker Adjustment and Retraining Notification Act	Requires employers to provide 60 days' notice before a facility closing or mass layoff
1990	Americans with Disabilities Act	Prohibits employers from discriminating against individuals with physical or mental disabilities or the chronically ill
1991	Civil Rights Act of 1991	Reaffirms and tightens prohibition of discrimination; permits individuals to sue for punitive damages in cases of intentional discrimination

bona fide occupational qualifications (BFOQ)
A criterion such as sex, age, or national origin may be used as a basis for hiring if it can be clearly demonstrated to be job related.

affirmative action programs
Programs that enhance the organizational status of members of protected groups.

be hired, for example, or which employees will be chosen for a management training program must be made without regard to race, sex, religion, age, color, or national origin. Exceptions can occur only for requirements that are **bona fide occupational qualifications (BFOQ).** This explains why, for instance, airlines today have flight attendants of both sexes and of varying ages. In the early 1960s, airlines hired almost exclusively flight attendants who were young, attractive females. But age, beauty, and gender are not BFOQs for this job; and so such criteria had to be dropped.

Many organizations have **affirmative action programs** to ensure that decisions and practices enhance the employment, upgrading, and retention of members from protected groups, such as minorities and females. That is, not only will the organization refrain from discrimination, but it will actively seek to enhance the status of members from protected groups. Why are organizations taking this affirmative

In 1992, State Farm Insurance Companies paid $157 million to settle with 814 California women who claimed to have been denied sales jobs in the 1980s and late 1970s because of gender bias. State Farm had previously paid $33 million to other California women who won or settled sex-discrimination cases against the insurer. State Farm appears to be correcting its past mistake: More than 50 percent of all State Farm agents appointed in recent years have been women.

stance? On the ethical side, they have a social responsibility to improve the status of protected group members. On the economic side, the cost of defending the organization against charges of discrimination can be enormous. As an example, Sears, Roebuck spent over twelve years and $20 million in legal fees and employed 250 full-time people to defend itself successfully against accusations by the Equal Employment Opportunity Commission that its past hiring practices had discriminated against females.[2]

Our conclusion is that managers are not completely free to choose who they hire, promote, or fire. While these regulations have significantly helped to reduce discrimination and unfair employment practices in organizations, they have, at the same time, also reduced management's discretion over human resource decisions.

Human Resource Planning

human resource planning
The process by which management ensures that it has the right personnel, who are capable of completing those tasks that help the organization reach its objectives.

Human resource planning is the process by which management ensures that it has the right number and kinds of people in the right places, and at the right times, who are capable of effectively and efficiently completing those tasks that will help the organization achieve its overall objectives. Human resource planning, then, translates the organization's objectives into terms of the workers needed to meet those objectives.[3]

Human resource planning can be condensed into three steps: (1) assessing current human resources, (2) assessing future human resource needs, and (3) developing a program to meet future human resource needs.

Current Assessment

Management begins by reviewing its current human resource status. This is typically done by generating a *human resource inventory*. In an era of sophisticated computer systems, it is not too difficult a task for most organizations to generate a human resource inventory report. The input for this report is derived from forms completed by employees. Such reports might list the name, education, training, prior employment, languages spoken, capabilities, and specialized skills of each employee in the organization. This inventory allows management to assess what talents and skills are available.

job analysis
An assessment that defines jobs and the behaviors necessary to perform them.

Another part of the current assessment is the **job analysis.** While the human resource inventory is concerned with telling management what individual employees can do, job analysis is more fundamental. It defines the jobs within the organization and the behaviors that are necessary to perform those jobs. For instance, what are the duties of a purchasing specialist, grade 3, who works for Boise Cascade? What minimal knowledge, skills, and abilities are necessary for the adequate performance of a grade 3 purchasing specialist's job? How do the requirements for a purchasing specialist, grade 3, compare with those for a purchasing specialist, grade 2, or for a purchasing analyst? These are questions that job analysis can answer. It seeks to determine the kind of people needed to fill each job and culminates in job descriptions and job specifications.

There are several methods for analyzing jobs. There is the observation method, in which employees are either watched directly or filmed on the job. Employees can also be interviewed individually or in a group. A third method is the use of structured questionnaires on which employees check or rate the items they perform in their jobs from a long list of possible task items. A fourth method is the use of a technical conference, at which "experts"—usually supervisors with extensive knowledge of a job—identify its specific characteristics. A fifth method is to have employees record their daily activities in a diary or notebook, which can then be reviewed and structured into job activities.

job description
A written statement of what a jobholder does, how it is done, and why it is done.

job specification
A statement of the minimum acceptable qualifications that an incumbent must possess to perform a given job successfully.

Information gathered by using one or more of these methods allows management to draw up a **job description** and **job specification.** The former is a written statement of what a jobholder does, how it is done, and why it is done. It typically portrays job content, environment, and conditions of employment. The job specification states the minimum acceptable qualifications that an incumbent must possess to perform a given job successfully. It identifies the knowledge, skills, and abilities needed to do the job effectively.

The job description and specification are important documents when managers begin recruiting and selecting. The job description can be used to describe the job to potential candidates. The job specification keeps the manager's attention on the list of qualifications necessary for an incumbent to perform a job and assists in determining whether candidates are qualified.

Future Assessment

Future human resource needs are determined by the organization's objectives and strategies.

Demand for human resources is a result of demand for the organization's products or services. On the basis of its estimate of total revenue, management can attempt to establish the number and mix of human resources needed to reach these revenues. In some cases, the situation may be reversed. Where particular skills are necessary and in scarce supply, the availability of satisfactory human resources determines revenues. This might be the case, for example, in a tax consulting firm that finds it has more business opportunities than it can handle. Its only limiting factor in building revenues might be its ability to locate and hire staff with the qualifications necessary to satisfy the consulting firm's clients. In most cases, however, the overall organizational goals and the resulting revenue forecast provide the major input determining the organization's human resource demand requirements.

Developing a Future Program

After it has assessed both current capabilities and future needs, management is able to estimate shortages—both in number and in kind—and to highlight areas in which the organization will be overstaffed. A program can then be developed that can match these estimates with forecasts of future labor supply. So human resource planning not only provides information to guide current staffing needs, but also provides projections of future personnel needs and availability.

Recruitment and Decruitment

recruitment
The process of locating, identifying, and attracting capable applicants.

decruitment
Techniques for reducing the labor supply within an organization.

Once managers know their current personnel status (whether they are understaffed or overstaffed), they can begin to do something about it. If one or more vacancies exist, they can use the information gathered through job analysis to guide them in **recruitment**—that is, the process of locating, identifying, and attracting capable applicants.[4] On the other hand, if human resource planning indicates a surplus, management will want to reduce the labor supply within the organization. This activity is called **decruitment.**[5]

Where does a manager look to recruit potential candidates? Table 12–2 offers some guidance. The source that is used should reflect the local labor market, the type or level of position, and the size of the organization.

TABLE 12–2　Major Sources of Potential Job Candidates

Source	Advantages	Disadvantages
Internal search	Low cost; builds employee morale; candidates are familiar with organization	Limited supply; may not increase proportion of employees from protected groups
Advertisements	Wide distribution; can be targeted to specific groups	Generates many unqualified candidates
Employee referrals	Knowledge about the organization provided by current employee; can generate strong candidates because a good referral reflects on the recommender	May not increase the diversity and mix of employees
Public employment agencies	Free or nominal cost	Candidates tend to be unskilled or minimally trained
Private employment agencies	Wide contacts; careful screening; short-term guarantees often given	High cost
School placement	Large, centralized body of candidates	Limited to entry-level positions
Temporary help services	Fills temporary needs	Expensive; generally limited to routine or narrowly defined skills

Simon & Schuster publishers offers a $600 finders fee for referring job applicants that are eventually hired.

For filling senior executive jobs—like Linda Rice's position as Chief Operating Officer at Johnson Publications—organizations often rely on executive search firms with national contacts. A wider set of candidates is justified because of the potential impact the decisions of such managers will have on an organization's future.

Regardless of the type of position or its attractiveness, it is generally easier to recruit in large labor markets than in small ones. If for no other reasons, large labor markets like New York or Chicago have a greater supply of workers. Of course, this generalization has to be moderated by unemployment levels, wage rates, and other factors. But in large markets, recruitment efforts can be directed locally—to newspapers, employment agencies, colleges, or referrals by current employees.

The type or level of a position influences recruitment methods. The greater the skill required or the higher the position in the organization's hierarchy, the more the recruitment process will expand to become a regional or national search.

The scope of recruitment and the amount of effort devoted to it will also be influenced by the size of the organization. Generally, the larger the organization, the easier it is to recruit job applicants. Larger organizations have a larger pool of internal candidates from which to choose to fill positions above the lowest level. They have more visibility and, typically, more prestige. Also, larger organizations are often perceived as offering greater opportunities for promotions and increased responsibility.

Are certain recruiting sources superior to others? More specifically, do certain recruiting sources produce superior candidates? The answer is yes. The majority of studies find that employee referrals prove to be superior.[6] The explanation for this finding is intuitively logical. First, applicants referred by current employees are prescreened by these employees. Because the recommenders know both the job and the person being recommended, they tend to refer applicants who are better qualified for the job. Second, because current employees often feel their reputation in the organization is at stake with a referral, they tend to refer others only when they are reasonably confident that the referral won't make them look bad.

In the past decade, most large U.S. corporations, as well as many government agencies and small businesses, have been forced to engage in some decruitment activities. The decline in many manufacturing industries, market changes, foreign competition, and mergers have been the primary causes of personnel cutbacks.

Decruitment is not a pleasant task for any manager to perform. But as many organizations are forced to shrink the size of their work force or restructure their skill composition, decruitment is becoming an increasingly important part of human resource management.

What are a manager's decruitment options? Obviously, people can be fired. But other choices may be more beneficial to the organization and/or the employee.[7] Table 12–3 summarizes a manager's major options.

TABLE 12–3   Decruitment Options

Option	Description
Firing	Permanent involuntary termination.
Layoffs	Temporary involuntary termination; may last only a few days or extend to years.
Attrition	Not filling openings created by voluntary resignations or normal retirements.
Transfers	Moving employees either laterally or downward; usually does not reduce costs but can reduce intra-organizational supply-demand imbalances.
Reduced workweeks	Having employees work fewer hours per week, share jobs, or perform their jobs on a part-time basis.
Early retirements	Providing incentives to older and more senior employees for retiring before their normal retirement date.

Selection

selection process
The process of screening job applicants to ensure that the most appropriate candidates are hired.

A new college graduate with a degree in accounting walked into the personnel office of a medium-sized corporation not long ago in search of a job. Immediately, she was confronted by two doors, one of which displayed the sign "Applicants With College Degree" and the other, "Applicants Without College Degree." She opened the first door. As soon as she did so, she was confronted by two more doors. The first said, "Applicants with Grade Point Average of 3.0 or Greater," and the other, "Applicants with Grade Point Average of Less Than 3.0." Having achieved a 3.6 average, she again chose the first door—and was once again faced by two doors, one reading, "Applicants with Management Majors," and the other, "Applicants with Nonmanagement Majors." Having an accounting degree, she opened the second of these doors—and found herself out in the street.[8]

Although this story is fictitious, it does convey the essence of the selection process. When human resource planning identifies a personnel shortage and develops a pool of applicants, it needs some method for screening the applicants to ensure that the most appropriate candidate is awarded the job. That screening method is the **selection process.**

Foundations of Selection

Selection is a prediction exercise. It seeks to predict which applicants will be successful if hired. "Successful" in this case means performing well on the criteria the organization uses to evaluate personnel. In filling a sales position, for example, the selection process should be able to predict which applicants will generate a high volume of sales; for a position as a high school teacher, it should predict which applicants will be effective educators.

Prediction Consider, for a moment, that any selection decision can result in four possible outcomes. As shown in Figure 12–2, two of these outcomes would indicate correct decisions, but two would indicate errors.

A decision is correct when the applicant was predicted to be successful and later proved to be successful on the job or when the applicant was predicted to be unsuccessful and would perform accordingly if hired. In the former case, we have successfully accepted; in the latter case, we have successfully rejected.

Problems occur when we make errors by rejecting candidates who would later perform successfully on the job (reject errors) or accepting those who subsequently perform poorly (accept errors). These problems are, unfortunately, far from insignifi-

FIGURE 12–2
Selection Decision Outcomes

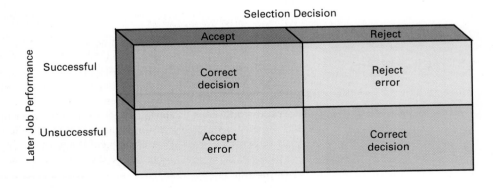

Julie Stasch at Stein & Company

Julie Stasch is president of Stein & Company, a major real estate developer in Chicago.[9] She joined the company in 1976 and rose through the ranks to become president in 1991. Among her accomplishments has been her role in creating the Female Employment Initiative (FEI).

Stasch was unhappy with the low number of women in high-paid, skilled construction jobs. Contractors would rationalize the situation by arguing that, although they'd love to hire women, unions didn't have any women in their ranks. The unions would argue that, although they too would love to admit more women, contractors didn't want to hire them. Instead of seeking change through the courts, Stasch, with the full support of her company, created FEI in 1988 as a committee of ten influential women from Chicago contracting and nonprofit groups. As consultants paid by Stein & Company, committee members encouraged women to seek skilled construction jobs, helped train these women, and worked with employers to make job sites more woman-friendly.

Through Stasch's efforts, eighty-five of the 500 tradespeople who built the thirty-story Ralph H. Metcalfe Federal Building in Chicago were women, as were seventy-five of the workers who built U.S. Gypsum's headquarters. Additionally, more than 200 women are working on Stein & Company's new projects in Chicago—a convention center and a sports arena.

cant. A generation ago reject errors meant only that the costs of selection would be increased because more candidates would have to be screened. Today, selection techniques that result in reject errors can open the organization to charges of discrimination, especially if applicants from protected groups are disproportionately rejected. Accept errors, on the other hand, have very obvious costs to the organization, including the cost of training the employee, the costs generated or profits forgone because of the employee's incompetence, and the cost of severance and the subsequent costs of further recruiting and selection screening. The major thrust of any selection activity is therefore to reduce the probability of making reject errors or accept errors, while increasing the probability of making correct decisions.

validity
The proven relationship that exists between a selection device and some relevant criterion.

Validity   Any selection device that a manager uses—such as application forms, tests, interviews, or background investigations—must demonstrate **validity.** That is, there must be a proven relationship between the selection device and some relevant criterion. For example, the law prohibits management from using a test score as a selection device unless there is clear evidence that, once on the job, individuals with high scores on this test outperform individuals with low test scores.

The burden is on management to support that any selection device it uses to differentiate applicants is related to job performance. While management can give applicants an intelligence test and use the results to help make selection decisions, it must be prepared to demonstrate, if challenged, that this intelligence test is a valid measure; that is, that scores on the test are positively related to later job performance.

reliability
The ability of a selection device to measure the same thing consistently.

Reliability In addition to being valid, a selection device must also demonstrate reliability. **Reliability** indicates whether the device measures the same thing consistently. For example, if a test is reliable, any single individual's score should remain fairly stable over time, assuming that the characteristics it is measuring are also stable.

The importance of reliability should be evident. No selection device can be effective if it is low in reliability. That is equivalent to weighing yourself everyday on an erratic scale. If the scale is unreliable—randomly fluctuating, say, ten to fifteen pounds every time you step on it—the results will not mean much. To be effective predictors, selection devices must possess an acceptable level of consistency.

Selection Devices

Managers can use a number of selection devices to reduce accept and reject errors. The best-known devices include an analysis of the prospects' completed application form, written and performance-simulation tests, interviews, background investigations, and in some cases a physical examination. Let us briefly review each of these devices, giving particular attention to the validity of each in predicting job performance. After we review the devices, we will discuss when each should be used.

The trend in recent years has been towards shorter application forms essentially focusing on education and experience.

The Application Form Almost all organizations require candidates to fill out an application. It may be only a form on which a prospect gives his or her name, address, and telephone number. At the other extreme, it might be a comprehensive personal history profile, detailing the applicant's activities, skills, and accomplishments.

Hard and relevant biographical data that can be verified—for example, rank in high school graduating class—have shown to be valid measures of performance for some jobs.[10] Additionally, when application form items have been appropriately weighted to reflect job relatedness, the device has proven a valid predictor for such diverse groups as salesclerks, engineers, factory workers, district managers, clerical employees, and technicians.[11] But, typically, only a couple of items on the application prove to be valid predictors, and then only for a specific job. Use of weighted applications for selection purposes is difficult and expensive because the weights have to be validated for each specific job and must be continually reviewed and updated to reflect changes in weights over time.

Written Tests Typical written tests include tests of intelligence, aptitude, ability, and interest. Such tests have long been used as selection devices, although their popularity has run in cycles. Written tests were widely used for twenty years following World War II. Beginning in the late 1960s, however, they fell into disfavor. Written tests were frequently characterized as discriminatory, and many organizations couldn't validate that their written tests were job related.[12] But since the late 1980s, written tests have made a comeback.[13] Managers have become increasingly aware that poor hiring decisions are costly, and that properly designed tests could reduce the likelihood of these decisions occurring. In addition, the cost of developing and validating a set of written tests for a specific job has come down markedly. "Ten years ago," says an executive at Personnel Decisions Inc., "if an employer called us and wanted to put together a test battery for salespeople or copywriters . . . we told him [or her] it would take $100,000 and six months. Now we're talking about $6,000 and a couple of weeks."[14]

A review of the evidence finds that tests of intellectual ability, spatial and mechanical ability, perceptual accuracy, and motor ability are moderately valid predictors for many semiskilled and unskilled operative jobs in industrial organizations.[15] And intelligence tests are reasonably good predictors for supervisory positions.[16] However, an enduring criticism of written tests is that intelligence, and other tested

An applicant for a paint-sealer position at Mazda participates in a performance simulation test.

characteristics, can be somewhat removed from the actual performance of the job itself. For example, a high score on an intelligence test is not necessarily a good indicator that the applicant will perform well as a computer programmer. This criticism has led to an increased use of performance simulation tests.

Performance Simulation Tests   What better way to find out whether an applicant for a technical-writing position at McDonnell-Douglas can write technical manuals than by having him or her do it? The logic of this question has led to the expanding interest in performance simulation tests. Undoubtedly, the enthusiasm for these tests lies in the fact that they are based on job analysis data and therefore should more easily meet the requirement of job relatedness than do written tests. Performance simulation tests are made up of actual job behaviors rather than surrogates.

The best-known performance simulation tests are work sampling and assessment centers. The former is suited to routine jobs, the latter to selecting managerial personnel.

work sampling

A personnel selection device in which job applicants are presented with a miniature replica of a job and are asked to perform tasks central to that job.

Work sampling involves presenting applicants with a miniature replica of a job and having them perform a task or set of tasks that are central to the job. Applicants demonstrate that they possess the necessary talents by actually doing the tasks. By carefully devising work samples based on job analysis data, management can determine the knowledge, skills, and abilities needed for each job. Each work sample element is then matched with a corresponding job performance element. For instance, a work sample for a job that involves computations on a calculator would require applicants to make similar computations.

The results from work sample experiments have generally been impressive. They have almost always yielded validity scores that are superior to those of written aptitude, personality, or intelligence tests.[17]

assessment centers

Places in which job candidates undergo performance simulation tests that evaluate managerial potential.

A more elaborate set of performance simulation tests, specifically designed to evaluate a candidate's managerial potential, is administered in **assessment centers.** In assessment centers, line executives, supervisors, or trained psychologists evaluate candidates as they go through two to four days of exercises that simulate real problems they would confront on the job. Based on a list of descriptive dimensions that the actual job incumbent has to meet, activities might include interviews, in-basket problem-solving exercises, group discussions, and business decision games.

The evidence for the effectiveness of assessment centers is extremely impressive. They have consistently demonstrated results that predict later job performance in managerial positions.[18] Although they are not cheap, the selection of an ineffective manager is undoubtedly far more costly.

Interviews   The interview, along with the application form, is an almost universal selection device.[19] Not many of us have ever gotten a job without one or more interviews. The irony of this is that the value of the interview as a selection device has been the subject of considerable debate.[20]

Interviews *can* be valid and reliable selection tools, but too often they're not. When interviews are structured and well-organized, and when interviewers are held to common questioning, interviews are effective predictors.[21] But those conditions don't characterize most interviews. The typical interview—in which applicants are asked a varying set of essentially random questions in an informal setting—usually provide little in the way of valuable information.

There are all kinds of potential biases that can creep into interviews if they are not well structured and standardized. To illustrate, a review of the research leads us to the following conclusions:

1. Prior knowledge about the applicant will bias the interviewer's evaluation.
2. The interviewer tends to hold a stereotype of what represents a "good" applicant.
3. The interviewer tends to favor applicants who share his or her own attitudes.
4. The order in which applicants are interviewed will influence evaluations.
5. The order in which information is elicited during the interview will influence evaluations.
6. Negative information is given unduly high weight.
7. The interviewer often makes a decision concerning the applicant's suitability within the first four or five minutes of the interview.
8. The interviewer forgets much of the interview's content within minutes after its conclusion.
9. The interview is most valid in determining an applicant's intelligence, level of motivation, and interpersonal skills.[22]

What can managers do to make interviews more valid and reliable? Specifically, we suggest: (1) structuring a fixed set of questions for all applicants; (2) having detailed information about the job for which applicants are interviewing; (3) minimizing any foreknowledge of applicants' background, experience, interests, test scores, or other characteristics; (4) asking behavioral questions that require applicants to give detailed accounts of actual job behaviors (for example: Give me a specific example of a time you had to reprimand an employee, tell me what action you took, and describe the result); (5) using a standardized evaluation form; (6) taking notes during the interview; and (7) avoiding short interviews that encourage premature decision making.[23]

Background Investigation   Background investigations are of two types: verifications of application data and reference checks. The first type has proven to be a valuable source of selection information, whereas the latter is essentially worthless. Let's briefly review each.

Several studies indicate that verifying "facts" given on the application form pays dividends. A significant percentage of job applicants—upwards of 15 percent—exaggerate or misrepresent dates of employment, job titles, past salaries, or reasons for leaving a prior position.[24] Confirmation of hard data on the application with prior employers is therefore a worthwhile endeavor.

The reference check is used by many organizations but is extremely difficult to justify. Whether they are work related or personal, references provide little valid information for the selection decision.[25] Employers are frequently reluctant to give candid evaluations of a former employee's job performance for fear of legal repercussions. In fact, a survey found that only 55 percent of human resource executives would "always" provide accurate references to a prospective employer. Moreover, 7 percent said they would never give an accurate reference.[26] Personal likes and dislikes also heavily influence the type of recommendation given. Personal references are likely to provide biased information. Who among us doesn't have three or four friends who will speak in glowing terms about our integrity, work habits, positive attitudes, knowledge, and skills?

Physical Examination For jobs with certain physical requirements, the physical examination has some validity. However, this includes a very small number of jobs today. In almost all cases, the physical examination is done for insurance purposes. Management wants to eliminate insurance claims for injuries or illnesses contracted prior to being hired.

Great care must be taken to ensure that physical requirements are job related and do not discriminate. Some physical requirements may exclude certain disabled persons, when, in fact, such requirements do not affect job performance.

What Works Best and When

Many selection devices are of limited value to managers in making selection decisions. An understanding of strengths and weaknesses of each will help you to determine when each should be used. We offer the following advice to guide your choices.

Since the validity of selection devices varies for different types of jobs, you should use only those devices that predict for a given job. (See Table 12–4.) The application form offers limited information. Traditional written tests are reasonably effective devices for routine jobs. Work samples, however, are clearly preferable to written tests. For managerial selection, the assessment center is strongly recommended. If the interview has a place in the selection decision, it is most likely among less-routine jobs, particularly middle- and upper-level managerial positions. The interview is a

TABLE 12–4 Quality of Selection Devices as Predictors

Selection Device	Position[a]			
	Senior Management	Middle and Lower Management	Complex Nonmanagerial	Routine Operative
Application Form	2	2	2	2
Written tests	1	1	2	3
Work samples	—	—	4	4
Assessment center	5	5	—	—
Interviews	4	3	2	2
Verification of application data	3	3	3	3
Reference checks	1	1	1	1
Physical exam	1	1	1	2

[a] Validity is measured on a scale from 5 (highest) to 1 (lowest).

Is It Wrong to Write a "Creative" Résumé?

Almost all of us have written, or will write, a résumé to give to prospective employers. It summarizes our background, experiences, and accomplishments. Should it be 100 percent truthful? Let's take a few examples.

Person A leaves a job where his title was "Credit Clerk." When looking for a new job, he describes his previous title as "Credit Analyst." He thinks it sounds more impressive. Is this retitling of a former job wrong?

Person B made $2700 a month when she left her previous job. On her résumé, she says that she was making $2900. Is that wrong?

Person C, about eight years ago, took nine months off between jobs to travel overseas. Afraid that people might consider her unstable or lacking in career motivation, she puts down on her résumé that she was engaged in "independent consulting activities" during the period. Was she wrong?

Person D is fifty years old with an impressive career record. He spent five years in college thirty years ago, but he never got a degree. He is being considered for a $150,000-a-year vice presidency at another firm. He knows that he has the ability and track record to do the job, but he won't get the interview if he admits to not having a college degree. He knows that the probability that anyone would check his college records is very low. Should he put on his résumé that he completed his degree?

Falsehoods on résumés are widespread. A recent survey of 200 applicants found that 30 percent reported incorrect dates of employment.[28] Eleven percent misrepresented reasons for leaving a previous job to cover up the fact that they were fired. Some falsely claimed college degrees or totally fabricated work histories. In a larger study of 11,000 applicants, 488 failed to disclose criminal records; most of these were drug or alcohol offenses, but some were as serious as rape or attempted murder.

Is it wrong to write a "creative" résumé? What deviations from the truth, if any, would *you* make?

reasonably good device for discerning intelligence and interpersonal skills.[27] These are more likely to be related to job performance in nonroutine activities, especially in senior managerial positions. Verification of application data is valuable for all jobs. Conversely, reference checks are generally worthless for all jobs. Finally, physical examinations rarely provide any valid selection information.

Orientation

orientation
The introduction of a new employee into his or her job and the organization.

Once a job candidate has been selected, he or she needs to be introduced to the job and organization. This introduction is called **orientation.**

The major objectives of orientation are to reduce the initial anxiety all new employees feel as they begin a new job; to familiarize new employees with the job, the work unit, and the organization as a whole; and to facilitate the outsider–insider transition. Job orientation expands on the information the employee obtained during the recruitment and selection stages. The new employee's specific duties and responsibilities are clarified, as well as how his or her performance will be evaluated. This is

All new Disney World employees go through an eight-hour orientation program, followed by forty hours of apprenticeship training on park grounds. The purpose is to familiarize the employees with Disney's history, traditions, policies, expectations, and ways of doing things.

also the time to rectify any unrealistic expectations new employees might hold about the job. Work unit orientation familiarizes the employee with the goals of the work unit, makes clear how his or her job contributes to the unit's goals, and includes introduction to his or her co-workers. Organization orientation informs the new employee about the organization's objectives, history, philosophy, procedures, and rules. This should include relevant personnel policies and benefits such as work hours, pay procedures, overtime requirements, and fringe benefits. A tour of the organization's physical facilities is often part of the organization orientation.

Many organizations, particularly large ones, have formal orientation programs. Such a program might include a tour of the offices or plant, a film describing the history of the organization, and a short discussion with a representative of the personnel department, who describes the organization's benefit programs. Other organizations utilize an informal orientation program in which, for instance, the manager assigns the new employee to a senior member of the unit, who introduces the new employee to immediate co-workers and shows him or her the locations of the rest rooms, cafeteria, coffee machine, and the like.

Management has an obligation to make the integration of the new employee into the organization as smooth and as free of anxiety as possible. Successful orientation, whether formal or informal, results in an outsider–insider transition that makes the new member feel comfortable and fairly well adjusted, lowers the likelihood of poor work performance, and reduces the probability of a surprise resignation by the new employee only a week or two into the job.

Employee Training

On the whole, planes don't cause airline accidents, people do. Most collisions, crashes, and other mishaps—about 74 percent to be exact—result from errors by the pilot or air traffic controller or inadequate maintenance. Weather and structural failures cause only 15 percent of accidents.[29] We cite these statistics to illustrate the importance of training in the airline industry. These maintenance and human errors could be prevented or significantly reduced by better employee training.

As job demands change, employee skills have to be altered and updated. It has been estimated, for instance, that U.S. business firms alone spend an astounding $30 billion a year on formal courses and training programs to build workers' skills. And that figure might go to $47 billion if President Clinton is successful in implementing his proposal, which will require that all firms with more than 100 employees either spend the equivalent of 1.5 percent of their payroll on training or pay those sums into a public training fund.[30] Management, of course, is responsible for deciding when subordinates are in need of training and what form that training should take.

Skill Categories

We can dissect employee skills into three categories: technical, interpersonal, and problem solving. Most employee training activities seek to modify one or more of these skills.

Technical   Most training is directed at upgrading and improving an employee's technical skills. This includes basic skills—the ability to read, write, and perform mathematical computations—as well as job-specific competencies.[31]

In the past ten years, the majority of jobs have become more complex. Computerized factories and offices, digitally controlled machines, and other types of sophisticated technology require that employees have math, reading, and computer skills. How, for example, can employees master statistical process control or the careful measurement and self-inspection needed for tool changes in flexible manufacturing systems if they can't make basic math calculations or read detailed operating manuals? Or how can most clerical personnel do their jobs effectively without the ability to understand word processing programs and electronic mail systems?

Interpersonal   Almost every employee belongs to a work unit. To some degree, work performance depends on the employee's ability to interact effectively with his or her co-workers and boss. Some employees have excellent interpersonal skills. Others require training to improve theirs. This includes learning how to be a better listener, how to communicate ideas more clearly, and how to reduce conflict.

One employee who had had a history of being difficult to work with found that a

These accountants are participating in Arthur Andersen Worldwide's professional development training program. This firm recently spent $322 million in one year on the education and training of its employees.

three-hour group session in which she and co-workers openly discussed how each perceived the other significantly changed the way she interacted with her peers. Her co-workers were unanimous in describing her as arrogant. They all interpreted her requests as sounding like orders. Now aware of this tendency, she began to make conscious efforts to change the tone and content of her requests, and this had very positive results in her relationships with her colleagues.

Problem Solving   Many employees find that they have to solve problems on their job. This is particularly true in jobs that are of the nonroutine variety. When the problem-solving skills of employees are deficient, management might want to improve these skills through training. This would include participating in activities to sharpen logic, reasoning, and skills at defining problems; assessing causation; developing alternatives; analyzing alternatives; and selecting solutions.

Training Methods

Most training takes place on the job. This can be attributed to the simplicity of such methods and their usually lower cost. However, on-the-job training can disrupt the workplace and result in an increase in errors while learning takes place. Also, some skill training is too complex to learn on the job. In such cases, it should take place outside the work setting.

On-the-Job Training   Popular on-the-job training methods include job rotation and understudy assignments. Job rotation involves lateral transfers that enable employees to work at different jobs. Employees get to learn a wide variety of jobs while gaining increased insight into the interdependency between jobs and a wider perspective on organizational activities. New employees frequently learn their jobs by understudying a seasoned veteran. In the trades, this is usually called an *apprenticeship*. In white-collar jobs, it is called a *coaching*, or *mentor*, relationship. In each, the understudy works under the observation of an experienced worker, who acts as a model whom the understudy attempts to emulate.

Both job rotation and understudy assignments apply to the learning of technical skills. Interpersonal and problem-solving skills are acquired more effectively by training that takes place off the job.

vestibule training
Training in which employees learn on the same equipment they will be using but in a simulated work environment.

Off-the-Job Training   There are a number of off-the-job training methods that managers may want to make available to employees. The more popular are classroom lectures, films, and simulation exercises. *Classroom lectures* are well suited for conveying specific information. They can be used effectively for developing technical and problem-solving skills. *Films and videos* can also be used to explicitly demonstrate technical skills that are not easily presented by other methods. Interpersonal and problem-solving skills may be best learned through *simulation exercises* such as case analyses, experiential exercises, role playing, and group interaction sessions. However, complex computer models, such as those used by airlines in the training of pilots, are another kind of simulation exercise, which in this case is used to teach technical skills. So, too, is **vestibule training,** in which employees learn their jobs on the same equipment they will be using, only the training is conducted in a simulated work environment, not on the actual work floor. Most airplane maintenance trainees learn to repair engines and correct maintenance problems in specially created vestibule labs containing actual aircraft that simulate real working conditions. This provides for careful control of learning experiences—allowing trainees to handle every conceivable problem—while minimizing interference with an airline's actual ongoing maintenance operations.

Performance Appraisal

performance appraisal
The evaluation of an individual's work performance in order to arrive at objective personnel decisions.

Performance appraisal is a process of evaluating individuals in order to arrive at objective personnel decisions. As shown in Table 12–5, organizations use performance appraisals to make a number of human resource decisions. Performance appraisals are used to decide who gets merit pay increases and other rewards. They provide feedback to employees on how the organization views their performance. Appraisals also identify training and development needs; they pinpoint employee skills and competencies that are currently inadequate but for which remedial programs can be developed. They provide input into human resource planning and guide promotion, transfer, and termination decisions. Finally, performance appraisals are occasionally used for personnel research—specifically, as a criterion against which to validate selection and development programs.

Performance Appraisal Methods

Obviously, performance appraisals are important. But how do you evaluate an employee's performance? That is, what are the specific techniques for appraisal? The following discussion reviews the major performance appraisal methods.[32]

written essay
A performance appraisal technique in which an evaluator writes out a description of an employee's strengths, weaknesses, past performance, and potential and then makes suggestions for improvement.

Written Essays   Probably the simplest method of appraisal is to write a narrative describing an employee's strengths, weaknesses, past performance, and potential and then to provide suggestions for improvement. The **written essay** requires no complex forms or extensive training to complete. However, a "good" or "bad" appraisal may be determined as much by the evaluator's writing skill as by the employee's actual level of performance.

critical incidents
A performance appraisal technique in which an evaluator lists key behaviors that separate effective from ineffective job performance.

Critical Incidents   The use of **critical incidents** focuses the evaluator's attention on those critical or key behaviors that separate effective from ineffective job performance. The appraiser writes down little anecdotes that describe what the employee did that was especially effective or ineffective. The key here is that only specific behaviors are cited, not vaguely defined personality traits. A list of critical incidents for a given employee provides a rich set of examples from which to point out to the employee his or her desirable and undesirable behaviors.

graphic rating scales
A performance appraisal technique in which an evaluator rates a set of performance factors on an incremental scale.

Graphic Rating Scales   One of the oldest and most popular methods of appraisal is **graphic rating scales.** This method lists a set of performance factors such as quantity and quality of work, job knowledge, cooperation, loyalty, attendance,

TABLE 12–5   Primary Uses for Performance Appraisals

Use	Percent[a]
Compensation	85.6
Performance feedback	65.1
Training	64.3
Promotion	45.3
Personnel planning	43.1
Retention/discharge	30.3
Research	17.2

[a] Based on responses from 600 organizations.

Source: "Performance Appraisal: Current Practices and Techniques," *Personnel*, May–June 1984, p. 57, © 1984 American Management Association, New York. By permission of the publisher. All rights reserved.

honesty, and initiative. The evaluator then goes down the list and rates each on an incremental scale. The scales typically specify five points; a factor such as job knowledge might be rated from 1 ("poorly informed about work duties") to 5 ("has complete mastery of all phases of the job").

Why are graphic ratings scales so popular? Though they don't provide the depth of information that essays or critical incidents do, they are less time consuming to develop and administer. They also allow for quantitative analysis and comparison.

Behaviorally Anchored Rating Scales An approach that has received a great deal of attention in recent years involves **behaviorally anchored rating scales (BARS).**[33] These scales combine major elements from the critical incident and graphic rating scale approaches: The appraiser rates an employee according to items along a numerical scale, but the items are examples of actual behavior on a given job rather than general descriptions or traits.

Behaviorally anchored rating scales focus on specific and measurable job behaviors. Key elements of jobs are broken down into performance dimensions, and then specific illustrations of effective and ineffective behaviors are identified for each performance dimension. The result is behavioral descriptions such as "anticipates," "plans," "executes," "solves immediate problems," "carries out orders," and "handles emergency situations." So, for example, a manager might rate one of her subordinate supervisors on a five-point scale of 0 (almost never) to 4 (almost always) for statements such as: "Distributes overtime equally taking seniority into account" or "Tells workers that if they have questions or problems to feel free to come and talk to him or her."

Multiperson Comparisons **Multiperson comparisons** compare one individual's performance to those of one or more others. It is a relative, not an absolute, measuring device. The three most popular uses of this method are group order rankings, individual ranking, and paired comparisons.

The **group order ranking** requires the evaluator to place employees into a particular classification such as "top one-fifth" or "second one-fifth." This method is often used in recommending a student for graduate school. Evaluators are asked to rank the student in the top 5 percent, the next 5 percent, the next 15 percent, and so forth. When this method is used to appraise employees, managers rank all their subordinates. If a rater has twenty subordinates, only four can be in the top fifth, and, of course, four must be relegated to the bottom fifth.

The **individual ranking** approach requires the evaluator merely to list the employees in order from highest to lowest. Only one can be "best." In an appraisal of thirty subordinates, the difference between the first and second employee is assumed to be the same as that between the twenty-first and twenty-second. Even though some employees may be closely grouped, there can be no ties.

In the **paired comparison** approach, each employee is compared to every other employee in the comparison group and rated as either the superior or weaker member of the pair. After all paired comparisons are made, each employee is assigned a summary ranking based on the number of superior scores he or she achieved. While this approach ensures that each employee is compared against every other, it can become unwieldy when large numbers of employees are being assessed.

Multiperson comparisons can be combined with other methods to yield a blend of the best from both absolute and relative standards. For example, a college could use the graphic rating scale and the individual ranking methods to provide more accurate information about its students' performance. An absolute grade (A, B, C, D, or F) could be assigned and a student's relative rank in a class ascertained. A prospective employer or graduate school admissions committee could then look at two students who each got a "B" in financial accounting and draw considerably different conclusions about each when next to one grade it says "ranked fourth out of twenty-six,"

behaviorally anchored rating scales (BARS)
A performance appraisal technique in which an evaluator rates employees on specific job behaviors derived from performance dimensions.

multiperson comparison
A performance appraisal technique in which individuals are compared to one another.

group order ranking
A performance appraisal approach that groups employees into ordered classifications.

individual ranking
A performance appraisal approach that ranks employees in order from highest to lowest.

paired comparison
A performance appraisal approach in which each employee is compared to every other employee and rated as either the superior or weaker member of the pair.

while next to the other it says "ranked seventeenth out of thirty." Obviously, the latter instructor gives out many more high grades.

Objectives We previously introduced Management by Objectives in our discussion on planning. MBO, however, is also a mechanism for appraising performance. In fact, it is the preferred method for assessing managers and professional employees.[34]

With MBO, employees are evaluated by how well they accomplish a specific set of objectives that have been determined to be critical in the successful completion of their jobs. As you'll remember from our discussion in Chapter 7, these objectives need to be tangible, verifiable, and measurable.

MBO's popularity among managerial personnel is probably due to its focus on end goals. Managers tend to emphasize such results-oriented outcomes as profit, sales, and costs. This emphasis aligns with MBO's concern with quantitative measures of performance. Because MBO emphasizes ends rather than means, this appraisal method allows managers the discretion to choose the best path for achieving their goals.

Providing Feedback in the Appraisal Review

Many managers are reluctant to give a formal performance appraisal review for each employee. Why? Probably the two main reasons are that (1) they lack complete confidence in the appraisal method used and (2) they fear a confrontation with the employee or an unpleasant reaction from him or her if the results are not overwhelmingly positive. Nevertheless, managers should conduct such reviews because they are the primary means by which employees gain feedback on their performance.

An effective review—in which the employee perceives the appraisal as fair, the manager as sincere, and the climate as constructive—is likely to result in the employee leaving the interview in an upbeat mood, informed about the performance areas in which he or she needs to improve and determined to correct the deficiencies. Unfortunately, this is not the usual outcome of appraisal reviews.

The problem is that performance appraisal reviews have a built-in barrier. Statistically speaking, half of all employees must be below-average performers. But evidence tells us that the *average* employee's estimate of his or her own performance level generally falls around the seventy-fifth percentile.[35] In other words, employees tend to form inflated assessments of their own performances. The good news the manager does convey may be perceived as not good enough. In Chapter 16, where we discuss feedback skills, we'll provide suggestions for making the best of a tough situation.

Career Development

career
The sequence of positions occupied by a person during the course of a lifetime.

The term *career* has a number of meanings. In popular usage, it can mean advancement ("his career is progressing nicely"), a profession ("she has chosen a career in medicine"), or a lifelong sequence of jobs ("his career has included fifteen jobs in six different organizations"). For our purposes, we define a **career** as the "sequence of positions occupied by a person during the course of a lifetime."[36] By this definition, it is apparent that we all have, or will have, careers. Moreover, the concept is as relevant to transient, unskilled laborers as to engineers or physicians.

Why should an organization be concerned with careers? More specifically, why should management spend time on career development? Focusing on careers forces management to adopt a long-term perspective on its human resources. An effective career development program ensures that needed talent will be available and that minorities and women get opportunities for growth and development. It also improves the organization's ability to attract and retain highly talented personnel.

Career Stages

The most popular way of analyzing and discussing careers is to view them as a series of stages.[37] In this section, we'll develop a five-stage model that is generalizable to most people during their adult years, regardless of the type of work they do.

Most individuals begin to form ideas about their careers during their elementary and secondary school years. Their careers begin to wind down as they reach retirement age. We can identify five career stages that most people will go through during these years: exploration, establishment, midcareer, late career, and decline. These stages are depicted in Figure 12–3.

Exploration   Individuals make critical choices about their careers even before they enter the work force on a paid basis. The influence of relatives, teachers, and friends, as well as television programs and films, begins to narrow alternatives very early in people's lives and leads them in certain directions.

The exploration period ends for most people when they are in their mid-20s and make the transition from school to work. From an organizational standpoint, this stage has the least relevance, since it occurs prior to employment. It is relevant, however. The exploration period is a time when a person develops a number of expectations about his or her career, many of which are unrealistic. Such expectations may, of course, lie dormant for years and then pop up later to frustrate both employee and employer.

Establishment   The establishment period begins with the search for work and includes getting the first job, being accepted by one's peers, learning the job, and gaining the first tangible evidence of success or failure in the real world. This stage is characterized by steadily improving performance, making mistakes, and learning from mistakes.

Career development has become increasingly important for employees as the environment has become more turbulent. Captain Jeffrey Davis, a seven-year Army veteran, is one of more than half a million soldiers whose jobs will be eliminated by 1997. While he dreamed of a long-term career in the Army, he now has to look at how he can transfer the skills he learned in the military to civilian life.

FIGURE 12–3
Stages in Career Development

Source: D. T. Hill, *Careers in Organization* (Glenview, IL: Scott, Foresman and Company, 1976), p. 57. With permission of author.

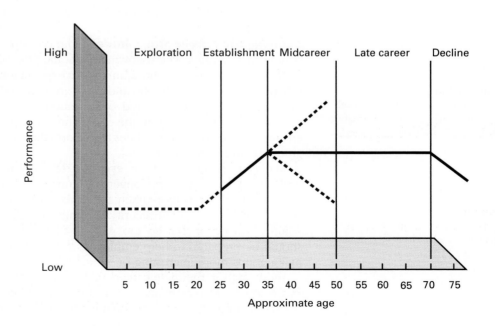

Midcareer   Most people don't face their first severe career dilemmas until they reach the midcareer stage. This is a time when a person's performance may continue to improve, level off, or begin to deteriorate. An important fact about this stage is that the individual is no longer seen as a "learner." Mistakes carry greater penalties. Individuals who successfully make the transition to this stage receive greater responsibilities and rewards. For others, it may be a time of reassessment, job changes, adjustment of priorities, or pursuit of alternative life-styles (for example, divorce, going back to school, making a major geographical move).

This stage has become, and will continue to be, particularly relevant to baby boomers—those people born between 1946 and 1964—because of career plateauing.[38] The enormous size of this group, coupled with the unprecedented restructuring of organizations to make them flatter and more efficient, translates into significantly reduced advancement prospects for employees now in their 30s and 40s. While the mid-career stage was typically just a step on an upwardly moving promotion path for previous generations, it is increasingly becoming a time of anxiety and frustration for much of today's work force.

Late Career   For people who continue to grow through the midcareer stage, the late career usually is a pleasant time when they can relax a bit and play the part of elder statesperson. Their value to the organization lies in their judgment, built up over many years and through varied experiences, and their ability to share their knowledge with others.

For those whose performances have stagnated or deteriorated during the previous stage, the late career brings the reality that they will not have an everlasting impact or change the world as they had once thought. It is a time when individuals recognize that they have decreased work mobility and might be locked into their current jobs.

Decline   The final stage in a career is difficult for everyone but, ironically, it is probably hardest on those who have had continued success in the earlier stages. After several decades of achievement and high levels of performance, the time has come for retirement. One is forced to step out of the limelight and give up a major component of one's identity. For modest performers or those who have seen their performance deteriorate over the years, it may be a pleasant time. The frustrations that have been associated with work will be left behind.

Applying the Career Stage Model   The concept of career stages can be of great benefit to managers. The following are some possible insights.

New employees often hold unrealistic expectations about their work. A **realistic job preview**—in which job candidates are exposed to negative as well as positive information about the job and organization—can reduce the number of surprise resignations.[39] Employees in the establishment stage need training and mentoring to ensure that they have the abilities to perform their jobs well and to provide them with guidance and encouragement.

Managers should keep an eye out for employees who, in midcareer, fail to understand that they are no longer apprentices and that mistakes now carry penalties. Disciplinary action is more likely to be necessary at this stage, when employees first start to show signs of insecurity. Younger employees may be threats. Midcareer failures will occur, but so too will frustration, boredom, and burnout. Managers should be prepared to help employees with their insecurities and consider ways of making jobs more interesting or varied.

Individuals in their late careers make excellent mentors. Managers should exploit this resource. Managers also need to recognize that people in the late career stage frequently undergo significant changes in personal priorities. They may become less interested in work or prefer more free time or a less stressful position instead of more money.

realistic job preview
Exposing job candidates to both negative and positive information about a job and an organization.

Finally, managers should recognize that the decline stage is difficult for every employee to confront. Periods of depression are not uncommon. Employees may also become more hostile and aggressive.

Keys to a Successful Management Career

If you choose a career in management, there are certain keys to success you should consider (see Figure 12–4). The following discussion makes some suggestions based on proven tactics that managers have used to advance their careers.[40]

Select your first job judiciously   All first jobs are not alike. Where managers begin in the organization has an important effect on their subsequent career progress. Specifically, the evidence suggests that, if you have a choice, you should select a powerful department as the place to start your management career.[41] Managers who start out in departments that are high in power within the organization are more likely to advance rapidly throughout their careers.

Do Good Work   Good work performance is a necessary (but not sufficient) condition for managerial success. The marginal performer may be rewarded in the short term, but his or her weaknesses are bound to surface eventually and cut off career advancement. Good work performance is no guarantee of success, but without it the probability of a successful management career is low.

Present the Right Image   Assuming that a particular set of managers are all performing well, the ability to align one's image with that sought by the organization is certain to be interpreted positively.

The manager should evaluate the organization's culture so that he or she understands what the organization wants and values from its managers. Then the manager is equipped to project the appropriate image in terms of style of dress; associates one

FIGURE 12–4
Steps to a Successful
Management Career

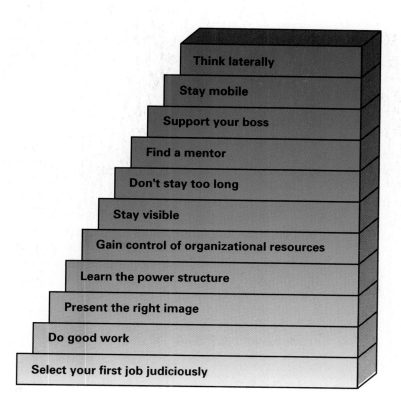

should and should not cultivate; whether one should project a risk-taking or risk-aversive stance; the organization's preferred leadership style; whether conflict should be avoided, tolerated, or encouraged; the importance attributed to getting along well with others; and so forth.

Learn the Power Structure   The authority relationships defined by the organization's formal structure explain only part of the influence patterns within an organization. It's of equal or greater importance to know and understand the organization's power structure. The effective manager needs to learn "who is really in charge, who has the goods on whom, what are the major debts and dependencies—all things that are not reflected by the neat boxes in the table of organization. Once he [or she] has this knowledge he [or she] can navigate with more skill and ease.⁴²

Gain Control of Organizational Resources   The control of organizational resources that are scarce and important is a source of power. Knowledge and expertise are particularly effective resources to control. They make you more valuable to the organization and therefore more likely to gain security and advancement.

Stay Visible   Because the evaluation of managerial effectiveness can be very subjective, it is important that your boss and those in power in the organization be made aware of your contribution. If you are fortunate enough to have a job that brings your accomplishments to the attention of others, taking direct measures to increase your visibility might not be needed. But your job may require you to handle activities that are low in visibility, or your specific contribution may be indistinguishable because you are part of a group endeavor. In such cases—without creating the image of being a braggart—you will want to call attention to yourself by giving progress reports to your boss and others, being seen at social functions, being active in your professional associations, developing powerful allies who speak positively about you, and engaging in other similar tactics.

Don't stay too long in your first job   The evidence indicates that, given a choice between staying in your first management job until you've "really made a difference" or accepting an early transfer to a new job assignment, you should go for the early transfer.⁴³ By moving quickly through different jobs, you signal to others that you're on the fast track. This, then, often becomes a self-fulfilling prophesy. The message to aspiring managers is to start fast by seeking early transfers or promotions from the first management job.

Find a Mentor   A **mentor** is an individual, typically someone higher up in the organization, who takes on a protégé as an ally. A mentor is someone from whom you can learn and who can encourage and help you. The evidence indicates that acquiring a sponsor who is part of the organization's power core is essential for managers who aspire to make it to the top.⁴⁴

Where do employees get a mentor? Some organizations have formal mentoring programs. Young managers for whom the organization has high expectations are assigned to senior managers who play mentoring roles. More typically, you are informally selected to become a protégé by your boss or someone in the organization with whom you share similar interests. If your mentor is someone other than your boss, be sure that you do nothing through your mentor–protégé relationship that threatens your boss or suggests disloyalty on your part.

Support Your Boss   Your immediate future is in the hands of your current boss. He or she evaluates your performance, and few young managers are powerful

Sherry Lansing, the recently named head of Paramount Pictures, has been mentored throughout her career by Stanley R. Jaffe. When Jaffe took over as president of Paramount Communications, he confidently turned to Ms. Lansing to improve performance at the company's film studio.

mentor
A person who sponsors or supports another employee who is lower in the organization.

enough to challenge their boss and survive. You should make the effort to help your boss succeed, be supportive if your boss is under siege, and find out what criteria he or she will be using to assess your effectiveness. Don't undermine your boss. Don't speak negatively of your boss to others. If your boss is competent, visible, and in possession of a power base, he or she is likely to be on the way up in the organization. By being perceived as supportive, you might find yourself pulled along too. At worst, you will have established an ally higher up in the organization. If your boss's performance is poor and his or her power is low, you should use your mentor (if you have one) to arrange a transfer. It's hard to have your competence recognized or your positive performance evaluation taken seriously if your boss is perceived as incompetent.

Stay Mobile   Managers are likely to move upward more rapidly if they indicate a willingness to move to different geographical locations and across functional lines within the organization. Career advancement may also be facilitated by a willingness

MANAGING FROM A GLOBAL PERSPECTIVE

Selecting Managers for Global Assignments

William Stewart is a thirty-year-old American bachelor who worked for computer giant NEC in Tokyo.[46] He understands the Japanese way of doing business: sixteen-hour days six days a week, heavy-duty golfing, and after-work drinking. He also recognizes that Japanese work demands would make it nearly impossible for him to have an American wife and hold his job in Tokyo. "Japanese wives and kids understand Dad is not going to be seen much. American families wouldn't stand for it."

Most global organizations have made significant strides since the 1970s, when it was widely believed that "working abroad is working abroad."[47] Transferring managers into new and different national cultures, without careful thought and proper selection, sets those managers up to fail.

Most research on the transfer of managers between diverse countries—particularly the moving of U.S. executives overseas—indicates a fairly high failure rate. Of particular interest is the finding that U.S. executives seem to fail at a rate that is considerably higher than those of European and Japanese managers transferred to new countries.

Why don't more managers succeed when they are placed in foreign countries? One possible reason is that most organizations still select transfer candidates on the basis of technical competence alone, ignoring other predictors of success such as language skills, flexibility, and family adaptability.[48]

A contingency approach to selecting managers for foreign assignments in subsidiaries has been proposed, based on the type of information and control required.[49] When jobs are largely technical, information is objective, and control is bureaucratic, organizations will probably do best by selecting technically competent outsiders for relatively short tours to foreign subsidiaries. However, for longer-term assignments in posts where social information and an understanding of organizational norms are more important, long-time insiders steeped in the organization's culture should be more effective both working in the subsidiary and communicating what they learn back to headquarters.

to change organizations. In slow-growth, stagnant, or declining organizations, mobility should be of even greater importance to the ambitious manager.

The appearance of maintaining interorganizational mobility, when coupled with control of organizational resources, can be particularly effective. If senior management needs what you have and is fearful that you might leave, it is not likely to ignore your needs. One fast-rising manager was very competent, possessed some unique skills, but also took great strides to keep himself visible in his industry. He made a habit of regularly mentioning to those in the powerful inner circle of his firm that he received a steady stream of job offers from competitors (which was true) but that as long as he continued to receive increasingly responsible positions and large salary increases, he had no intention of leaving his firm. This strategy has continued to pay dividends for this manager. He has received three promotions in five years and increased his salary fourfold.

Think Laterally   Our final suggestion acknowledges the changing world of management in the 1990s. Because of management restructuring and the flattening of hierarchies, there are fewer rungs on the promotion ladder in many organizations. To survive in this environment, it's a good idea to think in terms of lateral career moves.[45]

In the 1960s and 1970s, people who made lateral moves were assumed to be mediocre performers. Not anymore. Lateral shifts are now a viable career consideration. They give individuals a wider range of experiences, which enhances long-term mobility. In addition, these moves help to energize people by making work more interesting and satisfying. So if you're not moving ahead in your organization, consider a lateral move internally or a lateral shift to another organization.

Labor–Management Relations

labor union
An organization that represents workers and seeks to protect their interests through collective bargaining.

As we mentioned at the beginning of this chapter, approximately 16 percent of the U.S. labor force belongs to a **labor union.** These unions represent workers and seek to protect and promote their members' interests through collective bargaining (see Table 12–6 for why employees join unions). Even though almost one-in-six Americans belong to a union, the figures are considerably higher in other countries. For

TABLE 12–6   Why Do Employees Join Unions?

1. *Unions influence the wage and effort outcome.* Unions bargain for their members over wages, hours, and working conditions. The result of this bargaining determines the amount of pay, the hours of employment, the amount of work required during a given period, and the conditions of employment.

2. *Unions establish a security system with employers.* Unions have a security agreement with employers that, in effect, defines the union's power. It can control, for example, whom the employer may hire and whether employees must join the union. It may also restrict the employer from contracting out work to other organizations.

3. *Unions influence the administration of rules.* Unions provide workers with an opportunity to participate in determining the conditions under which they work; unions also have specific grievance procedures by which they can protest conditions they believe to be unfair.

4. *Unions have political power in the state and over the economy.* Unions have not been reluctant to exert political muscle to gain through legislation what they have been unable to win at the bargaining table. Unions use their lobbying efforts to support legislation that is in labor's interests.

Michigan Pontiac autoworkers discuss job concerns at a union meeting.

example, in Japan and Germany, respectively, 28 percent and 43 percent of the labor force belongs to a union.[50]

U.S. labor unions did not do well in the 1980s.[51] In response to intense global competition, particularly in the manufacturing sector, management both reduced the size of its unionized work force and imposed high concessionary demands on those union jobs that remained. The steel division of USX Corp., for instance, slashed its unionized work force from 50,000 in 1982 to 18,000 by 1991.[52] As a whole, few union members in the United States were able to keep their pay increases equal to increases in the Consumer Price Index.[53]

The 1990s may be a different story. The prospects for organized labor look relatively upbeat largely because union workers have already given up so much.[54] There is little indication that U.S. unions will regain the clout they had back in the 1950s or 1960s, but the precipitous decline may be over.

In this section, we want to briefly discuss **labor–management relations**—that is, the formal interactions between labor unions and the organization's management.

labor-management relations
The formal interactions between unions and an organization's management.

Why Good Labor-Management Relations Are Important

For many managers in unionized organizations, the management of human resources is largely composed of following procedures and policies laid out in the labor contract. Decisions about where recruitment is done, how employees are selected, who is trained, how compensation is determined, and how disciplinary procedures are carried out are no longer unilateral prerogatives of management for jobs within the union's province. Such decisions are substantially made at the time the labor contract is negotiated. The development of good labor–management relations can produce a number of positive outcomes for management during these negotiations: for instance, work rules that don't place unreasonable constraints on managerial decision options and reduced threats of costly strikes and work stoppages.[55]

collective bargaining
A process for negotiating a union contract and for administrating the contract after it has been negotiated.

The Collective Bargaining Process

The negotiation, administration, and interpretation of a labor contract are achieved through **collective bargaining.** The following discussion summarizes how the process typically flows in the private sector among U.S. firms.

Organizing and Certification Efforts to organize a group of employees may begin when employee representatives ask union officials to visit the employees' organization and solicit members or when the union itself initiates a membership drive. Either way, the law requires that a union must secure signed authorization cards from at least 30 percent of the employees that it desires to represent. If the 30 percent goal is achieved, either the union or management will file a petition with a federal agency—the National Labor Relations Board (NLRB)—requesting a representation election.

When the NLRB receives the required number of authorization cards, it evaluates them, verifies that legal requirements have been satisfied, and then clarifies the appropriate bargaining unit—that is, it identifies which employees the union will represent if it wins the election.

A secret ballot election is usually called within twenty-five days after the NLRB receives the authorization cards. If the union gets a majority in this election, the NLRB certifies the union and recognizes it as the exclusive bargaining representative for all employees within the specified bargaining unit. Should the union fail to get a majority, another election cannot be held for one year.

Occasionally, employees become dissatisfied with a certified union. In such instances, employees may request a decertification election by the NLRB. If a majority of the members vote for decertification, the union is out.

Preparation for Negotiation Once a union has been certified, management will begin preparing for negotiations. It will gather information on the economy, copies of recently negotiated contracts between other unions and employers, cost-of-living data, labor market statistics, and similar environmental concerns. It will also gather internal information on grievance and accident records, employee performance reports, and overtime figures.

This information will tell management their organization's current labor-performance status, what similar organizations are doing, and what it can anticipate from the economy in the near term. Management then uses these data to determine what it can expect to achieve in the negotiation. What can it expect the union to ask for? What is management prepared to acquiesce on?

Negotiation Negotiation customarily begins when the union delivers a list of demands to management. These are typically ambitious in order to create room for trading in the later stages of negotiation. Not surprisingly, management's initial response is typically to counter by offering little more than the terms of the previous contract. In recent years, some managements have even begun by proposing a reduction in wages and benefits and demanding that the union take a lesser role in the organization's decision-making process.

These introductory proposals usually initiate a period of long and intense bargaining. Compromises are made, and after an oral agreement is achieved, it is converted into a written contract. Finally, negotiation concludes with the union's representatives submitting the contract to its members for ratification.

Contract Administration Once a contract is agreed upon and ratified, it must be administered. The way in which it will be administered is included in the contract itself.

Probably the most important element of contract administration has to do with the spelling out of a procedure for handling contractual disputes. Almost all collective bargaining agreements contain formal procedures for resolving grievances over the interpretation and application of the contract.

Current Issues in Human Resource Management

We conclude by discussing several contemporary issues facing today's managers. These include managing work force diversity, dual career couples, and sexual harassment.

Managing Work Force Diversity

We've previously discussed the changing makeup of the work force in several places in this book. Let's now consider how work force diversity will affect such basic HRM concerns as recruitment, selection, and orientation and training.

Recruitment   Improving work force diversity requires managers to widen their recruiting net. For example, the popular practice of relying on current employee referrals as a source of new job applicants tends to result in candidates who have similar characteristics to present employees. So managers have to look for applicants in places where they haven't typically looked before.

To increase diversity, managers are increasingly turning to nontraditional recruitment sources. This includes women's job networks, over-fifty clubs, urban job banks, disabled peoples' training centers, ethnic newspapers, and gay-rights organizations.

Selection   Once a diverse set of applicants exists, efforts must be made to ensure that the selection process doesn't discriminate. Moreover, applicants need to be made comfortable with the organization and be made aware of management's desire to accommodate their needs.

Orientation and Training   The outsider–insider transition is often more difficult for women and minorities. Many organizations provide special workshops to raise diversity consciousness among current employees as well as programs for new employees that focus on diversity issues. For example, Hewlett-Packard conducts training on cultural differences between American-Anglos and Mexicans, Indochinese, and Filipinos at a San Diego plant; and Monsanto's two-day diversity program directly addresses racial, ethnic, and gender stereotypes.[56] In addition, a number of companies have instituted special mentoring programs to deal with the reality that lower-level female and minority managers have few role models with whom to identify.

Dual-Career Couples

dual-career couples
Couples in which both partners have a professional, managerial, or administrative occupation.

The number of **dual-career couples**—couples in which both partners have a professional, managerial, or administrative occupation[57]—have expanded dramatically in the United States in recent years as married women have gained professional credentials and sought jobs outside the home. An organization's human resource management policies need to reflect this trend and the special problems it creates for couples. Special attention needs to be specifically given to the organization's policies regarding nepotism, transfers, and conflicts of interest.[58]

The issue of nepotism concerns spouses who both work for the same employer. Recent evidence indicates that only about 10 percent of organizations have a strict no-relatives-allowed policy. However, most organizations prohibit spouses from working in the same department or one directly supervising the other.[59]

Dual-career couples have become a major factor affecting organizations' relocation policies. Promotions represent a good illustration. When managers were pre-

Conduct that many men consider unobjectionable may offend women. As such, it becomes sexual harassment.

sexual harassment
Behavior marked by sexually suggestive remarks, unwanted touching and sexual advances, requests for sexual favors, or other verbal or physical conduct of a sexual nature.

dominantly male and their wives either were not employed or held low-skilled jobs, organizations could design development programs entailing extensive transfers and correctly assume that their managers would readily accept such moves. However, dual-career couples have shown far greater reluctance to pull up roots for one member's promotion opportunity. For dual-career couples, a promotion of one member that requires a geographical move becomes a joint decision that must consider the financial implications for both members and job opportunities for the other member in the new location. As a result, organizations will have to expand formal spouse relocation policies to include assuming a portion of the spouse's job search costs, giving the spouse priority on jobs at the new location, and providing career counseling that includes assessment, planning, and placement assistance.[60]

Another challenge that dual-career couples create for organizations is the conflict of interest created by a partner who holds a key position in a competing organization. Such situations can allow confidential information to find its way easily into the competitor's hands. Most organizations will probably continue to trust their employees to use good judgment in handling potential conflicts of interest. However, we can expect to see an increasing number of organizations requiring employees to sign loyalty statements or even developing policies that prohibit spouses from working for or holding key positions with major competitors.[61]

Sexual Harassment

Professor Anita Hill's widely publicized allegations of sexual harassment against the U.S. Supreme Court nominee Clarence Thomas in the fall of 1991 single-handedly moved the topic of sexual harassment to the top of many organizations' education agendas.[62]

Since 1980, U.S. courts generally have used guidelines from the federal Equal Employment Opportunity Commission to define **sexual harassment.** Sexual harassment generally encompasses sexually suggestive remarks, unwanted touching and sexual advances, requests for sexual favors, and other verbal and physical conduct of a sexual nature. It is considered illegal, a violation of the federal civil rights law.[63]

From management's standpoint, sexual harassment is a growing concern because it intimidates employees, interferes with job performance, and exposes the organization to liability. On this last point, the courts have ruled that if the employee who is guilty of sexual harassment is a supervisor or agent for an organization, then the organization is liable for sexual harassment, regardless of whether the act was authorized or forbidden by the organization or whether the organization knew of the act.

To avoid liability, management must establish a clear and strong policy against sexual harassment.[64] That policy should then be reinforced by regular discussion sessions in which managers are reminded of the rule and carefully instructed that even the slightest sexual overture to another employee will not be tolerated. At AT&T, for instance, all employees have been specifically advised that they can be fired for making repeated unwelcome sexual advances, using sexually degrading words to describe someone, or displaying sexually offensive pictures or objects at work.

Summary

This summary is organized by the chapter-opening learning objectives found on page 339.

1. The human resource management process seeks to staff the organization and sustain high employee performance through human resource planning, recruitment or decruitment, selection, orientation, training, performance appraisal, career development, and labor–management relations.

2. Since the mid-1960s, the U.S. government has greatly expanded its influence over HRM decisions by enacting new laws and regulations. Because of the government's effort to provide equal employment opportunities, management must ensure that key HRM decisions—such as recruitment, selection, training, promotions, and terminations—are made without regard to race, sex, religion, age, color, or national origin. Extensive financial penalties can be imposed on organizations that fail to follow these laws and regulations.

3. A job description is a written statement of what a jobholder does, how it's done, and why it's done. A job specification states the minimum acceptable qualifications that an incumbent must possess to perform a given job successfully.

4. Recruitment seeks to develop a pool of potential job candidates. Typical sources include an internal search, advertisements, employee referrals, employment agencies, school placement centers, and temporary help services. Decruitment reduces the labor supply within an organization through options such as firing, layoffs, attrition, transfers, reduced workweeks, and early retirements.

5. The quality of a selection device is determined by its validity and reliability. If a device is not valid, then no proven relationship exists between it and relevant job criteria. If a selection device isn't reliable, then it cannot be assumed to be a consistent measure.

6. Selection devices must match the job in question. Work samples work best with low-level jobs. Assessment centers work best for managerial positions. The validity of the interview as a selection device increases at progressively higher levels of management.

7. Employee training can be on-the-job or off-the-job. Popular on-the-job methods include job rotation, understudying, and apprenticeships. The more popular off-the-job methods are classroom lectures, films, and simulation exercises.

8. Six performance appraisal methods are: (a) written essays—written descriptions of an employee's strengths, weaknesses, past performance, potential, and areas in need of improvement; (b) critical incidents—lists of key behaviors that separate effective from ineffective job performances; (c) graphic rating scales—ratings of performance factors on an incremental scale; (d) BARS—rating employees on specific job behaviors derived from performance dimensions of the job; (e) multiperson comparisons—comparing individual employees against one another; and (f) objectives—evaluating employees against tangible, verifiable, and measurable objectives.

9. The five career stages are exploration, establishment, midcareer, late career, and decline.

10. The collective bargaining process begins with a union organizing effort and attainment of NLRB certification. Once a union has been certified, management begins preparation for negotiations by reviewing internal documents and environmental data. Negotiations then proceed, which often involve long and intense bargaining, leading to a written contract. Once a contract is agreed upon and ratified, it must be administered, and a procedure must be spelled out for handling contract disputes.

11. HRM practices can facilitate work force diversity by widening the recruitment net, eliminating any discriminatory practices in the selection process, making applicants aware of the willingness to accommodate their needs, and providing programs that focus on diversity issues.

12. Sexual harassment is a growing concern for management because it intimidates employees, interferes with job performance, and exposes the organization to liability.

Review Questions

1. How does HRM affect all managers?
2. What are the possible sources for finding new employees?
3. Contrast reject errors and accept errors. Which one is most likely to open an employer to charges of discrimination? Why?
4. Why is decruitment now a major concern for managers?
5. What are the major problems of the interview as a selection device?
6. Identify three skill categories for which organizations do employee training.
7. What is the goal of orientation?
8. How does MBO affect performance appraisals?
9. Contrast the advantages and disadvantages of written essays, graphic rating scales, and BARS.
10. What constitutes sexual harassment?

Discussion Questions

1. What is the relationship between selection, recruitment, and job analysis?
2. Do you think there are moral limits on how far a prospective employer should delve into an applicant's life by means of interviews and tests?
3. Assume that you are the human resources director for a company that has 75 employees and is expanding rapidly. What specific practices would you institute to facilitate the hiring of females and minorities?
4. Do you feel that the government should be able to influence the HRM process of organizations through legislation and regulations? Support your position.
5. Assuming that management is already responsive to employee needs, do you think that labor unions benefit employees? Support your position.

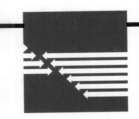

SELF-ASSESSMENT EXERCISE

How do You Define Life Success?

People have different ideas about what it means to be successful. Please rate each of the following ideas on life success by circling the number that best represents its importance to you.

	Always Important	Very Often Important	Fairly Often Important	Occasionally Important	Never Important
1. Getting others to do what I want	5	4	3	2	1
2. Having inner peace and contentment	5	4	3	2	1

	Always Important	Very Often Important	Fairly Often Important	Occasionally Important	Never Important
3. Having a happy marriage	5	4	3	2	1
4. Having economic security	5	4	3	2	1
5. Being committed to my organization	5	4	3	2	1
6. Being able to give help, assistance, advice, and support to others	5	4	3	2	1
7. Having a job that pays more than peers earn	5	4	3	2	1
8. Being a good parent	5	4	3	2	1
9. Having good job benefits	5	4	3	2	1
10. Having a rewarding family life	5	4	3	2	1
11. Raising children to be independent adults	5	4	3	2	1
12. Having people work for me	5	4	3	2	1
13. Being accepted at work	5	4	3	2	1
14. Enjoying my non-work activities	5	4	3	2	1
15. Making or doing things that are useful to society	5	4	3	2	1
16. Having high income and the resulting benefits	5	4	3	2	1
17. Having a sense of personal worth	5	4	3	2	1
18. Contributing to society	5	4	3	2	1
19. Having long-term job security	5	4	3	2	1
20. Having children	5	4	3	2	1
21. Getting good performance evaluations	5	4	3	2	1
22. Having opportunities for personal creativity	5	4	3	2	1
23. Being competent	5	4	3	2	1
24. Having public recognition	5	4	3	2	1
25. Having children who are successful emotionally and professionally	5	4	3	2	1
26. Having influence over others	5	4	3	2	1

	Always Important	Very Often Important	Fairly Often Important	Occasionally Important	Never Important
27. Being happy with my private life	5	4	3	2	1
28. Earning regular salary increases	5	4	3	2	1
29. Having personal satisfaction	5	4	3	2	1
30. Improving the well-being of the work force	5	4	3	2	1
31. Having a stable marriage	5	4	3	2	1
32. Having the confidence of my bosses	5	4	3	2	1
33. Having the resources to help others	5	4	3	2	1
34. Being in a high-status occupation	5	4	3	2	1
35. Being able to make a difference in something	5	4	3	2	1
36. Having money to buy or do anything	5	4	3	2	1
37. Being satisfied with my job	5	4	3	2	1
38. Having self-respect	5	4	3	2	1
39. Helping others to achieve	5	4	3	2	1
40. Having personal happiness	5	4	3	2	1
41. Being able to provide quality education for my children	5	4	3	2	1
42. Making a contribution to society	5	4	3	2	1

Turn to page SK-4 for scoring directions and key.

Source: Barbara Parker and Leonard H. Chusmir, *Development and Validation of the Life Success Measures Scale.* Miami: Florida International University, 1991. Used with permission.

To: Sandra Gillies; Director of Human Resources
From: L. William Mullane; Chairman
Subject: Sexual Harassment

It has come to my attention that some of our people are not clear on what practices do or do not constitute sexual harassment. This is an area that cannot be ambiguous. We need to take immediate action toward developing training for all our employees and developing a workable procedure to handle complaints.

I want to make the issue of sexual harassment the primary topic of next month's executive board meeting. To facilitate discussion, I'd like you to develop a working paper (not to exceed two pages) that would describe (1) the content of an initial two-hour workshop on sexual harassment and (2) an appropriate procedure that all employees can follow if they believe that they have been sexually harassed.

This is a fictionalized account of a potentially real problem. It was written for academic purposes only and is not meant to reflect either positively or negatively on actual management practices at Western Massachusetts Power & Light.

CASE APPLICATION

Von's Supermarkets

Susan Chapman is southern regional manager for Von's Supermarkets, a chain in the western United States. Five district supervisors report to her. Each of the district supervisors, in turn, oversees the activities of eight to twelve stores.

One spring morning, as Susan was going over her morning reports, her secretary buzzed her on the intercom. "Ms. Chapman, did you see the business section in this morning's paper?" "No, why?" Susan responded. "Well, it says here that Chuck Bailey has accepted the position of Arizona regional manager for Safeway." Leaping to her feet, Susan went to see the article for herself.

Susan's concern was not unwarranted. Chuck Bailey was one of her district supervisors. He had been in his current job with Von's for four years. Von's had hired him away from Alpha Beta Markets, where he had been a store manager. Susan felt hurt that she had to learn of Chuck's departure through the newspaper, but she knew she'd get over that quickly. What was more relevant was that Chuck was a very effective supervisor—his district consistently outperformed her other four. Where was she going to find a competent replacement?

Several days passed. She talked with Chuck and sincerely wished him well in his new job. She also discussed with him the problem of finding a replacement. Her final decision was to transfer one of the supervisors from a smaller district in her region into Chuck's district and to begin an immediate search for someone to fill the smaller district's supervisory vacancy.

Susan went to her files and pulled out the job description for a district supervisor's position (no job specification was available). The job's duties included ensuring the maintenance of corporate standards of cleanliness, service, and product quality; supervising store managers and evaluating their performance; preparing monthly, quarterly, and annual revenue and expense forecasts for the district; making cost-savings suggestions to head office and/or store managers; coordinating buying; negotiating cooperative advertising programs with suppliers; and participating in union negotiations.

Questions

1. What recruitment sources would you recommend that Susan use? Why?
2. Define the factors that should predict success in this job.
3. Which selection devices would you recommend that Susan use to screen applicants? Why?
4. In terms of career development, what might Susan have done to ensure Chuck's continued employment with Von's?

VIDEO CASE

Forced Retirement for Airline Pilots

Imagine that you're in a commercial airliner 39,000 feet above the earth and a serious emergency arises. Who would you want to be at the controls of that plane? Undoubtedly, most of us would choose someone with many years' experience, a clean bill of health, and an excellent flight record. Well, if a pilot is sixty or over, no matter how experienced, healthy, or qualified that person may be, he or she won't be at the controls. The Federal Aviation Administration mandates that commercial airline pilots retire at the relatively young age of sixty. Is this age restriction the best approach to controlling safety in the airline industry?

The FAA's "Age 60 Rule," which has existed for thirty years, prohibits anyone sixty years or older from sitting in the front of the cockpit as pilot or co-pilot of any commercial airliner carrying more than thirty passengers. The agency's concern is safety. It defends its use of the Age 60 Rule by citing a 1983 study that found that pilots in their forties and fifties had much lower accident rates than pilots in their sixties. However, as critics have pointed out, this study had nothing to do with airline pilots. It focused on private pilots, who had much less training and were flying much smaller planes. Also, critics say that the study was biased against older pilots to begin with because of the way that flying time was calculated. In fact, pilots challenging the Age 60 Rule had the study's accident rates recalculated and found that the accident rate for active pilots in their forties and fifties was *higher* than that for pilots in their sixties and that pilots in their seventies had the lowest accident rates of all. Nevertheless, FAA officials continue to defend the Age 60 Rule. One administrator said, "You must draw the line somewhere for safety reasons and you must apply it fairly across the board."

With more than one million U.S. passengers taking off and landing in commercial airliners every day, safety would seem to require experienced captains with exceptional skills and reflexes. Yet, in 1990, 700 experienced commercial pilots were grounded because they had reached age sixty. In 1991, 800 more were forced out, and in 1992, another 1,000 were compelled to retire. A number of experienced pilots have been challenging the FAA's mandatory retirement age. Says one captain, a pilot for thirty-seven years and about to reach age sixty, "It's almost a paradox because I feel I'm reaching the peak of my professional capabilities; and physically, I'm working probably as hard, if not harder, than I even did ten years ago to maintain a good physical profile." In fact, when a concerned group of thirty older captains put themselves through a series of physical and psychological tests far more extensive than those the FAA requires for younger pilots, they were all certified fit to fly by a panel of experts. Yet the FAA has refused to make a single exception to the Age 60 Rule. Pilots who have reached sixty and wish to continue their flying careers have three options: Become a corporate pilot, fly commuter planes (those with 30 or fewer passengers), or take a demotion to flight engineer.

Questions

1. What are HRM implications of the Age 60 Rule for airlines?

2. Design a test or series of tests that would allow airlines to take advantage of pilot experience without compromising safety.

3. How does the Age 60 Rule fit into the career stage model?

Source: "Too Old Too Soon," *ABC's 20/20,* June 28, 1991.

CHAPTER 13

Managing Change and Innovation

LEARNING OBJECTIVES

After Reading This Chapter, You Should Be Able To:

1. Contrast the "calm waters" and "white-water rapids" metaphors of change.
2. Explain why people are likely to resist change.
3. List techniques for reducing resistance.
4. Describe what it is that managers can change in organizations.
5. Describe the situational factors that facilitate cultural change.
6. Explain how management should go about enacting cultural change.
7. Describe how managers can implement TQM.
8. Describe the techniques for reducing employee stress.
9. Explain how organizations can stimulate innovation.

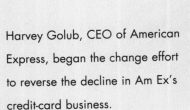

Harvey Golub, CEO of American Express, began the change effort to reverse the decline in Am Ex's credit-card business.

"Where did all the Yuppies go?" That's what the top managers at American Express must have been asking themselves in the fall of 1992.[1] While sales in the company's credit-card division boomed during the status-conscious 1980s, the company was forced to rethink its market and introduce significant changes to adjust to the value-oriented customer of the 1990s.

The American Express card built its reputation on status. It was perceived as a high-priced card carried by the affluent and accepted by upscale merchants. While Visa and MasterCard sought to appeal to the masses, the green American Express card was marketed as evidence that its holder had "made it." The addition of the AmEx gold and platinum cards sought to add new rungs to the prestige-card ladder.

But the increasingly value-conscious consumer has been rejecting American Express' upscale image. While customers appreciate the extra service AmEx offers, they don't like the $50 to $300 a year fees AmEx charges. Also, many customers don't look favorably on the requirement that they must pay off their entire card balance every month. With hordes of competitors aggressively offering special deals, rebates, and other promotions to get people to use their charge cards, AmEx has been losing customers in droves. From late 1991 to late 1992, its number of card holders dropped at the rate of half a million a quarter. What once had been a profit machine for American Express became a major source of corporate losses.

Harvey Golub, current company CEO and former president of the credit-card division of American Express, has implemented a number of changes in an attempt to arrest the decline in the company's credit-card business. First, he gave new emphasis to Optima, the company's revolving-credit card. Golub hopes to build the customer base of Optima card holders and greatly expand the number of merchants who will accept the card. Second, the company is reassessing and lowering its fee to merchants. Historically, American Express discounted merchants' charge receipts by 2.5 to 4.5 percent as a cost of handling. But with Visa and MasterCard typically charging half as much, many merchants have stopped taking American Express cards. Third, lower rates to merchants and a declining number of card users translate into significantly lower revenues. So Golub has cut 4800 jobs, or 9 percent of the company's work force. He expects these cuts to result in savings of $350 million a year beginning in 1994. Finally, Golub took the controversial step of signing up lower-end merchants such as Kmart. This, of course, is a risky strategy. It potentially could undermine the image of the American Express card as a premium product.

The challenge for American Express is: Can the credit card division change with the times? Can it simultaneously cut costs, reposition itself in the marketplace, and maintain what Golub calls American Express' "world-class global service?"

The problems faced by American Express' credit-card division certainly are not unique in the 1990s. Big companies, small businesses, school districts, state and city governments, hospitals, and even the military are being forced to change the way they do things significantly. While change has always been a part of the manager's job, it has become more so in recent years. We'll describe why in this chapter. We'll also discuss ways in which managers can stimulate innovation and increase their organization's adaptability.

What is Change?

change
An alteration in people, structure, or technology.

If it weren't for **change,** the manager's job would be relatively easy. Planning would be without problems because tomorrow would be no different from today. The issue of organizational design would be solved. Since the environment would be free from uncertainty and there would be no need to adapt, all organizations would be tightly structured. Similarly, decision making would be dramatically simplified because the outcome of each alternative could be predicted with almost certain accuracy. It would, indeed, simplify the manager's job if, for example, competitors didn't introduce new products or services, if customers didn't make new demands, if government regulations were never modified, or if employees' needs didn't change.

However, change is an organizational reality. Handling that change is an integral part of every manager's job. In this chapter of the book we address the key issues related to managing change.

Forces for Change

In Chapter 3, we pointed out that there are both external and internal forces that constrain managers. These same forces also bring about the need for change. Let's briefly look at the factors that can create the need for change.

External Forces

The external forces that create the need for change come from various sources. In recent years, the *marketplace* has affected firms like BMW and Domino's by introducing new competition. BMW now has upscale Japanese cars produced by Lexus and Infiniti to compete against, and Domino's must now contend with Pizza Hut, which recently moved into the home-delivery market. *Government laws and regulations* are a frequent impetus for change. The passage of a major tax revision in 1986, which included the phasing out of interest deductibility except for home mortgages, created huge opportunities to sell home equity loans for firms like Citicorp and Bank One almost overnight. In 1990, the passage of the Americans with Disabilities Act required thousands of businesses to widen doorways, reconfigure restrooms, add ramps, and take other actions to improve accessibility.

Technology also creates the need for change. Recent developments in sophisticated and extremely expensive diagnostic equipment have created significant economies of scale for hospitals and medical centers. The assembly line in many industries is undergoing dramatic changes as employers replace human labor with technologically advanced mechanical robots. The fluctuation in *labor markets* forces managers to initiate change. For instance, the current shortage of registered nurses has forced hospitals to redesign jobs and alter their reward and benefit packages.

Economic changes, of course, affect almost all organizations. The dramatic drop in Japanese real estate prices during the early 1990s forced many of Japan's largest companies to sell off assets and cut back ambitious growth plans. Meanwhile, in the United States, record low interest rates were stimulating an unprecedented demand for the services of mortgage loan brokers.

Internal Forces

In addition to the external forces noted above, internal forces can also stimulate the need for change. These internal forces tend to originate primarily from the internal operations of the organization or from the impact of external changes.

When management redefines or modifies its *strategy,* it often introduces a host of changes. As noted at the beginning of this chapter, American Express's new strategy of competing more aggressively in the nonpremium card market has required a major reorganization of its work force. An organization's *work force* is rarely static. Its composition changes in terms of age, education, sex, and so forth. In a stable organization with an increasing number of older executives, there might be a need to restructure jobs in order to retain the younger and more ambitious managers who occupy the lower ranks. The compensation and benefits systems might also need to be reworked to reflect the needs of an older work force. The introduction of new *equipment* represents another internal force for change. Employees may have their jobs redesigned, need to undergo training to operate the new equipment, or be required to establish new interaction patterns within their formal group. *Employee attitudes,* such as increased job dissatisfaction, may lead to increased absenteeism, more voluntary resignations, and even strikes. Such events will, in turn, often lead to changes in management policies and practices.

Many U.S. defense contractors are responding to government cutbacks by changing their strategy. Westinghouse Electronic Systems, for example, is using its defense technology to make home and commercial security gear, airport and weather radar, mail-sorting equipment, and systems for tracking mass-transit buses (pictured).

The Manager as Change Agent

change agents
People who act as catalysts and manage the change process.

Changes within an organization need a catalyst. People who act as catalysts and assume the responsibility for managing the change process are called **change agents.**

Any manager can be a change agent. As we review the topic of change, we assume that it is initiated and carried out by a manager within the organization. However, the change agent can be a nonmanager—for example, an internal staff specialist or outside consultant whose expertise is in change implementation. For major system-wide changes, internal management will often hire outside consultants to provide advice and assistance. Because they are from the outside, they can offer an objective perspective usually lacking in insiders. However, outside consultants are usually at a disadvantage because they have an inadequate understanding of the organization's history, culture, operating procedures, and personnel. Outside consultants are also often prone to initiate more drastic changes than insiders—which can be either a benefit or a disadvantage—because they do not have to live with the repercussions after the change is implemented. In contrast, internal managers who act as change agents may be more thoughtful (and possibly more cautious) because they must live with the consequences of their actions.

Two Different Views on the Change Process

We can use two very different metaphors to describe the change process.[2] One envisions the organization as a large ship crossing a calm sea. The ship's captain and crew know exactly where they're going because they've made the trip many times before. Change surfaces as the occasional storm, a brief distraction in an otherwise calm and predictable trip. In the other metaphor, the organization is seen as a small raft navigating a raging river with uninterrupted white-water rapids. Aboard the raft are half-a-dozen people who've never worked together before, who are totally unfamiliar with the river, who are unsure of their eventual destination and, as if things

MANAGING FROM A GLOBAL PERSPECTIVE

The Global Economy Intensifies the Need for Change

Probably no single external stimulus for change has been more influential in the past decade than the emergence of the global economy.

As we have discussed throughout this book, few organizations are so insulated that they can ignore foreign competition.[3] In many cases, economies of scale dictate that firms either expand or merge with other organizations in order to compete effectively in world markets. A number of the major U.S. public accounting firms, for instance, have merged in recent years in order to better handle the rise of multinationals and the consolidation going on in western Europe.

Additionally, as trade barriers are lessened, organizations find that their rivals are just as likely to come from 15,000 miles away as from across town. Remember that less than twenty-five years ago, Xerox owned almost 100 percent of the copier market; no one, including Kodak, had ever heard of Fuji Photofilm; and General Motors sold one of every two automobiles bought in the United States.

weren't bad enough, who are traveling in the pitch-dark of night. In the white-water rapids metaphor, change is a natural state and managing change is a continual process.

These two metaphors present very different approaches to understanding and responding to change. Let's take a closer look at each one.

The "Calm Waters" Metaphor

Until very recently, the "calm waters" metaphor dominated the thinking of practicing managers and academics. It is best illustrated in Kurt Lewin's three-step description of the change process[4] (see Figure 13–1).

According to Lewin, successful change requires *unfreezing* the status quo, *changing* to a new state, and *refreezing* the new change to make it permanent. The status quo can be considered an equilibrium state. To move from this equilibrium, unfreezing is necessary. It can be achieved in one of three ways:

1. The *driving forces,* which direct behavior away from the status quo, can be increased.

2. The *restraining forces,* which hinder movement from the existing equilibrium, can be decreased.

3. The two approaches can be *combined.*

Once unfreezing has been accomplished, the change itself can be implemented. However, the mere introduction of change does not ensure that it will take hold. The new situation therefore needs to be *refrozen* so that it can be sustained over time. Unless this last step is attended to, there is a very strong chance that the change will be short-lived and employees will revert to the previous equilibrium state. The objective of refreezing, then, is to stabilize the new situation by balancing the driving and restraining forces.

Note how Lewin's three-step process treats change as a break in the organization's equilibrium state. The status quo has been disturbed, and change is necessary to establish a new equilibrium state. This view might have been appropriate to the relatively calm environment that most organizations faced in the 1950s, 1960s, and early 1970s. But the "calm waters" metaphor is increasingly obsolete as a way to describe the kind of seas that current managers have to navigate.

The "White-Water Rapids" Metaphor

The "white-water rapids" metaphor is consistent with our discussion of uncertain and dynamic environments in Chapter 3. It is consistent with Mintzberg's observation,

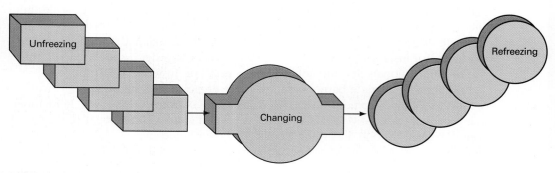

FIGURE 13–1
The Change Process

discussed in Chapter 1, that the manager's job is one of constant interruptions. It is also consistent with the dynamics associated with going from an industrial society to a world dominated by information and ideas.

To get a feeling for what managing change might be like when you have to continually maneuver in uninterrupted rapids, consider attending a college that had the following curriculum: Courses vary in length. Unfortunately, when you sign up, you don't know how long a course will last. It might go for two weeks or thirty weeks. Furthermore, the instructor can end a course any time he or she wants, with no prior warning. If that isn't bad enough, the length of the class changes each time it meets—sometimes it lasts twenty minutes, while other times it runs for three hours—and determination of the time of the next class meeting is set by the instructor during the previous class. Oh yes, there's one more thing. The exams are all unannounced, so you have to be ready for a test at any time.

To succeed in this college, you would have to be incredibly flexible and able to respond quickly to every changing condition. Students who were overstructured or slow on their feet wouldn't survive.

A growing number of managers are coming to accept that their job is much like what a student would face in such a college. The stability and predictability of the "calm water" metaphor don't exist. Disruptions in the status quo are not occasional and temporary, followed by a return to calm waters. Many of today's managers never get out of the rapids. They face constant change, bordering on chaos. These managers are being forced to play a game they've never played before and that is governed by rules that are created as the game progresses.[5]

Is the "white-water rapids" metaphor merely hyperbole? No! Take the case of Harry Quadracci, founder and president of Quad/Graphics Inc.[6] His firm is a commercial printer based in Wisconsin. Founded in 1971, the company is one of the largest and fastest-growing printers in the United States. It prints such magazines as *Time, People,* and *Architectural Digest.* The company now employs more than 3,500 people and has sales in excess of $400 million a year.

Quadracci attributes his company's success to its ability to act fast when opportunities arise. Change and growth are among the few constants at Quad/Graphics. He encourages his people to "act now, think later." The company has no budgets because it is moving too fast—its annual growth rate during the past decade has been an astounding 40 percent! As Quadracci points out, when every department looks 30 percent different every six months, budgets aren't much use. Instead of budgets, each of the company's ten divisions is measured against its own previous performance.

Putting the Two Views in Perspective

Does *every* manager face a world of constant and chaotic change? No, but the set of managers who don't is dwindling rapidly.

Managers in such businesses as women's high-fashion clothing and computer software have long confronted a world of white-water rapids. These managers used to look with envy at their counterparts in industries such as auto manufacturing, oil exploration, banking, publishing, telecommunications, and air transportation, who historically faced a stable and predictable environment. That might have been true in the 1960s, but it's not true in the 1990s!

Few organizations today can treat change as the occasional disturbance in an otherwise peaceful world. Even these few do so at great risk. Too much is changing too fast for any organization or its managers to be complacent.[7] Most competitive advantages last less than eighteen months. A firm like People Express—a no-frills, no-reservations airline—was described in business periodicals as the model "new look" firm, then went bankrupt a short time later. As Tom Peters has aptly noted, the old saying "If it ain't broke, don't fix it" no longer applies. In its place, he suggests "If it ain't broke, you just haven't looked hard enough. Fix it anyway."[8]

The Increasing Need for the Agent of Revolutionary Change

The historical role of change agents in organizations was to fix and improve things bit by bit. When the environment changed slowly, organizations could respond to those changes in an incremental fashion. However, in today's dynamic "white-water rapids" world, where victory increasingly goes to the flexible and adaptive, there is a need for a new kind of change agent: Someone who can throw out the conventional wisdom about how things have always been done and initiate radical change.[9]

Harvey Golub tried to be such a change agent at American Express' credit-card division. Jack Welch plays that role at General Electric. Ted Turner did it in the cable news business.

Lesser-known Dick Hackborn, executive vice president for desktop computer products at Hewlett-Packard, has built a reputation as an architect of revolutionary change. He oversaw the introduction of HP's first LaserJet printer with a price tag of $3495. Using emerging technology, and ignoring critics who said such printers had to sell for $100,000 or more to be profitable, the LaserJet totally destroyed the competition. HP now owns 70 percent of the U.S. market for desktop laser printers, and Hackborn is helping to spread the lessons learned from the LaserJet throughout the rest of HP.

Turbulent times require revolutionary, not incremental, change. Therefore, organizations are increasingly looking for managers who can introduce and successfully implement quantum change.

Organizational Inertia and Resistance to Change

As change agents, managers should be motivated to initiate change because they're concerned with improving their organization's effectiveness. However, change can be a threat to managers. Of course, change can be a threat to nonmanagerial personnel as well. Organizations can build up inertia that propels them to resist changing their status quo, even if that change might be beneficial. In this section, we want to review why people in organizations resist change and what can be done to lessen this resistance.

Resistance to Change

It has been said that most people hate any change that doesn't jingle in their pockets. This awareness of resistance to change is well documented.[10] But why do people resist change? An individual is likely to resist change for three reasons: uncertainty, concern over personal loss, and the belief that the change is not in the organization's best interest.[11]

Changes substitute ambiguity and uncertainty for the known. Regardless of how much you may dislike attending college, at least you know the ropes. You understand what is expected of you. When you leave college and venture out into the world of full-time employment, regardless of how anxious you are to get out of college, you will have to trade the known for the unknown. Employees in organizations hold the

Individuals who spent twenty years as mail sorters for the post office were likely to resist automatic letter sorters more actively than recent hires. The latter had less personal investment in the old system and were less threatened by automation.

same dislike for uncertainty. For example, the introduction in manufacturing plants of quality-control methods based on sophisticated statistical models means that many quality-control inspectors will have to learn these new methods. Some inspectors may fear that they will be unable to do so. They may, therefore, develop a negative attitude toward statistical control techniques or behave dysfunctionally if required to use them.

The second cause of resistance is the fear of losing something already possessed. Change threatens the investment one has already made in the status quo. The more people have invested in the current system, the more they resist change. Why? They fear the loss of status, money, authority, friendships, personal convenience, or other benefits that they value. This explains why older employees resist change more than do younger ones. Older employees have generally invested more in the current system and therefore have more to lose by adapting to a change.

A final cause of resistance is a person's belief that the change is incompatible with the goals and best interests of the organization. If an employee believes that a new job procedure proposed by a change agent will reduce productivity or product quality, that employee can be expected to resist the change. If the employee expresses his or her resistance positively (clearly expressing it to the change agent, along with substantiation), this form of resistance can be beneficial to the organization.

Techniques for Reducing Resistance

When management sees resistance to change as dysfunctional, what actions can it take? Six tactics have been suggested for use by managers or other change agents in dealing with resistance to change.[12]

Education and Communication   Resistance can be reduced through communicating with employees to help them see the logic of a change. This tactic assumes that the source of resistance lies in misinformation or poor communication: If employees receive the full facts and have their misunderstandings cleared up, their resistance will subside. This can be achieved through one-on-one discussions, memos, group presentations, or reports. Does it work? It does, provided that the source of resistance is inadequate communication and that management–employee relations are characterized by mutual trust and credibility. If these conditions do not exist, it is unlikely to succeed. Moreover, the time and effort that this tactic involves must be weighed against its advantages, particularly when the change affects a large number of people.

Participation   It's difficult for individuals to resist a change decision in which they participated. Before a change is made, those who are opposed can be brought into the decision process. Assuming that the participants have the expertise to make a meaningful contribution, their involvement can reduce resistance, obtain commitment, and increase the quality of the change decision. However, this technique has its disadvantages: the possibility of a poor solution and the consumption of a lot of time.

Facilitation and Support   Change agents can offer a range of supportive efforts to reduce resistance. When employee fear and anxiety are high, employee counseling and therapy, new skills training, or a short paid leave of absence might facilitate adjustment. The drawback of this tactic, as of the others, is that it is time consuming. Furthermore, it is expensive, and its implementation offers no assurance of success.

Negotiation   Another way for the change agent to deal with potential resistance to change is to exchange something of value for a lessening of the resistance. For instance, if the resistance is centered in a few powerful individuals, a specific reward package can be negotiated that will meet their individual needs. Negotiation as a tactic may be necessary when resistance comes from a powerful source, such as a union. Yet one cannot ignore its potentially high costs. There is also the risk that, once a change agent negotiates to avoid resistance, he or she is open to the possibility of being blackmailed by others with power.

Manipulation and Cooptation *Manipulation* refers to covert attempts to influence. Twisting and distorting facts to make them appear more attractive, withholding damaging information, and creating false rumors to get employees to accept a change are all examples of manipulation. A corporate management that threatens to close a particular manufacturing plant if the employees fail to accept an across-the-board pay cut, when it actually has no intention of doing so, is using manipulation. *Cooptation* is a form of both manipulation and participation. It seeks to "buy off" the leaders of a resistance group by giving them a key role in the change decision. The leaders' advice is sought, not to arrive at a better decision but to get their endorsement. Both manipulation and cooptation are relatively inexpensive and easy ways to gain the support of adversaries, but the tactics can backfire if the targets become aware that they are being tricked or used. Once the deception has been discovered, the change agent's credibility may drop to zero.

Coercion Last on the list of tactics is *coercion*—that is, the use of direct threats or force upon the resisters. A corporate management that is really determined to close a manufacturing plant if employees do not agree to a pay cut is using coercion. Other examples of coercion include threats of transfer, loss of promotions, negative performance evaluations, or a poor letter of recommendation. The advantages of coercion are approximately the same as those of manipulation and cooptation. However, the major disadvantage of this method is that coercion is very often illegal. Even legal coercion tends to be seen as bullying and can completely undermine a change agent's credibility.

Techniques for Managing Change

What *can* a manager change? The manager's options essentially fall into one of three categories: structure, technology, or people. (See Figure 13–2.) Changing *structure* includes any alteration in authority relations, coordination mechanisms, degree of centralization, job redesign, or similar structural variables. Changing *technology* encompasses modifications in the way work is processed or the methods and

FIGURE 13–2
Three Categories of Change

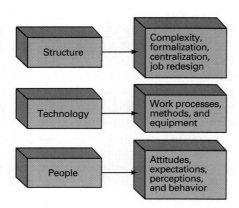

Structure	→	Complexity, formalization, centralization, job redesign
Technology	→	Work processes, methods, and equipment
People	→	Attitudes, expectations, perceptions, and behavior

equipment are used. Changing *people* refers to changes in employee attitudes, expectations, perceptions, or behavior.

Changing Structure

In Chapters 10 and 11, we discussed structural issues. Managers were described as having responsibility for such activities as choosing the organization's formal design, allocating authority, determining the degree of decentralization that would prevail, and designing jobs. Once those structural decisions have been made, however, they are not set in concrete. Changing conditions demand changes in the structure. As a result, the manager, in his or her role as a change agent, might need to modify the structure.

What options does the manager have for changing structure? Essentially the same ones we introduced in our discussion of structure and design. A few examples should make these options clearer.

An organization's structure is defined in terms of its degree of complexity, formalization, and centralization. Managers can alter one or more of these *structural components*. For instance, departmental responsibilities can be combined, vertical layers removed, and spans of control widened to make the organization flatter and less bureaucratic. More rules and procedures can be implemented to increase standardization. An increase in decentralization can be made to speed up the decision-making process. AT&T's top management, for example, has eliminated a fourth of the company's payroll, cut several levels out of the hierarchy, widened spans, and decentralized decision making into twenty new operating units.

Another option would be to introduce major changes in the actual *structural design*. This might include a shift from a functional to a product structure or the creation of a matrix design. Managers might consider redesigning jobs or work schedules. Job descriptions can be redefined, jobs enriched, or flexible work hours introduced. Still another option is to modify the organization's compensation system. Motivation could be increased, for example, by introducing performance bonuses or profit sharing. Polaroid, for instance, has replaced its traditional functional structure with a new design that arranges work around cross-disciplinary teams and rewards individuals for their team's accomplishments.

Changing Technology

Managers can also change the technology used to convert inputs into outputs. Most of the early studies in management—such as the work of Frederick Taylor and Frank Gilbreth—dealt with efforts aimed at technological change. Scientific management sought to implement changes that would increase production efficiency based on time-and-motion studies. Today, major technological changes usually involve the introduction of new equipment, tools, or methods; automation; or computerization.

Competitive factors or new innovations within an industry often require management to introduce *new equipment, tools,* or *operating methods*. As an example, U.S. aluminum companies like Alcoa and Reynolds have significantly modernized their plants in recent years in order to compete more effectively against foreign manufacturers. More efficient handling equipment, furnaces, and presses have been installed to reduce the cost of manufacturing a ton of aluminum.

Automation is a technological change that replaces people with machines. It began in the Industrial Revolution and continues as a management option today. Automation has been introduced (and sometimes resisted) in the U.S. Postal Service in the form of automatic mail sorters and in automobile assembly lines in the form of robots.

Probably the most visible technological change in recent years has come through management's efforts at expanding *computerization*. Many organizations now have sophisticated management information systems. Large supermarkets have converted their cash registers into input terminals and linked them to computers to provide instant inventory data. The office of 1994 is dramatically different from its counterpart of 1974, predominantly because of computerization. This is typified by desktop microcomputers that can run hundreds of business software packages and network systems that allow these computers to communicate with each other.

Changing People

The last thirty years have seen a dramatic increase in interest by academic researchers and practicing managers in helping individuals and groups within organizations to work more effectively together. The term **organizational development (OD)**, though occasionally referring to all types of change, essentially focuses on techniques or programs to change people and the nature and quality of interpersonal work relationships.[13] The more popular OD techniques include sensitivity training, survey feedback, process consultation, team building, and intergroup development (see Figure 13–3). The common thread running through these techniques is that each seeks to bring about changes in or among the organization's personnel.

Sensitivity training is a method of changing behavior through unstructured group interaction. The group is made up of a professional behavioral scientist and a set of participants. There is no specified agenda, and the professional —who accepts no leadership role—merely creates the opportunity for participants to express their ideas and feelings. The forum is free and open: Participants can discuss anything they like. What evolves is discussion that focuses on the individual participants and their interactive processes.

The research evidence on the effectiveness of sensitivity training as a change technique indicates mixed results. On the positive side, it appears to stimulate short-term improvement in communication skills, improve perceptual accuracy, and increase one's willingness to use participation.[14] However, the impact of these changes

organizational development (OD)
Techniques to change people and the quality of interpersonal work relationships.

sensitivity training
A method of changing behavior through unstructured group interaction.

FIGURE 13–3
Organizational Development Techniques

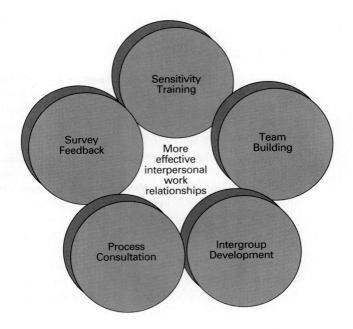

Corporate executives participate in a team building exercise.

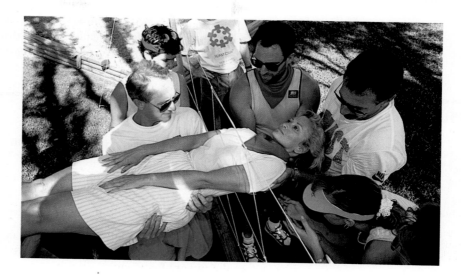

on job performance is inconclusive,[15] and the technique is not devoid of psychological risks.[16]

survey feedback

A technique for assessing attitudes, identifying discrepancies between these attitudes and perceptions, and resolving the differences by using survey information in feedback groups.

Survey feedback is a technique for assessing the attitudes of organizational members, identifying discrepancies in these attitudes and perceptions, and resolving the differences by using survey information in feedback groups. A questionnaire is typically completed by all members of the organization or unit. It asks members for their perceptions and attitudes on a broad range of topics such as decision-making practices, communication effectiveness, coordination between units, and satisfaction with the organization, job, peers, and immediate manager. The data from the questionnaire are tabulated and distributed to the relevant employees, and the information obtained becomes the springboard for identifying problems and clarifying issues that may be creating difficulties for people.

process consultation

Help given by an outside consultant to a manager in perceiving, understanding, and acting upon process events.

In **process consultation,** an outside consultant helps the manager to "perceive, understand, and act upon process events" with which he or she must deal.[17] These might include, for example, work flow, informal relationships among unit members, and formal communication channels. The consultant gives the manager insight into what is going on around and within him or her and between the manager and other people. The consultant is not there to solve the manager's problem. Rather, the consultant acts as a coach to help the manager diagnose which processes need improvement. If the manager, with the help of the consultant, cannot solve the problem, the consultant will help the manager to locate an expert who has the appropriate technical knowledge.

team building

Interaction among members of work teams to learn how each member thinks and works.

In **team building,** work-team members interact to learn how each member thinks and works. Through high interaction, team members learn to develop increased trust and openness. Activities that might be included in a team-building program include group goal setting, development of interpersonal relations among team members, role analysis to clarify each member's role and responsibilities, and team process analysis.

intergroup development

Changing the attitudes, stereotypes, and perceptions that work groups have of each other.

The attempt to change the attitudes, stereotypes, and perceptions that members of work groups have about each other is called **intergroup development.** For example, if two groups have a history of difficult work relationships, they can meet independently to develop lists of their perceptions of themselves, of the other group, and of how they believe the other group perceives them. The groups then share their lists, after which similarities and differences are discussed. Differences are clearly articulated, the groups look for the causes of the disparities, and efforts are made to develop solutions that will improve relations between the groups.

Contemporary Issues in Managing Change

- What can management do to change an organizational culture when that culture no longer supports the organization's mission?
- How does management implement a continuous change program such as TQM?
- Finally, today's competitive environment has made the workplace more stressful. What can managers do to help employees better handle this stress?

These change issues—altering organizational cultures, implementing TQM, and handling employee stress—will be critical concerns to managers leading their organizations into the twenty-first century. In this section, we'll look at each of these issues and discuss what actions managers should consider for dealing with them.

Changing Organizational Cultures

The fact that an organization's culture is made up of relatively stable and permanent characteristics (see Chapter 3) tends to make that culture very resistant to change.[18] A culture takes a long time to form and once it is established it tends to become entrenched. Strong cultures, such as General Motors and AT&T, are particularly resistant to change because employees have become so committed to them. If over time a given culture becomes inappropriate to an organization and a handicap to management, there might be little management can do to change it. This is especially true in the short run. Even under the most favorable conditions, cultural changes have to be measured in years, not weeks or months.

Understanding the Situational Factors What "favorable conditions" *might* facilitate cultural change? The evidence suggests that cultural change is most likely to take place where most or all of the following conditions exist:

A dramatic crisis occurs. This can be the shock that undermines the status quo and calls into question the relevance of the current culture. Examples are a surprising financial setback, the loss of a major customer, or a dramatic technological breakthrough by a competitor.

Leadership changes hands. New top leadership, which can provide an alternative set of key values, may be perceived as more capable of responding to the crisis. Top leadership would encompass the organization's chief executive but might need to include all senior management positions.

The organization is young and small. The younger the organization, the less entrenched its culture. Similarly, it's easier for management to communicate its new values when the organization is small.

The culture is weak. The more widely held a culture is and the higher the agreement among members on its overall value, the more difficult it will be to change. Conversely, weak cultures are more malleable than strong ones.[19]

These situational factors help to explain why a company like General Motors has had difficulty in reshaping its culture. For the most part, employees didn't see their company's day-to-day problems as being of crisis proportions. "New" leadership has been more in name than in substance. Until 1993, CEOs have been long-term veterans of the company, seeped in the organization's established culture. And, finally, GM is neither young nor small, and its culture is not weak.

How Can Cultural Change Be Accomplished? Now we ask the question: If conditions are right, how does management go about enacting the cultural change?

The challenge is to unfreeze the current culture. No single action is likely to have the impact necessary to unfreeze something that is so entrenched and highly valued. Therefore there needs to be a comprehensive and coordinated strategy for managing culture, as is illustrated in Table 13–1.

The best place to begin is with a cultural analysis.[20] This would include a cultural audit to assess the current culture, a comparison of the present culture with the culture that is desired, and a gap evaluation to identify what cultural elements specifically need changing.

We have discussed the importance of a dramatic crisis as a means to unfreeze an entrenched culture. Unfortunately, crises are not always evident to all members of the organization. It might be necessary for management to make the crisis more visible. It is important that it be clear to everyone that the organization's survival is legitimately threatened. If employees don't see the urgency for change, it's unlikely that a strong culture will respond to change efforts.

The appointment of a new top executive is likely to dramatize that major changes are going to take place. He or she can offer a new role model and new standards of behavior. However, this executive needs to introduce his or her new vision of the organization quickly and to staff key management positions with individuals who are loyal to this vision. A large part of Lee Iacocca's success in changing Chrysler's culture was undoubtedly due to his rapid and wholesale shakeup of Chrysler's senior management, in which he brought in loyal associates with whom he had worked before at Ford.

Along with a shakeup among key management personnel, it also makes sense to initiate a reorganization. The creation of new units, the combining of some, and the elimination of others convey, in very visible terms, that management is determined to move the organization in new directions.

The new leadership will want to move quickly also to create new stories and rituals to replace those that were previously used to convey to employees the organization's dominant values. This needs to be done rapidly. Delays will allow the current culture to become associated with the new leadership, thus closing the window of opportunity for change.

Finally, management will want to change the selection and socialization processes and the evaluation and reward systems to support employees who espouse the new values that are sought.

TABLE 13–1 The Road to Cultural Change

Conduct a cultural analysis to identify cultural elements needing change.

Make it clear to employees that the organization's survival is legitimately threatened if change is not forthcoming.

Appoint new leadership with a new vision.

Initiate a reorganization.

Introduce new stories and rituals to convey the new vision.

Change the selection and socialization processes and the evaluation and reward systems to support the new values.

D. Wayne Calloway, CEO of PepsiCo, has successfully reshaped his company's culture since taking over in 1987. For instance, the new culture rewards risk taking, even if the idea fails.

The previous suggestions, of course, provide no guarantee that change efforts will succeed. Organizational members don't quickly let go of values that they understand and that have worked well for them in the past. Managers must therefore show patience. Change, if it comes, will be slow. And management must keep on a constant alert to protect against reversion to old, familiar practices and traditions. Yet, there is an expanding set of success stories. For instance, Bankers Trust, British Airways, First Chicago, Nissan, and GE have effectively achieved dramatic cultural change.[21] Three points about these success stories are worth noting. First, these turnarounds tended to take seven to ten years, confirming our call for patience. Second, in every case of successful cultural change, the change agents—the corporate CEOs—were essentially outsiders. They were either brought in directly from outside the organization or from a division not in the corporate mainstream. And, finally, all of the CEOs started their new jobs by trying to create an atmosphere of perceived crisis.

Implementing TQM

Total Quality Management is essentially a continuous, incremental change program. It is compatible with the white-water metaphor of change that we discussed earlier. In this section, we want to draw on our knowledge of change processes to consider how managers can effectively implement TQM.

First, let's briefly review the key components of TQM. You'll remember that it focuses on customer needs, emphasizes participation and teamwork, and seeks to create a culture in which all employees strive to improve continuously not only the quality of the organization's products or services, but also such factors as work processes and customer response time. It might be helpful if we look at TQM in terms of the three areas toward which management can direct its change efforts: structure, technology, and people (see Figure 13–4).

Focusing the Change Effort   As first discussed in Chapter 11, the *structure* of an organization that expects to implement TQM effectively will be decentralized; will have reduced vertical differentiation, wider spans of control, and reduced division of labor; and will support cross-functional teams. These structural components give employees the authority and means to implement process improvements. For instance, the creation of work teams that cut across departmental lines allows those people who understand a problem best to solve that problem. Additionally, cross-functional teams encourage cooperative problem solving rather than "us vs. them" blame placing.

The primary focus on *technology* change in TQM is directed at developing flexible processes to support continuous improvement. Employees committed to TQM are constantly looking for things to fix. Thus, work processes must be adaptable to continual change and fine tuning. To achieve this, TQM requires an extensive commitment to educating and training workers. The organization must provide employees with skills training in problem solving, decision making, negotiation,

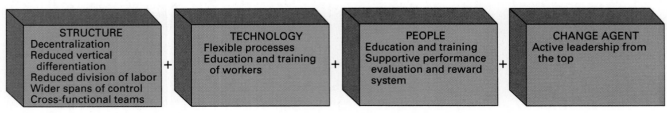

FIGURE 13–4
Factors That Facilitate Continuous Incremental Improvements

Jan Timmer at Philips Electronics

Philips Electronics is the last big, integrated electronics manufacturer. This Dutch giant is the only survivor left to battle the Japanese companies in the highly competitive European market.[22]

Philips has long been renowned for its product technology. This is the company that invented the videocassette recorder and the audio compact disc. But success in consumer electronics is nowadays more a function of marketing agility and price than of technological superiority. For Philips, this means head-to-head competition with the Japanese.

In 1990, Jan Timmer was brought in as president to change Philips' culture. In his first two years, he cut 45,000 jobs and sold off appliances, computers, and other businesses in which the company had no comparative advantage. He then put Philips on the offensive with a series of innovative consumer electronic products such as the Imagination Machine, which uses a compact disc to reproduce sound and pictures off an ordinary TV, and a digital compact cassette that records and plays music with the same fidelity as compact discs.

Despite the changes Timmer has brought, he's found it tough to quickly revamp Philips' slow-moving, bureaucratic culture. "You just can't change a deep-rooted corporate culture in one or two years. It takes at least five years or longer," says Timmer.

Timmer knows what he *wants* to do, but changes in a company with sales in excess of $30 billion a year come slowly. He can only hope his shake-up will make his organization nimble enough to overcome his Japanese foes.

statistical analysis, and team building.[23] For example, employees need to be able to analyze and act on data. An organization with a TQM program should provide work teams with quality data such as failure rates, reject rates, and scrap rates. It should provide feedback data on customer satisfaction. It should give the teams the necessary information to create and monitor process control charts. And, of course, the structure should allow the work teams to make continual improvements in the operations based on process control data.

The *people* dimension of TQM requires a work force committed to the organization's objectives of quality and continual improvement. Again, this necessitates proper education and training. It also demands a performance evaluation and reward system that supports and encourages TQM objectives. For example, successful programs put quality objectives into bonus plans for executives and incentives for operating employees.[24]

Role of the Change Agent   Studies of successful TQM programs consistently demonstrate that these programs require active and unwavering leadership from the CEO.[25] It is he or she who sets the vision and continually conveys the message. For instance, James Houghton, chairman of Corning Inc., says that he repeats the same list of buzzwords fifty or more times a year, at one factory or office after another: "Quality, quality, quality. World-class. Customer focus. Worker participation."[26]

It has taken Bruce Woolpert, CEO of Granite Rock Co., five years, but his company has become the industry's low-cost producer of crushed rock by using TQM concepts such as decentralized decision making, teams, open communications, and extensive employee training. The company's quality and service levels allow it to charge a 6 percent premium and still gain market share. Woolpert's goal for the firm: Focus every day on being better.

stress
A dynamic condition in which an individual is confronted with an opportunity, constraint, or demand related to what he or she desires and for which the outcome is perceived to be both uncertain and important.

A Philosophical Dilemma   The observant reader may have noted a potential philosophical conflict between TQM's incremental approach to change and our previous discussion of revolutionary change. This dilemma is real. Polaroid, for example, has yet to resolve this conflict. Manufacturing executives embrace the incremental changes that TQM tends to produce, while executives in research and development argue that the structure imposed by continuous, incremental change is likely to inhibit the dramatic, revolutionary changes that can make or break a technology company.[27]

TQM is a commitment to continuous, incremental change. But for many organizations, incrementalism isn't good enough. These organizations need a dramatic and radical shift in the way they operate. What this suggests is that, for some organizations, TQM should be the second phase of a two-phase change process. Before TQM's approach to change is implemented, management first needs to oversee a revolution. Alcoa's management has decided that it needs massive quality improvements if the company is to meet world standards.[28] Only after this is achieved will Alcoa be ready to implement TQM's incremental approach to change.

Handling Employee Stress

For many employees, change creates stress. A dynamic and uncertain environment characterized by takeovers, mergers, restructurings, forced retirements, and mass layoffs has created a large number of employees who are overworked and stressed out.[29] In this section, we want to review what specifically is meant by the term *stress*, what causes it, how to identify it, and what managers can do to reduce it.

What Is Stress?   **Stress** is a dynamic condition in which an individual is confronted with an opportunity, constraint, or demand related to what he or she desires and for which the outcome is perceived to be both uncertain and important.[30] This is a complicated definition. Let's look at its components more closely.

Stress is not necessarily bad in and of itself. While stress is often discussed in a negative context, it also has a positive value, particularly when it offers a potential gain. Functional stress allows an athlete or stage performer to perform at his or her highest level in critical situations.

However, stress is more often associated with constraints and demands. A constraint prevents you from doing what you desire; demands refer to the loss of something desired. When you take a test at school or undergo your annual performance review at work, you feel stress because you confront opportunity, constraints, and demands. A good performance review may lead to a promotion, greater responsibilities, and a higher salary. But a poor review may prevent you from getting the promotion. An extremely poor review might cause you to be fired.

Because the conditions are right for stress to surface doesn't mean it always will. Two conditions are necessary for *potential* stress to become *actual* stress.[31] There must be uncertainty over the outcome, and the outcome must be important. Regardless of the conditions, a stressful condition exists only when there is doubt or uncertainty regarding whether the opportunity will be seized, whether the constraint will be removed, or whether the loss will be avoided. That is, stress is highest for individuals who are uncertain whether they will win or lose and lowest for individuals who think that winning or losing is a certainty. The importance of the outcome is also a critical factor. If winning or losing is unimportant, there is no stress. If a subordinate feels that keeping a job or earning a promotion are unimportant, he or she will experience no stress before a performance review.

Causes of Stress   As illustrated in Figure 13–5, the causes of stress can be found in issues related to the organization or in personal factors that evolve out of the employee's private life.

FIGURE 13-5
Sources of Stress

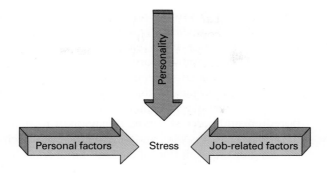

Personality

Personal factors → Stress ← Job-related factors

Clearly, change of any kind has the potential to cause stress. It can present opportunities, constraints, or demands. Moreover, changes are frequently created in a climate of uncertainty and around issues that are important to employees. It's not surprising, then, for change to be a major stressor.

An employee's job and the organization's structure are also pervasive causes of stress. Excessive work loads create stress, as do pressures to maintain a machine-regulated pace. At the other extreme, job boredom can also create stress. Individuals with more challenging jobs have less anxiety, depression, and physical illness than those with less challenging jobs.[32] Role conflict and ambiguity create stress.[33] The former imposes contradictory demands on the employee, whereas the latter foists unclear expectations and uncertain job requirements on the employee. A classic structural source of stress is when the unity of command is broken and employees must deal with more than one boss. Additional organizational factors that cause employee stress include excessive rules and regulations, an unresponsive and unsupportive boss, ambiguous communications, and unpleasant physical working conditions such as extreme temperatures, poor lighting, or distracting noises.

The death of a family member, a divorce, and personal financial difficulties are examples of private matters that can create personal stress.[34] Because employees bring their personal problems with them to work, a full understanding of employee stress requires consideration of these personal factors.

There is evidence that an employee's personality acts as a moderator to accentuate or diminish the impact of both organizational and personal stressors.[35] The most attention has been given to what has been called the Type A–Type B dichotomy.[36] Individuals exhibiting **Type A behavior** are characterized by a chronic sense of time urgency and an excessive competitive drive. They are impatient, do everything fast, and have great difficulty coping with leisure time. **Type B behavior** is just the opposite—relaxed, easygoing, and noncompetitive. Type As live with moderate to high levels of stress; they are more susceptible to heart disease than Type Bs. From a manager's standpoint, Type As are more likely to show symptoms of stress, even if organizational and personal stressors are low.

Symptoms of Stress   What signs indicate that an employee's stress level might be too high? Stress shows itself in a number of ways. For instance, an employee who is experiencing a high level of stress may become depressed, accident-prone, or argumentative, have difficulty making routine decisions, be easily distracted, and the like. These symptoms can be subsumed under three general categories: physiological, psychological, and behavioral.[37]

Most of the early concern with stress was directed at physiological symptoms. This was predominantly because the topic was researched by specialists in the health and medical sciences. This research led to the conclusion that stress could create changes in metabolism, increase heart and breathing rates, increase blood pressure, bring on headaches, and induce heart attacks.

The link between stress and particular physiological symptoms is not clear. There

Type A behavior
Behavior marked by a chronic sense of time urgency and an excessive competitive drive.

Type B behavior
Behavior that is relaxed, easygoing, and noncompetitive.

Dr. Reed Moskowitz (right), director of the stress disorder clinic at New York University Hospital Medical Center, reported seeing a 50 percent increase in bankers, brokers, managers, and other professionals during the 1991-2 economic recession.

are few, if any, consistent relationships.[38] This is attributed to the complexity of the symptoms and the difficulty in measuring them objectively. But physiological symptoms have the least direct relevance to managers.

Of greater importance are the psychological symptoms. Stress can cause dissatisfaction. Job-related stress can cause job-related dissatisfaction. Job dissatisfaction, in fact, is "the simplest and most obvious psychological effect" of stress.[39] But stress has other psychological manifestations—for instance, tension, anxiety, irritability, boredom, and procrastination. Behaviorally related stress symptoms include changes in productivity, absence, and turnover, as well as changes in eating habits, increased smoking or consumption of alcohol, rapid speech, fidgeting, and sleep disorders.

Reducing Stress   As we have seen before, not all stress is dysfunctional. Moreover, realistically, stress can never be totally eliminated from a person's life, either off the job or on. As we review stress reduction techniques, keep in mind that our concern is with reducing the part of stress that is dysfunctional.

In terms of organizational factors, any attempt to lower stress levels has to begin with employee *selection*. Management needs to make sure that an employee's abilities match the requirements of the job. When employees are "in over their heads," their stress levels typically will be high. A realistic job preview during the selection process will also lessen stress by reducing ambiguity. Improved organizational communications will keep ambiguity-induced stress to a minimum. Similarly, a performance planning program such as MBO will clarify job responsibilities, provide clear performance objectives, and reduce ambiguity through feedback. Job redesign is also a way to reduce stress. If stress can be traced directly to boredom or work overload, jobs should be redesigned to increase challenge or reduce the work load. Redesigns that increase opportunities for employees to participate in decisions and to gain social support have also been found to lessen stress.[40]

Stress that arises from an employee's personal life creates two problems. First, it is difficult for the manager to control directly. Second, there are ethical considerations. Specifically, does the manager have any right to intrude—even in the most subtle ways—in the employee's personal life? If a manager believes it is ethical and the employee is receptive, there are a few approaches the manager can consider. Employee *counseling* can provide stress relief. Employees often want to talk to someone about their problems, and the organization—through its managers, in-house personnel counselors, or free or low-cost outside professional help—can meet that need. Companies such as Citicorp, AT&T, and Johnson & Johnson provide extensive counseling services. For employees whose personal lives suffer from a lack of planning and organization that, in turn, creates stress, the offering of a *time management program* may prove beneficial in helping them to sort out their priorities.[41] Honeywell, for example, provides such a service. And still another approach is organizationally sponsored *physical activity programs*.[42] American Express, for instance, has a fitness center in New York and sponsors teams in basketball, volleyball and softball. New York Telephone's stress-management program includes meditation and relaxation techniques. At Apple Computer, in Cupertino, California, employees are encouraged to go for lunch-time fitness walks and join the company's running club.

Stimulating Innovation

"Innovate or die!" That has increasingly become the rallying cry of today's contemporary managers. In the dynamic world of global competition, organizations must create new products and services and adopt state-of-the-art technology if they are to compete successfully. The standard of innovation to which many organizations strive is that achieved by the 3M Co.[43] 3M has developed a reputation for being able to stimulate innovation over a long period of time. One of its stated objectives is that 25 percent of each division's profits are to come from products less than five years old. Toward that end, 3M typically launches more than 200 new products each year. During one recent five-year period, 3M generated better than 30 percent of its $13 billion in revenues from products introduced during the previous five years.

What's the secret to 3M's success? What, if anything, can other managers do to make their organizations more innovative? In the following pages, we'll try to answer these questions as we discuss the factors behind innovation.

Creativity versus Innovation

creativity

The ability to combine ideas in a unique way or to make unusual associations between ideas.

innovation

The process of taking a creative idea and turning it into a useful product, service, or method of operation.

In general usage, **creativity** means the ability to combine ideas in a unique way or to make unusual associations between ideas.[44] An organization that stimulates creativity is one that develops novel approaches to things or unique solutions to problems. **Innovation** is the process of taking a creative idea and turning it into a useful product, service, or method of operation. Thus the innovative organization is characterized by the ability to channel its creative juices into useful outcomes. When managers talk about changing an organization to make it more creative, they usually mean that they want to stimulate innovation. The 3M company is aptly described as innovative because it has taken novel ideas and turned them into profitable products such as cellophane tape, Scotch-Guard protective coatings, Post-it note pads, and diapers with elastic waistbands. So, too, is the highly successful microchip manufacturer Intel. It leads all chip manufacturers in miniaturization, and the success of its 386 and 486 chips gives the company a 75 percent share of the microprocessor market for IBM-compatible PC machines. With $5 billion a year in sales, Intel's commitment to staying ahead of the competition by introducing a stream of new and more powerful products is supported by annual expenditures of $1.2 billion for its plant and equipment and $800 million on research and development.

Fostering Innovation

There are three sets of variables that have been found to stimulate innovation. They pertain to the organization's structure, culture, and human resource practices. (See Figure 13–6.)

FIGURE 13–6
Innovation Variables

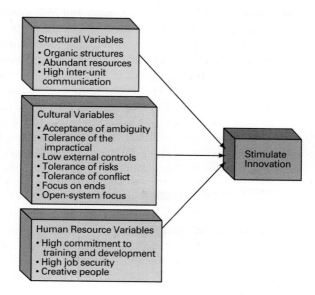

What Would You Do If You Had Details on a Competitor's Trade Secret?

A disgruntled employee who works for one of your key competitors mails you samples of a top-secret new product that your competitor is working on. He even offers, for a small fee, to help you unravel its ground-breaking technology. You realize that this new technology will make your competition's new products unbeatable. Should you send the samples back to the employee and turn him in to his employer? Or should you turn the samples over to your research and development team for analysis and encourage them to break the code? Sound far-fetched? Not really. This dilemma was actually faced by managers at Johnson & Johnson.[45]

Philip A. Stegora, a disgruntled employee at 3M Co., got hold of some samples of a new casting tape that 3M developed for doctors to use to set broken bones. He mailed the tape to Johnson & Johnson and offered to help them unravel 3M's technology for a fee of only $20,000. As the manager at J&J who received the package, you'd love to understand the technology that 3M has developed. The new products that might evolve from this technology could be unbeatable in the $200 million market for casting tapes.

What would *you* do? Throw the samples away? Send them to your company's research department for analysis? Notify 3M about what Stegora has done? Call the Federal Bureau of Investigation?

Structural Variables Based on extensive research, we can make three statements regarding the effect of structural variables on innovation.[46] First, organic structures positively influence innovation. Because they're lower in vertical differentiation, formalization, and centralization, organic structures facilitate the flexibility, adaptation, and cross-fertilization that make the adoption of innovations easier. Second, the easy availability of plentiful resources provides a key building block for innovation. An abundance of resources allows management to afford to purchase innovations, bear the cost of instituting innovations, and absorb failures. Finally, frequent inter-unit communication helps to break down possible barriers to innovation.[47] Committees, task forces, and other such mechanisms facilitate interaction across departmental lines and are widely used in successfully innovative organizations. 3M, for instance, is highly decentralized and takes on many of the characteristics of small, organic organizations. The company also has the "deep pockets" needed to support its policy of allowing scientists and engineers to use up to 15 percent of their time on projects of their own choosing.

Cultural Variables Innovative organizations tend to have similar cultures.[48] They encourage experimentation. They reward both successes and failures. They celebrate mistakes. An innovative culture is likely to have the following characteristics:

- *Acceptance of ambiguity:* Too much emphasis on objectivity and specificity constrains creativity.
- *Tolerance of the impractical:* Individuals who offer impractical, even foolish,

The 486 microprocessor is just one product in a long line of innovative products developed at Intel. This company has successfully created a structure and culture that stimulates innovation.

answers to "what if" questions are not stifled. What seems impractical at first might lead to innovative solutions.

- *Low external controls:* Rules, regulations, policies, and similar controls are kept to a minimum.

- *Tolerance of risk:* Employees are encouraged to experiment without fear of consequences should they fail. Mistakes are treated as learning opportunities.

- *Tolerance of conflict:* Diversity of opinions is encouraged. Harmony and agreement between individuals and/or units are *not* assumed to be evidence of high performance.

- *Focus on ends rather than means:* Goals are made clear, and individuals are encouraged to consider alternative routes toward their attainment. Focusing on ends suggests that there might be several right answers to any given problem.

- *Open systems focus:* The organization closely monitors the environment and responds rapidly to changes as they occur.

Human Resource Variables

Within the *human resources* category, we find that innovative organizations actively promote the training and development of their members so that their knowledge remains current, offer their employees high job security to reduce the fear of getting fired for making mistakes, and encourage individuals to become champions of change. Once a new idea is developed, champions of change actively and enthusiastically promote the idea, build support, overcome resistance, and ensure that the innovation is implemented. Recent research finds that champions have common personality characteristics: extremely high self-confidence, persistence, energy, and a tendency to risk-taking. Champions also display characteristics associated with dynamic leadership. They inspire and energize others with their vision of the potential of an innovation and through their strong personal conviction in their mission. They are also good at gaining the commitment of others to support their mission. Additionally, champions have jobs that provide considerable decision-making discretion. This autonomy helps them introduce and implement innovations in organizations.[49]

Summary

This summary is organized by the chapter-opening learning objectives found on page 379.

1. The "calm waters" metaphor views change as a break in the organization's equilibrium state. Organizations are seen as stable and predictable, disturbed by an occasional crisis. The "white-water rapids" metaphor views change as continual and unpredictable. Managers must deal with ongoing and almost chaotic change.

2. Change is often resisted because of the uncertainty it creates, concern for personal loss, and a belief that it might not be in the organization's best interest.

3. Six tactics reduce resistance to change: education and communication, participation, facilitation and support, negotiation, manipulation and cooptation, and coercion.

4. Managers can change the organization's *structure* by altering complexity, formalization, or centralization variables or by redesigning jobs; changing the organization's *technology* by altering work processes, methods, and equipment; or changing *people* by altering attitudes, expectations, perceptions, or behavior.

5. Dramatic crises and changes in top leadership facilitate cultural change by providing major shocks to employees and the status quo. Having a small or young organization and a weak culture facilitates cultural change by providing a more malleable base with which to work.

6. Management should enact cultural change by beginning with a cultural analysis. This can be followed by taking action to make a crisis more visible; appointing new personnel in top positions; reorganizing key functions; creating new stories, symbols, and rituals to replace ones that reflect the old culture; and altering the organization's selection and socialization processes and evaluation and reward systems to reflect the new cultural values.

7. Managers can implement TQM by providing the right structure, technology, and human resources. The structure should be decentralized, have reduced vertical differentiation and wide spans of control, and support cross-functional teams. The technology must be flexible to support continuous improvement. The work force must be committed to the objectives of quality and continual improvement.

8. Techniques for reducing employee stress include carefully matching applicants with jobs in the selection process, having clear performance objectives, redesigning jobs to increase challenge and reduce the work load, counseling employees, providing time management programs, and sponsoring physical activity programs.

9. Organizations that stimulate innovation will have structures that are flexible, easy access to resources, and fluid communication; a culture that is relaxed, supportive of new ideas, and encourages monitoring of the environment; and creative people who are well trained, current in their fields, and secure in their jobs.

Review Questions

1. Why is handling change an integral part of every manager's job?

2. What internal and external forces create the need for organizations to change?

3. Who are change agents?

4. Describe Lewin's three-step change process.

5. What is OD and what are some of the techniques it involves?

6. Why might an organization such as General Electric have more trouble changing its culture than a small software company?

7. Is TQM consistent with the goal of introducing revolutionary change into an organization? Discuss.

8. What signs would indicate to a manager that an employee's stress level might be too high?

9. List the characteristics of organizational culture that encourage innovation.

Discussion Questions

1. Do you think that a low-level employee could act as a change catalyst? Explain.

2. Contrast management practices in a retail electronics store where management followed the "calm waters" view of change versus one where management followed the "white-water rapids" view.

3. How can an innovative culture make an organization more effective? Could such an innovative culture make an organization less effective? Explain.

4. Do you think a TQM program could be developed that consisted of continual revolutionary change as opposed to continual gradual change?

5. Assuming that employees are well informed about the jobs they are getting themselves into, do you think it is the manager's responsibility to try to alleviate work-related stress on employees, or is this stress just a normal part of the job with which employees will just have to cope?

SELF-ASSESSMENT EXERCISE

How Ready Are You For Managing in a Turbulent World?

Instructions: Listed below are some statements a thirty-seven-year-old manager made about his job at a large, successful corporation. If your job had these characteristics, how would you react to them? After each statement are five letters, A to E. Circle the letter that best describes how you think you would react according to the following scale:

A *I would enjoy this very much; it's completely acceptable.*
B *This would be enjoyable and acceptable most of the time.*
C *I'd have no reaction to this feature one way or another, or it would be about equally enjoyable and unpleasant.*
D *This feature would be somewhat unpleasant for me.*
E *This feature would be very unpleasant for me.*

1. I regularly spend 30 to 40 percent of my time in meetings.   A B C D E

2. A year and a half ago, my job did not exist, and I have been essentially inventing it as I go along.   A B C D E

3. The responsibilities I either assume or am assigned consistently exceed the authority I have for discharging them.   A B C D E

4. At any given moment in my job, I have on the average about a dozen phone calls to be returned.   A B C D E

5. There seems to be very little relation in my job between the quality of my performance and my actual pay and fringe benefits.   A B C D E

6. About two weeks a year of formal management training is needed in my job just to stay current.   A B C D E

7. Because we have very effective equal employment opportunity (EEO) in my company and because it is thoroughly multinational, my job consistently brings me into close working contact at a professional level with people of many races, ethnic groups, and nationalities and of both sexes.
A B C D E

8. There is no objective way to measure my effectiveness.   A B C D E

9. I report to three different bosses for different aspects of my job, and each has an equal say in my performance appraisal.   A B C D E

10. On average, about a third of my time is spent dealing with unexpected emergencies that force all scheduled work to be postponed.   A B C D E

11. When I have to have a meeting of the people who report to me, it takes my secretary most of a day to find a time when we are all available, and even then, I have yet to have a meeting where everyone is present for the entire meeting.   A B C D E

12. The college degree I earned in preparation for this type of work is now obsolete, and I probably should go back for another degree.   A B C D E

13. My job requires that I absorb 100–200 pages per week of technical materials.
A B C D E

14. I am out of town overnight at least one night per week.   A B C D E

15. My department is so interdependent with several other departments in the company that all distinctions about which departments are responsible for which tasks are quite arbitrary.   A B C D E

16. I will probably get a promotion in about a year to a job in another division that has most of these same characteristics.   A B C D E

17. During the period of my employment here, either the entire company or the division I worked in has been reorganized every year or so.   A B C D E

18. While there are several possible promotions I can see ahead of me, I have no real career path in an objective sense.   A B C D E

19. While there are several possible promotions I can see ahead of me, I think I have no realistic chance of getting to the top levels of the company.
A B C D E

20. While I have many ideas about how to make things work better, I have no direct influence on either the business policies or the personnel policies that govern my division.   A B C D E

21. My company has recently put in an "assessment center" where I and all other managers will be required to go through an extensive battery of psychological tests to assess our potential.   A B C D E

22. My company is a defendant in an antitrust suit, and if the case comes to trial, I will probably have to testify about some decisions that were made a few years ago.   A B C D E

23. Advanced computer and other electronic office technology is continually being introduced into my division, necessitating constant learning on my part.
A B C D E

24. The computer terminal and screen I have in my office can be monitored in my bosses' offices without my knowledge.   A B C D E

Turn to page SK-4 for scoring directions and key.

Source: From Peter B. Vaill, *Managing as a Performing Art: New Ideas for a World of Chaotic Change* (San Francisco: Jossey-Bass, 1989), pp. 8–9. With permission.

To: T. Bob Carter, President
From: J.J. Williams, Jr.; Store Manager, Shawnee
Subject: Responding to the Wal-Mart Assault

The heat's on, Bobby. Wal-Mart just announced plans to build a store only five miles from town. All the small-business people here are scared. We haven't had to compete against Wal-Mart in our other three locations so I'm at a loss about what we should do here in Shawnee.

We should expect the Wal-Mart to carry similar merchandise to our own—modestly-priced clothing for the whole family. It's going to be hard, maybe impossible, for us to match their prices. What do we do?

I figure we've got eight to ten months to come up with an aggressive strategy. We grew and prospered here, beginning in 1966, by offering a wide selection of value-priced merchandise. We had little competition in our town of 30,000, and we built a loyal following. Unfortunately, I think we got a bit complacent. The average tenure among employees in our store is twenty-one years. When I talk about the Wal-Mart threat, our people seem unconcerned. They seem to think we're immortal. They just don't see that Wal-Mart might put us out of business. Hey, Wal-Mart has single-handedly led to the closing of thousands of small businesses in hundreds of small towns. We'll be next unless we come up with something. Maintaining the status quo is certain death.

Can you rough out a competitive strategy and a plan for implementing it that can help me compete against Wal-Mart?

This is a fictionalized account of a potentially real problem. It was written for academic purposes only and is not meant to reflect either positively or negatively on actual management practices by Carter's Family Stores.

CASE APPLICATION

Wang Labs vs. Hewlett-Packard: Contrasting Approaches to Change

With more than $3 billion in annual sales, Wang Laboratories ranked No. 146 on the Fortune 500 list of major corporations in 1989. The pioneer in word-processing computers, Wang employed 27,000 people worldwide. Three years later, the company had filed for Chapter 11 bankruptcy, sales were down to $1.9 billion, its work force was around 8,000, and the company was reeling from a string of devastating losses. Wang lost $716 million in 1990, $386 million in 1991, and $357 million in 1992. The company's stock-market value, once $5.6 billion, had shrunk to $70 million.

Now take a look at Hewlett-Packard (H-P). In 1989, the computer and electronics firm was facing slowing sales and experiencing its first earnings decline in years. But instead of entering a period of massive decline like Wang, H-P has staged an impressive comeback. Sales are up, although its work force has been trimmed from 92,000 to 89,000 (without any forced layoffs). First and second quarter earnings for 1992 were up 49 percent and 40 percent, respectively, and the market value of the company has surged past $19 billion. What did H-P do that led to such very different results from Wang?

Since the late 1980s, the computer business has been the quintessential example of an industry facing tremendous change. It has adversely affected such major players as IBM, Digital Equipment, and Unisys. Customer needs have changed from large mainframe computers to smaller and more versatile personal computers (PCs). Much of the hardware has become a commodity-like product, with market share growth going to firms that can either offer low price, outstanding service, or consistent innovation. During this time, Wang's management acted as if they operated in a stable environment. An Wang, the company's founder, was resistant to change. He envisioned himself as having revolutionized the office by freeing secretaries from their typewriters. Dr. Wang and his entire management cadre failed to see how rapidly PCs would supercede Wang's one-function word processors and expensive minicomputers.

It was a different story at Hewlett-Packard. Management saw what was happening and made a commitment to embrace change. They empowered their people, streamlined decision making, and vigorously cut costs. While H-P would continue to be big, management was determined that it would not be slow moving. Senior executives traveled the country, visiting H-P facilities and soliciting the opinions and ideas of employees on the front lines of manufacturing and sales. What they heard were consistent complaints about H-P's bureaucracy and how difficult it was to get approvals for new projects. So management reorganized. They streamlined the decision-making process by eliminating two senior management committees and put in place a team structure that cut across functional and organizational boundaries. The teams were given unprecedented freedom to design and deliver new products. And top management spent considerable time explaining to employees that they needed to accept a higher sense of urgency and to take risks. Further, recognizing that good products weren't enough when competitors were pushing down prices, management encouraged employees to seek out innovative ways to keep costs down in every area from research and development to administration and sales. The result has been that, in spite of low gross margins on many of its products, H-P has been able to achieve high profitability.

Questions

1. Relate the calm-waters and white-water-rapids metaphors to the computer industry in the late 1980s. Which of these metaphors applies to Hewlett-Packard? To Wang?

2. Contrast Wang's and H-P's culture. How did they influence management's response to a changing environment?

3. Could the same managerial actions taken at H-P in the late 1980s have worked at Wang? Support your position.

4. How does H-P epitomize the concepts discussed in this chapter?

This case is based on William M. Bulkeley and John R. Wilke, "Filing in Chapter 11, Wang Sends Warning to High-Tech Circles," *Wall Street Journal,* August 19, 1992, p. A1; Tim Noonan, "The Agile Giant: How Hewlett-Packard Climbed Back to the Top," *Hemispheres,* October 1992, pp. 28–30; and Glenn Rifkin, "Wang Turnaround Artist Quits Work in Progress," *New York Times,* January 22, 1993, p. C1.

VIDEO CASE

Daddy Track: Corporate Response to Changing Roles

In the old days it was so simple. Dad went to work and mom stayed home and cared for the kids. As we know, those traditional roles are now the exception. Today's mom is likely to hold a full-time job outside the home and dad is likely to play a major role in doing household chores and raising the children. But have organizational policies changed to reflect these new roles? In a number of companies, the answer seems to be "no." Ironically, today's organizational policies may better reflect the needs of working mothers than the needs of fathers who want to balance family and work responsibilities. There are risks for fathers who choose "the daddy track."

Take the case of Jeff Coulter. Jeff had a sales job with Microsoft, a company known for expecting long hours from its employees. This is illustrated by the story of a Microsoft programmer who ran into the company's CEO, Bill Gates, one evening when the former was leaving for home. It was 8 p.m. Gates asked the employee where he was going. "Home," he replied. "I've been here for twelve hours." "Oh," responded Gates, "only working half-day?"

Coulter put in fifty hour work weeks at Microsoft. But, in order to get his work completed and get home in time for dinner, he would come in early. His co-workers and boss, who came in after he did in the mornings, only noticed that Coulter was leaving at 5 or 5:30 each evening. Coulter was eventually fired. The company said it was for inadequate performance. Coulter thinks otherwise. He says Microsoft discriminated against him because of his family status.

The following excerpts from Coulter's boss were secretly recorded by him during conversations with her: "Microsoft hires everybody who's killing themselves, so everyone who's killing themselves is competing against other people who are killing themselves and it's like survival of the fittest . . . You picked a company where it's a disadvantage to be married. It's a disadvantage to have any other priority other than work." Microsoft's position is that these comments were taken out of context. Coulter, meanwhile, continues to believe that his family cost him his job.

Questions

1. Is it unrealistic for a company like Microsoft to expect employees to put their careers ahead of their families? Do you think organizations need to change in response to changing family roles and values?

2. Working long hours is a widely recognized part of Microsoft's culture. Do you think that Microsoft needs to change its culture to meet the needs of family-oriented employees like Jeff Coulter or do you think that workers like Jeff need to change to fit into Microsoft's culture?

3. Is there a new double standard where organizations provide flextime, child care, and other options to reduce career-family conflicts for women while men put their careers at risk if they want to spend time with their family?

4. Describe how the demands placed on employees that undermine their family responsibilities can cause stress.

Source: "Joys and Risks of the Daddy Track," *ABC's Nightline*, August 14, 1991.

INTEGRATIVE EXERCISE FOR PART IV

ORGANIZATION CHARTS

PURPOSE

To analyze different organization charts.

REQUIRED KNOWLEDGE

1. Components in an organization structure.
2. Organization design options.

TIME REQUIRED

Approximately 30 minutes.

INSTRUCTIONS

1. Study the three organization charts in Figures IV-A, IV-B, and IV-C.
2. Determine what type of organization might use each and why.
3. Analyze the method of organizing for each.
4. Predict the management problems you think might surface from each.

Based on Judith R. Gordon, *A Diagnostic Approach to Organizational Behavior,* 2nd ed. (Boston: Allyn & Bacon, Inc., 1987), pp. 571–72.

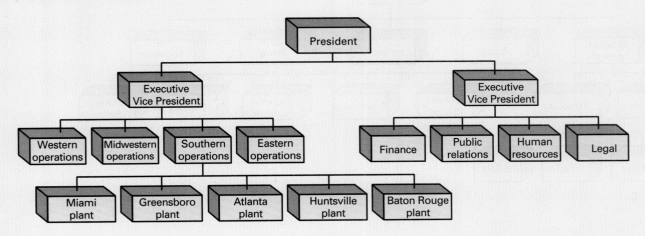

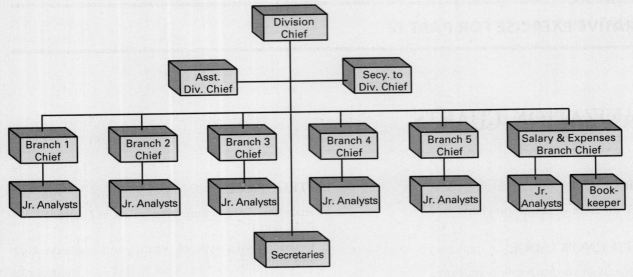

FIGURE IV-B

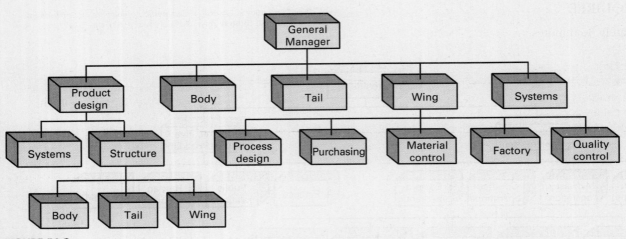

FIGURE IV-C

INTEGRATIVE CASE FOR PART IV

SATURN CORPORATION: IS IT A SUCCESS?

When General Motors' top management originally conceived the Saturn, they viewed it as the company's chance to prove it could efficiently build high-quality cars that were every bit as good as those made by the Japanese. The fact is—somewhat surprisingly given GM's recent dismal record at implementing change and responding to changing consumer tastes—the Saturn has proven to be a car that the public loves. Customers like the car's design and quality. The car has won wide praise for its low price, reliability, and courteous dealer service. Buyers rank Saturn sixth in customer satisfaction—just below cars such as Lincoln and Mercedes, which cost three to five times Saturn's average $11,000 sticker price. Meanwhile, Saturn dealers are able to sell all the cars they get—and without discounting them. Unfortunately, as you'll see, while Saturn is a design and sales success, the company can't seem to produce the cars profitably. While Saturn wasn't expected to make money for several years, it is losing far more than envisioned. In 1991, for example, the Saturn subsidiary lost more than $700 million.

Planning for Saturn began in the early 1980s. By the time the first cars came off the assembly line in the fall of 1990, at the company's brand-new Spring Hill, Tennessee, plant, GM had invested over $3.5 billion in the project. But during that decade, management took an approach to developing the Saturn that was unheard of for GM. A team of ninety-nine people from the United Auto Workers union and GM joined together and literally designed the company from scratch. Workers and managers scoured the world, examining successful manufacturing operations to learn what they could to improve quality and cut costs. What they finally settled on was a new-age production facility. The plant was designed with flexible equipment so that one assembly line could make different car models in response to changing market demands. Competitors' products were carefully studied to find the "best in class" worldwide with the goal of surpassing these efforts. And the actual jobs on the production floor were designed unlike any GM auto plant.

Saturn's 4500 workers share decision making with the company's managers on every issue from how workers are to perform their jobs to the development of budgets. A joint-management structure has union members sitting on Saturn's major committees and having a voice at every level. Workers are given full responsibility for how jobs are done. Managers act as advisers and cheerleaders. Jobs are done in teams of fifteen or so workers who have been trained to perform all of their team's tasks. And in contrast to the typical assembly line where workers stay put and the line moves, Saturn's teams of assembly workers ride along with the car bodies on a slowly moving platform—which can be raised and lowered—so they remain engaged with the evolving automobile shell. This latter innovation alone helped Saturn save $60 million.

Now to Saturn's problems. The company has consistently been unable to produce the quantity of high quality cars that it needs to be profitable. Every time management increases production levels, quality suffers. Employees have become outspoken in their belief that management is willing to trade off quality for increased output. They are becoming increasingly concerned that this could put the entire company at risk. Further, in management's desire to meet increased consumer demand, employees are complaining that the cooperative spirit between management and labor is being seriously threatened.

Saturn has had trouble from the beginning with reaching its production goals. For instance, in the first year management's goal was 150,000 units. It built only 50,000. By 1993, production was increased to 240,000 units a year by using two shifts. Yet management was adding still a third shift to boost production to 310,000. Management claims it needs these higher production goals to satisfy consumer demand and to make Saturn profitable. The fact that Saturn's parent, General Motors, is losing tens-of-billions-of-dollars a year additionally means GM's top executives are running out of patience for money-losing operations. Unfortunately, the pattern at Saturn has been that increased production leads to increased defects. In October 1991, workers briefly donned armbands in a silent expression of their frustration that quality was being sacrificed for greater output. Workers know that their jobs, in the long run, depend on making a top-notch product. "We're not going to sacrifice quality to get productivity," says the plant's UAW president.

To reduce its losses and meet the high demand, the Saturn plant has gone to fifty-hour workweeks that are taking a toll on workers. In addition, recent hires tend to be less gung ho about cooperation. As a result of a labor pact GM and the UAW signed in 1990, Saturn can hire only workers laid off from other GM plants. Many of the 1800 who have transferred into Saturn since late 1990 are bitter toward GM and prefer an adversarial relationship with management rather than a cooperative one. To make matters worse, employee training has been drastically cut at Saturn to cut costs. The extensive training for new workers that helped the original work force learn cooperative work methods and team skills has been dropped. Management wants new arrivals to immediately start producing in order to help relieve workers who have been putting in the fifty-hour weeks for more than a year. So new employees get just 175 hours of initial training, compared with up to 700 hours before. And instead of first learning basic skills that are crucial to the smooth operation of Saturn's teams, such as conflict management, new hires initially focus on such job-specific skills as power-tool operation.

Not too surprisingly, some of the GM transfers have not adjusted to Saturn's teamwork approach. To help deal with these disgruntled workers, Saturn's management has agreed to an expensive option. They are offering severance pay of between $15,000 and $50,000,

depending on length of service at GM, to those who are unhappy and want to leave. Saturn officials figure that 25 to 100 of the plant's workers will opt to go. Management has decided that harmony is worth the price.

Questions

1. What are the reasons behind the structural changes that GM implemented at Saturn?

2. Analyze the production jobs at Saturn in terms of the job characteristics model.

3. What are the implications of this case for an organization's selection of employees and labor-management relations?

4. What are the implications of this case for managing change and innovation?

5. What TQM concepts is Saturn applying?

6. Do you think high production volume and high quality are incompatible goals? Discuss.

Source: Based on William J. Cook, "Ringing in Saturn," *U.S. News & World Report,* October 22, 1990, pp. 51–54; Joseph B. White, "GM Struggles to Get Saturn Car on Track After Rough Launch," *Wall Street Journal,* May 24, 1991, p. A1; David Woodruff, "At Saturn, What Workers Want Is . . . Fewer Defects," *Business Week,* December 2, 1991, pp. 117–18; Doron P. Levin, "G.M. Woes Add to Pressure on Saturn," *New York Times,* December 17, 1991, p. C1; Joseph B. White, "For Saturn, Copying Japan Yields Hot Sales But No Profits," *Wall Street Journal,* October 1, 1992, p. A6; and David Woodruff, "Saturn: Labor's Love Lost?" *Business Week,* February 8, 1993, pp. 122–24.

CHAPTER 14

Foundations
of Behavior

LEARNING OBJECTIVES

After Reading This Chapter, You Should Be Able To:

1. Define the focus and goals of organizational behavior.
2. Identify the role consistency plays in attitudes.
3. Explain the relationship between satisfaction and productivity.
4. Describe Holland's personality-job fit theory.
5. Describe attribution theory.
6. Explain how managers can shape employee behavior.

Hyatt's Myrna Hellerman learns firsthand that cooking is no piece of cake on In-Touch Day.

Doesn't it seem logical that top executives who spend time in the trenches—doing the day-to-day activities of operating employees—will have a better understanding of their employees and the problems those employees face than executives who stay cloistered in their headquarters offices? It does, but very few organizations do anything about it. One exception is Hyatt Hotels.[1]

Hyatt's president came up with the idea of "in-touch day" in 1989. On this day, once a year, the company closes its headquarters office and the firm's senior management staff spreads out to a hundred Hyatt hotels in the United States and Canada. There, they take jobs as bellhops, chambermaids, cooks, carpenters, and similar frontline positions. Myrna Hellerman, Hyatt's vice president of human resources, oversees the program.

Ms. Hellerman notes that even though most Hyatt executives visit company hotels about thirty-five times a year, there's a big difference between seeing hotel operations from the vantage point of a guest and seeing them from the point of view of a desk clerk or a waiter. Actually performing such jobs allows managers to learn, first hand, the problems that employees confront. For instance, the head of employee training recently spent her day in a hotel kitchen and saw, up close and personal, problems with her new training manuals. Specifically, they were designed for lengthy training sessions, which don't take place because of the constant demands of the kitchen, and the manuals were unclear to many of those to whom English was not their first language. In response, the training manager had her department produce several shorter booklets to get the information across more quickly and create multi-language versions of training materials.

Additionally, the in-touch day concept provides tangible evidence to employees that management cares about them and their job problems. It's one thing to talk about improving employee jobs, but another to put yourself in the shoes of your employees and work right alongside them.

Hyatt's in-touch day illustrates one way for managers to better understand their employees. This chapter looks at a number of factors that influence employee behavior and their implications for management practice.

Toward Explaining and Predicting Behavior

behavior
The actions of people.

organizational behavior
The study of the actions of people at work.

The material in this and the following four chapters draws heavily on the field of study that has come to be known as *organizational behavior* (OB). While it is concerned with the subject of **behavior**—that is, the actions of people—**organizational behavior** is concerned more specifically with the actions of people at work.

One of the challenges to understanding organizational behavior is that it addresses a number of issues that are not obvious. Like an iceberg, a lot of organizational behavior is not visible to the naked eye. (See Figure 14–1.) What we tend to see when we look at organizations are their formal aspects—strategies, objectives, policies and procedures, structure, technology, formal authority, and chains of command. But just under the surface there lie a number of informal elements that managers need to understand. As we'll show, OB provides managers with considerable insight into these important, but hidden, aspects of the organization.

FIGURE 14–1
The "Organization as an Iceberg" Metaphor

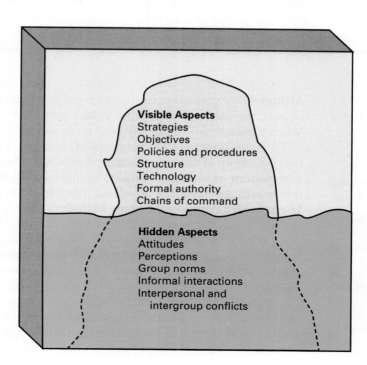

Visible Aspects
Strategies
Objectives
Policies and procedures
Structure
Technology
Formal authority
Chains of command

Hidden Aspects
Attitudes
Perceptions
Group norms
Informal interactions
Interpersonal and
　　intergroup conflicts

Focus of Organizational Behavior

Organizational behavior focuses primarily on two major areas. First, OB looks at *individual behavior*. Based predominantly on contributions from psychologists, this area includes such topics as attitudes, personality, perception, learning, and motivation. Second, OB is concerned with *group behavior,* which includes norms, roles, team building, and conflict. Our knowledge about groups comes basically from the work of sociologists and social psychologists. Unfortunately, the behavior of a group of employees cannot be understood by merely summing up the actions of each individual, because individuals in groups behave differently from individuals acting alone. You see this characteristic when a street gang in a large city harasses innocent citizens. The gang members, acting individually, might never engage in such behavior. Put them together, and they act differently. Therefore, because employees in an organization are both individuals and members of groups, we need to study them at two levels. In this chapter, we'll provide the foundation for understanding individual behavior. In the next chapter, we'll introduce basic concepts related to understanding group behavior.

Goals of Organizational Behavior

The goals of OB are to *explain* and to *predict behavior.* Why do managers need this skill? Simply, in order to manage their employees' behavior. We know that a manager's success depends on getting things done through other people. Toward this goal, the manager needs to be able to explain why employees engage in some behaviors rather than others and to predict how employees will respond to various actions the manager might take.

What employee behaviors are we specifically concerned about explaining and predicting? The emphasis will be on employee productivity, absenteeism, and turnover. In addition, we'll also look at job satisfaction. While job satisfaction is an attitude rather than a behavior, it is an outcome about which many managers are concerned.

In the following pages, we'll address how an understanding of employee attitudes, personality, perception, and learning can help us to predict and explain employee productivity, absence and turnover rates, and job satisfaction.

Attitudes

attitudes
Evaluative statements concerning objects, people, or events.

cognitive component of an attitude
The beliefs, opinions, knowledge, or information held by a person.

affective component of an attitude
The emotional or feeling segment of an attitude.

behavioral component of an attitude
An intention to behave in a certain way toward someone or something.

Attitudes are evaluative statements—either favorable or unfavorable—concerning objects, people, or events. They reflect how an individual feels about something. When a person says "I like my job," he or she is expressing an attitude about work.

To better understand the concept of attitudes, we should look at an attitude as being made up of three components: Cognition, affect, and behavior.[2] The **cognitive component of an attitude** makes up the beliefs, opinions, knowledge, or information held by a person. The belief that "discrimination is wrong" illustrates a cognition. The **affective component of an attitude** is the emotional or feeling segment of an attitude. Using our example, this component would be reflected in the statement, "I don't like Jon because he discriminates against minorities." Finally, affect can lead to behavioral outcomes. The **behavioral component of an attitude** refers to an intention to behave in a certain way toward someone or something. So, to continue our example, I might choose to avoid Jon because of my feelings about him.

Looking at attitudes as being made up of three components—cognition, affect, and behavior—helps to show the complexity of attitudes. But for the sake of clarity, keep in mind that the term *attitude* usually refers only to the affective component.

Naturally, managers aren't interested in every attitude an employee might hold.

job satisfaction
A person's general attitude toward his or her job.

job involvement
The degree to which an employee identifies with his or her job, actively participates in it, and considers his or her job performance important to his or her self-worth.

organizational commitment
An employee's orientation toward the organization in terms of his or her loyalty to, identification with, and involvement in the organization.

They're specifically interested in job-related attitudes. The three most popular of these are job satisfaction, job involvement, and organizational commitment.[3] **Job satisfaction** is an employee's general attitude toward his or her job. When people speak of employee attitudes, more often than not they mean job satisfaction. **Job involvement** is the degree to which an employee identifies with his or her job, actively participates in it, and considers his or her job performance important to his or her self-worth. Finally, **organizational commitment** represents an employee's orientation toward the organization in terms of his or her loyalty to, identification with, and involvement in the organization.

Attitudes and Consistency

Did you ever notice how people change what they say so it doesn't contradict what they do? Perhaps a friend of yours has consistently argued that American cars are poorly built and that he'd never own anything but a foreign import. But his dad gives him a late-model American-made car, and suddenly they're not so bad. Or, when going through sorority rush, a new freshman believes that sororities are good and that pledging a sorority is important. If she fails to make a sorority, however, she may say: "I recognized that sorority life isn't all it's cracked up to be, anyway!"

Research has generally concluded that people seek consistency among their attitudes and between their attitudes and their behavior.[4] This means that individuals try to reconcile differing attitudes and align their attitudes and behavior so they appear rational and consistent. When there is an inconsistency, individuals will take steps to correct it. This can be done by altering either the attitudes or the behavior or by developing a rationalization for the discrepancy.

For example, a recruiter for Ontario Electronics Ltd. (OEL), whose job it is to visit college campuses, identify qualified job candidates, and sell them on the advantages of OEL as a place to work, would be in conflict if he personally believed OEL had poor working conditions and few opportunities for new college graduates. This recruiter could, over time, find his attitudes toward OEL becoming more positive. He may, in effect, convince himself by continually articulating the merits of working for OEL. Another alternative would be for the recruiter to become overtly negative about OEL and the opportunities within the firm for prospective candidates. The original enthusiasm that the recruiter may have shown would dwindle, probably to be replaced by open cynicism toward the company. Finally, the recruiter might acknowledge that OEL is an undesirable place to work, but as a professional recruiter his obligation is to present the positive side of working for the company. He might further rationalize that no work place is perfect; therefore, his job is not to present both sides of the issue, but rather to present a rosy picture of the company.

Cognitive Dissonance Theory

Can we additionally assume from this consistency principle that an individual's behavior can always be predicted if we know his or her attitude on a subject? The answer to this question is, unfortunately, more complex than merely a "Yes" or "No."

cognitive dissonance
Any incompatibility between two or more attitudes or between behavior and attitudes.

Leon Festinger, in the late 1950s, proposed the theory of **cognitive dissonance.**[5] This theory sought to explain the relation between attitudes and behavior. Dissonance in this case means inconsistency. Cognitive dissonance refers to any incompatibility that an individual might perceive between two or more of his or her attitudes, or between his or her behavior and attitudes. Festinger argued that any form of inconsistency is uncomfortable and that individuals will attempt to reduce the dissonance and, hence, the discomfort. Therefore, individuals will seek a stable state where there is a minimum of dissonance.

Of course, no individual can completely avoid dissonance. You know that cheating on your income tax is wrong, but you "fudge" the numbers a bit every year, and hope you're not audited. Or you tell your children to brush after every meal, but *you* don't. So how do people cope? Festinger proposed that the desire to reduce dissonance is determined by the importance of the elements creating the dissonance, the degree of influence the individual believes he or she has over the elements, and the rewards that may be involved in dissonance.

If the elements creating the dissonance are relatively unimportant, the pressure to correct this imbalance will be low. However, say that a corporate manager—Mrs. Smith—believes strongly that no company should pollute the air or water. Unfortunately, Mrs. Smith, because of the requirements of her job, is placed in the position of having to make decisions that would trade off her company's profitability against her attitudes on pollution. She knows that dumping the company's sewage into the local river (which we shall assume is legal) is in the best economic interest of her firm. What will she do? Clearly, Mrs. Smith is experiencing a high degree of cognitive dissonance. Because of the importance of the elements in this example, we cannot expect Mrs. Smith to ignore the inconsistency. There are several paths that she can follow to deal with her dilemma. She can change her behavior (stop polluting the river). Or she can reduce dissonance by concluding that the dissonant behavior is not so important after all ("I've got to make a living, and in my role as a corporate decision maker, I often have to place the good of my company above that of the environment or society"). A third alternative would be for Mrs. Smith to change her attitude ("There is nothing wrong in polluting the river"). Still another choice would be to seek out more consonant elements to outweigh the dissonant ones ("The benefits to society from our manufacturing our products more than offset the cost to society of the resulting water pollution").

The degree of influence that individuals believe they have over the elements will have an impact on how they will react to the dissonance. If they perceive the dissonance to be an uncontrollable result—something over which they have no choice—they are less likely to be receptive to attitude change. If, for example, the dissonance-producing behavior was required as a result of the boss's directive, the pressure to reduce dissonance would be less than if the behavior was performed voluntarily. While dissonance exists, it can be rationalized and justified.

Rewards also influence the degree to which individuals are motivated to reduce dissonance. High dissonance, when accompanied by high rewards, tends to reduce the tension inherent in the dissonance. The reward acts to reduce dissonance by increasing the consistency side of the individual's balance sheet.

These moderating factors suggest that just because individuals experience dissonance they will not necessarily move directly toward consistency; that is, toward reduction of this dissonance. If the issues underlying the dissonance are of minimal importance, if an individual perceives that the dissonance is externally imposed and is substantially uncontrollable by him or her, or if rewards are significant enough to offset the dissonance, the individual will not be under great tension to reduce the dissonance.

Attitude Surveys

An increasing number of organizations are regularly surveying their employees in order to keep informed of their attitudes.

Figure 14–2 illustrates what an attitude survey might look like. Typically, **attitude surveys** present the employee with a set of statements or questions. Ideally, the items will be tailor-made to obtain the specific information that management desires. An attitude score is achieved by summing up responses to individual questionnaire items. These scores can then be averaged for job groups, departments, divisions, or the organization as a whole. General Electric, for example, in surveying more than

attitude surveys
Eliciting responses from employees through questionnaires about how they feel about their jobs, work groups, supervisors, and/or the organization.

FIGURE 14-2
Sample Attitude Survey

Please answer each of the following statements using the following rating scale:
  5 = Strongly agree
  4 = Agree
  3 = Undecided
  2 = Disagree
  1 = Strongly disagree

Statement	Rating
1. This company is a pretty good place to work.	____
2. I can get ahead in this company if I make the effort.	____
3. This company's wage rates are competitive with those of other companies.	____
4. Employee promotion decisions are handled fairly.	____
5. I understand the various fringe benefits the company offers.	____
6. My job makes the best use of my abilities.	____
7. My work load is challenging but not burdensome.	____
8. I have trust and confidence in my boss.	____
9. I feel free to tell my boss what I think.	____
10. I know what my boss expects of me.	____

20,000 of its employees, found that over half of the respondents were dissatisfied with the information and the recognition they received from the company and with their opportunities for advancement.[6] As a result, management instituted regular monthly information meetings, brought in experts to answer questions, and began printing a newsletter. One year later, a follow-up survey found that the number of employees dissatisfied with the information they received had dropped to zero, while the number dissatisfied with promotional opportunities fell from 50 to 20 percent.

The Satisfaction-Productivity Controversy

From the 1930s to the mid-1960s, it was taken as a truism that happy workers were productive workers. As a result of the Hawthorne studies (discussed in Chapter 2), managers generalized that if their employees were satisfied with their jobs, they would then transfer their satisfaction into high productivity. Much of the paternalism shown by managers in the 1930s, 1940s, and 1950s—by forming company bowling teams and credit unions, holding company picnics, and training supervisors to be sensitive to the concerns of subordinates—was supposed to make workers happy. But belief in the happy worker thesis was based more on wishful thinking than on hard evidence.

A careful review of the research indicates that if satisfaction does have a positive effect on productivity, that effect is fairly small.[7] However, the introduction of contingency variables has improved the relationship.[8] For example, the relationship is stronger when the employee's behavior is not constrained or controlled by outside factors. An employee's productivity on machine-paced jobs, for instance, is going to be much more influenced by the speed of the machine than by his or her level of satisfaction. Job level also seems to be an important moderating variable. The satisfaction–performance correlations are stronger for higher-level employees. Thus, we might expect the relationship to be more relevant for individuals in professional, supervisory, and managerial positions.

Unfortunately, most of the studies on the relationship between satisfaction and productivity used research designs that could not prove cause and effect. Studies that have controlled for this possibility indicate that the more valid conclusion is that productivity leads to satisfaction rather than the other way around.[9] If you do a good job, you intrinsically feel good about it. Additionally, assuming that the organization rewards productivity, your higher productivity should increase verbal recognition,

J. W. Kisling at Multiplex, Inc.

J. W. Kisling is CEO at Multiplex, Inc., a St. Louis-based manufacturer of automatic beverage dispenser machines.[10] The company employs 150 people, eighty of them operating personnel who work on the factory floor. Kisling recently decided to survey the eighty line workers to see how their attitudes aligned with national data and to identify areas where management could make improvements.

Kisling and his personnel manager used a fifty-two question survey covering nine areas: Attitude toward top management; work and safety conditions; supervisory effectiveness; pay and employee benefits; communication and recognition; job security and promotion; attitude toward fellow workers; attitude toward the survey; and quality. Space was also provided for suggestions. The fifty-two items in the questionnaire were based on a survey developed by the National Association of Manufacturers. This allowed Multiplex to compare its results with those of thousands of other manufacturers.

Much of what Kisling found was encouraging. For instance, 82 percent of the employees agreed with the statement, "I would recommend employment in Multiplex to my friends." But the survey also uncovered a number of trouble spots. One plant manager was severely criticized for his autocratic style. He was let go. Top management was criticized for being unavailable. Kisling responded with a voice-mailbox system that allows line employees to send him messages confidentially. And some people wrote that they had become bored with their jobs. Results were broken down by departments to find those who were frustrated. In response to this concern, Multiplex's management has redesigned a number of jobs and has begun cross-training workers at different positions on the line.

---

your pay level, and probabilities for promotion. These rewards, in turn, increase your level of satisfaction with the job.

Implications for Managers

We know that employees can be expected to try to reduce dissonance. Therefore, not surprisingly, there is relatively strong evidence that committed and satisfied employees have lower rates of turnover and absenteeism.[11] Because most managers want to minimize the number of resignations and absences—especially among their more productive employees—they should do those things that will generate positive job attitudes. Dissonance, however, can be managed. If employees are required to engage in activities that appear inconsistent to them or that are at odds with their attitudes, managers should remember that pressure to reduce the dissonance is lessened when the employee perceives that the dissonance is externally imposed and uncontrollable. The pressure is also lessened if rewards are significant enough to offset the dissonance.

The findings about the satisfaction–productivity relationship have important implications for managers. They suggest that the goal for making employees happy on the assumption that this will lead to high productivity is probably misdirected. Managers

Employees doing machine-paced work, such as these at a Gillette razor manufacturing plant, often reduce their dissonance by perceiving that their work behavior is largely determined by externally imposed and uncontrollable forces.

who follow this strategy could end up with a very happy but poorly performing group of employees. Managers would get better results by directing their attention primarily to what will help employees to become more productive. Successful job performance should then lead to feelings of accomplishment, increased pay, promotions, and other rewards—all desirable outcomes—which then lead to satisfaction with the job.

Personality

personality
A combination of psychological traits that classifies a person.

Some people are quiet and passive, while others are loud and aggressive. When we describe people using terms such as quiet, passive, loud, aggressive, ambitious, extroverted, loyal, tense, or sociable, we are categorizing them in terms of *personality traits*. An individual's **personality** is the combination of the psychological traits we use to classify that person.

Predicting Behavior from Personality Traits

There are literally dozens of personality traits. However, six have received the bulk of attention in the search to link personality traits to behavior in organizations. They include *locus of control, authoritarianism, Machiavellianism, self-esteem, self-monitoring,* and *risk propensity.*

Locus of Control   Some people believe that they control their own fate. Others see themselves as pawns of fate, believing that what happens to them in their lives is due to luck or chance. The locus of control in the first case is *internal;* these people believe that they control their destiny. In the second case it is *external;* these people believe that their lives are controlled by outside forces.[12] The evidence indicates that employees who rate high in externality are less satisfied with their jobs, more alienated from the work setting, and less involved in their jobs than those who rate high in internality.[13] A manager might also expect to find that externals blame a poor performance evaluation on their boss's prejudice, their co-workers, or other events outside their control, whereas internals explain the same evaluation in terms of their own actions.

authoritarianism
A measure of a person's belief that there should be status and power differences among people in organizations.

Authoritarianism **Authoritarianism** refers to a belief that there should be status and power differences among people in organizations.[14] The extremely high authoritarian personality is intellectually rigid, judgmental of others, deferential to those above, exploitative of those below, distrustful, and resistant to change. Because few people are extreme authoritarians, our conclusions must be guarded. It seems reasonable to postulate, however, that possessing a high authoritarian personality would be negatively related to the performance of a job that demands sensitivity to the feelings of others, tact, and the ability to adapt to complex and changing situations.[15] On the other hand, in a job that is highly structured and in which success depends on close conformance to rules and regulations, the highly authoritarian employee should perform quite well.

Machiavellianism
A measure of the degree to which people are pragmatic, maintain emotional distance, and believe that ends can justify means.

Machiavellianism Closely related to authoritarianism is the characteristic of **Machiavellianism** ("Mach"), named after Niccolo Machiavelli, who wrote in the sixteenth century on how to gain and manipulate power. An individual who is high in Machiavellianism—in contrast to someone who is low—is pragmatic, maintains emotional distance, and believes that ends can justify means.[16] "If it works, use it" is consistent with a high Mach perspective. Do high Machs make good employees? That answer depends on the type of job and whether you consider ethical implications in evaluating performance. In jobs that require bargaining skills (such as labor negotiator) or that have substantial rewards for winning (such as a commissioned salesperson), high Machs are productive. In jobs in which ends do not justify the means or that lack absolute standards of performance, it is difficult to predict the performance of high Machs.

self-esteem
An individual's degree of like or dislike for him or herself.

Self-Esteem People differ in the degree to which they like or dislike themselves. This trait is called **self-esteem.**[17]

The research on self-esteem (SE) offers some interesting insights into organizational behavior. For example, self-esteem is directly related to expectations for success. High SEs believe that they possess more of the ability they need in order to succeed at work. Individuals with high SEs will take more risks in job selection and are more likely to choose unconventional jobs than people with low SEs.

The most common finding on self-esteem is that low SEs are more susceptible to external influence than are high SEs. Low SEs are dependent on the receipt of positive evaluations from others. As a result, they are more likely to seek approval from others and more prone to conform to the beliefs and behaviors of those they respect than are high SEs. In managerial positions, low SEs will tend to be concerned with pleasing others and, therefore, less likely to take unpopular stands than are high SEs.

Not surprisingly, self-esteem has also been found to be related to job satisfaction. A number of studies confirm that high SEs are more satisfied with their jobs than low SEs.

self-monitoring
A personality trait that measures an individual's ability to adjust his or her behavior to external situational factors.

Self-Monitoring Another personality trait that has recently received increased attention is called **self-monitoring.**[18] It refers to an individual's ability to adjust his or her behavior to external, situational factors.

Individuals high in self-monitoring can show considerable adaptability in adjusting their behavior to external, situational factors. They are highly sensitive to external cues and can behave differently in different situations. High self-monitors are capable of presenting striking contradictions between their public persona and their private selves. Low self-monitors can't deviate their behavior. They tend to display their true dispositions and attitudes in every situation; hence there is high behavioral consistency between who they are and what they do.

The research on self-monitoring is in its infancy, thus predictions are hard to make. However, preliminary evidence suggests that high self-monitors tend to pay closer attention to the behavior of others and are more capable of conforming than are low self-monitors.[19] We might also hypothesize that high self-monitors will be more successful in managerial positions where individuals are required to play multiple, and even contradicting, roles. The high self-monitor is capable of putting on different "faces" for different audiences.

Risk Taking   People differ in their willingness to take chances. This propensity to assume or avoid risk has been shown to have an impact on how long it takes managers to make a decision and how much information they require before making their choice. For instance, in a recent study, a group of managers worked on simulated personnel exercises that required them to make hiring decisions.[20] High-risk-taking managers made more rapid decisions and used less information in making their choices than did the low-risk-taking managers. Interestingly, the decision accuracy was the same for both groups.

While it is generally correct to conclude that managers in organizations are risk aversive,[21] there are still individual differences on this dimension.[22] As a result, it makes sense to recognize these differences and even to consider aligning risk-taking propensity with specific job demands. For instance, a high-risk-taking propensity may lead to more effective performance for a stock trader in a brokerage firm. This type of job demands rapid decision making. On the other hand, this personality characteristic might prove a major obstacle to accountants performing auditing activities. This latter job might be better filled by someone with a low-risk-taking propensity.

Matching Personalities and Jobs

Obviously, individual personalities differ. So, too, do jobs. Following this logic, efforts have been made to match the proper personalities with the proper jobs.

The best documented personality–job fit theory has been developed by psychologist John Holland.[23] His theory states that an employee's satisfaction with his or her job, as well as his or her propensity to leave that job, depends on the degree to which the individual's personality matches his or her occupational environment. Holland has identified six basic personality types an organization's employees might possess. Table 14–1 describes each of the six types, their personality characteristics, and examples of congruent occupations.

Holland's research strongly supports the hexagonal diagram in Figure 14–3.[24] This figure shows that the closer two fields or orientations are in the hexagon, the more compatible they are. Adjacent categories are quite similar, while those diagonally opposite are highly dissimilar.

What does all this mean? The theory argues that satisfaction is highest and turnover lowest where personality and occupation are in agreement. Social individuals should be in social jobs, conventional people in conventional jobs, and so forth. A realistic person in a realistic job is in a more congruent situation than is a realistic person in an investigative job. A realistic person in a social job is in the most incongruent situation possible. The key points of this model are that (1) there do appear to be intrinsic differences in personality among individuals, (2) there are different types of jobs, and (3) people in job environments congruent with their personality types should be

Donald Trump's high-risk-propensity personality fits well with his businesses: real estate development and gaming enterprises.

Donald Trump's high-risk-taking personality might be a major obstacle for an accountant who has to perform auditing activities.

TABLE 14-1   Holland's Typology of Personality and Sample Occupations

Type	Personality Characteristics	Sample Occupations
Realistic - Prefers physical activities that require skill, strength, and coordination	Shy, genuine, persistent, stable, conforming, practical	Mechanic, drill press operator, assembly line worker, farmer
Investigative - Prefers activities involving thinking, organizing, and understanding	Analytical, original, curious, independent	Biologist, economist, mathematician, news reporter
Social - Prefers activities that involve helping and developing others	Sociable, friendly, cooperative, understanding	Social worker, teacher, counselor, clinical psychologist
Conventional - Prefers rule-regulated, orderly, and unambiguous activities	Conforming, efficient, practical, unimaginative, inflexible	Accountant, corporate manager, bank teller, file clerk
Enterprising - Prefers verbal activities where there are opportunities to influence others and attain power	Self-confident, ambitious, energetic, domineering	Lawyer, real estate agent, public relations specialist, small business manager
Artistic - Prefers ambiguous and unsystematic activities which allow creative expression	Imaginative, disorderly, idealistic, emotional, impractical	Painter, musician, writer, interior decorator

Source: Based on John L. Holland, *Making Vocational Choices: A Theory of Vocational Personalities and Work Environments,* 2nd ed. Englewood Cliffs, NJ; Prentice Hall, 1985.

more satisfied and less likely to resign voluntarily than should people in incongruent jobs.

Implications for Managers

The major value of a manager's understanding personality differences probably lies in selection. Managers are likely to have higher-performing and more satisfied employees if consideration is given to matching personality types with compatible jobs. In addition, there may be other benefits. For instance, managers can expect that individuals with an external locus of control may be less satisfied with their jobs than internals and also that they may be less willing to accept responsibility for their actions.

FIGURE 14-3
Relationships Among Occupational Personality Types

Source: J. L. Holland, *Making Vocational Choices: A Theory of Vocational Personalities and Work Environments,* 2nd ed. (Englewood Cliffs, NJ: Prentice Hall, 1985). Used by permission. This model originally appeared in J. L. Holland et al., "An Empirical Occupational Classification Derived from a Theory of Personality and Intended for Practice and Research," ACT Research Report No. 29 (Iowa City: The American College Testing Program, 1969).

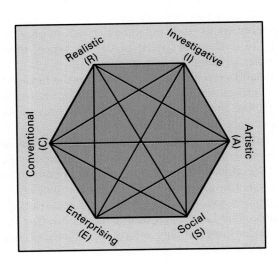

Dominant Personality Attributes Should Vary Across National Cultures

There are certainly no common personality types for a given country. You can, for instance, find high risk takers and low risk takers in almost any culture. Yet a country's culture should influence the dominant personality characteristics of its population. We can see this by looking at two personality traits—locus of control and authoritarianism.

National cultures differ in terms of the degree to which people believe they control their environment. North Americans, for example, believe that they can dominate their environment while other societies, such as Middle Eastern countries, believe that life is essentially preordained. Notice the close parallel to internal and external locus of control. We should expect a larger proportion of internals in the U.S. and Canadian work force than in the work forces of Saudi Arabia or Iran.

Authoritarianism is closely related to the concept of power distance. In high power-distance societies, such as Mexico or Venezuela, there should be a large proportion of individuals with authoritarian personalities, especially among the ruling class. In contrast, because the United States rates below average on this dimension, we'd expect authoritarian personalities to be less prevalent there than in the high power-distance countries.

Perception

perception
The process of organizing and interpreting sensory impressions in order to give meaning to the environment.

Perception is a process by which individuals organize and interpret their sensory impressions in order to give meaning to their environment. Research on perception consistently demonstrates that individuals may look at the same thing, yet perceive it differently. One manager, for instance, can interpret the fact that her assistant regularly takes several days to make important decisions as evidence that the assistant is slow, disorganized, and afraid to make decisions. Another manager, with the same assistant, might interpret the same action as evidence that the assistant is thoughtful, thorough, and deliberate. The first manager would probably evaluate her assistant negatively, while the second manager would probably evaluate the person positively. The point is that none of us actually sees reality. We interpret what we see and call it *reality*. And, of course, as the above example illustrates, we act according to our perceptions.

Factors Influencing Perception

How do we explain the fact that people can perceive the same thing differently. A number of factors operate to shape and sometimes distort perception. These factors can reside in the *perceiver;* in the object, or *target,* being perceived; or in the context of the *situation* in which the perception is made.

When an individual looks at a target and attempts to interpret what he or she sees, the individual's personal characteristics are going to heavily influence the interpretation. These personal characteristics include attitudes, personality, motives, interests, past experiences, and expectations.

FIGURE 14–4
Perception Challenges

Do you see a vase or two profiles face-to-face? It depends on what you choose as a background.

The characteristics of the target being observed can also affect what is perceived. Loud people are more likely than quiet people to be noticed in a group. So, too, are extremely attractive or unattractive individuals. Because targets are not looked at in isolation, the relationship of a target to its background also influences perception (see Figure 14–4), as does our tendency to group close things and similar things together.

The context in which we see objects or events is also important. The time at which an object or event is seen can influence attention, as can location, light, heat, and any number of other situational factors.

Attribution Theory

Much of research on perception is directed at inanimate objects. Managers, though, are more concerned with human beings. So our discussion of perception should focus on person perception.

Our perceptions of people differ from our perceptions of such inanimate objects as desks, machines, or buildings because we make inferences about the actions of people that we don't make about inanimate objects. Nonliving objects have no beliefs, motives, or intentions; people do. The result is that when we observe people, we attempt to develop explanations of why they behave in certain ways. Our perception and judgment of a person's actions, therefore, will be significantly influenced by the assumptions we make about the person's internal state.

attribution theory
A theory used to develop explanations of how we judge people differently depending on the meaning we attribute to a given behavior.

Attribution theory has been proposed to develop explanations of how we judge people differently depending on what meaning we attribute to a given behavior.[25] Basically, the theory suggests that when we observe an individual's behavior, we attempt to determine whether it was internally or externally caused. Internally caused behaviors are those that are believed to be under the personal control of the individual. Externally caused behavior results from outside causes; that is, the person is seen as forced into the behavior by the situation. That determination, however, depends on three factors: (1) distinctiveness, (2) consensus, and (3) consistency.

Distinctiveness refers to whether an individual displays a behavior in many situations or whether it is particular to one situation. Is the employee who arrives late today also the source of complaints by co-workers for being a "goof-off"? What we want to know is if this behavior is unusual or not. If it is, the observer is likely to give the behavior an external attribution. If this action is not unique, it will probably be judged as internal.

If everyone who is faced with a similar situation responds in the same way, we can say the behavior shows *consensus*. Our tardy employee's behavior would meet this criterion if all employees who took the same route to work were also late. From an attribution perspective, if consensus is high you would be expected to give an external attribution to the employee's tardiness; whereas if other employees who took the same route made it to work on time, your conclusion for causation would be internal.

Finally, an observer looks for *consistency* in a person's actions. Does the person engage in the behaviors regularly and consistently? Does the person respond the same way over time? Coming in ten minutes late for work is not perceived in the same way if for one employee it represents an unusual case (she hasn't been late for several months), while for another it is part of a routine pattern (she is regularly late two or three times a week). The more consistent the behavior, the more the observer is inclined to attribute it to internal causes.

Figure 14–5 summarizes the key elements in attribution theory. It would tell us, for instance, that if an employee—let's call her Ms. Smith—generally performs at about the same level on other related tasks as she does on her current task (low distinctiveness), if other employees frequently perform differently—better or worse—than Ms. Smith does on that current task (low consensus), and if Ms. Smith's performance on this current task is consistent over time (high consistency), her manager or anyone else who is judging Ms. Smith's work is likely to hold her primarily responsible for her task performance (internal attribution).

One of the more interesting findings drawn from attribution theory is that there are errors or biases that distort attributions. For instance, there is substantial evidence to support that when we make judgments about the behavior of other people, we have a tendency to underestimate the influence of external factors and overestimate the influence of internal or personal factors.[26] This is called the **fundamental attribution error** and can explain why a sales manager may be prone to attribute the poor performance of her sales agents to laziness rather than the innovative product line introduced by a competitor. There is also a tendency for individuals to attribute *their own* successes to internal factors like ability or effort while putting the blame for failure on external factors like luck. This is called the **self-serving bias** and suggests that feedback provided to employees in performance reviews will be predictably distorted by recipients depending on whether it is positive or negative.

fundamental attribution error
The tendency to underestimate the influence of external factors and overestimate the influence of internal factors when making judgments about the behavior of others.

self-serving bias
The tendency for individuals to attribute their own successes to internal factors while putting the blame for failures on external factors.

FIGURE 14–5
Attribution Theory

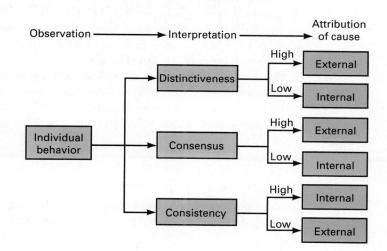

Frequently Used Shortcuts in Judging Others

We use a number of shortcuts when we judge others. Perceiving and interpreting what others do is burdensome. As a result, individuals develop techniques for making the task more manageable. These techniques are frequently valuable—they allow us to make accurate perceptions rapidly and provide valid data for making predictions. However, they are not foolproof. They can and do get us into trouble. An understanding of these shortcuts can be helpful toward recognizing when they can result in significant distortions.

selectivity
The process by which people assimilate certain bits and pieces of what they observe, depending on their interests, background, and attitudes.

Individuals cannot assimilate all they observe, so they engage in **selectivity.** They take in bits and pieces. These bits and pieces are not chosen randomly; rather, they are selectively chosen depending on the interests, background, experience, and attitudes of the observer. Selective perception allows us to "speed read" others, but not without the risk of drawing an inaccurate picture.

assumed similarity
The belief that others are like oneself.

It is easy to judge others if we assume that they are similar to us. In **assumed similarity,** or the "like me" effect, the observer's perception of others is influenced more by the observer's own characteristics than by those of the person observed. For example, if you want challenge and responsibility in your job, you will assume that others want the same. People who assume that others are like them can, of course, be right, but most of the time they're wrong.

stereotyping
Judging a person on the basis of one's perception of a group to which he or she belongs.

When we judge someone on the basis of our perception of a group to which he or she belongs, we are using the shortcut called **stereotyping.** "Married people are more stable employees than singles" and "union people expect something for nothing" are examples of stereotyping. To the degree that a stereotype is based on fact, it may produce accurate judgments. However, many stereotypes have no foundation in fact. In such cases, stereotypes distort judgments.

halo effect
A general impression of an individual based on a single characteristic.

When we form a general impression about an individual based on a single characteristic such as intelligence, sociability, or appearance, we are being influenced by the **halo effect.** This effect frequently occurs when students evaluate their classroom instructor. Students may isolate a single trait such as enthusiasm and allow their entire evaluation to be tainted by their perception of this one trait. An instructor might be quiet, assured, knowledgeable, and highly qualified, but if his style lacks zeal, he or she will be rated lower on a number of other characteristics.

Implications for Managers

Managers need to recognize that their employees react to perceptions, not reality. So whether a manager's appraisal of an employee is *actually* objective and unbiased or whether the organization's wage levels are *actually* among the highest in the industry is less relevant than what employees perceive them to be. If individuals perceive appraisals to be biased or wage levels as low, they will behave as if these conditions actually exist. Employees organize and interpret what they see; this creates the potential for perceptual distortion.

The message to managers should be clear: Close attention needs to be paid to how employees perceive both their jobs and management practices. Remember, the valuable employee who quits because of an *incorrect perception* is just as great a loss to an organization as the valuable employee who quits for a *valid reason.*

Learning

The last individual-behavior concept we want to introduce in this chapter is learning. It is included for the obvious reason that almost all complex behavior is learned. If we want to explain and predict behavior, we need to understand how people learn.

learning
Any relatively permanent change in behavior that occurs as a result of experience.

operant conditioning
A type of conditioning in which desired voluntary behavior leads to a reward or prevents a punishment.

What is **learning?** A psychologist's definition is considerably broader than the layperson's view that "it's what we did when we went to school." In actuality, each of us is continuously "going to school." Learning occurs all the time. We continually learn from our experiences. A workable definition of learning is, therefore, any relatively permanent change in behavior that occurs as a result of experience.

Operant Conditioning   **Operant conditioning** argues that behavior is a function of its consequences. People learn to behave to get something they want or to avoid something they don't want. Operant behavior means voluntary or learned behavior in contrast to reflexive or unlearned behavior. The tendency to repeat such behavior is influenced as a result of the reinforcement or lack of reinforcement brought about by the consequences of the behavior. Reinforcement, therefore, strengthens a behavior and increases the likelihood that it will be repeated.

Building on earlier work in the field, the late Harvard psychologist B. F. Skinner's research has extensively expanded our knowledge of operant conditioning.[27] Even his staunchest critics, who represent a sizable group, admit that his operant concepts work.

Behavior is assumed to be determined from without—that is, learned—rather than from within—reflexive or unlearned. Skinner argued that by creating pleasing consequences to follow specific forms of behavior, the frequency of that behavior will increase. People will most likely engage in desired behaviors if they are positively reinforced for doing so. Rewards, for example, are most effective if they immediately follow the desired response. Additionally, behavior that is not rewarded, or is punished, is less likely to be repeated.

You see illustrations of operant conditioning everywhere. For example, any situation in which it is either explicitly stated or implicitly suggested that reinforcements are contingent on some action on your part involves the use of operant learning. Your instructor says that if you want a high grade in the course you must supply correct answers on the test. A commissioned salesperson wanting to earn a sizable income finds that this is contingent on generating high sales in his or her territory. Of course, the linkage can also work to teach the individual to engage in behaviors that work against the best interests of the organization. Assume that your boss tells you that if you will work overtime during the next three-week busy season, you will be compen-

Mary Kay Cosmetics understands the value of operant conditioning. The use of visible rewards for high sales performance reinforces and strengthens this behavior.

sated for it at the next performance appraisal. However, when performance appraisal time comes, you find that you are given no positive reinforcement for your overtime work. The next time your boss asks you to work overtime, what will you do? You will probably decline! Your behavior can be explained by operant conditioning: If a behavior fails to be positively reinforced, the probability that the behavior will be repeated declines.

social learning theory
People can learn through observation and direct experience.

Social Learning   Individuals can also learn by observing what happens to other people and just by being told about something, as well as by direct experiences. So, for example, much of what we have learned comes from watching models—parents, teachers, peers, television and movie performers, bosses, and so forth. This view that we can learn both through observation and direct experience has been called **social learning theory.**[28]

While social learning theory is an extension of operant conditioning—that is, it assumes that behavior is a function of consequences—it also acknowledges the existence of observational learning and the importance of perception in learning. People respond to how they perceive and define consequences, not to the objective consequences themselves.

The influence of models is central to the social learning viewpoint. Four processes have been found to determine the influence that a model will have on an individual:

1. *Attentional processes.* People learn from a model only when they recognize and pay attention to its critical features. We tend to be most influenced by models that are attractive, repeatedly available, we think are important, or we see as similar to us.

2. *Retention processes.* A model's influence will depend on how well the individual remembers the model's action, even after the model is no longer readily available.

3. *Motor reproduction processes.* After a person has seen a new behavior by observing the model, the watching must be converted to doing. This process then demonstrates that the individual can perform the modeled activities.

Arthur Andersen uses social learning concepts in the development of its in-house training programs.

4. *Reinforcement processes*. Individuals will be motivated to exhibit the modeled behavior if positive incentives or rewards are provided. Behaviors that are reinforced will be given more attention, learned better, and performed more often.

Shaping: A Managerial Tool

shaping behavior
Systematically reinforcing each successive step that moves an individual closer to the desired response.

Because learning takes place on the job as well as prior to it, managers will be concerned with how they can teach employees to behave in ways that most benefit the organization. Thus managers will often attempt to mold individuals by guiding their learning in graduated steps. This process is called **shaping behavior.**

Consider the situation in which an employee's behavior is significantly different from that sought by management. If management only reinforced the individual when he or she showed desirable responses, there might be very little reinforcement taking place. In such a case, shaping offers a logical approach toward achieving the desired behavior.

We *shape* behavior by systematically reinforcing each successive step that moves the individual closer to the desired response. If an employee who has chronically been a half-hour late for work comes in only twenty minutes late, we can reinforce this improvement. Reinforcement would increase as responses more closely approximate the desired behavior.

There are four ways in which to shape behavior: through positive reinforcement, negative reinforcement, punishment, or extinction. When a response is followed with something pleasant, such as when a manager praises an employee for a job well done, it is called *positive reinforcement*. Rewarding a response with the termination or withdrawal of something unpleasant is called *negative reinforcement*. Managers who habitually criticize their subordinates for taking extended coffee breaks are using negative reinforcement. The only way these employees can stop the criticism is to shorten their breaks. *Punishment* penalizes undesirable behavior. Suspending an employee for two days without pay for showing up drunk is an example of punishment. Eliminating any reinforcement that is maintaining a behavior is called *extinction*. When the behavior is not reinforced, gradually it tends to be extinguished. In meetings, managers who wish to discourage employees from continually asking distracting or irrelevant questions can eliminate this behavior by ignoring these employees when they raise their hands to speak. Hand-raising will become extinct when it is invariably met with an absence of reinforcement.

Both positive and negative reinforcement result in learning. They strengthen a desired response and increase the probability of repetition. Both punishment and extinction also result in learning; however, they weaken behavior and tend to decrease its subsequent frequency.

Implications for Managers

Managers can very clearly benefit from understanding the learning process. Because employees continually learn on the job, the only issue is whether managers are going to let employee learning occur randomly or whether they are going to manage learning through the rewards they allocate and the examples they set. If marginal employees are rewarded with pay raises and promotions, they will have little reason to change their behavior. If managers want a certain type of behavior but reward a different type of behavior, it shouldn't surprise them to find employees learning to engage in the other type of behavior. Similarly, managers should expect that employees will look to them as models. Managers who are constantly late to work, or take two hours for lunch, or help themselves to company office supplies for personal

Is Shaping Behavior a Form of Manipulative Control?

Animal trainers use rewards—typically food—to get dogs, porpoises, and whales to perform extraordinary stunts. Behavioral psychologists have put rats through thousands of experiments by manipulating their food supply. These trainers and researchers have shaped the behavior of these animals by controlling conse- quences. Such learning techniques may be appropriate for animals performing in zoos, circuses, or laboratories, but are they appropriate for managing the behavior of people at work?

Critics argue that human beings are not rats in an experiment. Human beings should be treated with respect and dignity. To explicitly use rewards as a learning device—to encourage the repetition of desired behaviors—is manipulative. Human beings in organizations should act of free will and not be subjected to manipulative control techniques by their bosses.

No well-schooled behavioral scientist would argue that shaping isn't a powerful tool for controlling behavior. But when used by managers, is it a form of manipu- lation? If an employee engages in behaviors that the organization later judges "wrong" but that were motivated by a manager's control of rewards, is that employee any less responsible for his or her actions than if such rewards were not involved? What do *you* think?

use, should expect employees to read the message they're sending and model their behavior accordingly.

Summary

This summary is organized by the chapter-opening learn- ing objectives found on page 413.

1. The field of organizational behavior is concerned with the actions of people— managers and operatives alike—in organizations. By focusing on individual- and group-level concepts, OB seeks to explain and predict behavior. Because they get things done through other people, managers will be more effective leaders if they have an understanding of behavior.

2. People seek consistency among their attitudes and between their attitudes and their behavior. They seek to reconcile divergent attitudes and align their attitudes and behavior so they appear rational and consistent.

3. The correlation between satisfaction and productivity tends to be low. The best evidence suggests that productivity leads to satisfaction rather than, as was popu- larly believed, the other way around.

4. Holland identified six basic personality types and six sets of congruent occupa- tions. He found that when individuals were properly matched with occupations that were congruent with their personality types, they experienced high satisfac- tion with their job and lower turnover rates.

5. Attribution theory proposes that we judge people differently depending on whether we attribute their behavior to internal or external causation. This deter- mination, in turn, depends on three factors: distinctiveness, consensus, and consis- tency.

6. Managers can shape or mold employee behavior by systematically reinforcing

each successive step that moves the employee closer to the response desired by the manager.

Review Questions

1. How is an organization like an iceberg? Use the "iceberg metaphor" to describe the field of organizational behavior.
2. What are the three components of an attitude?
3. Clarify how individuals reconcile inconsistencies between attitudes and behaviors.
4. What are attitude surveys and how do they help managers?
5. What behavioral predictions might you make if you knew that an employee had (a) an external locus of control? (b) a low Mach score? (c) low self-esteem? (d) high self-monitoring tendencies?
6. Name four different shortcuts used in judging others. What effect does each of these have on perception?
7. What is the self-serving bias?
8. What is social learning theory? What are its implications for managing people at work?

Discussion Questions

1. How could you use personality traits to improve employee selection?
2. Given that perception affects behavior, do you think there is anything management can do to reduce employee perceptual distortion.
3. What factors do you think might create the fundamental attribution error?
4. "Managers should never use discipline with a problem employee." Do you agree or disagree? Discuss.
5. How important do you think knowledge of OB is to low-, middle-, and upper-level managers? What type of OB knowledge do you think is most important to each?

SELF-ASSESSMENT EXERCISE

Who Controls Your Life?

Instructions: Read the following statement and indicate whether you agree more with choice A or choice B.

A	B
1. Making a lot of money is largely a matter of getting the right breaks.	1. Promotions are earned through hard work and persistence. _____

A	B
2. I have noticed that there is usually a direct connection between how hard I study and the grades I get.	2. Many times the reactions of teachers seem haphazard to me. _____
3. The number of divorces indicates that more and more people are not trying to make their marriages work.	3. Marriage is largely a gamble. _____
4. It is silly to think that one can really change another person's basic attitudes.	4. When I am right I can convince others. _____
5. Getting promoted is really a matter of being a little luckier than the next person.	5. In our society a person's future earning power depends upon his or her ability. _____
6. If one knows how to deal with people, they are really quite easily led.	6. I have little influence over the way other people behave. _____
7. The grades I make are the result of my own efforts; luck has little or nothing to do with it.	7. Sometimes I feel that I have little to do with the grades I get. _____
8. People like me can change the course of world affairs if we make ourselves heard.	8. It is only wishful thinking to believe that one can really influence what happens in our society at large. _____
9. A great deal that happens to me is probably a matter of chance.	9. I am the master of my fate. _____
10. Getting along with people is a skill that must be practiced.	10. It is almost impossible to figure out how to please some people. _____

Turn to page SK-4 for scoring directions and key.

Source: Adapted from Julian B. Rotter, "External Control and Internal Control," *Psychology Today*, June 1971, p. 42. Copyright 1971 by the American Psychological Association. Adapted with permission.

Palomino Publishers

To: Jane Lopez, Director of Human Resources
From: W. H. Luden, Director of Sales

I'm excited about the Executive Committee's recent decision to create our own national sales force. During our first three years of business, with our financial capabilities limited, it made sense to contract with Paramount Publishing to use their sales staff to sell our book titles. But our sales are now approaching $10 million a year, and we need our own sales organization.

It is my intention to hire six to ten new college graduates this spring to staff these new sales positions. Upon joining our company, I want to put them through a four-day, intensive sales-training program. I have a good idea of what the content of that program should be. Where I need some help is in suggesting how to present that content. That's why I'm writing you this memo.

Based on your knowledge of learning theories, could you please provide me with a short report (not to exceed two pages), giving me specific suggestions on how best to design a thirty-hour sales-training program. For example, would learning be more effective if I exclusively lectured to the trainees or should I also use group discussion or some type of role-play exercises?

This is a fictionalized account of a potentially real problem. It was written for academic purposes only and is not meant to reflect either positively or negatively on actual management practices at Palomino Publishers.

CASE APPLICATION

Lettuce Entertain You Enterprises Inc.

Richard Melman's Lettuce Entertain You Enterprises Inc. is becoming the preeminent operator of unique restaurants in America. His restaurants offer cuisines ranging from seafood to Italian and from Greek to Spanish. And he covers the full range of ambiance—from Ed Debevic's 1950s-style diner to Chicago's elegant Pump Room. Lettuce, in fact, has turned dining into theatre by developing restaurant chains such as Lawrence of Oregano, Scoozi's, Need Some Dim Some, and Tucci Benucch. Behind these restaurants, however, is a cadre of happy, loyal employees. To Melman's credit, he has worked hard to inspire his 4000 employees.

Melman runs Lettuce as tightly as McDonald's, but without the stifling standardization. His restaurants thrive on individuality. Equity stakes, extensive employee training, generous benefits, and expanding promotion opportunities have kept the company devoutly entrepreneurial while developing employee loyalty that is unusual in an industry notorious for high turnover. Employees participate in each concept's development. Chefs, managers, designers, and artists are all involved in concocting a "history" of each new eatery. Each restaurant also has its own set of partners, usually longtime Lettuce employees rewarded with the opportunity of ownership.

Melman trusts his workers to be partners because Lettuce has trained them. Nobody is promoted unless he or she has prepared a replacement, and many people started at the bottom and rose through management. For instance, Luis Garcia started at Tucci Benucch in 1987 as a dishwasher who spoke no English. Lettuce adjusted his work schedule so he could take English classes and promoted him through a series of jobs. Today he's a manager at Tucci.

For Melman, treating employees well is simply good business. "If people are happy and able to make a decent living, you can have teamwork," he says. "That falls apart when individuals are unhappy."

Questions

1. Compare Melman's view on the satisfaction-productivity relationship with the research evidence presented in this chapter. Explain any differences.

2. Why do you think Lettuce's turnover rate is so low? Shouldn't it have costs far greater than its competition, which would make it difficult for Lettuce's restaurants to compete? What implications might your explanation have for managers in other businesses?

3. Why does Melman's formula for managing his employees work?

Based on Lois Therrien, "Why Rich Melman Is Really Cooking," *Business Week*, November 2, 1992, pp. 127–28.

VIDEO CASE

Are There Individual Differences Between Men and Women?

Are men and women different? If so, are the differences relevant to work-related performance variables?

At birth, males and females are much the same. But as they mature, males become larger, stronger, and more aggressive. Much of this is directly related to higher levels of testosterone. Meanwhile, the average woman acquires better senses—taste, sight, hearing—than the typical male. Of course, we know that females live approximately seven years longer than males.

One behavior that men tend to exhibit much more than women is aggression. Every year in the United States, 15,000 males commit murder compared to only 2000 females. Why? We don't know. It could be biological or environmental.

A great deal of the differences that exist between men and women is the result of the way each is socialized. Women, for instance, are socialized to value affiliation and attachment. Men, on the other hand, are shaped to value power and competition. This is most explicitly visible in the communication process.

Deborah Tannen's research finds that men use talk to emphasize status, while women use it to create connection. Tannen states that communication is a continual balancing act, juggling the conflicting needs for intimacy and independence. Intimacy emphasizes closeness and commonalities. Independence emphasizes separateness and differences. But here's the most important finding: Women speak and hear a language of connection and intimacy; men speak and hear a language of status and independence. So, for many men, conversations are primarily a means to preserve independence and maintain status in a hierarchical social order. For many women, conversations are negotiations for closeness in which people try to seek and give confirmation and support. For example, men frequently complain that women talk on and on about their problems. Women criticize men for not listening. What's happening is that when men hear a problem, they frequently assert their desire for independence and control by providing solutions. Many women, on the other hand, view telling a problem as a means to promote closeness. The women present the problem to gain support and connection, not to get the male's advice.

Questions

1. In what jobs, if any, would gender be relevant to performance variables such as productivity or absenteeism?

2. "The fact that women have better honed senses, are less aggressive, and use communication to facilitate connection would suggest that they have superior qualities for managing in the 1990s than do men." Do you agree or disagree with this statement? Support your position.

3. How might managing men and women differ in terms of attitudes, personality, perception, and learning? What suggestions would you have managers keep in mind to handle those differences?

Source: "What Are the Differences Between Men and Women?, *ABC Nightline,* July 31, 1991; and Deborah Tannen, *You Just Don't Understand: Women and Men in Conversation* (New York: Ballantine Books, 1991).

CHAPTER 15

Understanding Groups and Teamwork

LEARNING OBJECTIVES

After Reading This Chapter, You Should Be Able To:

1. Contrast formal and informal groups.
2. Explain why people join groups.
3. State how roles and norms influence an employee's behavior.
4. Describe the key components in the group behavior model.
5. Explain the increased popularity of work teams in organizations.
6. Describe the characteristics of effective teams.
7. Identify how managers can build trust.
8. Describe the role of teams in TQM.

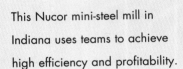

This Nucor mini-steel mill in Indiana uses teams to achieve high efficiency and profitability.

W̲e hear a lot about people being turned off by their jobs. Friends tell us that their work is boring or their boss treats them like an idiot. We see interviews on television with auto and steel workers grumbling about pressures by management to increase productivity while, at the same time, pushing employees to take wage cuts. The good news is that managers in a number of organizations are learning that there are ways to cut costs, improve productivity, and *increase* employee commitment. Take, for instance, the management at Nucor Corp.[1]

Nucor decided to build a mini-mill in Indiana to make sheet steel. They processed 3000 job applicants and eventually hired 400 in 1988. The first hundred people hired actually built the mill with their own hands, alongside the contractors. This gave the new employees a degree of involvement and commitment to their new employer that is often missing in many jobs. Once the mill was up, workers were placed into five- to ten-person teams. Team members were trained to do most jobs on their teams. This expanded management's flexibility and increased skill variety for team members. While each team has a supervisor, these supervisors are more like co-workers than bosses. Supervisors relay information from plant management, but they're essentially members of their respective teams.

The team format at Nucor has proved beneficial for both management and workers. The plant is highly efficient and profitable. The use of teams fosters a sense of family among employees. Teams let employees feel that they're part of the company and that what they do directly contributes to the company's success. Additionally, Nucor workers enjoy lucrative bonuses based on their group's performance. Members of one group, for instance, recently earned annual wages of $50,000 to $59,000 each.

Nucor's team-based organiza-

tion isn't unique. Thousands of organizations have recently made the move to restructure work around groups rather than individuals. Why has this occurred? What do these teams look like? How can interested managers build effective teams? We'll answer these questions in this chapter. First, however, let's begin by developing our understanding of group behavior.

Understanding Group Behavior

The behavior of individuals in groups is not the same as the sum total of each individual's behavior. This is because individuals act differently in groups than they do when they are alone. Therefore, if we want to understand organizational behavior more fully, we need to study groups.

What is a Group?

group

Two or more interacting and interdependent individuals who come together to achieve particular objectives.

A **group** is defined as two or more interacting and interdependent individuals who come together to achieve particular objectives. Groups can be either formal or informal. *Formal groups* are work groups established by the organization and have designated work assignments and established tasks. In formal groups, the behaviors in which one should engage are stipulated by and directed toward organizational goals. Table 15–1 provides some examples of different types of formal groups used in organizations today.

In contrast, *informal* groups are of a social nature. These groups are natural formations that appear in the work environment in response to the need for social contact. Informal groups tend to form around friendships and common interests.

TABLE 15–1   Examples of Formal Groups

Command groups. These are the basic, traditional work groups determined by formal authority relationships and depicted on the organizational chart. They typically include a manager and those subordinates that report directly to him or her.

Cross-functional teams. These bring together the knowledge and skills of individuals from various work areas in order to come up with solutions to operational problems. Cross-functional teams also include groups whose members have been trained to do each other's jobs.

Self-managed teams. These are essentially independent groups that, in addition to doing their operating jobs, take on traditional management responsibilities such as hiring, planning and scheduling, and performance evaluations.

Task forces. These are temporary groups created to accomplish a specific task. Once the task is complete, the group is disbanded.

Why People Join Groups

There is no single reason why individuals join groups. Because most people belong to a number of groups, it's obvious that different groups provide different benefits to their members. Most people join a group out of needs for security, status, self-esteem, affiliation, power, or goal achievement.

Security "There's strength in numbers." By joining a group we can reduce the insecurity of "standing alone"—we feel stronger, have fewer self-doubts, and are more resistant to threats. New employees are particularly vulnerable to a sense of isolation; they turn to the group for guidance and support. However, whether we are talking about new employees or those with years on the job, we can state that few individuals like to stand alone. Human beings get reassurances from interacting with others and being part of a group. This often explains the appeal of unions. If management creates a climate in which employees feel insecure, they are likely to turn to unionization to reduce their feelings of insecurity.

Status "I'm a member of our company's running team. Last month, at the National Corporate Relays, we won the national championship. Didn't you see our picture in the company newsletter?" Comments like this demonstrate the power of a group to give prestige. Inclusion in a group that others view as important provides recognition and status for its members.

Self-Esteem "Before I was asked to pledge Phi Omega Chi, I felt like a nobody. Being in a fraternity makes me feel a lot more important." This quote demonstrates that groups can increase people's feelings of self-worth. That is, in addition to conveying status to those outside the group, membership can also raise feelings of self-esteem. Our self-esteem is bolstered, for example, when we are accepted into a highly valued group. Being assigned to a task force to review and make recommen-

Employees at Amgen, a California bio-tech firm, participate on the company's bowling team. This group helps meet members' needs for affiliation. When the team wins, it also enhances member status and self-esteem.

dations for the location of the company's new corporate headquarters can fulfill one's needs for competence and growth as well as for status.

Affiliation   "I'm independently wealthy, but I wouldn't give up my job. Why? Because I really like the people I work with!" This quote, from a $35,000-a-year purchasing agent who inherited several million dollars' worth of real estate, verifies that groups can fulfill our social needs. People enjoy the regular interaction that comes with group membership. For many people, these on-the-job interactions are their primary means of fulfilling their need for affiliation. For almost all people, work groups significantly contribute to fulfilling their need for friendships and social relations.

Power   "I tried for two years to get the plant management to increase the number of female restrooms on the production floor to the same number as the men have. It was like talking to a wall. But I got about fifteen other women who were production employees together and we jointly presented our demands to management. The construction crews were in here adding female restrooms within ten days!"

One of the appealing aspects of groups is that they represent power. What often cannot be achieved individually becomes possible through group action. Of course, this power might not be sought only to make demands on others. It might be desired merely as a countermeasure. To protect themselves from unreasonable demands by management, individuals may align with others.

Informal groups additionally provide opportunities for individuals to exercise power over others. For individuals who desire to influence others, groups can offer power without a formal position of authority in the organization. As a group leader, you might be able to make requests of group members and obtain compliance without any of the responsibilities that traditionally go with formal managerial positions. For people with a high power need, groups can be a vehicle for fulfillment.

Goal Achievement   "I'm part of a three-person team studying how we can cut our company's transportation costs. Since they've been going up at over 30 percent a year for several years now, the corporate controller assigned representatives from cost accounting, shipping, and marketing to study the problem and make recommendations."

This task group was created to achieve a goal that would be considerably more difficult if pursued by a single person. There are times when it takes more than one person to accomplish a particular task; there is a need to pool talents, knowledge, or power in order to get a job completed. In such instances, management will rely on the use of a formal group.

Stages of Group Development

Group development is a dynamic process. Most groups are in a continual state of change. But even though groups probably never reach complete stability, there is a general pattern that describes how most groups evolve. There is strong evidence that groups pass through a standard sequence of five stages.[2] As shown in Figure 15–1, these five stages have been labeled *forming, storming, norming, performing,* and *adjourning.*

forming
The first stage in group development, characterized by much uncertainty.

The first stage, **forming,** is characterized by a great deal of uncertainty about the group's purpose, structure, and leadership. Members are "testing the waters" to determine what types of behavior are acceptable. This stage is complete when members have begun to think of themselves as part of a group.

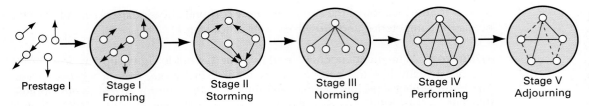

FIGURE 15–1
Stages of Group Development

storming
The second stage of group development, characterized by intragroup conflict.

norming
The third stage of group development, characterized by close relationships and cohesiveness.

performing
The fourth stage in group development, when the group is fully functional.

adjourning
The final stage in group development for temporary groups, characterized by concern with wrapping up activities rather than task performance.

The **storming** stage is one of intragroup conflict. Members accept the existence of the group, but there is resistance to the control that the group imposes on individuality. Further, there is conflict over who will control the group. When stage II is complete, there will be a relatively clear hierarchy of leadership within the group.

The third stage is one in which close relationships develop and the group demonstrates cohesiveness. There is now a strong sense of group identity and comaraderie. This **norming** stage is complete when the group structure solidifies and the group has assimilated a common set of expectations of what defines correct member behavior.

The fourth stage is **performing.** The structure at this point is fully functional and accepted. Group energy has moved from getting to know and understand each other to performing the task at hand.

For permanent work groups, performing is the last stage in their development. However, for temporary committees, task forces, teams, and similar groups that have a limited task to perform, there is an **adjourning** stage. In this stage the group prepares for its disbandment. High levels of task performance are no longer the group's top priority. Instead, attention is directed toward wrapping-up activities. Responses of group members vary in this stage. Some are upbeat, basking in the group's accomplishments. Others may be depressed over the loss of comaraderie and friendships gained during the work group's life.

Most of you have probably encountered each of these stages in a group project for a class. Group members are selected and then meet for the first time. There is a "feeling out" period to assess what the group is going to do and how it is going to do it. This is usually rapidly followed by the battle for control: Who is going to lead us? Once this is resolved and a hierarchy is agreed upon, the group identifies specific aspects of the task, who is going to do them, and dates by which the parts need to be completed. General expectations become set and agreed upon for each member. This forms the foundation for what you hope will be a coordinated group effort culminating in a job well done. Once the group project is complete and turned in, the group breaks up. Of course, groups occasionally don't get much beyond the first or second stage, which typically results in disappointing projects and grades.

Should one assume from the foregoing that a group becomes more effective as it progresses through the first four stages? Some argue that effectiveness of work units increases at advanced stages, but it is not that simple.[3] While this assumption may be generally true, what makes a group effective is a complex issue. Under some conditions, high levels of conflict are conducive to high levels of group performance. We might expect to find situations in which groups in stage II outperform those in stages III or IV. Similarly, groups do not always proceed clearly from one stage to the next. Sometimes, in fact, several stages are going on simultaneously, as when groups are storming and performing at the same time. Groups even occasionally regress to previous stages. Therefore one should not always assume that all groups precisely follow this developmental process or that stage IV is always the most preferable. It is better to think of this model as a general framework. It reminds you that groups are

The students at Brooklyn College behave differently in class on Monday morning than they do when they're partying on Saturday night. They understand that role expectations in college classrooms differ from those in a night club.

role

A set of behavior patterns expected of someone occupying a given position in a social unit.

norms

Acceptable standards shared by a group's members.

dynamic entities and can help you better understand the problems and issues that are most likely to surface during a group's life.

Basic Group Concepts

In this section we introduce the foundation concepts upon which an understanding of group behavior can be built. These are *roles, norms* and *conformity, status systems,* and *group cohesiveness.*

Roles   We introduced the concept of roles in Chapter 1 when we discussed what managers do. Of course, managers are not the only individuals in an organization who have roles. The concept of roles applies to all employees in organizations and to their life outside the organization as well.

A **role** refers to a set of expected behavior patterns attributed to someone who occupies a given position in a social unit. Individuals play multiple roles, adjusting their roles to the group to which they belong at the time. In an organization, employees attempt to determine what behaviors are expected of them. They'll read their job descriptions, get suggestions from their boss, and watch what their co-workers do. An individual who is confronted by divergent role expectations experiences *role conflict*. Employees in organizations often face such role conflicts. The credit manager expects her credit analysts to process a minimum of thirty applications a week, but the work group pressures members to restrict output to twenty applications a week so that everyone has work to do and no one gets laid off. A young college instructor's colleagues want him to give out very few high grades in order to maintain the department's "tough standards" reputation, whereas students want him to give out lots of high grades to enhance their grade point averages. To the degree that the instructor sincerely seeks to satisfy the expectations of both his colleagues and his students, he faces role conflict.

Norms and Conformity   All groups have established **norms,** or acceptable standards that are shared by the group's members. Norms dictate things like output levels, absenteeism rates, promptness or tardiness, and the amount of socializing allowed on the job.

Norms, for example, dictate the "arrival ritual" among scheduling clerks at one National Steel plant. The workday begins at 8:00 a.m. Most employees typically arrive a few minutes before; put their jackets, purse, lunch bag, or similar personal evidence on their chairs or desks to prove they're "at work"; then proceed down to the company cafeteria to get coffee and chat. Employees who violate this norm by starting work sharply at eight are teased and pressured until their behavior conforms to the group's standard.

Although each group will have its own unique set of norms, there are common classes of norms that appear in most organizations. These focus on effort and performance, dress, and loyalty.

Probably the most widespread norms relate to levels of effort and performance. Work groups typically provide their members with very explicit cues on how hard to work, what level of output to have, when to look busy, when it's acceptable to goof off, and the like. These norms are extremely powerful in affecting an individual employee's performance. They are so powerful that performance predictions that are based solely on an employee's ability and level of personal motivation often prove to be wrong.

Some organizations have formal dress codes. However, even in their absence, norms frequently develop to dictate the kind of clothing that should be worn to work. College seniors, interviewing for their first postgraduate job, pick up this norm quickly. Every spring on college campuses throughout the country, those interviewing for jobs can usually be spotted—they're the ones walking around in the dark gray or blue pinstriped suits. They are enacting the dress norms they have learned are expected in professional positions. Of course, what connotes acceptable dress in one organization may be very different from another.

Few managers appreciate employees who disparage the organization. Similarly, professional employees and those in the executive ranks recognize that most employers view those who actively look for another job unfavorably. If such people are unhappy, they know to keep their job searches secret. These examples demonstrate that loyalty norms are widespread in organizations. This concern for demonstrating loyalty, by the way, often explains why ambitious aspirants to top management positions in an organization willingly take work home at night, come in on weekends, and accept transfers to cities where they would otherwise not prefer to live.

Because individuals desire acceptance by the groups to which they belong, they are susceptible to conformity pressures. The impact that group pressures for conformity can have on an individual member's judgment and attitudes was demonstrated in the now-classic studies by Solomon Asch.[4] Asch made up groups of seven or eight people who sat in a classroom and were asked to compare two cards held by the experimenter. One card had one line, the other had three lines of varying length. As shown in Figure 15–2, one of the lines on the three-line card was identical to the line on the one-line card. Also, as shown in Figure 15–2, the difference in line length was quite obvious; under ordinary conditions, subjects made less than 1 percent errors. The object was to announce aloud which of the three lines matched the single line. But what happens if all the members in the group begin to give incorrect answers? Will the pressures to conform result in the unsuspecting subject (USS) altering his or her answers to align with the others? That was what Asch wanted to know. So he arranged the group so only the USS was unaware that the experiment was "fixed." The seating was prearranged so that the USS was the last to announce his or her decision.

The experiment began with several sets of matching exercises. All the subjects gave the right answers. On the third set, however, the first subject gave an obviously wrong answer—for example, saying "C" in Figure 15–2. The next subject gave the same wrong answer, and so did the others until it got to the unsuspecting subject. He knew "B" was the same as "X," yet everyone had said "C." The decision confronting the USS was this: Do you state a perception publicly that differs from the preannounced position of the others? Or do you give an answer that you strongly believe is incorrect in order to have your response agree with the other group members?

The results obtained by Asch demonstrated that over many experiments and many trials, subjects conformed in about 35 percent of the trials; that is, the subjects gave answers that they knew were wrong but that were consistent with the replies of other group members.

What can we conclude from this study? The results suggest that there are group norms that press us toward conformity. We desire to be one of the group and avoid

FIGURE 15–2
Examples of Cards Used in the ASCH Study

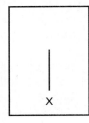
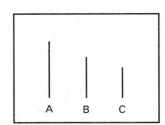

being visibly different. We can generalize further to say that when an individual's opinion of objective data differs significantly from that of others in the group, he or she feels extensive pressure to align his or her opinion to conform with those of the others.

status

A prestige grading, position, or rank within a group.

Status Systems   **Status** is a prestige grading, position, or rank within a group. As far back as scientists have been able to trace human groupings, they have found status hierarchies: tribal chiefs and their followers, nobles and peasants, the haves and the have-nots. Status systems are an important factor in understanding behavior. Status is a significant motivator and has behavioral consequences when individuals see a disparity between what they perceive their status to be and what others perceive it to be.

Status may be informally conferred by characteristics such as education, age, skill, or experience. Anything can have status value if others in the group evaluate it as such. Of course, just because status is informal does not mean that it is less important or that there is less agreement on who has it or who does not. Members of groups have no problem placing people into status categories, and they usually agree closely about who is high, low, and in the middle.

It is important for employees to believe that the organization's formal status system is congruent. That is, there should be equity between the perceived ranking of an individual and the status accoutrements he or she is given by the organization. For instance, incongruence occurs when a supervisor is earning less than his or her subordinates, a desirable office is occupied by a lower-ranking individual, or paid country club membership is provided by the company for division managers but not for vice presidents. Employees expect the things an individual has and receives to be congruent with his or her status. When they are not congruent, employees are likely to reject the authority of their superiors, the motivation potential of promotions decreases, and the general pattern of order and consistency in the organization is disturbed.

Group Size   Does the size of a group affect the group's overall behavior? The answer to this question is a definite yes, but the effect depends upon which outcomes you focus.[5]

The office of Stanley Gault, CEO of Goodyear, conveys the high status of his position.

The evidence indicates, for instance, that small groups are faster at completing tasks than are larger ones. However, if the group is engaged in problem solving, large groups consistently get better marks than their smaller counterparts. Translating these results into specific numbers is a bit more hazardous, but we can offer some parameters. Large groups—with a dozen or more members—are good for gaining diverse input. Thus if the goal of the group is finding facts, larger groups should be more effective. On the other hand, smaller groups are better at doing something productive with those facts. Groups of approximately seven members tend to be more effective for taking action.

One of the more disturbing findings related to group size is that, as groups get incrementally larger, the contribution of individual members often tends to lessen.[6] That is, while the total productivity of a group of four is generally greater than that of a group of three, the individual productivity of each group member declines as the group expands. Thus a group of four will tend to produce at a level less than four times the average individual performance. The best explanation for this reduction of effort in groups is that dispersion of responsibility encourages individuals to slack off. When the results of the group cannot be attributed to any single person, the relationship between an individual's input and the group's output is clouded. In such situations, individuals may be tempted to become "free riders" and coast on the group's efforts. In other words, there will be a reduction in efficiency where individuals think that their contributions cannot be measured. The obvious conclusion from this finding is that when managers use work teams they should also provide means by which individual efforts can be identified.

ETHICAL DILEMMAS IN MANAGEMENT

Should Managers Agree With Their Boss When They Don't?

Asch's studies looked at how group norms press individuals toward conformity. This suggests an ethical dilemma that many managers face: Whether it is ethical to outwardly agree with their boss when, in actuality, they think he or she is wrong.

Are managers who disagree with their boss acting unethically by claiming to agree? Are they compromising personal standards of integrity? Would it be unethical merely to suppress their disagreement? Open agreement may be the politically astute thing to do, but does it display a lack of moral character?

The norms of conformity can be very strong in an organization. Individuals who openly challenge long-condoned but questionable practices may be labeled as disloyal or lacking in commitment. Another perspective is that conformance with group and organizational norms acts to bond people together. Conformity facilitates cooperation and cohesiveness. It also contributes toward standardizing behavior. These are qualities that can enhance organizational effectiveness. Still another argument might be that suppression of dissent and the appearance of conformity doesn't improve organizational effectiveness; it merely plants the seeds for later hostilities and conflicts.

What should a manager do when he or she disagrees with the boss? What can organizations do to avoid encouraging individuals from unethically conforming while, at the same time, maintaining cohesiveness and commitment?

group cohesiveness
The degree to which members are attracted to one another and share the group's goals.

Group Cohesiveness   Intuitively, it makes sense that groups in which there is a lot of internal disagreement and lack of cooperation are less effective in completing their tasks than groups in which individuals generally agree, cooperate, and like each other. Research on this position has focused on **group cohesiveness,** or the degree to which members are attracted to one another and share the group's goals. The more the members are attracted to one another and the more the group's goals align with their individual goals, the greater the group's cohesiveness.

Research has generally shown that highly cohesive groups are more effective than those with less cohesiveness,[7] but the relationship between cohesiveness and effectiveness is more complex. A key moderating variable is the degree to which the group's attitude aligns with its formal goals or those of the larger organization of which it is a part.[8] The more cohesive a group is, the more its members will follow its goals. If these goals are favorable (for instance, high output, quality work, cooperation with individuals outside the group), a cohesive group is more productive than a less cohesive group. But if cohesiveness is high and attitudes are unfavorable, productivity decreases. If cohesiveness is low and goals are supported, productivity increases but not as much as when both cohesiveness and support are high. When cohesiveness is low and goals are not supported, cohesiveness has no significant effect upon productivity. These conclusions are summarized in Figure 15–3.

Toward Understanding Work Group Behavior

Why are some groups more successful than others? The answer to that question is complex, but it includes variables such as the abilities of the group's members, the size of the group, the level of conflict, and the internal pressures on members to conform to the group's norms. Figure 15–4 presents the major components that determine group performance and satisfaction.[9] It can help you to sort out the key variables and their interrelationships.

External Conditions Imposed on the Group   To begin understanding the behavior of a formal work group, we need to view it as a subsystem embedded in a larger system.[10] When we realize that formal groups are subsets of a larger organization system, we can extract part of the explanation of the group's behavior from an explanation of the organization to which it belongs. For instance, a design team in General Dynamics' Convair Division in San Diego must live within the rules and policies dictated from the division's headquarters and GD's corporate offices in St. Louis. Every work group is influenced by external conditions imposed from outside it.

What are some of these external conditions? They include the organization's

FIGURE 15–3
The Relationship Between Cohesiveness and Productivity

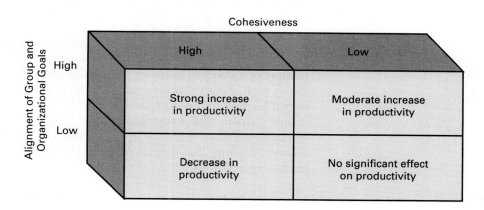

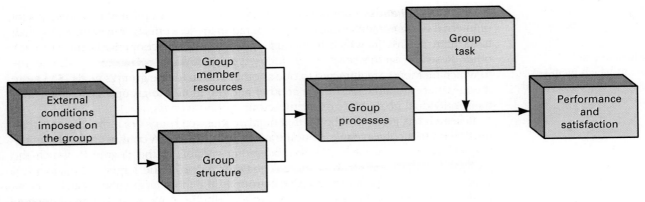

FIGURE 15-4
Group Behavior Model

overall strategy, authority structures, formal regulations, the abundance or absence of organizationwide resources, personnel selection criteria, the organization's performance evaluation and reward system, the organization's culture, and the general physical layout of the group's work space set by the organization's industrial engineers and office designers.

Group Member Resources A group's potential level of performance depends to a large extent on the resources that its members individually bring to the group. This would include member abilities and personality characteristics.

Part of a group's performance can be predicted by assessing the task-relevant and intellectual abilities of its individual members. We do occasionally read about an athletic team composed of mediocre players who, because of excellent coaching, determination, and precision teamwork, beat a far more talented group of players. Such cases make the news precisely because they are aberrations. Group performance is not merely the summation of its individual members' abilities. However, these abilities set parameters for what members can do and how effectively they will perform in a group.

There has been a great deal of research on the relationship between personality traits and group attitudes and behavior. The general conclusion is that attributes that tend to have a positive connotation in our culture tend to be positively related to group productivity and morale. These include traits such as sociability, self-reliance, and independence. In contrast, negatively evaluated characteristics such as authoritarianism, dominance, and unconventionality tend to be negatively related to productivity and morale.[11] These personality traits affect group performance by strongly influencing how the individual will interact with other group members.

Group Structure Work groups are not unorganized mobs. They have a structure that shapes members' behavior and makes it possible to explain and predict a larger portion of individual behavior within the group as well as the performance of the group itself. These structural variables include roles, norms, status, group size, and formal leadership. Because we have already discussed roles, norms, status, and size in this chapter, and leadership will be covered in Chapter 17, we don't need to elaborate on these variables here. Just keep in mind that every work group has an internal structure that defines member roles, norms, status, group size, and formal leadership positions.

Group Processes   The next component in our group behavior model concerns the processes that go on within a work group—the communication patterns used by members to exchange information, group decision processes, leader behavior, power dynamics, conflict interactions, and the like.

Why are processes important to understanding work group behavior? Because in groups, one and one do not necessarily add up to two. Every group begins with a potential defined by the group's constraints, resources, and structure. Then you need to add in process gains and losses created within the group itself. Four people on a research team, for instance, may be able to generate far more ideas as a group than the members could produce individually. This positive synergy results in a process gain. You also have to subtract out process losses. High levels of conflict, for example, may hinder group effectiveness.

To determine a group's *actual* effectiveness, you need to *add* in process gains and *subtract* out process losses from the group's *potential* effectiveness.

Group Tasks   The final box in our model points out that the impact of group processes on the group's performance and member satisfaction depends on the task that the group is doing. More specifically, the *complexity* and *interdependence* of tasks influence the group's effectiveness.[12]

Tasks can be generalized as being either simple or complex. Simple tasks are routine and standardized. Complex tasks are ones that tend to be novel or non-routine. We would hypothesize that the more complex the task, the more the group will benefit from discussion among members about alternative work methods. If the task is simple, group members don't need to discuss such alternatives. They can rely on standardized operating procedures. Similarly, if there is a high degree of interdependence among the tasks that group members must perform, they'll need to interact more. Effective communication and controlled levels of conflict should therefore be more relevant to group performance when tasks are interdependent.

Turning Groups Into Effective Teams

work teams

Formal groups made up of interdependent individuals, responsible for the attainment of a goal.

A recent survey of 476 large U.S. corporations found that 7 percent of their employees were organized into teams.[13] If we can generalize from this sample to the overall population, somewhere between 8 and 9 million people are currently doing their jobs as part of a team. This same study also found that half the companies surveyed planned to rely significantly more on work teams in the coming years.

What are **work teams?** They're formal groups, made up of interdependent individuals, responsible for the attainment of a goal.[14] Thus all work teams are groups, but only formal groups can be work teams.

In this section, we'll discuss why organizations are increasingly designing work around teams rather than individuals, and consider the various characteristics that are associated with effective work teams.

Why Use Teams?

There's no *single* explanation for the recent increased popularity of teams. We propose that there are a number of reasons.

Creates Esprit de Corps   Team members expect and demand a lot from each other. In so doing, they facilitate cooperation and improve employee morale. So we

G. Glenn Gardner at Chrysler Corporation

G. Glenn Gardner, Chrysler Corp.'s senior product-development engineer, is a thirty-three-year veteran of the company.[15] He spent most of those years developing cars in Detroit's traditional, sequential way. First design draws it, then engineering makes it work, then manufacturing figures out how to build it, then service looks for some way to fix it. And every time the job is handed to the next department, the new people discover something they don't like and make changes. But in 1985, Chrysler sent Gardner to Illinois as chairman of Diamond–Star Motors, a joint venture between Chrysler and Mitsubishi Motors Corp. There he saw the Japanese system of team development and became an immediate convert.

When Gardner took over the development of Chrysler's "LH" line of midsized cars in 1989, he instituted the Japanese system. He became the team leader and put together a team that included people from every different department and discipline: body engineering, interior design, purchasing, manufacturing, marketing, finance, and the like. All team members reported to him, no matter what department they came from.

Gardner attributes much of the LH program's success to the team development process. The first LH prototypes were ready ninety-five weeks before the scheduled launch date. This was some thirty weeks faster than it typically took at Chrysler and allowed for more testing to catch flaws. In addition, Gardner's team did their work with nearly half as many people as Chrysler usually needed to bring new models to market. Finally, the cost savings and streamlined decision-making brought about by using cross-functional teams allowed Chrysler to give the LH cars features that otherwise would have been rejected as too costly. The result? Early evidence indicates that the LH line of Intrepid-Vision-Concorde cars are a hit with both critics and consumers.

find that team norms tend to encourage members to excel and, at the same time, create a climate that increases job satisfaction.

Allows Management to Think Strategically   The use of teams, especially self-managed ones, frees up managers to do more strategic planning. When jobs are designed around individuals, managers often spend an inordinate amount of their time supervising their people and "putting out fires." They're too busy to do much strategic thinking. Implementing work teams allows managers to redirect their energy toward bigger issues such as long-term plans.

Speeds Decisions   Moving decision-making vertically down to teams allows the organization greater flexibility for faster decisions. Team members frequently know more about work-related problems than do managers. Moreover, team members are closer to those problems. As a result, decisions are often made more quickly when teams exist than when jobs are designed around individuals.

Facilitates Work Force Diversity   Two heads are frequently better than one. Groups made up of individuals from different backgrounds and with different experiences often see things that homogeneous groups don't. Therefore, the use of diverse teams may result in more innovative ideas and better decisions than might arise if individuals alone made the decisions.

Increases Performance   Finally, all the above factors can combine to make team performance higher than might be achieved by the same individuals working alone. Organizations as varied as Federal Express, Chrysler Corporation, U.S. Steel, and the Naval Aviation Depot Operations Center have found that teams eliminate waste, slash bureaucratic overhead, stimulate ideas for improvements, and generate more output-per-worker-hour than more traditional, individual-focused work designs.[16]

Characteristics of Effective Teams

Teams are not automatic productivity enhancers. They can also be disappointments for management. Fortunately, recent research provides insight into the primary characteristics related to effective teams.[17] Let's take a look at these characteristics as summarized in Figure 15–5.

Clear Goals   High performance teams have both a clear understanding of the goal to be achieved and a belief that the goal embodies a worthwhile or important result. Moreover, the importance of these goals encourages individuals to sublimate personal concerns to these team goals. In effective teams, members are committed to the team's goals, know what they are expected to accomplish, and understand how they will work together to achieve these goals.

Relevant Skills   Effective teams are composed of competent individuals. They have the necessary technical skills and abilities to achieve the desired goals and the

Companies such as L-S Electro-Galvanizing in Cleveland are getting on the self-managing-team bandwagon. These rank-and-file, unionized, L-SE team members switch shifts without telling their boss. They keep track of their own overtime. They do the scheduling of their work. They also do the hiring for their team.

FIGURE 15–5
Characteristics of Effective Teams

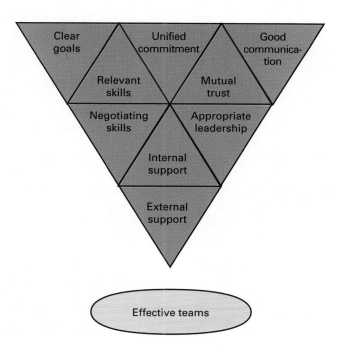

Factory workers at Saturn Corp. are organized into teams of about ten members, who share decisions on everything from hiring co-workers to buying equipment for the plant.

personal characteristics required to achieve excellence while working well with others. This second point is important and often overlooked. Not everyone who is technically competent has the skills to work well as a team member. High-performing teams have members who possess both technical and interpersonal skills.

Mutual Trust Effective teams are characterized by high mutual trust among members. That is, members believe in the integrity, character, and ability of one another. But as you probably know from personal relationships, trust is fragile. It takes a long time to build and can be easily destroyed. Also, because trust begets trust and distrust begets distrust, maintaining trust requires careful attention by management.

The climate of trust within a group tends to be strongly influenced by the organization's culture and the actions of management. Organizations that value openness, honesty, and collaborative processes and that additionally encourage employee involvement and autonomy are likely to create trusting cultures. Table 15–2 lists six recommended actions that can help managers build and maintain trust.

Unified Commitment Members of an effective team exhibit intense loyalty and dedication to the team. They're willing to do anything that has to be done to help their team succeed. We call this loyalty and dedication *unified commitment*.

Studies of successful teams have found that members identify with their teams.[18] Members redefine themselves to include membership in the team as an important aspect of the self. Unified commitment, then, is characterized by dedication to the team's goals and a willingness to expend extraordinary amounts of energy to achieve it.

Good Communication Not surprisingly, effective teams are characterized by good communication. Members are able to convey messages between each other in a form that is readily and clearly understood. This includes nonverbal as well as spoken messages. Good communication is also characterized by a healthy dose of feedback from team members and management. This helps to guide team members and to correct misunderstandings. Like a couple who have been together for many years, members on high-performing teams are able to quickly and efficiently share ideas and feelings.

TABLE 15–2 Six Suggestions for Helping Managers Build Trust

1. *Communicate.* Keep team members and subordinates informed by explaining decisions and policies and providing accurate feedback. Be candid about your own problems and limitations.

2. *Be supportive.* Be available and approachable. Encourage and support team members' ideas.

3. *Be respectful.* Delegate real authority to team members and listen to their ideas.

4. *Be fair.* Give credit where it's due, be objective and impartial in performance evaluations, and be generous with your praise.

5. *Be predictable.* Be consistent in your daily affairs. Make good on your explicit and implied promises.

6. *Demonstrate competence.* Develop the admiration and respect of team members by demonstrating technical and professional ability and good business sense.

Source: Adapted from Fernando Bartolomé, "Nobody Trusts the Boss Completely—Now What?" *Harvard Business Review,* March–April 1989, pp. 135–42.

Negotiating Skills When jobs are designed around individuals, job descriptions, rules and procedures, and other types of formalized documentation clarify employee roles. Effective teams, on the other hand, tend to be flexible and continually making adjustments. This requires team members to possess adequate negotiating skills. Problems and relationships are regularly changing in teams, requiring members to confront and reconcile differences.

Appropriate Leadership Effective leaders can motivate a team to follow them through the most difficult situations. How? They help clarify goals. They demonstrate that change is possible by overcoming inertia. And they increase the self-confidence of team members, helping members to realize their potential more fully.

Importantly, the best leaders are not necessarily directive or controlling. Increas-

MANAGING FROM A GLOBAL PERSPECTIVE

Organizing Work Around Teams: A Global Analysis

The popularity of teams is influenced by cultural factors. The fact that the Japanese and Israelis were organizing around teams decades before their American and Canadian counterparts can be largely explained in cultural teams: Japanese and Israelis are oriented more toward collectivism than are North Americans. Of course, this doesn't mean you can't introduce groups into highly individualistic societies. But it does suggest that acceptance may be longer in coming and managers will need to provide adequate training, encouragement, and rewards to overcome potential resistance.

Suzuki's efforts at introducing teams into its new plant in Hungary provide an excellent illustration of challenges related to national culture.[19] In 1990, Suzuki made the decision to build an automobile plant on the site of a former Soviet military testing area in northern Hungary. The plant, which opened in 1992, began with the modest objective of producing 16,000 subcompact cars in its first year. However, Suzuki's management has set a far more ambitious goal of 50,000 cars a year by 1994, with the expectation that Hungarian workers will have adjusted to Suzuki's very non-Hungarian way of doing things by then. Remember, these Hungarian workers developed their skills and attitudes under the Communist system. They are used to hierarchically dominated organizations. Bosses make decisions and employees follow orders.

Suzuki is determined to bring the Japanese industrial culture to its Hungarian operation. Every Hungarian worker has been flown to the company's headquarters in Hamamatsu for instruction in the ways of Japan's industrial success. "Team spirit was the phrase I heard in every second sentence," says Tibor Ivanov, a production engineer. "That was the thing they most wanted to impress on us: everybody together for the good of the company. But I am afraid such dedication is generally foreign to us."

It'll take some time to see if the Japanese team concept can be exported to Hungary. But as with most Japanese firms that operate in foreign countries, Suzuki is strongly committed to bringing Japanese-style management to Hungary rather than adjusting its practices to the Hungarian culture.

ingly, effective team leaders are taking the role of coach and facilitator. They help guide and support the team, but they don't control it. This obviously applies to self-managed teams but also increasingly applies to task forces and cross-functional teams in which the members themselves are empowered. For some traditional managers, changing their role from boss to facilitator—from giving orders to working *for* the team—is a difficult transition. While most managers relish the new-found shared authority or come to understand its advantages through leadership training, some hard-nosed dictatorial managers are just ill-suited to the team concept and must be transferred or replaced.

Internal and External Support The final condition necessary to making an effective team is a supportive climate. Internally, the team should be provided with a sound infrastructure. This includes proper training, an understandable measurement system with which team members can evaluate their overall performance, an incentive program that recognizes and rewards team activities, and a supportive human-resource system. The right infrastructure should support members and reinforce behaviors that lead to high levels of performance. Externally, management should provide the team with the resources needed to get the job done.

Teams and TQM

One of the central characteristics of total quality management is the use of teams. But why teams?

The essence of TQM is process improvement, and employee participation is the linchpin of process improvement. In other words, TQM requires management to give employees the encouragement to share ideas and act on what they suggest. Problem-solving teams provide the natural vehicle for employees to share ideas and to implement improvements. As stated by Gil Mosard, a TQM specialist at McDonnell Douglas: "When your measurement system tells you your process is out of control, you need teamwork for structured problem-solving. Not everyone needs to know how to do all kinds of fancy control charts for performance tracking, but everybody does need to know where their process stands so they can judge if it is improving.[20]

Employee involvement and teamwork are key ingredients in Motorola's dramatic success at improving quality through process improvement.

Examples from Ford Motor Co. and Amana Refrigeration, Inc. illustrate how teams are being used in TQM programs.[21]

Ford began its TQM efforts in the early 1980s with teams as the primary organizing mechanism. "Because this business is so complex, you can't make an impact on it without using a team approach," noted one Ford manager. In designing their quality problem-solving teams, Ford's management identified five goals. The teams should (1) be small enough to be efficient and effective; (2) be properly trained in the skills their members will need; (3) be allocated enough time to work on the problems they plan to address; (4) be given the authority to resolve the problems and implement corrective action; and (5) each have a designated "champion" whose job it is to help the team get around roadblocks that arise.

At Amana, task forces made up of people from different levels within the company are used to deal with quality problems that cut across various functional areas. The various task forces each have a unique area of problem-solving responsibility. For instance, one handles in-plant products, another deals with items that arise outside the production facility, and still another focuses its attention specifically on supplier problems. Amana claims the use of these task forces has improved vertical and horizontal communication within the company and substantially reduced both the number of units that don't meet company specifications and the number of service problems in the field.

quality circles
Work groups that meet regularly to discuss, investigate, and correct quality problems.

Another team application to TQM is **quality circles.** These are work groups of eight to ten employees and supervisors who share an area of responsibility. They meet regularly (typically once a week on company time and on company premises) to discuss their quality problems, investigate causes of the problems, recommend solutions, and take corrective actions. They assume responsibility for solving quality problems, and they generate and evaluate their own feedback. However, management usually makes the final decision about the implementation of recommended solutions. Figure 15–6 describes a typical quality circle process.

FIGURE 15–6
How a Typical Quality Circle Operates

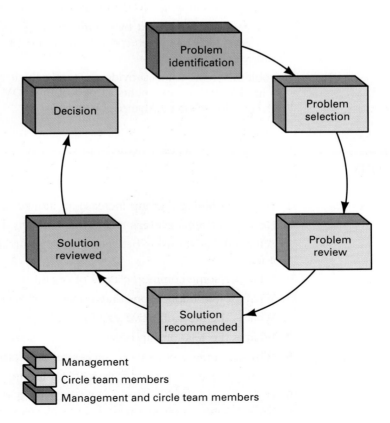

Summary

This summary is organized by the chapter-opening learning objectives found on page 439.

1. *Formal* groups are defined by the organization's structure, with designated work assignments establishing tasks. *Informal* groups are social alliances that are neither structured nor organizationally determined.

2. People join groups because of their needs for security, status, self-esteem, affiliation, power, or achievement.

3. A role refers to a set of behavior patterns expected of someone occupying a given position in a social unit. At any given time, employees adjust their role behaviors to the group of which they are a part. Norms are standards shared by group members. They informally convey to employees which behaviors are acceptable and which are unacceptable.

4. There are five variables in the group behavior model that, in aggregate, explain the group's performance and satisfaction. First, a group is influenced by the larger organization of which it is a part. Second, a group's potential level of performance depends to a large extent on the resources that its members individually bring to the group. Third, there is a group structure that shapes the behavior of members. Fourth, there are internal processes within the group that aid or hinder interaction and the ability of the group to perform. Finally, the impact of group processes on the group's performance and member satisfaction depends on the task that the group is doing.

5. Teams have become increasingly popular in organizations because they build esprit de corps, free up management to think more strategically, permit faster decision making, facilitate work force diversity, and usually increase performance.

6. Effective work teams are characterized by clear goals, members with relevant skills, mutual trust among members, unified commitment, good communication, adequate negotiating skills, and appropriate leadership.

7. Managers can build trust by communicating openly; providing support to team members' ideas; being respectful, fair, and predictable; and by demonstrating competence.

8. Problem-solving teams provide a natural vehicle for employees to share ideas and to implement improvements as part of the TQM process. Teams are particularly effective for resolving complex problems.

Review Questions

1. How can joining a group increase an individual's sense of power?

2. How might organizations create role conflicts for an employee?

3. What is the relationship between a work group and the organization of which it is a part?

4. What are some common classes of organizational norms?

5. What are the implications drawn from Asch's conformity studies?

6. What is the most effective size for a group?

7. What is the relationship between *group cohesiveness* and *effectiveness?*

8. Why are some groups more successful than others?

9. How can managers build trust within a group?

10. How do you explain the rapidly increasing popularity of work teams in the United States when American culture places such high value on individualism?

Discussion Questions

1. Identify five roles you play. What behaviors do they require? Are any of these roles in conflict? If so, in what way? How do you resolve these conflicts?

2. What do you think the behavioral consequences of status incongruence might be?

3. How do you think scientific management theorists would react to the increased reliance on teams in organizations? How about the behavioral science theorists?

4. When might individuals, acting independently, outperform teams in an organization?

5. In North America, historically we have built organizations around individuals. What would happen if we used teams as the basic building block for an organization? What if we *selected* teams rather than individuals, *trained* teams rather than individuals, *paid* teams rather than individuals, *promoted* teams rather than individuals, *fired* teams rather than individuals, and so forth?

SELF-ASSESSMENT EXERCISE

How Trustworthy Are You?

Answer these eight questions using the following scale:

Strongly Disagree									Strongly Agree
1	2	3	4	5	6	7	8	9	10

1. People can expect me to play fair.   _____

2. People can confide in me and know that I will listen.   _____

3. People can expect me to tell the truth.   _____

4. People know that I would never intentionally misrepresent their points of view to others.   _____

5. People can confide in me and know that I will not discuss it with others.   _____

6. People know that if I promised to do them a favor, I would carry out that promise.   _____

7. If I had an appointment with someone, he or she could count on me showing up.   _____

8. If I borrowed money from someone, he or she could count on getting it back as soon as possible.   _____

Total score = _____

Turn to page SK-5 for scoring directions and key.

Source: Based on Cynthia Johnson-George and Walter C. Swap, "Measurement of Specific Interpersonal Trust: Construction and Validation of a Scale to Assess Trust in a Specific Other," *Journal of Personality and Social Psychology,* December 1982, pp. 1306–17.

THE ANN ARBOR NEWS HERALD

To: Dana Reynolds, Director of Human Resources
From: John Savin, Editor-in-Chief
Subject: Reorganization of Departments

It seems as if every business periodical I've picked up recently has had an article on work teams. Also, I just got back from a meeting of the Midwestern Newspaper Publishers group and found that the issue of "using teams to improve productivity" was a major topic of cocktail-party conversation. I think it's time for us to consider whether we could benefit by reorganizing our departments—the national news desk, local news, editorial, sports, business, lifestyles, commercial advertising, classified, and operations—around teams rather than individuals.

Please provide me with a two- or three-page concise summary of the advantages and disadvantages that might result from such a reorganization. You should also address whether teams make more sense in some departments than in others.

CASE APPLICATION

The San Diego Zoo

The San Diego Zoo is trying an experiment. It is introducing self-managed teams in a pilot project. If the project works, the zoo expects to completely replace its traditional departments with teams by 1995.

The zoo has been transforming its operation to reflect the modern zoo's ultimate imperative: To preserve and protect the earth's wildlife. The San Diego Zoo is leading the way in creating innovative natural environments for every species in its care. These "bioclimatic zones" are slices of nature that group flora and fauna in cageless enclosures that closely resemble their native habitats. So far, four zones have been completed: Kopje Corner, Tiger River, Sun Bear Forest, and Gorilla Tropics.

The bioclimatic zone concept is also the driving force behind a radical redesign of the zoo's human organization. The original organization structure—fifty functional departments that specialize in everything from mammal-keeping to information systems—"is neither fast enough nor flexible enough for the new setup," according to a consultant who is helping with the transition.

Each of the four zones is staffed by a permanent, self-managing team of seven to ten people who come from a cross-section of old departments. Together, they share responsibility for running the whole area. Management plans to transport the most successful parts of the team experiment to new zones as they open, until all the functional departments have vanished. In the meantime, there is considerable redundancy, because most of the functional departments are still up and running.

Questions

1. If you were on one of these zone teams, do you think it would increase or decrease your job satisfaction? Why? Do you think you'd be more productive as a team member than as part of a functional department? Explain.
2. Under what conditions would the introduction of teams possibly fail and lead to lower group performance?
3. "Here's a classic example of management responding to the latest fad. Zoos have always worked well when organized by functional departments. The kind of work they do doesn't require, nor is it likely to benefit by, the use of teams." Do you agree or disagree with this criticism? Discuss.

Based on Nancy K. Austin, "Making Teamwork Work," *Working Woman*, January 1993, p. 28.

VIDEO CASE

Self-Managed Work Teams at Rockwell Tactical Systems

One company that has enjoyed resounding success with self-managed work teams is Rockwell Tactical Systems (RTS), a division of Rockwell International. In 1988, the RTS plant outside of Atlanta that manufactured the high-tech Hellfire missile used on attack helicopters was losing money. Its parent company decided to take drastic action to turn the plant around.

General manager Paul Smith was sent to a week-long seminar on the teachings of Edward Deming and the Japanese style of management Deming inspired. Smith came back a convert. He says, "They were talking just to the kind of problems we were having, and that was improving our quality, getting the cost down." So Smith implemented some changes in the way the plant was managed. Instead of supervisors calling all the shots on the shop floor, the work force was divided into self-managing teams composed of ten to fifteen workers.

The work groups were put in charge of deciding on acceptable quality within their group. One early decision made by the teams was to use new assembly machines to reduce the number of defects in the circuit boards being produced. After the new machines were brought in, the number of circuit boards without defects climbed to close to 100 percent. Says one Rockwell employee, "If I've got an idea that will make something better, something like that, we all discuss it."

Another example of the workers' new self-management was a decision made in one of the assembly areas to close for two weeks because the group determined there were not enough orders to operate economically. The Rockwell workers are willing to take this kind of initiative because a percentage of any cost savings is passed back to them in the form of a bonus. In 1990, this "gainshare" program amounted to $1,000 per worker.

Has this "boss-less" approach worked? At this plant, employment dropped from 2,100 workers to 1,300, while missile production and profits went up.

Questions

1. Based on the group concepts you learned in this chapter, why do you think self-managed work teams are successful in general? Why do you think self-managed teams worked at the Hellfire plant?

2. Why might self-managed teams not be appropriate for all jobs? Name some specific jobs for which these teams would not be beneficial.

3. Would you prefer to work on a self-managed team? Explain.

Source: "Self-Directed Work Teams," *ABC's Business World,* March 10, 1991.

CHAPTER 16

Motivating Employees

LEARNING OBJECTIVES

After Reading This Chapter, You Should Be Able To:

1. Define the motivation process.
2. Explain the hierarchy of needs theory.
3. Differentiate Theory X from Theory Y.
4. Explain the motivational implications of the motivation-hygiene theory.
5. Identify the characteristics that high achievers seek in a job.
6. Explain how goals motivate people.
7. Differentiate reinforcement theory from goal-setting theory.
8. Describe the motivational implications of equity theory.
9. Explain the key relationships in expectancy theory.
10. Identify management practices that are likely to lead to more motivated employees.

Tina Irwin thought all her employees would prefer more leisure time over more money. She learned she was wrong.

In 1986, when Tina Irwin started Friendship Cards, she wanted to use her degree in commercial design to make and sell greeting cards. Of course, she hoped to make a decent living, too. Today, Tina's firm employs twelve people and provides her with an annual income that exceeds $100,000.

In March, 1993, Tina decided to share her firm's success with her employees. She announced that, during the upcoming months of June, July, and August, Friendship Cards would close on Fridays. All employees could therefore enjoy a three-day weekend. Of course, they would continue to be paid as if they had worked a full five-day week.

The three-day weekend had been in place about a month when one of Tina's most trusted employees confided to her that he would have preferred a pay increase instead of the extra days off. He was sure that several others felt the same way.

Tina was surprised. Most of her employees were under 30 years of age, yet they were paid an average of $35,000 a year. This was a good 20 percent more than other employers in town were paying for comparable jobs. Tina knew that if *she* were making $35,000 a year and were given the choice of more money or more free time, she would have no trouble deciding. She'd take the free time. She thought her employees would too. But Tina had an open mind. At the next staff meeting she polled all twelve employees. She asked, "What's your preference? Do you want the four-day workweek for the summer months, or would you rather have a $4,000 cash bonus? How many want to continue the four-day week?" Six hands rose. "How many would prefer the money instead?" The other six hands went up.

This incident taught Tina something about rewarding and motivating her employees. Moreover, Tina's lesson can be generalized to all students of management. Successful managers understand that what motivates them may have little or no effect on others. Effective managers who want their employees to make a maximum effort know that they should tailor their motivational practices to satisfy the needs and wants of those employees.[1]

What is Motivation?

motivation
The willingness to exert high levels of effort to reach organizational goals, conditioned by the effort's ability to satisfy some individual need.

need
An internal state that makes certain outcomes appear attractive.

Companies such as Trump's Taj Mahal and Bally's have profited handsomely by recognizing that the same employee who is quickly bored when pulling the lever on his or her drill press might pull the lever on a slot machine for hours on end without the slightest hint of boredom. Can you explain these differences in individual behavior?

To understand what motivation *is,* let us begin by pointing out what motivation *isn't.* Why? Because many people incorrectly view motivation as a personal trait—that is, some have it and others don't. In practice, this would characterize the manager who labels a certain employee as unmotivated. Our knowledge of motivation, though, tells us that this just isn't true. What we know is that motivation is the result of the interaction between the individual and the situation. Certainly, individuals differ in motivational drive, but overall motivation varies from situation to situation. As we analyze the concept of motivation, keep in mind that level of motivation varies both between individuals and within individuals at different times.

We'll define **motivation** as the willingness to exert high levels of effort to reach organizational goals, conditioned by the effort's ability to satisfy some individual need. While general motivation refers to effort toward *any* goal, here it will refer to *organizational goals* because our focus is on work-related behavior. The three key elements in our definition are effort, organizational goals, and needs.

The *effort* element is a measure of intensity. When someone is motivated, he or she tries hard. But high levels of effort are unlikely to lead to favorable job performance outcomes unless the effort is channeled in a direction that benefits the organization.[2] Therefore we must consider the quality of the effort as well as its intensity. Effort that is directed toward, and consistent with, the organization's goals is the kind of effort that we should be seeking. Finally, we will treat motivation as a need-satisfying process. This is depicted in Figure 16–1.

A **need,** in our terminology, means some internal state that makes certain outcomes appear attractive. An unsatisfied need creates tension that stimulates drives within an individual. These drives generate a search behavior to find particular goals that, if attained, will satisfy the need and reduce the tension.

We can say that motivated employees are in a state of tension. To relieve this tension, they exert effort. The greater the tension, the higher the effort level. If this effort successfully leads to the satisfaction of the need, it reduces tension. Since we are interested in work behavior, this tension-reduction effort must also be directed toward organizational goals. Therefore, inherent in our definition of motivation is the requirement that the individual's needs be compatible and consistent with the organization's goals. When this does not occur, individuals may exert high levels of effort that run counter to the interests of the organization. Incidentally, this is not so unusual. Some employees regularly spend a lot of time talking with friends at work in

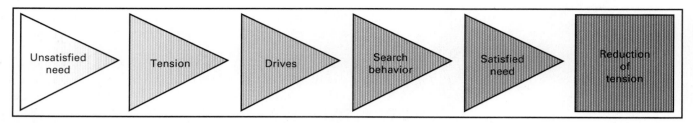

FIGURE 16–1
The Motivation Process

order to satisfy their social needs. There is a high level of effort, but it's being unproductively directed.

Early Theories of Motivation

hierarchy of needs theory
Maslow's theory that there is a hierarchy of five human needs: physiological, safety, social, esteem, and self-actualization. As each need is substantially satisfied, the next becomes dominant.

physiological needs
Basic food, drink, shelter, and sexual needs.

safety needs
A person's needs for security and protection from physical and emotional harm.

social needs
A person's needs for affection, belongingness, acceptance, and friendship.

esteem needs
Internal factors such as self-respect, autonomy, and achievement; and external factors such as status, recognition, and attention.

self-actualization needs
A person's drive to become what he or she is capable of becoming.

The 1950s were a fruitful time for the development of motivation concepts. Three specific theories were formulated during this period that, although heavily attacked and now considered questionably valid, are probably still the best-known explanations for employee motivation. These are the *hierarchy of needs theory, Theories X and Y,* and the *motivation-hygiene theory.* While more valid explanations of motivation have been developed, you should know these theories for at least two reasons: (1) They represent the foundation from which contemporary theories grew, and (2) practicing managers regularly use these theories and their terminology in explaining employee motivation.

Hierarchy of Needs Theory

The best-known theory of motivation is probably Abraham Maslow's **hierarchy of needs theory.**[3] He hypothesized that within every human being there exists a hierarchy of five needs. These are:

1. **Physiological needs:** food, drink, shelter, sexual satisfaction, and other bodily requirements
2. **Safety needs:** security and protection from physical and emotional harm
3. **Social needs:** affection, belongingness, acceptance, and friendship
4. **Esteem needs:** internal esteem factors such as self-respect, autonomy, and achievement; and external esteem factors such as status, recognition, and attention
5. **Self-actualization needs:** growth, achieving one's potential, and self-fulfillment; the drive to become what one is capable of becoming

As each need is substantially satisfied, the next need becomes dominant. In terms of Figure 16–2, the individual moves up the hierarchy. From the standpoint of motivation, the theory says that although no need is ever fully gratified, a substantially satisfied need no longer motivates. If you want to motivate someone, according to Maslow, you need to understand where that person is in the hierarchy and focus on satisfying needs at or above that level.

Maslow separated the five needs into higher and lower levels. Physiological and safety needs were described as *lower-order needs*, and social, esteem, and self-actualization were described as *higher-order needs*. The differentiation between the two orders was made on the premise that higher-order needs are satisfied internally, whereas lower-order needs are predominantly satisfied externally. In fact, the natural conclusion to be drawn from Maslow's classification is that, in times of economic plenty, almost all permanently employed workers have their lower-order needs substantially met.

Maslow's need theory has received wide recognition, particularly among practicing managers. This can be attributed to the theory's intuitive logic and ease of understanding. Unfortunately, however, research does not generally validate the theory. Maslow provided no empirical substantiation for his theory, and several studies that sought to validate it found no support.[4]

Theory X and Theory Y

As discussed in Chapter 2, Douglas McGregor proposed two distinct views of the nature of human beings: a basically negative view, labeled *Theory X,* and a basically positive view, labeled *Theory Y.*[5] After viewing the way managers dealt with employees, McGregor concluded that a manager's view of human nature is based on a group of assumptions and that the manager molds his or her behavior toward subordinates according to these assumptions.

Under **Theory X,** the four assumptions held by a manager are the following: (1) Employees inherently dislike work and, whenever possible, will attempt to avoid it; (2) because employees dislike work, they must be coerced, controlled, or threatened with punishment to achieve desired goals; (3) employees will shirk responsibilities and seek formal direction whenever possible; and (4) most workers place security above all other factors associated with work and will display little ambition.

In contrast to these negative views of human nature, McGregor listed four other assumptions, which he called **Theory Y:** (1) Employees can view work as being as natural as rest or play; (2) men and women will exercise self-direction and self-control if they are committed to the objectives; (3) the average person can learn to accept, even seek, responsibility; and (4) the ability to make good decisions is widely dispersed throughout the population and is not necessarily the sole province of managers.

What does McGregor's analysis imply about motivation? The answer is best expressed in the framework presented by Maslow. Theory X assumes that lower-order needs dominate individuals. Theory Y assumes that higher-order needs dominate individuals. McGregor himself held to the belief that the assumptions of Theory Y were more valid than those of Theory X. Therefore he proposed that participation in decision making, responsible and challenging jobs, and good group relations would maximize job motivation.

Unfortunately, there is no evidence to confirm that either set of assumptions is valid or that accepting Theory Y assumptions and altering one's actions accordingly

Theory X
The assumption that employees dislike work, are lazy, seek to avoid responsibility, and must be coerced to perform.

Theory Y
The assumption that employees are creative, seek responsibility, and can exercise self-direction.

FIGURE 16–2
Maslow's Hierarchy of Needs

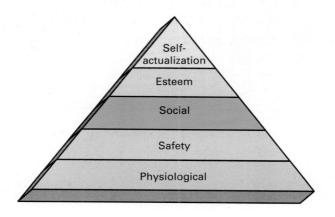

motivation-hygiene theory
The theory that intrinsic factors are related to job satisfaction, while extrinsic factors are associated with dissatisfaction.

will make one's employees more motivated. In the real world, there are examples of effective managers who make Theory X assumptions. For instance, Bob McCurry, vice-president of Toyota's U.S. marketing operations, essentially follows Theory X. He drives his staff hard and uses a "crack-the-whip" style. Yet he has been extremely successful at increasing Toyota's market share in a highly competitive environment.

Motivation-Hygiene Theory

The **motivation-hygiene theory** was proposed by psychologist Frederick Herzberg.[6] Believing that an individual's relation to his or her work is a basic one and that his or her attitude toward work can very well determine success or failure, Herzberg investigated the question, "What do people want from their jobs?" He asked people to describe in detail situations in which they felt exceptionally good or bad about their jobs. These responses were then tabulated and categorized. Figure 16–3 represents Herzberg's findings.

From analyzing the responses, Herzberg concluded that the replies people gave when they felt good about their jobs were significantly different from the replies given when they felt bad. As seen in Figure 16–3, certain characteristics were consistently related to job satisfaction (factors on the left side of the figure), and others to job dissatisfaction (the right side of the figure). Intrinsic factors such as achievement, recognition, and responsibility were related to job satisfaction. When those questioned felt good about their work, they tended to attribute these characteristics to themselves. On the other hand, when they were dissatisfied, they tended to cite extrinsic factors such as company policy and administration, supervision, interpersonal relationships, and working conditions.

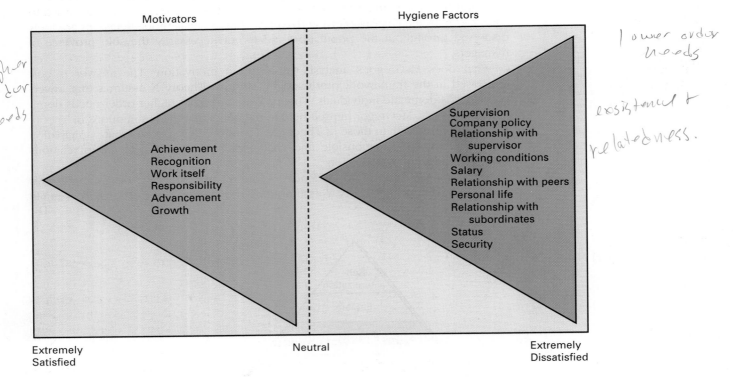

FIGURE 16–3
Herzberg's Motivation-Hygiene Theory

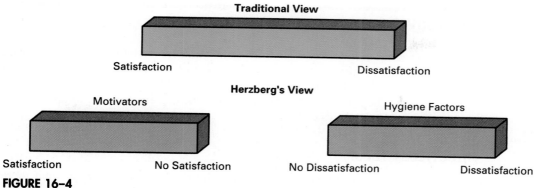

FIGURE 16–4
Contrasting Views of Satisfaction-Dissatisfaction

The data suggest, said Herzberg, that the opposite of satisfaction is not dissatisfaction, as was traditionally believed. Removing dissatisfying characteristics from a job does not necessarily make the job satisfying. As illustrated in Figure 16–4, Herzberg proposed that his findings indicate the existence of a dual continuum: The opposite of "satisfaction" is "no satisfaction," and the opposite of "dissatisfaction" is "no dissatisfaction."

According to Herzberg, the factors leading to job satisfaction are separate and distinct from those that lead to job dissatisfaction. Therefore managers who seek to eliminate factors that create job dissatisfaction can bring about peace, but not necessarily motivation. They are placating their work force rather than motivating it. Because they don't motivate employees, the factors that create job dissatisfaction were characterized by Herzberg as **hygiene factors.** When these factors are adequate, people will not be dissatisfied; however, neither will they be satisfied. To motivate people on their jobs, Herzberg suggested emphasizing **motivators,** the factors that increase job satisfaction.

The motivation-hygiene theory is not without its detractors. The criticisms of the theory include the following:

1. The procedure that Herzberg used was limited by its methodology. When things are going well, people tend to take the credit themselves. They blame failure on extrinsic factors.

2. The reliability of Herzberg's methodology was questionable. Since raters had to make interpretations, they might have contaminated the findings by interpreting one response in one manner while treating another similar response differently.

3. No overall measure of satisfaction was utilized. A person may dislike part of his or her job yet still think the job is acceptable.

4. The theory is inconsistent with previous research. The motivation-hygiene theory ignores situational variables.

5. Herzberg assumed that there is a relationship between satisfaction and productivity, but the research methodology he used looked only at satisfaction, not at productivity. To make such research relevant, one must assume a close relationship between satisfaction and productivity.[7]

Regardless of these criticisms, Herzberg's theory has been widely popularized, and few managers are unfamiliar with his recommendations. Much of the enthusiasm for job enrichment, discussed in Chapter 11, can be attributed to Herzberg's findings and recommendations.

hygiene factors
Factors that eliminate dissatisfaction.

motivators
Factors that increase job satisfaction.

Contemporary Theories of Motivation

three-needs theory
The needs for achievement, power, and affiliation are major motives in work.

need for achievement
The drive to excel, to achieve in relation to a set of standards, to strive to succeed.

need for power
The need to make others behave in a way that they would not have behaved otherwise.

need for affiliation
The desire for friendly and close interpersonal relationships.

While the previous theories are well known, they unfortunately have not held up well under close examination. However, all is not lost. A number of contemporary theories have one thing in common: each has a reasonable degree of valid supporting documentation. The following theories represent the current "state-of-the-art" explanations of employee motivation.

Three-Needs Theory

David McClelland and others have proposed the **three-needs theory**—that there are three major relevant motives or needs in work situations:

1. **Need for achievement *(nAch)*:** the drive to excel, to achieve in relation to a set of standards, to strive to succeed
2. **Need for power *(nPow)*:** the need to make others behave in a way that they would not have behaved otherwise
3. **Need for affiliation *(nAff)*:** the desire for friendly and close interpersonal relationships.[8]

Some people have a compelling drive to succeed, but they are striving for personal achievement rather than for the rewards of success per se. They have a desire to do something better or more efficiently than it has been done before. This drive is the need for achievement. From research concerning the achievement need, McClelland found that high achievers differentiate themselves from others by their desire to do things better.[9] They seek situations in which they can attain personal responsibility for finding solutions to problems, in which they can receive rapid and unambiguous feedback on their performance in order to tell whether they are improving or not, and in which they can set moderately challenging goals. (See Figure 16–5.) High achievers are not gamblers; they dislike succeeding by chance. They prefer the challenge of working at a problem and accepting the personal responsibility for success or failure, rather than leaving the outcome to chance or the actions of others. An important point is that they avoid what they perceive to be very easy or very difficult tasks.

High achievers perform best when they perceive their probability of success as being 0.5—that is, when they estimate that they have a fifty–fifty chance of success. They dislike gambling when the odds are high because they get no achievement satisfaction from happenstance success. Similarly, they dislike low odds (high probability of success) because then there is no challenge to their skills. They like to set goals that require stretching themselves a little. When there is an approximately equal chance of success or failure, there is the optimum opportunity to experience feelings of successful accomplishment and satisfaction from their efforts.

The need for power is the desire to have impact and to be influential. Individuals high in *nPow* enjoy being "in charge," strive for influence over others, and prefer to be in competitive and status-oriented situations.

The third need isolated by McClelland is affiliation, which is the desire to be liked

FIGURE 16–5
Matching Achievers and Jobs

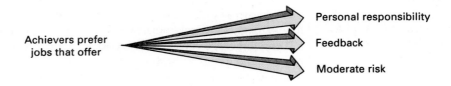

Achievers prefer jobs that offer

Personal responsibility

Feedback

Moderate risk

This is a sample of the test McClelland used to measure achievement. Individuals look at ambiguous pictures and create stories based on those pictures. McClelland and his associates then analyze the stories to assess the degree of achievement they project.

and accepted by others. This need has received the least attention by researchers. Individuals with high *nAff* strive for friendships, prefer cooperative situations rather than competitive ones, and desire relationships involving a high degree of mutual understanding.

How do you find out if someone is, for instance, a high achiever? All three motives typically are measured by a projective test in which subjects respond to a set of pictures. Each picture is briefly shown to a subject who then writes a story based on the picture.

Based on an extensive amount of research, some reasonably well-supported predictions can be made between the relationship of the achievement need and job performance. Though less research has been done on power and affiliation needs, there are consistent findings here too. First, individuals with a high need to achieve prefer job situations with personal responsibility, feedback, and an intermediate degree of risk. When these characteristics are prevalent, high achievers are strongly motivated. The evidence consistently demonstrates, for instance, that high achievers are successful in entrepreneurial activities like running their own business, managing a self-contained unit within a large organization, and many sales positions.[10] Second, a high need to achieve does not necessarily lead to being a good manager, especially in large organizations. A high *nAch* salesperson at Pfizer does not necessarily make a good sales manager, and good managers in large organizations like Exxon, AT&T, or Sears do not necessarily have a high need to achieve.[11] Third, the needs for affiliation and power are closely related to managerial success.[12] The best managers are high in the need for power and low in the need for affiliation. Last, employees can be trained successfully to stimulate their achievement need.[13] If a job calls for a high achiever, management can select a person with a high *nAch* or develop its own candidate through achievement training.

Goal-Setting Theory

In Chapter 7, in our discussion of MBO, we found substantial support for the thesis that specific goals increase performance and that difficult goals, when accepted, result in higher performance than do easy goals. This thesis has been labeled **goal-setting theory.** It's not necessary to review the evidence again, but the results are important, so let's summarize what we know about goals as motivators.

Intention to work toward a goal is a major source of job motivation. Studies on goal setting have demonstrated the superiority of specific and challenging goals as motivating forces.[14] While we can't state that having employees participate in the

goal-setting theory
Specific goals increase performance and difficult goals, when accepted, result in higher performance than easy goals.

goal-setting process is always desirable, participation is probably preferable to assigning goals when you expect resistance to accepting more difficult challenges.

The highly astute reader may have noted what appears to be a contradiction between the research findings on achievement motivation and goal setting. Is it a contradiction that achievement motivation is stimulated by moderately challenging goals, whereas goal-setting theory says that motivation is maximized by difficult goals? The answer is no. The explanation is twofold.[15] First, goal-setting theory deals with people in general. The conclusions on achievement motivation are based only on people who have a high *nAch*. Given the probability that not more than 10 to 20 percent of North Americans are naturally high achievers, difficult goals are still recommended for the majority of workers. Second, the conclusions of goal-setting theory apply to those who accept and are committed to the goals. Difficult goals will lead to higher performance only if they are accepted.

Reinforcement Theory

reinforcement theory
Behavior is a function of its consequences.

reinforcer
Any consequence immediately following a response that increases the probability that the behavior will be repeated.

A counterpoint to goal-setting theory is **reinforcement theory.** Goal-setting theory proposes that an individual's purpose directs his or her actions. Reinforcement theory argues that behavior is externally caused. What controls behavior are **reinforcers,** consequences that, when immediately following a response, increase the probability that the behavior will be repeated. Hence, reinforcement theorists argue that behavior is a function of its consequences.

The key to reinforcement theory is that it ignores factors such as goals, expectations, and needs. Instead, it focuses solely on what happens to a person when he or she takes some action. This helps explain, for instance, why publishers such as Simon & Schuster provide incentive clauses in their authors' contracts. If every time an author submits a completed chapter, the company sends her an advance check against future royalties for $10,000, she is motivated to keep working and submitting chapters.

In Chapter 14 we showed how reinforcers condition behavior and help people to learn. But the concept of reinforcement is also widely believed to explain motivation. According to B.F. Skinner, reinforcement theory can be explained as follows: People will most likely engage in desired behavior if they are rewarded for doing so; these

Michael Milken (center) was sentenced to three years in jail for illegal junk-bond dealings. The compensation arrangement he had with his employer, Drexel Burnham—which in one year paid him more than half-a-billion dollars—coupled with positive media attention and his growing power in global finance, encouraged and reinforced practices that broke the law.

Pay-for-Performance Gains in Popularity

Pay-for-performance is increasingly replacing the annual cost-of-living raise for managers and operating employees alike. In 1991, 35 percent of Fortune 500 companies had some form of pay-for-performance program—up from only 7 percent ten years earlier.[16] Another survey of 1708 companies found that 51 percent were practicing some form of pay-for-performance for employees other than top management, up from 44 percent two years earlier.[17]

Piece-rate pay plans, wage incentive plans, profit sharing, and lump-sum bonuses are all examples of pay-for-performance options. The common thread that differentiates these forms of pay from more traditional bonus plans is that instead of paying people for *time* on the job, managers are adjusting people's pay to reflect some performance measure. That measure might be individual productivity, work-group or departmental productivity, unit profitability, or the overall organization's profit performance. At Chaparral Steel, for example, workers receive a salary and bonus based on individual performance, company profits, and new skills learned.[18]

The growing popularity of pay-for-performance can be explained in terms of both motivation and cost control. From a motivation perspective, making some or all of a worker's pay conditional on some performance measure focuses his or her attention and effort toward that measure, then reinforces the continuation of the effort with a reward. Performance-based bonuses and other incentive rewards avoid the fixed expense of permanent salary boosts, and so save money; and if the employee or organization's performance declines, so does the reward. For instance, workers at a Monsanto plant for mining and refining phosphorous in Idaho saw their annual performance bonuses drop from $1800 to $255 when business slowed as a result of an economic recession.[19]

rewards are most effective if they immediately follow a desired response; and behavior that is not rewarded, or is punished, is less likely to be repeated.[20]

Following reinforcement theory, managers can influence others' behavior by reinforcing acts they deem favorable. However, because the emphasis is on positive reinforcement, not punishment, managers should ignore, not punish, unfavorable behavior. Even though punishment eliminates undesired behavior faster than non-reinforcement does, its effect is often only temporary and may later have unpleasant side effects such as dysfunctional conflictual behavior, absenteeism, or turnover.

The evidence indicates that reinforcement is undoubtedly an important influence on work behavior. But reinforcement is not the *only* explanation for differences in employee motivation.[21] Goals, for instance, also affect motivation, as do levels of achievement motivation, inequities in rewards, and expectations.

Equity Theory

Employees don't work in a vacuum. They make comparisons. If someone offered you $40,000 a year on your first job upon graduation from college, you'd probably grab the offer and report to work enthusiastic and certainly satisfied with your pay. How would you react if you found out a month or so into the job that a co-worker—another recent graduate, your age, with comparable grades from a comparable

TABLE 16-1 Equity Theory

Perceived Ratio Comparison*	Employee's Assessment
$\dfrac{\text{Outcomes A}}{\text{Inputs A}} < \dfrac{\text{Outcomes B}}{\text{Inputs B}}$	Inequity (underrewarded)
$\dfrac{\text{Outcomes A}}{\text{Inputs A}} = \dfrac{\text{Outcomes B}}{\text{Inputs B}}$	Equity
$\dfrac{\text{Outcomes A}}{\text{Inputs A}} > \dfrac{\text{Outcomes B}}{\text{Inputs B}}$	Inequity (overrewarded)

*Person A is the employee, and Person B is a relevant other or referent.

equity theory
The theory that an employee compares his or her job's inputs –outcomes ratio to that of relevant others and then corrects any inequity.

referents
The persons, systems, or selves against which individuals compare themselves to assess equity.

college—was getting $45,000 a year? You would probably be upset! Even though, in absolute terms, $40,000 is a lot of money for a new graduate to make (and you know it!), that suddenly would not be the issue. The issue would now center on relative rewards and what you believe is fair. There is considerable evidence that employees make comparisons of their job inputs and outcomes relative to others and that inequities influence the degree of effort that employees exert.[22]

Developed by J. Stacey Adams, **equity theory** says that employees perceive what they get from a job situation (outcomes) in relation to what they put into it (inputs) and then compare their inputs–outcomes ratio with the inputs–outcomes ratio of relevant others. This is shown in Table 16–1. If they perceive their ratio to be equal to those of the relevant others with whom they compare themselves, a state of equity exists. They perceive that their situation is fair—that justice prevails. If the ratios are unequal, inequity exists; that is, they view themselves as underrewarded or over-rewarded. When inequities occur, employees attempt to correct them.

The **referent** with whom employees choose to compare themselves is an important variable in equity theory.[23] The three referent categories have been classified as "other," "system," and "self." The "other" category includes other individuals with similar jobs in the same organization and also includes friends, neighbors, or professional associates. On the basis of information they receive through word of mouth, newspapers, and magazine articles on issues such as executive salaries or a recent union contract, employees compare their pay with that of others.

The "system" category considers organizational pay policies and procedures and the administration of this system. It considers organizationwide pay policies, both implied and explicit. Precedents by the organization in terms of allocation of pay are major determinants in this category.

The "self" category refers to inputs–outcomes ratios that are unique to the individual. It reflects past personal experiences and contacts. This category is influenced by criteria such as past jobs or family commitments.

The choice of a particular set of referents is related to the information available about referents as well as to their perceived relevance. On the basis of equity theory, when employees perceive an inequity, they might: (1) distort either their own or others' inputs or outcomes; (2) behave in some way to induce others to change their inputs or outcomes; (3) behave in some way to change their own inputs or outcomes; (4) choose a different comparison referent; and/or (5) quit their jobs.

Equity theory recognizes that individuals are concerned not only with the absolute rewards they receive for their efforts, but also with the relationship of these rewards to what others receive. They make judgments concerning the relationship between their inputs and outcomes and the inputs and outcomes of others. On the basis of one's inputs, such as effort, experience, education, and competence, one compares outcomes such as salary levels, raises, recognition, and other factors. When people perceive an imbalance in their inputs–outcomes ratio relative to those of others, they

Executives tend to be equity-sensitive. Roy Vagelos (pictured), CEO of Merck, is likely to compare his compensation with that of the CEOs at Eli Lilly, Upjohn, Pfizer, Abbott Laboratories, and other large health and drug companies.

experience tension. This tension provides the basis for motivation as people strive for what they perceive as equity and fairness.

Specifically, the theory establishes the following four propositions relating to inequitable pay:

1. *Given payment by time, overrewarded employees will produce more than equitably paid employees.* Hourly and salaried employees will generate a high quantity or quality of production in order to increase the input side of the ratio and bring about equity.

2. *Given payment by quantity of production, overrewarded employees will produce fewer but higher-quality units than equitably paid employees.* Individuals paid on a piece-rate basis will increase their effort to achieve equity, which can result in greater quality or quantity. However, increases in quantity will only increase inequity, since every unit produced results in further overpayment. Therefore effort is directed toward increasing quality rather than quantity.

3. *Given payment by time, underrewarded employees will produce less or poorer-quality output.* Effort will be decreased, which will bring about lower productivity or poorer-quality output than equitably paid subjects.

4. *Given payment by quantity of production, underrewarded employees will produce a large number of low-quality units in comparison with equitably paid employees.* Employees on piece-rate pay plans can bring about equity because trading off quality of output for quantity will result in an increase in rewards with little or no increase in contributions.

The propositions listed above have generally proven to be correct.[24] A review of the research consistently confirms the equity thesis: Employee motivation is influenced significantly by relative rewards as well as absolute rewards. Whenever employees perceive inequity, they will act to correct the situation.[25] The result might be lower or higher productivity, improved or reduced quality of output, increased absenteeism, or voluntary resignation.

From the discussion above, however, we should not conclude that equity theory is without problems. The theory leaves some key issues still unclear.[26] For instance, how do employees define inputs and outcomes? How do they combine and weigh their inputs and outcomes to arrive at totals? When and how do the factors change over time? Regardless of these problems, equity theory has an impressive amount of research support and offers us some important insights into employee motivation.

ETHICAL
DILEMMAS IN
MANAGEMENT

The Ethics of CEO Compensation

The chief executive officers of America's largest companies earn, on average, 160 times as much as the typical blue-collar worker.[27] Some say this represents a classic economic response to a situation in which the demand is great for high-quality top-executive talent and the supply is low. Other arguments in favor of paying CEOs $1 million a year or more are: the need to compensate people for the tremendous responsibilities and stress that go with such jobs, the motivating potential that seven- and eight-figure annual incomes provide to both the CEOs and those who might aspire to the position, and the CEO's influence on the company's bottom line.

Critics describe the astronomical pay packages given to American CEO's as indicative of "rampant greed." They note, for instance, that during the 1980s, CEO compensation jumped by 212 percent, while factory workers saw their pay increase by just 53 percent. During the same decade, the average earnings per share of the Standard & Poor's 500 companies grew by only 78 percent. In 1990, the average chief executive's salary and bonus *rose* by 3.5 percent to $1,214,000, yet profits *dropped* 7 percent. Moreover, in the year 1990, all twenty of the highest-paid U.S. CEO's earned in excess of $5.8 million.

Executive pay is considerably higher in the United States than in most other countries. American CEOs typically make two or three times as much as their counterparts in Canada and Europe. In Japan, CEOs earn only seventeen times the pay of an ordinary worker. For example, in 1990, the top three U.S. auto-company chiefs were paid a total of $7.3 million. By contrast, the combined income for the heads of Japan's top three automakers in that same year was $1.8 million. Critics of executive pay practices in the United States argue that CEOs choose board members who can be counted on to support ever-increasing pay for top management. If board members fail to "play along," they risk losing their positions, their fees, and the prestige and power inherent in board membership.

Does the blame for the problem lie with CEOs or with the shareholders and boards that knowingly allow the practice? Should we fault a Stephen Wolf, chairman of UAL Corp., for collecting $18,301,000 in salary, bonuses, and stock-based incentive plans in 1990 while, during that same year, his company's profits dropped 71 percent?

Are American CEOs greedy? Are these CEOs acting unethically? What do *you* think?

Expectancy Theory

expectancy theory
The theory that an individual tends to act in a certain way based on the expectation that the act will be followed by a given outcome and on the attractiveness of that outcome to the individual.

The most comprehensive explanation of motivation is Victor Vroom's **expectancy theory.**[28] Though it has its critics,[29] most of the research evidence is supportive of the theory.[30]

The expectancy theory states that an individual tends to act in a certain way based on the expectation that the act will be followed by a given outcome and on the attractiveness of that outcome to the individual. It includes three variables or relationships.

1. *Effort–performance linkage:* the probability perceived by the individual that exerting a given amount of effort will lead to performance.

2. *Performance–reward linkage:* the degree to which the individual believes that performing at a particular level will lead to the attainment of a desired outcome.

3. *Attractiveness:* the importance that the individual places on the potential outcome or reward that can be achieved on the job. This considers the goals and needs of the individual.[31]

While this might sound complex, it really is not that difficult to visualize. It can be summed up in the questions: How hard do I have to work to achieve a certain level of performance and can I actually achieve that level? What reward will performing at that level get me? How attractive is this reward to me and does it help achieve my goals? Whether one has the desire to produce at any given time depends on one's particular goals and one's perception of the relative worth of performance as a path to the attainment of these goals.

Figure 16–6 shows a very simple version of the expectancy theory that expresses its major contentions. The strength of a person's motivation to perform (effort) depends on how strongly that individual believes that he or she can achieve what is being attempted. If this goal is achieved (performance), will he or she be adequately rewarded by the organization? If so, will the reward satisfy his or her individual goals? Let us consider the four steps inherent in the theory and then attempt to apply it.

First, what perceived outcomes does the job offer the employee? Outcomes may be positive: pay, security, companionship, trust, fringe benefits, a chance to use talent or skills, or congenial relationships. On the other hand, employees may view the outcomes as negative: fatigue, boredom, frustration, anxiety, harsh supervision, or threat of dismissal. Reality is not relevant here; the critical issue is what the individual employee *perceives* the outcome to be, regardless of whether his or her perceptions are accurate.

Second, how attractive do employees consider these outcomes to be? Are they valued positively, negatively, or neutrally? This obviously is an internal issue and considers the individual's personal attitudes, personality, and needs. The individual who finds a particular outcome attractive—that is, values it positively—would rather attain it than not attain it. Others may find it negative and therefore prefer not attaining it to attaining it. Still others may be neutral.

Third, what kind of behavior must the employee exhibit to achieve these outcomes? The outcomes are not likely to have any effect on an individual employee's performance unless the employee knows, clearly and unambiguously, what he or she must do to achieve them. For example, what is "doing well" in terms of performance appraisal? What criteria will be used to judge the employee's performance?

Fourth and last, how does the employee view his or her chances of doing what is asked? After the employee has considered his or her own competencies and ability to control those variables that will determine success, what probability does he or she place on successful attainment?[32]

Let's use the classroom organization as an illustration of how one can use the expectancy theory to explain motivation.

Most students prefer an instructor who tells them what is expected of them in the

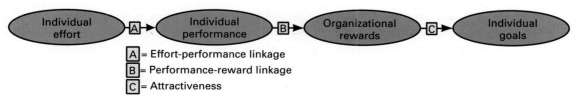

= Effort-performance linkage
= Performance-reward linkage
= Attractiveness

FIGURE 16–6
Simplified Expectancy Model

These Lincoln Electric employees participate in what is probably the most lucrative bonus system for factory workers in U.S. manufacturing. In Lincoln's pay-for-performance system, factory workers can earn as much as $100,000 a year.

course. They want to know what the assignments and examinations will be like, when they are due or to be taken, and how much weight each carries in the final term grade. They also like to think that the amount of effort they exert in attending classes, taking notes, and studying will be reasonably related to the grade they will make in the course. Let us assume that you, as a student, feel this way. Consider that five weeks into a class you are really enjoying (we'll call it MGT 301), an examination is given back to you. You studied hard for this examination, and you have consistently made As and Bs on examinations in other courses to which you have expended similar effort. The reason you work so hard is to make top grades, which you believe are important for getting a good job upon graduation. Also, you are not sure, but you might want to go on to graduate school. Again, you think grades are important for getting into a good graduate school.

Well, the results of that five-week examination are in. The class median was 72. Ten percent of the class scored an 85 or higher and got an A. Your grade was 46; the minimum passing mark was 50. You're mad. You're frustrated. Even more, you're perplexed. How could you possibly have done so poorly on the examination when you usually score in the top range in other classes by preparing as you did for this one?

Several interesting things are immediately evident in your behavior. Suddenly, you are no longer driven to attend MGT 301 classes regularly. You find that you do not study for the course either. When you do attend classes, you daydream a lot—the result is an empty notebook instead of several pages of notes. One would probably be correct in describing you as "lacking in motivation" in MGT 301. Why did your motivation level change? You know and I know, but let's explain it in expectancy terms.

If we use Figure 16–6 to understand this situation, we might say the following: Studying and preparing for MGT 301 (effort) are conditioned by their resulting in correctly answering the questions on the examination (performance), which will produce a high grade (reward), which will lead, in turn, to the security, prestige, and other benefits that accrue from obtaining a good job (individual goal).

The attractiveness of the outcome, which in this case is a good grade, is high. But what about the performance–reward linkage? Do you feel that the grade you received truly reflects your knowledge of the material? In other words, did the test fairly measure what you know? If the answer is yes, then this linkage is strong. If the answer is no, then at least part of the reason for your reduced motivational level is your belief that the test was not a fair measure of your performance. If the test was of an essay type, maybe you believe that the instructor's grading method was poor. Was too much weight placed on a question that you thought was trivial? Maybe the instructor does not like you and was biased in grading your paper. These are examples of perceptions that influence the performance–reward linkage and your level of motivation.

Another possible demotivating force may be the effort–performance relationship. If, after you took the examination, you believe that you could not have passed it regardless of the amount of preparation you had done, then your desire to study will drop. Possibly the instructor wrote the examination under the assumption that you had a considerably broader background in the subject matter. Maybe the course had several prerequisites that you did not know about, or possibly you had the prerequisites but took them several years ago. The result is the same: You place a low value on your effort leading to answering the examination questions correctly; hence your motivational level decreases, and you lessen your effort.

The key to the expectancy theory is therefore understanding an individual's goal—and the linkage between effort and performance, between performance and rewards, and, finally, between rewards and individual goal satisfaction. As a contingency model, the expectancy theory recognizes that there is no universal principle for explaining everyone's motivations. In addition, knowing what needs a person seeks to satisfy does not ensure that the individual will perceive that high performance will necessarily lead to the satisfaction of these needs. If you desire to take MGT 301 in order to meet new people and make social contacts, but the instructor organizes the class on the assumption that you want to make a good grade in the course, the instructor may be personally disappointed should you perform poorly on the examinations. Unfortunately, most instructors assume that their ability to allocate grades is a potent force in motivating students. It will be so only if students place a high importance on grades, if students know what they must do to achieve the grade desired, and if the students consider that there is a high probability of their performing well should they exert a high level of effort.

Let us summarize some of the issues surrounding the expectancy theory. First, it emphasizes payoffs, or rewards. As a result, we have to believe that the rewards the organization is offering align with what the employee wants. It is a theory based on self-interest, wherein each individual seeks to maximize his or her expected satisfaction. Second, expectancy theory stresses that managers understand why employees view certain outcomes as attractive or unattractive. We shall want to reward individuals with those things they value positively. Third, the expectancy theory emphasizes expected behaviors. Do individuals know what is expected of them and how they will be appraised? Finally, the theory is concerned with perceptions. What is realistic is irrelevant. An individual's own perceptions of performance, reward, and goal satisfaction outcomes will determine his or her level of effort, not the objective outcomes themselves.

Integrating Contemporary Theories of Motivation

We have presented a number of theories in this chapter. There is a tendency, at this point, to view them independently. This is a mistake. The fact is that many of the ideas underlying the theories are complementary, and your understanding of how to motivate people is maximized when you see how the theories fit together.[35]

Figure 16–7 presents a model that integrates much of what we know about motivation. Its basic foundation is the simplified expectancy model shown in Figure 16–6. Let's work through Figure 16–7, beginning at the left.

FIGURE 16-7
Integrating Contemporary
Theories of Motivation

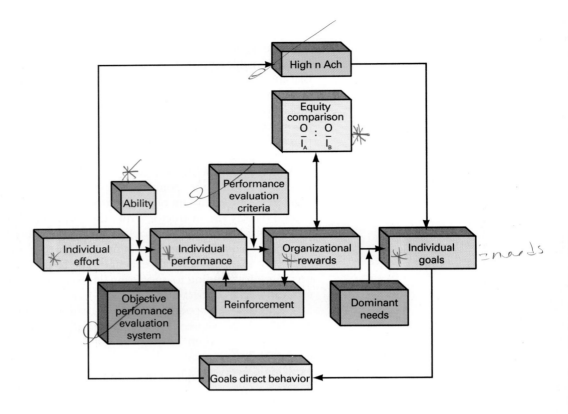

The individual effort box has an arrow leading into it. This arrow flows out of the individual's goals. Consistent with goal-setting theory, this goals-effort loop is meant to remind us that goals direct behavior.

Expectancy theory predicts that an employee will exert a high level of effort if he or she perceives that there is a strong relationship between effort and performance, performance and rewards, and rewards and satisfaction of personal goals. Each of these relationships, in turn, is influenced by certain factors. For effort to lead to good performance, the individual must have the requisite ability to perform, and the performance evaluation system that measures the individual's performance must be perceived as being fair and objective. The performance–reward relationship will be strong if the individual perceives that it is performance (rather than seniority, personal favorites, or other criteria) that is rewarded. The final link in expectancy theory is the rewards–goals relationship. Need theories would come into play at this point. Motivation would be high to the degree that the rewards an individual received for his or her high performance satisfied the dominant needs consistent with his or her individual goals.

A closer look at Figure 16–7 will also reveal that the model considers the achievement-need and reinforcement and equity theories. The high achiever is not motivated by the organization's assessment of his or her performance or organizational rewards; hence the jump from effort to individual goals for those with a high *nAch*. Remember that high achievers are internally driven as long as the jobs they are doing provide them with personal responsibility, feedback, and moderate risks. They are not concerned with the effort–performance, performance–rewards, or rewards–goal linkages.

Reinforcement theory enters our model by recognizing that the organization's rewards reinforce the individual's performance. If management has designed a reward system that is seen by employees as "paying off" for good performance, the rewards will reinforce and encourage continued good performance.

Modifying Motivation Theories for Different Cultures

The theories of motivation we have been studying were developed largely by U.S. psychologists and validated by studying American workers. These theories need to be modified for different cultures.[33]

The self-interest concept is consistent with capitalism and the extremely high value placed on individualism in the United States. Because almost all the motivation theories presented in this chapter are based on the self-interest motive, they should be applicable to organizations in such countries as Great Britain and Australia, where capitalism and individualism are highly valued. In more collectivist nations—Venezuela; Singapore, Japan, and Mexico—the link to the organization is the individual's *loyalty* to the organization or society, rather than his or her self-interest. Employees in collectivist cultures should be more receptive to team-based job design, group goals, and group performance evaluations. Reliance on the fear of being fired in such cultures is likely to be less effective, even if the laws in these countries allow managers to fire employees.

The need-achievement concept provides another example of a motivation theory with a U.S. bias. The view that a high need for achievement acts as an internal motivator presupposes the existence of two cultural characteristics: a willingness to accept a moderate degree of risk and a concern with performance. These characteristics would exclude countries with high uncertainty avoidance scores and high quality-of-life ratings. The remaining countries are exclusively Anglo-American countries such as New Zealand, South Africa, Ireland, the United States, and Canada.

Keep in mind that the road goes two ways. Motivation techniques that work well in China, for instance, may be inappropriate in North America. A large department store in Xian, China, selects its forty *worst* sales clerks each year.[34] They have to write self-criticisms and analyze their shortcomings. Management then hangs a plaque over their work stations, complete with picture, proclaiming them as members of the "Forty Worst." This approach was a response to the generally poor service that management felt its clerks were giving customers and the fact that lifetime employment is guaranteed for Chinese employees. The store's management has found that those employees selected for the "Forty Worst" are strongly motivated to improve their performances and to get the plaques removed from their work areas. Motivation through humiliation might be acceptable and effective in China, but it isn't likely to work in North America.

Finally, rewards also play the key part in equity theory. Individuals will compare the rewards (outcomes) they receive from the inputs they make with the inputs–outcomes ratio of relevant others ($O/I_A : O/I_B$), and inequities may influence the effort expended.

Motivating a Diversified Work Force

To maximize motivation among today's diversified work force, management needs to think in terms of *flexibility*. For instance, studies tell us that men place considerably more importance on having a lot of autonomy in their jobs than do women. In

In today's diversified work force, males are increasingly combining parental and job responsibilities. This manager enjoys the flexibility of being able to handle correspondence using his company's electronic mail system that is networked to his home.

contrast, the opportunity to learn, convenient work hours, and good interpersonal relations are more important to women than to men.[36] Managers need to be aware that what motivates the single mother with two dependent children who's working full-time to support her family may be very different from the needs of a young, single, part-time worker or the older employee who is working to supplement his or her pension income. The following examples, which link the issue of motivation with our previous discussion of job design in Chapter 11, illustrate the importance of designing flexible work schedules and benefit programs to respond to employees' varied needs.

Ann works for DuPont. As a mother of two preschool children, she finds that the company's family-friendly benefits—day care, flextime, job sharing, flexible benefits, and personal leaves of absence—increase her commitment to her job and to DuPont.

Mark also works for DuPont. He is among the company's 2000 or so employees who work part-time. This DuPont option allows Mark to gain valuable experience and meet his financial obligations, while at the same time allowing him to pursue his graduate studies in chemistry.

Jack is seventy-two years old. Unfortunately, his Social Security check provides an inadequate income. In order to make ends meet, Jack works full-time at a local plant nursery. One of the firm's hardest-working and enthusiastic employees, he regularly praises management for providing him with flexible work hours and an excellent health plan that supplements Medicare.

From Theory to Practice: Suggestions for Motivating Employees

If you're a manager concerned with motivating your employees, what specific recommendations can you draw from the theories presented in this chapter? While there is no simple, all-encompassing set of guidelines, the following suggestions draw on the essence of what we know about motivating employees.

Recognize Individual Differences   Almost every contemporary motivation theory recognizes that employees are not homogeneous. They have different needs.

MANAGERS WHO MADE A DIFFERENCE

F. Suzanne Jenniches at Westinghouse Electronic Systems

In 1971, F. Suzanne Jenniches was a high school biology teacher. In 1975, she joined Westinghouse as an associate test engineer. Today, she's general manager of Westinghouse's Civil Systems Division. Jenniches' comments on work-force diversity and motivation offer some insights into why she has succeeded at Westinghouse.[37]

"I believe in the strength of diversity. It's a passion of mine. I value diverse opinions, diverse skills, and diverse personalities all working in harmony in a team. . . . People [of diverse backgrounds] each bring their special skills and the ability to see a problem from a different angle, and that's important.

"I don't like 'yes' men, and I don't like everyone marching in step and saluting together. Of course, ultimately we must arrive at a common goal or approach, but we arrive at a better one by coming at it from different angles."

Ms. Jenniches encourages diversity through careful recruitment efforts, by teaming diverse employees, and by allowing open communication. "We look for people from all different social and academic backgrounds and try to mix quiet with talky people, electrical engineers with software and quality-assurance engineers. It's a tremendously energizing and often chaotic atmosphere. We allow employees to have a say here and to make a contribution. That builds respect and teamwork."

On motivation, Ms. Jenniches recognizes the need to individualize rewards. For example, she believes that the practice of promoting top performers into management and then transferring them into a new area often isn't the best approach for rewarding them. "I believe the best thing you can do for people in terms of recognizing and rewarding them is to give them a higher level of responsibility and authority. That doesn't necessarily mean a promotion to management, because many people don't want that kind of responsibility—many of them want more technical responsibility, more recognition of their technical expertise, or to be a team leader."

They also differ in terms of attitudes, personality, and other important individual variables. For instance, expectancy predictions are more accurate with individuals who have an internal rather than external locus of control.[38] Why? The former believe that events in their lives are largely under their own control, which is consistent with the expectancy theory's self-interest assumptions.

Match People to Jobs   There is a great deal of evidence showing the motivational benefits of carefully matching people to jobs. For example, high achievers should be sought for a job of running a small business or an autonomous unit within a larger business. However, if the job to be filled is a managerial slot in a large bureaucratic organization, a candidate high in *nPow* and low in *nAff* should be selected. Along these same lines, don't put a high achiever into a job that is inconsistent with his or her needs. Achievers will do best in jobs that provide opportunities to participate in setting moderately challenging goals and in which there is autonomy and feedback.

Keep in mind that not everybody is motivated by jobs that are high in autonomy, variety, and responsibility. Such jobs are most attractive and motivating to employees with a high growth need.

Use Goals   The literature on goal-setting theory suggests that managers should ensure that employees have hard, specific goals and feedback on how well they are doing in pursuit of those goals. For those with high achievement needs, typically a minority in any organization, the existence of external goals is less important because high achievers are already internally motivated.

Should the goals be assigned by a manager, or should employees participate in setting goals? The answer depends on your perception of goal acceptance and the organization's culture. If you expect resistance to goals, the use of participation should increase acceptance. If participation is inconsistent with the culture, use assigned goals. When participation and the culture are incongruous, employees are likely to perceive the participative process as manipulative and be turned off by it.

Ensure that Goals are Perceived as Attainable   Regardless of whether goals are actually attainable, employees who see these goals as unattainable will reduce their effort. Managers must be sure, therefore, that employees feel confident that increased efforts *can* lead to performance goals. For managers, this means that employees must be capable of doing the job and must perceive the performance appraisal process as both reliable and valid.

Individualize Rewards   Because employees have different needs, what acts as a reinforcer for one may not for another. Managers should use their knowledge of employee differences to individualize the rewards over which they have control. Some of the more obvious rewards that managers allocate include pay, promotions, autonomy, and the opportunity to participate in goal setting and decision making.

Link Rewards to Performance   Managers need to make rewards contingent on performance. Rewarding factors other than performance will only reinforce those other factors. Key rewards such as pay increases and promotions should be given for the attainment of the employee's specific goals. Managers should also look for ways to increase the visibility of rewards. Eliminating the secrecy surrounding pay by openly communicating everyone's compensation, publicizing performance bonuses, and allocating annual salary increases in a lump sum rather than spreading them out over the entire year are examples of actions that will make rewards more visible and potentially more motivating.

Check the System for Equity   Employees should perceive that rewards or outcomes are equal to the inputs given. On a simplistic level, experience, ability, effort, and other obvious inputs should explain differences in pay, responsibility, and other obvious outcomes. The problem, however, is complicated by the existence of dozens of both inputs and outcomes and by the fact that employee groups place different degrees of importance on them. For instance, a study comparing clerical and production workers identified nearly twenty inputs and outcomes.[39] The clerical workers considered factors such as quality of work performed and job knowledge near the top of their input list, but these factors were at the bottom of the production workers' list. Similarly, production workers thought the most important inputs were intelligence and personal involvement with the task to be accomplished, two factors that were quite low in the clerks' importance ratings. There were also important, though less dramatic, differences on the outcome side. For example, production workers rated advancement very high, whereas clerical workers rated advancement in the lower third on their list. Such findings suggest that one person's equity is another's inequity,

By linking increases in pay to increases in productivity, the management at Whirlpool's Benton Harbor, Michigan, washing machine factory has reduced costs and bolstered profits. In 1991, improvement in the aging plant's productivity translated into an average bonus of $2,700 for each of the plant's 265 employees.

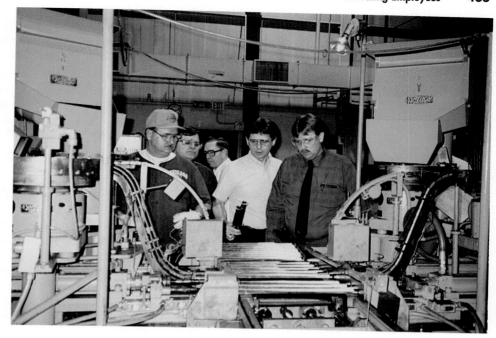

so an ideal reward system should probably weight inputs differently in arriving at the proper rewards for each job.

Don't Ignore Money It's easy to get so caught up in setting goals, creating interesting jobs, and providing opportunities for participation that one forgets that money is a major reason why most people work. Thus the allocation of performance-based wage increases, piecework bonuses, and other pay incentives is important in determining employee motivation. A review of eighty studies evaluating motivational methods and their impact on employee productivity supports this point.[40] Goal setting alone produced, on the average, a 16 percent increase in productivity; redesign efforts to enrich jobs yielded 8 to 16 percent increases; employee participation in decision making produced a median increase of less than 1 percent; whereas monetary incentives led to an average increase of 30 percent. We're not saying that management should focus solely on money. Rather, we're simply stating the obvious—that is, if money is removed as an incentive, people aren't going to show up for work. The same can't be said for removing goals, enriched work, or participation.

Summary

This summary is organized by the chapter-opening learning objectives found on page 463.

1. Motivation is the willingness to exert high levels of effort toward organizational goals, conditioned by the effort's ability to satisfy some individual need. The motivation process begins with an unsatisfied need, which creates tension and drives an individual to search for goals that, if attained, will satisfy the need and reduce the tension.

2. The hierarchy of needs theory states that there are five needs—physiological, safety, social, esteem, and self-actualization—that individuals attempt to satisfy in a steplike progression. A substantially satisfied need no longer motivates.

3. Theory X is basically a negative view of human nature, assuming that employees

dislike work, are lazy, seek to avoid responsibility, and must be coerced to perform. Theory Y is basically positive, assuming that employees are creative, seek responsibility, and can exercise self-direction.

4. The motivation–hygiene theory states that not all job factors can motivate employees. The presence or absence of certain job characteristics, or hygiene factors, can only placate employees and not lead to satisfaction or motivation. Factors that people find intrinsically rewarding, such as achievement, recognition, responsibility, and growth, act as motivators and produce job satisfaction.

5. High achievers prefer jobs that offer personal responsibility, feedback, and moderate risks.

6. Goals motivate employees by providing specific and challenging bench marks to guide and stimulate performance.

7. Reinforcement theory emphasizes the pattern in which rewards are administered. It states that only positive, not negative, reinforcement be used, and then only to reward desired behavior. The theory assumes that behavior is environmentally caused. Goal-setting theory views motivation as coming from an individual's internal statements of purpose.

8. In equity theory, individuals compare their job's inputs–outcomes ratio to those of relevant others. If they perceive that they are underrewarded, their work motivation declines. When individuals perceive that they are overrewarded, they often are motivated to work harder in order to justify their pay.

9. The expectancy theory states that an individual tends to act in a certain way based on the expectation that the act will be followed by a given outcome and on the attractiveness of that outcome to the individual. Its prime components are the relationships between effort and performance, performance and rewards, and rewards and individual goals.

10. Management practices that are likely to lead to more motivated employees include recognizing individual differences, matching people to jobs, using goals, ensuring that employees perceive goals as attainable, individualizing rewards, linking rewards to performance, checking the reward system for equity, and realizing that money is an important incentive.

Review Questions

1. What role do *needs* play in motivation?

2. What role would money play in (a) the hierarchy of needs theory, (b) motivation-hygiene theory, (c) equity theory, (d) expectancy theory, and (e) employees with a high *nAch*?

3. Contrast lower-order and higher-order needs in Maslow's need hierarchy.

4. If you accept Theory Y assumptions, how would you be likely to motivate employees?

5. Describe the three needs in the three-needs theory.

6. According to reinforcement theory, why should managers never punish employees?

7. How can we explain the apparent contradiction between the difficult goals called for by goal-setting theory and the moderate goals sought by high achievers?

8. What are some of the possible consequences of employees perceiving an inequity between their inputs and outcomes and those of others?

9. What role does perception play in (a) expectancy theory, (b) equity theory, and (c) reinforcement theory?

10. Explain the motivation implications of expectancy theory for management practice.

Discussion Questions

1. If you had to develop an incentive system for a company, which elements from which theories would you use? Why?

2. What part, if any, do you see goal setting playing in reinforcement and expectancy theories?

3. Would an individual with a high *nAch* be a good candidate for a management position? Explain.

4. What difficulties do you think work force diversity causes managers trying to use equity theory?

5. List five criteria (for example, pay, recognition, challenging work) that are most important to you in a job. Rank them by importance. Break into small groups and compare your responses. What patterns, if any, did you find?

SELF-ASSESSMENT EXERCISE

What Needs Are Most Important to You?

Instructions: Rank your responses for each of the following questions. The response that is most important or most true for you should receive a 5; the next should receive a 4; the next a 3; the next a 2; and the least important or least true should receive a 1.

Example

The work I like best involves:

A __4__ Working alone.
B __3__ A mixture of time spent with people and time spent alone.
C __1__ Giving speeches.
D __2__ Discussion with others.
E __5__ Working outdoors.

1. Overall, the most important thing to me about a job is whether or not:
   A _____ The pay is sufficient to meet my needs.
   B _____ It provides the opportunity for fellowship and good human relations.
   C _____ It is a secure job with good employee benefits.
   D _____ It allows me freedom and the chance to express myself.
   E _____ There is opportunity for advancement based on my achievements.

2. If I were to quit a job, it would probably be because:
   A _____ It was a dangerous job, such as working with inadequate equipment or poor safety procedures.

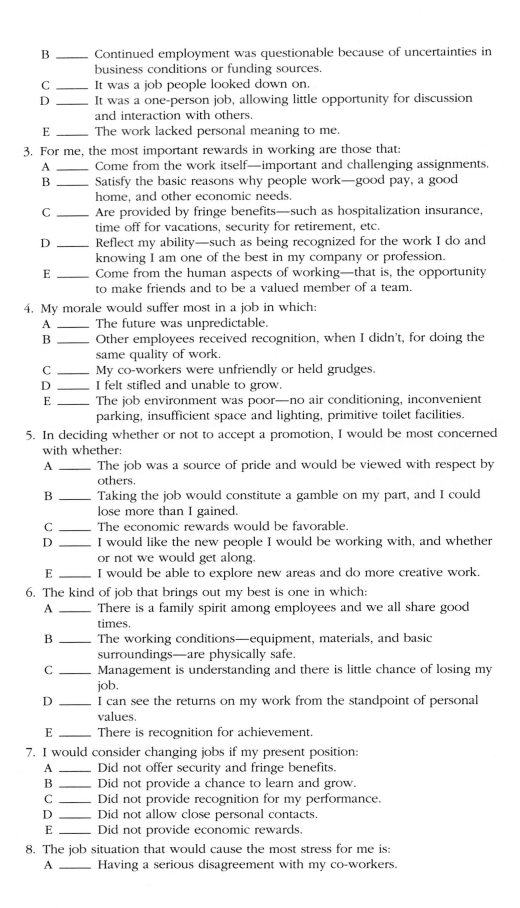

B _____ Continued employment was questionable because of uncertainties in business conditions or funding sources.

C _____ It was a job people looked down on.

D _____ It was a one-person job, allowing little opportunity for discussion and interaction with others.

E _____ The work lacked personal meaning to me.

3. For me, the most important rewards in working are those that:

A _____ Come from the work itself—important and challenging assignments.

B _____ Satisfy the basic reasons why people work—good pay, a good home, and other economic needs.

C _____ Are provided by fringe benefits—such as hospitalization insurance, time off for vacations, security for retirement, etc.

D _____ Reflect my ability—such as being recognized for the work I do and knowing I am one of the best in my company or profession.

E _____ Come from the human aspects of working—that is, the opportunity to make friends and to be a valued member of a team.

4. My morale would suffer most in a job in which:

A _____ The future was unpredictable.

B _____ Other employees received recognition, when I didn't, for doing the same quality of work.

C _____ My co-workers were unfriendly or held grudges.

D _____ I felt stifled and unable to grow.

E _____ The job environment was poor—no air conditioning, inconvenient parking, insufficient space and lighting, primitive toilet facilities.

5. In deciding whether or not to accept a promotion, I would be most concerned with whether:

A _____ The job was a source of pride and would be viewed with respect by others.

B _____ Taking the job would constitute a gamble on my part, and I could lose more than I gained.

C _____ The economic rewards would be favorable.

D _____ I would like the new people I would be working with, and whether or not we would get along.

E _____ I would be able to explore new areas and do more creative work.

6. The kind of job that brings out my best is one in which:

A _____ There is a family spirit among employees and we all share good times.

B _____ The working conditions—equipment, materials, and basic surroundings—are physically safe.

C _____ Management is understanding and there is little chance of losing my job.

D _____ I can see the returns on my work from the standpoint of personal values.

E _____ There is recognition for achievement.

7. I would consider changing jobs if my present position:

A _____ Did not offer security and fringe benefits.

B _____ Did not provide a chance to learn and grow.

C _____ Did not provide recognition for my performance.

D _____ Did not allow close personal contacts.

E _____ Did not provide economic rewards.

8. The job situation that would cause the most stress for me is:

A _____ Having a serious disagreement with my co-workers.

B _____ Working in an unsafe environment.

C _____ Having an unpredictable supervisor.

D _____ Not being able to express myself.

E _____ Not being appreciated for the quality of my work.

9. I would accept a new position if:

A _____ The position would be a test of my potential.

B _____ The new job would offer better pay and physical surroundings.

C _____ The new job would be secure and offer long-term fringe benefits.

D _____ The position would be respected by others in my organization.

E _____ Good relationships with co-workers and business associates were probable.

10. I would work overtime if:

A _____ The work is challenging.

B _____ I need the extra income.

C _____ My co-workers are also working overtime.

D _____ I must do it to keep my job.

E _____ The company recognizes my contribution.

Turn to page SK-5 for scoring directions and key.

Source: George Manning and Kent Curtis, *Human Behavior: Why People Do What They Do* (Cincinnati, Ohio: Vista Systems/Southwestern Publishing, 1988), pp. 17–20. With permission.

⊔ herman miller

To: Members of the Board of Directors
From: Max DePree, Chairman of the Board
Subject: Reevaluation of our Salary Rule

With Richard Ruch's recent announcement that he plans to retire, we will begin our search for a new CEO. After speaking with several executive search firms, I think we should reevaluate our salary rule.

As most of you know, our current salary rule—limiting an executive's cash compensation, including salary and bonus, to twenty times our average employee's paycheck—has been in effect since 1984. At that time I was our chief executive officer. I relinquished the CEO position to Richard in 1988. Last year, he earned $409,000 as president and chief executive.

On the plus side, our current rule is socially responsible and has been good for employee morale. But the executive recruiters point out several potential problems. Most specifically, we risk getting stuck with mediocre managers by curbing pay scales and we are vulnerable to raids from competitors who pay higher salaries. Naturally, filling our CEO position will be harder because of our pay restriction.

We're a Fortune 500 company with annual sales in excess of $900 million. We're one of the largest office-furniture makers in the world. Do we want to hinder our ability to attract top-flight management talent with our current salary rule? Perhaps we should consider raising the multiple beyond twenty or calculating it on the basis of the average white-collar salary?

I would appreciate if each of you would write up a short (not to exceed three pages) position paper reviewing the pros and cons of our current rule in terms of both motivation and social responsibility. Regarding the motivation issue, be sure to consider the effects on both management and our factory workers.

Source: This fictionalized memorandum is based on Jacqueline Mitchell, "Herman Miller Links Worker–CEO Pay," *Wall Street Journal,* May 7, 1992, p. B1. It was written for academic purposes only and is not meant to reflect either positively or negatively on actual management practices at Herman Miller Inc.

CASE APPLICATION

Lincoln Electric

Lincoln Electric is a Cleveland-based firm with sales of $440 million a year, 2,400 employees, and a very unusual way of motivating its employees.* What is its business? About 90 percent of its sales come from manufacturing arc-welding equipment and supplies.

Factory workers at Lincoln receive piece-rate wages with no guaranteed minimum hourly pay. After working for the firm for two years, employees begin to participate in the year-end bonus plan. Determined by a formula that considers the company's gross profits and the employees' base piece rate and merit rating, it might be the most lucrative bonus system for factory workers in U.S. manufacturing. The *average* size of the bonus over the past fifty-six years has been 95.5 percent of base wages. A handful of Lincoln factory workers make more than $100,000 a year! In recent good years, average employees have earned about $44,000 a year, well above the $17,000 average for U.S. manufacturing workers as a whole. But in a bad year, as during the 1982 recession, Lincoln employees' average fell to $27,000—still not bad, but a significant drop from the better years.

The company has a guaranteed-employment policy that it put in place in 1958. Since that time, it has not laid off a single worker. In return for job security, however, employees agree to several things. During slow times they will accept reduced work periods. They also agree to accept work transfers, even to lower-paid jobs, if that is necessary to maintain a minimum of 30 hours of work per week.

Lincoln Electric is extremely cost and productivity conscious. If a worker produces a part that does not meet quality standards, he or she is not paid for that part until it is fixed. The piece-rate wage system and a highly competitive merit rating system create a high-pressure atmosphere that some workers might find stressful. But the pressure has been good for productivity. One company executive estimates that Lincoln's overall productivity is about double that of its domestic competitors. The company has earned a profit every year since the depths of the 1930s depression and has never missed a quarterly dividend. Lincoln has one of the lowest employee turnover rates in U.S. industry. Recently, *Fortune* magazine cited Lincoln's two U.S. plants as among the ten best-managed in the country.

Questions

1. Which motivation theories discussed in this chapter—if any—do you feel Lincoln is using in motivating its employees?
2. Why does Lincoln's approach to motivating employees work?
3. What problems, if any, do you think this system might create for management?

---

*Based on "Why This 'Obsolete' Company is a 'Great Place to Work'," *International Management*, April 1986, pp. 46–51; Bruce G. Posner, "Right From the Start," *INC.*, August 1988, pp. 95–96; and Gene Epstein, "Inspire Your Team," *Success*, October 1989, p. 12.

VIDEO CASE

Executive Compensation: Are U.S. Executives Overpaid?

It's a basic tenet of most contemporary motivation programs—link rewards to performance. How, then, has it happened in recent years that dozens of executives' pay have gone up while their companies profits have gone down?

The answer seems to be lack of CEO accountability. Shareholders, who actually own the company, by law have no direct say in how much their chief executive is paid. The decision lies with the company's board of directors. But the typical board is made up of individuals handpicked by the CEO. As such, there are few checks and balances to prevent excessive compensation of CEOs.

Among the top thirty corporations in the United States, the average CEO compensation is now more than $3 million. Is that a lot? It depends on whom you're comparing against. Relative to chief executives in most other countries, it seems excessive. For instance, it's four times higher than what comparable executives are paid in Germany and six times higher than in Japan. The rate of increase also could be argued to be out of line. During the 1980s, the average worker's pay went up 53 percent. The average CEO pay, during the same period, rose 212 percent.

But is $3 million too much for running a company with 100,000 or more employees? Is it too much when baseball players earn $5 million a year and singers make $30 million?

A study of the largest 1000 companies in corporate America found that only 4 percent of the difference in executive pay could be attributed to differences in performance. This seems to support that performance has little bearing on executive compensation. What, then, is it related to? Some argue that it is based substantially on the industry in which the firm operates. The entertainment industry, for example, pays considerably more than the utility industry. Others suggest that pay is a function of organization size—larger companies pay more than smaller ones. Still others claim that compensation is purely a function of a CEO's power and control of his or her board. Those with the most power get the most bucks.

Questions

1. Can you make an argument, in terms of motivation, to justify increases in CEO pay when his or her organization's profits decline?

2. How would you structure a CEO's compensation to maximize both executive motivation and shareholder interest?

3. Should there be a ratio—say 20:1 or 30:1—between a CEO's pay and the lowest paid employee in his or her company, that defines an upper limit to the CEO's compensation?

4. How do you think excessive CEO compensation affects low-level employees in terms of motivation?

Source: "The U.S.'s Overpaid Executives," *ABC News Nightline,* April 17, 1992.

CHAPTER 17

Leadership

LEARNING OBJECTIVES

After Reading This Chapter, You Should Be Able To:

1. Explain the difference between managers and leaders.
2. Summarize the conclusions of trait theories.
3. Identify the two underlying leadership styles in the Managerial Grid.
4. Describe the Fiedler Contingency Model.
5. Explain the Hersey-Blanchard Situational Theory.
6. Summarize the Path-Goal Model.
7. Explain when leaders may not be that important.
8. Identify the key characteristics of charismatic leaders.
9. Contrast transactional and transformational leadership.
10. Explain gender differences in leadership styles.

Ted Turner (pictured with wife Jane Fonda) personifies the public's image of the bold, self-assured leader.

The sign on Ted Turner's desk reads, "Either lead, follow, or get out of the way." In Turner's case, it's clear that he's chosen to lead. He has spent his entire adult life taking on one bold risk after another—and succeeded when all the "experts" seemed assured that he'd fail.[1]

A dropout from Brown University, Ted Turner took over the family's nearly bankrupt billboard business in 1963 when he was twenty-four years old. In a few quick years, Turner turned the business around. Then he bought a small independent television station in Atlanta and arrogantly dubbed it the SuperStation. A year later he purchased the Atlanta Braves baseball team, then perennial losers, so that he'd have something to televise on his station besides old reruns of "Leave It to Beaver" and "Father Knows Best." Combining new satellite transmission technology with the unexploited cable television market, his WTBS SuperStation became a runaway success. Oh yes, and the Braves made it to the World Series in 1992.

In 1981, convinced that there was a market for twenty-four-hour news, which no one else acknowledged, Turner leveraged all his assets to launch the Cable News Network. CNN has proven to be incredibly profitable and has won numerous awards for its coverage of the 1989 Chinese revolution at Tiananmen Square and the 1991 war in the Persian Gulf. In 1986, Ted Turner bet the company again to buy the MGM/United Artists' film library. As usual, the critics thought he was nuts. But once again he proved them wrong, creating the highly successful Turner Network Television as a vehicle for showing his classic films.

The ability to see opportunities that others don't and to boldly "go for the victory" differentiates Ted Turner from your typical business executive. This is the man who, wanting to prove his worth as a sailor, took on the establishment and led his boat to a win in the 1979 America's Cup race. This is the person who, to facilitate world peace in the 1980s, created the Goodwill Games, an Olympic-style contest featuring U.S. and then-Soviet athletes. This is the guy who decided to call up Jane Fonda when he heard she was getting a divorce—they married two years later. This is the man *Time* magazine dubbed "Man of the Year" in January 1992.

Ted Turner reminds us of the importance of leadership. It's the leaders in organizations who make things happen. But if leadership is so important, it's only natural to ask: Are leaders born or made? What differentiates leaders from nonleaders? What can *you* do if you want to be seen as a leader? In this chapter we'll try to answer such questions.

Managers Versus Leaders

Let's begin by clarifying the distinction between managers and leaders. Writers frequently confuse the two, although they are not necessarily the same.

Managers are appointed. They have legitimate power that allows them to reward and punish. Their ability to influence is founded upon the formal authority inherent in their positions. In contrast, leaders may either be appointed or emerge from within a group. Leaders can influence others to perform beyond the actions dictated by formal authority.

Should all managers be leaders? Conversely, should all leaders be managers? Because no one yet has been able to demonstrate through research or logical argument that leadership ability is a handicap to a manager, we can state that all managers should *ideally* be leaders. However, not all leaders necessarily have the capabilities in other managerial functions, and thus not all should hold managerial positions. The fact that an individual can influence others does not tell whether he or she can also plan, organize, and control. Given (if only ideally) that all managers should be leaders, we will pursue the subject from a managerial perspective. Therefore **leaders** in this chapter mean those who are able to influence others and who possess managerial authority.

leaders
Those who are able to influence others and who possess managerial authority.

Trait Theories

Ask the average person on the street what comes to mind when he or she thinks of leadership. You're likely to get a list of qualities such as intelligence, charisma, decisiveness, enthusiasm, strength, bravery, integrity, and self-confidence. These responses represent, in essence, **trait theories** of leadership. The search for traits or characteristics that differentiate leaders from nonleaders, though done in a more sophisticated manner than our on-the-street survey, dominated the early research efforts in the study of leadership.

trait theories
Theories isolating characteristics that differentiate leaders from nonleaders.

Is it possible to isolate one or more traits in individuals who are generally acknowledged to be leaders—for instance, Martin Luther King, Jr., Joan of Arc, Ted Turner, Nelson Mandela, Margaret Thatcher, Mahatma Gandhi—that nonleaders do not possess? We may agree that these individuals meet our definition of a leader, but they represent individuals with utterly different characteristics. If the concept of traits was to prove valid, there had to be found specific characteristics that all leaders possess.

What traits characterize leaders like Jesse Jackson? The research has identified six: drive, the desire to lead, honesty and integrity, self-confidence, intelligence, and job-relevant knowledge.

Research efforts at isolating these traits resulted in a number of dead ends. Attempts failed to identify a set of traits that would always differentiate leaders from followers and effective leaders from ineffective leaders. Perhaps it was a bit optimistic to believe that a set of consistent and unique personality traits could apply across the board to all effective leaders, whether they were in charge of the Hell's Angels, New York Yankees, Federal Express, Shell Oil, Massachusetts General Hospital, Church of Jesus Christ of Latter-Day Saints, or Playboy Enterprises.

However, attempts to identify traits consistently *associated* with leadership have been more successful. Six traits on which leaders are seen to differ from nonleaders include: drive, the desire to lead, honesty and integrity, self-confidence, intelligence, and job-relevant knowledge.[2] These traits are briefly described in Table 17–1.

Yet traits alone are not sufficient for explaining leadership. Explanations based solely on traits ignore situational factors. Possessing the appropriate traits only makes it more likely that an individual will be an effective leader. He or she still has to take the right actions. And what is right in one situation is not necessarily right for a different situation. So while there has been some resurgent interest in traits during the past decade, a major movement away from trait theories began as early as the 1940s. Leadership research from the late 1940s through the mid-1960s emphasized the preferred behavioral styles that leaders demonstrated.

Behavioral Theories

behavioral theories
Theories identifying behaviors that differentiate effective from ineffective leaders.

The inability to strike gold in the trait mines led researchers to look at the behavior that specific leaders exhibited. Researchers wondered whether there was something unique in the *behavior* of effective leaders. For example, do leaders tend to be more democratic than autocratic?

It was hoped that not only would the **behavioral theories** approach provide more definitive answers about the nature of leadership, but, if successful, it would have practical implications quite different from those of the trait approach. If trait research had been successful, it would have provided a basis for *selecting* the "right"

TABLE 17-1   Six Traits That Differentiate Leaders from Nonleaders

1. *Drive.* Leaders exhibit a high effort level. They have a relatively high desire for achievement, they're ambitious, they have a lot of energy, they're tirelessly persistent in their activities, and they show initiative.

2. *Desire to lead.* Leaders have a strong desire to influence and lead others. They demonstrate the willingness to take responsibility.

3. *Honesty and integrity.* Leaders build trusting relationships between themselves and followers by being truthful or nondeceitful and by showing high consistency between word and deed.

4. *Self-confidence.* Followers look to leaders for an absence of self-doubt. Leaders, therefore, need to show self-confidence in order to convince followers of the rightness of goals and decisions.

5. *Intelligence.* Leaders need to be intelligent enough to gather, synthesize, and interpret large amounts of information; and to be able to create visions, solve problems, and make correct decisions.

6. *Job-relevant knowledge.* Effective leaders have a high degree of knowledge about the company, industry, and technical matters. In-depth knowledge allows leaders to make well-informed decisions and to understand the implications of those decisions.

Source: Shelly A. Kirkpatrick and Edwin A. Locke, "Leadership: Do Traits Really Matter?," *Academy of Management Executive,* May 1991, pp. 48–60.

people to assume formal positions in organizations requiring leadership. In contrast, if behavioral studies were to turn up critical behavioral determinants of leadership, we could *train* people to be leaders.

A number of studies looked at behavioral styles. We shall briefly review the two most popular studies: the Ohio State group and the University of Michigan group. Then we shall see how the concepts that these studies developed could be used to create a grid for looking at and appraising leadership styles.

The Ohio State Studies

The most comprehensive and replicated of the behavioral theories resulted from research that began at Ohio State University in the late 1940s.[3] These studies sought to identify independent dimensions of leader behavior. Beginning with over 1,000 dimensions, they eventually narrowed the list down to two categories that accounted for most of the leadership behavior described by subordinates. They called these two dimensions *initiating structure* and *consideration.*

initiating structure
The extent to which a leader defines and structures his or her role and those of subordinates to attain goals.

Initiating structure refers to the extent to which a leader is likely to define and structure his or her role and those of subordinates in the search for goal attainment. It includes behavior that attempts to organize work, work relationships, and goals. For example, the leader who is characterized as high in initiating structure assigns group members to particular tasks, expects workers to maintain definite standards of performance, and emphasizes the meeting of deadlines.

consideration
The extent to which a person has job relationships characterized by mutual trust, respect for subordinates' ideas, and regard for their feelings.

Consideration is defined as the extent to which a person has job relationships characterized by mutual trust and respect for subordinates' ideas and feelings. A leader who is high in consideration helps subordinates with personal problems, is friendly and approachable, and treats all subordinates as equals. He or she shows concern for his or her followers' comfort, well-being, status, and satisfaction.

high–high leader
A leader high in both initiating structure and consideration.

Extensive research based on these definitions found that a leader who is high in initiating structure *and* consideration (a **"high–high"** leader) achieved high subordinate performance and satisfaction more frequently than one who rated low on either consideration, initiating structure, or both. However, the high–high style did

James G. Kaiser at Corning Inc.

James G. Kaiser joined Corning Inc. as a sales representative in 1968, a short time after graduating from UCLA. Today, Kaiser is senior vice president and general manager of Corning's technical products division and Latin America, Asia-Pacific Exports.[4] He's directly responsible for a $200 million business that develops, produces, and sells 40,000 products and technologies—everything from high-priced Serengeti sunglasses to space shuttle windows.

Associates describe Kaiser as "a bulldog," yet "a fair-minded and caring manager." As one put it, "he's tenacious, a bold risk-taker and very concerned about his people." Kaiser believes in giving decision authority to his staff: "I'm a very people-oriented manager and I believe you can't be smart enough—particularly with the span of control that I have—to know the answers for everything. . . . So there's a participatory process and an empowerment process where my staff can literally run the business."

Kaiser's record of accomplishment at Corning is impressive. For instance, he's played an instrumental role in Corning's cultural diversity initiative and its TQM program. His division was one of the first within Corning to integrate his business strategy with the company's quality strategy. But James Kaiser is a leader in the community as well as in his place of employment. He recently spent two years as president of the Executive Leadership Council, a national organization based in Washington, D.C., and made up of sixty senior-level black managers that has helped hundreds of black executives gain contacts and information to enhance their careers. Says Kaiser, "As an African-American, I have a role in the community in making sure that black people come along, that they are taught and that the system works for them."

not *always* yield positive results. For example, leader behavior characterized as high on initiating structure led to greater rates of grievances, absenteeism, and turnover and lower levels of job satisfaction for workers performing routine tasks. Other studies found that high consideration was negatively related to performance ratings of the leader by his or her superior. In conclusion, the Ohio State studies suggested that the high–high style generally produced positive outcomes, but enough exceptions were found to indicate that situational factors needed to be integrated into the theory.

The University of Michigan Studies

Leadership studies undertaken at the University of Michigan's Survey Research Center, at about the same time as those being done at Ohio State, had similar research objectives: to locate behavioral characteristics of leaders that were related to performance effectiveness.

The Michigan group also came up with two dimensions of leadership behavior that they labeled employee oriented and production oriented.[5] Leaders who were *employee oriented* were described as emphasizing interpersonal relations; they took a

Roberto Suarez, publisher of the *El Nuevo Herald* in Miami, is an employee-oriented leader. He takes a strong personal interest in the concerns of his people. His low-key, nonthreatening style encourages people to get work done on their own.

personal interest in the needs of their subordinates and accepted individual differences among members. The *production-oriented* leaders, in contrast, tended to emphasize the technical or task aspects of the job, were concerned mainly with accomplishing their group's tasks, and regarded group members as a means to that end.

The conclusions of the Michigan researchers strongly favored leaders who were employee oriented. Employee-oriented leaders were associated with higher group productivity and higher job satisfaction. Production-oriented leaders were associated with low group productivity and lower worker satisfaction.

The Managerial Grid

managerial grid
A two-dimensional portrayal of leadership based on concerns for people and for production.

A two-dimensional view of leadership style was developed by Blake and Mouton.[6] They proposed a **managerial grid** based on the styles of "concern for people" and "concern for production," which essentially represent the Ohio State dimensions of consideration and initiating structure and the Michigan dimensions of employee orientation and production orientation.

The grid, depicted in Figure 17–1, has nine possible positions along each axis, creating eighty-one different positions into which a leader's style may fall. The grid does not show the results produced, but rather the dominating factors in a leader's thinking in regard to getting results.

Although there are eighty-one positions on the grid, the five key positions identified by Blake and Mouton are as follows:

1,1: *Impoverished:* The leader exerts a minimum effort to accomplish the work.

9,1: *Task:* The leader concentrates on task efficiency but shows little concern for the development and morale of subordinates.

1,9: *Country-club:* The leader focuses on being supportive and considerate of subordinates to the exclusion of concern for task efficiency.

5,5: *Middle-of-the-road:* The leader maintains adequate task efficiency and satisfactory morale.

FIGURE 17-1
The Managerial Grid

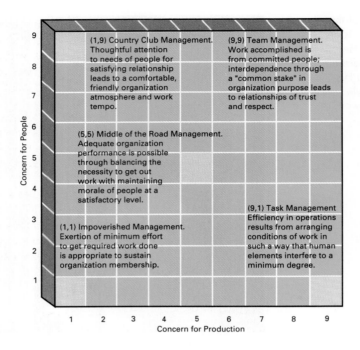

9,9: *Team:* The leader facilitates task efficiency and high morale by coordinating and integrating work-related activities.

From these findings, Blake and Mouton concluded that managers perform best using a 9,9 style. Unfortunately, the grid offers no answers to the question of what makes a manager, but only a framework for conceptualizing leadership style. In fact, there is little substantive evidence to support the conclusion that a 9,9 style is most effective in all situations.[7]

Summary of Behavioral Theories

We have described the most popular and important attempts to explain leadership in terms of behavior. There were other efforts,[8] but they faced the same problem that confronted the Ohio State and Michigan researchers: They had very little success in identifying consistent relationships between patterns of leadership behavior and successful performance. General statements could not be made because results would vary over different ranges of circumstances. What was missing was consideration of the situational factors that influence success or failure. For example, would Mother Teresa have been a great leader of the downtrodden at the turn of the century? Would Ralph Nader have risen to lead a consumer activist group had he been born in 1834 rather than in 1934 or in Costa Rica rather than in Connecticut? It seems quite unlikely, yet the behavioral approaches we have described could not clarify such situational factors.

Contingency Theories

It became increasingly clear to those studying the leadership phenomenon that predicting leadership success involved something more complex than isolating a few traits or preferable behaviors. The failure to obtain consistent results led to a new focus on situational influences. The relationship between leadership style and effectiveness suggested that under condition *a,* style *x* would be appropriate, whereas style *y* would be more suitable for condition *b,* and style *z* for condition *c.* But what were the conditions *a, b, c,* and so forth? It was one thing to say that leadership effectiveness depended on the situation and another to be able to isolate those situational conditions.

There has been no shortage of studies attempting to isolate critical situational factors that affect leadership effectiveness. One author, in reviewing the literature, found that the task being performed (that is, the complexity, type, technology, and size of the project) was a significant moderating variable; but he also uncovered studies that isolated situational factors such as style of the leader's immediate supervisor, group norms, span of control, external threats and stress, and organizational culture.[9]

Several approaches to isolating key situational variables have proven more successful than others and, as a result, have gained wider recognition. We shall consider four of these: the Fiedler model, Hersey and Blanchard's situational theory, path-goal theory, and the leader-participation model.

The Fiedler Model

The first comprehensive contingency model for leadership was developed by Fred Fiedler.[10] The **Fiedler contingency model** proposes that effective group performance depends upon the proper match between the leader's style of interacting with his or her subordinates and the degree to which the situation gives control and influence to the leader. Fiedler developed the **least-preferred co-worker (LPC) questionnaire** which purports to measure whether a person is task or relationship oriented. Further, he isolated three situational criteria—leader–member relations, task structure, and position power—that he believes can be manipulated to create the proper match with the behavioral orientation of the leader. In a sense the Fiedler model is an outgrowth of trait theory, since the LPC questionnaire is a simple psychological test. However, Fiedler goes significantly beyond trait and behavioral approaches by isolating situations, relating an individual's personality to the situation, and then predicting leadership effectiveness as a function of the two.

The above description of the Fiedler model can appear somewhat abstract. Let us now look at the model in more pragmatic detail.

Fiedler believes a key factor in leadership success to be an individual's basic leadership style. Thus he first tries to find out what that basic style is. Fiedler created the LPC questionnaire for this purpose. As shown in Figure 17–2, it contains sixteen pairs of contrasting adjectives. Respondents are asked to think of all the co-workers they have ever had and to describe the one person they *least enjoyed* working with by rating him or her on a scale of 1 to 8 for each of the sixteen sets of adjectives. Fiedler believes that, on the basis of the respondents' answers to this LPC questionnaire, you can determine most people's basic leadership style.

If the least preferred co-worker is described in relatively positive terms (a high LPC score), then the respondent is primarily interested in good personal relations with this co-worker. That is, if you describe the person you are least able to work with in favorable terms, Fiedler would label you *relationship oriented.* In contrast, if you see the least preferred co-worker in relatively unfavorable terms (a low LPC score), you are primarily interested in productivity and thus would be labeled *task oriented.* Using the LPC instrument, Fiedler is able to place most respondents into either of these two leadership styles. A small group of people has been found to fall in between for whom Fiedler acknowledges that it is difficult to draw a personality sketch.

It's important to note that Fiedler assumes that an individual's leadership style is

Fiedler contingency model
The theory that effective groups depend on a proper match between a leader's style of interacting with subordinates and the degree to which the situation gives control and influence to the leader.

least-preferred co-worker (LPC) questionnaire
A questionnaire that measures whether a person is task or relationship oriented.

FIGURE 17–2
Fiedler's LPC Scale

Source: From Fred E. Fiedler and Martin M. Chemers, *Leadership and Effective Management* (Scott, Foresman & Co., 1974). Reprinted by permission of authors.

	8	7	6	5	4	3	2	1	
Pleasant	8	7	6	5	4	3	2	1	Unpleasant
Friendly	8	7	6	5	4	3	2	1	Unfriendly
Rejecting	1	2	3	4	5	6	7	8	Accepting
Helpful	8	7	6	5	4	3	2	1	Frustrating
Unenthusiastic	1	2	3	4	5	6	7	8	Enthusiastic
Tense	1	2	3	4	5	6	7	8	Relaxed
Distant	1	2	3	4	5	6	7	8	Close
Cold	1	2	3	4	5	6	7	8	Warm
Cooperative	8	7	6	5	4	3	2	1	Uncooperative
Supportive	8	7	6	5	4	3	2	1	Hostile
Boring	1	2	3	4	5	6	7	8	Interesting
Quarrelsome	1	2	3	4	5	6	7	8	Harmonious
Self-assured	8	7	6	5	4	3	2	1	Hesitant
Efficient	8	7	6	5	4	3	2	1	Inefficient
Gloomy	1	2	3	4	5	6	7	8	Cheerful
Open	8	7	6	5	4	3	2	1	Guarded

fixed. As we'll show in a moment, this means that if a situation requires a task-oriented leader and the person in that leadership position is relationship oriented, either the situation has to be modified or the leader has to be removed and replaced if optimum effectiveness is to be achieved. Fiedler argues that leadership style is innate—you *can't* change your style to fit changing situations!

After an individual's basic leadership style has been assessed through the LPC, it is necessary to evaluate the situation and match the leader with the situation. Fiedler has identified three contingency dimensions that, he argues, define the key situational factors for determining leadership effectiveness. These are *leader–member relations, task structure,* and *position power.* They are defined as follows:

leader–member relations
The degree of confidence, trust, and respect subordinates have in their leader.

task structure
The degree to which the job assignments are procedurized.

position power
The degree of influence a leader has over power variables such as hiring, firing, discipline, promotions, and salary increases.

1. **Leader–member relations:** The degree of confidence, trust, and respect subordinates have in their leader
2. **Task structure:** The degree to which the job assignments are procedurized (that is, structured or unstructured)
3. **Position power:** The degree of influence a leader has over power variables such as hiring, firing, discipline, promotions, and salary increases

The next step in the Fiedler model is to evaluate the situation in terms of these three contingency variables. Leader-member relations are either good or poor, task structure either high or low, and position power either strong or weak. Altogether, by mixing the three contingency variables, there are potentially eight different situations or categories in which a leader could find him- or herself.

FIGURE 17–3
The Findings of the Fiedler Model

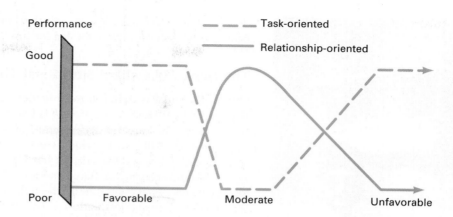

Category								
	I	II	III	IV	V	VI	VII	VIII
Leader-member relations	Good	Good	Good	Good	Poor	Poor	Poor	Poor
Task structure	High	High	Low	Low	High	High	Low	Low
Position power	Strong	Weak	Strong	Weak	Strong	Weak	Strong	Weak

The Fiedler model proposes matching an individual's LPC and an assessment of the three contingency variables to achieve maximum leadership effectiveness. In his studies of over 1,200 groups, in which he compared relationship- versus task-oriented leadership styles in each of the eight situational categories, Fiedler concluded that task-oriented leaders tend to perform better in situations that were *very favorable* to them and in situations that were *very unfavorable* (see Figure 17–3). Fiedler would predict that, when faced with a category I, II, III, VII, or VIII situation, task-oriented leaders perform better. Relationship-oriented leaders, however, perform better in moderately favorable situations—categories IV through VI.

Remember that according to Fiedler an individual's leadership style is fixed. Therefore there are really only two ways in which to improve leader effectiveness. First, you can change the leader to fit the situation. As in a baseball game, management can reach into its bullpen and put in a right-handed pitcher or a left-handed pitcher, depending on the situational characteristics of the hitter. For example, if a group situation rates as highly unfavorable but is currently led by a relationship-oriented manager, the group's performance could be improved by replacing that manager with one who is task oriented. The second alternative would be to change the situation to fit the leader. That could be done by restructuring tasks or increasing or decreasing the power that the leader has to control factors such as salary increases, promotions, and disciplinary actions. To illustrate, assume that a task-oriented leader is in a category IV situation. If this leader could significantly increase his or her position power, then the leader would be operating in category III, and the leader-situation match would be compatible for high group performance.

As a whole, reviews of the major studies undertaken to test the overall validity of the Fiedler model lead to a generally positive conclusion. That is, there is considerable evidence to support the model.[11] But additional variables are probably needed if an improved model is to fill in some of the remaining gaps. Moreover, there are problems with the LPC and the practical use of the model that need to be addressed. For instance, the logic underlying the LPC is not well understood, and studies have shown that respondents' LPC scores are not stable.[12] Also, the contingency variables are complex and difficult for practitioners to assess. It's often difficult in practice to

According to Fiedler, the leadership style of this prison guard at the Marion Federal Penitentiary is fixed. If his style doesn't fit the situation, either the situation has to be changed or he needs to be replaced by a guard with a different style.

situational leadership theory
A contingency theory that focuses on followers' maturity.

maturity
The ability and willingness of people to take responsibility for directing their own behavior.

determine how good the leader–member relations are, how structured the task is, and how much position power the leader has.[13]

The Hersey-Blanchard Situational Theory

One of the most widely followed leadership models is the **situational leadership theory** of Paul Hersey and Kenneth Blanchard.[14] Situational leadership is a contingency theory that focuses on followers. Successful leadership is achieved by selecting the right leadership style, which Hersey and Blanchard argue is contingent on the level of the followers' maturity. It has been used as a major training device at such *Fortune* 500 companies as BankAmerica, Caterpillar, IBM, Mobil Oil, and Xerox; it has also been widely accepted in all the military services.[15] Although the theory has not undergone extensive evaluation to test its validity, we include it here because of its wide acceptance and its strong intuitive appeal.

The emphasis on followers in leadership effectiveness reflects the reality that it is they who accept or reject the leader. Regardless of what the leader does, effectiveness depends on the actions of his or her followers. This is an important dimension that has been overworked or underemphasized in most leadership theories.

The term **maturity,** as defined by Hersey and Blanchard, is the ability and willingness of people to take responsibility for directing their own behavior. It has two components: job maturity and psychological maturity. The first encompasses one's knowledge and skills. Individuals who are high in job maturity have the knowledge, ability, and experience to perform their job tasks without direction from others. Psychological maturity relates to the willingness or motivation to do something. Individuals who are high in psychological maturity don't need much external encouragement; they are already intrinsically motivated.

Situational leadership uses the same two leadership dimensions that Fiedler identified: task and relationship behaviors. However, Hersey and Blanchard go a step further by considering each as either high or low and then combining them into four specific leadership styles: telling, selling, participating, and delegating. They are described as follows:

Telling (high task–low relationship): The leader defines roles and tells people what, how, when, and where to do various tasks.

Selling (high task–high relationship): The leader provides both directive behavior and supportive behavior.

Participating (low task–high relationship): The leader and follower share in decision making, the main role of the leader being facilitating and communicating.

Delegating (low task–low relationship): The leader provides little direction or support.

The final component in Hersey and Blanchard's theory is defining four stages of maturity:

M1: People are both unable and unwilling to take responsibility for doing something. They are neither competent nor confident.

M2: People are unable but willing to do the necessary job tasks. They are motivated but currently lack the appropriate skills.

M3: People are able but unwilling to do what the leader wants.

M4: People are both able and willing to do what is asked of them.

Figure 17–4 integrates the various components into the situational leadership model. As followers reach high levels of maturity, the leader responds not only by continuing to decrease control over activities, but also by continuing to decrease

FIGURE 17–4
The Situational Leadership Model

Source: Adapted from P. Hersey and K. Blanchard, *Management of Organizational Behavior: Utilizing Human Resources,* 4th ed. © 1982, p. 152. Adapted by permission of Prentice-Hall, Inc., Englewood Cliffs, NJ.

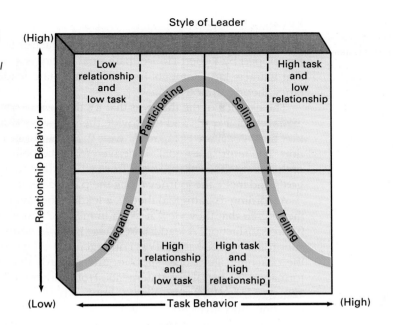

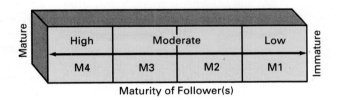

Maturity of Follower(s)

relationship behavior. At stage M1, followers need clear and specific directions. At stage M2, both high-task and high-relationship behavior is needed. The high-task behavior compensates for the followers' lack of ability, and the high-relationship behavior tries to get the followers psychologically to "buy into" the leader's desires. M3 creates motivational problems that are best solved by a supportive, nondirective, participative style. Finally, at stage M4 the leader doesn't have to do much because followers are both willing and able to take responsibility.

The astute reader might have noticed the high similarity between Hersey and Blanchard's four leadership styles and the four "corners" in the managerial grid. Is situational leadership, then, merely the managerial grid with one major difference: the replacement of the 9,9 ("one style for all occasions") contention with the recommendation that the "right" style should align with the maturity of the followers? Hersey and Blanchard say no.[16] They argue that the grid emphasizes *concern* for production and people, which are attitudinal dimensions. Situational leadership, in contrast, emphasizes task and relationship *behavior.* In spite of Hersey and Blanchard's claim, this is a pretty minute differentiation. The situational leadership theory is probably better understood by being considered as a fairly direct adaptation of the grid framework to reflect four stages of follower maturity.

Finally, we come to the critical question: Is there evidence to support situational leadership theory? As was noted earlier, the theory has received little attention from researchers.[17] Thus on the basis of the research to date, conclusions must be guarded. Some researchers claim that evidence provides partial support for the theory,[18] while other researchers find no support for its assumptions.[19] As a result, any enthusiastic endorsement at this time should be cautioned against.

path-goal theory
The theory that a leader's behavior is acceptable to subordinates insofar as they view it as a source of either immediate or future satisfaction.

Path-Goal Theory

Currently, one of the most respected approaches to leadership is path-goal theory. Developed by Robert House, path-goal theory is a contingency model of leadership that extracts key elements from the Ohio State leadership research and the expectancy theory of motivation.[20]

The essence of the theory is that it's the leader's job to assist his or her followers in attaining their goals and to provide the necessary direction and/or support to ensure that their goals are compatible with the overall objectives of the group or organization. The term "path-goal" is derived from the belief that effective leaders clarify the path to help their followers get from where they are to the achievement of their work goals and make the journey along the path easier by reducing roadblocks and pitfalls.

According to path-goal theory, a leader's behavior is *acceptable* to subordinates to the degree that they view it as an immediate source of satisfaction or as a means of future satisfaction. A leader's behavior is *motivational* to the degree that it (1) makes subordinate need-satisfaction contingent on effective performance and (2) provides the coaching, guidance, support, and rewards that are necessary for effective performance. To test these statements, House identified four leadership behaviors. The *directive leader* lets subordinates know what is expected of them, schedules work to be done, and gives specific guidance as to how to accomplish tasks. This type of leadership closely parallels the Ohio State dimension of initiating structure. The *supportive leader* is friendly and shows concern for the needs of subordinates. This type of leadership is essentially synonymous with the Ohio State dimension of consideration. The *participative leader* consults with subordinates and uses their suggestions before making a decision. The *achievement-oriented leader* sets challenging goals and expects subordinates to perform at their highest level. In contrast to Fiedler's view of a leader's behavior, House assumes that leaders are flexible. Path-goal theory implies that the same leader can display any or all of these leadership styles depending on the situation.

As Figure 17–5 illustrates, path-goal theory proposes two classes of situational or contingency variables that moderate the leadership behavior–outcome relationship—those in the *environment* that are outside the control of the subordinate (task structure, the formal authority system, and the work group) and those that are part of the personal characteristics of the *subordinate* (locus of control, experience, and perceived ability). Environmental factors determine the type of leader behavior

FIGURE 17–5
Path-Goal Theory

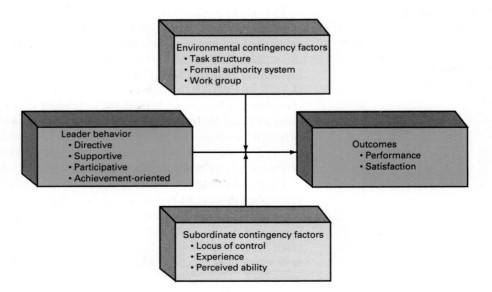

required as a complement if subordinate outcomes are to be maximized, while personal characteristics of the subordinate determine how the environment and leader behavior are interpreted. The theory proposes that leader behavior will be ineffective when it is redundant with sources of environmental structure or incongruent with subordinate characteristics.

The following are some examples of hypotheses that have evolved out of path-goal theory:

- Directive leadership leads to greater satisfaction when tasks are ambiguous or stressful than when they are highly structured and well laid out.

- Supportive leadership results in high employee performance and satisfaction when subordinates are performing structured tasks.

- Directive leadership is likely to be perceived as redundant among subordinates with high perceived ability or with considerable experience.

- The more clear and bureaucratic the formal authority relationships, the more leaders should exhibit supportive behavior and deemphasize directive behavior.

- Directive leadership will lead to higher employee satisfaction when there is substantive conflict within a work group.

- Subordinates with an internal locus of control (those who believe they control their own destiny) will be more satisfied with a participative style.

- Subordinates with an external locus of control will be more satisfied with a directive style.

- Achievement-oriented leadership will increase subordinates' expectancies that effort will lead to high performance when tasks are ambiguously structured.

Research to validate hypotheses such as these is generally encouraging.[21] The evidence supports the logic underlying the theory. That is, employee performance and satisfaction are likely to be positively influenced when the leader compensates for shortcomings in either the employee or the work setting. However, if the leader spends time explaining tasks when those tasks are already clear or the employee has the ability and experience to handle them without interference, the employee is likely to see such directive behavior as redundant or even insulting.

Leader-Participation Model

leader-participation model
A leadership theory that provides a set of rules to determine the form and amount of participative decision making in different situations.

Back in 1973, Victor Vroom and Phillip Yetton developed a **leader participation model** that related leadership behavior and participation to decision making.[22] Recognizing that task structures have varying demands for routine and nonroutine activities, these researchers argued that leader behavior must adjust to reflect the task structure. Vroom and Yetton's model was normative—it provided a sequential set of rules that should be followed in determining the form and amount of participation in decision making, as determined by different types of situations. The model was a decision tree incorporating seven contingencies (whose relevance could be identified by making "yes" or "no" choices) and five alternatives leadership styles.

The model assumes that any of five behaviors may be feasible in a given situation—Autocratic I (AI), Autocratic II (AII), Consultative I (CI), Consultative II (CII), and Group II (GII). These are described as follows:

- AI. You solve the problem or make a decision yourself using information available to you at that time.

- AII. You obtain the necessary information from subordinates and then decide on the solution to the problem yourself. You may or may not tell subordinates what the problem is in getting the information from them. The role played by your

Jim Muller is president of the Muller advertising agency, which does about $85 million a year in business. Muller has found that the group approach works best with the professionals in his firm. "When you come to terms with the fact that your employees know more than you do, it's one short step to accepting that, in their area of expertise, they're quite likely to make better decisions than you will."

subordinates in making the decision is clearly one of providing the necessary information to you rather than generating or evaluating alternative solutions.

- CI. You share the problem with relevant subordinates individually, getting their ideas and suggestions without bringing them together as a group. Then *you* make the decision that may or may not reflect your subordinates' influence.

- CII. You share the problem with your subordinates as a group, collectively obtaining their ideas and suggestions. Then, you make the decision that may or may not reflect your subordinates' influence.

- GII. You share the problem with your subordinates as a group. Together you generate and evaluate alternatives and attempt to reach an agreement (consensus) on a solution.

More recent work by Vroom and Arthur Jago has resulted in a revision of this model.[23] The new model retains the same five alternative leadership styles but expands the contingency variables to twelve, ten of which are answered along a five-point scale. Table 17–2 lists the twelve variables.

Vroom and Jago have developed a computer program that cuts through all the complexity of the new model. But managers can still use decision trees to select their leadership style, assuming that there are no "shades of gray" (that is, when the status of a variable is clear-cut so a "yes" or "no" response is accurate), that there are no critically severe time constraints, and that subordinates are not geographically dispersed. Figure 17–6 on page 511 illustrates one of these decision trees.

Research testing the original leader-participation model was very encouraging.[24] Because the revised model is new, its validity still needs to be assessed. But the new model is a direct extension of the 1973 version, and it's also consistent with our current knowledge of the benefits and costs of participation. So, at this time, we have every reason to believe that the revised model provides an excellent guide to help managers choose the most appropriate leadership style in different situations.

The leader-participation model confirms that leadership research should be directed at the situation rather than at the person. It probably makes more sense to talk about autocratic and participative *situations* rather than autocratic and participative *leaders*. As did House in his path-goal theory, Vroom, Yetton, and Jago argue against the notion that leader behavior is inflexible. The leader-participation model assumes that the leader can adapt his or her style to different situations.

Sometimes Leadership Is Irrelevant!

In keeping with the contingency spirit, we want to conclude this section by offering this notion: The belief that some leadership style will always be effective regardless of the situation may not be true. Leadership may not always be important. Data from numerous studies demonstrate that, in many situations, any behaviors a leader exhibits are irrelevant. Certain individual, job, and organizational variables can act as "substitutes for leadership," negating the influence of the leader.[25]

For instance, characteristics of subordinates such as experience, training, "professional" orientation, or need for independence can neutralize the effect of leadership. These characteristics can replace the need for a leader's support or ability to create structure and reduce task ambiguity. Similarly, jobs that are inherently unambiguous and routine or that are intrinsically satisfying may place fewer demands on the leadership variable. Finally, such organizational characteristics as explicit formalized goals, rigid rules and procedures, or cohesive work groups can act in the place of formal leadership.

TABLE 17-2 Contingency Variables in the Revised Leader-Participation Model

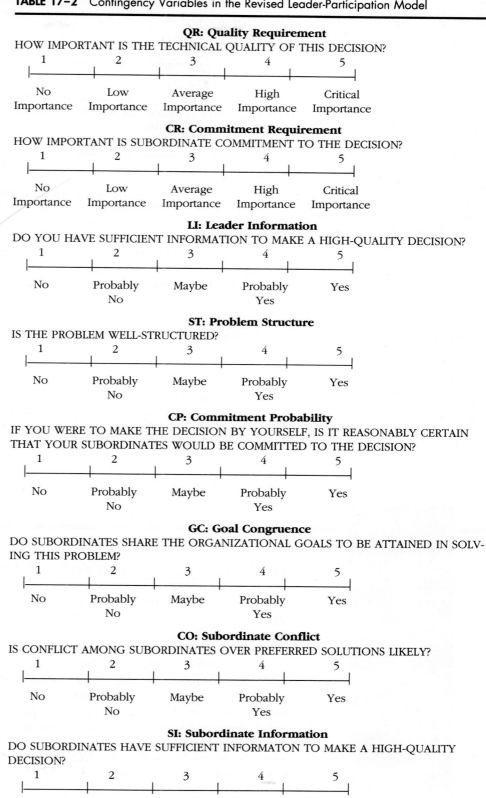

QR: Quality Requirement
HOW IMPORTANT IS THE TECHNICAL QUALITY OF THIS DECISION?

1	2	3	4	5
No Importance	Low Importance	Average Importance	High Importance	Critical Importance

CR: Commitment Requirement
HOW IMPORTANT IS SUBORDINATE COMMITMENT TO THE DECISION?

1	2	3	4	5
No Importance	Low Importance	Average Importance	High Importance	Critical Importance

LI: Leader Information
DO YOU HAVE SUFFICIENT INFORMATION TO MAKE A HIGH-QUALITY DECISION?

1	2	3	4	5
No	Probably No	Maybe	Probably Yes	Yes

ST: Problem Structure
IS THE PROBLEM WELL-STRUCTURED?

1	2	3	4	5
No	Probably No	Maybe	Probably Yes	Yes

CP: Commitment Probability
IF YOU WERE TO MAKE THE DECISION BY YOURSELF, IS IT REASONABLY CERTAIN THAT YOUR SUBORDINATES WOULD BE COMMITTED TO THE DECISION?

1	2	3	4	5
No	Probably No	Maybe	Probably Yes	Yes

GC: Goal Congruence
DO SUBORDINATES SHARE THE ORGANIZATIONAL GOALS TO BE ATTAINED IN SOLVING THIS PROBLEM?

1	2	3	4	5
No	Probably No	Maybe	Probably Yes	Yes

CO: Subordinate Conflict
IS CONFLICT AMONG SUBORDINATES OVER PREFERRED SOLUTIONS LIKELY?

1	2	3	4	5
No	Probably No	Maybe	Probably Yes	Yes

SI: Subordinate Information
DO SUBORDINATES HAVE SUFFICIENT INFORMATON TO MAKE A HIGH-QUALITY DECISION?

1	2	3	4	5
No	Probably No	Maybe	Probably Yes	Yes

TC: Time Constraint

DOES A CRITICALLY SEVERE TIME CONSTRAINT LIMIT YOUR ABILITY TO INVOLVE SUBORDINATES?

No   Yes

GD: Geographical Dispersion

ARE THE COSTS INVOLVED IN BRINGING TOGETHER GEOGRAPHICALLY DISPERSED SUBORDINATES PROHIBITIVE?

No   Yes

MT: Motivation-Time

HOW IMPORTANT IS IT TO YOU TO MINIMIZE THE TIME IT TAKES TO MAKE THE DECISION?

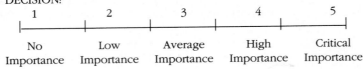

| No | Low | Average | High | Critical |
| Importance | Importance | Importance | Importance | Importance |

MD: Motivation-Development

HOW IMPORTANT IS IT TO YOU TO MAXIMIZE THE OPPORTUNITIES FOR SUBORDINATE DEVELOPMENT?

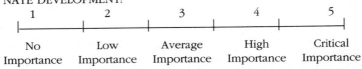

| No | Low | Average | High | Critical |
| Importance | Importance | Importance | Importance | Importance |

Source: V.H. Vroom and A.G. Jago, *The New Leadership: Managing Participation in Organizations* (Englewood Cliffs, N.J.: Prentice-Hall, 1988), pp. 111–12. With permission.

The Case Against the Universal Leader

One general conclusion that surfaces from the leadership literature is that effective leaders don't use any single style. They adjust their style to the situation. While not mentioned explicitly, national culture is certainly an important situational variable determining which leadership style will be most effective.

National culture affects leadership style by way of the subordinate. A leader cannot choose his or her style at will. "What is feasible depends to a large extent on the cultural conditioning of a leader's subordinates."[26] For example, a manipulative or autocratic style is compatible with high power distance, and we find high power distance scores in Arab, Far Eastern, and Latin countries. Power distance rankings should also be good indicators of employee willingness to accept participative leadership. Participation is likely to be most effective in low-power-distance cultures such as those in Norway, Finland, Denmark, and Sweden.

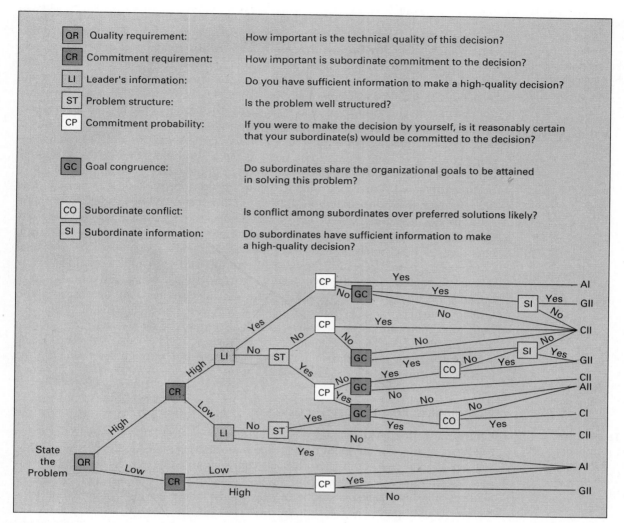

QR	Quality requirement:	How important is the technical quality of this decision?
CR	Commitment requirement:	How important is subordinate commitment to the decision?
LI	Leader's information:	Do you have sufficient information to make a high-quality decision?
ST	Problem structure:	Is the problem well structured?
CP	Commitment probability:	If you were to make the decision by yourself, is it reasonably certain that your subordinate(s) would be committed to the decision?
GC	Goal congruence:	Do subordinates share the organizational goals to be attained in solving this problem?
CO	Subordinate conflict:	Is conflict among subordinates over preferred solutions likely?
SI	Subordinate information:	Do subordinates have sufficient information to make a high-quality decision?

FIGURE 17–6

The Revised Leader-Participation Model (Time-Driven Decision Tree—Group Problems)

Source: V.H. Vroom and A.G. Jago, *The New Leadership: Managing Participation in Organizations* (Englewood Cliffs, N.J.: Prentice-Hall, 1988), p. 184. With permission.

Emerging Approaches to Leadership

We conclude our review of leadership theories by presenting three emerging approaches to the subject: an attribution theory of leadership, charismatic leadership, and transactional versus transformational leadership. If there is one theme that underlies the approaches in this section, it is that they take a more practical view of leadership than previous theories have, with the exception of trait theories. The following approaches to leadership look at the subject the way the average "person on the street" does.

Attribution Theory of Leadership

In Chapter 14, we discussed attribution theory in relation to perception. Attribution theory has also been used to help explain the perception of leadership.

**attribution theory
of leadership**
Proposes that leadership is
merely an attribution that people
make about other individuals.

Attribution theory, as you remember, deals with trying to make sense out of cause–effect relationships. When an event happens, people want to attribute it to a certain cause. The **attribution theory of leadership** says that leadership is merely an attribution that people make about other individuals.[27] Using the attribution framework, researchers have found that people tend to characterize leaders as having traits such as intelligence, outgoing personality, strong verbal skills, aggressiveness, understanding, and industriousness.[28] Similarly, the model of the high–high leader of the Ohio State study has been found to be consistent with people's attributions of what makes a good leader.[29] That is, regardless of the situation, a high–high leadership style tends to be perceived as best. At the organizational level, the attribution framework explains why people are prone to attribute either the extremely negative or the extremely positive performance of an organization to its leadership.[30] It also helps explain the vulnerability of CEOs when their organizations suffer major financial setbacks, regardless of whether they had much to do with it. It also clarifies why these CEOs tend to be given credit for extremely positive financial results, again regardless of how much or how little they contributed.

One of the more interesting themes in the attribution theory of leadership literature is the perception that effective leaders are generally considered consistent or unwavering in their decisions. One of the explanations for why Lee Iacocca and Ronald Reagan (during his first term as President) were perceived as leaders was that both were fully committed, steadfast, and consistent in the decisions they made and the goals they set. Evidence indicates that a "heroic" leader is perceived as being someone who takes up a difficult or unpopular cause but, through determination and persistence, ultimately succeeds.[31]

Charismatic Leadership Theory

Charismatic Leadership
Followers make attributions of
heroic or extraordinary leadership abilities when they observe
certain behaviors.

Charismatic leadership theory is an extension of attribution theory. It says that followers make attributions of heroic or extraordinary leadership abilities when they observe certain behaviors.[32] Studies on charismatic leadership have, for the most part, been directed at identifying those behaviors that differentiate charismatic leaders—the Jesse Jacksons and John F. Kennedys of the world—from their noncharismatic counterparts.

Several authors have attempted to identify personal characteristics of the charismatic leader. Robert House (of path–goal fame) has identified three: extremely high confidence, dominance, and strong convictions in his or her beliefs.[33] Warren Bennis, after studying ninety of the most effective and successful leaders in the United States, found that they had four common competencies: They had a compelling vision or sense of purpose; they could communicate that vision in clear terms that their followers could readily identify with; they demonstrated consistency and focus in the pursuit of their vision; and they knew their own strengths and capitalized on them.[34] The most recent and comprehensive analysis, however, has been completed by Jay Conger and Rabindra Kanungo at McGill University.[35] Among their conclusions, they propose that charismatic leaders have an idealized goal that they want to achieve and a strong personal commitment to that goal, are perceived as unconventional, are assertive and self-confident, and are perceived as agents of radical change rather than managers of the status quo. Table 17–3 summarizes the key characteristics that appear to differentiate charismatic leaders from noncharismatic ones.

What can we say about the charismatic leader's effect on his or her followers? There is an increasing body of research that shows impressive correlations between charismatic leadership and high performance and satisfaction among followers.[36] People working for charismatic leaders are motivated to exert extra work effort and, because they like their leader, express greater satisfaction.

If charisma is desirable, can people learn to be charismatic leaders? Or are

TABLE 17–3   Key Characteristics of Charismatic Leaders

1. *Self-confidence.* Charismatic leaders have complete confidence in their judgment and ability.

2. *Vision.* They have an idealized goal that proposes a future better than the status quo. The greater the disparity between this idealized goal and the status quo, the more likely that followers will attribute extraordinary vision to the leader.

3. *Ability to articulate the vision.* They are able to clarify and state the vision in terms that are understandable to others. This articulation demonstrates an understanding of the followers' needs and, hence, acts as a motivating force.

4. *Strong convictions about the vision.* Charismatic leaders are perceived as being strongly committed, and willing to take on high personal risk, incur high costs, and engage in self-sacrifice to achieve their vision.

5. *Behavior that is out of the ordinary.* They engage in behavior that is perceived as being novel, unconventional, and counter to norms. When successful, these behaviors evoke surprise and admiration in followers.

6. *Appearance as a change agent.* Charismatic leaders are perceived as agents of radical change rather than as caretakers of the status quo.

7. *Environment sensitivity.* They are able to make realistic assessments of the environmental constraints and resources needed to bring about change.

Based on Jay A. Conger and R. N. Kanungo, "Behavioral Dimensions of Charismatic Leadership," in Jay A. Conger and R. N. Kanungo, *Charismatic Leadership* (San Francisco: Jossey-Bass, 1988), p. 91.

charismatic leaders born with their qualities? While a small minority still think that charisma cannot be learned, most experts believe that individuals can be trained to exhibit charismatic behaviors.[37] For example, researchers have succeeded in actually scripting undergraduate business students to "play" charismatic.[38] The students were taught to articulate an overarching goal, communicate high performance expectations, exhibit confidence in the ability of subordinates to meet these expectations, and empathize with the needs of their subordinates; they learned to project a powerful, confident, and dynamic presence; and they practiced using a captivating and engaging voice tone. To further capture the dynamics and energy of charisma, the leaders were trained to evoke charismatic nonverbal characteristics: They alternated between pacing and sitting on the edges of their desks, leaned toward the subordinate, maintained direct eye contact, and had a relaxed posture and animated facial expressions. These researchers found that these students could *learn* how to project charisma. Moreover, subordinates of these leaders had higher task performance, task adjustment, and adjustment to the leader and to the group than did subordinates who worked under groups led by noncharismatic leaders.

One last point on this topic: Charismatic leadership may not always be needed to achieve high levels of employee performance. It may be most appropriate when the follower's task has an ideological component.[39] This may explain why, when charismatic leaders surface, it is more likely to be in politics, religion, or a business firm that is introducing a radically new product or facing a life-threatening crisis. Franklin D. Roosevelt offered a vision out of the Great Depression. Martin Luther King Jr. was unyielding in his desire to bring about social equality through peaceful means. Steve Jobs achieved unwavering loyalty and commitment from the technical staff he oversaw at Apple Computer during the late 1970s and early 1980s by articulating a vision of personal computers which would dramatically change the way people lived. Charismatic leaders, in fact, may become a liability to an organization once the crisis and need for dramatic change subsides.[40] Why? Because the charismatic leader's overwhelming self-confidence often becomes problematic. He or she is unable to

Now chairman of NeXT Computer, Steve Jobs became rich and famous as co-founder of Apple Computer. His charismatic leadership at Apple came out of his vision that personal computers would dramatically change the way people lived their lives. And he was able to convince Apple employees that they weren't just building computers, but that they were changing the world.

listen to others, becomes uncomfortable when challenged by aggressive subordinates, and begins to hold an unjustifiable belief in his or her "rightness" on issues.

Transactional versus Transformational Leadership

The final branch of research we'll touch on is the recent interest in differentiating transformational leaders from transactional leaders.[41] As you'll see, because transformational leaders are also charismatic, there is some overlap between this topic and our previous discussion of charismatic leadership.

Most of the leadership theories presented in this chapter—for instance, the Ohio State studies, Fiedler's model, path-goal theory, and the leader-participation model—have been addressing **transactional leaders.** These leaders guide or motivate their followers in the direction of established goals by clarifying role and task requirements. But there is another type of leader who inspires followers to transcend their own self-interests for the good of the organization and is capable of having a profound and extraordinary effect on his or her followers. These are **transformational leaders,** and include Leslie Wexner of The Limited retail chain and Bill Gates of Microsoft. They pay attention to the concerns and developmental needs of individual followers; they change followers' awareness of issues by helping those followers to look at old problems in new ways; and they are able to excite, arouse, and inspire followers to put out extra effort to achieve group goals.

Transactional and transformational leadership should not be viewed as opposing approaches to getting things done.[42] Transformational leadership is built on top of transactional leadership. Transformational leadership produces levels of subordinate effort and performance that go beyond what would occur with a transactional approach alone. Moreover, transformational leadership is more than charisma. "The purely charismatic [leader] may want followers to adopt the charismatic's world view and go no further; the transformational leader will attempt to instill in followers the ability to question not only established views but eventually those established by the leader."[43]

The evidence supporting the superiority of transformational leadership over the transactional variety is overwhelmingly impressive. For instance, a number of studies with U.S., Canadian, and German military officers found, at every level, that transformational leaders were evaluated as being more effective than their transactional counterparts.[44] Managers at Federal Express who were rated by their followers as exhibiting more transformational leadership were evaluated by their immediate

transactional leaders
Leaders who guide or motivate their followers in the direction of established goals by clarifying role and task requirements.

transformational leaders
Leaders who provide individualized consideration, intellectual stimulation, and possess charisma.

Is It Unethical to Create Charisma?

In 1993, no list of charismatic business leaders would have been complete without the names of John Sculley, Jack Welch, and Ted Turner. They personified the contemporary idea of charisma in the corporate world. But are these men authentically charismatic figures or self-created images?

Each of these men employs a public relations firm or has public relations specialists on his staff to shape and hone his image. John Sculley has promoted the vision of the take-charge executive who came to Apple Computer from PepsiCo and introduced marketing expertise and professional management into a company that had been run by a group of "techies" who wanted to change the world. Jack Welch relishes his reputation for reshaping General Electric by buying and selling dozens of businesses. Ted Turner has worked hard to project his "to hell with tradition" image in the popular press.

One view of these men is that they are authentically charismatic leaders whose actions and achievements have caught the fancy of the media. This view assumes that these leaders couldn't hide their charismatic qualities. It was just a matter of time before they were found out and gained the public's eye. Another view—certainly a more cynical one—proposes that these men consciously created an image that they wanted to project and then purposely went about doing things that would draw attention to, and confirm, that image. They are not inherently charismatic individuals but rather highly astute manipulators of symbols, circumstances, and the media. In support of this latter position, one can identify leaders such as Sandra Kurtzig at Ask Computer Systems, Max DePree at Herman Miller, and Chuck Knight at Emerson Electric, who are widely viewed as charismatic in their firms and industries but relatively unknown in the popular press.

Is charismatic leadership an inherent quality within a person, a label thrust upon an individual, or a purposely and carefully molded image? If charisma can be derived from the media, is it unethical for a person to engage in practices whose primary purposes are to create or enhance this perception? Is it unethical to *create* charisma? What do *you* think?

supervisors as higher performers and more promotable.[45] In summary, the overall evidence indicates that transformational, as compared with transactional, leadership is more strongly correlated with lower turnover rates, higher productivity, and higher employee satisfaction.[46]

Gender and Leadership: Do Males and Females Lead Differently?

Twenty years ago, the question "Do males and females lead differently?" could be accurately characterized as a purely academic issue—interesting but not very relevant. That's certainly not true today! Millions of women are now in management positions. Millions more will join the management ranks in the next few years. Gender myths about leadership can adversely affect hiring, performance evaluation, promotion, and other personnel decisions for both men and women. So this timely topic needs to be addressed.

First, however, a warning: This topic is controversial.[47] If male and female styles differ, does this imply that one is inferior? Moreover, if there is a difference, does labeling leadership styles by gender encourage stereotyping? These are not easily dismissed questions, and they should be considered. We'll come back to them later in this section.

The Evidence

A number of studies that have focused on gender and leadership style have been conducted in recent years.[48] Their general conclusion is that males and females *do* use different styles. Specifically, women tend to adopt a more democratic or participative style and a less autocratic or directive style than do men. Women are more likely to encourage participation, share power and information, and attempt to enhance followers' self-worth. They lead through inclusion and rely on their charisma, expertise, contacts, and interpersonal skills to influence others. Women tend to use transformational leadership, motivating others by transforming their self-interest into the goals of the organization.[49]

Men are more likely to use a directive, command-and-control style. They rely on the formal authority of their position for their influence base. Men use transactional leadership, handing out rewards for good work and punishment for bad.[50]

There is an interesting qualifier to the above findings. This tendency for female leaders to be more democratic than males declines when women are in male-dominated jobs. Apparently group norms and stereotypes of male roles override personal preferences so that women abandon their natural styles in such jobs and act more autocratically.

Is Different Better?

Given that males have historically held the majority of leadership positions in organizations, it may be tempting to assume that the existence of differences between males and females would automatically favor males. Not necessarily! In today's organizations, flexibility, teamwork, trust, and information sharing are rapidly replacing rigid structures, competitive individualism, control, and secrecy. The best managers listen,

ASK Computer Systems' CEO, Sandra Kurtzig, admits to using a more open and inclusive style than her male contemporaries. "Whenever possible, I try to compliment them in front of their peers and go up to them and hug them. A woman can show the warmth that a man often can't."

motivate, and provide support to their people. They inspire and influence rather than control. And, generally speaking, women seem to do these things better than men. As a specific example, the expanded use of cross-functional teams in organizations means that effective managers must become skillful negotiators. Women's leadership style makes them better at negotiating. They don't focus on wins, losses, and competition as do men. Women treat negotiations in the context of a continuing relationship—trying hard to make the other party a winner in its own and other's eyes.[51]

A Few Concluding Thoughts

The research evidence we've presented suggests a general relationship between gender and leadership style. But certainly gender doesn't imply destiny. Not all female leaders prefer a democratic style. And many men use transformational leadership. Thus we need to show caution in labeling leadership styles by gender. To refer to a "feminine style of leadership," for example, may create more confusion than clarity. Additionally, the research we've reviewed has looked at leadership *styles,* not leadership *effectiveness.* Which style is effective will depend on the situation. So even if men and women differ in their leadership styles, we should be careful not to assume that one is always preferable to the other. There are, for instance, organizations with inexperienced and unmotivated workers performing ambiguous tasks in which directive leadership is likely to be most effective.

One last point. Some people are more flexible in adjusting their leadership behaviors to different situations than are others.[52] That said, it is probably best to think of gender as providing a behavioral *tendency* in leadership. A person may, for instance, tend toward a participative style but use an autocratic one because the situation required the latter.

Leading Through Empowerment

One final note before we leave the topic of leadership. As we described in Chapter 2, managers are increasingly leading by empowering their employees. Millions of individual employees and teams of employees are making the key operating decisions that directly affect their work. They're developing budgets, scheduling work loads, controlling inventories, solving quality problems, and engaging in similar activities that until very recently were viewed as exclusively part of management's job.

The empowerment movement is being driven by two forces. First is the need for quick decisions by those people who are most knowledgeable about the issues. That requires moving decisions to lower levels. If organizations are to successfully compete in a global economy, they have to be able to make decisions and implement changes quickly. Second is the reality that the large layoffs in the middle-management ranks during the late 1980s and early 1990s have left many managers with considerably larger spans of control than they had a decade earlier. The same manager who today oversees a staff of thirty-five, can't micro-manage in the ways that were possible when his or her span was only ten. For instance, one manager at AT&T, a company that has undergone extensive downsizing, had to assume managerial responsibilities for three areas that had previously been handled by three people. This manager had to empower her people "because you can't know every data system and every policy. It's been a letting-go process and a stretching."[53]

Is the empowerment movement inconsistent with the contingency perspective on leadership? Yes and no! It is being sold, in some circles, as a universal panacea. That is, that empowerment will work anywhere. This universal perspective is an anticontingency approach to leadership. On the other hand, where a work force has the knowledge, skills, and experience to do their jobs competently, and where employees seek autonomy and possess an internal locus of control, empowering people through delegation and participation would be consistent with contingency theories such as situational leadership and path-goal. For instance, it is not a coincidence that empowerment efforts are almost always coupled with extensive training. By giving employees enhanced skills, abilities, and confidence, management increases the likelihood that the empowerment process will succeed.

Summary

This summary is organized by the chapter-opening learning objectives found on page 493.

1. Managers are appointed. They have legitimate power that allows them to reward and punish. Their ability to influence is founded upon the formal authority inherent in their positions. In contrast, leaders may either be appointed or emerge from within a group. Leaders can influence others to perform beyond the actions dictated by formal authority.

2. Six traits have been found on which leaders differ from nonleaders—drive, the desire to lead, honesty and integrity, self-confidence, intelligence, and job-relevant job knowledge. Yet possession of these traits is no guarantee of leadership because they ignore situational factors.

4. Fiedler's contingency model identifies three situational variables: leader–member relations, task structure, and position power. In situations that are highly favorable or highly unfavorable, task-oriented leaders tend to perform best. In moderately favorable or unfavorable situations, relations-oriented leaders are preferred.

5. Hersey and Blanchard's situational theory proposes that there are four leadership styles—telling, selling, participating, and delegating. Which style a leader chooses depends on the follower's job maturity and psychological maturity. As followers reach higher levels of maturity, the leader responds by reducing control and involvement.

6. The path-goal model proposes two classes of contingency variables—those in the environment and those that are part of the personal characteristics of the subordinate. Leaders select a specific behavior—directive, supportive, participative, or achievement-oriented—that is congruent with the demands of the environment and the characteristics of the subordinate.

7. Leaders might not be important when individual variables replace the need for a leader's support or ability to create structure and reduce task ambiguity; when jobs are unambiguous, routine, or intrinsically satisfying; or when such organizational characteristics as explicit goals, rigid rules and procedures, or cohesive work groups act in place of formal leadership.

8. Charismatic leaders are self-confident, possess a vision of a better future, have a strong belief in that vision, engage in unconventional behaviors, and are perceived as agents of radical change.

9. Transactional leaders guide their followers in the direction of established goals by clarifying role and task requirements. Transformational leaders inspire followers to transcend their own self-interests for the good of the organization and are capable of having a profound and extraordinary effect on their followers.

10. Research finds that women tend to adopt a more democratic or participative style of leadership, while men are more likely to use a directive, command-and-control style.

Review Questions

1. What is the managerial grid? Contrast its approach to leadership with that of the Ohio State and Michigan groups.
2. Is "high–high" the most effective leadership style? Explain.
3. Contrast the Hersey-Blanchard situational leadership theory with the managerial grid.
4. According to the leader-participation model, what contingencies dictate the degree of participation a leader should exercise?
5. What is the attribution theory of leadership?
6. Can people learn to be charismatic leaders? Explain.
7. Is charisma always appropriate in organizations?
8. Can we say whether male or female leadership styles are better? Why or why not?

Discussion Questions

1. What style of leadership, if any, does your instructor for this course use? Is it effective? If not, what would be more effective?
2. Which leadership theories, or parts of theories, appear to demonstrate reasonable predictive capability?
3. What similarities, if any, can you find among all the behavioral theories?
4. Do you think most managers use a contingency approach to increase leader effectiveness in practice? Discuss.
5. When average people on the street are asked to explain why a given individual is a leader, they tend to describe the person in terms such as competent, consistent, self-assured, inspiring a shared vision, invoking enthusiasm for goal-attainment, and supportive of his or her followers. Can you reconcile this description with leadership concepts presented in this chapter?

SELF-ASSESSMENT EXERCISE

What Kind of Leader Are You?

Instructions: The following items describe aspects of leadership behavior. Respond to each item according to the way you would be most likely to act if you were the leader of a work group. Circle whether you would be likely to behave in the described way Always (A), Frequently (F), Occasionally (O), Seldom (S), or Never (N).

If I Were the Leader of a Work Group . . .

A F O S N _____ 1. I would most likely act as the spokesperson of the group.

A F O S N _____ 2. I would encourage overtime work.

A F O S N _____ 3. I would allow members complete freedom in their work.

A F O S N _____ 4. I would encourage the use of uniform procedures.

A F O S N _____ 5. I would permit the members to use their own judgment in solving problems.

A F O S N _____ 6. I would stress being ahead of competing groups.

A F O S N _____ 7. I would speak as a representative of the group.

A F O S N _____ 8. I would needle members for greater effort.

A F O S N _____ 9. I would try out my ideas in the group.

A F O S N _____ 10. I would let the members do their work the way they think best.

A F O S N _____ 11. I would be working hard for a promotion.

A F O S N _____ 12. I would be able to tolerate postponement and uncertainty.

A F O S N _____ 13. I would speak for the group when visitors were present.

A F O S N _____ 14. I would keep the work moving at a rapid pace.

A F O S N _____ 15. I would turn the members loose on a job and let them go to it.

A F O S N _____ 16. I would settle conflicts when they occur in the group.

A F O S N _____ 17. I would get swamped by details.

A F O S N _____ 18. I would represent the group at outside meetings.

A F O S N _____ 19. I would be reluctant to allow the members any freedom of action.

A F O S N _____ 20. I would decide what shall be done and how it shall be done.

A F O S N _____ 21. I would push for increased production.

A F O S N _____ 22. I would let some members have authority that I could keep.

A F O S N _____ 23. Things would usually turn out as I predict.

A F O S N _____ 24. I would allow the group a high degree of initiative.

A F O S N _____ 25. I would assign group members to particular tasks.

A F O S N _____ 26. I would be willing to make changes.

A F O S N _____ 27. I would ask the members to work harder.

A F O S N _____ 28. I would trust the group members to exercise good judgment.

A F O S N _____ 29. I would schedule the work to be done.

A F O S N _____ 30. I would refuse to explain my actions.

A F O S N _____ 31. I would persuade others that my ideas are to their advantage.

A F O S N _____ 32. I would permit the group to set its own pace.

A F O S N _____ 33. I would urge the group to beat its previous record.

A F O S N _____ 34. I would act without consulting the group.

A F O S N _____ 35. I would ask that group members follow standard rules
and regulations.

Turn to page SK-6 for scoring directions and key.

_____

Source: From J. William Pfeiffer and John E. Jones, eds., *A Handbook of Structural Experiences for Human Relations Training,* Vol. 1 (San Diego, CA: University Associates, Inc., 1974). With permission.

THE
WOLLENBERG
BROADCASTING
GROUP

To: Alison LaRosa; Vice President, Corporate Human Resources
From: Veronica Taylor; Special Assistant to the President
Subject: Leadership Training

I concur with your recommendation that we develop an in-house leadership training program. Like you, I think our managers need some formal training to help them be more effective leaders. This includes all our managerial personnel in operations, programming, sales, and general administration.

Before we commit a budget to this program, I'd like to see a proposal. Assuming we put together a twenty-hour leadership course, what content should we include? And what training methods do you think would be most effective for helping our managers learn this content?

Please provide me with a two-page proposal responding to the above concerns.

CASE APPLICATION

Sue Reynolds at Connecticut Mutual

Sue Reynolds is twenty-two years old and will be receiving her B.S. degree in human resource management from the University of Hartford at the end of this semester. She has spent the past two summers working for Connecticut Mutual (CM), filling in on a number of different jobs while employees took their vacations. She has received and accepted an offer to join CM as a supervisor in the policy renewal department on a permanent basis upon graduation.

Connecticut Mutual is a large insurance company. In the headquarters office alone, where Sue will work, 5,000 employees are employed. The company believes strongly in the personal development of its employees. This translates into a philosophy, emanating from the top executive offices, of trust and respect for all CM employees.

The job Sue will be assuming requires her to direct the activities of twenty-five clerks. Their jobs require little training and are highly routine. A clerk's responsibility is to ensure that renewal notices are sent on current policies, to tabulate any changes in premiums from a standardized table, and to advise the sales division if a policy is to be canceled as a result of nonresponse to renewal notices.

Sue's group is composed of all females, ranging from nineteen to sixty-two years of age, with a median age of twenty-five. For the most part they are high school graduates with little prior working experience. The salary range for policy renewal clerks is $1,420 to $2,070 per month. Sue will be replacing a long-time CM employee, Mabel Fincher. Mabel is retiring after thirty-seven years with CM, the last fourteen spent as a policy renewal supervisor. Because Sue spent a few weeks in Mabel's group last summer, she is familiar with Mabel's style and knows most of the group members. She anticipates no problems from any of her soon-to-be employees, except possibly for Lillian Lantz. Lillian is well into her fifties, has been a policy renewal clerk for over a dozen years, and—as the "grand old lady"—carries a lot of weight with group members. Sue has concluded that her job could prove very difficult without Lantz's support.

Sue is determined to get her career off on the right foot. As a result, she has been doing a lot of thinking about the qualities of an effective leader.

Questions

1. What critical factors will influence Sue's success as a leader? Would these factors be the same if success were defined as group satisfaction rather than group productivity?

2. Do you think that Sue can choose a leadership style? If so, describe the style you think would be most effective for her. If not, why?

3. What suggestions might you make to Sue to help her win over or control Lillian Lantz?

VIDEO CASE

Richard Branson of the Virgin Group

Richard Branson is Great Britain's answer to Ted Turner. Brash, confident, unconventional, a self-promoter, a bold risk taker, a man with big ideas. Each is a billionaire who made his fortune through entrepreneurial activities. Both are also sportsmen. Turner made a reputation for himself in sailing. Branson made his in trans-Pacific ballooning.

Branson never graduated from high school. But he understood the taste of music consumers. He created Virgin Records and built it into a megacorporation. From there he ventured into producing music videos, running an island hotel, and creating an airline. His sale of Virgin Records for nearly a billion dollars gave him the deep pockets to pursue his current interest—Virgin Atlantic Airlines.

Virgin Atlantic has only eight 747s, but it has redefined trans-Atlantic service. First class is out, replaced by upper class—which includes free limo service. Branson's airline has aggressively sought and captured a large share of the trans-Atlantic business-traveler market. He's gotten it by merging technology with service. He was the first, for instance, to install a six-channel video monitor for every seat on his planes.

Branson is a fighter. He won't be intimidated by bigger foes. As a case in point, he went to court and charged British Airways with dirty tricks like dumping tickets on the market and calling Virgin customers at home. In February 1993, he won his case—receiving a multi-million dollar settlement and a public apology from BA.

Branson has a unique philosophy about business. Counter to current norms, he *doesn't* put the customer first. "Almost 100 percent of running a business is motivating your staff and the people around you. And if you can motivate them, then you can achieve anything. And too many companies have put shareholders first, customers second, staff way last. If you reverse that and you put your staff first, very quickly you find that the customers come first as well, and the shareholders come first, as well."

Questions

1. Contrast the leadership styles of Ted Turner and Richard Branson. Why do you think they have both been successful?

2. Would you call Branson's leadership style charismatic? Describe the aspects of Branson's leadership philosophy that you think make that philosophy work.

3. Who would you rather work for—Turner or Branson? Why?

Source: "Richard Branson," *ABC News Business World*, November 22, 1992.

CHAPTER 18

Communication and Interpersonal Skills

LEARNING OBJECTIVES

After Reading This Chapter, You Should Be Able To:

1. Define communication and explain why it is important to managers.
2. Describe the communication process.
3. List techniques for overcoming communication barriers.
4. Identify behaviors related to effective active listening.
5. Identify behaviors related to providing effective feedback.
6. Describe the contingency factors in delegation.
7. Identify behaviors related to effective delegating.
8. Explain the "hot stove" rule.
9. Identify behaviors related to effective disciplining.
10. Describe the steps in analyzing and resolving conflict situations.
11. Explain when a manager might want to stimulate conflict.
12. Contrast distributive and integrative bargaining.

Part of Jenny Jankovich's effectiveness in communicating with her staff is choosing the right medium for delivering her message.

A s Jenny Jankovich related the experience, she knew she had made a major mistake soon after arriving at work on Monday, July 9th.

As director of nursing at Scripps Memorial Hospital in San Diego, Jenny oversees nine shift supervisors and 115 registered nurses and nursing aides.

When Jenny came into the hospital around 6:05 a.m., she saw a number of nurses—from both the shift going off duty and the new shift coming on—in scattered groups, talking in a very animated fashion. But when the group members saw Jenny, they immediately stopped talking. The sudden silence and the cold stares told her that *she* was the object of discussion and what they'd been saying wasn't likely to be complimentary.

About thirty seconds after Jenny had settled into her office, one of her supervisors, Dee Marcos, came in. Dee didn't mince words.

"Jenny, you really blew it with those letters you sent out last week. Everyone is upset."

"What's the problem?" asked Jenny. "We had agreed at the supervisory staff meeting that we would notify everyone in our unit about the budget problems and the possibility of layoffs. All I did was carry that decision out."

"What are you talking about?" replied Dee. She was obviously upset. "We're dealing with people's livelihoods here. We [the supervisors] assumed that you'd talk to all the nurses directly, in small groups, tell them about the problem, break it to them gently, and allow them to ask questions. In that way, we'd cushion a large part of the blow. But you sent them this form letter, to their homes! My God, Jenny, they got those letters on Friday and have spent all weekend anguishing, calling friends and colleagues, spreading rumors. We've had a near riot on our hands all weekend. I've never seen staff morale this low."

Jenny Jankovich had made a mistake. Maybe two. First, she clearly failed to communicate to her staff her intention to mail letters. Second, those letters were the wrong medium for delivering her message. Some communications are effectively handled in the written form. Others are better relayed orally. When Jenny later reflected on her action, she came to the conclusion that—like many individuals—she tends to avoid oral communications. She suffers from oral communication apprehension.[1] Unfortunately, in this case, her apprehension acted as a barrier to selecting the right medium for communicating a message that she knew was likely to create fear and uncertainty for her staff. In such a situation, Jenny needed to convey her message in a manner that would allow for maximum clarity and that would allow her and her supervisors to quickly manage the potential damage. And the best way to do that is orally. The decision to mail letters to employees' homes with the unexpected bad news proved to be an unfortunate mistake.

Jenny Jankovich's mistake illustrates an important point: Communication is fundamentally linked to managerial performance.[2] In this chapter, we will present basic concepts in interpersonal communication. We'll explain the communication process, methods of communicating, barriers to effective communication, and ways to overcome those barriers. Additionally, because most interpersonal skills rely heavily on effective communication, we'll also use this chapter to review the basic interpersonal skills in which every manager needs to become proficient. These include active listening, providing feedback, delegating, disciplining, managing conflict, and negotiating.

Understanding Communication

The importance of effective communication for managers can't be overemphasized for one specific reason: Everything a manager does involves communicating. Not *some* things, but everything! A manager can't make a decision without information. That information has to be communicated. Once a decision is made, communication must again take place. Otherwise, no one will know that a decision has been made. The best idea, the most creative suggestion, or the finest plan cannot take form without communication. Managers therefore need effective communication skills. We are not suggesting, of course, that good communication skills alone make a successful manager. We can say, however, that ineffective communication skills can lead to a continuous stream of problems for the manager.

What Is Communication?

Communication involves the transfer of meaning. If no information or ideas have been conveyed, communication has not taken place. The speaker who is not heard or the writer who is not read does not communicate. The philosophical question, "If a tree falls in a forest and no one hears it, does it make any noise?" must, in a communicative context, be answered negatively.

communication
The transferring and understanding of meaning.

However, for communication to be successful, the meaning must be not only imparted, but also understood. A letter addressed to me but written in Portuguese (a language of which I am totally ignorant) cannot be considered a communication until I have it translated. **Communication** is the *transferring* and *understanding* of meaning. Perfect communication, if such a thing were possible, would exist when a transmitted thought or idea was perceived by the receiver exactly as it was envisioned by the sender.

Another point to keep in mind is that *good* communication is often erroneously defined by the communicator as *agreement* instead of clarity of understanding.[3] If someone disagrees with us, many of us assume that the person just didn't fully understand our position. In other words, many of us define good communication as having someone accept our views. But I can understand very clearly what you mean and *not* agree with what you say. In fact, when observers conclude that a lack of communication must exist because a conflict has continued for a prolonged time, a

interpersonal communication
Communication between two or more people in which the parties are treated as individuals rather than objects.

message
A purpose to be conveyed.

encoding
Converting a message into symbols.

channel
The medium by which a message travels.

decoding
Retranslating a sender's message.

communication process
The seven stages in which meaning is transmitted and understood.

noise
Disturbances that interfere with the transmission of a message.

close examination often reveals that there is plenty of effective communication going on. Each fully understands the other's position. The problem is one of equating effective communication with agreement.

A final point before we move on: Our attention in this chapter will be on **interpersonal communication.** This is communication between two or more people in which the parties are treated as individuals rather than objects. Organizationwide communication—which encompasses topics such as the flow of organizational communication, communication networks, and the development of management information systems—will be covered in our discussion of information control systems in Chapter 20.

The Communication Process

Before communication can take place, a purpose, expressed as a **message** to be conveyed, must exist. It passes between a source (the sender) and a receiver. The message is converted to symbolic form (called **encoding**) and passed by way of some medium (**channel**) to the receiver, who retranslates the sender's message (called **decoding**). The result is the transfer of meaning from one person to another.[4]

Figure 18–1 depicts the **communication process.** This model is made up of seven stages: (1) the communication source, (2) the message, (3) encoding, (4) the channel, (5) decoding, (6) the receiver, and (7) feedback. In addition, the entire process is susceptible to **noise**—that is, disturbances that interfere with the transmission of the message (depicted in Figure 18–1 as lightning bolts). Typical examples of noise include illegible print, telephone static, inattention by the receiver, or the background sounds of machinery on the production floor. Remember that anything that interferes with understanding—whether internal (such as the low speaking voice of the speaker/sender) or external (like the loud voices of co-workers talking at an adjoining desk)—represents noise. Noise can create distortion at any point in the communication process. Because the impact of external noise on communication effectiveness is self-evident, let's look at some potential internal sources of distortion in the communication process.

A source initiates a message by encoding a thought. Four conditions affect the encoded message: skill, attitudes, knowledge, and the social-cultural system.

If textbook authors are without the requisite skills, their message will not reach students in the form desired. My success in communicating to you depends upon my

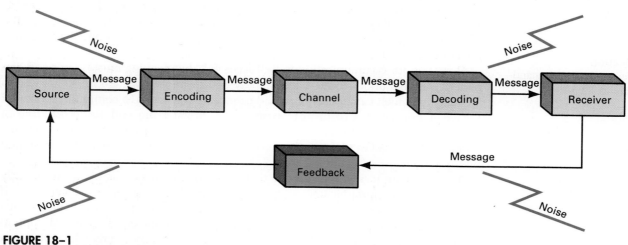

FIGURE 18–1
The Communication Process

writing skills. One's total communicative success also includes speaking, reading, listening, and reasoning skills. As we discussed in Chapter 14, our attitudes influence our behavior. We hold preformed ideas on numerous topics, and these ideas affect our communications. Furthermore, we are restricted in our communicative activity by the extent of our knowledge of a particular topic. We cannot communicate what we do not know; and should our knowledge be too extensive, it is possible that our receiver will not understand our message. Clearly, the amount of knowledge we have about a subject affects the message we seek to transfer. Finally, just as our attitudes influence our behavior, so does our position in the social-cultural system in which we exist. Our beliefs and values (all part of our culture) act to influence us as communication sources.

The message itself can cause distortion in the communication process, regardless of the supporting apparatus used to convey it. Our message is the actual physical product encoded by the source. "When we speak, the speech is the message. When we write, the writing is the message. When we paint, the picture is the message. When we gesture, the movements of our arms, the expressions on our face are the message."[5] Our message is affected by the code or group of symbols we use to transfer meaning, the content of the message itself, and the decisions that the source makes in selecting and arranging both codes and content. Each of these three segments can act to distort the message.

The *channel* is the medium through which the message travels. It is selected by the sender. Common channels are air for the spoken word and paper for the written word. If you decide to convey to a friend something that happened to you during the day in a face-to-face conversation, you're using spoken words and gestures to transmit your message. But you have choices. A specific message—an invitation to a party, for example—can be communicated orally or in writing. In an organization, certain channels are more appropriate for certain messages. Obviously, if the building is on fire, a memo to convey the fact is inappropriate! If something is important, such as an employee's performance appraisal, a manager might want to use multiple channels—for instance, an oral review followed by a summary letter. This decreases the potential for distortion.

The *receiver* is the individual to whom the message is directed. But before the message can be received, the symbols in it must be translated into a form that can be understood by the receiver. This is the *decoding* of the message. Just as the encoder was limited by his or her skills, attitudes, knowledge, and social-cultural system, so is the receiver equally restricted. Just as the source must be skillful in writing or speaking, the receiver must be skillful in reading or listening, and both must be able to reason. A person's level of knowledge influences his or her ability to receive, just as it does his or her ability to send. Moreover, the receiver's preformed attitudes and cultural background can distort the message being transferred.

The final link in the communicative process is a feedback loop. "If a communication source decodes the message that he encodes, if the message is put back into the system, we have feedback."[6] That is, *feedback* returns the message to the sender and provides a check on whether understanding has been achieved.

Methods of Communicating

The most popular communication methods used by people in organizations are verbal or oral interaction, written communications, nonverbal communication, and electronic media. In this section we'll briefly describe each method.

Oral People communicate with each other most often by talking, or oral communication. Popular forms of oral communication include speeches, formal one-on-one and group discussions, informal discussions, and the rumor mill or grapevine.

Most managers are like Joseph Vittoria, CEO at Avis. They rely heavily on face-to-face communication to get their job done.

The advantages of oral communications are quick transmission and quick feedback. A verbal message can be conveyed and a response received in a minimum amount of time. If the receiver is unsure of the message, rapid feedback allows the sender to detect the uncertainty and to correct it.

The major disadvantage of oral communication surfaces whenever a message has to be passed through a number of people. The more people who are involved, the greater the potential for distortion. Each person interprets the message in his or her own way. The message's content, when it reaches its destination, is often very different from the original. In an organization where decisions and other communiqués are verbally passed up and down the authority hierarchy, considerable opportunity exists for messages to become distorted.

Written   Written communications include memos, letters, organizational periodicals, bulletin boards, or any other device that transmits written words or symbols.

Why would a sender choose to use written communications? Because they're permanent, tangible, and verifiable. Typically, both sender and receiver have a record of the communication. The message can be stored for an indefinite period of time. If there are questions about the content of the message, it is physically available for later reference. This is particularly important for complex or lengthy communications. The marketing plan for a new product is likely to contain a number of tasks spread out over several months. By putting it in writing, those who have to initiate the plan can readily refer to it over the life of the plan. A final benefit of written communication comes from the process itself. Except in rare instances, such as when presenting a formal speech, more care is taken with the written word than with the oral word. Having to put something in writing forces a person to think more carefully about what he or she wants to convey. Therefore written communications are more likely to be well thought out, logical, and clear.

Of course, written messages have their drawbacks. While writing may be more precise, it also consumes a great deal more time. You could convey far more information to your college instructor in a one-hour oral exam than in a one-hour written exam. In fact, you could probably say the same thing in ten to fifteen minutes that takes you an hour to write. The other major disadvantage is feedback or lack of it. Oral communications allow the receivers to respond rapidly to what they think they hear. However, written communications do not have a built-in feedback mechanism.

The result is that sending a memo is no assurance that it will be received: if it is received, there is no guarantee that the recipient will interpret it as the sender meant. The latter point is also relevant in oral communiqués, except that it's easier in such cases merely to ask the receiver to summarize what you've said. An accurate summary presents feedback evidence that the message has been received and understood.

nonverbal communication
Communication transmitted without words.

Nonverbal Some of the most meaningful communications are neither spoken nor written. These are **nonverbal communications.** A loud siren or a red light at an intersection tells you something without words. When a college instructor is teaching a large lecture class, she doesn't need words to tell her that her students are bored when eyes get glassy or students begin to read the school newspaper. Similarly, when papers start to rustle and notebooks begin to close, the message is clear: Class time is about over. The size of a person's office and desk or the clothes a person wears also conveys messages to others. However, the best-known areas of nonverbal communication are body language and verbal intonation.

body language
Gestures, facial configurations, and other movements of the body that convey meaning.

Body language refers to gestures, facial configurations, and other movements of the body. A snarled face, for example, says something different from a smile. Hand motions, facial expressions, and other gestures can communicate emotions or temperaments such as aggression, fear, shyness, arrogance, joy, and anger.

verbal intonation
An emphasis given to words or phrases that conveys meaning.

Verbal intonation refers to the emphasis someone gives to words or phrases. To illustrate how intonations can change the meaning of a message, consider the student who asks the instructor a question. The instructor replies, "What do you mean by that?" The student's reaction will vary, depending on the tone of the instructor's response. A soft, smooth tone creates a different meaning from one that is abrasive and puts a strong emphasis on the last word. Most of us would view the first intonation as coming from someone who sincerely sought clarification, whereas the second suggests that the person is aggressive or defensive.

The fact that every oral communication also has a nonverbal message cannot be overemphasized. Why? Because the nonverbal component is likely to carry the greatest impact. One researcher found that 55 percent of an oral message is derived from facial expression and physical posture, 38 percent from verbal intonation, and only 7 percent from the actual words used.[7] Most of us know that animals respond to how we say something rather than what we say. Apparently, people aren't much different.

electronic mail
Instantaneous transmission of written messages on computers that are linked together.

Electronic Media Today we rely on a number of sophisticated electronic media to carry our communications. In addition to the more common media—the telephone and public address system—we have closed-circuit television, voice-activated computers, xerographic reproduction, fax machines, and a host of other electronic devices that we can use in conjunction with speech or paper to create more effective communication. Maybe the fastest growing is **electronic mail**. Electronic mail allows individuals to instantaneously transmit written messages on computers that are linked together with the appropriate software. Messages sit at the receiver's terminal to be read at the receiver's convenience. Electronic mail is fast and cheap and can be used to send the same message to dozens of people at the same time. Its other strengths and weaknesses generally parallel those of written communications.

Barriers to Effective Communication

In our discussion of the communication process, we noted the consistent potential for distortion. What causes such distortions? In addition to the general distortions identified in the communication process, there are other barriers to effective communication.

MANAGING FROM A GLOBAL PERSPECTIVE

Cross-Cultural Insights Into Communication Processes

Interpersonal communication is not conducted in the same way around the world. For example, compare countries that place a high value on individualism (such as the United States) with countries where the emphasis is on collectivism (such as Japan).[8]

Owing to the emphasis on the individual in countries such as the United States, communication patterns there are individual-oriented and rather clearly spelled out. For instance, U.S. managers rely heavily on memoranda, announcements, position papers, and other formal forms of communication to stake out their positions in intra-organizational negotiations. Supervisors in the United States often hoard secret information in an attempt to promote their own advancement and as a way of inducing their subordinates to accept decisions and plans. For their own protection, lower-level employees also engage in this practice.

In collectivist countries such as Japan, there is more interaction for its own sake and a more informal manner of interpersonal contact. The Japanese manager, in contrast to U.S. managers, will engage in extensive verbal consultation over an issue first and only draw up a formal document later to outline the agreement that was made. Face-to-face communication is encouraged. Additionally, open communication is an inherent part of the Japanese work setting. Work spaces are open and crowded with individuals at different levels in the work hierarchy. U.S. organizations emphasize authority, hierarchy, and formal lines of communication.

These cultural differences between the United States and Japan can make negotiations difficult between executives from these countries.[9] Research on negotiations has found, for example, that executives from these countries come to the negotiating table with two different objectives. Americans come to make a deal, while their Japanese counterparts come to start a relationship. Americans want to begin talking immediately about numbers and details. Japanese executives start the process by talking in generalities. Americans tend to be blunt and forthright in their refusals. Many Japanese find this aggressiveness and frankness offensive.

---

filtering
The deliberate manipulation of information to make it appear more favorable to the receiver.

Filtering   **Filtering** is the deliberate manipulation of information to make it appear more favorable to the receiver. For example, when a manager tells his or her boss what the boss wants to hear, the manager is filtering information.

The extent of filtering tends to be a function of the height of the structure and the organizational culture. The more vertical levels there are in an organization's hierarchy, the more opportunities there are for filtering. The organizational culture encourages or discourages filtering by the type of behavior it emphasizes through rewards. The more rewards emphasize style and appearance, the more managers are motivated to alter communications in their favor.

Selective Perception   We've mentioned selective perception several times throughout this book. The receiver in the communication process selectively sees and hears communications depending on his or her needs, motivations, experience, background, and other personal characteristics. The receiver also projects his or her interests and expectations into communications in decoding them. The employment interviewer who expects a female job candidate to put family before career is likely to *see* that in female candidates, regardless of whether the candidates feel that way. As we said in Chapter 14, we don't see reality; instead, we interpret what we see and call it reality.

Emotions How the receiver feels when a message is received influences how he or she interprets it. You will often interpret the same message differently, depending on whether you are happy or distressed. Extreme emotions such as jubilation or depression are most likely to hinder effective communication. In such instances, we often disregard our rational and objective thinking processes and substitute emotional judgments. It's best to avoid making decisions when you're upset because you're not likely to be thinking clearly.

Language Words mean different things to different people. Age, education, and cultural background are three of the more obvious variables that influence the language a person uses and the definitions he or she gives to words. The language of William F. Buckley, Jr., is clearly different from that of the typical high-school-educated factory worker. The latter, in fact, would undoubtedly have trouble understanding much of Buckley's vocabulary. In an organization, employees usually come from diverse backgrounds. Furthermore, horizontal differentiation creates specialists who develop their own jargon or technical language. In large organizations, members are often widely dispersed geographically (some even work in different countries), and employees in each locale will use terms and phrases that are unique to their area. Vertical differentiation can also cause language problems. For instance, differences in the meaning of words such as *incentives* and *quotas* occur at different levels of management.[10] Top managers often speak about the need for incentives and quotas, yet these terms imply manipulation and create resentment among lower managers.

The point is that while you and I might both speak the same language (English), our use of that language is far from uniform. A knowledge of how each of us modifies the language would minimize communication difficulties. The problem is that members in an organization usually don't know how others with whom they interact have modified the language. Senders tend to assume that their words and terms will be appropriately interpreted by the receiver. This, of course, is often incorrect and creates communication difficulties.

Nonverbal Cues Earlier, we noted the nonverbal communication is an important way in which people convey messages to others. But nonverbal communication is almost always accompanied by oral communication. As long as the two are in agreement, they act to reinforce each other. My boss's words tell me that he is angry; his tone of voice and body movements indicate anger. I can conclude—probably correctly—that he is angry. When nonverbal cues are inconsistent with the oral message, the receiver becomes confused, and the clarity of the message suffers. The boss who tells you that she sincerely wants to hear about your problem and then proceeds to read her mail while you talk is sending conflicting signals.

Overcoming the Barriers

Given these barriers to communication, what can managers do to overcome them? The following suggestions should help to make communication more effective.

Use Feedback Many communication problems can be directly attributed to misunderstandings and inaccuracies. These problems are less likely to occur if the manager uses the feedback loop in the communication process. This feedback can be verbal or nonverbal.

If a manager asks a receiver, "Did you understand what I said?" the response

When Rosetta Riley was hired in 1986 as director of customer satisfaction at the Cadillac division of General Motors, she was frustrated by the lack of feedback from customers. She recruited key dealerships across the United States to serve as "listening posts" and had the dealers call a team of technical specialists directly with comments. Riley also convinced everyone at the company, from plant workers to executives, to call new Cadillac buyers for feedback. Her program proved highly successful. Her work helped Cadillac win the highly prized Baldridge quality award.

active listening
Listening for full meaning without making premature judgments or interpretations.

represents feedback. Also, feedback should include more than yes and no answers. The manager can ask a set of questions about a message in order to determine whether or not the message was received as intended. Better yet, the manager can ask the receiver to restate the message in his or her own words. If the manager then hears what was intended, understanding and accuracy should be enhanced. Feedback includes subtler methods than the direct asking of questions or the summarizing of messages. General comments can give a manager a sense of the receiver's reaction to a message. In addition, performance appraisals, salary reviews, and promotions represent important forms of feedback.

Of course, feedback does not have to be conveyed in words. Actions *can* speak louder than words. The sales manager who sends out a directive to his or her staff describing a new monthly sales report that all sales personnel will need to complete receives feedback if some of the salespeople fail to turn in the new report. This feedback suggests that the sales manager needs to clarify further the initial directive. Similarly, when you give a speech to a group of people, you watch their eyes and look for other nonverbal clues to tell you whether they are getting your message or not.

Simplify Language   Because language can be a barrier, managers should choose words and structure their messages in ways that will make those messages clear and understandable to the receiver. The manager needs to simplify his or her language and consider the audience to whom the message is directed so that the language will be tailored to the receivers. Remember, effective communication is achieved when a message is both received and *understood*. Understanding is improved by simplifying the language used in relation to the audience intended. This means, for example, that a hospital administrator should always try to communicate in clear, easily understood terms and that the language used in messages to the surgical staff should be purposely different from that used with office employees. Jargon can facilitate understanding when it is used within a group of those who know what it means, but it can cause innumerable problems when used outside that group.

Consistent with the previous discussion on feedback, language problems in an important message can be minimized by trying out the message on someone who is unfamiliar with the issue. For example, having a friend read a speech or letter before it is officially communicated can be an effective device for identifying confusing terminology, unclear assumptions, or discontinuous logic flows.

Listen Actively   When someone talks, we hear. But too often we don't listen. Listening is an active search for meaning, whereas hearing is passive. In listening, two people are thinking: the receiver and the sender.

Many of us are poor listeners. Why? Because it's difficult, and it's usually more satisfying to be on the offensive. Listening, in fact, is often more tiring than talking. It demands intellectual effort. Unlike hearing, **active listening** demands total concentration. The average person speaks at a rate of about 150 words per minute, whereas we have the capacity to listen at the rate of nearly 1,000 words per minute.[11] The difference obviously leaves idle time for the brain and opportunities for the mind to wander.

Active listening is enhanced by developing empathy with the sender—that is, by placing yourself in the sender's position. Because senders differ in attitudes, interests, needs, and expectations, empathy makes it easier to understand the actual content of a message. An empathetic listener reserves judgment on the message's content and carefully listens to what is being said. The goal is to improve one's ability to receive the full meaning of a communication without having it distorted by premature

ETHICAL DILEMMAS IN MANAGEMENT

Is It Unethical to Purposely Distort Information?

The issue of "ethics in lying" was introduced in Chapter 1. Since then, you've had ample time to think about this issue. Because lying is such a broad concern and so closely intertwined with interpersonal communication, this might be a good time to think again about dilemmas that managers face relating to the intentional distortion of information.

You have just seen your division's sales report for last month. Sales are down considerably. Your boss, who works 2,000 miles away in another city, is unlikely to see last month's sales figures. You're optimistic that sales will pick up this month and next so that your overall quarterly numbers will be acceptable. You also know that your boss is the type of person who hates to hear bad news. You're having a phone conversation today with your boss. He happens to ask, in passing, how last month's sales went. Do you tell him the truth?

A subordinate asks you about a rumor she's heard that your department and all its employees will be transferred from New York to Dallas. You know the rumor to be true, but you would rather not let the information out just yet. You're fearful that it could hurt departmental morale and lead to premature resignations. What do you say to your employee?

These two incidents illustrate dilemmas that managers face relating to evading the truth, distorting facts, or lying to others.

It might not always be in a manager's best interest or those of his or her unit to provide full and complete information. In fact, a strong argument can be made for managers to purposely keep their communications vague and unclear.[12] Keeping communications fuzzy can cut down on questions, permit faster decision making, minimize objections, reduce opposition, make it easier to deny one's earlier statements, preserve the freedom to change one's mind, permit one to say "No" diplomatically, help to avoid confrontation and anxiety, and provide other benefits that work to the advantage of the manager.

Is it unethical to purposely distort communications to get a favorable outcome? Is distortion acceptable but lying not? What about "little white lies" that really don't hurt anybody? What do *you* think?

judgments or interpretations. Active listening skills are discussed in considerable detail beginning on the next page.

Constrain Emotions   It would be naive to assume that managers always communicate in a fully rational manner. We know that emotions can severely cloud and distort the transference of meaning. A manager who is emotionally upset over an issue is more likely to misconstrue incoming messages and fail to express his or her outgoing messages clearly and accurately. What can the manager do? The simplest answer is to desist from further communication until he or she has regained composure.

Watch Nonverbal Cues   If actions speak louder than words, then it's important to watch your actions to make sure that they align with and reinforce the words that go along with them. We noted that nonverbal messages carry a great deal of weight.

Given this fact, the effective communicator watches his or her nonverbal cues to ensure that they too convey the desired message.

Developing Interpersonal Skills

Would it surprise you to know that more managers are probably fired because of poor interpersonal skills than for lack of technical ability on the job?[13] A survey of 191 top executives at six *Fortune* 500 companies found that, according to these executives, the single biggest reason for failure was poor interpersonal skills.[14] The Center for Creative Leadership in North Carolina estimates that half of all managers and 30 percent of all senior managers have some type of difficulty with people.[15]

If you need any further evidence of the importance of interpersonal skills, we would point to a recent comprehensive study of the people who hire students with undergraduate business degrees and depend on these hires to fill future management vacancies. This study found that the area in which these graduates were most deficient was in leadership and interpersonal skills.[16] Of course, these overall findings are consistent with our view of the manager's job. Because managers ultimately get things done through others, competencies in leadership, communication, and other interpersonal skills must be a prerequisite to managerial effectiveness.

In the rest of this chapter, we'll review the key interpersonal skills that every manager needs to develop.[17]

Active Listening Skills

The ability to be an effective listener is too often taken for granted. We confuse hearing with listening. Hearing is merely picking up sound vibrations. Listening is making sense of what we hear. Listening requires paying attention, interpreting, and remembering sound stimuli.

Active Versus Passive Listening

Effective listening is active rather than passive. In passive listening, you're much like a tape recorder. You absorb the information given. If the speaker provides you with a clear message and makes his or her delivery interesting enough to keep your attention, you'll probably get most of what the speaker is trying to communicate. But active listening requires you to get inside the speaker so that you can understand the communication from his or her point of view. As you'll see, active listening is hard work. You have to concentrate, and you have to want to fully understand what a speaker is saying. Students who use active listening techniques for an entire fifty-minute lecture are as tired as their instructor when the lecture is over because they have put as much energy into listening as the instructor put into speaking.

There are four essential requirements for active listening. You need to listen with (1) intensity, (2) empathy, (3) acceptance, and (4) a willingness to take responsibility for completeness.[18]

As noted previously, the human brain is capable of handling a speaking rate that is about six times as fast as that of the average speaker. That leaves a lot of time for idle mind wandering while listening. The active listener concentrates intensely on what the speaker is saying and tunes out the thousands of miscellaneous thoughts (about money, sex, vacations, parties, friends, getting the car fixed, and the like) that create distractions. What do active listeners do with their idle brain time? Summarize and

Patricia Carrigan, a former plant manager for General Motors, used her finely-honed interpersonal skills to break down the traditionally antagonistic relationship between management and the union at GM's Lakewood assembly plant in Atlanta.

integrate what has been said! They put each new bit of information into the context of what has preceded it.

Empathy requires you to put yourself in the speaker's shoes. You try to understand what the *speaker* wants to communicate rather than what *you* want to understand. Notice that empathy demands both knowledge of the speaker and flexibility on your part. You need to suspend your own thoughts and feelings and adjust what you see and feel to your speaker's world. In that way you increase the likelihood that you will interpret the message being spoken in the way the speaker intended.

An active listener demonstrates acceptance. He or she listens objectively without judging content. This is no easy task. It is natural to be distracted by the content of what a speaker says, especially when we disagree with it. When we hear something we disagree with, we begin formulating our mental arguments to counter what is being said. Of course, in doing this we miss the rest of the message. The challenge for the active listener is to absorb what is being said and to withhold judgment on content until the speaker is finished.

The final ingredient of active listening is taking responsibility for completeness. That is, the listener does whatever is necessary to get the full intended meaning from the speaker's communication. Two widely used active listening techniques to achieve this end are listening for feelings as well as for content and asking questions to ensure understanding.

Developing Effective Active Listening Skills

From a review of the active listening literature, we can identify eight specific behaviors that effective listeners demonstrate.[19] As you review these behaviors, ask yourself the degree to which they describe your listening practices. If you're not currently using these techniques, there is no better time than today to begin developing them.

Make Eye Contact   How do you feel when somebody doesn't look at you when you're speaking? If you're like most people, you're likely to interpret this as aloofness or disinterest. It's ironic that while "you listen with your ears, people judge whether you are listening by looking at your eyes."[20] Making eye contact with the speaker focuses your attention, reduces the likelihood that you will become distracted, and encourages the speaker.

Exhibit Affirmative Nods and Appropriate Facial Expressions   The effective listener shows interest in what is being said. How? Through nonverbal signals. Affirmative nods and appropriate facial expressions, when added to good eye contact, convey to the speaker that you're listening.

Avoid Distracting Actions or Gestures   The other side of showing interest is avoiding actions that suggest that your mind is somewhere else. When listening, *don't* look at your watch, shuffle papers, play with your pencil, or engage in similar distractions. They make the speaker feel that you're bored or uninterested. Furthermore, they indicate that you *aren't* fully attentive and might be missing part of the message that the speaker wants to convey.

Ask Questions   The critical listener analyzes what he or she hears and asks questions. This behavior provides clarification, ensures understanding, and assures the speaker that you're listening.

paraphrasing
Restating what a speaker has said but in your own words.

Paraphrase   **Paraphrasing** means restating *in your own words* what the speaker has said. The effective listener uses phrases as: "What I hear you saying is . . ." or "Do you mean . . . ?" Why rephrase what's already been said? There are two reasons.

First, it's an excellent control device to check on whether you're listening carefully. You can't paraphrase accurately if your mind is wandering or if you're thinking about what you're going to say next. Second, it's a control for accuracy. By rephrasing in your own words what the speaker has said and feeding it back to the speaker, you verify the accuracy of your understanding.

Avoid Interrupting the Speaker   Let the speaker complete his or her thought before you try to respond. Don't try to second-guess where the speaker's thoughts are going. When the speaker is finished, you'll know it.

Don't Overtalk   Most of us would rather speak our own ideas than listen to what someone else says. Too many of us listen only because it's the price we have to pay to get people to let us talk. While talking might be more fun and silence might be uncomfortable, you can't talk and listen at the same time. The good listener recognizes this fact and doesn't overtalk.

Make Smooth Transitions Between the Roles of Speaker and Listener   As a student sitting in a lecture hall, you probably find it relatively easy to get into an effective listening frame of mind. Why? Because communication is essentially one-way; the instructor talks and you listen. But the instructor–student dyad is atypical. In most work situations you're continually shifting back and forth between the roles of speaker and listener. The effective listener makes transitions smoothly from speaker to listener and back to speaker. From a listening perspective this means concentrating on what a speaker has to say and practicing not thinking about what you're going to say as soon as you get your chance.

Feedback Skills

Ask a manager about the feedback he or she gives subordinates, and you're likely to get a qualified answer. If the feedback is positive, it's likely to be given promptly and enthusiastically. Negative feedback is often treated very differently. Like most of us, managers don't particularly enjoy being the bearers of bad news. They fear offending or having to deal with the recipient's defensiveness. The result is that negative feedback is often avoided, delayed, or substantially distorted.[21] The purposes of this section are to show you the importance of providing both positive and negative feedback and to identify specific techniques to make your feedback more effective.

Positive Versus Negative Feedback

We said that managers treat positive and negative feedback differently. So, too, do recipients. You need to understand this fact and adjust your style accordingly.

Positive feedback is more readily and accurately perceived than negative feedback. Furthermore, while positive feedback is almost always accepted, negative feedback often meets resistance.[22] Why? The logical answer seems to be that people want to hear good news and block out the bad. Positive feedback fits what most people wish to hear and already believe about themselves.

Does this mean that you should avoid giving negative feedback? No! What it means is that you need to be aware of potential resistance and learn to use negative feedback in situations in which it is most likely to be accepted.[23] What are those situations? Research indicates that negative feedback is most likely to be accepted when it comes from a credible source or if it is objective in form. Subjective impressions carry weight only when they come from a person with high status and credibility.[24] This suggests that negative feedback that is supported by hard data—numbers, specific examples, and the like—has a good chance of being accepted. Negative feedback that is subjective can be a meaningful tool for experienced managers, particularly those high in the organization who have earned the respect of their employees. From less experienced managers, those in the lower ranks of the organization, and those whose reputations have not yet been established, negative feedback that is subjective in nature is not likely to be well received.

Developing Effective Feedback Skills

There are six specific suggestions that we can make to help you be more effective in providing feedback.

Focus on Specific Behaviors   Feedback should be specific rather than general.[25] Avoid such statements as "You have a bad attitude" or "I'm really impressed with the good job you did." They're vague, and while they provide information, they don't tell the recipient enough to correct the "bad attitude" or *on what basis* you concluded that a "good job" had been done.

Suppose you said something like "Bob, I'm concerned with your attitude toward your work. You were a half hour late to yesterday's staff meeting and then told me you hadn't read the preliminary report we were discussing. Today you tell me you're taking off three hours early for a dental appointment"; or "Jan, I was really pleased with the job you did on the Phillips account. They increased their purchases from us by 22 percent last month, and I got a call a few days ago from Dan Phillips complimenting me on how quickly you responded to those specification changes for the MJ-7 microchip." Both of these statements focus on specific behaviors. They tell the recipient *why* you are being critical or complimentary.

Keep Feedback Impersonal   Feedback, particularly the negative kind, should be descriptive rather than judgmental or evaluative.[26] No matter how upset you are, keep the feedback job-related and never criticize someone personally because of an inappropriate action. Telling people they're "stupid," "incompetent," or the like is almost always counterproductive. It provokes such an emotional reaction that the performance deviation itself is apt to be overlooked. When you're criticizing, remember that you're censuring a job-related behavior, not the person. You might be tempted to tell someone he or she is "rude and insensitive" (which might well be true); however, that's hardly impersonal It's better to say something like "You interrupted me three times, with questions that were not urgent, when you knew I was talking long-distance to a customer in Scotland."

Keep Feedback Goal-Oriented   Feedback should not be given primarily to "dump" or "unload" on another.[27] If you have to say something negative, make sure it's directed toward the recipient's goals. Ask yourself whom the feedback is supposed to help. If the answer is essentially *you*—"I've got something I just want to get off my chest"—bite your tongue. Such feedback undermines your credibility and lessens the meaning and influence of future feedback.

Make Feedback Well-Timed   Feedback is most meaningful to a recipient when there is a very short interval between his or her behavior and the receipt of feedback about that behavior.[28] To illustrate, a new employee who makes a mistake is more likely to respond to his manager's suggestions for improvement right after the mistake or at the end of that working day, rather than during a performance-review session several months later. If you have to spend time recreating a situation and refreshing someone's memory of it, the feedback you're providing is likely to be ineffective.[29]

Moreover, if you are particularly concerned with *changing* behavior, delays in providing feedback on the undesirable actions lessen the likelihood that the feedback will be effective in bringing about the desired change.[30] Of course, making feedback prompt merely for promptness' sake can backfire if you have insufficient information, if you're angry, or if you're otherwise emotionally upset. In such instances, "well-timed" could mean "somewhat delayed."

Ensure Understanding   Is your feedback concise and complete enough that the recipient clearly and fully understands your communication? Remember that every successful communication requires both transference and understanding of meaning. If feedback is to be effective, you need to ensure that the recipient understands it.[31] Consistent with our discussion of listening techniques, you should have the recipient rephrase the content of your feedback to find out whether it fully captures the meaning you intended.

Direct Negative Feedback Toward Behavior That the Recipient Can Control
There's little value in reminding a person of some shortcoming over which he or she has no control. Negative feedback should be directed toward behavior the recipient can do something about.[32] For example, to criticize an employee who is late because she forgot to set her wake-up alarm is valid. To criticize her for being late when the subway she takes to work every day had a power failure, trapping her underground for half an hour, is pointless. There is nothing she could have done to correct what happened.

Additionally, when negative feedback is given concerning something that the recipient can control, it might be a good idea to indicate specifically what can be done to improve the situation. This takes some of the sting out of the criticism and offers guidance to recipients who understand the problem but don't know how to resolve it.

Delegation Skills

Managers get things done through other people. This description recognizes that there are limits to any manager's time and knowledge. Effective managers, therefore, need to understand the value of delegating and know how to do it.[33]

What Is Delegation?

delegation
The assignment of authority and responsibility to another person to carry out specific activities.

Delegation is the assignment of authority to another person to carry out specific activities. It allows a subordinate to make decisions—that is, it's a shift of decision-making authority from one organizational level to another, lower one.[34] (See Figure 18-2.)

Delegation should not be confused with participation. In participative decision making, there is a sharing of authority. With delegation, subordinates make decisions on their own.

Is Delegation Abdication?

When done properly, delegation is *not* abdication. The key word here is "properly." If you dump tasks on a subordinate without clarifying the exact job to be done, the range of the subordinate's discretion, the expected level of performance, the time the tasks are to be completed, and similar concerns, you are abdicating responsibility and inviting trouble.[35]

FIGURE 18–2
Effective Delegation

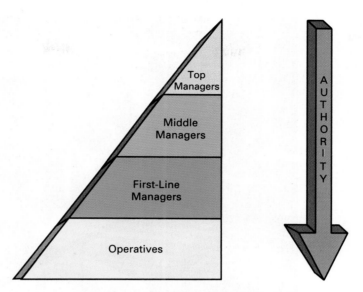

Effective delegation pushes authority down vertically
through the ranks of an organization.

Don't fall into the trap of assuming that, to avoid the appearance of abdicating, you should minimize delegation. Unfortunately, this is the approach taken by many new and inexperienced managers. Lacking confidence in their subordinates or fearful that they will be criticized for their subordinates' mistakes, these managers try to do everything themselves.

It might very well be true that you're capable of doing the tasks better, faster, or with fewer mistakes. The catch is that your time and energy are scarce resources. It's not possible for you to do everything yourself. You need to learn to delegate if you're going to be effective in your job.[36] This fact suggests two important points. First, you should expect and accept some mistakes by your subordinates. Mistakes are part of delegation. They are often good learning experiences for your subordinates, as long as their costs are not excessive. Second, to ensure that the costs of mistakes don't exceed the value of the learning, you need to put adequate controls in place. As we'll discuss later in this section, delegation without feedback controls that let you know when there are serious problems *is* abdication.

Contingency Factors in Delegation

How much authority should a manager delegate? Should he or she keep authority centralized, delegating only the least number of duties? If not, what contingency factors should be considered in determining the degree to which authority is delegated? The following contingency factors provide some guidance.

The Size of the Organization   The larger the organization, the greater the number of decisions that have to be made. Because the top managers in an organization have only so much time and can obtain only so much information, they become increasingly dependent in larger organizations on the decision making of lower-level managers. Therefore, managers in large organizations resort to increased delegation.

The Importance of the Duty or Decision   The more important a duty or decision is (as expressed in terms of cost and impact on the future of the organization), the less likely it is to be delegated. For instance, a department head may be delegated

In large companies such as Citibank, effective managers have to delegate authority or decision making will become slow and unresponsive.

authority to make expenditures up to $5,000, and division heads and vice presidents up to $25,000 and $100,000, respectively.

Task Complexity The more complex the task, the more difficult it is for top management to possess current and sufficient technical information to make effective decisions. Complex tasks require greater expertise, and decisions about them should be delegated to the individuals who possess the necessary technical knowledge.

Organizational Culture If management has confidence and trust in subordinates, the culture will support a greater degree of delegation. However, if top management does not have confidence in the abilities of lower-level managers, it will delegate authority begrudgingly. In such instances, as little authority as possible will be delegated.

Qualities of Subordinates A final contingency consideration is the qualities of subordinates. Delegation requires subordinates with the skills, abilities, and motivation to accept authority and act on it. If this is lacking, top management will be reluctant to relinquish authority.

Developing Effective Delegating Skills

A number of actions differentiate the effective from the ineffective delegator.[37]

Clarify the Assignment The place to begin is to determine *what* is to be delegated and to *whom*. You need to identify the person who is best capable of doing the task and then determine whether he or she has the time and motivation to do the job.

Assuming that you have a willing and able subordinate, it is your responsibility to provide clear information on what is being delegated, the results you expect, and any time or performance expectations you hold.

Unless there is an overriding need to adhere to specific methods you should delegate only the results. That is, get agreement on what is to be done and the results

Debbi Fields at Mrs. Fields Inc.

Debbi Fields' desire to do it all—to be involved in every decision—was almost the undoing of her cookie empire. Fortunately for her company, she recognized the problem in time and has learned the importance of delegating.[38]

The Debbi Fields story is well known. She began selling chocolate chip cookies in 1977, at the age of twenty. Annual sales rocketed from $200,000 in 1977 to more than $100 million in 1988. But along the way she remained fixed to a style that has destroyed many growing companies: She wouldn't delegate. Says Fields, " . . . I used to ask managers what they needed, and then I did it for them. 'Your ice machine is broken? Your milk delivery is off? I'll take care of it.' If I saw something I didn't like, I fixed it myself, right then and there."

Her micromanagement style worked when she had one or two stores. It didn't work when she had 600. Insistent on doing everything herself, Fields didn't pay attention to the big picture. The company's aggressive growth strategy—which included the purchase of the La Petite Boulangerie bakery chain from PepsiCo and expansion into Europe—demanded her time, but she was too busy trying to make all the decisions. And her failure to delegate began to show by the late 1980s. Profits plummeted. Costs got out of hand. In 1988, the company closed eighty-five stores.

Although it hasn't been easy for Debbi Fields, she's learned her lesson. The company reorganized by adding another layer of management. And she is delegating real decision authority to lower-level managers.

One of the more pleasant surprises for Mrs. Fields is that by delegating authority she is actually more accessible to her employees. She now has more opportunity to visit stores, meet the stores' staffs, and get involved in the company's employee training and development program.

---

expected, but let the subordinate decide on the means. By focusing on goals and allowing the employee the freedom to use his or her own judgment as to how those goals are to be achieved, you increase trust between you and the employee, improve the employee's motivation, and enhance accountability for the results.

Specify the Subordinate's Range of Discretion Every act of delegation comes with constraints. You are delegating authority to act, but not *unlimited* authority. What you are delegating is authority to act on certain issues within certain parameters. You need to specify what those parameters are so that subordinates know, in no uncertain terms, the range of their discretion. When this has been successfully communicated, both you and the subordinate will have the same idea of the limits to the latter's authority and how far he or she can go without further approval.

Allow the Subordinate to Participate One of the best ways to decide how much authority will be necessary to accomplish a task is to allow the subordinate who will be held accountable for that task to participate in that decision. Be aware, however, that participation can present its own set of potential problems as a result of subordinates' self-interest and biases in evaluating their own abilities. Some subordinates might be personally motivated to expand their authority beyond what they need and beyond what they are capable of handling. Allowing such people too much participation in deciding what tasks they should take on and how much authority they must have to complete those tasks can undermine the effectiveness of the delegation process.

Inform Others That Delegation Has Occurred   Delegation should not take place in a vacuum. Not only do the manager and subordinate need to know specifically what has been delegated and how much authority has been granted, but anyone else who is likely to be affected by the delegation act also needs to be informed. This includes people outside the organization as well as inside it. Essentially, you need to convey what has been delegated (the task and amount of authority) and to whom. Failure to inform others makes conflict likely and decreases the chances that your subordinate will be able to accomplish the delegated task efficiently.

Establish Feedback Controls   To delegate without instituting feedback controls is to invite problems. There is always the possibility that a subordinate will misuse the discretion that he or she has been delegated. The establishment of controls to monitor the subordinate's progress increases the likelihood that important problems will be identified early and that the task will be completed on time and to the desired specifications.

Ideally, controls should be determined at the time of the initial assignment. Agree on a specific time for completion of the task and then set progress dates when the subordinate will report back on how well he or she is doing and any major problems that have surfaced. These controls can be supplemented with periodic spot checks to ensure that authority guidelines are not being abused, organization policies are being followed, proper procedures are being met, and the like.

Too much of a good thing can be dysfunctional. If the controls are too constraining, the subordinate will be deprived of the opportunity to build self-confidence and much of the motivational aspects of delegation will be lost. A well-designed control system, which we'll elaborate on in detail in Chapter 19, permits your subordinates to make small mistakes but quickly alerts you when big mistakes are imminent.

Discipline Skills

It has been fashionable in management circles for years to talk about rewards and downplay punishment or discipline. This tendency has essentially derived from the research on learning, which was discussed in Chapter 14. According to learning theorists, punishment can decrease or eliminate an undesirable behavior, but it will not necessarily lead to desirable behaviors. The negative connotation of punishment and discipline is not a sufficient reason to dismiss it as a management skill for modifying employee behavior.[39] As most practicing managers have learned, the use of discipline is sometimes necessary in dealing with problem employees.

discipline
Actions taken by a manager to enforce the organization's standards and regulations.

What specifically do we mean when we use the term **discipline?** It refers to actions taken by a manager to enforce the organization's standards and regulations. Table 18–1 lists the most common types of discipline problems.

TABLE 18-1   Types of Discipline Problems and Examples of Each

Attendance
   Absenteeism, tardiness, abuse of sick leave

On-the-Job Behaviors
   Insubordination, failure to use safety devices, alcohol or drug abuse

Dishonesty
   Theft, lying to superiors, falsifying information on employment applications

Outside Activities
   Working for a competing organization, criminal activities, unauthorized strike activities

The "Hot Stove" Rule

"hot stove" rule
Discipline should immediately follow an infraction, provide ample warning, be consistent, and impersonal.

The **"hot stove" rule** is a frequently cited set of principles that can guide you in effectively disciplining an employee.[40] The name comes from the similarities between touching a hot stove and administering discipline. Both are painful, but the analogy goes further. When you touch a hot stove, you get an *immediate* response. The burn you receive is instantaneous, leaving no doubt in your mind about the relation between cause and effect. You have ample *warning*. You know what happens if you touch a hot stove. Furthermore, the result is *consistent*. Every time you touch a hot stove, you get the same result—you get burned. Finally, the result is *impersonal*. Regardless of who you are, if you touch a hot stove, you will be burned.

The analogy with discipline should be apparent, but let's briefly expand on each of these four points, since they are central tenets in developing your disciplining skills.

Immediacy   The effect of a disciplinary action will be reduced as the time between the infraction and the penalty lengthens. The more quickly the discipline follows the offense, the more likely it is that the employee will associate the discipline with the offense rather than with you as the imposer of the discipline. Therefore it is best to begin the disciplinary process as soon as possible after you notice a violation. Of course, the immediacy requirement should not result in undue haste. Fair and objective treatment should not be compromised for expediency.

Advance Warning   As a manager, you have an obligation to give advance warning before initiating formal disciplinary action. This means that the employee must be aware of the organization's rules and accept its standards of behavior. Disciplinary action is more likely to be interpreted as fair by employees when they have received clear warning that a given violation will lead to discipline and when they know what that discipline will be.

Consistency   Fair treatment of employees demands that disciplinary action be consistent. If you enforce rule violations in an inconsistent manner, the rules will lose their impact, morale will decline, and employees will question your competence. Productivity will suffer as a result of employee insecurity and anxiety. Your employees will want to know the limits of permissible behavior, and they will look to your actions for guidance. Consistency, by the way, need not result in treating everyone exactly alike because that ignores mitigating circumstances. It does, however, put the responsibility on you to clearly justify disciplinary actions that might appear inconsistent to employees.

Impersonal Nature   The last guideline that flows from the "hot stove" rule is to keep the discipline impersonal. Penalties should be connected with a given violation, not with the personality of the violator. That is, discipline should be directed at what the employee has done, not at the employee. You are penalizing the rule violation, not the individual. Once the penalty has been imposed, you must make every effort to forget the incident. You should attempt to treat the employee just as you did before the infraction.

Developing Effective Discipline Skills

The essence of effective disciplining can be summarized by the following seven behaviors:[41]

Confront the Employee in a Calm, Objective, and Serious Manner   Managers can facilitate many interpersonal situations by a loose, informal, and relaxed manner. The idea in such situations is to put the employee at ease. Administering discipline is not one of those situations. Avoid anger or other emotional responses, and convey your comments in a calm, serious tone. But do *not* try to lessen the tension by cracking jokes or making small talk. Such actions are likely to confuse the employee because they send conflicting signals.

State the Problem Specifically   When you sit down with the employee, indicate that you have documentation and be specific about the problem. Give the date, time, place, individuals involved, and any mitigating circumstances surrounding the violation. Be sure to define the violation in exact terms instead of just citing company regulations or the union contract. It's not the breaking of the rules per se about which you want to convey concern. It's the effect that the rule violation has on the work unit's performance. Explain why the behavior can't be continued by showing how it specifically affects the employee's job performance, the unit's effectiveness, and the employee's colleagues.

Keep the Discussion Impersonal   As we stated in our discussion of feedback skills, criticism should focus on the employee's behavior rather than on the individual personally. For instance, if an employee has been late for work several times, point out how this behavior has increased the workload of others or has lowered departmental morale. Don't criticize the person for being thoughtless or irresponsible.

Allow the Employee to Explain His or Her Position   Regardless of what facts you have uncovered, even if you have the proverbial "smoking gun" to support your accusations, due process demands that you give the employee the opportunity to explain his or her position. From the employee's perspective, what happened? Why did it happen? What was his or her perception of the rules, regulations, and circumstances? If there are significant discrepancies between your version of the violation and the employee's, you might need to do more investigating.

Maintain Control of the Discussion   In most interpersonal exchanges, you want to encourage open dialogue. You want to give up control and create a climate of open communication between equals. This won't work in administering discipline. Why? Because violators are prone to use any opportunity to put you on the defensive. In other words, if you don't take control, they will. Disciplining an employee is, by definition, an authority-based act. You are *enforcing* the organization's standards and regulations, so take control. Ask the employee for his or her side of the story. Get the facts. But don't let the employee interrupt you or divert you from your objective.

Obtain Agreement on How Mistakes Can Be Prevented in the Future
Disciplining should include guidance and direction for correcting the problem. Let the employee state what he or she plans to do in the future to ensure that the violation isn't repeated. For serious violations, have the employee draft a step-by-step plan to change the problem behavior. Then set a timetable with follow-up meetings in which progress can be evaluated.

Select Disciplinary Action Progressively, Considering Mitigating Circumstances   Choose a punishment that is appropriate to the crime.[42] Penalties should get progressively stronger if, or when, an offense is repeated. Typically, progressive disciplinary action begins with a verbal warning and then proceeds through a written reprimand, suspension, a demotion or pay cut, and finally, in the most serious cases, dismissal. The punishment you select should be viewed as fair and consistent. This means acknowledging mitigating circumstances. For example, how severe is the problem? Have there been other disciplinary problems with this employee? If so, for how long? To what extent has the employee been previously warned about the offense? How have similar infractions been dealt with in the past? Answers to questions such as these can help to ensure that mitigating circumstances are considered.

Disciplinary action should fit the offense. In the case of William Aramony, head of the United Way, the board bypassed progressive discipline and immediately fired him when it discovered that he was misusing the organization's funds.

Conflict Management Skills

The ability to manage conflict is undoubtedly one of the most important skills a manager needs to possess. A study of middle- and top-level executives by the American Management Association revealed that the average manager spends approximately 20 percent of his or her time dealing with conflict.[43] The importance of conflict management is reinforced by a survey of what topics practicing managers consider most important in management development programs; conflict management was rated as being more important than decision making, leadership, or communication skills.[44] In further support of our claim, one researcher studied a group of managers and looked at twenty-five skill and personality factors to determine which, if any, were related to managerial success (defined in terms of ratings by one's boss, salary increases, and promotions).[45] Of the twenty-five measures, only one—the ability to handle conflict—was positively related to managerial success.

What Is Conflict?

conflict
Perceived incompatible differences that result in interference or opposition.

When we use the term **conflict,** we are referring to perceived incompatible differences resulting in some form of interference or opposition. Whether the differences are real or not is irrelevant. If people perceive that differences exist, then a conflict state exists. In addition, our definition includes the extremes, from subtle, indirect, and highly controlled forms of interference to overt acts such as strikes, riots, and wars.

traditional view of conflict
The view that all conflict is bad and must be avoided.

human relations view of conflict
The view that conflict is a natural and inevitable outcome in any organization.

Over the years, three differing views have evolved toward conflict in organizations.[46] One argues that conflict must be avoided, that it indicates a malfunctioning within the organization. We call this the **traditional view of conflict.** A second, the **human relations view of conflict,** argues that conflict is a natural and inevitable outcome in any organization and that it need not be evil but, rather, has the potential to be a positive force in contributing to an organization's performance. The third and most recent perspective proposes not only that conflict can be a positive force in an organization, but also that some conflict is *absolutely necessary* for an organization or

interactionist view of conflict
The view that some conflict is necessary for an organization to perform effectively.

units within the organization to perform effectively. We label this third approach the **interactionist view of conflict.**

The Traditional View   The early approach assumed that conflict was bad and would *always* have a negative impact on an organization. Conflict became synonymous with violence, destruction, and irrationality. Because conflict was harmful, it was to be avoided. Management had a responsibility to rid the organization of conflict. This traditional view dominated management literature during the late nineteenth century and continued until the mid-1940s.

The Human Relations View   The human relations position argued that conflict was a natural and inevitable occurrence in all organizations. Because conflict was inevitable, the human relations approach advocated acceptance of conflict. This approach rationalized the existence of conflict; conflict cannot be eliminated, and there are times when it may even benefit the organization. The human relations view dominated conflict thinking from the late 1940s through the mid-1970s.

The Interactionist View   The current theoretical perspective on conflict is the interactionist approach. While the human relations approach accepts conflict, the interactionist approach *encourages* conflict on the grounds that a harmonious, peaceful, tranquil, and cooperative organization is prone to becoming static, apathetic, and nonresponsive to needs for change and innovation. The major contribution of the interactionist approach, therefore, is that it encourages managers to maintain an ongoing minimum level of conflict—enough to keep units viable, self-critical, and creative.

Functional Versus Dysfunctional Conflict

functional conflicts
Conflicts that support an organization's goals.

dysfunctional conflicts
Conflicts that prevent an organization from achieving its goals.

The interactionist view does not propose that *all* conflicts are good. Rather, some conflicts support the goals of the organization; these are **functional conflicts** of a constructive form. However, some conflicts prevent an organization from achieving its goals; these are **dysfunctional conflicts** and are destructive forms.

Of course, it is one thing to argue that conflict can be valuable, but how does a manager tell whether a conflict is functional or dysfunctional? Unfortunately, the

Digital Equipment Corp. is one of an increasing number of firms that have learned the value of functional conflict. DEC openly encourages all employees "to push back against the system," and the company rewards those that do.

FIGURE 18-3
Conflict and Organizational
Performance

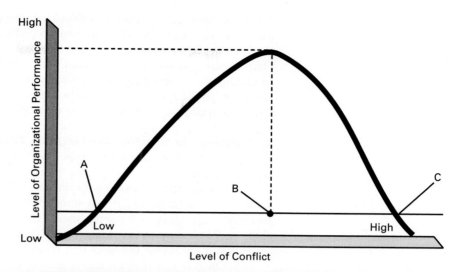

Situation	Level of Conflict	Type of Conflict	Organization's Internal Characteristics	Level of Organizational Performance
A	Low or none	Dys-functional	Apathetic Stagnant Unresponsive to change Lack of new ideas	Low
B	Optimal	Functional	Viable Self-critical Innovative	High
C	High	Dys-functional	Disruptive Chaotic Uncooperative	Low

demarcation is neither clear nor precise. No one level of conflict can be adopted as acceptable or unacceptable under all conditions. The type and level of conflict that promote a healthy and positive involvement toward one department's goals may, in another department or in the same department at another time, be highly dysfunctional. Functionality or dysfunctionality, therefore, is a matter of judgment. Figure 18–3 illustrates the challenge facing managers. They want to create an environment within their organization or organizational unit in which conflict is healthy but not allowed to run to pathological extremes. Neither too little nor too much conflict is desirable. Managers should stimulate conflict to gain the full benefits of its functional properties, yet reduce its level when it becomes a disruptive force. Because we have yet to devise a sophisticated measuring instrument for assessing whether a given conflict level is functional or dysfunctional, it remains for managers to make intelligent judgments concerning whether conflict levels in their units are optimal, too high, or too low.

Developing Effective Conflict Resolution Skills

If conflict is dysfunctional, what can a manager do? In this section, we'll review conflict resolution skills. Essentially, you need to know your basic conflict-handling style, as well as those of the conflicting parties, to understand the situation that has created the conflict and to be aware of your options.

What Is Your Underlying Conflict-Handling Style?   While most of us have the ability to vary our conflict response according to the situation, each of us has a preferred style for handling conflicts.[47] The self-assessment exercise at the end of this chapter can help you to identify your basic conflict handling style. You might be able to change your preferred style to suit the context in which a certain conflict exists; however, your basic style tells you how you're *most likely* to behave and the conflict-handling approaches on which you *most often* rely.

Be Judicious in Selecting the Conflicts That You Want to Handle   Not every conflict justifies your attention. Some might not be worth the effort; others might be unmanageable.

Not every conflict is worth your time and effort to resolve. While avoidance might appear to be a "cop-out," it can sometimes be the most appropriate response. You can improve your overall management effectiveness, and your conflict-management skills in particular, by avoiding trivial conflicts. Choose your battles judiciously, saving your efforts for the ones that count.

Regardless of our desires, reality tells us that some conflicts are unmanageable.[48] When antagonisms are deeply rooted, when one or both parties wish to prolong a conflict, or when emotions run so high that constructive interaction is impossible, your efforts to manage the conflict are unlikely to meet with much success.

Don't be lured into the naive belief that a good manager can resolve every conflict effectively. Some aren't worth the effort. Some are outside your realm of influence. Still others may be functional and, as such, are best left alone.

Evaluate the Conflict Players   If you choose to manage a conflict situation, it's important that you take the time to get to know the players. Who is involved in the conflict? What interests does each party represent? What are each player's values, personality, feelings, and resources? Your chances of success in managing a conflict will be greatly enhanced if you can view the conflict situation through the eyes of the conflicting parties.

Assess the Source of the Conflict   Conflicts don't pop out of thin air. They have causes. Because your approach to resolving a conflict is likely to be determined largely by its causes, you need to determine the source of the conflict. Research indicates that while conflicts have varying causes, they can generally be separated into three categories: Communication differences, structural differences, and personal differences.[49]

Communication differences are disagreements arising from semantic difficulties, misunderstandings, and noise in the communication channels. People are often quick to assume that most conflicts are caused by lack of communication but, as one author has noted, there is usually plenty of communication going on in most conflicts.[50] As we pointed out at the beginning of this chapter, the mistake many people make is equating good communication with having others agree with their views. What might at first look like an interpersonal conflict based on poor communication is usually found, upon closer analysis, to be a disagreement caused by different role requirements, unit goals, personalities, value systems, or similar factors. As a source of conflict for managers, poor communication probably gets more attention than it deserves.

As we discussed in Chapter 10, organizations are horizontally and vertically differentiated. This *structural differentiation* creates problems of integration. The frequent result is conflicts. Individuals disagree over goals, decision alternatives, performance criteria, and resource allocations. These conflicts are not due to poor communication or personal animosities. Rather, they are rooted in the structure of the organization itself.

The third conflict source is *personal differences*. Conflicts can evolve out of individual idiosyncrasies and personal value systems. The chemistry between some people makes it hard for them to work together. Factors such as background, education, experience, and training mold each individual into a unique personality with a particular set of values. The result is people who may be perceived by others as abrasive, untrustworthy, or strange. These personal differences can create conflict.

Know Your Options   What resolution tools or techniques can a manager call upon to reduce conflict when it is too high? Managers essentially can draw upon five conflict-resolution options: Avoidance, accommodation, forcing, compromise, and collaboration.[51] Each has particular strengths and weaknesses, and no one option is ideal for every situation. You should consider each a "tool" in your conflict-management "tool chest." While you might be better at using some tools than others, the skilled manager knows what each tool can do and when each is likely to be most effective.

As we noted earlier, not every conflict requires an assertive action. Sometimes **avoidance**—just withdrawing from or suppressing the conflict—is the best solution. When is avoidance a desirable strategy? When the conflict is trivial, when emotions are running high and time is needed to cool them down, or when the potential disruption from a more assertive action outweighs the benefits of resolution.

The goal of **accommodation** is to maintain harmonious relationships by placing another's needs and concerns above your own. You might, for example, yield to another person's position on an issue. This option is most viable when the issue under dispute isn't that important to you or when you want to build up credits for later issues.

In **forcing**, you attempt to satisfy your own needs at the expense of the other party. In organizations this is most often illustrated by a manager using his or her formal authority to resolve a dispute. Forcing works well when you need a quick resolution on important issues where unpopular actions must be taken, and when commitment by others to your solution is not critical.

A **compromise** requires each party to give up something of value. Typically this is the approach taken by management and labor in negotiating a new labor contract. Compromise can be an optimum strategy when conflicting parties are about equal in power, when it is desirable to achieve a temporary solution to a complex issue, or when time pressures demand an expedient solution.

Collaboration is the ultimate win–win solution. All parties to the conflict seek to satisfy their interests. It is typically characterized by open and honest discussion among the parties, active listening to understand differences, and careful deliberation over a full range of alternatives to find a solution that is advantageous to all. When is collaboration the best conflict option? When time pressures are minimal, when all parties seriously want a win–win solution, and when the issue is too important to be compromised.

What About Conflict Stimulation?

What about the other side of conflict management—situations that require managers to *stimulate* conflict? The notion of stimulating conflict is often difficult to accept. For almost all of us the term "conflict" has a negative connotation, and the idea of purposely creating conflict seems to be the antithesis of good management. Few of us personally enjoy being in conflict situations. Yet the evidence demonstrates that there are situations in which an increase in conflict is constructive.[52] Given this reality and the fact that there is no clear demarcation between functional and dysfunctional conflict, we have listed in Table 18–2 a set of questions that might help you. While there is no definitive method for assessing the need for more conflict, an affirmative

avoidance
Withdrawal from or suppression of conflict.

accommodation
Resolving conflicts by placing another's needs and concerns above one's own.

forcing
Satisfying one's own needs at the expense of another's.

compromise
A solution to conflict in which each party gives up something of value.

collaboration
Resolving conflict by seeking a solution advantageous to all parties.

TABLE 18–2   Is Conflict Stimulation Needed?*

1. Are you surrounded by "yes people"?
2. Are subordinates afraid to admit ignorance and uncertainties to you?
3. Is there so much concentration by decision makers on reaching a compromise that they lose sight of values, long-term objectives, or the organization's welfare?
4. Do managers believe that it is in their best interest to maintain the impression of peace and cooperation in their unit, regardless of the price?
5. Is there an excessive concern by decision makers for not hurting the feelings of others?
6. Do managers believe that popularity is more important for obtaining organizational rewards than competence and high performance?
7. Are managers unduly enamored of obtaining consensus for their decisions?
8. Do employees show unusually high resistance to change?
9. Is there a lack of new ideas?
10. Is there an unusually low level of employee turnover?

---

* An affirmative answer to any or all of these questions suggests the need for conflict stimulation.

Source: From Stephen P. Robbins, "'Conflict Management' and 'Conflict Resolution' Are Not Synonymous Terms," *California Management Review*, Winter 1978, p. 71. With permission of the Regents.

answer to one or more of the questions in Table 18–2 suggests a need for conflict stimulation.

We know a lot more about resolving conflict than about stimulating it. That's only natural, because human beings have been concerned with the subject of conflict reduction for hundreds, maybe thousands, of years. The dearth of ideas on conflict stimulation techniques reflects the very recent interest in the subject. The following are some preliminary suggestions that managers might want to utilize.[53]

Change the Organization's Culture   The initial step in stimulating functional conflict is for managers to convey to subordinates the message, supported by actions, that conflict has its legitimate place. Individuals who challenge the status quo, suggest innovative ideas, offer divergent opinions, and demonstrate original thinking need to be rewarded visibly with promotions, salary increases, and other positive reinforcers.

Use Communication   As far back as Franklin Roosevelt's administration, and probably before, the White House consistently has used communication to stimulate conflict. Senior officials "plant" possible decisions with the media through the infamous "reliable source" route. For example, the name of a prominent judge is "leaked" as a possible Supreme Court appointment. If the candidate survives the public scrutiny, his or her appointment will be announced by the president. However, if the candidate is found lacking by the press, media, and public, the president's press secretary or other high-level official will make a formal statement such as, "At no time was this candidate under consideration." Regardless of party affiliation, occupants of the White House have regularly used the reliable source as a conflict stimulation technique. It is all the more popular because of its handy escape mechanism. If the conflict level gets too high, the source can be denied and eliminated.

Ambiguous or threatening messages also encourage conflict. Information that a plant might close, that a department is likely to be eliminated, or that a layoff is imminent can reduce apathy, stimulate new ideas, and force reevaluation—all positive outcomes that result from increased conflict.

Bring in Outsiders   A widely used method for shaking up a stagnant unit or organization is to bring in—either by hiring from outside or by internal transfer—

individuals whose backgrounds, values, attitudes, or managerial styles differ from those of present members. Many large corporations have used this technique during the last decade in filling vacancies on their boards of directors. Women, minority group members, consumer activists, and others whose backgrounds and interests differ significantly from those of the rest of the board have been purposely selected to add a fresh perspective.

devil's advocate

A person who purposely presents arguments that run counter to those proposed by the majority.

Restructure the Organization   We know that structural variables are a source of conflict. It is therefore only logical that managers look to structure as a conflict stimulation device. Centralizing decisions, realigning work groups, increasing formalization, and increasing interdependencies between units are all structural devices that disrupt the status quo and act to increase conflict levels.

Appoint a Devil's Advocate   A **devil's advocate** is a person who purposely presents arguments that run counter to those proposed by the majority or against current practices. He or she plays the role of the critic, even to the point of arguing against positions with which he or she actually agrees.

A devil's advocate acts as a check against groupthink and practices that have no better justification than "that's the way we've always done it around here." When thoughtfully listened to, the advocate can improve the quality of group decision making. On the other hand, others in the group often view advocates as time wasters, and their appointment is almost certain to delay any decision process.

Negotiation Skills

negotiation

A process in which two or more parties exchange goods or services and attempt to agree upon the exchange rate for them.

We know that lawyers and car salesmen spend a lot of their time negotiating. But so, too, do managers. They have to negotiate salaries for incoming employees, cut deals with superiors, work out differences with associates, and resolve conflicts with subordinates.

For our purposes, we'll define **negotiation** as a process in which two or more parties exchange goods or services and attempt to agree upon the exchange rate for them.[54] Additionally, we'll use the terms *negotiation* and *bargaining* interchangeably.

Bargaining Strategies

There are two general approaches to negotiation—*distributive bargaining* and *integrative bargaining*.[55] These are compared in Table 18–3.

TABLE 18–3   Distributive versus Integrative Bargaining

Bargaining Characteristic	Distributive Bargaining	Integrative Bargaining
Available resources	Fixed amount of resources to be divided	Variable amount of resources to be divided
Primary motivations	I win, you lose	I win, you win
Primary interests	Opposed to each other	Convergent or congruent with each other
Focus of relationships	Short-term	Long-term

Source: Based on R.J. Lewicki and J.A. Litterer, *Negotiation* (Homewood, IL: Irwin, 1985), p. 280.

This tourist in Panama is practicing distributive bargaining when haggling over price with a street vendor.

distributive bargaining
Negotiations that seek to divide up a fixed amount of resources: a win–lose situation.

Distributive bargaining　You see a used car advertised for sale in the newspaper. It appears to be just what you've been looking for. You go out to see the car. It's great and you want it. The owner tells you the asking price. You don't want to pay that much. The two of you then negotiate over the price. The negotiating process you are engaging in is called **distributive bargaining.** Its most identifying feature is that it operates under zero-sum conditions. That is, any gain I make is at your expense, and vice versa. Referring back to the used car example, every dollar you can get the seller to cut from the car's price is a dollar you save. Conversely, every dollar more he or she can get from you comes at your expense. Thus the essence of distributive bargaining is negotiating over who gets what share of a fixed pie.

Probably the most widely cited example of distributive bargaining is in labor-management negotiations over wages. Typically, labor's representatives come to the bargaining table determined to get as much money as possible out of management. Because every cent more that labor negotiates increases management's costs, each party bargains aggressively and treats the other as an opponent who must be defeated.

Figure 18–4 depicts the distributive bargaining strategy. Parties A and B represent the two negotiators. Each has a *target point* that defines what he or she would like to achieve. Each also has a *resistance point,* which marks the lowest outcome that is acceptable—the point below which he or she would break off negotiations rather than accept a less favorable settlement. The area between their resistance points is the settlement range. As long as there is some overlap in their aspiration ranges, there exists a settlement area where each one's aspirations can be met.

When engaged in distributive bargaining, your tactics should focus on trying to get your opponent to agree to your specific target point or to get as close to it as possible. Examples of such tactics are persuading your opponent of the impossibility of getting to his or her target point and the advisability of accepting a settlement near yours; arguing that your target is fair, while your opponent's isn't; and attempting to get your opponent to feel emotionally generous toward you and thus accept an outcome close to your target point.

Integrative bargaining　A sales representative for a women's sportswear manufacturer has just closed a $15,000 order from a small clothing retailer. The sales rep calls in the order to her firm's credit department. She is told that the firm can't approve credit to this customer because of a past slow-pay record. The next day, the sales rep and the firm's credit manager meet to discuss the problem. The sales rep doesn't want to lose the business. Neither does the credit manager, but he also doesn't want to get

FIGURE 18-4
Staking Out the Bargaining Zone

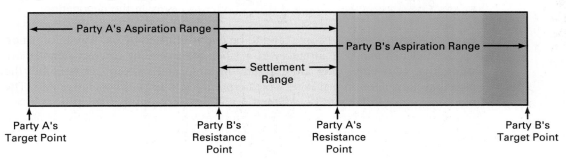

stuck with an uncollectable debt. The two openly review their options. After considerable discussion, they agree on a solution that meets both their needs: The credit manager will approve the sale, but the clothing store's owner will provide a bank guarantee that will assure payment if the bill isn't paid within sixty days.

integrative bargaining
Negotiation that seeks one or more settlements that can create a win–win solution.

The sales–credit negotiation is an example of **integrative bargaining**. In contrast to distributive bargaining, integrative problem solving operates under the assumption that there is at least one settlement that can create a win–win solution.

In general, integrative bargaining is preferable to distributive bargaining. Why? Because the former builds long-term relationships and facilitates working together in the future. It bonds negotiators and allows each to leave the bargaining table feeling that he or she has achieved a victory. Distributive bargaining, on the other hand, leaves one party a loser. It tends to build animosities and deepen divisions between people who have to work together on an ongoing basis.

Why, then, don't we see more integrative bargaining in organizations? The answer lies in the conditions necessary for this type of negotiation to succeed. These conditions include openness with information and frankness between parties; a sensitivity by each party to the other's needs; the ability to trust one another; and a willingness by both parties to maintain flexibility.[56] Because many organizational cultures and intra-organizational relationships are not characterized by openness, trust, and flexibility, it isn't surprising that negotiations often take on a win-at-any-cost dynamic.

Decision-Making Biases That Hinder Effective Negotiations

Recent research has identified a set of seven decision-making biases that blind people to opportunities and prevent individuals from getting as much as possible out of a negotiation.[57]

Irrational Escalation of Commitment   People tend to continue a previously selected course of action beyond what rational analysis would recommend. Such misdirected persistence can lead to wasting a great deal of time, energy, and money. Time and money already invested are "sunk costs." They *cannot* be recovered and should *not* be considered when selecting future courses of action.

The Mythical Fixed Pie   Bargainers assume that their gain must come at the expense of the other party. As noted with integrative bargaining, that needn't be the case. There are often win–win solutions. But assuming a zero-sum game means missed opportunities for trade-offs that could benefit both sides.

Anchoring and Adjustments   People often have a tendency to anchor their judgments upon irrelevant information, such as an initial offer. Many factors influence the initial positions people take when entering a negotiation. These factors are often meaningless. Effective negotiators don't let an initial anchor minimize the amount of information and the depth of thinking they use to evaluate a situation, and don't give too much weight to their opponent's initial offer too early in the negotiation.

Framing Negotiations   People tend to be overly affected by the way information is presented to them. For instance, in a labor–management contract negotiation, assume that your employees are currently making fifteen dollars an hour but the union is seeking a four dollar raise. You are prepared to go to seventeen dollars. The union's response is likely to be different if you can successfully frame this as a two dollar an hour gain (in comparison to the current wage) rather than a two dollar an hour loss (when compared against the union's demand).

Availability of Information   Negotiators often rely too much on readily available information, while ignoring more relevant data. Facts or events that people have encountered more often are usually easy to remember—they're more "available" in their memories. It's also easier to remember or imagine more vivid events. Information that is easily recalled because it's familiar or vivid may be interpreted as being reliable when it's not. Thus effective negotiators learn to distinguish what's emotionally familiar to them from what's reliable and relevant.

The Winner's Curse   In most negotiations, one side (usually the seller) has much better information than the other. Yet people in a negotiation tend to act as if their opponent is inactive and ignore the valuable information that can be learned by thinking about the other side's decisions. The "winner's curse" reflects the regret one often feels after closing a negotiation. Your opponent has accepted your offer, which might suggest that you offered too much. You can reduce the "curse" by gaining as much information as possible and putting yourself in your opponent's shoes.

Overconfidence   Many of the previous biases can combine to inflate a person's confidence in his or her judgment and choices. When people hold certain beliefs and expectations, they tend to ignore contradictory information. The result is that negotiators tend to be overconfident. This, in turn, lessens the incentive to compromise. Considering the suggestions of qualified advisers and seeking objective assessment about your position from a neutral party are two ways to temper this tendency.

Developing Effective Negotiation Skills

The essence of effective negotiation can be summarized in the following six recommendations.[58]

Research Your Opponent   Acquire as much information as you can about your opponent's interests and goals. What constituencies must he or she appease? What is his or her strategy? This will help you better to understand your opponent's behavior, to predict his or her responses to your offers, and to frame solutions in terms of his or her interests.

Begin with a Positive Overture   Research shows that concessions tend to be reciprocated and lead to agreements. As a result, begin bargaining with a positive overture—perhaps a small concession—and then reciprocate your opponent's concessions.

Address Problems, Not Personalities   Concentrate on the negotiation issues, not on the personal characteristics of your opponent. When negotiations get tough, avoid the tendency to attack your opponent. It's your opponent's ideas or position that you disagree with, not him or her personally. Separate the people from the problem, and don't personalize differences.

Pay Little Attention to Initial Offers   Treat an initial offer as merely a point of departure. Everyone has to have an initial position. They tend to be extreme and idealistic. Treat them as such.

Emphasize Win–Win Solutions   If conditions are supportive, look for an integrative solution. Frame options in terms of your opponent's interests and look for solutions that can allow your opponent, as well as yourself, to declare a victory.

Be Open to Accepting Third-Party Assistance   When stalemates are reached, consider the use of a neutral third party. *Mediators* can help parties come to an agreement, but they don't impose a settlement. *Arbitrators* hear both sides of this dispute, then impose a solution. *Conciliators* are more informal, and act as a communication conduit, passing information between the parties, interpreting messages, and clarifying misunderstandings.

Summary

This summary is organized by the chapter-opening learning objectives found on page 525.

1. Communication is the transference and understanding of meaning. It is important because everything a manager does—decision making, planning, leading, and all other activities—require that information be communicated.

2. The communication process begins with a communication source (a sender) who has a message to convey. The message is converted to symbolic form (encoding) and passed by way of a channel to the receiver, who decodes the message. To ensure accuracy, the receiver should provide the sender with feedback as a check on whether understanding has been achieved.

3. Some techniques for overcoming communication barriers include using feedback, simplifying language, listening actively, constraining emotions, and watching nonverbal cues.

4. Behaviors related to effective active listening are making eye contact, exhibiting affirmative nods and appropriate facial expressions, avoiding distracting actions or gestures, asking questions, paraphrasing, avoiding interruption of the speaker, not overtalking, and making smooth transitions between the roles of speaker and listener.

5. Behaviors related to providing effective feedback are focusing on specific behaviors; keeping feedback impersonal, goal-oriented, and well-timed; ensuring understanding; and directing negative feedback toward behavior that the recipient can control.

6. Contingency factors guide managers in determining the degree to which authority should be delegated. These factors include the size of the organization (larger organizations are associated with increased delegation), the importance of the duty or decision (the more important a duty or decision is, the less likely it is to be delegated), task complexity (the more complex the task is, the more likely it is that decisions about the task will be delegated), organizational culture (confidence and trust in subordinates are associated with delegation), and qualities of subordinates (delegation requires subordinates with the skills, abilities, and motivation to accept authority and act on it).

7. Behaviors related to effective delegating are clarifying the assignment, specifying the subordinate's range of discretion, allowing the subordinate to participate,

informing others that delegation has occurred, and establishing feedback controls.

8. The "hot stove" rule proposes that effective disciplining should be equivalent to touching a hot stove. The response should be immediate, there should be ample warning, and enforcement of rules should be consistent and impersonal.

9. Behaviors related to effective disciplining are confronting the employee in a calm, objective, and serious manner; stating the problem specifically; keeping the discussion impersonal; allowing the employee to explain his or her position; maintaining control of the discussion; obtaining agreement on how mistakes can be prevented in the future; and selecting disciplinary action progressively, considering mitigating circumstances.

10. The steps to be followed in analyzing and resolving conflict situations begin by finding out your underlying conflict-handling style. Then select only conflicts that are worth the effort and that can be managed. Third, evaluate the conflict players. Fourth, assess the source of the conflict. Finally, choose the conflict-resolution option that best reflects your style and the situation.

11. A manager might want to stimulate conflict if his or her unit suffers from apathy, stagnation, a lack of new ideas, or unresponsiveness to change.

12. Distributive bargaining creates a win–lose situation because the object of negotiation is treated as fixed in amount. Integrative bargaining treats available resources as variable, and hence creates the potential for win–win solutions.

Review Questions

1. Why isn't *effective communication* synonymous with *agreement?*
2. Where in the communication process is distortion likely to occur?
3. What are the most popular communication methods used by people in organizations?
4. What are the four essential requirements for active listening?
5. What qualities would characterize an effective disciplinary program?
6. Contrast the traditional, human relations, and interactionist views of conflict.
7. What are the five primary conflict-resolution techniques?
8. Describe seven decision-making biases that hinder effective negotiation.
9. What can a manager do if he or she wants to be a more effective negotiator?

Discussion Questions

1. "Ineffective communication is the fault of the sender." Do you agree or disagree with this statement? Support your position.
2. Why are effective interpersonal skills so important to a manager's success?
3. Using what you've learned about listening in this chapter, are you a good listener? Where are you deficient? How could you improve your listening skills? Be specific.
4. What view of conflict—traditional, human relations, or interactionalist—do you think most managers have? Do you think this view is appropriate?
5. Assume you found an apartment that you wanted to rent and the ad had said: "$450/month negotiable." What could you do to improve the likelihood that you would negotiate the lowest possible price?

SELF-ASSESSMENT EXERCISE

Conflict-Handling Style Questionnaire

Indicate how often you do the following when you differ with someone.

When I Differ With Someone:	Usually	Sometimes	Seldom
1. I explore our differences, not backing down, but not imposing my view either.	☐	☐	☐
2. I disagree openly, then invite more discussion about our differences.	☐	☐	☐
3. I look for a mutually satisfactory solution.	☐	☐	☐
4. Rather than let the other person make a decision without my input, I make sure I am heard and also that I hear the other out.	☐	☐	☐
5. I agree to a middle ground rather than look for a completely satisfying solution.	☐	☐	☐
6. I admit I am half wrong rather than explore our differences.	☐	☐	☐
7. I have a reputation for meeting a person halfway.	☐	☐	☐
8. I expect to get out about half of what I really want to say.	☐	☐	☐
9. I give in totally rather than try to change another's opinion.	☐	☐	☐
10. I put aside any controversial aspects of an issue.	☐	☐	☐
11. I agree early on, rather than argue about a point.	☐	☐	☐
12. I give in as soon as the other party gets emotional about an issue.	☐	☐	☐
13. I try to win the other person over.	☐	☐	☐
14. I work to come out victorious, no matter what.	☐	☐	☐
15. I never back away from a good argument.	☐	☐	☐
16. I would rather win than end up compromising.	☐	☐	☐

Turn to page SK-6 for scoring directions and key.

Source: From Thomas J. Von Der Embse, *Supervision: Managerial Skills for a New Era.* Copyright © 1987 by Macmillan Publishing Co. With permission.

STONE, HARTWICK, MUELLER, AND GIBSON
CERTIFIED PUBLIC ACCOUNTANTS

To: Chris Richards; Senior Partner and Manager, Atlanta Office
From: Dana Gibson; Partner, Charleston Office

Chris, I'm writing this because I need your advice. We've been friends for many years. I guess I've come to consider you my mentor since you hired me back in 1979. Most of all, I respect your opinion. Let me tell you my problem.

A number of employees have complained in recent months about having money and personal items stolen while here at the office. Last week, for example, one female associate reported $70 missing from her purse. Another associate said that a bank credit card—which he kept in his desk drawer—had disappeared. Office gossip has recently been revolving around the theft problem, with people advancing various theories as to who the culprit is.

This morning, two of our senior tax specialists—Jim Cisco and Karla Lindsay—came into my office. They told me that late yesterday afternoon, while Pam Staw (a secretary) was in the restroom, they observed Lee Reeves going through Pam's purse. They saw Lee take money and some other things out of her wallet and return the wallet to the purse. Jim and Karla know that Lee didn't see them.

I immediately called in Pam and asked her if she had any problems yesterday. She volunteered that when she got home she found that $25 and three credit cards were missing from her purse. She said she had no idea what happened to them. I asked her if she was sure about the amount of money. She replied that she was certain because she had taken the money from the bank that afternoon.

I've considered Lee a potential problem almost from the day he joined the firm fourteen months ago. Lee is not an open person and seems manipulative and untrustworthy. While Lee was an excellent student in college and is a competent tax accountant, I've observed him looking through papers on other people's desks, blaming others for errors that were clearly his, and calling in sick when I knew he had gone boating with friends. In addition, about a month ago, Lee told me that he'd come in and worked the previous Saturday. I had been in the office that Saturday, so I knew that Lee hadn't come in.

What should I do now?

[In 400 words or less, give your response to Dana]

This is a fictionalized account of a potentially real management issue. It is meant for academic purposes only and is not meant to reflect positively or negatively on the firm of Stone, Hartwick, Mueller, and Gibson or any of its employees.

CASE APPLICATION

Avianca Flight 52

At 7:40 p.m. on January 25, 1990, Avianca Flight 52 was cruising at thirty-seven thousand feet above the southern New Jersey coast. The aircraft had enough fuel to last nearly two hours—a healthy cushion considering the plane was less than half an hour from touchdown at New York's Kennedy airport. Then a series of delays began. First, at 8 p.m., the air traffic controllers at Kennedy told the pilots on Flight 52 that they would have to circle in a holding pattern because of heavy traffic. At 8:45, the Avianca co-pilot advised Kennedy that they were "running low on fuel." The controller at Kennedy acknowledged the message but the plane was not cleared to land until 9:24. In the interim, the Avianca crew relayed no information to Kennedy that an emergency was imminent, yet the cockpit crew spoke worriedly among themselves about their dwindling fuel supplies.

Flight 52's first attempt to land at 9:24 was aborted. The plane had come in too low and poor visibility made a safe landing uncertain. When the Kennedy controllers gave Flight 52's pilot new instructions for a second attempt, the crew again mentioned that they were running low on fuel, but the pilot told the controllers that the newly assigned flight path was "O.K." At 9:32, two of Flight 52's engines lost power. A minute later, the other two cut off. The plane, out of fuel, crashed on Long Island at 9:34 p.m. All seventy-three people on board were killed.

When investigators reviewed the cockpit tapes and talked with the controllers involved, they learned that a communication breakdown caused this tragedy. A closer look at the events of that evening help to explain why a simple message was neither clearly transmitted nor adequately received.

First, the pilots kept saying they were "running low on fuel." Traffic controllers told investigators that it is fairly common for pilots to use this phrase. In times of delay, controllers assume that everyone has a fuel problem. However, had the pilots uttered the words "fuel emergency," the controllers would have been obligated to direct the jet ahead of all others and clear it to land as soon as possible. As one controller put it, if a pilot "declares an emergency, all rules go out the window and we get the guy to the airport as quickly as possible." Unfortunately, the pilots of Flight 52 never used the word "emergency," so the people at Kennedy never understood the true nature of the pilots' problem.

Second, the vocal tone of the pilots on Flight 52 didn't convey the severity or urgency of the fuel problem to the air traffic controllers. Many of these controllers are trained to pick up subtle tones in a pilot's voice in such situations. While the crew of Flight 52 expressed considerable concern among themselves about the fuel problem, their voice tones in communicating to Kennedy were cool and professional.

Finally, the culture and traditions of pilots and airport authorities may have made the pilot of Flight 52 reluctant to declare an emergency. A pilot's expertise and pride can be at stake in such a situation. Declaration of a formal emergency requires the pilot to complete a wealth of paperwork. Moreover, if a pilot has been found to be negligent in calculating how much fuel was needed for a flight, the Federal Aviation Administration can suspend his license. These negative reinforcers strongly discourage pilots from calling an emergency.

Questions

1. Analyze the communications between the pilots on Flight 52 and the traffic controllers at Kennedy using the seven step model presented in this chapter.

2. How could active listening skills have prevented this crash? Be specific.

3. Avianca is a Colombian airline. A large number of flights into major world airports are foreign carriers. How is it possible for world air traffic controllers to be as generally effective as they are given that pilots and controllers often speak different languages?

Based on J. Cusman, "Avianca Flight 52: The Delays That Ended in Disaster," *The New York Times*, February 5, 1990, p. B-1; and E. Weiner, "Right Word is Crucial in Air Control," *The New York Times*, January 29, 1990, p. B-5.

VIDEO CASE

Kansas City Police Chief Steven Bishop

"I want our officers to treat the citizens that we must serve and those that we must be accountable to with dignity and respect." Those words, spoken by Kansas City Police Chief Steven Bishop, reflect an attitude toward police work and communication that is changing the way the Kansas City police are doing their jobs.

Steven Bishop joined the KC Police Department in 1970. He spent the majority of his career on SWAT teams. In 1990, he was promoted to police chief, the first cop on the beat in Kansas City to make chief. He is determined to change the way his officers do their jobs.

When Bishop took over as chief, citizen complaints of excessive force were coming in at the rate of fifty per month. Bishop's position: Enough is enough. KC had had its share of use of excessive force by police officers when suspects offered little or no resistance. It had to stop. When a local religious leader was mistaken for a bank robber, taken from his car, and beaten senseless even though he offered no resistance, Bishop acted swiftly. He suspended the officer in question for six months without pay. He was determined not to have a Rodney King-type incident in his department.

All of Bishop's officers now must take part in an eight-hour seminar designed to help them communicate better with the people they deal with every day. His goal: To change these officers' behavior. His program of strong talk coupled with harsh discipline for unacceptable behavior and supported by skill-improvement seminars seems to be working. Complaints of police brutality, after Bishop's first eighteen months on the job, were down 33 percent.

Questions

1. Describe how police officers can use nonverbal communication to intimidate citizens.

2. How are effective interpersonal skills necessary for the cop on the beat? For a police chief?

3. Chief Bishop believes you can teach improved communication skills to police officers. Others say that the selection process and group norms in these jobs work against open, sensitive communication with citizens. What do you think?

Source: "Friday Profile: Steven Bishop," *ABC World News Tonight,* September 20, 1991.

INTEGRATIVE EXERCISE FOR PART V

Active Listening

PURPOSE

1. To contrast passive and active listening.
2. To apply paraphrasing skills

REQUIRED KNOWLEDGE

The skills of paraphrasing what others have said.

TIME REQUIRED

Approximately 15 minutes

INSTRUCTIONS

Most of us are pretty poor listeners. This is probably because active listening is very demanding. This exercise is specifically designed to dramatize how difficult it is to listen actively and to accurately interpret what is being said. It also points out how emotions can distort communication.

Break the class into pairs. In each pair, Person A is to choose a contemporary issue. Some examples include business ethics, stiffer college grading practices, gun control, legalization of abortion, on-site employee drug-testing, money as a motivator, and company-paid maternity benefits. Person B is then to select a position on that issue. Person A must automatically take the opposing position. The two individuals are now to debate the issue.

But not so fast! There's a catch. Before each speaks, he or she must first summarize, in his or her *own* words and without notes, what the other has said. If the summary doesn't satisfy the speaker, it must be corrected until it does.

INTEGRATIVE CASE FOR PART V

Concrete Products

Concrete Products is a subsidiary of the Premix Company and is located in Bellevue, Washington. The main product of Concrete Products is building blocks. The firm is made up of about 150 unskilled production employees, twenty skilled metal workers, fifteen first-line supervisors, and a staff of twenty office and management personnel.

The president of Concrete Products was concerned about the company's profitability and hired a management consultant, Pete Thompson, who specializes in OB to prepare a study. As a preliminary investigation, it was agreed that Pete Thompson would carefully evaluate three diverse positions in the firm. The individuals and jobs selected for evaluation were Mike Phillips (a production worker), Carol Hunt (a sales dispatcher), and Gary Riley (the company's sales manager). Their place in Concrete Products' organization can be seen in Figure V–1.

MIKE PHILLIPS

Mike Phillips had been employed by Tacoma Block and Concrete until 1989. In that year, Tacoma Block and Concrete was bought by Concrete Products, and Mike was transferred to the Bellevue location. He operates the off-bearer, a fork attachment that removes masonry blocks from a conveyor and places them in racks to be forwarded to the autoclave for curing. The job might be

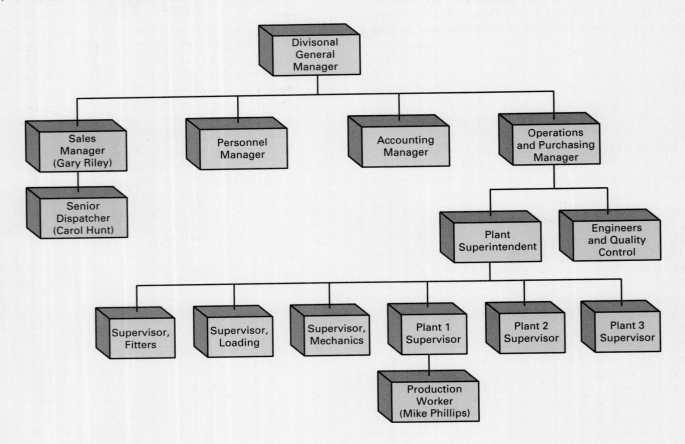

described as undesirable for two reasons. First, the surroundings are very noisy because the job is done in close proximity to the compaction equipment. Second, the job is monotonous because the production line has been designed to produce at a constant rate.

The Job

Mike's day begins at 7:00 a.m. He begins work on the production line almost immediately, because plant setup, repairs, and preventive maintenance are completed overnight by fitters. The job itself is quite straightforward. As the concrete blocks are pressed, Mike removes them from the conveyor and places them into special steel racks. He does this by swivelling the fork into position parallel to the racks. The procedure, while sounding simple, actually requires considerable skill. Mike has to adjust his methods according to the size and weight of each type of block.

Mike also acts as a control point on the production line, and this enables him to take corrective action in case of delays. These delays are usually caused by the failure of the forklift drivers to replace the steel shelving quickly. This, in turn, is caused by breakdowns, slowness of the strippers to empty the racks, general "orneriness" of the lift drivers, and absenteeism on any of these jobs. Other factors causing delays in Mike's job are poor quality control in batching, deflection of the block molds, and poor compaction of the blocks due to machine failure. Another increasing problem Mike faces is sabotage—specifically, employees who throw foreign materials into the batching system. This results in the fracturing or bending of molds and almost always requires a number of employees (including Mike) to work overtime. Mike estimates that, on average, at least one hour per day is lost due to delays. When a big job is on, Mike has noted that sabotage tends to increase and, with it, the length of delays.

Job Satisfaction

Mike describes himself as "reasonably satisfied" with his pay. This is probably due to the way in which his pay is calculated. He gets a basic wage rate plus a group bonus. The group bonus requires that each supervisor decide on performance rankings, and thus the bonus differentials, of the employees in his group of ten to twelve workers. Mike is consistently one of the highest bonus earners, and while money is probably not as much of an incentive to Mike as it once was, it still remains an important measure of success for him. Mike told Pete Thompson that 'the worth of a job is determined by how much money you're paid for doing that job."

The work group of which Mike is a part also gives him satisfaction. Mike's experience and skill level provide him with relatively high status in his work group. This status compensates for some of the job's disadvantages like limited opportunities for promotion or personal growth, poor working conditions, and the frustration from performing highly repetitive tasks.

When Mike was asked to talk about things that "turn him off" about his job, he mentioned three. There are the occasional verbal confrontations with the forklift drivers. Mike thinks this may be due to the fact that these drivers are not included in the bonus system. Another frustration is that "new workers are here one day and disappear the next." This lack of continuity makes it hard to develop smooth coordination. But Mike's biggest beef concerns the company's philosophy. "This place, like every other place I've ever worked, doesn't care about helping people to do a better job. Nothing gets done to make our jobs more meaningful unless it increases profits or benefits someone in management."

Contact with Superiors

Mike's contacts with the "higher-ups" are limited to those with his supervisor. That relationship, however, is fairly positive. Mike considers his supervisor "reasonably objective" and "receptive to change." Mike's supervisor often gives him the opportunity to participate in efforts to improve block-handling methods. For instance, the redesign of the racking system and twin off-bearer are two of Mike's suggestions now in operation.

Mike has almost no contact with upper management except for passing "hello's." The president often walks through the factory but seldom talks with production people. Mike noted that this distancing works both ways. Few workers take any interest in the president. This, he surmised, is a result of frequent changes of company presidents. It has become generally accepted by production personnel that because Concrete Products is one of the smaller subsidiaries of Premix, it suffers from turnover in chief executives. The presidents take "little interest in the detailed operations here so we take little interest in presidents."

Contact with Peers

High turnover has resulted in the creation of two production groups:"Newcomers" and "old pros." Each group tends to go its own way at break time, during lunch and after work. Within his peer group, Mike's ability and competence is generally recognized, though occasionally new members within the group will question his skills, which "burns me to no end." Members of the "old pros" often rely on Mike for both personal and work-related advice. Pete Thompson noted, with interest, that there was little social interaction between the production workers and people such as fitters, mechanics, and forklift drivers.

CAROL HUNT

Carol Hunt has been with Concrete Products since 1987. Initially, she was employed as a salesclerk, but in the last two years she has been responsible for dispatching orders throughout the Seattle metropolitan area. As senior sales dispatcher, she also supervises three clerks involved in order taking.

The Job

Carol's day begins at 8:00 A.M., when she ensures that all orders allocated the previous day have been dispatched and checks on breakdowns and the number of trucks and cranes available for the day. She receives and prices orders, checks on pallet returns, and follows up on claims for waiting time, additional cartage, and credit. Claims for credit are forwarded to the accounts department and, occasionally, to the sales manager for consideration. By midmorning, the first set of drivers is returning for second loads. New orders are distributed to the drivers as they pass the dispatch office on their way to the loading areas.

This pattern continues throughout the day until approximately 3:00 P.M., when the transactions for the day are totalled for the sales manager's review. It is at this time that the allocation of orders for the next day begins and delivery lists are forwarded to the loading docks for use early the following day. Carol also handles all minor customer complaints and forwards details on these to the sales manager. On a typical day, Carol will make one or two trips to the loading docks to check on delays and driver complaints. Occasionally she has found as many as eight or ten trucks sitting idle. Such incidents occur, according to Carol, because forklifts break down or are reallocated to production areas.

Job Satisfaction

Carol says she likes her job "when everything runs smoothly." Unfortunately, this isn't too often. She tends to be confronted continually with problems related to loading and delivery. This does, of course, add challenge to her daily activities; and when she successfully solves a problem, she feels "a sense of satisfaction."

Carol's job allows her a considerable degree of freedom and responsibility. Seldom are her decisions questioned by more senior staff. When discussing the satisfying aspects of her job, she talks about autonomy, responsibility, and achievement.

On the negative side, Carol becomes frustrated and dissatisfied when she is accused of favoring some drivers over others. The drivers are subcontractors and she is regularly accused of allocating "easy runs" to certain of these. Carol also spoke negatively about job pressures and the lack of rewards. Carol says sometimes the pressure of the job becomes so great that she feels that she is "running around in circles." She is disappointed by the lack of verbal recognition of her performance by her superiors. She also thinks the company is "exploiting" her by paying her less than a male would receive for doing the same job.

Contact with Superiors

Communication with her immediate boss, Gary Riley—the sales manager, is inhibited because of "personality differences." In Carol's opinion, the sales manager "likes to talk rather than listen." This has eroded her belief that any suggestions regarding improvements in her area of responsibility would be heeded. Contact with other members of management is limited. She commented that this is probably due to her occupying "what was once regarded as a man's job."

Contact with Peers

All Carol's social contacts with her work peers occur on the job. Carol does not believe in socializing with colleagues outside working hours. "I have little in common with the people around here." Carol was described by the order clerks as "abrasive," "arrogant," and "self-centered."

GARY RILEY

Gary Riley has been with Concrete Products since 1985. He was initially an industrial salesman but has been sales manager since 1989.

The Job

Gary's work involves a diverse pattern of activity. Most of his time is occupied by reading and sending mail, by handling telephone calls, and by meeting with customers, subordinates, and superiors. Gary does not work to a plan in the accepted sense of the word, and the pressures of the job leave little room for reflection. Other activities during the day include delegating "calls" to sales representatives and informing sales reps of trade gossip, customer problems, promotional programs, and production and delivery problems. Gary is also responsible for supervising and coordinating all the activities in the sales department.

Gary devotes a major part of his day to immediate issues such as daily production analysis and calling personally on major customers. He also disseminates information returned by representatives—information on the quality of the blocks, credits, color range, competitive activity, and new process technology. In this way he attempts to piece together some tangible details of what products are being sold.

Job Satisfaction

The prior sales managers had been perceived as resistant to change and highly autocratic. "Middle management just didn't participate in the running of the company; the skills were there but in most cases were underutilized." Since becoming sales manager, Gary has greatly enjoyed the challenge of reorganizing and rejuvenating the sales department.

Gary believes he has developed a climate in the sales department that affords his staff the opportunity to develop their knowledge and skills to contribute to the department's success. This development is a continual source of satisfaction to Gary.

Gary's goal has been to remove any social barriers within his department. Yet he is worried about how much control he should maintain and how much he should delegate.

Gary is also dissatisfied because he is often criticized by senior managers for his lack of decision-making ability and his "easygoing" manner. Gary admits his style is very different from that of most other managers. "Historically, this has been an extremely autocratic company," he says. Gary's estimate of his own abilities doesn't generally coincide with that of senior management, with the notable exception of the current president. Other senior executives are regularly questioning "my competence as a manager."

Contact with Superiors

Gary communicates well with his immediate superior, the president, which is a direct result of the president's participative management style. This is a major depar-

ture from the highly autocratic style of the previous presidents appointed from the Premix group. Gary has been able to discuss many of his problems and ideas with the president, and the president regularly seeks Gary out for his opinions. The two-way interaction has given Gary access to information not available to previous sales managers, and he feels that this information has been extremely beneficial to his decision making.

Contact with Peers

Gary is generally liked by his peers, but some are suspicious of his motives. Gary's close contact with the current president has caused some resentment, especially in the operational and engineering departments. Organizational changes are being made in both areas, and Gary acknowledges that some of them are a result of his suggestions. He is concerned that he might be earning a reputation as a hatchetman. Because of the organizational changes that are taking place, Gary has noticed that his position within his peer group is also changing.

QUESTIONS

1. What motivates Mike Phillips? Carol Hunt? Gary Riley? Do you think that Concrete Products could do more to motivate these employees effectively?

2. How is each person's job performance influenced by interactions with others in and around his or her work groups? Discuss.

3. What general communication problems do you see at Concrete Products? What special problems in communication and interpersonal skills do you see between Gary Riley and Carol Hunt? How can these problems be overcome?

4. Analyze the conflicts that exist at Concrete Products. Are these functional or dysfunctional?

5. If you were Pete Thompson, what changes would you suggest the president make to improve the company's profitability? Be specific.

This case was prepared by Dr. Graham Kenny. Reprinted, with modifications, by permission of the author.

CHAPTER 19

Foundations of Control

LEARNING OBJECTIVES

After Reading This Chapter, You Should Be Able To:

1. Define control.
2. Explain why control is important.
3. Describe the control process.
4. Distinguish between the three types of control.
5. Define the factors that managers can control.
6. Contrast the organizational goals and systems approaches to organizational effectiveness.
7. Explain the strategic constituencies approach to organizational effectiveness.
8. Describe the qualities of an effective control system.
9. Explain how controls can become dysfunctional.

After much anticipation, when the Hubble Space Telescope was finally launched it was found to have a flaw in its primary mirror. Better controls could have prevented this problem.

The Hubble Space Telescope was planned for more than fifteen years and cost more than $1.5 billion.[1] Yet when it was finally launched in April 1990, the National Aeronautics and Space Administration (NASA) found that there was a flaw in the telescope's primary mirror. The 94.5-inch diameter primary mirror was too flat in the center, and so it produced blurry images. The result: Because the telescope could not focus on distant stars nearly as sharply as had been expected, it threatened as many as half of the planned experiments, and many observations might not be able to be carried out.

The sad part about the Hubble story is that, with better controls, it could have been prevented. The mirror's maker, Perkins-Elmer, used a flawed optical template to achieve the exacting specifications. An optical verification test that was used in making the mirror—a reflective null corrector—had not been set up correctly. A spacing error of 1.3 millimeters in this device—about the diameter of the tip of a ballpoint pen—caused the mirror's surface to be ground and polished in the wrong shape. But no one caught the mistake. Ironically, in contrast with many NASA projects, time pressures were not the issue. There was more than enough time to catch the telescope's flaws. Rough grinding of the mirror began in 1978, and final polishing was not finished until 1981. Then the completed telescope sat on the ground for two years after the space shuttle program was disrupted by the *Challenger* disaster, in which barely two minutes after liftoff a flame from one of the solid rocket boosters ignited the massive liquid-fuel tank in the shuttle. In a spectacular explosion, all seven of the crew were killed.

Managers at NASA who had responsibility for the Hubble project paid little attention to the details of the telescope's construction. A NASA executive who headed up a six-member investigating committee on the Hubble debacle said, "There were at least three cases where there was clear evidence that a problem had developed, and it was missed all three times."

The Hubble example illustrates what can happen when an organization has inadequate controls. Regardless of the thoroughness of the planning, an idea still may be poorly or improperly implemented without a satisfactory control system. Effective management, therefore, needs to consider the benefits of a well-designed control system.

What Is Control?

control
The process of monitoring activities to ensure they are being accomplished as planned and of correcting any significant deviations.

Control can be defined as the process of monitoring activities to ensure that they are being accomplished as planned and of correcting any significant deviations. All managers should be involved in the control function even if their units are performing as planned. Managers cannot really know whether their units are performing properly until they have evaluated what activities have been done and have compared the actual performance with the desired standard.[2] An effective control system ensures that activities are completed in ways that lead to the attainment of the organization's goals. The criterion that determines the effectiveness of a control system is how well it facilitates goal achievement. The more it helps managers achieve their organization's goals, the better the control system.[3]

The Importance of Control

Planning can be done, an organization structure can be created to efficiently facilitate the achievement of objectives, and employees can be directed and motivated. Still, there is no assurance that activities are going as planned and that the goals managers are seeking are, in fact, being attained. Control is important, therefore, because it is the final link in the functional chain of management. However, the value of the control function lies predominantly in its relation to planning and delegating activities.

In Chapter 7, we described objectives as the foundation of planning. Objectives give specific direction to managers. However, just stating objectives or having subordinates accept your objectives is no guarantee that the necessary actions have been accomplished. "The best-laid plans of mice and men oft go awry." The effective manager needs to follow up to ensure that the actions that others are supposed to take and the objectives they are supposed to achieve are, in fact, being taken and achieved.

In our discussion of interpersonal skills we noted that many managers find it difficult to delegate. A major reason given was the fear that subordinates would do something wrong for which the manager would be held responsible. Thus many managers are tempted to do things themselves and avoid delegating. This reluctance to delegate, however, can be reduced if managers develop an effective control system. Such a control system can provide information and feedback on the performance of subordinates to whom they have delegated authority. An effective control system is therefore important because managers need to delegate authority; but because they are held ultimately responsible for the decisions that their subordinates make, managers also need a feedback mechanism.

The Control Process

control process
The process of measuring actual performance, comparing it against a standard, and taking managerial action to correct deviations or inadequate standards.

The **control process** consists of three separate and distinct steps: (1) *measuring* actual performance; (2) *comparing* actual performance against a standard; and (3) taking *managerial action* to correct deviations or inadequate standards. Before we consider each step in detail, you should be aware that the control process assumes that standards of performance *already exist*. These standards are the specific objectives against which progress can be measured. They are created in the planning function. If managers use MBO, then objectives are, by definition, tangible, verifiable, and measurable. In such instances, these objectives are the standards against which progress is measured and compared. If MBO is not practiced, then standards are the specific performance indicators that management uses. Our point is that these standards are developed in the planning function; planning must *precede* control.

Measuring

To determine what actual performance is, a manager must acquire information about it. The first step in control, then, is measuring. Let us consider *how* we measure and *what* we measure.

How We Measure   Four common sources of information, frequently used by managers to measure actual performance, are personal observation, statistical reports, oral reports, and written reports. Each has particular strengths and weaknesses; however, a combination of them increases both the number of input sources and the probability of receiving reliable information.

An increasing number of managers, such as Ralph Stayer of Johnsonville Foods, are using personal observation as a means of control. Management-by-walking-around provides a richness of information often lost in formal reports.

activity—information that is not filtered through others. It permits intensive coverage because minor as well as major performance activities can be observed as well as opportunities for the manager to "read between the lines." Management-by-walking-around can pick up omissions, facial expressions, and tones of voice that may be missed by other sources. Unfortunately, in a time when quantitative information suggests objectivity, personal observation is often considered an inferior information source. It is subject to perceptual biases—what one manager sees, another might not. Personal observation also consumes a good deal of time. Finally, this method suffers from obtrusiveness. Employees might interpret a manager's overt observation as a sign of a lack of confidence in them or of mistrust.

The current wide use of computers in organizations has made managers rely increasingly on *statistical reports* for measuring actual performance. This measuring device, however, is not limited to computer outputs. It also includes graphs, bar charts, and numerical displays of any form that managers may use for assessing performance. Although statistical data is easy to visualize and effective for showing relationships, it provides limited information about an activity. Statistics report on only a few key areas and often ignore other important factors.

Information can also be acquired through *oral reports*—that is, through conferences, meetings, one-to-one conversations, or telephone calls. The advantages and disadvantages of this method of measuring performance are similar to those of personal observation. Although the information is filtered, it is fast, allows for feedback, and permits language expression and tone of voice, as well as words themselves, to convey meaning. Historically, one of the major drawbacks of oral reports was the problem of documenting information for later references. However, our technological capabilities have progressed in the last couple of decades to the point at which oral reports can be efficiently taped and become as permanent as if they were written.

Actual performance may also be measured by *written reports*. As with statistical reports, they are slower yet more formal than first- or secondhand oral measures. This formality also often means greater comprehensiveness and conciseness than is found in oral reports. In addition, written reports are usually easy to catalogue and reference.

Given the varied advantages and disadvantages of each of these four measurement techniques, comprehensive control efforts by managers should use all four.

What We Measure   *What* we measure is probably more critical to the control process than *how* we measure. The selection of the wrong criteria can result in serious dysfunctional consequences. Besides, what we measure determines, to a great extent, what people in the organization will attempt to excel at.[4]

Some control criteria are applicable to any management situation. For instance, because all managers, by definition, direct the activities of others, criteria such as employee satisfaction or turnover and absenteeism rates can be measured. Most managers have budgets for their area of responsibility set in dollar costs. Keeping costs within budget is therefore a fairly common control measure. However, any comprehensive control system needs to recognize the diversity of activities among managers. A production manager in a manufacturing plant might use measures of the quantity of units produced per day, units produced per labor hour, scrap per unit of output, or percent of rejects returned by customers. The manager of an administrative unit in a government agency might use number of document pages typed per day, number of orders processed per hour, or average time required to process service calls. Marketing managers often use measures such as percent of market captured, average dollar value per sale, or number of customer visits per salesperson.

The performance of some activities is difficult to measure in quantifiable terms. It is more difficult, for instance, for an administrator to measure the performance of a research chemist or an elementary school teacher than of a person who sells life insurance. But most activities can be broken down into objective segments that allow for measurement. The manager needs to determine what value a person, department, or unit contributes to the organization and then convert the contribution into standards.

Most jobs and activities can be expressed in tangible and measurable terms. When a performance indicator cannot be stated in quantifiable terms, managers should look for and use subjective measures. Certainly, subjective measures have significant limitations. Still, they are better than having no standards at all and ignoring the control function. If an activity is important, the excuse that it is difficult to measure is inadequate. In such cases, managers should use subjective performance criteria. Of course, any analysis or decisions made based on subjective criteria should recognize the limitations of the data.

Comparing

range of variation
The acceptable parameters of variance between actual performance and the standard.

The comparing step determines the degree of variation between actual performance and the standard. Some variation in performance can be expected in all activities; it is therefore critical to determine the acceptable **range of variation.** (See Figure 19–1.) Deviations in excess of this range become significant and receive the manager's attention. In the comparison stage, managers are particularly concerned with the size and direction of the variation. An example should make this clearer.

Rich Tanner is sales manager for Eastern States Distributors. The firm distributes imported beers in several states on the east coast. Rich prepares a report during the first week of each month that describes sales for the previous month, classified by brand name. Table 19–1 displays both the standard and actual sales figures (in hundreds of cases) for the month of July.

Should Rich be concerned about the July performance? Sales were a bit higher than he had originally targeted, but does that mean that there were no significant deviations? Even though overall performance was generally quite favorable, several brands might deserve the sales manager's attention. However, the number of brands that

FIGURE 19–1
Defining an Acceptable Range of Variation

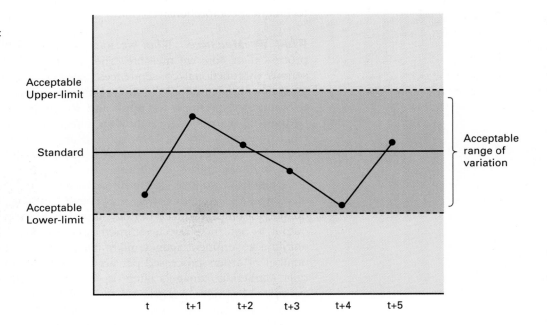

TABLE 19–1   Eastern States Distributors' Sales Performance for July (hundreds of cases)

Brand	Standard	Actual	Over (Under)
Heineken	1,075	913	(162)
Molson	630	634	4
Beck's	800	912	112
Moosehead	620	622	2
Labatt's	540	672	132
Corona	160	140	(20)
Amstel Light	225	220	(5)
Dos Equis	80	65	(15)
Tecate	170	286	116
Total Cases	4,300	4,464	164

deserve attention depends on what Rich believes to be *significant*. How much variation should Rich allow before he takes corrective action?

The deviation on several brands is very small and undoubtedly not worthy of special attention. These include Molson, Moosehead, and Amstel Light. Are the shortages for Corona and Dos Equis brands significant? That's a judgment Rich must make. Heineken sales were 15 percent below Rich's goal. This needs attention. Rich should look for a cause. In this case, Rich attributed the loss to aggressive advertising and promotion programs by the big domestic producers, Anheuser-Busch and Miller. Because Heineken is the number one selling import, it is most vulnerable to the promotion clout of the big domestic producers. If the decline in Heineken is more than a temporary slump, Rich will need to reduce his orders with the brewery and lower his inventory stock.

An error in understating sales can be as troublesome as an overstatement. For instance, is the surprising popularity of Tecate a one-month aberration, or is this

Eastern States Distributors uses monthly sales reports to identify problem areas. Significant deviations between actual sales and the budgeted standard will require attention from the company's sales manager.

brand increasing its market share? Our Eastern States' example illustrates that both overvariance and undervariance require managerial attention.

Taking Managerial Action

The third and final step in the control process is taking managerial action. Managers can choose among three courses of action: They can do nothing; they can correct the actual performance; or they can revise the standard. Because "doing nothing" is fairly self-explanatory, let's look more closely at the latter two.

immediate corrective action
Correcting an activity at once in order to get performance back on track.

basic corrective action
Determining how and why performance has deviated and correcting the source of deviations.

Correct Actual Performance   If the source of the variation has been deficient performance, the manager will want to take corrective action. Examples of such corrective action might include changes in strategy, structure, compensation practices, or training programs; the redesign of jobs; or the replacement of personnel.

A manager who decides to correct actual performance has to make another decision: Should he or she take immediate or basic corrective action? **Immediate corrective action** corrects problems at once and gets performance back on track. **Basic corrective action** asks how and why performance has deviated and then proceeds to correct the source of deviation. It is not unusual for managers to rationalize that they do not have the time to take basic corrective action and therefore must be content to perpetually "put out fires" with immediate corrective action. Effective managers, however, analyze deviations and, when the benefits justify it, take the time to permanently correct significant variances between standard and actual performance.

To return to our example of Eastern States Distributors, Rich Tanner might take basic corrective action on the negative variance for Heineken. He might increase promotion efforts, increase the advertisement budget for this brand, or reduce future orders with the manufacturer. The action he takes will depend on his assessment of each brand's potential effectiveness.

Revise the Standard   It is possible that the variance was a result of an unrealistic standard—that is, the goal may be too high or too low. In such cases it's the standard that needs corrective attention, not the performance. In our example, the sales manager might need to raise the standard for Tecate to reflect its increasing popularity. This frequently happens in sports when athletes adjust their performance goals upward during a season if they achieve their season goal early.

The more troublesome problem is the revising of a performance standard downward. If an employee or unit falls significantly short of reaching its target, the natural response is to shift the blame for the variance to the standard. For instance, students who make a low grade on a test often attack the grade cutoff points as too high. Rather than accept the fact that their performance was inadequate, students argue that the standards are unreasonable. Similarly, salespeople who fail to meet their monthly quota may attribute the failure to an unrealistic quota. It may be true that standards are too high, resulting in a significant variance and acting to demotivate those employees being assessed against it. But keep in mind that if employees or managers don't meet the standard, the first thing they are likely to attack is the standard itself. If you believe the standard is realistic, hold your ground. Explain your position, reaffirm to the employee or manager that you expect future performance to improve, and then take the necessary corrective action to turn that expectation into reality.

Summary

Figure 19–2 summarizes the control process. Standards evolve out of objectives, but because objectives are developed during planning, they are tangential to the control process. The process is essentially a continuous flow between measuring, comparing,

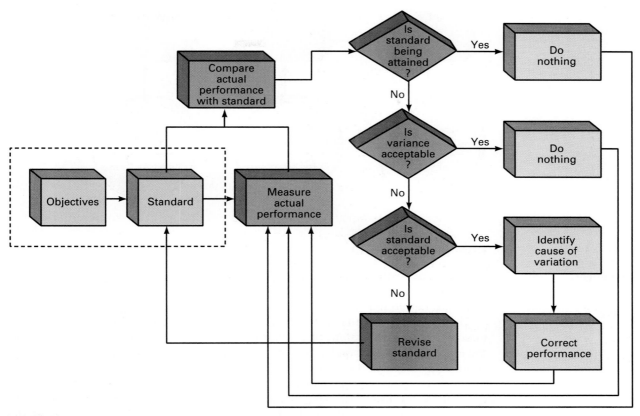

FIGURE 19–2
The Control Process

and managerial action. Depending on the results of the comparing stage, management's courses of action are to do nothing, revise the standard, or correct the performance.

Types of Control

Management can implement controls before an activity commences, while the activity is going on, or after the activity has been completed. The first type is called *feedforward control,* the second is *concurrent control,* and the last is *feedback control.* (See Figure 19–3.)

Feedforward Control

feedforward control

Control that prevents anticipated problems.

The most desirable type of control—**feedforward control**—prevents anticipated problems. It is called feedforward control because it takes place in advance of the actual activity. It is future-directed.[5] For instance, managers at Lockheed Corp. may hire additional personnel as soon as the government announces that the firm has won a major military contract. The hiring of personnel ahead of time prevents potential delays. The key to feedforward controls, therefore, is taking managerial action before a problem occurs.

Feedforward controls are desirable because they allow management to prevent problems rather than having to cure them later. Unfortunately, these controls require timely and accurate information that is often difficult to develop. As a result, managers frequently have to use one of the other two types of control.

FIGURE 19–3
Types of Control

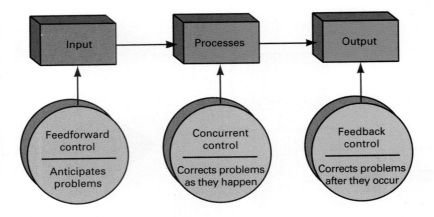

Concurrent Control

concurrent control
Control that occurs while an activity is in progress.

Concurrent control, as its name implies, takes place while an activity is in progress. When control is enacted while the work is being performed, management can correct problems before they become too costly.

The best-known form of concurrent control is direct supervision. When a manager directly oversees the actions of a subordinate, the manager can concurrently monitor the employee's actions and correct problems as they occur. While there is obviously some delay between the activity and the manager's corrective response, the delay is minimal. Technical equipment can be designed to include concurrent controls. Most computers, for instance, are programmed to provide operators with immediate response if an error is made. If you input the wrong command, the program's concurrent controls reject your command and may even tell you why it is wrong.

Feedback Control

The most popular type of control relies on feedback. The control takes place after the action. The control report that Rich Tanner used for assessing beer sales is an example of a **feedback control.**

feedback control
Control imposed after an action has occurred.

The major drawback of this type of control is that, by the time the manager has the information the damage is already done. It's analogous to the proverbial closing the barn door after the horse has been stolen. But for many activities, feedback is the only viable type of control available.

We should note that feedback has two advantages over feedforward and concurrent control.[6] First, feedback provides managers with meaningful information on how effective its planning effort was. If feedback indicates little variance between standard and actual performance, this is evidence that planning was generally on target. If the deviation is great, a manager can use this information when formulating new plans to make them more effective. Second, feedback control can enhance employee motivation. People want information on how well they have performed. Feedback control provides that information.

The Focus of Control

What do managers control? Most control efforts are directed at one of five areas: people, finances, operations, information, or the performance of the overall organization.

People

Managers accomplish goals by working through other people. To achieve their unit goals, managers need and depend on subordinates. It is therefore important for managers to ensure that employees are performing as they are supposed to. The most explicit way managers do this is by direct supervision and performance appraisals.

On a day-to-day basis, managers oversee employees' work and correct problems as they occur. The supervisor who spots an employee taking an unnecessary risk when operating his or her machine may point out the correct way to perform the task and tell the employee to do it the correct way in the future.

Managers assess the work of their employees in a more formal way by means of systematic performance appraisals. An employee's recent performance is evaluated. If performance is positive, the employee's behavior can be reinforced with a reward such as a pay increase. If performance is below standard, managers will seek to correct it or, depending on the nature of the deviation, discipline the employee.

As Table 19–2 illustrates, management has a great many behavioral control devices at its disposal. In actual practice, managers use almost all of the options described in Table 19–2 to increase the likelihood that employees will perform as desired.

Finances

The primary purpose of every business firm is to earn a profit. In pursuit of this objective, managers seek financial controls. Managers might, for instance, carefully search quarterly income statements for excessive expenses. They might also perform several financial ratio tests to ensure that sufficient cash is available to pay ongoing expenses, that debt does not become too large and burdensome, and that assets are being productively used. These are examples of how financial controls can be used to reduce costs and make the best use of financial resources.

TABLE 19–2   Behavioral Control Devices

Selection. Identify and hire people whose values, attitudes, and personality fit with what management desires.

Goals. When employees accept specific goals, the goals then direct and limit behavior.

Job design. The way jobs are designed determines, to a large degree, the tasks that a person does, the pace of the work, the people with whom he or she interacts, and similar activities.

Orientation. New-employee orientation defines which behaviors are acceptable and which aren't.

Direct supervision. The physical presence of supervisors acts to constrain employee behavior and allows for rapid detection of deviant behavior.

Training. Formal training programs teach employees desired work practices.

Mentoring. Informal and formal mentoring activities by senior employees convey to junior employees "the ropes to skip and the ropes to know."

Formalization. Formal rules, policies, job descriptions, and other regulations define acceptable practices and constrain behavior.

Performance appraisals. Employees will behave in ways so as to look good on the criteria by which they will be appraised.

Organizational rewards. Rewards act as reinforcers to encourage desired behaviors and to extinguish undesirable ones.

Organizational culture. Through stories, rituals, and top-management practices, culture conveys what constitutes proper behavior.

ETHICAL DILEMMAS IN MANAGEMENT

Behavioral Control and Employees' Right to Privacy

When does management's effort to control the actions of its employees become an invasion of privacy? Consider two cases.[7]

Daniel Winn made nearly nine dollars an hour setting up machinery at Best Lock Corp. in Indiana. He was fired after he testified in a relative's legal hearing that he drank socially from time to time. Unfortunately for Mr. Winn, Best Lock forbids alcohol consumption by its employees, even after work. It should be noted that in a test of the company's no-drinking rule, a state court in Indiana determined the rule to be valid and upheld the firing decision.

Employees at General Electric's Answering Center handle telephone inquiries from customers all day long. Those conversations are taped by GE and occasionally reviewed by its management.

Are either of the above practices—firing someone for drinking off the job or listening in on telephone conversations—an invasion of privacy? These questions actually touch two larger issues: Does management have the right to tell employees how they can or cannot spend their time off the job, and on the job, when does management overstep the bounds of decency and privacy by silently (even covertly) scrutinizing the behavior of its employees?

How does management defend such practices? In the case of Best Lock, the argument essentially is based on keeping medical costs down. In recent years, corporate insurance plan premiums have risen an average of 17 percent annually. And employees who engage in unhealthy habits—such as drinking, smoking, or overeating—file more claims. General Electric can point to U.S. government statistics estimating that six million workers are being electronically monitored on their jobs. And silent surveillance of telephone calls can be used to help employees do their jobs better. Managers can review employee performance and provide feedback that can improve the quality of the employees' work.

But once management starts regulating off-the-job behavior, where does it stop? What about employees who eat lots of greasy food? Is that grounds for disciplinary action? Similarly, when does management's need for more information about employee performance cross over the line and interfere with a worker's right to privacy? What do *you* think?

Financial controls, of course, are used not only by managers in the private sector. Managers of not-for-profit organizations have objectives, one of the most important being efficiency. Financial controls such as budgets are an important tool for controlling costs in hospitals, schools, and government agencies.

In Chapter 9, we discussed budgets as a planning tool. As we noted, they are used for both planning and control. Budgets provide managers with quantitative standards against which to measure and compare resource consumption. And by pointing out deviations between standard and actual consumption, they become control devices.

Table 19–3 summarizes some of the most popular financial ratios used in organizations. Taken from the organization's financial statements (the balance sheet and income statement), they compare two significant figures and express them as a percentage, or ratio. Because you undoubtedly have encountered these ratios in introductory accounting and finance courses, or you will in the near future, we needn't elaborate on them. We mention them, however, to remind you that managers

TABLE 19-3 Popular Financial Ratios

Objective	Ratio	Calculation	Meaning
Liquidity test	Current ratio	$\dfrac{\text{Current assets}}{\text{Current liabilities}}$	Tests the organization's ability to meet short-term obligations
	Acid test	$\dfrac{\text{Current assets less inventories}}{\text{Current liabilities}}$	Tests liquidity more accurately when inventories turn over slowly or are difficult to sell
Leverage test	Debt-to-assets	$\dfrac{\text{Total debt}}{\text{Total assets}}$	The higher the ratio, the more leveraged the organization
	Times-interest-earned	$\dfrac{\text{Profits before interest and taxes}}{\text{Total interest charges}}$	Measures how far profits can decline before the organization is unable to meet its interest expenses
Operations test	Inventory turnover	$\dfrac{\text{Sales}}{\text{Inventory}}$	The higher the ratio, the more efficiently inventory assets are being used
	Total asset turnover	$\dfrac{\text{Sales}}{\text{Total assets}}$	The fewer assets used to achieve a given level of sales, the more efficiently management is using the organization's total assets
Profitability	Profit-margin-on-sales	$\dfrac{\text{Net profit after taxes}}{\text{Total sales}}$	Identifies the profits that various products are generating
	Return-on-investment	$\dfrac{\text{Net profit after taxes}}{\text{Total assets}}$	Measures the efficiency of assets to generate profits

use such ratios as internal control devices for monitoring how efficiently the organization uses its assets, debt, inventories, and the like.

Operations

The success of an organization depends to a large extent on its ability to produce goods and services effectively and efficiently. Operations control techniques are designed to assess how effectively and efficiently an organization's transformation processes are working.

Operations control typically encompasses monitoring production activities to ensure that they are on schedule; assessing purchasing's ability to provide the proper quantity and quality of supplies needed at the lowest cost possible; monitoring the

Sears, Roebuck chairman, Edward A. Brennan, recently took personal control of Sears' retail operations. "We must get costs under control," said Brennan. Expenses consumed 30 cents of every dollar of retail sales at Sears compared to 23 cents and 16 cents at rivals Kmart and Wal-Mart, respectively.

quality of the organization's products or services to ensure that they meet pre-established standards; and making sure that equipment is well maintained. These concerns will be elaborated upon in Chapter 21 in our discussion of operations management.

Information

Managers need information to do their job. Inaccurate, incomplete, excessive, or delayed information will seriously impede their performance. It's therefore necessary to develop a management information system that provides the right data in the right amount to the right person at the right time.

The technology for managing information has changed dramatically in recent years. Fifteen years ago, for instance, managers in large organizations relied on a centralized data-processing department to service their information needs. If they wanted a breakdown of weekly sales by regional sales territory, they requested the report from the data-processing manager. A lucky manager might get a computer printout of the sales figures early the following week. Today's managers usually have computers on their desks. They can type in their request at any time and call up the latest sales figures by territory. What used to take days to get can now be accessed in seconds.

Few areas of the manager's job have changed, and will continue to change, as rapidly as has management information systems. Technology is creating new options for managers at an unprecedented pace. Today's state-of-the-art system will almost certainly be antiquated in two or three years. The importance of management information systems and their rapid development are further discussed in Chapter 20.

Organization Performance

Evaluations of an organization's overall performance or effectiveness are made regularly by a number of constituencies. Managers, of course, are concerned with their organization's performance, but they're not the only group that evaluates organizational effectiveness. Customers and clients make effectiveness judgments when they choose to do business with one firm rather than another. Security analysts, potential investors, potential lenders, and suppliers (especially those extending credit terms) also have to make effectiveness evaluations. In government, decisions as to which departments get budget increases or cuts are essentially effectiveness determinations. Even employees and potential employees evaluate an organization's effectiveness. When you decide to accept or reject a job offer from an organization, you undoubtedly consider effectiveness factors.

The facts above support the idea that managers should be concerned with controlling in order to maintain or improve their organization's overall effectiveness. But there is no singular measure of an organization's effectiveness. Productivity, efficiency, profit, morale, quality of output, flexibility, stability, and employee absenteeism are criteria that undoubtedly have an important bearing on an organization's overall effectiveness.[8] None, however, is synonymous with organizational effectiveness.[9] An organization's effectiveness can be assessed by any of three basic approaches.

organizational goals approach
Appraising an organization's effectiveness according to whether it accomplishes its goals.

The Organizational Goals Approach The **organizational goals approach** states that an organization's effectiveness is appraised in terms of the accomplishment of ends rather than means.[10] It is the bottom line that counts. Popular organizational goals criteria include maximizing profits, educating students efficiently, bringing the enemy to surrender, winning the basketball game, and restoring patients to good health. On the assumption that organizations are deliberately created to achieve one or more specified goals, the organizational goals approach makes a great deal of sense.

The problem with goals in the organization was elaborated upon in Chapter 7. Do we use official goals or actual goals? Whose goals? Short-term or long-term? Because organizations have multiple goals, how should these goals be ranked in importance? These problems are not insurmountable. If managers are willing to confront the complexities inherent in the organizational goals approach, they can obtain reasonably valid information for assessing an organization's effectiveness. However, it has been argued that there is more to organizational effectiveness than identifying and measuring specific ends. When managers give their sole attention to ends, they are likely to overlook the long-term health of the organization. An alternative is the systems approach.

The Systems Approach   We introduced the systems framework in Chapter 2. It was used to describe the organization as an entity that acquires inputs, engages in transformation processes, and generates outputs. Consistent with the systems perspective, it can be said that an organization should be judged on its ability to acquire inputs, process these inputs, channel the outputs, and maintain stability and balance. Outputs are the ends, whereas acquisition of inputs and processing efficiencies are means. If an organization is to survive over the long term, it must remain adaptive and healthy. The **systems approach to organizational effectiveness** focuses on those factors—means and ends—that can and do affect survival.[11]

The relevant criteria in the systems approach include market share, stability of earnings, employee absenteeism and turnover rates, growth in research and development expenditures, level of interunit conflicts, degree of employee satisfaction, and clarity of internal communications. Notice that the systems approach emphasizes factors that are important to the long-term health and survival of the organization but may not be critical in the short term. Research and development expenditures, for instance, are an investment in the future. Management can cut costs here and immediately increase profits or reduce losses. But the effect of this action will reduce the organization's viability in later years.

The major advantage to the systems approach is that it discourages management from looking for immediate results at the expense of future successes. Another advantage of the systems approach is its applicability where goals are either very vague or defy measurement. Managers of public organizations, for instance, frequently use "ability to acquire budget increases" as a measure of effectiveness—that is, they substitute an input criterion for an output criterion.

The Strategic Constituencies Approach   The third approach proposes that an effective organization satisfies the demands of those constituencies in its environment from whom it requires support for its continued existence.[12] We call this the **strategic constituencies approach.**

Most public universities consider effectiveness in terms of acquiring students but feel that they need not be concerned with potential *employers* of their graduates. Why? Because these universities' survival does not depend on whether or not their graduates get jobs. Administrators in public universities devote considerable effort to wooing state legislators. Failure to win legislators' support is sure to have adverse effects on the budget of a public university. In contrast, a private university's effectiveness is hardly affected by whether or not it has a favorable relationship with the key people in the state capital. Administrators in private universities direct their energies to lobbying for increased federally subsidized student loans and to romancing alumni, wealthy philanthropists, and foundations who might donate money to their schools. These are constituencies who significantly determine whether private universities survive.

systems approach to organizational effectiveness
Appraising an organization's effectiveness in terms of both means and ends.

strategic constituencies approach
Appraising an organization's effectiveness according to how well the organization satisfies the demands of its key constituencies.

Using the strategic constituencies approach, managers at Goodyear Tire & Rubber would pay particular attention to the demands of suppliers of critical petroleum products used in the tire-manufacturing process; officers of the United Rubber Workers union; officials at banks where the company has sizable short-term loans; government regulatory agencies that grade tires and inspect facilities for safety violations; security analysts at major brokerage firms who specialize in the tire-and-rubber industry; regional tire jobbers and distributors; and purchasing agents responsible for the acquisition of tires at Ford, Mack Truck, Caterpillar, and other vehicle manufacturers.

The strategic constituencies approach is just as applicable to business firms as it is to universities. A corporation with a very strong cash position, for instance, need not be concerned with the effectiveness criteria that bankers use. However, assume that the company you head has $200 million in bank loans coming due in the next quarter and that you will have to ask the consortium of banks with whom these loans were made to restructure this indebtedness because your firm can't meet this deadline. In such a situation, the criteria these bankers use to measure your organization's effectiveness will undoubtedly be the ones you will emphasize. To do otherwise would threaten your organization's survival. So the effective organization is defined as one that successfully identifies its critical constituencies—customers, government agencies, financial institutions, security analysts, labor unions, and so forth—and then satisfies their demands.

Notice the assumptions underlying the strategic constituencies approach. It assumes that an organization is faced with frequent and competing demands from a variety of interest groups. Because these interest groups are of unequal importance, effectiveness is determined by the organization's ability to identify its critical or strategic constituencies and to satisfy the demands they place upon the organization. Further, this approach assumes that managers pursue a number of goals and that the goals selected represent a response to those interest groups who control the resources necessary for the organization to survive.

While the strategic constituencies approach makes a lot of sense, it is not easy for managers to put into action. The task of separating the strategic constituencies from the larger environment is very difficult in practice. Because the environment changes rapidly, what was critical to the organization yesterday might not be so today. Even if the constituencies in the environment can be identified and are assumed to be relatively stable, what separates the "strategic" constituencies from the "almost strategic" constituencies? Regardless of the difficulty of the task, identifying and satisfying strategic constituencies can pay big dividends. By using the strategic constituencies approach, managers decrease the likelihood that they might ignore or severely upset a group whose power could significantly hinder the organization's operations. If management knows whose support is necessary to the health of the organization, it can modify its preference ordering of goals to reflect the changing power relationships with its strategic constituencies.

Preston Smith at S-K-I Ltd.

Running ski resorts is no vacation nowadays. In 1980 there were 1100 ski area operators in the United States. In 1992 there were only half that many. Industry problems have included reduced growth because of the aging of the baby boomers, rapidly escalating costs for ski lift tickets and lodging, a number of mild winters in recent years, and the management challenge of keeping tabs on employees spread over several square miles of mountainside. One person who has weathered the industry's problems is Preston Smith, chief executive officer of S-K-I Ltd.[13] His firm operates popular Vermont ski areas at Killington and Mt. Snow, as well as Southern California's largest ski area, at Bear Mountain.

Smith has invested heavily to develop special snow-making equipment that covers a lot more terrain than the average resort. "We've virtually eliminated our dependence on snow," says Smith. He has also devised a computerized control system that allows S-K-I's management to closely monitor operations, to quickly identify problems and just as quickly to move to correct them. For example, his control system provides him both with up-to-the-minute details of conditions on each major trail and with the ability to create snow on any specific trail by regulating the valves and pumps that control the flow of air and water to the snow-making guns.

Smith's actions have paid handsome dividends. While many of his competitors lose money, he has remained profitable. In 1992, company revenues hit a record $89 million, with earnings of $3.7 million.

Qualities of an Effective Control System

Effective control systems tend to have certain qualities in common.[14] The importance of these qualities varies with the situation, but we can generalize that the following characteristics should make a control system more effective.

1. *Accuracy.* A control system that generates inaccurate information can result in management failing to take action when it should or responding to a problem that doesn't exist. An accurate control system is reliable and produces valid data.

2. *Timeliness.* Controls should call management's attention to variations in time to prevent serious infringement on a unit's performance. The best information has little value if it is dated. Therefore, an effective control system must provide timely information.

3. *Economy.* A control system must be economically reasonable to operate. Any system of control has to justify the benefits that it gives in relation to the costs it incurs. To minimize costs, management should try to impose the least amount of control that is necessary to produce the desired results.

4. *Flexibility.* Effective controls must be flexible enough to adjust to adverse change or to take advantage of new opportunities. Few organizations face environments

Every item that goes on board the NASA Space Shuttle has to be of the highest quality within the tightest of tolerances. The importance of this activity and the enormous costs inherent in failure justify the imposition of extensive controls by both NASA and its subcontractors.

so stable that there is no need for flexibility. Even highly mechanistic structures require controls that can be adjusted as times and conditions change.

5. *Understandability.* Controls that cannot be understood have no value. It is sometimes necessary, therefore, to substitute less complex controls for sophisticated devices. A control system that is difficult to understand can cause unnecessary mistakes, frustrate employees, and eventually be ignored.

6. *Reasonable criteria.* Control standards must be reasonable and attainable. If they are too high or unreasonable, they no longer motivate. Because most employees don't want to risk being labeled incompetent by accusing superiors of asking too much, employees may resort to unethical or illegal shortcuts. Controls should, therefore, enforce standards that challenge and stretch people to reach higher performance levels without being demotivating or encouraging deception.

7. *Strategic placement.* Management can't control everything that goes on in an organization. Even if it could, the benefits couldn't justify the costs. As a result, managers should place controls on those factors that are strategic to the organization's performance. Controls should cover the critical activities, operations, and events within the organization. That is, they should focus on places where variations from standard are most likely to occur or where a variation would do the greatest harm. In a department where labor costs are $20,000 a month and postage costs are $50 a month, a 5 percent overrun in the former is more critical than a 20 percent overrun in the latter. Hence we should establish controls for labor and a critical dollar allocation, whereas postage expenses would not appear to be critical.

8. *Emphasis on the exception.* Because managers can't control all activities, they should place their strategic control devices where those devices can call attention only to the exceptions. An exception system ensures that a manager is not overwhelmed by information on variations from standard. For instance, if management policy gives supervisors the authority to give annual raises up to $200 a month, approve individual expenses up to $500, and make capital expenditures

up to $5,000, then only deviations above these amounts require approval from higher levels of management. These checkpoints become controls that are part of the authority constraints and free higher levels of management from reviewing routine expenditures.

9. *Multiple criteria.* Managers and employees alike will seek to "look good" on the criteria that are controlled. If management controls by using a single measure such as unit profit, effort will be focused only on looking good on this standard. Multiple measures of performance decrease this narrow focus.

   Multiple criteria have a dual positive effect. Because they are more difficult to manipulate than a single measure, they can discourage efforts to merely look good. Additionally, because performance can rarely be objectively evaluated from a single indicator, multiple criteria make possible more accurate assessments of performance.

10. *Corrective action.* An effective control system not only indicates when a significant deviation from standard occurs, but also suggests what action should be taken to correct the deviation. That is, it ought to both point out the problem and specify the solution. This is frequently accomplished by establishing *if—then guidelines*; for instance, *if* unit revenues drop more than 5 percent, *then* unit costs should be reduced by a similar amount.

The Dysfunctional Side of Controls

Larry Boff called the Dallas Fire Department's emergency number to get immediate help for his stepmother, who was having trouble breathing.[15] The nurse/dispatcher, Billie Myrick, spent fifteen minutes arguing with Mr. Boff because he wouldn't bring his stepmother to the phone. He told Ms. Myrick that his stepmother was in the bedroom and couldn't speak. Myrick insisted that she was required to talk to the person in question so she could determine if the situation was a true emergency. Boff insisted that his stepmother was unable to speak on the phone and pleaded with Ms. Myrick to send an ambulance. Myrick continually responded that she could not send an ambulance until she spoke to Boff's stepmother. After getting nowhere for fifteen minutes, Boff hung up the phone. His stepmother was dead.

Three managers at a big General Motors truck plant in Flint, Michigan, installed a secret control box in a supervisor's office to override the control panel that governed the speed of the assembly line.[16] The device allowed the managers to speed up the assembly line—a serious violation of GM's contract with the United Auto Workers. When caught, the managers explained that, while they knew that what they had done was wrong, the pressure from higher-ups to meet unrealistic production goals was so great that they felt the secret control panel was the only way they could meet their targets. As described by one manager, senior GM executives would say, "I don't care *how* you do it—just *do* it."

Did you ever notice that the people who work in the college registrar's office often don't seem to care much about the problems of students? They become so fixated on ensuring that every rule is followed that they lose sight of the fact that their job is to *serve* students, not *hassle* them!

These examples illustrate what can happen when controls are inflexible or control standards are unreasonable. People lose sight of the organization's overall goals.[17] Instead of the organization running the controls, sometimes the controls run the organization.

Because any control system has imperfections, problems occur when individuals or organizational units attempt to look good exclusively in terms of the control

MANAGING FROM A GLOBAL PERSPECTIVE

Adjusting Controls for National Differences

Methods of controlling people and operations can be quite different in foreign countries. For the multinational corporation, managers of foreign operations tend to be less closely controlled by the head office, if for no other reason than that distance precludes direct controls. The head office of a multinational must rely on extensive formal reports to maintain control. But collecting data that are comparable between countries introduces problems for multinationals. A company's factory in Mexico might produce the same products as its factory in the United States. The Mexican factory, however, might be much more labor intensive than its counterpart in the United States (to take advantage of low labor costs in Mexico). If headquarters' executives were to control costs by, for example, calculating labor costs per unit or output per worker, the figures would not be comparable. Therefore distance creates a tendency to formalize controls, and technological differences often make control data uncomparable.

Technology's impact on control is most evident in comparing technologically advanced nations with more primitive countries. Organizations in technologically advanced nations such as the United States, Japan, Canada, Great Britain, Germany, and Australia use indirect control devices—particularly computer-related reports and analyses—in addition to standardized rules and direct supervision to ensure that activities are going as planned. In Tanzania, Zambia, Lebanon, and other less advanced countries, direct supervision and highly centralized decision making are the basic means of control.

Constraints on managerial corrective action may also affect managers in foreign countries. For example, laws in some countries do not allow management the options of closing plants, laying off personnel, taking money out of the country, or bringing in a new management team from outside the country.

devices. The result is dysfunctional in terms of the organization's goals. More often than not, this dysfunctionality is caused by incomplete measures of performance. If the control system evaluates only the quantity of output, people will ignore quality. Similarly, if the system measures activities rather than results, people will spend their time attempting to look good on the activity measures.

To avoid being reprimanded by managers because of the control system, people can engage in behaviors that are designed solely to influence the information system's data output during a given control period. Rather than actually performing well, employees can manipulate measures to give the appearance that they are performing well. Evidence indicates that the manipulation of control data is not a random phenomenon. It depends on the importance of an activity. Organizationally important activities are more likely to make a difference in a person's rewards; therefore, there is a greater incentive to look good on these particular measures.[18] When rewards are at stake, individuals tend to manipulate data to appear in a favorable light by, for instance, distorting actual figures, emphasizing successes, and suppressing evidence of failures. On the other hand, only random errors occur when the distribution of rewards is unaffected.[19]

Our conclusion is that controls have both an up side and a down side. Failure to design flexibility into a controls system can create problems more severe than those the controls were implemented to prevent.

When personnel in a college registrar's office become more concerned with every rule and procedure being followed rigidly, regardless of the possible negative consequences on a student's enrollment or personal life, the control imposed by the rules and procedures can become dysfunctional.

Summary

This summary is organized by the chapter-opening learning objectives found on page 569.

1. Control is the process of monitoring activities to ensure that they are being accomplished as planned and of correcting any significant deviations.

2. Control is important because it monitors whether objectives are being accomplished as planned and delegated authority is being abused.

3. In the control process, management must first have standards of performance from the objectives it formed in the planning stage. Management must then measure actual performance and compare that performance to the standards. If a variance exists between standards and performance, management must either adjust performance, adjust the standards, or do nothing, according to the situation.

4. There are three types of control: Feedforward control is future-directed and prevents anticipated problems. Concurrent control takes place while an activity is in progress. Feedback control takes place after the activity.

5. Most control efforts are directed at one of these areas: people, finances, operations, information, or total organization performance.

6. The goals approach assesses effectiveness in terms of the accomplishment of ends. If the organization achieves its goals, it is effective. The systems approach assesses both means and ends. The systems approach is more comprehensive and takes a longer-term perspective than the goals approach.

7. The strategic constituencies approach requires the organization to satisfy the demands of those constituencies in the environment from whom the organization requires support for its continued existence. Management must identify its strategic constituencies, determine their effectiveness criteria, and then ensure that the organization satisfies these criteria.

8. An effective control system is accurate, timely, economical, flexible, and understandable. It uses reasonable criteria, has strategic placement, emphasizes the exception, uses multiple criteria, and suggests corrective action.

9. Controls can be dysfunctional when they redirect behavior away from an organi-

zation's goals. This can occur as a result of inflexibility or unreasonable standards. Additionally, when rewards are at stake, individuals are more likely to manipulate data so that their performance will be perceived positively.

Review Questions

1. What is the role of control in management?
2. How are planning and control linked?
3. Why is *what* is measured in the control process probably more critical to the control process than *how* it is measured?
4. Name four methods managers can use to acquire information about actual performance.
5. Contrast *immediate* and *basic* corrective action.
6. What are the advantages and disadvantages of feedback control?
7. What behavioral control devices does management have at its disposal?
8. What is the importance of financial controls?
9. How can management determine whether or not the organization is effective?
10. What can management do to reduce the dysfunctionality of controls?

Discussion Questions

1. In what ways might the functional area in which a manager works (for example, production, sales, or accounting) affect the emphasis he or she divides between people, finances, operations, and information controls?
2. Describe how you might design a performance evaluation system that would minimize the dysfunctional aspects of this behavioral control device.
3. In Chapter 13 we discussed the white-water-rapids view of change. Do you think it's possible to establish and maintain effective standards and controls in this type of atmosphere? Explain.
4. Do you think MBO and TQM programs facilitate the control process? Explain your answer.
5. Using the strategic constituencies approach, what criteria would you expect the following organizations to emphasize:
   a. A local grocery store chain
   b. Mobil Oil
   c. The New York Public Library
   d. The U.S. Department of Defense

SELF-ASSESSMENT EXERCISE

How Willing Are You to Give Up Control?

Instructions: You can get a good idea of whether you are willing to give up enough control to be effective in delegating by responding to the following items. If you have limited work experience, base your answers on what you know about yourself and your personal beliefs. Indicate the extent to which you agree or disagree by circling the number following each statement.

	Strongly Agree				Strongly Disagree
1. I'd delegate more, but the jobs I delegate never seem to get done the way I want them to be done.	5	4	3	2	1
2. I don't feel I have the time to delegate properly.	5	4	3	2	1
3. I carefully check on subordinates' work without letting them know I'm doing it, so I can correct their mistakes if necessary before they cause too many problems.	5	4	3	2	1
4. I delegate the whole job—giving the opportunity for the subordinate to complete it without any of my involvement. Then I review the result.	5	4	3	2	1
5. When I have given clear instructions and the task isn't done right, I get upset.	5	4	3	2	1
6. I feel the staff lacks the commitment that I have. So any task I delegate won't get done as well as I'd do it.	5	4	3	2	1
7. I'd delegate more, but I feel I can do the task better than the person I might delegate it to.	5	4	3	2	1
8. I'd delegate more, but if the individual I delegate the task to does an incompetent job, I'll be severely criticized.	5	4	3	2	1
9. If I were to delegate a task, my job wouldn't be nearly as much fun.	5	4	3	2	1
10. When I delegate a task, I often find that the outcome is such that I end up doing the task over again myself.	5	4	3	2	1
11. I have not really found that delegation saves any time.	5	4	3	2	1
12. I delegate a task clearly and concisely, explaining exactly how it should be accomplished.	5	4	3	2	1
13. I can't delegate as much as I'd like to because my subordinates lack the necessary experience.	5	4	3	2	1
14. I feel that when I delegate I lose control.	5	4	3	2	1
15. I would delegate more but I'm pretty much a perfectionist.	5	4	3	2	1
16. I work longer hours than I should.	5	4	3	2	1
17. I can give subordinates the routine tasks, but I feel I must do nonroutine tasks myself.	5	4	3	2	1
18. My own boss expects me to keep very close to all details of my job.	5	4	3	2	1

Turn to page SK-7 for scoring directions and key.

Source: Adapted from Theodore J. Klein, "How to Improve Delegation Habits," *Management Review,* May 1982, p. 59. With permission. © 1982 American Management Association, New York. All rights reserved.

STEP UP SHOES, INC.

To: Joyce Rothschild; Assistant to the President
From: Jason Lyman; President
Subject: Assessing our effectiveness

I just came back from a meeting of the Young President's Association. Over lunch, a small group of us got to talking about how well our companies were doing. One YPA member seemed extremely concerned with defining success in terms of his stock's price. Another thought that return-on-investment was the true measure of her firm's performance. But then this guy Ron tells us that he uses something called the "strategic constituencies" approach to assess his company's overall performance. I had no idea what he was talking about.

I want you to review this approach to assessing organizational effectiveness. Then I want you to give me a short summary on how it would apply to a public company like ours that manufactures women's shoes for the upper-middle part of the market. Specifically, tell me: (a) who are our strategic constituencies and (b) what criteria would each use in assessing our company's effectiveness? I hope to use your analysis to help focus in on these people and organizations that we need to satisfy.

CASE APPLICATION

Chuck's Parking

If you were having a party in Hollywood or Beverly Hills, you would want to be sure the "name people" were there: Jack Nicholson, Madonna, Tom Cruise, Cher, Chuck Pick. Chuck Pick? Of course! You can't have a party without parking attendants, and Chuck Pick is *the* name in parking in southern California. Chuck's Parking employs more than 100 people, mostly part time, to park cars at the dozens of parties he handles in any given week. On a busy Saturday night, his service might be handling half a dozen parties simultaneously, with three to fifteen attendants working each.

Chuck's Parking is a small business, but it grosses nearly a million dollars a year. It is composed of two elements: parking for private parties, and an ongoing contract to handle the parking concession at an exclusive country club. The country club requires two to three attendants, seven days a week. However, the bulk of Chuck's business comes from the private parties. He spends his days visiting the homes of the rich and famous, evaluating their driveways and parking facilities and then telling them how many attendants he will need to handle their get-together. A small party might require only three or four attendants, with a bill of $400 or so. However, it's not unusual for a large party to run up a $2,000 parking tab.

While the private parties and the country club concession both involve the parking of cars, the ways they generate revenues for Chuck are very different. The parties are done on a bid basis. Chuck estimates the number of attendants necessary to do the job right, prices them out at so much an hour, and gives the customer his total price. If the customer "buys" his service, Chuck mails a bill for payment after the party. At the country club, Chuck's contract calls for him to pay the club a fixed monthly rent to operate his concession. His income is derived solely from the tips his attendants receive. Thus, while he absolutely forbids his attendants at private parties from accepting tips, tips are the only source of revenue for his country club operation.

Questions

1. Do you think Chuck's control problems differ in the two operations? If so, how?
2. For the country club, give examples of each type of control that Chuck might use, as follows:
   a. feedforward
   b. concurrent
   c. feedback
3. For the private parties, give examples of each type of control that Chuck might use, as follows:
   a. feedforward
   b. concurrent
   c. feedback

VIDEO CASE

Health-Care Controls

Joe Akin worked for Augmentation, Inc. a Birmingham, Alabama, agency that supplies nurses to hospitals on a temporary basis. He was sent out to hospitals to work as a critical care nurse. There is nothing especially unique about this arrangement. Because of nurse shortages and the desire to keep their costs down by minimizing the number of permanent employees, hospitals regularly call agencies to temporarily fill their nursing needs.

But you wouldn't want Joe Akin as your nurse. He's accused of murdering one of his patients by deliberately injecting him with a fatal dose of medication. Akin's also being investigated for fifteen suspicious fatalities in hospitals where he worked in critical-care units and was twice fired for lying about his credentials. Augmentation never checked Akin's credentials and only fabricated references after the county district attorney began an investigation into Akin's record.

Hospitals are increasingly relying on outside agencies to fill the gaps in their medical staffs and handle the background checks. They are putting blind trust in these agencies. But some of these agencies—in actuality, only a small minority—aren't checking the backgrounds of the people they're sending out. Investigations have found all kinds of abuses—from imposters to people with drug records to people carrying drugs in their purses. One agency sent a house painter and an eighteen-year-old former Kmart employee, both with no medical training whatsoever, out as certified nurses' aids.

How does this occur? Hospitals have demands that require immediate staffing. They also assume that the temp agencies are checking credentials. Additionally, temporary nursing agencies are a fast-growing industry that is completely unregulated in forty-three states. Anyone with a Rolodex full of nurses' telephone numbers can open up shop. There's no license required, no regulations to follow. And business is good for most agencies. One small agency filled 1,200 nursing shifts a week at hospitals in South Florida. If agencies pay their people $12 an hour and bill the hospitals at $25, you can see that this can be a very profitable business.

Questions

1. Should the government place regulations on temporary nursing agencies? If so, what types of controls should be implemented?

2. Assume you are a hospital administrator? Specifically describe the control system you would implement to protect your hospital against hiring people like Joe Akin.

***

Source: "Rent a Nurse," *ABC News 20/20,* November 1, 1991.

CHAPTER 20

Information Control Systems

LEARNING OBJECTIVES

After Reading This Chapter, You Should Be Able To:

1. Explain the purpose of a management information system (MIS).
2. Differentiate between data and information.
3. Contrast the four directions in which communication can flow.
4. Identify five common communication networks.
5. Compare centralized and end-user systems.
6. Explain the value of networking.
7. Explain why more information is not always better.
8. Outline the key elements in designing an MIS.
9. Explain how an MIS can relate to an organization's strategy.
10. Describe how an MIS changes power relationships in an organization.
11. Explain how MIS's are changing communication in organizations.

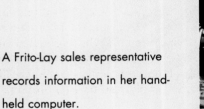

A Frito-Lay sales representative records information in her hand-held computer.

All day long, each working day of the week, salespeople at Frito-Lay (a division of PepsiCo) punch information into their hand-held computers (see photo).[1] At the end of each workday, these salespeople "download" the collected information into minicomputers at local sales offices or through modems in their homes. This downloaded data is then relayed to corporate headquarters in Dallas, Texas. The company's CEO, Robert Beeby, will have a complete report within twenty-four hours. Information on one hundred Frito-Lay product lines in 400,000 stores is available on his computer screen in easy-to-read, color-coded charts: Red means a sales drop, yellow a slowdown, and green an advance. This system allows problems to be quickly identified and corrected..

Frito-Lay's management information system helped the company solve a recent problem in San Antonio and Houston. Sales were slumping in area supermarkets. Beeby turned on his computer, called up data for south Texas, and quickly isolated the cause. A regional competitor had just introduced El Galindo, a white-corn tortilla chip. The chip was getting good word of mouth, and store managers were giving it more shelf space than Frito's traditional Tostitos tortilla chips. Using this information, Beeby sprung into action. He immediately directed his product development people to produce a white-corn version of Tostitos. Within three months his new product was on the shelves, and his company successfully won back lost market share.

Interestingly, this computerized information system at Frito-Lay is relatively new. Prior to its installation, Beeby would have needed at least three months just to pinpoint the problem. But this new system gathers data daily from supermarkets, scans it for important clues about local trends, and warns executives about problems and opportunities in all of Frito-Lay's markets. As Beeby's boss, the chairman of PepsiCo International Foods, Michael H. Jordan, noted, before the company installed the new system, "if I asked how we did in Kansas City on July Fourth weekend, I'd get five partial responses three weeks later." Now he can get that information in a day and act on it immediately.

As Frito-Lay illustrates, sophisticated information systems are changing the way managers manage and organizations do business. In this chapter, we'll introduce the concept of management information systems, explain how they have evolved in organizations and what's entailed in designing an effective information system, and show the dramatic ways in which they are affecting the manager's job and changing organizational communication. As you'll see, technology is changing the way managers receive, apply, and transmit information.

What is a Management Information System?

management information system (MIS)
A system that provides management with needed information on a regular basis.

While there is no universally agreed-upon definition for a **management information system (MIS),** we'll define the term as a system used to provide management with needed information on a regular basis.[2] In theory, this system can be manual or computer based, although all current discussion, including ours, focuses on computer-supported applications.

The term *system* in MIS implies order, arrangement, and purpose. Further, an MIS focuses specifically on providing management with *information,* not merely *data.* These two points are important and require elaboration.

A library provides a good analogy. Although it can contain millions of volumes, a library doesn't do users much good if they can't *find* what they want *quickly.* That's why libraries spend a lot of time cataloging their collections and ensuring that volumes are returned to their proper locations. Organizations today are like well-stocked libraries. There is no lack of data. There is, however, a lack of ability to process that data so that the right information is available to the right person when he or she needs it.[3] A library is almost useless if it has the book you want, but either you can't find it or the library takes a week to retrieve it from storage. An MIS, on the other hand, has organized data in some meaningful way and can access the information in a reasonable amount of time. **Data** are raw, unanalyzed facts, such as numbers, names, or quantities. But as data, these facts are relatively useless to managers.[4] When data are analyzed and processed, they become **information.** An MIS collects data and turns them into relevant information for managers to use. Figure 20-1 summarizes these observations.

data
Raw, unanalyzed facts.

information
Analyzed and processed data.

Linking Information and Organizational Communication

Management information systems are obviously closely linked with the topic of communication. In Chapter 18, we reviewed *interpersonal* communication, but there is still the important subject of *organizational* communication to consider. Before we discuss the evolution and current status of management information systems, let's review several key terms and concepts related to organizational communication. As

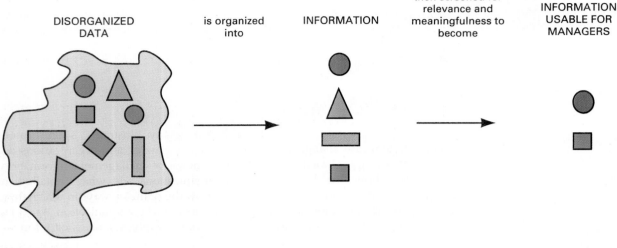

DISORGANIZED DATA   is organized into   INFORMATION   then screened for relevance and meaningfulness to become   INFORMATION USABLE FOR MANAGERS

FIGURE 20-1
MIS Makes Data Usable

Yosi Amram, president of Individual, Inc., publishes a personalized newspaper called *First!*, which refines and summarizes information for people in high-technology industries. His daily newspaper, sent by electronic mail or fax, helps decision makers who suffer from information overload by turning data into information.

formal communication
Communication that follows the authority chain of command or that is necessary to do a job.

informal communication
Communication that is not approved by management and not defined by the structural hierarchy.

you'll see by the end of this chapter, an MIS is an essential element in organizational communications, and computerization is significantly changing organizational communication practices.[5]

Formal Versus Informal Communication

In Chapter 15, we differentiated between formal and informal groups. We can do the same with communication. **Formal communication** refers to communication that follows the authority chain of command or is part of the communications required to do one's job. When a boss makes a request of a subordinate, he or she is communicating formally, as is the employee who takes a problem to his or her superior. Formal communication also occurs when two shipping clerks must interact to coordinate a customer's order.

Informal communications arise to meet needs that are not satisfied by formal communication. These communications are not approved by management, and there is no predetermined structural hierarchy by which they are defined. However, the lack of management sanction does not mean that informal communications do not exist. Employees form friendships, and cliques develop. These in turn allow employees to fill in communication gaps within the formal channels. The informal communication system therefore serves two purposes. It permits employees to satisfy their need for social interaction. It can also improve an organization's performance by creating alternative, and frequently faster and more efficient, channels of communication.

Direction of Communication Flow

Organizational communication can flow downward, upward, laterally, or diagonally. Let's look at each.

Downward Any communication that flows from a manager down the authority hierarchy is **downward communication.** When we think of managers communicating with subordinates, we usually think of a downward pattern. Downward communication is used to inform, direct, coordinate, and evaluate subordinates. When managers assign goals to subordinates, they are using downward communica-

downward communication

Communication that flows from a manager down the authority hierarchy.

upward communication

Communication that flows from subordinates to higher-level managers.

Like many successful managers, Linda Wachner, CEO at Warnaco, relies on the telephone to get information fast from sources throughout her organization.

lateral communication

Communication among any horizontally equivalent personnel.

diagonal communication

Communication that cuts across functions and levels in an organization.

tion. Managers are also using downward communication by providing subordinates with job descriptions, informing them of organizational policies and procedures, pointing out problems that need attention, or evaluating their performance. But downward communication doesn't have to involve oral or face-to-face contact. The sending of letters to employees' homes to advise them of the organization's new sick leave policy is also a downward communication.

Upward   Managers rely on those below them for information. Reports are sent upward in the authority hierarchy to inform higher management of progress toward goals and current problems. **Upward communication** keeps managers aware of how employees feel about their jobs, their co-workers, and the organization in general. Managers also rely on upward communication for ideas on how things can be improved.

The extent of upward communication, particularly that which is initiated at the lowest level, depends on the organizational culture. If management has created a climate of trust and respect and uses participative decision making, there will be considerable upward communication as employees provide input to decisions. In a highly authoritarian environment, upward communication still takes place, but it is limited to the managerial ranks and to providing control information to upper management.

Some examples of upward communication include performance reports prepared by lower management for review by middle and upper management, suggestion boxes, employee attitude surveys, grievance procedures, superior–subordinate discussions, and informal "gripe" sessions in which employees have the opportunity to identify and discuss problems with their boss or representatives of upper management.

Lateral   Communication that takes place among any horizontally equivalent personnel is called **lateral communication.**

As implied in our discussion of formal and informal communication, horizontal communications are often necessary to save time and facilitate coordination. In some cases, these lateral relationships are formally sanctioned. In others, they are informally created to bypass the vertical hierarchy and expedite action. Lateral communications can, from management's viewpoint, be good or bad. Because strict adherence to the formal vertical structure for all communications can impede the efficient and accurate transfer of information, lateral communications can be beneficial. In such cases, they occur with the knowledge and support of superiors. However, they can create dysfunctional conflicts when the formal vertical channels are breached, when members go above or around their superiors to get things done, or when bosses find out that actions have been taken or decisions made without their knowledge.

Diagonal   **Diagonal communication** cuts across functions and levels in an organization. When a supervisor in the credit department communicates directly with a regional marketing manager, who is not only in a different department but also at a higher level in the organization, they are engaged in diagonal communication.

A major problem with this form of communication is that it departs from the normal chain of command. In the above example, the credit supervisor should notify his or her boss in order to avoid later surprises and to adhere to the chain of command. To minimize gaps, most diagonal communications also encompass a vertical communication to superiors or subordinates who have been bypassed.

Given the potential for problems, why would individuals resort to diagonal communication? The answer is efficiency and speed. In some situations, bypassing vertical and horizontal channels expedites action and prevents others from being used merely as conduits between senders and receivers.

communication networks
Vertical and horizontal communication patterns.

Communication Networks

The vertical and horizontal dimensions in organizational communications can be combined into a variety of patterns, or into what is referred to as **communication networks.** Most studies of communication networks have taken place in groups created in a laboratory setting. As a result, the research conclusions have limited application because of the artificial settings and the small groups used. Five common networks are shown in Figure 20-2; these are the chain, Y, wheel, circle, and all-channel networks. To treat the networks shown in the figure in an organizational context, let's assume that the organization has only five members.

Five Common Networks   As shown in Figure 20-2, the *chain network* represents a five-level vertical hierarchy in which communications can move only upward or downward. In an organization, this type of network woud be found in direct-line authority relations with no deviations. For example, the payroll clerk reports to the payroll supervisor, who in turn reports to the general accounting manager, who reports to the plant controller, who reports to the plant manager. These five individuals would represent a chain network.

If we turn the *Y network* upside down, we can see two subordinates reporting to a manager, with two levels of authority above the manager. This is, in effect, a four-level hierarchy.

Looking at the *wheel diagram* as if we were standing above the network, we see that the wheel represents four subordinates who report to a manager. There is no interaction between the subordinates. All communications are channeled through the manager.

The *circle network* allows members to interact with adjoining members, but no further. It would represent a three-level hierarchy in which there is vertical communication between superiors and subordinates and lateral communication only at the lowest level.

Finally, the *all-channel network* allows each of the members to communicate freely with the other four. Of the networks discussed, it is the least structured. There are no restrictions; all members are equal. This network is best illustrated by a committee in which no one member formally or informally assumes a dominant or take-charge position. All members are free to share their viewpoints.

Evaluation of Network Effectiveness   As a manager, which network should you use? The answer depends on your goal.

Table 20-1 summarizes the effectiveness of the various networks according to four criteria: speed, accuracy, the probability that a leader will emerge, and the level of morale among members. One observation is immediately apparent: No single net-

FIGURE 20-2
Common Communication Networks

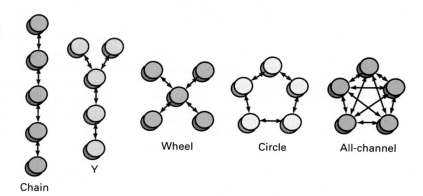

Chain   Y   Wheel   Circle   All-channel

TABLE 20-1 Networks and Evaluation Criteria

	Networks				
Criteria	**Chain**	**Y**	**Wheel**	**Circle**	**All-Channel**
Speed	Moderate	Moderate	Fast	Slow	Fast
Accuracy	High	High	High	Low	Moderate
Emergence of leader	Moderate	Moderate	High	None	None
Morale	Moderate	Moderate	Low	High	High

Source: Adapted from Alex Bavelas and Dermot Barrett, "An Experimental Approach to Organizational Communication," *Personnel,* March 1951, p. 370.

work is best for all occasions. If speed is important, the wheel and all-channel networks are preferred. The chain, Y, and wheel score high on accuracy. The structure of the wheel facilitates the emergence of a leader. The circle and all-channel networks promote high employee satisfaction.

An Informal Network: The Grapevine   The previous discussion of networks emphasized formal communication patterns. Let's take a look at how communications travel along the informal network—more specifically, the well-known **grapevine.**

The grapevine is active in almost all organizations, and there appear to be patterns to this form of communication. Figure 20-3 illustrates four patterns that the grapevine can take. The *single strand* is the way in which most people view the grapevine. However, the evidence indicates that the *cluster* is the most popular pattern that grapevine communications take.[6] That is, a few people are active communicators on the grapevine. As a rule, only about 10 percent of the people in an organization act as

grapevine
The informal communication network.

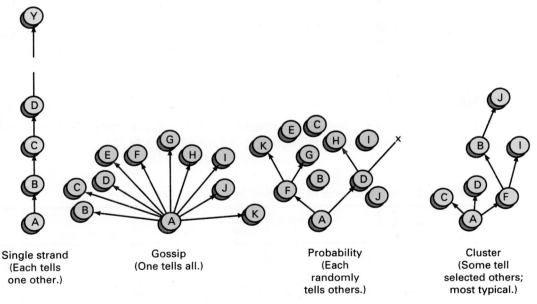

Single strand
(Each tells
one other.)

Gossip
(One tells all.)

Probability
(Each
randomly
tells others.)

Cluster
(Some tell
selected others;
most typical.)

FIGURE 20-3
Grapevine Patterns

Source: Keith Davis and John W. Newstrom, *Human Behavior at Work: Organizational Behavior,* 7th ed. (New York: McGraw-Hill, 1985), p. 317. Reproduced with permission.

liaisons who pass on information to more than one other person. Which individuals are active on the grapevine often depends on the message. A message that sparks the interest of an employee may stimulate him or her to tell someone else. However, another message that is perceived to be of lesser interest may never be transmitted further.

Can the grapevine be used to managements's benefit? The answer is yes. Given that only a small number of employees typically pass information to more than one other person, managers can analyze grapevine information and predict its flow. Certain messages are likely to follow predictable patterns. Managers might even consider using the grapevine informally to transmit information to specific individuals by "planting" messages with key people who are active on the grapevine and are likely to find a given message worth passing on.

Managers should not lose sight of the grapevine's value for identifying issues that employees consider important and that create anxiety among them. It acts as both a filter and feedback mechanism, picking up issues that employees consider relevant and planting messages that employees want passed on to upper management. For instance, the grapevine can tap employee concerns. If a rumor of a mass layoff is spreading along the grapevine and management knows the rumor to be totally false, the message still has meaning. It reflects the fears and concerns of employees and hence should not be ignored by management.

The Evolution of Management Information Systems

MIS have come a long way in the last four-plus decades. Most of this progress is a direct result of improvements in computing power. The trend has been toward smaller, faster, and cheaper technology. In 1946, there was one computer in the United States. It weighed 30 tons and had 18,000 vacuum tubes and 70,000 resistors. The computing power that in 1966 took a roomful of equipment and cost $15 million is available today on a $10 microprocessor chip that's only a quarter of an inch square.[7]

Table 20-3 describes the four-stage evolution of MIS. Beginning in 1954, it reflects extraordinary changes. In fact, only in stage four have MIS reached their full potential as integrated and coordinated information systems.

Stage 1: Centralized Data Processing

The first computer was installed for a business application in 1954.[8] For all intents and purposes, that date marks the beginning of what is now MIS.

TABLE 20-2   The Evolution of Management Information Systems

Stage	Approximate Time Period	Description
1. Centralized data processing	1954–1964	Accounting and clerical applications
2. Management-focused data processing	1965–1979	Direct support for management and operational functions
3. Decentralized end-user computing	1980–1985	Personal computers under the direct control of users
4. Interactive networks	1986–	Linking of individual end-users

Until the mid-1960s, management information systems involved the processing of routine data for payroll, billing, accounting, and similar clerical functions. Because of its narrow focus, responsibility for overseeing an MIS tended to lie with an organization's financial controller's office.

batch processing
Storing data and processing them all at the same time.

real-time processing
The continuous updating of data as transactions occur.

Centralized data processing was characterized by **batch processing**—that is, transactions were stored and processed all at one time. This, of course, limited any MIS usage. Centralized data processing was fine for producing monthly accounting reports, but it was incapable of giving managers any current information on organizational activities. It wasn't until Stage 2 that organizations began to use **real-time processing,** which allowed data to be continually updated as transactions occurred for

Stage 2: Management-Focused Data Processing

The period between 1965 and 1979 saw centralized data processing expand by providing support information for management and operational activities. Information systems were now being designed specifically to help managers in diverse functions to make better decisions. Not only were managers in the accounting area involved with information control, but also managers in purchasing, personnel, marketing, engineering, research and development, and production and operations. In this second stage, separate data systems departments were created, and remote terminals were introduced.

By the mid-1960s, managers of every type had begun to see how computers could help them to do their jobs better and more efficiently. Computers could accumulate and analyze large quantities of data that could never be analyzed economically on a manual basis. Marketing executives, for instance, could now not only review weekly sales reports broken down by each salesperson, but also have those data analyzed by product groups. If the sales of a particular product line suddenly dropped, computer-generated information could alert management quickly and allow for rapid corrective action. This contrasts with information controls in Stage 1, when a similar report would have to be produced by a clerk or a group of clerks and might take a month or longer to complete. Thus Stage 2 marks the real beginning of *management* information systems.

The expanding role of computerized information control created the need for

Mainframe computers, like this IBM ES/9000, are playing an increasingly smaller role in processing information for management. They're being replaced by decentralized personal computers.

What's Wrong with Pirating Software?

The court officers and lawyers walked into the Milan headquarters of Montedison, Italy's chemical giant. Employees at computer workstations were ordered to step away from their keyboards while the investigators punched in commands to test the programs. Their suspicions were confirmed. The employees were using pirated copies of Lotus 1–2–3, the popular spreadsheet program. Workers were bewildered. They asked, "Why are you here for this? Everybody does it!" Maybe so, but, as the chairman of Lotus Development Corp. puts it, "We spend $100 million a year on creating new software. We can't just give our stuff away!"[9]

The duplicating of software programs has become a widespread practice. It's been estimated that, worldwide, software companies (which include firms such as Lotus Development and Microsoft) lose $10 to $12 billion a year to software pirates. Yet almost all of these duplicated programs are protected by copyright law. Copying them is punishable by fines of up to $100,000 and five years in jail. How is it, then, that this lawbreaking has become such a common practice? Part of the answer is due to cultural differences. A lot of piracy occurs in places like Hong Kong and Singapore, where copyright laws don't apply and *sharing* rather than *protecting* creative work is the norm. In the United States, employees and managers who pirate software defend their behavior by giving such answers as: "Everybody does it!" "I won't get caught!" "The law isn't enforced!" "No one really loses!" or "Our departmental budget isn't large enough to handle buying dozens of copies of the same program!"

Contrast software to other forms of intellectual property. Ask the same employees who copy software if it is similarly acceptable to steal a book from the library or a tape from a video store. Most are quick to condemn such practices. However, some think that there's nothing wrong with checking out a video, making a copy, and returning it—despite the copyright statement at the beginning of the tape that specifically states that the act of copying that tape is in violation of the law.

Is reproducing copyrighted software ever an acceptable practice? Is it wrong for employees of a corporation to do it but permissible for struggling college students? What do *you* think?

---

reorganization. As MIS became less an accounting control device and more a management tool, it needed to be separated from its accounting origins. In Stage 2, therefore, MIS units came into their own. Organizations created new departments with titles like Data Systems or Information Systems, run by MIS professionals. When managers in an organization had an information control problem, they now had a specific department to which they could go for a solution.

Finally, Stage 2 also saw the introduction of remote terminals that provided access to a computer's central processing unit from external locations. Remote terminals, for example, would allow a production supervisor to review and modify a production schedule by communicating directly with the central computer through a terminal on the production floor. Remote terminals not only made information more readily available, they also allowed managers who knew what information they needed to get it without going through the data systems department.

Computers are changing the way everybody does business, legal or otherwise. Consider the following quotation from Colombia's fugitive drug lord Pablo Escobar on the hardships he endured in a prison where he spent thirteen months awaiting trial before escaping: "We were fifteen prisoners, and there were only three computers."

end-user
The person who uses information and assumes responsibility for its control.

data base management
A computerized system that allows the user to organize, get at easily, and select and review a precise set of data from a larger base of data.

spreadsheets
Software packages that allow users to turn a computer's memory into a large worksheet in which data and formulas can be entered to perform a variety of calculations.

Stage 3: Decentralized End-User Computing   The next major breakthrough in MIS was the decentralization of information control. Centralized data processing was being rapidly replaced by decentralized systems in which part or all of the computer logic functions were performed outside the central computer. During Stage 3, managers became end-users, personal computers became overwhelmingly popular, managers found themselves enmeshed in software decisions, and data systems departments evolved into information support centers.

When a manager becomes an **end-user,** he or she takes responsibility for information control.[10] It is no longer delegated to some other department or staff assistant. When managers became end-users, they had to become knowledgeable about their own needs and the systems that were available to meet those needs, and had to accept responsibility for their systems' failures. If they didn't have the information they wanted, there was no one to blame but themselves.

In Stage 3, whether they liked it or not, managers had to come face to face with computer technology and all that it could offer. Some were enthusiastic about the opportunity to bypass the data-processing technicians who spoke "computerese." Other managers—and they were the majority—initially resisted. Terrified of learning how to operate a personal computer, they continued to rely on others for their information needs. But increased amounts of "user friendly" software and the reality that end-user computing was here to stay essentially has resulted in turning most managers into converts. Managers have come to realize that they now have a better information base from which to make more timely decisions. By developing their computer skills and judiciously selecting the right software, managers are able to get the exact information they want, literally in seconds.

Table 20-3 describes the five types of personal computer software packages that are most relevant for managers. The packages a manager uses, of course, depend on what tasks he or she is trying to accomplish. For information control purposes, use of **data base management** is going to be very important. For developing an annual budget, the **spreadsheet** becomes invaluable. The point to keep in mind is that managers who have an extensive library of software packages can make their computers *flexible.* They can use their hardware to the maximum extent. In minutes,

TABLE 20-3   Five Types of Personal Computer Software Packages

word processing   Allows the user to write, change, edit, revise, delete, or print letters, reports, and manuscripts. For example, a user can write a report and then correct it or update it without having to retype the whole thing.

spreadsheets   Allows a user to turn the computer's memory into a large worksheet in which data and formulas can be entered to perform a variety of calculations. The spreadsheet defines a structure and then allows the user to change a number within that structure to see how the change will affect other numbers. Permits managers to ask a series of what-if questions. For example, a manager could use a spreadsheet to see what effect a 5 percent increase in costs would have on monthly profitability.

data base management   Allows the user to organize, easily obtain, and select and review a precise set of data from a larger base of data. A manager could use a data base for keeping an up-to-date record of each customer's purchases.

graphics   Allows the user to display (and often print) numerical findings in the form of charts or graphs. Managers can use these to present financial analyses, budgets, sales projections, and similar numerical data.

communication   Allows computers to communicate and transfer data to and from each other. Managers can use this software to transfer messages from their terminals to other managers' terminals rather than use telephones to relay the same message.

Source: Based on James P. Morgan, "Software Buying: A New Purchasing Frontier," *Purchasing,* September 20, 1984, p. 71; and Lawrence J. Magid, "Software," *1988 Inc. Office Guide,* pp. 51–54.

word processing
Software packages that allow users to write, change, edit, revise, delete, or print letters, reports, and manuscripts.

for instance, they can change from "crunching numbers" on a spreadsheet to writing a perfectly prepared report based on those numbers using a **word-processing** program.

A final outcome of Stage 3 has been the transformation of data systems departments into information support centers.[11] Rather than generating information for managers, these departments are helping managers become more effective end-users. For instance, they are advising managers on the availability of software, training them in using it, showing them how to access data base information from centralized mainframes, and overseeing user service hotlines. Thus as managers have become end-users, data-processing professionals have had to switch from *providing* managers with information to *helping* them get their own information.

Stage 4: Interactive Networks

The fourth and current stage of MIS development relies heavily on communication software packages to fully achieve the *systems* objective of MIS. In Stage 4, the emphasis is on creating and implementing mechanisms to link end-users. By means of an interactive network, a manager's computer can communicate with other computers.[12] This is opening up opportunities for electronic mail, teleconferencing, and interorganizational linkages.

networking
Linking computers so that they can communicate with each other.

Networking interconnects computer hardware. By networking, the user of a personal computer can communicate with other personal computers, turn the computer into a terminal and gain access to an organization's mainframe system, share the use of expensive printers, and tap into outside data bases.

The biggest computer network is also the oldest: our national telephone system. Run almost entirely by computers, it connects 100 million homes and businesses through 1 billion circuit miles of wires, cables, microwave relays, and satellites.[13] Organizations are now installing networking systems, only on a smaller scale. To illustrate, Digital Equipment Corporation has designed a network system that integrates the company's 27,000 computers in twenty-six different countries.[14] Engineers in Israel, Japan, and the United States, for example, can collaborate on design work by exchanging memos, circuit diagrams, and even software. The network also facilitates open and flexible communication by allowing people to leapfrog levels in the organization. With this network, for instance, a DEC programmer in Australia can send a message directly to the corporate CEO in Massachusetts, essentially bypassing more than a half a dozen levels in the organization. Of course, key people in the hierarchy can still be kept informed by merely ensuring that they receive "copies" of communications.

As we'll demonstrate later, networks are reshaping the manager's job. Electronic mail is lessening the manager's dependence on the telephone and traditional mail delivery service.[15] Electronic messages can be communicated in seconds, and if the receiver isn't at the terminal, there's no need for the sender to call back. Teleconferencing, introduced in Chapter 11, is reducing the need for travel. Group meetings can now take place among people thousands of miles apart. Telecommuting permits some employees, including managers, to do their jobs at home and connect to the workplace by means of a personal computer. (See Figure 20-4.) Networks are also enabling managers to monitor their subordinates' work closely. For employees who perform their tasks on a terminal, software packages are available that can summarize, in detail, each employee's hourly productivity, error rate, and the like.

We also shouldn't overlook the effect that networks are having on interorganizational communications.[16] They are making it possible for an organization's computers to interact with computers in other organizations. The computers at General Motors, for example, are also linked to those of primary suppliers and major dealers. These linkages are dramatically cutting paperwork and speeding up communications.

Networks are increasingly being used to facilitate group meetings. Here, Boeing executives participate in an electronic meeting with networked computers.

Interorganizational networks are also widening the scope of data base management. If you want to know what other companies are doing in regard to strategic planning, for instance, you can get your answer through a computer search of outside data bases. Companies like Dow Jones and Mead Corporation have developed extensive data bases that are available on a fee basis. Just as college students are researching their term papers by means of data base searches at a library instead of going through periodical indexes or journals manually, managers can now tap into a multitude of data bases without leaving the office.

FIGURE 20-4
The Telecommuting Workplace

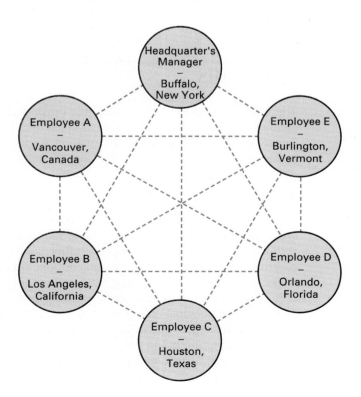

The Next Stage: Expert Systems and Cellular Communications

What will the next stage of development of MIS be? We're certain to see more personal computers, more end-users, and a much larger maze of interlocking grids linking them together. This, in turn, will reshape the way offices look and work. And, as we'll show, the office itself may soon become obsolete.

One of the most far-reaching MIS developments will be the application of artificial intelligence to managerial decision making.[17] These **expert systems** use software programs to encode the relevant experience of a human expert and allow a system to act like that expert in analyzing and solving unstructured problems.[18] Managerial expertise in handling complex decisions is a natural candidate for such systems.

The essence of expert systems is that they (1) use specialized knowledge about a particular problem area rather than general knowledge that would apply to all problems, (2) use qualitative reasoning rather than numerical calculations, and (3) perform at a level of competence that is higher than that of nonexpert humans.[19] In the not-too-distant future, we might see computers making unstructured decisions that were previously made by middle- and upper-level managers. For instance, IDS Financial Services, the financial planning subsidiary of American Express, has already encoded the expertise of its best account managers in an expert-systems program. "Now even the worst of our 6,500 planners is better than our average planner used to be," says Chairman Harvey Golub.[20]

Another exciting development is evolving out of cellular technology.[21] Cellular modems are vastly expanding the reach of computer networks. Up to now, anyone who wasn't connected to a wire or telephone was "out of touch." But with the wireless communication that cellular technology makes possible, networks will soon link people and their computers around the clock and around the world. In just a few years, we can expect that managers will each carry a pocket-sized phone and a lightweight, full-featured computer as well. The computer will have a cellular modem, allowing it to stay in touch with its parent at the office. Moreover, as computers become attached to people rather than locations, the idea of a fixed office will be replaced by the more fluid concept of a 24-hour, mobile decision maker.

expert systems
Software programs that encode the relevant experience of a human expert.

Debunking a Few Myths About MIS

There is no shortage of myths and misconceptions about management information systems. In this section, we want to challenge three widely circulated myths: (1) formal MIS will replace other information sources, (2) more information is always better, and (3) managers need the latest technology available.

The Replacement Myth

Sophisticated, computer-based information systems have significantly improved the ability of managers to monitor and control organizational activities. But these formal systems *add to* rather than *replace* other sources of information for managerial controls. Meetings, chance encounters, one-on-one conversations, unscheduled walks around facilities, social activities, telephone calls, and the like continue to be important sources of information for managers.[22]

Verbal and personal communications are a very real part of every manager's job. As leaders, managers inevitably receive sizable quantities of rich information about how well things are going and what is or could be a problem. Often, such informal information can alert a manager more quickly to a potential problem than can any formal MIS. An MIS is not necessarily a panacea. It has not and will not replace other, less formal means of gaining information about organizational activities.

The "More Is Better" Myth

The "more is better" myth has two themes. The first is that a greater quantity of information will lead to better decisions. The second is that managers need all the information they request. Neither statement holds up under close scrutiny.

An increased quantity of information might not improve decisions for at least three reasons: (1) the manager can become overwhelmed with information, (2) the value of any information depends on a lot more than just its quantity, and (3) a manager who has the relevant data might not understand how it fits together.

Too much information, even high-quality information, can hinder decision-making performance after some optimal point.[23] Why? Because of information overload. Up to a point, new information is beneficial, but decision makers can assimilate only so much information. Once that maximum point has been reached, additional information can actually decrease decision performance.

The value of information used in decision making is measured not only in quantity. *Quality* also needs to be considered. Is the information relevant, accurate, complete, reliable, and timely?[24] If it fails to meet these criteria, then more isn't necessarily better.

Regardless of the quantity and quality of information available, decision performance still depends on the decision maker's ability to understand a problem, what's causing it, and which solution is most preferred. This is particularly true of complex decision situations in which numerous variables have to be considered. Managers often have difficulty in understanding cause–effect relationships among these variables, and more information doesn't necessarily improve the decision. More and better information should lead to better decision performance only when managers can use it in a logical, meaningful way.

Even if these criteria are met, there is still another factor that shouldn't be ignored: Cost! The "more is better" argument overlooks the reality that increased information comes at an increased cost. Any request for more information therefore needs to be assessed in cost-benefit terms. What marginal improvement in decision performance can be expected as a result of the additional cost? Is that marginal improvement worth the extra cost?

Many managers fall into the habit of searching continually for more information, but they don't always need the information they request. In many organizational cultures, failure carries a very high price. In such organizations, managers often request more information as a security defense. Even if the decision later proves faulty, they at least cannot be attacked on the grounds that they acted hastily or with inadequate data. Some individuals, of course, are inherently risk aversive. Regardless of their organization's culture, they have a tough time making important decisions. When placed in managerial positions, they search for more information in order to put off making tough decisions.

The "New Is Better" Myth

The last myth that we want to dispel assumes that an effective information system requires the latest in technology. While teleconferencing, voice-activated input devices, cellular systems, supercomputers with enormous memory capacities, and the like *might* improve managerial effectiveness in some situations, it's dangerous to assume that all technological improvements should be adopted.

Like most consumers, managers are not immune to fashion. As computers have become faster and more powerful and innovative peripherals and software have been developed, many managers assume that the newest technological breakthrough is best. That is often not the case. Managers often don't need the greater power, speed, or other advantages offered by a new system. Whether new is better depends on the user's needs and the cost of the improved technology. Moreover, improved technology almost always requires change. A new system requires managers to learn how to use it. Even "user-friendly" systems often require fifty or more hours before the user is fully up to speed. When managers often earn in excess of $50 an hour (including benefits), bringing a new system on-line just to have the latest technology is certain to be both costly and disruptive. Before managers jump to purchase the latest MIS technological innovation, they need to consider the full repercussions of the decision.

Designing the MIS

While there is no universally agreed-upon approach to designing a management information system, the following steps represent the key elements in putting an MIS together.

Analyze the Decision System

The decisions that managers make should drive the design of any MIS. Therefore, the first step is to identify all the management decisions for which information is needed. This should encompass all the functions within the organization and every management level from first-level supervisor to the chief executive officer.

This step should also consider whether each decision is being made by the right person. Is it being made at the right level? By the right department? Failure to ask these questions can misdirect the entire MIS design. If the wrong people are making the decision and this problem isn't corrected before a sophisticated information system is put in place, then these people will continue to make the wrong decision, only faster.

Analyze Information Requirements

Once the decisions are isolated, we need to know the exact information required to effectively make these decisions.

Information needs differ according to managerial function in the organization. The information that a marketing manager needs differs from that required by a financial manager. Thus the MIS has to be tailored to meet the varying needs of different functional managers.

As Figure 20-5 illustrates, a manager's information needs also vary by organizational level. Top-level managers are looking for environmental data and summary reports. At the other extreme, lower-level supervisors want detailed reports of operating problems. The well-designed MIS must consider these diverse requirements if it is to satisfy the varied needs of managers.

Aggregate the Decisions

After each functional area and manager's needs have been identified, those that have the same or largely overlapping informational requirements should be located. Even though needs vary up and down and across the organization, redundancies often occur. Both sales and production executives, for example, may want feedback data

FIGURE 20–5
Matching Information Requirements with Managerial Level

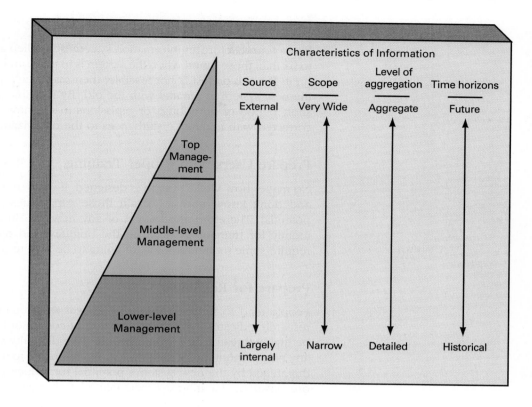

on a given product's quality level. One, however, wants the feedback to ensure customer satisfaction, while the other wants it to control for variances in the production processes. By identifying these redundancies, management can create systems that contain the least amount of duplication and that group together similar decisions under a single manager.

Design Information Processing

In this step, internal technical specialists or outside consultants are utilized to develop the actual system for collecting, storing, transmitting, and retrieving information. A detailed flowchart of the desired system will be drawn up. It will include, among other things, sources and types of data, locations of users, and storage requirements. The precise hardware and software requirements will also be determined.

Before the system is implemented, it is carefully evaluated to ensure that it will do what management wants it to do. That is, the bottom-line test of an MIS effectiveness is its ability to meet each manager's information needs. A design that meets all of most managers' needs or most of all managers' needs will not provide the optimum quantity or quality of information for the organization as a whole.

Implementing the MIS

Once the MIS design has been resolved, the system needs to be implemented. The implementation phase should begin with pretesting the system and conclude with building in regular evaluations in the system. The following points highlight concerns that need to be addressed during the implementation phase.

Pretest the System Before Installation

Flaws found before an information system is installed are much easier and less costly to fix than those found when the system is in place and people have begun to depend on it. If a full pretest is not feasible, then management should consider introducing the new system in parallel with the old. By running two systems side by side for a short period of time, bugs or omissions in the new system can be identified and corrected with minimal disturbances to the organization's operations.

Prepare Users with Proper Training

No matter how well a system is designed, if users aren't aware of its full capabilities and don't know how to obtain those capabilities, it will never achieve its full potential. Therefore, the budget of any new MIS installation must cover time and money for training users. Even the brightest and most competent managers will require some training if they are going to be able to make full use of a new system.

Prepare for Resistance

People tend to resist changes that appear threatening to them. A sizable body of research indicates that the introduction of computer-based information systems can be highly threatening.[25] Some people have difficulty adapting to the introduction of any new technology. Some also fear being unable to learn the new system. Many are threatened by the new system's potential for reducing their power and status in the organization, changing interpersonal relationships, or lessening their job security.

Get Users Involved

One of the most effective ways of neutralizing resistance to an MIS is to have those who will be affected by the system participate fully in its design and implementation.[26] Participation will familiarize users with the system before they have to use it, increase their commitment to it because they were involved in its creation, and lessen the likelihood that their needs will be overlooked.

Check for Security

As information systems become decentralized, there is a critical need to ensure that unauthorized individuals do not gain access to valuable or privileged information. When information was centralized at a single source, only a few people could tap into important data bases such as production schedules, customer records, inventory accounts, credit data, and employee files. Today, however, such data bases are much more vulnerable to unauthorized access. The solution is to ensure that adequate security measures are included in the system. Access to the place where hardware is located should be controlled. Software should be locked up when not in use. A system should also have impossible-to-guess passwords or codes for gaining access, require users to identify themselves once into the system, and impose strict controls over telephone access.

Build in Regular Reviews

The information that a manager needed last year is not necessarily the same that he or she needs today. As customers, suppliers, government regulations, and other environmental factors change, so too will the informational needs of managers. Implementation should be viewed as the beginning of an ongoing process. If an information system is to be valuable to managers over time, it must be regularly evaluated and modified to adapt to the changing needs of its users.

Using Information Systems to Gain a Competitive Advantage

As we discussed in Chapter 8, managers seek to develop organizationwide strategies that will give them an advantage over their competition. We talked about gaining a competitive advantage through strategies such as being the cost-leader in a given market or by carefully differentiating your product from that of the competition. In recent years, managers at a number of organizations have come to the realization that information systems can be used as a tool to give their firms a competitive advantage.[27] Let's look at three of those organizations: American Airlines, Mrs. Fields, and Wal-Mart.

American Airlines developed a reservation system called Sabre in the 1960s. Its state-of-the-art capability at the time allowed it to get an early foothold in travel agencies. Today, 14,000 travel agencies keep up with some 45 million different fares of 281 airlines by subscribing to American's Sabre system.[28] The system not only brings in nearly $500 million annually for American, but it also allows American to control the display of flight information that travel agents see. For many years, for instance, the system was programmed so that American's flight information received more display screen prominence than did competitors' flights.

Mrs. Fields, the world's largest cookie retailer, uses its management information system to eliminate layers of management, keep in close touch with employees, and closely monitor store performance.[29] For instance, a computer in each cookie store tells the manager how much business is expected that day based on historical data. It tells the manager the amount of batter to mix and at what time. Later, the computer updates the projections based on that day's experience. Even though Mrs. Fields' headquarters is in Utah and its stores are spread across the country, this system allows the company to offer fresher and more consistent cookies than can most of its competitors, even those whose owners are present on site.

This satellite room at EDS Corporation, a wholly-owned subsidiary of General Motors that provides supportive computer and information systems to organizations, is the nerve center that allows the company to track its worldwide operations.

Networking the World

An Exxon executive in Dallas wants to redirect one of the company's tankers that's somewhere in the Persian Gulf. Fifteen years ago this would probably have been done by telephone. Today, this can be accomplished via networked computers. Without leaving his desk, the executive in Dallas can send his communique directly to the ship's captain and get an immediate response. The executive can even make a hard copy of the communique for the record in case any future questions arise.

A Sony executive in Japan is concerned about the inventory of Sony Watchman mini-televisions in Canada. Is there enough product in the company's Vancouver and Toronto warehouses to meet retailers' needs over the next three months? Fifteen years ago, that type of question might have taken two days and half a dozen phone calls to answer. Not any more! Because Sony's computers are networked to communicate with each other, tapping a few buttons on the executive's keyboard can immediately give the executive access to the inventory records at both Canadian warehouses. Today, the question about the status of Watchmans in Canada can be answered in two or three minutes.

As these examples illustrate, the networking of computers has important implications for management control in global organizations. Managers can now monitor activities halfway around the world with the speed and accuracy that were once available only through direct personal observation.

In the early 1980s, Wal-Mart Stores trailed Kmart in the discount-store market. With its greater purchasing power, Kmart could negotiate lower wholesale prices. But Wal-Mart capitalized on information technology to become the world's largest retailer,[30] and its computerized distribution system is now the standard among retailers. Between 1987 and 1991, Wal-Mart invested $600 million in inventory-management equipment and other computerized technology. A satellite communications system allows it to track inventory and handle accounting and payments. It can also electronically place orders with suppliers. And 1500 of its vendors can access Wal-Mart's point-of-sale terminals to track sales of their products and resupply a Wal-Mart store before merchandise runs out. Another 3800 vendors get daily sales data directly from Wal-Mart stores. This system has been a major factor in making Wal-Mart the low-cost operator in its industry.

Once an information system has been put in place and management gains a leg up on its competition, the trick—as with any competitive advantage—is to sustain that advantage. Kmart, for instance, has recently invested in an information system that seeks to duplicate the one at Wal-Mart. Similarly, Federal Express was able to deliver packages faster and with more detailed tracking than could its competition for many years because it was the first to computerize the process completely. But as UPS, the U.S. Postal Service, and other competitors introduced comparable systems, Federal Express's on-time delivery advantage based on its MIS has all but disappeared. So while MIS can provide a competitive edge, that edge is not permanent. The system must be regularly modified and updated if it is to give an organization a sustainable advantage. Nevertheless, the creative use of an organization's information system provides managers with another tool for differentiating its products and services from those of its competitors.

Robert Portante at Brooks Fashion Stores

Robert Portante is director of information systems at Brooks Fashion Stores, a chain of 543 retail specialty clothing shops headquartered in New York City. He recently oversaw the introduction of an executive information system (EIS) at Brooks.[31]

Prior to the implementation of the EIS, top managers at Brooks relied almost exclusively on reports generated from a number of personal computers. These multiple reporting sources created inconsistencies in data. In order to clear up these inconsistencies, Portante wanted a single, centralized, massive data base from which executives could derive the individual information they needed. An EIS could provide that. For example, the senior vice-president for distribution could look at store data while the general merchandise manager could review product data.

The final system that was installed includes data on 220 different variables. For instance, information is available on sales, markdowns, inventory transfers, returns-to-vendors, receipts at different levels, and costs. The data also break down sales by style item and color. By bar coding merchandise and linking scanners to each store's computerized register, executives can access information rapidly. This information is presented in color, with lots of graphs that are easy to use and easily understandable. The company's general merchandise manager, for example, uses the EIS to make up his weekly "Best Seller Report," "Worst Seller Report," and "Color Analysis Report." He has structured these reports to see exactly what he needs to see, allowing him to quickly identify items that should be reordered or marked down.

The new EIS has proven to be a highly effective management tool. Before its implementation, Portante estimates that Brooks' senior managers were spending 80 percent of their time gathering information and 20 percent of the time making the decisions. Now it's just the reverse. "Where Monday morning typically had everyone scrambling around to get the numbers together, now they are sitting down analyzing the numbers."

How MIS is Changing the Manager's Job

No discussion of management information systems would be complete without assessing their impact on the manager's job. In this section, we'll touch on several of the key areas that are changing as a result of computer-based MIS.

Hands-On Involvement

A few years ago, managers could avoid computers by claiming, "I don't have to know how to use computers. I can hire people to do that for me." Those days are gone.[32]

Today's younger managers, exposed to computers in college or even in high

NCR vice-president James E. Clark travels extensively on his job. Using his notebook computer, he is able to access messages anytime, anywhere, the result of his computer's "wireless mailbox" capability. It receives messages bounced off a SkyTel satellite.

school, feel at home in front of a keyboard. If anything, they have swung to the other extreme: They have become dependent on their computers and feel threatened when access is limited. By the late 1990s, the "Nintendo generation" will be filling many lower- and middle-level managerial positions in organizations. Managers who fail to fully learn their systems and take advantage of their MIS capabilities will find it increasingly difficult to perform as effectively as their peers.

How will hands-on use change what managers do? Among other things, managers will spend less time on the phone, traveling to conferences, and waiting for subordinates to provide progress reports. They'll be using networks for electronic mail, videoconferencing, and closely monitoring organizational activities.

Decision-Making Capability

Because managers rely on information to make decisions and because a sophisticated MIS significantly alters the quantity and quality of information, as well as the speed with which it can be obtained, we come to the natural conclusion that an effective MIS will improve management's decision-making capability.[33]

The effect will be seen in ascertaining the need for a decision, in the development and evaluation of alternatives, and in the final selection of the best alternative. On-line, real-time systems allow managers to identify problems almost as they occur. Gone are the long delays between the appearance of a serious discrepancy and a manager's ability to find out about it. Data base management programs allow managers to look things up or get to the facts without either going to other people or digging through piles of paper. This reduces a manager's dependence on others for data and makes fact gathering far more efficient. Today's manager can identify alternatives quickly, evaluate those alternatives by using a spreadsheet program and posing a series of what-if questions based on financial data, and finally select the best alternative on the basis of answers to those questions.

Organization Design

Sophisticated information systems are reshaping organizations. For instance, traditional departmental boundaries will be less confining as networks cut across departments, divisions, geographic locations, and levels in the organization. But the most evident change is probably that MIS is making organizations flatter and more organic.[34]

Managers can now handle more subordinates. Why? Because computer control substitutes for personal supervision. As a result, there are wider spans of control and fewer levels in the organization. The need for staff support is also reduced with an MIS. As was noted previously, hands-on involvment allows managers to tap information directly, thus making large staff support groups, which traditionally compiled, tabulated, and analyzed data, redundant.[35] Both forces—wider spans and reduced staff—lead to flatter organizations.

One of the more interesting phenomena created by sophisticated information systems is that they have allowed management to make organizations more organic without any loss in control.[36] Management tends to prefer bureaucracy because bureaucracy facilitates control.[37] But there's more than one way to skin a cat. Management can lessen formalization and become more decentralized—thus making its organization more organic—without giving up control. In this case, an MIS substitutes computer control for rules and decision discretion. Computer technology rapidly apprises top managers of the consequences of any decision and allows them to take corrective action if the decision is not to their liking. There's the appearance of decentralization without any commensurate loss of control.

Power

Information is power. Anything that changes the access to scarce and important information is going to change power relationships within an organization.[38]

An MIS changes the status hierarchy in an organization. Middle managers have less status because they carry less clout. They no longer serve as the vital link between operations and the executive suite. Similarly, staff units have less prestige because senior managers no longer depend on them for evaluation and advice.

Centralized computer departments, which were extremely influential units in organizations during the 1970s, have had their role modified and their power reduced.[39] Reconstituted as information support centers, they no longer control access to data bases.

In aggregate, probably the most important effect that computer-based control systems have had on the power structure has been to tighten the hand of top management. In earlier years, top management regularly depended on lower-level managers to feed information upward. Because information was filtered and "enhanced," managers knew what their subordinates wanted them to know. End-user systems have put the power of information into top management's hands by giving them direct access to data.

Organizational Communication: An MIS Update

Earlier in this chapter we presented the basics of organizational communications. But improvements in information technology—specifically, progress made in MIS that has enhanced our ability to gather, synthesize, organize, monitor, and disseminate information—are significantly changing the way communication takes place in organizations.[40] The following discussion provides an MIS update to our earlier discussion of organizational communication.

Patterns of Communication Flow Will Change

Traditional discussions of organizational communication focused on upward and downward communication. The primary flow of formal communication was vertical. The MIS, however, permits more lateral and diagonal communication on a formal basis.

Employees using intraorganizational networks can get their work done more efficiently by jumping levels in the organization and avoiding the obstacles involved in "going through channels." The direct accessing of data, rather than the traditional sequential passing of data up and down the hierarchy, also decreases the historical problem of distortion and filtering of information. The breaking down of sequential communication patterns allows managers to formally monitor information across the organization that previously was limited to informal channels like the grapevine.

Communication Overload Should Be Lessened

Overload occurs when an individual can't process information as rapidly as it is received. Because information systems can scan, filter, process, maintain, and distribute information, overload should be reduced. For instance, a sales manager needn't spend hours looking through dozens of reports and thousands of statistics—many of them irrelevant—to analyze why sales in a certain region have declined. A sophisticated management information system can do most of that in a few seconds and provide the sales manager with specific answers.

Face-to-Face Communication Will Take on a More Symbolic Role

Sophisticated information systems eliminate the need for many communications that previously had to be done face-to-face. Managers can get timely, accurate information without being at the site of the action. However, this won't make face-to-face communication extinct. Rather, such communication will have a different purpose. Face-to-face communication will still be practiced, but it will be important for its symbolic significance.

As a case in point, the head of Exxon was widely criticized in the spring of 1989 for not going to Alaska after one of the company's ships, the *Exxon Valdez,* ran aground and spilled millions of barrels of oil into Prince William Sound. His presence wasn't needed to manage the oil spill—he was able to communicate with Exxon personnel in Alaska via telecommunications—but his decision to stay in New York was viewed by many as a lack of concern. Managers will still need to visit company offices and go down to the shop floor to talk with employees about their problems because such behaviors are expected of caring managers, although these actions will contribute little to any objective measure of "better communications."

Summary

This summary is organized by the chapter-opening learning objectives found on page 595.

1. The purpose of an MIS is to provide managers with accurate and current information for decision making and control.

2. Data are raw, unanalyzed facts. Information is data that have been organized into a usable form.

3. Downward communication flows from a manager down the authority hierarchy. Upward communication flows from subordinates to higher-level managers. Lateral communication takes place among any horizontally equivalent personnel. Diagonal communication cuts across functions and levels in an organization.

4. Five common communication networks are the chain, Y, wheel, circle, and all-channel networks. The Y and all-channel facilitate rapid action, the chain and wheel facilitate accuracy, the wheel encourages the emergence of a leader, and the circle and all-channel encourage high morale.

5. Centralized systems are controlled by MIS departments while an end-user system is controlled by the actual user. The latter makes access easier for managers and allows them to get information faster.

6. The major value of networking is that it allows personal computers to be linked to peripherals and mainframes, provides access to outside data bases, and links end-users and computers within an organization.

7. More information is not always better information because it can overwhelm managers. Managers need to know how additional information fits into the whole decision framework.

8. Designing an MIS requires analyzing the decision system, analyzing information requirements, aggregating the decisions, and developing the actual information-processing capability.

9. MIS relates to an organization's strategy by its ability to provide a means for gaining a competitive advantage. Such advantages over rivals are hard to come by and even more difficult to sustain once obtained. The creative use of an

organization's information system provides managers with a tool for differentiating its products and services from those of its competitors.

10. Power in organizations accrues to those who possess scarce and important information. MIS changes power relationships because they change the access to scarce and important information.

11. MIS are increasing the flow of horizontal formal communications, lessening information overload, and making face-to-face communication more a symbolic gesture than a necessary requirement for effective communication.

Review Questions

1. Contrast formal and informal communication.
2. Explain how formal communications can move horizontally as well as vertically.
3. How can managers "manage" the grapevine?
4. What characterizes Stage 1 in the evolution of an MIS? Stage 2? Stage 3? Stage 4?
5. Contrast batch and real-time processing.
6. How is the executive's office likely to be different by the year 2000?
7. How do the information requirements of a supervisor and a senior executive differ?
8. What are the steps in implementing MIS?
9. How is MIS changing the manager's job?
10. What is an expert system?

Discussion Questions

1. In what ways is information a unique resource for organizations? Give examples.
2. In the past, managers have had the choice to use computers or not. To what extent do you feel computers are an integral part of modern business?
3. Does the use of MIS empower all employees, all managers, or only top managers? Discuss.
4. Why might top managers be highly resistant to computers?

SELF-ASSESSMENT EXERCISE

Are You Computer Literate?

The following questionnaire has been developed to determine your computer literacy. For each definition in Column A, choose the term from Column B that appropriately matches.

Column A
Definitions

_____ 1. Has four functional parts: Input, processing, storage (programs and data), and output.
_____ 2. Performs the mathematical operations and any comparisons required.
_____ 3. Physical parts of a computer.

Column B
Terms

A. Arithmetic/logical unit
B. Computer system
C. CPU
D. Firmware
E. Hardware

_____ 4. Standard method of representing a character with a number inside the computer.
_____ 5. The base 2 numbering system that uses digits 0 and 1.
_____ 6. Number system that uses the ten digits 0 through 9 and the six letters A through F to represent values in base 16.

A. Alphanumeric
B. ASCII
C. Binary
D. Hexadecimal
E. Numeric data

_____ 7. Technique for opening folders with a mouse.
_____ 8. Technique for moving an icon with a mouse.
_____ 9. Pointer similar to arrows.

A. Double-clicking
B. Dragging
C. Highlighting
D. I-beam
E. Scroll bar

_____ 10. A read-only memory whose contents are alterable by electrical means.
_____ 11. Internal memory which is erased when the computer's power is shut off.
_____ 12. Time it takes to find data stored externally.

A. Access
B. Clockrate
C. Memory
D. PROM
E. RAM

_____ 13. Number of characters printed per horizontal inch of space.
_____ 14. Set of characters in one typeface, style, and size.
_____ 15. Narrows the spacing between letters.

A. Font
B. Kerning
C. Leading
D. Pitch
E. Points

_____ 16. Operator that describes the quality that connects two data or expressions such as greater than, less than, or equal to.
_____ 17. Messages the user sends to the computer that make it perform specific operations.
_____ 18. The ability to run more than one program at one time without interrupting the execution of another program.

A. Commands
B. Distributed
C. Execute
D. Multitasking
E. Relational operator

_____ 19. Place to enlarge or shrink a window.
_____ 20. Place documents are saved.
_____ 21. Place you are typing.

A. Active window
B. Dialog box
C. Folders
D. Record box
E. Zoom box

Column A
Definitions

Column B
Terms

_____ 22. A term that refers to memory in which data or software is lost when the computer is turned off.

_____ 23. Program that moves the read/write head to a section of the disk that has no data.

_____ 24. Read/write comes into contact with the disk's surface.

A. Crash
B. Erasable
C. Pack
D. Park
E. Volatile

_____ 25. The smallest piece of data that can be recognized by computers.

_____ 26. Basic unit of measure of computer's storage.

_____ 27. Placed in a microcomputer to take the burden of manipulating numbers off the CPU.

A. Bit
B. Byte
C. Chip
D. Control unit
E. Coprocessor

_____ 28. Program that translates the mnemonics and symbols of low-level language into the opcodes and operands of machine language.

_____ 29. Software that translates a whole program into machine language.

_____ 30. Language designed so that machines and human beings can interact easily.

A. Assembler
B. Compiler
C. Interpreter
D. Natural
E. Pascal

Turn to page 665 for scoring directions and key.

Source: Based on the "Computer Literacy Questionnaire" developed by Floyd Brock and Wayne Thomsen; Department of Management/MIS; University of Nevada at Las Vegas. With permission.

THE FIRST-REPUBLIC INSURANCE GROUP

To: Jason Harvey, Special Assistant to the President
From: Randall Weinstein, President
Subject: Expert Systems

I've been reading a lot recently in business journals about expert systems. Quite frankly, I don't know much about them. But, from the articles I've read, a number of organizations are using them to supplement or replace managerial decision makers.

Last year alone, we spent over $1 million on salaries and benefits for our actuarial professional staff.* For instance, our typical actuary has an M.S. in statistics or mathematics, seven years experience, and earns $57,000 a year. My question to you: Could expert systems software effectively replace some or all of our actuarial staff?

I'd like you to research the topic of expert systems and write me a brief report on its current status and its application to insurance actuarial jobs.

---

*Actuaries compute insurance risks and premiums using statistical analysis techniques.

This is a fictionalized account of a potentially real management issue. It is meant for academic purposes only and is not meant to reflect positively or negatively on The First-Republic Insurance Group or any of its employees.

CASE APPLICATION

Springfield Remanufacturing Corp.

What would you think of a company that strives for totally open communication? We're not talking about lots of memos or regular meetings between operating personnel and top management. We're talking about aggressively opening the company's financial books and demanding that employees understand the company's financial statements. There is such a company. It's called Springfield Remanufacturing Corporation (SRC). And they're doing very well, thank you.[41]

SRC remanufactures engines and engine components. They take worn-out engines from cars, bulldozers, and eighteen-wheelers, and rebuild them from the ground up. It's a dirty business. The company had been part of International Harvester but was bought from IH by a group of the firm's managers in 1983. That year the company employed 119 people and lost $60,488.

SRC's managers decided on an innovative way to cut costs, improve efficiency, and motivate their people. They decided that they would teach every single employee how a business makes money. They would take ignorance out of the workplace and force people to get involved, not with threats and intimidation, but with education. Management treats business as a game—no more complicated than baseball or bowling. The game has two goals: to make money and to generate cash. Everything at SRC is geared toward getting people involved in the game. Employees are taught the rules. They have sessions with the accounting staff, tutoring with supervisors, instructional sheets, and the like. Then, once employees know the rules, management teaches them how to keep score and follow the action. They learn about after-tax profits, retained earnings, equity, cash flow, everything. Finally, management floods everyone with the information they need to know how things are going. Oh yes, and to encourage people to accept the new system, management proposed that approximately 20 percent of any pretax profits would be distributed as bonuses to employees.

Once a week, supervisors hold meetings throughout the company to go over updated financial statements. The numbers show how the company is doing in relation to annual goals and whether or not there will be quarterly bonuses.

SRC's management seems to have discovered a unique way to deal with employees. Today, the company employs 650 people, generates more than $6 million a year in pre-tax profits, and distributes around $1.3 million in bonuses.

Questions:

1. Describe communication at the Springfield Remanufacturing Corporation. How does this relate to the communications networks discussed in this chapter?

2. How might the wealth of information SRC's employees are flooded with hinder their performance?

3. How do you think the open communication and fully shared information might affect the power structure at SRC?

4. This example portrays the employees at SRC as being very well informed, but makes no mention of computers or MIS. Do you think the communication and information channels at SRC qualify as MIS? Support your answer.

VIDEO CASE

Virtual Reality: Applications for Management?

The potential seems unlimited. Just think of it. Using advanced computer graphics, a surgeon looks through a pair of special glasses at a 3-D image of someone's brain. The illusion is so real that it's tempting to reach out and pat the frontal lobe, stroke the occipital lobe or run a finger through the folds of the cerebral cortex. With key strokes on a computer, the surgeon is able to rotate and pivot the brain. With a few more key strokes, layers of the brain peel off to reveal the inside, part by part. The use of virtual-reality technology allows this brain surgeon to prepare for an operation, using the images as a road map to help her maneuver instruments to the exact site in the brain that she wants.

Virtual reality isn't a fantasy anymore. You can put on a helmet and gloves and walk through computer-generated buildings, travel to cities around the world, or create a variety of manufacturing-plant layouts and test each to see how they work. The potential is limited only by the imagination of the users—from entertainment, to medicine, to business decision making. Virtual reality allows you to be anywhere you want to be, anytime you want to be there.

Critics of virtual reality tend to focus on its isolation aspects. Will the public become addicted to an artificial world? Why go out for an evening when you can create that same experience in your own living room? Why socialize with friends when you can *create* those friends at home? Will virtual reality turn us into an anti-social community, cocooned at home, living in an imaginary world with imaginary friends and lovers? Is virtual reality progress or merely a computerized version of LSD?

Questions

1. What specific management applications can you identify for virtual reality? Elaborate on each.
2. What ethical dilemmas, if any, could you envision for managers who use this technology?
3. How is virtual reality the ultimate MIS? Conversely, how could virtual reality completely isolate a manager from the important day-to-day realities of business?

Source: "Virtual Reality," *ABC Primetime Live,* September 19, 1991.

CHAPTER 21

Operations Management

LEARNING OBJECTIVES

After Reading This Chapter, You Should Be Able To:

1. Describe the role of the transformation process in operations management.
2. Explain what factors determine organizational productivity.
3. Describe how adding a "manufacturing focus" to organizational strategy affects an organization.
4. Describe the four key decisions that provide the long-term strategic direction for operations planning.
5. Describe the three decisions that make up tactical operations planning.
6. Explain how to determine the most economic order quantity.
7. Identify the three approaches to maintenance control.
8. Explain how contingency factors affect the implementation of TQM.
9. Discuss the advantages and potential problems of just-in-time inventory systems.
10. Explain how flexible manufacturing systems could give an organization a competitive advantage.

Motorola's cellular phones and wristwatch-sized pagers utilize cutting-edge technology and are manufactured to the world's most exacting standards.

In the mid-1980s, Motorola was in trouble.[1] Japanese companies such as NEC, Toshiba, and Hitachi were gobbling up the company's markets in pagers, cellular phones, and semiconductor chips. Something had to be done, and fast. Motorola's management responded with a bold plan that included rapid product development, sharply upgraded quality, and a focused determination to reduce costs through fine-tuning manufacturing processes. A key element in this plan is a statistical way of measuring quality called "Six Sigma."

Launched in 1987, Motorola's Six Sigma (99.99966% perfect) program seeks to slash defects down to 3.4 per million components. To put that in perspective, in 1986 Motorola's components had 6,000 defects per million! By 1991, the company had improved 150-fold—to an impressive 40 per million. Yet when your goal is perfection, which it now is at Motorola, 40 defects per million is deemed to be still unacceptable.

Today, Motorola is number one in semiconductor chip sales in the United States, number three in Southeast Asia, and number four worldwide. Its pocket-size cellular phone, MicroTac, has become the industry's top seller. And the company has achieved impressive improvements in production efficiency. It has cut the time it takes two-way radios to go from order to shipment from thirty days to three. Cellular phone development—from design to start of production—was slashed from three years to fifteen months. The assembly time for portable cellular phones has gone from forty hours to two!

How did Motorola's management do it? There are no simple explanations. The company reassessed and reworked dozens of its operating practices. For example, it launched an education drive to reach all of its 105,000 employees. Motorola is now spending more than $60 million a year to teach its employees about global competition, risk taking, statistical process control, and techniques for reducing product cycle times. The company's CEO and all top executives began a series of regular visits to key customers in order to learn, first hand, how customers were reacting to Motorola's products. And structurally, Motorola has expanded spans of control, flattened the organization, integrated departments to break down artificial functional barriers, redesigned work around teams, and made quality the key component of performance reviews, compensation, and reward programs.

This chapter focuses on the importance of efficiency, productivity, and controls in the operations side of the organization. Managers who thoughtfully develop well-designed operating systems and tight controls—as Motorola's management has done—will be the survivors in the increasingly competitive global economy. They'll be able to produce higher-quality products and services at prices that meet or beat those of their rivals.

Operations Management and the Transformation Process

operations management
The design, operation, and control of the transformation process that converts resources into finished goods and services.

Operations management refers to the design, operation, and control of the transformation process that converts such resources as labor and raw materials into finished goods and services. Remember that every organization produces something. Unfortunately, however, this is often overlooked except in obvious cases such as in the manufacturing of telephones or automobiles. But hospitals produce medical services, airlines produce a transportation service that moves people from one location to another, the armed forces produce defense capabilities, and the list goes on. Take a university as a specific illustration. University administrators bring together instructors, books, academic journals, audio-visual material, and similar resources to transform "unenlightened" students into educated and skilled individuals.

Figure 21–1 portrays, in a very simplified fashion, the fact that every organization has an operations system that creates value by transforming inputs into outputs. The system takes inputs—people, capital, equipment, materials—and transforms them into desired finished goods and services. Thus the transformation process is as relevant to service organizations as to those in manufacturing.

Just as every organization produces something, every unit in an organization also produces something. Marketing, finance, research and development, personnel, and accounting convert inputs into outputs such as sales, increased market shares, high rates of return on capital, new and innovative products, productive and satisfied employees, and accounting reports. As a manager, you need to be familiar with operations management concepts—regardless of the area in which you manage—in order to achieve your objectives more efficiently.

FIGURE 21–1
The Operations System

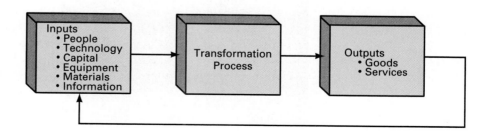

Managing Productivity

productivity
The overall output of goods and services produced, divided by the inputs needed to generate that output.

Improving productivity has become a major goal in virtually every organization. By **productivity,** we mean the overall output of goods or services produced, divided by the inputs needed to generate that output. For countries, higher productivity generates "costless growth."[2] Employees can receive higher wages and company profits can increase without causing inflation. For individual organizations, increased productivity means a more competitive cost structure and the ability to offer more competitive prices.

Increasing productivity is the key to global competitiveness. For instance, a great deal of Japan's prosperity in the 1980s can be explained in terms of its growth in manufacturing productivity. Between 1979 and 1986, Japan's productivity increased at an annual rate of 5.5. percent. During the same period, U.S. productivity gained only 2.8 percent annually.[3] But U.S. firms have responded in the last half-dozen years by making dramatic improvements to increase their efficiency. Xerox, for example, has halved the cost of producing a copier since the mid-1980s. Cummins Engine Co., the largest American manufacturer of heavy-duty diesel truck engines, has doubled its output per worker since 1985 and used this new efficiency to gain market share by cutting its engine prices by nearly a third.[4]

Contrary to what many American politicians claim, U.S. workers are now among the most productive in the world. They're an impressive 23 percent more productive than Japanese workers, for instance, and 25 percent more productive than British workers.[5] Where the Japanese are strongest in productivity is in automobile production and consumer electronics. Yet Japanese productivity in general merchandise retailing is 44 precent that of American workers, and Japanese factory workers overall produce 80 percent as much as Americans on an hourly basis.[6] Of course, this is not a static game. Managers in all countries are striving to improve the productivity of their

Ford's Taurus plant in Atlanta, Georgia, can match the best the Japanese have to offer in terms of both efficiency and quality. It takes 17.6 labor-hours to build a Taurus in this plant. That compares with 27 hours at a typical General Motors plant and 21 hours at a typical Japanese plant in the United States.

employees and organizations. In this competitive climate, organizations have no choice but to look for ways to significantly improve productivity.

How can organizations improve their productivity? Productivity is a composite of people and operations variables. To improve productivity, management needs to focus on both.

On the people side, techniques discussed in previous chapters should be considered. Participative decision making, management by objectives, team-based work groups, and equitable pay systems are examples of people-oriented approaches toward productivity improvement. Management consultant and quality expert W. Edwards Deming, who teaches that managers, not workers, are the primary source of increased productivity, outlined fourteen point for improving management's productivity. They are listed in Table 21–1.

A close look at Table 21–1 reveals Deming's understanding of the interplay between people and operations. High productivity cannot come solely from good "people management." The truly effective organization will maximize productivity by successfully integrating people into the overall operations system. This can explain, for instance, why in one recent year alone, U.S. companies spent $17 billion on computers and new process-control equipment.[7] Increased capital investment will make facilities more modern and efficient. It also explains why so many organizations have laid off employees and shrunk in size in recent years. These organizations aspire to get more output per labor hour—that is, to increase their productivity.

In this chapter, we'll demonstrate that factors such as size and layout of operating facilities, capacity utilization, inventory usage, and maintenance controls are important determinants of an organization's overall productivity performance.

TABLE 21–1 Deming's Fourteen Points for Improving Management's Productivity

---

1. Plan for the long-term future, not for next month or next year.
2. Never be complacent concerning the quality of your product.
3. Establish statistical control over your production processes and require your suppliers to do so as well.
4. Deal with the fewest number of suppliers—the best ones, of course.
5. Find out whether your problems are confined to particular parts of the production process or stem from the overall process itself.
6. Train workers for the job that you are asking them to perform.
7. Raise the quality of your line supervisors.
8. Drive out fear.
9. Encourage departments to work closely together rather than to concentrate on departmental or divisional distinctions.
10. Do not be sucked into adopting strictly numerical goals, including the widely popular formula of "zero defect."
11. Require your workers to do quality work, not just to be at their stations from 9 to 5.
12. Train your employees to understand statistical methods.
13. Train your employees in new skills as the need arises.
14. Make top managers responsible for implementing these principles.

Source: W. Edwards Deming, "Improvement of Quality and Productivity Through Action by Management," *National Productivity Review,* Winter 1981–82, pp. 12–22. With permission. Copyright 1981 by Executive Enterprises, Inc., 22 West 21st St., New York, NY 10010-6904. All rights reserved.

MANAGERS
WHO MADE A
DIFFERENCE

Herman Moore at Reynolds Metals Co.

Unlike many of his business-school classmates who chose careers in marketing or finance, Herman Moore has chosen to make his mark by making things.[8]

After graduating from the University of Dayton with a degree in industrial engineering, Herman Moore joined Reynolds Metals Co.'s management training program. After completing the program, he took a staff job with Reynolds at their Richmond, Virginia, headquarters. While there, he attended night classes at the University of Richmond and earned his M.B.A. in 1982. In 1985, Moore became superintendent at a Reynold's reclamation plant in Muscle Shoals, Alabama. He quickly realized that he had a talent for the manufacturing arena. The plant's scrap rate and its overall costs improved under Moore, and, after a year, he won a promotion to become manager of a newly opened plant that recycled cans.

In his new job, Moore found himself overseeing a plant that was operating at only 40 percent of capacity and with costs considerably higher than the competition. Moore lured top engineers from other company plants. He developed teams to cut costs and improve quality and safety. He upgraded equipment. Within two years, the plant was at 100 percent of capacity, and efficiency had been increased by 35 percent. The plant won a company award in 1989 in recognition of its setting records for productivity, shipments, energy conservation, and profits.

In 1990, Moore was promoted to his current job as plant superintendent at Reynold's Alloy Plant in Muscle Shoals. There he's second in command at the company's largest plant, where 2100 employees make aluminum sheets for cans, siding, and appliances. As in his prior job, Moore is making an impact at Alloys. He's overseeing a $430 million capital improvement project that will raise capacity by 30 percent, while cutting costs by 39 percent. Under Moore, the plant has also automated its process controls, which has helped to cut defects by almost two-thirds.

Herman Moore represents the new breed of operations manager. "Before, a manufacturing manager was responsible for getting a pound out the door," he says. "Now you have to get the pound out the door in a safe, quality, cost-effective, and environmental manner." And Moore seems to be thoroughly enjoying the challenges he faces. As he puts it, "I can't save American manufacturing, but at least I'm doing my part to make it possible."

Operations Management Includes Both Manufacturing and Services

manufacturing organizations
Organizations that produce physical goods such as steel, automobiles, textiles, and farm machinery.

For the first half of this century, **manufacturing organizations**—that is, organizations that produce physical goods such as steel, automobiles, textiles, and farm machinery—dominated most advanced industrialized nations. Today, in the United States, Canada, Australia, and Western Europe, **service organizations** dominate. They produce nonphysical outputs such as educational, medical, and transportation services that are intangible, can't be stored in inventory, and incorporate the customer or client in the actual production process.

service organizations
Organizations that produce non-physical outputs such as educational, medical, and transportation services that are intangible, can't be stored in inventory, and incorporate the customer or client in the actual production process.

deindustrialization
The conversion of an economy from dominance by manufacturing to dominance by service-oriented businesses.

Deindustrialization is taking place among advanced economies. Blue-collar jobs in manufacturing are being replaced by jobs in the service sector. The manufacturing firms that survive are becoming smaller and leaner. The bulk of new jobs are being created in services—from janitors to fast-food servers to computer repairers and programmers to accountants and physicians.

A major challenge for management in a deindustrialized society will be increasing productivity in the service sectors. Many managers and administrators in colleges, hospitals, airlines, government agencies, and similar service-sector organizations are responding to the challenge by transferring concepts and techniques that worked in manufacturing to services.

For example, state and local governments are increasingly using operations management techniques.[9] The city of Madison, Wisconsin, has used statistical process control and worker empowerment to improve the efficiency of its garbage collection operations. The Arkansas Department of Human Services cut the error rate on its nightly computer runs by 68 percent after a quality team figured out which programs were causing problems and why. Phoenix, Arizona, used quality teams and operations management techniques to cut the costs of the city's emergency ambulance service by 25 percent while, at the same time, cutting average response time from nineteen to just five minutes.

Strategic Operations Management

Modern manufacturing was born three-quarters of a century ago in the United States, primarily in Detroit's automobile factories. The success U.S. manufacturers experienced during World War II led executives of manufacturing firms to believe that the troublesome problems of production had been conquered. These executives directed their attention to other areas such as finance and marketing. From the late 1940s through the mid-1970s, manufacturing activities were slighted. With only the occasional exception (such as the aerospace industry), top management gave manufactur-

Sleep Inn is proving that significant productivity gains can be achieved in service firms. It employs 13 percent fewer people than comparably sized no-frills hotels. It was designed with the mind set of an industrial engineer laying out an assembly line. Among some of its features: the laundry room is almost completely automated; closets have no doors for maids to open and shut; and the shower stalls are round, eliminating corners that collect dust.

**MANAGING
FROM A
GLOBAL
PERSPECTIVE**

Global Operations Strategy

Japanese firms such as Sony and Panasonic could never produce the quality electronic products they do at the prices at which they sell them if they sold their products only in Japan. Why? Because the Japanese home market is very small. These companies are able to justify the investments they make in research, technology, and quality design only because they enjoy the economies of selling their products worldwide.

In the global marketplace, the place where goods are manufactured, the amount to be produced, and similar production and operations decisions must consider international comparative advantages.[10] Because of rapidly rising labor costs in Japan, Sony has moved some of its low-skill, labor-intensive manufacturing operations to Taiwan. The need for creative design skills encouraged Mazda executives to locate a design center in Southern California. The rise of the yen in relation to the dollar motivated Honda to set up manufacturing plants in Ohio. Low-interest loans by the Irish government led California-based semiconductor equipment manufacturer Western Digital Corporation to open a new plant in Ireland.

Global organizations no longer produce their goods in one country and then ship them around the world. Such companies as Ford, Procter & Gamble, and Royal Dutch Shell have manufacturing operations in countries throughout the world. They design products for world markets and use worldwide production and distribution systems, as well as vertical integration, to gain economies of scale. But many other benefits can accrue from pursuing a global operations strategy. Take, as examples, the ability to prolong life cycles and the benefits that can result from exploiting the volatility of economic factors. Companies can prolong product life cycles by manufacturing in developing nations. A tire retread manufacturer may face a declining market in the United States or Canada but a rapidly growing market in Latin American countries. Global firms can experience fluctuations of exchange rates, inflation rates, and similar volatile factors that provide advantages precisely because they do fluctuate, if the firms know how to benefit from the ups and downs. Firms that can accurately forecast economic fluctuations and adjust their manufacturing decisions accordingly, can outperform nonglobal organizations as well as global firms that forecast poorly or operate under the assumption of economic stability.

ing little attention, managers "on the way up" avoided it, and market leadership dwindled.

Meanwhile, with U.S. executives neglecting the production side of their business, managers in Japan, Germany, and other countries took the opportunity to develop modern, computer-assisted facilities that fully integrated manufacturing operations into strategic planning decisions. The competition's success realigned world manufacturing leadership. For example, U.S. manufacturers found that foreign goods were being made not only less expensively but also better. By the late 1970s, U.S. manufacturers were facing a true crisis, and a good percentage of them responded.[11] They invested heavily in improving manufacturing technology, increased the authority of manufacturing executives, and began incorporating existing and future production requirements into the organization's overall strategic plan. Today, successful manufacturers are taking a top-down approach to operations and implementing comprehensive manufacturing planning systems.[12]

Harvard University professor Wickham Skinner has been urging a "manufacturing focus" to strategy for a number of years.[13] He argues that too many important production decisions have been relegated to lower-level managers. Production needs to be managed from the top down rather than from the bottom up. According to Skinner, the organization's overall strategy should directly reflect its manufacturing capabilities and limitations and should include operations objectives and strategies. He points out, for example, that each organization's operations strategy needs to be unique and reflect the inherent trade-offs in any production process. Cost reduction and quality enhancement often work against each other. So, too, do short delivery times and limited inventory levels. Because there is no single "most efficient way" to produce things, top management needs to identify and emphasize its competitive advantage in operations. Some organizations are competing on the more traditional basis of low prices achieved through cost reduction. Others are competing on the basis of quality, reliable delivery, warranties, short lead times, customer service, rapid product introduction, or flexible capacity.

As we noted, Skinner's appeals have been heeded. The manufacturing organizations that expect to compete successfully in world markets are incorporating operations decisions in their strategic plans and returning manufacturing executives to a place of prominence in the organization's power structure.[14]

Planning Operations

As we've noted in several places throughout this book, planning must precede control. Therefore, before we can introduce operations-management control techniques, we need to review a few of the more important decisions related to planning operations.

Four key decisions—capacity, location, process, and layout—provide the long-term strategic direction for operations planning. They determine the proper size of an operating system, where the physical facilities should be located, the best methods for transforming inputs into outputs, and the most efficient layout of equipment and work stations. Once these decisions have been made, three short-term decisions—the aggregate plan, the master schedule, and a material requirements plan—need to be established. These provide the tactical plans for the operating system. In this section, we'll review each of these seven types of planning decisions. (See Figure 21-2.)

Capacity Planning

capacity planning
Assessing an operating system's ability to produce a desired number of output units for each type of product during a given time period.

Assume that you have decided to go into the boat-building business. On the basis of your analysis of the market and other environmental factors (see Chapter 8), you believe there is a market for a premium-quality 28-foot sailboat. You know *what* you want to produce. What's the next step? You need to determine *how many* boats you expect to build. This, in turn, will determine the proper size of your plant and other facility-planning issues. When managers assess their operating system's capabilities for producing a desired number of output units for each type of product anticipated during a given time period, they are engaged in **capacity planning.**

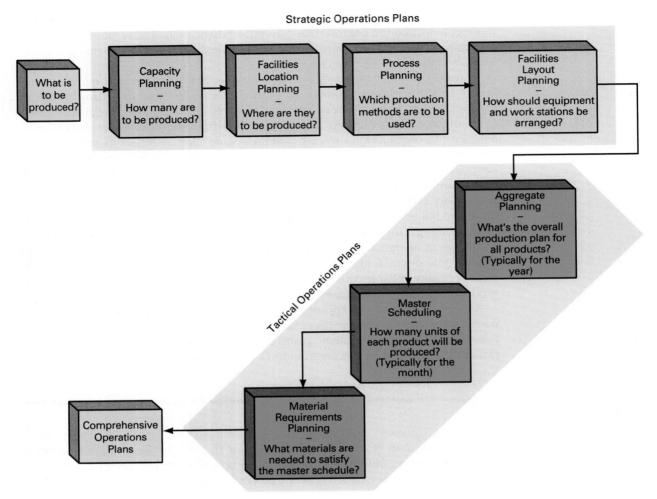

FIGURE 21-2
Planning Operations

Capacity planning begins by taking the forecasts of sales demand (see Chapter 9) and converting them into capacity requirements. If you produce only one type of boat, plan to sell the boats for an average of $50,000 each, and anticipate generating sales of $2.5 million during the first year, your physical capacity requirements need to handle fifty boats. This calculation is obviously much more complex if you're producing dozens of different products.

If your organization is already established, you compare this forecast against your existing production capacity. Then you can determine whether you'll need to add to or subtract from your existing capacity. Keep in mind that you don't have to be in a manufacturing business to use capacity planning. The following steps are just as relevant for determining the number of beds needed in a hospital or the maximum number of sandwiches that a Burger King can serve.

Once you have converted the forecast into physical capacity requirements, you will be able to develop a set of alternative capacity plans that will meet the requirements. You will often have to make some modifications—that is, you will have to expand or reduce capacity. In the long term, you can alter the size of your operation significantly and permanently by buying new equipment or selling off existing facilities. In the short term, however, you're forced to make more temporary modifications. You can add an extra shift, increase overtime, or reduce work hours;

temporarily shut down operations; or subcontract work out to other organizations. If you manufacture a product that can be stored (like sailboats), you can build inventories during slack periods to be used when demand exceeds capacity.

Facilities Location Planning

facilities location planning
The design and location of an operations facility.

When you determine the need for additional capacity, you must design and choose a facility. This process is called **facilities location planning.** Where you choose to locate will depend on which factors have the greatest impact on total production and distribution costs. These include availability of labor skills, labor costs, energy costs, proximity to suppliers or customers, and the like. Rarely are all these factors of equal importance. The kind of business you're in typically dictates your critical contingencies, which then dictate—to a large degree—the optimum location.

The need for skilled technical specialists has led an increasing number of high-tech firms to locate in the Boston area. The area's high concentration of colleges and universities makes it easier for firms who require employees with computer, engineering, and research skills to find and hold onto such people. Similarly, it's not by chance that many manufacturers whose conversion processes are labor intensive have moved their manufacturing facilities overseas to places such as Taiwan and South Korea. When labor costs are a critical contingency, organizations will locate their facilities where wage rates are low. Tire manufacturers chose their original locations in northern Ohio in order to be close to their major customers, the automobile manufacturers in Detroit. When customer convenience is critical, as it is for many retail outlets, the location decision is often dictated by concerns such as proximity to a highway or pedestrian traffic.

What contingencies are going to be critical in your sailboat business? You'll need employees with boat-building skills, and they're most likely to be plentiful in coastal areas such as New England, Florida, and southern California. Shipping costs of the final product are likely to be a major expenditure, thus, to keep your prices competitive you might want to locate close to your customers. That again suggests the east, west, or Gulf coasts, or possibly the Great Lakes. Weather might be a further factor. It

The building of this Reynolds Metals plant in Washington State is a clear response to low energy costs. Aluminum reduction mills require a great deal of energy, and Washington has cheap hydroelectric power.

might be less expensive to build boats outside in warm-weather climates than indoors during winter in the northeast. If labor availability, shipping costs, and weather are your critical contingencies, you still have a great deal of latitude in your location decision. After you choose a region, you still must select a community and a specific site.

Process Planning

process planning
Determining how a product or service will be produced.

In **process planning,** management determines how a product or service will be produced. Process planning encompasses evaluating the available production methods and selecting the set that will best achieve the operating objectives.

For any given production process, whether in manufacturing or the service sector, there are always alternative conversion methods. Designing a restaurant, for instance, allows for a number of process choices: to-inventory fast food (as served at McDonald's), limited-option fast food (as served at Burger King or Wendy's), cafeteria-style delivery, drive-in take out, a no-option fixed menu, and complex meals prepared to order. Key questions that ultimately determine how an organization's products or services will be produced include: Will the technology be routine or nonroutine? What degree of automation will be utilized? Should the system be developed to maximize efficiency or flexibility? How should the product or service flow through the operations system?[15]

In our sailboat-manufacturing example, the boats could be made by an assembly-line process. If you decide to keep them highly standardized, you will find a routine transformation process to be most cost efficient. But if you want each boat to be made to order, you will require a different technology and a different set of production methods.

Process planning is complex. Deciding on the best combinations of processes in terms of costs, quality, labor efficiency, and similar considerations is difficult because the decisions are intertwined. A change in one element of the production process often has spillover effects on a number of other elements. As a result, the detailed planning is usually left to production and industrial engineers under the overall guidance of top management.

Facilities Layout Planning

facilities layout planning
Assessing and selecting among alternative layout options for equipment and work stations.

process layout
Arranging manufacturing components together according to similarity of function.

product layout
Arranging manufacturing components according to the progressive steps by which a product is made.

fixed-position layout
A manufacturing layout in which the product stays in place while tools, equipment, and human skills are brought to it.

The final strategic decision in operations planning is to assess and select among alternative layout options for equipment and work stations. This is called **facilities layout planning.** The objective of layout planning is to find a physical arrangement that will best facilitate production efficiency and that is also appealing to employees.

Layout planning begins by assessing space needs. Space has to be provided for work areas, tools and equipment, storage, maintenance facilities, rest rooms, offices, lunch areas and cafeterias, waiting rooms, and even parking lots. Then, based on previous process plans, various layout configurations can be evaluated to determine how efficient each is for handling the work flow. To help make these decisions, a number of layout-planning devices are available, ranging from simple, scaled-to-size paper cutouts to sophisticated computer software programs that can manipulate hundreds of variables and print out alternative layout designs.[16]

There are basically three work-flow layouts.[17] The **process layout** arranges components (such as work centers, equipment, or departments) together according to similarity of function. Figure 21–3 illustrates the process layout at a medical clinic. In **product layout,** the components are arranged according to the progressive steps by which the product is made. Figure 21–4 illustrates a product layout in a plant that manufactures aluminum tubing. The third approach, the **fixed-position layout,** is used when, because of its size or bulk, the product remains at one location. The

FIGURE 21–3

A Process Layout at a Medical Clinic

Source: From Everett E. Adam, Jr. and Ronald J. Ebert, *Production and Operations Management: Concepts, Models, and Behavior,* 5th ed. (Englewood Cliffs, NJ: Prentice Hall, 1992), p. 254. With permission.

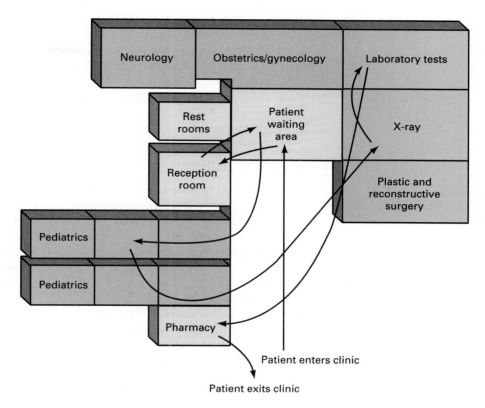

product stays in place, and tools, equipment, and human skills are brought to it. Sound stages on a movie lot or the manufacturing of airplanes illustrates the fixed-position layout. The building of your 28-foot sailboats is likely to use either a product or fixed-position layout.

Aggregate Planning

Once the strategic design decisions have been made, we move to the tactical operations decisions. The first of these deals with planning the overall production activities and their associated operating resources. This is called **aggregate planning** and often deals with a time frame of up to a year.

The aggregate plan provides a "big picture." On the basis of the demand forecast and capacity plan, the aggregate plan sets inventory levels and production rates and estimates the size of the total operation's labor force on a monthly basis for approximately the next twelve months. The focus is on *generalities,* not specifics. Families of items are considered, not individual items. A paint company's aggregate plan would look at the total number of gallons of house paint to be manufactured but avoid

aggregate planning

Planning overall production activities and their associated operating resources.

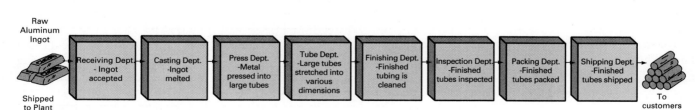

FIGURE 21–4

A Product Layout in an Aluminum Tubing Plant

decisions about color or size of container. As such, the aggregate plan is particularly valuable to large operations that have a varied product line. As you'll see in the next section, for the small, one-product firm, such as the sailboat-manufacturing operation, the aggregate plan will look like the master schedule, only it will cover a longer time frame.

When completed, the aggregate plan often yields two basic decisions: the best overall production rate to adopt and the overall number of workers to be employed during each period in the planning horizon.[18]

Master Scheduling

master schedule
A schedule that specifies quantity and type of items to be produced; how, when, and where they should be produced; labor force levels; and inventory.

The **master schedule** is derived from the aggregate plan. It specifies the quantity and type of each item to be produced; how, when, and where they should be produced for the next day, week, or month; labor force levels; and inventory.

The first requirement of master scheduling is *disaggregation*—that is, breaking the aggregate plan down into detailed operational plans for each of the products or services the organization produces.[19] After that, these plans need to be scheduled against one another in a master schedule.

Figure 21–5 depicts a master schedule for a manufacturer of automobile transmissions. The top portion of the figure informs lower-level managers (through the aggregate plan) that top management has authorized the capacity, inventory, and people to produce 100 heavy-duty transmissions in July, 125 in August, and so forth. The lower part of the figure illustrates a master schedule. For example, it shows how lower-level managers consider the July production for 100 heavy-duty transmissions and determine which models to make. Not only do they determine what specific models to make each week, they also state how many. During the first week of July, for instance, ten units of Model 1179 and fifteen units of Model 1180 will be assembled.

FIGURE 21–5
Developing a Master Schedule from an Aggregate Plan

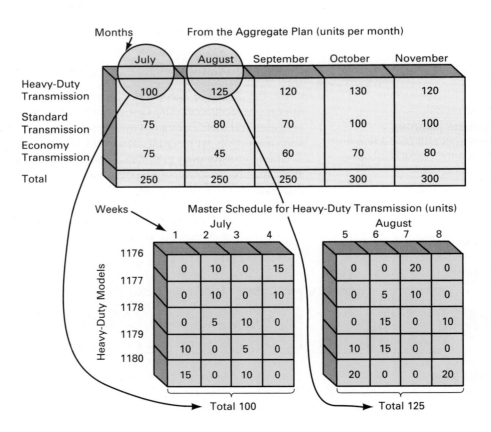

Material Requirements Planning

material requirements planning (MRP)
A system that dissects products into the materials and parts necessary for purchasing, inventorying, and priority-planning purposes.

After the specific products have been decided upon, each should be dissected to determine the precise materials and parts that it requires. **Material requirements planning (MRP)** is a system that uses this data for purchasing, inventorying, and priority-planning purposes.

With the assistance of a computer, product design specifications can be used to identify all the materials and parts necessary to produce the product. By merging this information with computerized inventory records, management will know the quantities of each part in inventory and when each is likely to be used up. When lead times and safety stock requirements are established and entered into the computer, MRP ensures that the right materials are available when needed.

Controlling Operations

Once the operating system has been designed and implemented, its key elements must be monitored. The following discussion offers guidance for controlling costs, purchasing, maintenance, and quality.

Cost Control

An automobile industry analyst has compared the U.S. and Japanese approaches to cost control: "The Japanese regard cost control as something you wake up every morning and do. Americans have always thought of it as a project. You cut costs 20 percent and say: 'Whew! That's over.' We can't afford to think that way anymore."[20]

U.S. managers have often treated cost control as an occasional crusade that is initiated and controlled by the accounting staff. Accountants establish cost standards per unit, and if deviations occur, management looks for the cause. Have material prices increased? Is labor being used efficiently? Do employees need additional training? However, as the previous annotation implies, cost control needs to play a central part in the design of an operating system, and it needs to be a continuing concern of every manager.

cost center
A unit in which managers are held responsible for all associated costs.

direct costs
Costs incurred in proportion to the output of a particular good or service.

indirect costs
Costs that are largely unaffected by changes in output.

Many organizations have adopted the cost-center approach to controlling costs. Work areas, departments, or plants are identified as distinct **cost centers,** and their managers are held responsible for the cost performance of these units. Any unit's total costs are made up of two types of costs: direct and indirect. **Direct costs** are costs incurred in proportion to the output of a particular good or service. Labor and materials typically fall into this category. On the other hand, **indirect costs** are largely unaffected by changes in output. Insurance expenses and the salaries of staff personnel are examples of typical indirect costs. This direct–indirect distinction is important. While cost-center managers are held responsible for all direct costs in their units, indirect costs are not necessarily within their control. However, because all costs are controllable at some level in the organization, top managers should identify where the control lies and hold lower managers accountable for costs under their control.[21]

Purchasing Control

It has been said that human beings *are* what they eat. Metaphorically, the same applies to organizations. Their processes and outputs depend on the inputs they "eat." It's difficult to make quality products out of inferior inputs. Highly skilled leather workers need quality cowhides if they are going to produce high-quality wallets. Gas station operators depend on a regular and dependable inflow of certain octane-rated gasolines from their suppliers in order to meet their customer's demands. If the gas isn't there, they can't sell it. If the gasoline is below the specified octane rating, customers may be dissatisifed and take their business somewhere else. Management must therefore monitor the delivery, performance, quality, quantity, and price of inputs from suppliers. Purchasing control seeks to ensure availablilty, acceptable quality, continued reliable sources, and, at the same time, reduced costs.

What can managers do to facilitate control of inputs? They need to gather information on the dates and conditions in which supplies arrive. They need to gather data about the quality of supplies and the compatibility of those supplies with operations processes. Finally, they need to obtain data on supplier price performance. Are the prices of the delivered goods the same as those quoted when the order was placed?

This information can be used to rate suppliers, identify problem suppliers, and guide management in choosing future suppliers. Trends can be detected. Suppliers can be evaluated, for instance, on responsiveness, service, reliability, and competitiveness.

Building Close Links with Suppliers   A rapidly growing trend in manufacturing is turning suppliers into partners.[22] Instead of using ten or twelve vendors and forcing them to compete against each other to gain the firm's business, manufacturers are using only two or three vendors and working closely with them to improve efficiency and quality.

Motorola, for instance, sends its design-and-manufacturing engineers to suppliers to help with any problem.[23] Other firms now routinely send inspection teams to rate suppliers' operations. They're assessing these suppliers' manufacturing and delivery techniques, statistical process controls that identify causes of defects, and ability to handle data electronically. Companies in the United States and around the world are doing what has long been a tradition in Japan—that is, they are developing long-term relationships with suppliers. As collaborators and partners, rather than adversaries, firms are finding that they can achieve better quality of inputs, fewer defects, and lower costs. Furthermore, when problems arise with suppliers, open communication channels facilitate quick resolutions.

economic order quantity model (EOQ)

A technique for balancing purchase, ordering, carrying, and stockout costs to derive the optimum quantity for a purchase order.

Economic Order Quantity Model   One of the best-known techniques for mathematically deriving the optimum quantity for a purchase order is the **economic order quantity model (EOQ).** The EOQ model seeks to balance four costs involved in ordering and carrying inventory: the *purchase costs* (purchase price plus delivery charges less discounts); the *ordering costs* (paperwork, follow-up, inspection when the item arrives, and other processing costs); *carrying costs* (money tied up in inventory, storage, insurance, taxes, and so forth); and *stockout costs* (profits forgone from orders lost, the cost of reestablishing goodwill, and additional expenses incurred to expedite late shipments).

The objective of the EOQ model, as shown in Figure 21–6, is to minimize the total costs of two of these four costs—carrying costs and ordering costs. As the amount ordered gets larger and larger, average inventory increases and so do carrying costs. But placing larger orders means fewer orders and thus lowers ordering costs. For example, if annual demand for an inventory item is 26,000 units, and we order 500 each time, we will place 52 (26,000/500) orders per year. This gives us an average inventory of 250 (500/2) units. However, if the order quantity is increased to 2,000 units, there will be fewer orders placed, 13 (26,000/2,000), but the average inventory on hand will increase to 1,000 (2,000/2) units. Thus as holding costs go up, ordering costs go down, and vice versa. As depicted in Figure 21–6, the lowest total cost—and thus the most economic order quantity—is reached at the lowest point on the total

FIGURE 21–6
Determining the Most Economic
Order Quantity

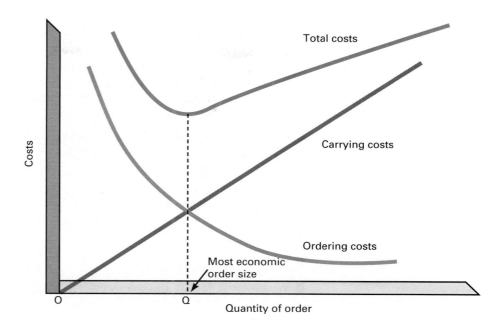

cost curve. That is the point at which ordering cost equals carrying cost. It is called the
economic order quantity.

To compute this optimal order quantity, you need the following data: forecasted
demand for the item during the period (D), the cost of placing each order (OC), the
value or purchase price of the item (V), and the carrying cost of maintaining the total
inventory expressed as a percentage (CC),, We can now present the standard EOQ
formula and demonstrate its use:

$$EOQ = \sqrt{\frac{2 \times D \times OC}{V \times CC}}$$

As an example, Playback Electronics, a retailer of high-quality sound and video
equipment, is trying to ascertain its economic order quantities. The item in question is
a Yamaha compact sound system. The company forecasts sales of 4,000 units a year.
Purchasing believes that the cost of each system will be $500. The accountants
estimate the cost of placing an order for the sound system at $75 per order and annual
insurance, taxes, and other carrying costs at 20 percent of the system's worth. Using
the EOQ formula and the information above, we find

$$EOQ = \sqrt{\frac{2 \times 4,000 \times 75}{500 \times 0.20}}$$
$$= \sqrt{6,000}$$
$$= 77.45 \text{ units} \cong 78 \text{ units}$$

The inventory model suggests to Playback's management that it is most economic
to order in quantities or lots of approximately 78 units; stated differently, they should
order about 52 (4,000/78) times a year.

What would happen if Yamaha offered Playback a 5 percent discount on purchases if Playback buys in minimum quantitites of 120 units? Should Playback's
management now purchase in quantities of 78 or 120? Without the discount, and
therefore ordering 78 each time, Playback's annual costs for this sound system would
be as follows:

Purchase cost: $500 × 4,000   = $2,000,000

Carrying cost: $\dfrac{78}{2}$ × $500 × 0.20   =   3,900

      (average inventory units) × (value of item) × (percentage)

Ordering cost: 52   ×   75   =   3,900

(Number of orders)   ×   (cost to place order)   _____

Total cost: $2,007,800

With the 5 percent discount for ordering 120 units, the item cost would be $475. The annual inventory costs would be as follows:

Purchase cost: $475 × 4,000   = $1,900,000

Carrying cost: $\dfrac{120}{2}$ × 475 × 0.20   =   5,700

Ordering cost: $\dfrac{4,000}{120}$ × 75   =   2,500

                                     _____

Total cost: $1,908,200

These computations suggest to Playback's management that it should take the 5 percent discount. Even though it has to stock larger quantities, the savings are almost $100,000 a year.

A word of caution should be added. The EOQ model assumes that demand and lead time are known and constant. If these conditions cannot be met, the model should not be used. For example, it generally should not be used for manufactured component inventory, because the components are taken out of stock all at once or in lumps or in lots rather than at a constant rate. Does this mean that the EOQ model is useless when demand is variable? No. The model can still be of some use in demonstrating trade-offs in costs and the need to control lot sizes. However, there are more sophisticated lot-sizing models for handling lumpy demand and special situations.

Inventory Ordering Systems   In many checkbooks, after you use up about 95 percent of the checks, you find a reorder form included among the few that remain; it reminds you that it's time to reorder. This is an example of a **fixed-point reordering system.** At some preestablished point in the operations process, the system is designed to "flag" the fact that the inventory needs to be replenished. The flag is triggered when the inventory reaches a certain point or level.

The goal of a fixed-point reordering system is to minimize inventory carrying costs and to ensure a reasonable level of customer service (limiting the probability of an item running out—a *stockout*). Therefore the reorder point should be established to equate the time remaining before a stockout and the lead time to receive delivery of the reordered quantity. In such cases, the newly ordered items would arrive at the same time as the last item in inventory was used up. More realistically, management does not usualy allow the inventory to fall below some safety stock level. (See Figure 21–7). By using certain statistical procedures, one can set a reorder point at a level that gives an organization enough inventory to get through the lead-time period and some reasonable insurance against a stockout. This buffer, or safety stock, gives protection against greater usage than expected during the lead time or an unexpected delay in receiving new stock.

As a simple example, to determine a check reorder point let's assume that the lead time averages three weeks and that we write about twenty checks a week. We would need sixty checks to get us through a "normal" reordering lead time. If we feel, on the basis of history, that a one-week safety stock would be sufficient to get us through most lead-time periods, the order should be placed when there are 80 (60 + 20) checks left. This is the reorder point. Another word of caution: The more safety stock,

fixed-point reordering system
A system that "flags" the fact that inventory needs to be replenished when it reaches a certain level.

FIGURE 21-7
Inventory Cycle with Safety Stock

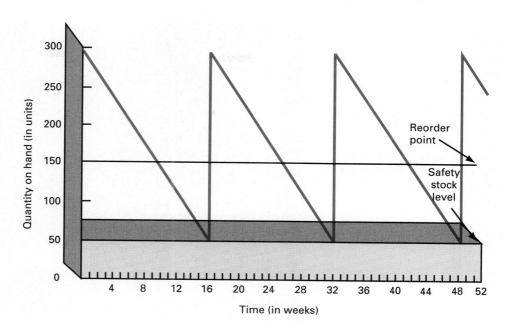

the less the risk of stockout. But the additional inventory will add to the carrying costs. Thus we again face a cost-benefit decision. At times it may be prudent (cost-wise) to run out of stock.

One of the most primitive but certainly effective uses of the fixed-point reordering system is to keep the item—for example, pens and duplicating paper in an office or boxes of shoes in a retail shoe store—in two separate containers. Inventory is drawn from one until it is empty. At that point, a reorder is placed, and items are drawn from the second container. If demand for an item has been estimated properly, the replacement order to replenish the stock should arrive before the second container is used up.

Another, more recent, version of the fixed-point reorder system relies on computer control. Sales are automatically recorded by a central computer that has been pro-grammed to initiate a purchase order for an item when its inventory reaches some critical fixed point. A number of retail stores have such systems. The cash registers are actually computers, and each sale automatically adjusts the store's inventory record. When the inventory of an item hits the critical point, the computer tells management to reorder or, in some systems, actually prints out the purchase order requisition.

fixed-interval reordering system

A system that uses time as the determining factor for reviewing and reordering inventory items.

Another common inventory system is the **fixed-interval reordering system.** The fixed-interval system uses time as the determining factor for inventory control. At a predetermined time—say, once a week or every ninety days—the inventory is counted, and an order is placed for the number of items necessary to bring the inventory back to the desired level. The desired level is established so that if demand and ordering lead time are average, consumption will draw the inventory down to zero (or some safety lead time can be added) just as the next order arrives. This system may have some transportation economies and quantity discount economies over the fixed-point system. For example, it may allow us to consolidate orders from one supplier if we review all the items we purchase from this source at the same time. This is not possible in the other system.

In the 1800s, economist Vilfredo Pareto found that 80 percent of the wealth was controlled by only 20 percent of the population. College instructors typically find that a few students cause most of their problems, and students have probably similarly found that a few instructors cause most of their problems. This concept, the vital few and the trivial many, can be applied to inventory control.

It might take a men's store three weeks to get an order for Levis 501 jeans filled by the manufacturer. If the store typically sells ten pairs of size 30-30 jeans a week, the store manager could set up two containers, keep thirty pairs of jeans in the second container, and initiate reorders whenever the first container is empty. This would be an application of the fixed-point reordering system.

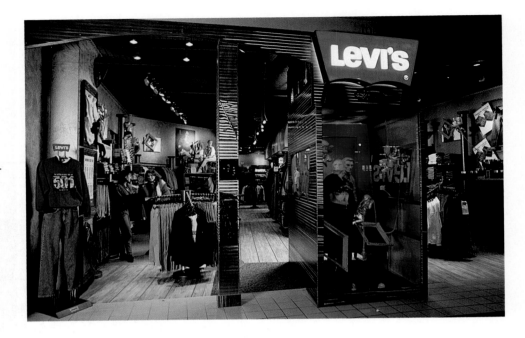

ABC system
A priority system for monitoring inventory items.

It is not unusual for a company to have thousands of items in inventory. However, evidence indicates that roughly 10 percent of the items in most organizations' inventory account for 50 percent of the annual dollar inventory value. Another 20 percent of the items account for 30 percent of the value. The remaining 70 percent of the items appear to account for only 20 percent of the value. These have been labeled as A, B, and C categories, respectively. Thus we have the name **ABC system.** (See Figure 21–8.)

Cost-benefit analysis would justify that A items receive the tightest control, B items moderate control, and C items the least control. This can be accomplished because there are so few A items and they represent a large dollar investment. Similarly, there are so many C items, but so little dollar investment, that tight control would not be justified. A items, for example, might be monitored weekly, B items monthly, and C items quarterly because they account for so little dollar value. Or C items might be controlled by using a simple form of order point.

Maintenance Control

Delivering goods or services in an efficient and effective manner requires operating systems with high equipment utilization and a minimum amount of downtime. Therefore managers need to be concerned with maintenance control. The importance of maintenance control, however, depends on the process technology used. For example, if a standardized assembly-line process breaks down, it can affect hundreds of employees. On an automobile or dishwasher assembly line, it's not unusual for a serious breakdown on one machine to bring an entire plant to a halt. In contrast, most systems using more general-purpose and redundant processes have less interdependency between activities, therefore a machine breakdown is likely to have less of an impact. Nevertheless, an equipment breakdown—like an inventory stockout—may mean higher costs, delayed deliveries, or lost sales.

preventive maintenance
Maintenance performed before a breakdown occurs.

remedial maintenance
Maintenance that calls for the overhaul, replacement, or repair of equipment when it breaks down.

conditional maintenance
Maintenance that calls for an overhaul or repair in response to an inspection.

There are three approaches to maintenance control.[24] **Preventive maintenance** is performed before a breakdown occurs. **Remedial maintenance** is a complete overhaul, replacement, or repair of the equipment when it breaks down. **Conditional maintenance** refers to overhaul or repair in response to an inspection and

FIGURE 21-8
Example of an ABC Inventory System

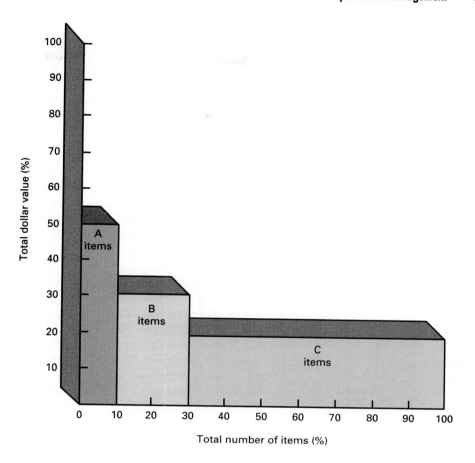

measurement of the equipment's state. When American Airlines tears down its planes' engines every 1,000 hours, it is engaging in preventive maintenance. When it inspects the planes' tires every twenty-four hours and changes them when conditions warrant it, it is performing conditional maintenance. Finally, if American Airlines' operations policy is to repair lavatory equipment on board its planes only after the equipment breaks down, then it is using remedial maintenance practices.

The American Airlines example points out that the type of maintenance control depends on the costs of a breakdown. The greater the cost in terms of money, time, liability, and goodwill, the greater the benefits from preventive maintenance. That is, the benefits can justify the costs.

Maintenance control should also be considered in the design of equipment. If downtime is highly inconvenient or costly, reliability can be increased by designing redundancy into the equipment. Nuclear power plants, for example, have elaborate backup systems built in. Similarly, equipment can be designed to facilitate fast or low-cost maintenance. Equipment that has fewer parts has fewer things to go wrong. High-failure items can also be placed in locations that are easily accessible or in independent modular units that can be quickly removed and replaced. Cable television operators follow these guidelines. Breakdowns infuriate customers, so when they occur management wants to be able to correct them quickly. Speed is facilitated by centralizing equipment in easy-access locations and making extensive use of modular units. If a piece of equipment fails, the whole module of which it is a part can be pulled or replaced in just a few minutes. Television service is resumed rapidly, and the pulled modular unit can be taken to the shop and repaired without time pressures.

Quality Control

We've discussed Total Quality Management throughout this book. We've described it as a comprehensive, customer-focused program to continuously improve the quality of the organization's processes, products, and services. In this section, we present the more limited and traditional approach to quality by focusing on its control. While TQM emphasizes actions to prevent mistakes, quality control emphasizes identifying mistakes that may have already occurred.

So what do we mean by *quality control?* It refers to monitoring quality—weight, strength, consistency, color, taste, reliability, finish, or any one of a myriad of characteristics—to ensure that it meets some preestablished standard. Quality control will probably be needed at one or more points beginning with the receipt of inputs. It will continue with work in process and all steps up to the final product. Assessments at intermediate stages of the transformation process typically are part of quality control. Early detection of a defective part or process can save the cost of further work on the item.

In imposing quality control, managers should begin by asking whether they expect to examine 100 percent of the items or whether a sample can be used. The inspection of each and every item makes sense if the cost of continuous evaluation is very low or if the consequences of a statistical error are very high (as in the manufacture of a drug used in open-heart surgery). Statistical samples are usually less costly, and sometimes they are the only viable option. For example, if the quality test destroys the product— as happens with bombs or flash bulbs—then sampling has to be utilized.

acceptance sampling
A quality control procedure in which a sample is taken and a decision to accept or reject a whole lot is based on a calculation of sample risk error.

process control
A quality control procedure in which sampling is done during the transformation process to determine whether the process itself is under control.

attribute sampling
A quality control technique that classifies items as acceptable or unacceptable on the basis of a comparison to a standard.

variable sampling
A quality control technique in which a measurement is taken to determine how much an item varies from the standard.

There are two categories of statistical quality control procedures: acceptance sampling and process control. **Acceptance sampling** refers to the evaluation of purchased or manufactured materials or products that already exist. A sample is taken, then the decision to accept or reject the whole lot is based on a calculation of sample risk error. **Process control** refers to sampling items during the transformation process to see whether the transformation process itself is under control. For example, a process control procedure at Coca-Cola would be able to detect if a bottling machine was out of adjustment because it was filling twenty-six ounce bottles with only twenty-three ounces of soda. Managers could then stop the process and readjust the machine.

A final consideration in quality control relates to whether the test is done by examining attributes or variables. The inspection and classification of items as acceptable or unacceptable is called **attribute sampling.** This is the way paint color and potato chips are evaluated. An inspector compares the items against some standard and rates their quality as acceptable or not acceptable. In contrast, **variable sampling** involves taking a measurement to determine how much an item varies from the standard. It involves a range rather than a dichotomy. Management typically identifies the standard and an acceptable deviation. Any sample that measures within the range is accepted, and those outside are rejected. Inland Steel might test some steel bar to see whether the average breaking strength is between 120 and 140 pounds per square inch. If it is not, the cause is investigated, and corrective action is initiated.

Current Issues in Operations Management

Capitalizing on new technology! Successfully implementing TQM! Reducing inventories! Utilizing flexibility and speed as competitive advantages! These issues currently top management's list for improving operations productivity. Because managers consider them to be essential for making products and services competitive in world markets, we review each of them in this section.

Technology and Product Development

Today's competitive marketplace has put tremendous pressure on manufacturers to deliver products with high quality and low cost and to significantly reduce time to market. Even if you have the proverbial "better mousetrap," customers won't be beating a path to your door if your competitor develops a mousetrap that is almost as good but is in stores a year or two ahead of yours. Two key ingredients to successfully accelerating the product-development process are organizational commitment to improving the development cycle and investment in the technology to make it happen.

computer-integrated manufacturing (CIM)

Combines the organization's strategic business plan and manufacturing plan with state-of-the-art computer applications.

One of the most effective tools that manufacturers have in meeting the time-to-market challenge is **computer-integrated manufacturing (CIM).** This brings together the organization's stratgic business plan and manufacturing plan with state-of-the-art computer applications.[25] The technologies of computer-aided design (CAD) and computer-aided manufacturing (CAM) typically are the basis for CIM.

CAD essentially has made manual drafting obsolete. Using computers to visually display graphics, CAD enables engineers to develop new product designs in about half the time required for manual drafting. Eagle Engine Manufacturing, for instance, used its CAD system to design a new race-car engine in nine months instead of the traditional two-plus years.[26]

CAM relies on computers to guide and control the manufacturing process. Numerically controlled programs can direct machines to cut patterns, shape parts, assemble units, and perform other complicated tasks.

In the not-too-distant future, CIM will permit the entire manufacturing process to be viewed as a continuum. Every step—from order entry to order shipping—will be expressed as data and computerized. It will allow management to respond rapidly to changing markets. It will give firms the ability to test hundreds of design changes in hours rather than months and then provide the flexibility to produce multiple variations of products efficiently in lot sizes as small as one or two. When manufacturing is computer-integrated, for example, it is no longer necessary to stop the assembly line and spend valuable time changing dies and equipment in order to produce a new or nonstandard product. A single change in the computer program—which can be done in seconds—immediately realigns the manufacturing process.

In the textile industry, computer-aided design (CAD) allows manufacturers to create and view cloth patterns in a fraction of the time it would have taken to prepare a preproduction sample for customer inspection.

THE CHANGING FACE OF MANAGEMENT PRACTICE

Small is Beautiful

"Bigger is better" was the rallying cry of management in the 1970s and 1980s. In the 1990s, that has been replaced by "small is beautiful."[27]

Managers long assumed that increases in size led to lower costs. This is what economists call "economies of scale." Larger size, the theory states, allows for an organization to distribute its fixed costs over more units of production, hence larger organizations have lower average costs. This belief led to the creation of large banks, huge steel mills, one-stop-shopping retail stores, and even mega-universities. But in recent years, something seemed to go wrong with the economies-of-scale argument. Big banks such as Citicorp and BankAmerica have been outperformed by smaller regional banks. Mini steel mills, run by companies such as Nucor and Chaparral, have become more efficient than the big ones operated by Bethlehem and U.S. Steel. Small niche retailers are grabbing market share from Sears and J.C. Penneys. And taxpayers are increasingly questioning whether small state colleges aren't doing a better job teaching students than the large research universities.

Why are smaller organizations increasingly able to outperform their larger rivals? They're flatter and often have less overhead. Smaller organizations are often more responsive and can react more quickly to changes in the market. Because they target narrower market segments, they can gain economies through specialization. Most importantly, however, technology now allows the little guys to do what only the big guys could do before. For an investment of less than $25,000, small firms can do computer-aided design. Similarly, use of computer-linked networks allows small companies to instantaneously coordinate with outside suppliers who provide the small firm with design, manufacturing, and sales services.

Implementing TQM Successfully

The list of organizations that have implemented TQM is long and impressive. It includes firms such as Motorola, Federal Express, Xerox, and IBM. In addition, public-sector organizations have recently gotten the message. Beginning with the class of '94, each high school graduate of the Los Angeles Unified School District will come with a written warranty assuring companies that he or she has the basic skills needed to enter the work force.[28] If an employer is not satisfied, the school district will provide remedial training at the district's expense. The governor of Ohio has created a statewide quality council to put TQM concepts to work throughout all state agencies.[29] Even the U.S. federal government is beginning to implement TQM.[30] A recent General Accounting Office study reports that 68 percent of the government's 2800 installations now use TQM.

Unfortunately, not all TQM efforts have been successful. A study of 584 companies in the United States, Canada, Germany, and Japan provides some important insights into factors that may hinder TQM effectiveness.[31] Consistent with the contingency approach to management, the survey found that the successful application of certain TQM concepts—including teams, benchmarking, training efforts, and empowering employees—depends on the company's current performance. The following suggestions highlight the study's recommendations for lower-, medium-, and higher-performing firms:[32]

The Stew Leonards, Jr. and Sr., understand that quality begins and ends with satisfying the customer. This five-ton piece of granite, with the company's motto, stands outside their monstrous Norwalk, Connecticut, food store. By listening to the customer, the Leonards have sales of $115 million a year and employ 650 people at this one store alone.

just-in-time (JIT) inventory system

A system in which inventory items arrive when they are needed in the production process instead of being stored in stock.

kanban

The Japanese name for a just-in-time inventory system.

For Lower-Performing Firms   Increase training of all types. Emphasize teams across and within departments. The formation of teams to help identify and solve small problems can help lower-performing companies as they begin their quality-improvement efforts. But teams lose their value and can distract from broader strategic issues once corporate performance improves. Don't use benchmarking because it tends to create unreasonable goals and thus can frustrate quality efforts. And don't empower employees yet because they usually don't have the training to make empowerment work.

For Medium-Performing Firms   Simplify corporate processes such as design and focus training on problem solving.

For Higher-Performing Firms   Use benchmarking to identify new processes, product, and services. Encourage companywide quality meetings. Actively disburse decision-making power by empowering employees. Don't increase departmental teams because this tends to inhibit cooperation across functions.

While the above contingency suggestions provide important limitations for the implementation of TQM, the survey also found some practices that tended to be universally effective. These included explaining the organization's strategy to all employees, customers, and suppliers; improving and simplifying operations and development processes; and shortening the time it takes from the design to the delivery of a product.

Reducing Inventories

A major portion of many companies' assets is tied up in inventories. For instance, General Electric recently reported its inventory assets at $7.4 billion and Boeing's inventory exceeds $13 billion.[33] Firms that can significantly cut their inventories of raw materials and of in-process and finished goods can reduce costs and improve their efficiency.

This fact has not been lost on management. In recent years, U.S. managers have been seeking ways to manage inventories better. On the output side, managers have been improving the information link between internal manufacturing schedules and forecasted customer demand. Marketing personnel are being increasingly relied on to provide accurate, up-to-date information on future sales. This is then being coordinated with operating systems data to get a better match between what is produced and what the customers want. Manufacturing resource planning systems are particularly well suited to this function. On the input side, they have been experimenting with another technique widely used in Japan: **just-in-time (JIT) inventory systems.**[34] This is a system in which inventory items arrive when they are needed in the production process instead of being stored in stock.

In Japan, JIT systems are called **kanban.** The derivation of the word gets to the essence of the just-in-time concept. *Kanban* is Japanese for "card" or "sign." Japanese suppliers ship parts to manufacturers in containers. Each container has a card, or kanban, slipped into a side pocket. When a production worker opens a container, he or she takes out the card and sends it back to the supplier. That initiates the shipping of a second container of parts that, ideally, reaches the production worker just as the last part in the first container is being used up. The ultimate goal of a JIT inventory system is to eliminate raw material inventories by coordinating production and supply deliveries precisely. When the system works as designed, it results in a number of positive benefits for a manufacturer: reduced inventories, reduced setup time, better work flow, shorter manufacturing time, less space consumption, and even higher quality. Of course, suppliers who can be depended on to deliver quality

JIT: Cost-Savings for Whom?

Just-in-time inventory systems reduce costs and increase efficiency for organizations that apply them. But what about the effect of these systems on suppliers? If Firestone builds a tire plant in the Detroit area to serve Chrysler better and to permit just-in-time deliveries to Chrysler, does Firestone benefit? Not if it has to stockpile an extensive tire inventory to meet Chrysler's needs.

An often overlooked side-effect of a JIT system is the burden it can place on suppliers. At the extreme, it can be argued that a JIT system is a self-serving device that merely pushes the costs and inefficiencies of carrying inventory back onto suppliers. If Chrysler's management demands that, to keep Chrysler as a customer, Firestone must be able to make daily deliveries of precisely the number and type of tires that Chrysler needs for each day's production, what options does Firestone have? It can impose JIT requirements on its own suppliers or it can manufacture for inventory and draw on those inventories, as needed, to meet Chrysler's demands.

One way out of this conundrum is for all firms in the supply chain to practice JIT. But that's unusual. In practice, companies that use JIT merely load their inventory problems onto the backs of their suppliers. Is that ethical? Are large companies that practice JIT abusing their power by exploiting suppliers who want and need their business? What do *you* think?

---

materials on time must be found. Because there are no inventories, there is no slack in the system to absorb defective materials or delays in shipment.

An illustration of JIT's benefits can be seen at Walgreen Laboratories, a manufacturer of health and beauty products for the Walgreen drugstore chain.[35] The firm calculated the cost of carrying and managing its inventory at about 25 percent of its total inventory costs. By introducing JIT, it cut its inventory levels by about $8 million. Of course, these benefits required additional work on the part of Walgreen's management. For instance, to allow its suppliers to plan their own production schedules, Walgreen had to project its supply needs six months in advance and commit itself to firm delivery dates weeks ahead of time.

A JIT system isn't for every manufacturer.[36] It requires that suppliers be located in close proximity to the manufacturer's production facility and that suppliers be capable of providing consistently defect-free materials. Such a system also requires reliable transportation links between suppliers and manufacturer; efficient receiving, handling, and distribution of materials; and precisely tuned production planning. Where these conditions can be met, JIT can help management to reduce inventory costs.

Flexibility as a Competitive Advantage

In today's changing world of business, firms that can't adjust rapidly won't survive. This is putting a premium on developing manufacturing flexibility.[37] As a result, many organizations are developing flexible manufacturing systems.[38]

They look like something out of a science-fiction movie in which remote-controlled carts deliver a basic casting to a computerized machining center. With

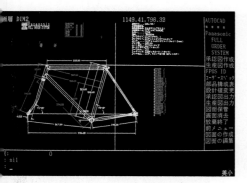

Using computer-aided design, Panasonic is able to produce separate blueprints for each bicycle it manufactures.

flexible manufacturing systems

Systems in which custom-made products can be mass produced by means of computer-aided design, engineering, and manufacturing.

robots positioning and repositioning the casting, the machining center calls upon its hundreds of tools to perform varying operations that turn the casting into a finished part. Completed parts, each a bit different from the others, are finished at a rate of one every ninety seconds. Neither skilled machinists nor conventional machine tools are used. Nor are there any costly delays for changing dies or tools in this factory. A single machine can make dozens or even hundreds of different parts in any order management wants.

The unique characteristic of **flexible manufacturing systems** is that by integrating computer-aided design, engineering, and manufacturing, they can produce low-volume, custom products at a cost comparable to what had been possible only through mass production. Flexible manufacturing systems are repealing the laws of economies of scale. Management no longer has to mass produce thousands of identical products to achieve low per-unit production costs. With a flexible manufacturing system, when management wants to produce a new part, it doesn't change machines—it just changes the computer program.

Some automated plants can build a wide variety of flawless products and switch from one product to another on cue from a central computer. John Deere, for instance, has a $1.5 billion automated factory that can turn out ten basic tractor models with as many as 3,000 options without plant shutdowns for retooling. These new flexible-factories are also proving to be cost effective. IBM's automated plant in Austin, Texas, can produce a laptop computer in less than two minutes without the help of a single worker. IBM's management has found the automated plant to be 75 percent more efficient than a conventional system.[39] National Bicycle Industrial Co., which sells its bikes under the Panasonic brand, uses flexible manufacturing to produce any of 11,231,862 variations on eighteen models of racing, road, and mountain bikes in 199 color patterns and an almost unlimited number of sizes.[40]

Speed as a Competitive Advantage

For years we have heard that on the highway, speed kills. Managers are now learning that the same principle works in business: Speed kills, only this time it's the competition's speed.[41] By quickly developing, making, and distributing products and services, organizations can gain a competitive advantage. Just as customers may select one organization over another because its products or services are less expensive, uniquely designed, or of superior quality, customers also choose organizations because they can get the product or service they want fast. In essence, Domino's has created a billion-dollar business by using speed as a competitive advantage, guaranteeing delivery of its pizzas in thirty minutes or less.

A number of companies have made incredible improvements in the time it takes them to design and produce their products.[42] AT&T used to need two years to design a new phone. Now it does the job in one year. General Electric used to take three weeks after an order to deliver a custom-made industrial circuit-breaker box. They've cut that down to three *days*. Kingston Technology Corp., founded in 1987, has become one of the fastest-growing companies in America by capitalizing on speed. The firm designs and manufactures memory upgrades for computers. In a market where customers want their upgrades yesterday, Kingston has achieved a remarkable 45 percent market share by being able to fill orders the same day they are received while its competitors continue to take four to six weeks. These firms and many others are cutting red tape; flattening their organization structures; adding cross-functional teams; redesigning their distribution chains; and using JIT, CIM, and flexible manufacturing systems to speed up their operations and put increased pressure on their competitors.

Summary

This summary is organized by the chapter-opening learning objectives found on page 625.

1. The transformation process is the essence of operations management. Operations management takes inputs, including people and materials, and then acts on them by transforming them into finished goods and services. This applies in service organizations as well as in manufacturing firms.

2. United States managers are increasingly concerned with improving productivity. How people are integrated into the overall operations system determines how productive an organization will be. Factors such as the size and layout of operating facilities, capacity utilization, inventory usage, and maintenance controls are operations management concepts that have a critical bearing on overall productivity.

3. A manufacturing focus to strategy pushes important production decisions to the top of the organization. It recognizes that an organization's overall strategy should directly reflect its manufacturing capabilities and limitations and should include operations objectives and strategies.

4. Four key decisions—capacity, location, process, and layout—provide the long-term strategic direction for operations planning. They determine the proper size of an operating system, the location of physical facilities, the best methods for transforming inputs into outputs, and the most efficient layout of equipment and work stations.

5. The three decisions that make up the tactical operations plans are the aggregate plan, the master schedule, and the material requirements plan. The aggregate plan determines the overall production plan, the master schedule determines how many units of each product will be produced, and the material requirements plan determines what materials are needed to satisfy the master schedule.

6. The economic order quantity model balances the costs of ordering and carrying inventory. To calculate the optimal order quantity, you need to know the forecasted demand for an item during a specific period, the cost of placing each order, the value or purchase price of the item, and the carrying cost of maintaining the total inventory.

7. The three types of maintenance control are preventive, remedial, and conditional. Preventive maintenance is performed before a breakdown occurs. Remedial maintenance is performed when the equipment breaks down. Conditional maintenance is a response to an inspection.

8. Evidence demonstrates that the application of certain TQM concepts should reflect whether the organization is a low, medium, or high performer. Low-performing firms, for instance, should emphasize team creation and downplay benchmarking and empowerment. High-performing firms, on the other hand, should encourage benchmarking and empowerment and deemphasize departmental teams.

9. Just-in-time inventory systems seek to reduce inventories, reduce setup time, improve work flow, cut manufacturing time, reduce space consumption, and raise the quality of production by coordinating the arrival of inventory items to their demand in the production process. However, they require precise coordination; if this is lacking, they can threaten the smooth, continuous operation of a production system.

10. A flexible manufacturing system can give an organization a competitive advantage by allowing it to produce a wider variety of products, at a lower cost, and in considerably less time than the competition.

Review Questions

1. What is the operations system?
2. What does W. Edwards Deming have to say about increasing productivity?
3. What is the role of critical contingencies in facilities location planning?
4. Contrast process, product, and fixed-position layouts.
5. How is cost control transferred from accountants to managers?
6. Contrast acceptance sampling and process control.
7. What is the ABC system? Why is it a contingency approach to inventory control?
8. How do CAD and CAM speed the product-development process?
9. Explain why benchmarking is inappropriate in low-performing firms.
10. What TQM practices are universally effective despite contingencies?

Discussion Questions

1. How might operations management apply to other managerial functions besides control? Discuss.
2. Demonstrate how capacity, facilities location, process, and facilities layout planning concepts can apply to a service organization.
3. Would you see any potential problems with implementing both CIM and TQM in the same organization? Discuss.
4. We have seen that increasing productivity is a concern of service organizations, but what about individuals? In what ways could you improve your own productivity?

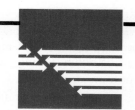

SELF-ASSESSMENT EXERCISE

How's Your Knowledge of Japanese Manufacturing?

The following questions test your awareness of Japanese business and manufacturing practices:

1. In the typical large Japanese company, how many employee suggestions for improvement of operations would there be in a year?
   a. 1000
   b. 10,000
   c. 100,000
   d. a million
   e. 10 million
2. Compared to the United States, Japan has _____ as many industrial robots in operation.
   a. half
   b. the same number
   c. twice
   d. five times
   e. ten times

3. The term *kaizen* refers to:
   a. an inventory control system
   b. continuous improvement
   c. highest quality
   d. a decision-making process
   e. ethnocentric policies

4. The term *kanban* refers to:
   a. an inventory control system
   b. continuous improvement
   c. highest quality
   d. a decision-making process
   e. ethnocentric policies

5. Which group is discriminated against in Japanese companies?
   a. Younger workers
   b. All workers with children
   c. Elderly workers
   d. Women
   e. None of the above

6. A fishbone diagram most directly addresses:
   a. causes of problems
   b. cost controls
   c. scrap reduction planning
   d. process planning
   e. facilities layout planning

7. The typical career path in a Japanese manufacturing company emphasizes:
   a. finance experience
   b. manufacturing experience
   c. sales experience
   d. any specialization
   e. generalization

8. A new hiree in a Japanese company would typically expect to receive his or her first promotion in:
   a. six months
   b. one year
   c. two years
   d. five years
   e. ten years

9. Which one of the following *best* describes Japanese decision making?
   a. the manager makes the decision and tells his subordinates
   b. the manager makes the decision and then gets input from all employees affected by the decision before implementing it
   c. the manager asks for input from all affected employees before making a decision
   d. the manager and his employees share in making the decision equally
   e. the manager delegates the decision completely to his or her employees

10. Which of the following statements is true about the Japanese government's role in business:
    a. it pursues a laissez faire policy
    b. it owns most of the major industries
    c. it provides subsidies and incentives to certain firms
    d. the key executives in most Japanese corporations are political appointees
    e. it regularly appropriates the assets of companies that make too much profit

Turn to page SK-8 for scoring directions and key.

FOR YOUR IMMEDIATE ACTION

◄‖‖ **WESTWOOD TRAVEL SERVICES**

To: Ron Crawford, Director of Operations
From: Anne Mendales, President
Subject: Applying TQM to our travel business

I just finished reading a fascinating book, *Total Quality Management in the Department of Defense* (by Jack Strickland and Peter Angiola; U.S. Government Printing Office, 1989). It made me realize that everything we read about TQM in manufacturing industries such as autos and computers should be applicable to service businesses like ours.

As you know, we've gone from one small agency to five offices and nearly forty employees by responding to the needs of the business traveler. However, in the last six months, we've lost several valuable clients to more aggressive competitors. Our competition, especially Chapman Travel and the American Express agency, are doing a better job at meeting customers' needs.

TQM might be able to help us. I'd like you to think about how we might be able to implement TQM in our travel agencies. Please prepare an analysis describing how we could apply the concepts of continuous process improvement, customer focus, benchmarking, training, teamwork, and empowerment to our travel business to make us more competitive.

This is a fictionalized account of a potentially real management issue. It is meant for academic purposes only and is not meant to reflect either positively or negatively on Westwood Travel Services or any of its employees.

CASE APPLICATION

Unimation and the Collapse of the U.S. Robot Industry

This is the story of how a U.S.-owned company—once the dominant player in a potentially huge market—failed and how the Japanese filled its void.

In the early 1980s, experts were predicting that robot sales in the United States would reach $2 billion by 1990. In actuality, they achieved only a small fraction of that goal. What happened? Such Japanese companies as Fanuc and Kawasaki were able to build better robots and to convince their homeland corporations of the value-added provided by robots. In contrast, the U.S. variety of robots were seen by most U.S. managers as novelties with serious design flaws.

Unimation was the major U.S. player in the robot market. Unimation's founder, Joseph Engleberger, essentially invented the industrial robot in 1967. In 1983, Westinghouse Electric Corp. bought Unimation with the intention of capitalizing on the perceived growing demand for robots. At the time of the purchase, there were sixty-two U.S. companies in the robot business—but Unimation dominated with 40 percent of the domestic market.

Unimation made a major strategic mistake in the early 1980s. In order to best Japanese competitors, Unimation had to excel in electrically driven gears and control systems. But Unimation's management stayed with their company's hydraulic robots, which moved their arms under fluid pressures. They sold for less than electric robots—$48,000 average versus more than $70,000 for the electric variety—which management thought gave it an advantage. But, ironically, Unimation was making big money off their robot's basic flaw—they leaked oil. Instead of trying to fix this design problem, they sold expensive drip pans. For instance, Ford gave Unimation an order for $5 million of robots that included $160,000 for drip pans. Unimation was turning a problem into a profit, which might have worked out all right if they didn't face competitors who had superior products.

The Japanese were perfecting electric robots. While it was true that they initially cost more, their annual operating cost was half of the hydraulic robots. And Unimation's entrepreneurial-type people were having terrific difficulties blending into Westinghouse's bureaucracy. Many of Unimation's top software programmers quit. In 1985, Unimation's sales plummeted 40 percent. It was now losing $15 million to $20 million a year—versus earnings of $7 million before it was acquired by Westinghouse.

The final nails in Unimation's coffin came from its Japanese competitors who understood that robots should be simplified and that robots were not mere replacements of people. Unimation's engineers kept making their robots more complicated while their Japanese counterparts looked for ways to reduce parts and make the robots simpler and less likely to break down. Additionally, the Japanese understood that robots had to be fully integrated into the manufacturing process. While Japanese robot makers helped customers redesign products and processes to make them "robot-friendly," Unimation was shipping robots out as a commodity.

Westinghouse sold the last parts of Unimation to a Swiss firm in 1987. The last major U.S. robot manufacturer, Cincinnati Milacron, left the business in 1990. The industrial robot business is now nonexistent in the United States. Robots in GM, Chrysler, IBM, and other U.S. manufacturing plants are made in places such as Switzerland and Japan. And, not surprisingly, many manufacturers in the United States are robot-shy, though such is not the case in Japan.

Questions

1. What implications can you draw from this case regarding the commercialization of new technology?

2. Do you think Unimation would have succeeded if it had stayed independent? If it had established a joint-venture with a Japanese robot manufacturer?

3. Compare Unimation and its Japanese competitors in terms of TQM practices.

4. Do you think that reluctance toward robots in the United States is indicative of the past U.S. reluctance to adopt other Japanese manufacturing practices? Explain.

Source: Based on Amal Kumar Naj, "How U.S. Robots Lost the Market to Japan in Factory Automation," *Wall Street Journal,* November 6, 1990, p. A1.

VIDEO CASE

Harley-Davidson

In the mid-1970s, America was going wild over motorcycles. Harley-Davidson, then owned by AMF Corp., responded by nearly tripling production to 75,000 units annually over a four-year period. Along with this growth, however, came problems. Engineering and design of Harleys had become dated. Quality had deteriorated so much that more than half the cycles coming off the assembly line had missing parts, and dealers had to fix them before they could be sold. Harleys leaked oil, vibrated badly, and couldn't match the performance of the flawlessly built Japanese bikes. Hardcore Harley enthusiasts were willing to tolerate these inconveniences, but newcomers had no such devotion and bought Japanese bikes.

In 1973, Harley had 75 percent of the super-heavyweight market. By 1980, its market share had plummeted to less than 25 percent. AMF was fast losing confidence in Harley and sold the company in 1981 to a group of Harley executives.

Harley's new owner-managers introduced a number of new products, redesigned and updated their basic product line, and greatly improved the company's marketing programs. However, none of these actions would have meant much if Harley hadn't dramatically revised its production and operations practices. The new managers visited Honda's assembly plant in Marysville, Ohio and realized what they were up against. In response, they initiated a number of changes on Harley's production floor. A new inventory system was introduced that eliminated the mountains of costly inventory parts. Management redesigned the entire production system, closely involving employees in planning and working out the details. Workers were taught statistical techniques for monitoring and controlling the quality of their own work. Harley's management even worked with its suppliers—as has long been done by Japanese manufacturers—to help them adopt the same efficiency and quality-improvement techniques that Harley had instituted in its plants.

Harley's management succeeded in pulling off one of America's most celebrated turnarounds. On the verge of bankruptcy in the early 1980s, ten years later Harley's share of the U.S. super-heavyweight market was almost 65 percent. The company was losing money in 1982, but now it's highly profitable.

Questions

1. What TQM concepts did Harley utilize as part of its turnaround?

2. What specific types of controls did Harley-Davidson implement? How do you think each of these controls contributed to Harley's turnaround?

3. What lessons can be drawn from Harley that might help a company, like General Motors, that has seen its market share eroded?

Source: "On the Road Again," *ABC News 20/20,* January 25, 1991.

INTEGRATIVE EXERCISE FOR PART VI

Paper Plane Corporation

PURPOSE

1. To integrate the management functions.
2. To apply planning and control concepts specifically to improve organizational performance.

REQUIRED KNOWLEDGE

1. Planning, organizing, and controlling concepts.

TIME REQUIRED

Approximately one hour.

INSTRUCTIONS

Any number of groups of six participants each are used in this exercise. These groups may be directed simultaneously in the same room. Each person should have assembly instructions (Figure VI–1) and a summary sheet, plus ample stacks of paper (8-1/2 by 11 inches). The physical setting should be a room that is large enough that individual groups of six can work without interference from other groups. A working space should be provided for each group.

- The participants are doing an exercise in production methodology.
- Each group must work independently of the other groups.
- Each group will choose a manager and an inspector, and the remaining participants will be employees.
- The objective is to make paper airplanes in the most profitable manner possible.

- The facilitator will give the signal to start. This is a ten-minute, timed event utilizing competition among the groups.
- After the first round, each group should report its production and profits to the entire group. Each group reports the manner in which it planned, organized, and controlled for the production of the paper airplanes.
- This same procedure is followed for as many rounds as there is time.

Your group is the complete work force for Paper Plane Corporation. Established in 1943, Paper Plane has led the market in paper plane production. Currently under new management, the company is contracting to make aircraft for the U.S. Air Force. You must establish a plan and organization to produce these aircraft. You must make your contract with the Air Force under the following conditions:

1. The Air Force will pay $20,000 per airplane.
2. The aircraft must pass a strict inspection.
3. A penalty of $25,000 per airplane will be subtracted for failure to meet the production requirements.
4. Labor and other overhead will be computed at $300,000.
5. Cost of materials will be $3,000 per bid plane. If you bid for ten but make only eight, you must pay the cost of materials for those you failed to make or that did not pass inspection.

FIGURE VI–1
Paper Plane Corporation:
Data Sheet

Instructions for aircraft assembly

 Step 1: Take a sheet of paper and fold it in half, then open it back up.

 Step 4: Fold in half.

 Step 2: Fold upper corners in the middle.

 Step 5: Fold both wings down.
Step 6: Fold tail fins up.

 Step 3: Fold the corners to the middle again.

 Completed aircraft

Summary Sheet

Round 1:
Bid: _____ Aircraft @ $20,000.00 per
aircraft = _____
Results: _____ Aircraft @ $20,000.00 per
aircraft = _____
Less: $300,000.000 overhead
_____ × $3,000 cost of raw
materials
_____ × $25,000 penalty
Profit: _____

Round 2:
Bid: _____ Aircraft @ $20,000.00 per
aircraft = _____
Results: _____ Aircraft @ $20,000.00 per
aircraft = _____
Less: $300,000.00 overhead
_____ × $3,000 cost of raw
materials
_____ × $25,000 penalty
Profit: _____

Round 3:
Bid: _____ Aircraft @ $20,000.00 per
aircraft = _____
Results: _____ Aircraft @ $20,000.00 per
aircraft = _____
Less: $300,000.00 overhead
_____ × $30,000 cost of raw
materials
_____ × $25,000 penalty
Profit: _____

Source: Based on an exercise in James H. Donnelly, Jr., James L. Gibson, and John M. Ivancevich, *Fundamentals of Management,* 8th ed. (Plano, Texas: Business Publications, Inc., 1992), pp. 285–89. With permission.

INTEGRATIVE CASE FOR PART VI

CASUAL TOGS

Casual Togs is a twenty-year old firm producing moderately-priced women's apparel. About 80 percent of production is sold to large and middle-sized department stores in cities throughout the country. The remaining 20 percent is sold to small women's specialty shops. All its clothes carry the firm's well-known brand label.

Cy Geldmark, the company's owner and principal stockholder, is an entrepreneur. Geldmark served a long apprenticeship in the New York garment district and saved part of his meager wages until he could open his own firm, staffed primarily with relatives and friends. An innovator, Geldmark pioneered in the "mix and/or match" coordinate idea of fashion ensembles. Designers with trend-setting styles and above average quality (considering the semi-mass-production methods employed) helped propel Casual Togs to a prominent position in the industry.

However, the mix-and-match coordinate idea was not patented, and intense fashion competition has now developed from larger firms as well as from new, smaller companies with fresh fashion ideas. In Geldmark's words, price competition is "deadly." The company has rapidly expanded in the last five years, setting up production plants in eight southern states to capitalize on low wage rates in these areas.

All facilities in these states are leased. Notwithstanding the use of the latest in large-capacity cutters and high-speed sewing machines, production hinges on a great expenditure of careful, personal effort by the individual worker. Many quality checks are necessary before a garment is finished.

In an attempt to coordinate production and delivery, the company is constructing a new multi-million-dollar central distribution plant at the present home office location, where all administrative and some production functions are performed. All production runs will be shipped to this new facility and then dispatched by a computer-programmed delivery-inventory scheduling method. This facility is planned to help cope with an increasingly serious problem of merchandise returned from customers who refuse acceptance because delivery is later than promised.

The industry is characterized by five distinct selling fashion "seasons"; consequently garments must be ordered, produced, and delivered within a relatively short time period. This five-season cycle produces unusual production and forecasting problems. Based on pilot sales during the first two weeks of each season, forecasts are developed regarding the quantity and styles to be produced for the entire season. Once the bolts of cloth are cut into a particular season's patterns, there is no turning back. If pilot sales are not indicative of the rest of the season or if the sales forecast is in error, the company is saddled with stock that can be disposed of only through "off-price" outlets, usually at a loss.

In an effort to increase the accuracy of sales forecasting and to pinpoint specific reasons for late deliveries, Geldmark instituted a computer printout of each day's sales, as reported by telephone by field salesmen. This printout was, initially, distributed to the president, the vice-president of sales, the sales forecast manager, the treasurer, the production manager, and the eight regional sales managers. All of these people were located at the firm's headquarters offices. The printout was voluminous, often running one hundred or more pages.

Geldmark relied a great deal on his "feel of the situation" for making decisions. Although he made all final important operating and policy decisions, he said that all department heads should feel free to act as "you see fit"; he said that he would back any decision made without consultation with him. Despite Geldmark's exhortations that he need not be consulted, almost all vice-presidents and departmental managers conferred daily with him, usually regarding the progress of the then current fashion season's products. During each fashion season many style modifications and quantity level changes were made. With rare exceptions Geldmark made all important daily decisions on these matters.

These daily decision sessions were marked by emotional outbursts by various management personnel. The meetings were informal and not scheduled, and different groups would meet at different times with Geldmark. The groups were not formal or even based on functional problem lines. If individuals felt that a daily printout indicated change "X," regardless of whether or not it affected their department, they would go to the president asking that the change be effected.

If another department manager or even a vice-president were present and disagreed, inevitably a shouting match developed in the president's office. Usually Geldmark remained impassive during these interchanges, giving his decision after all participants had finished.

Some management personnel said that Geldmark was "too lenient" and should curb these emotionally charged sessions because they were disruptive and led to erroneous decisions. These same critics pointed to Geldmark's reputation as an easy mark for suppliers, e.g., if a supplier had some previous tie from the old days or was remotely related to someone in Geldmark's family, he would be assured of at least some orders despite the fact that his prices were higher than those of competing suppliers.

For many years Geldmark's chief source of sales data and forecast was Andy Johnson, sales forecast-budget manager. Johnson prepared daily, hand-written recaps from telephone reports in the earlier years and from the printout in more recent years. Using intuition and a very thorough knowledge of the garment industry, Johnson would prepare the season's forecasts and modify them as the actual sales started coming in.

Johnson was given one new man to help with sales forecasts and budgets; the new man had an M.B.A. and was trained in statistical analysis. Johnson held a bachelor's degree in business. Smith, the new man, suggested to Johnson several new methods of collating and analyzing the daily printout, who abruptly rejected the ideas, saying, "Cy isn't used to getting data in that form; he would be confused by a change."

As the daily printout began to be more detailed and more widely distributed, Johnson became more critical of them than usual. He said that they didn't "really" show what styles were leading and that there were many errors. Johnson quoted personal conversations with field salesmen to prove his points. When Smith cited several instances in which, on the recap, Johnson was combining several new styles in what had previously been one category, Johnson replied that he was using horse sense to report data in a way that Geldmark and others would best understand.

The problem of returns was now most acute; on the average 40 percent of all shipments were being returned. Although all management personnel agreed that the reason for returns was late delivery, there was no agreement as to what caused the late deliveries. Some managers argued that forecasting by style line was inaccurate and resulted in erroneous production scheduling; others said that there was no coordination between the nine production centers and the shipping department, which was located at the home office site.

Still others said that shipping and/or production methods were not efficient. The production manager said that there was a disparity between the delivery dates given by customers and those on the salesman's order, which served as the basis of a production run. The sales manager maintained that poor quality was the real reason for returns; customers did not want to become embroiled in arguments with home office personnel over quality questions and therefore they wrote "late delivery" on sub-standard merchandise because it was simpler.

In an effort to solve the dilemma, Geldmark hired an experienced market analyst who had a strong computer-oriented background, Stan Levine. Levine was given a private office and the authority to effect any changes he deemed necessary. Several events happened immediately. A supplemental recap of the printout was published every day by Levine—in addition to Johnson's hand-written recap; the printout format was changed. Sol Green, manager of internal accounting and sales, objected strongly to the new format, saying that it did not provide accounting with the categorizations necessary for their work. Johnson referred to Levine as "this egotistical, snot-nosed kid."

At this same time, several new designers were hired, salesmen's commissions schedules were changed, many regional vice-presidents were put on the road "temporarily," and Johnson, backed by Geldmark, cut all department budgets by 15 percent (the company was in the middle of a twelve-month budget period).

Approximately four weeks after all of these changes had occurred, problems continued to arise. Returns had increased to an even higher level and many old customers had stopped ordering, saying that poor quality and late deliveries made Casual Togs too undependable. Performance of the nine plant centers fell, on the average 15 percent under previously established production goals. In addition, two of the new designers resigned. Johnson, Green and Levine would not speak to each other; Johnson began distributing two daily sales recap reports to a select group of top managers; and the computer services department complained directly to Geldmark that their new work load was too great because Levine now required them to produce a daily selling forecast, by week, month, and season.

1. What do you see as Cy Geldmark's biggest control problem at Casual Togs? What should Geldmark's focus of control be?

2. What organizational communication problems exist at Casual Togs?

3. How could Casual Togs benefit from using MIS?

In light of the general resistance to Stan Levine's changes, what would Geldmark have to do to implement MIS?

4. Do you think TQM would work at Casual Togs? If so, how would it have to be implemented? If not, why?

5. Could Casual Togs use JIT to help alleviate its returns problems? What other possible inventory controls could the company use?

6. "Responsibility for control ultimately rests on the shoulders of the head of an organization." Do you agree or disagree with this statement? How does this relate to Cy Geldmark?

Source: Adapted from Stephen J. Carroll, *Cases on Management* (Dubuque, Iowa: Kendall/Hunt, 1989), pp. 16–19. With permission.

SCORING KEYS FOR SELF-ASSESSMENT EXERCISES

Chapter 1: How Strong Is Your Motivation to Manage in a Large Organization?

Total your circled numbers. Your score will fall somewhere between 7 and 49. Arbitrary norms for comparison are: Scores of 7 to 21 = relatively low motivation to manage; 22–34 = moderate; 35–49 = relatively high.

Chapter 2: Are You the Quantitative Type?

Using the ratings (one through four) that you assigned to each of the fifteen items, add up your points. You can assess your level of math anxiety by comparing your scores to the following:

15–25 points = Math secure
26–40 points = Math wary
41–45 points = Math shy
46–60 points = Math anxious

Business students tend to score low (relatively math secure) on this exercise. This is probably due, in part, to self-selection. The fact that accounting, finance, statistics, and other quantitative courses are requirements for degrees in business is likely to discourage individuals with high math anxiety to pursue these majors.

Chapter 3: What Kind of Organizational Culture Fits You Best?

For items 5, 6, 7, and 9, score as follows:

Strongly agree	= +2
Agree	= +1
Uncertain	= 0
Disagree	= −1
Strongly disagree	= −2

For items 1, 2, 3, 4, 8, and 10, reverse the score (Strongly agree = −2, and so on). Add up your total. Your score will fall somewhere between +20 and −20.

What does your score mean? The higher your score (positive), the more comfortable you'll be in a formal, stable, rule-oriented, and structured culture. This is synonymous with large corporations in stable environments and government agencies. Negative scores indicate a preference for small, innovative, flexible, team-oriented cultures that are more likely to be found in research units or small businesses.

Chapter 4: The International Culture Quiz

The correct answers are:

1. a	6. a
2. b	7. d
3. e (Portuguese)	8. d
4. b	9. b
5. d	10. b

Scores of eight correct answers or more indicate that you are relatively knowledgeable about customs, practices, and facts regarding different countries. Scores of 4 or less suggest considerable room for expanding your knowledge of other people and lands.

Chapter 5: What Are Your Personal Value Preferences?

These 18 values have been labeled as *instrumental* values, which means they represent beliefs about near-term modes of conduct. Research studies have found that different groups have different ranked preferences. The following represent the highest ranked and lowest ranked values from three groups: 345 graduates of a university's Executive MBA program; a sample of 1000 members from a steelworker's union local; and a diverse set of 234 community activists.

	Executives	Unions	Activists
Top 5 responses			
1.	Honest	Responsible	Honest
2.	Responsible	Honest	Helpful
3.	Capable	Courageous	Courageous
4.	Ambitious	Independent	Responsible
5.	Independent	Capable	Capable
Bottom 5 responses			
14.	Helpful	Helpful	Ambitious
15.	Polite	Cheerful	Self-controlled
16.	Cheerful	Intellectual	Polite
17.	Clean	Forgiving	Clean
18.	Obedient	Imaginative	Obedient

What were your top 5 and bottom 5 responses? How do they compare with the three groups above?

Chapter 6: What's Your Intuitive Ability?

Total the number of "a" responses circled for questions 1, 3, 5, 6, 11; enter the score here [A=_____]. Total the number of "b" responses for questions, 2, 4, 7, 8, 9, 10, 12; enter the score here [B=_____]. Add your "a" and "b" scores and enter the sum here [A+B=_____]. This is your *intuitive score*. The highest possible intuitive score is 12; the lowest is 0.

The author of this scale states that traditional analytical techniques "are not as useful as they once were for guiding major decisions. . . . If you hope to be better prepared for tomorrow, then it only seems logical to pay some attention to the use and development of intuitive skills for decision making."

Chapter 7: Are You a Good Planner?

According to the author of this questionnaire, the "perfect" planner would have answered: (1) Yes, (2) No, (3) Yes, (4) Yes, (5) Yes, (6) Yes, (7) Yes, and (8) No.

Chapter 8: Are You an Entrepreneur?

Total up your score for the 22 characteristics. Your score will fall between +44 and −44. The higher your positive score, the more you share traits common to highly successful entrepreneurs.

Chapter 9: Do You Know Your Daily Productivity Cycle?

Calculate your score by adding up the points allocated to the response you checked:

1. a=5	6. a=4	11. a=1
b=4	b=3	b=2
c=3	c=2	c=3
d=2	d=1	d=4
e=1		

2. a=5	7. a=5	12. a=4
b=4	b=4	b=3
c=3	c=3	c=2
d=2	d=2	d=1
e=1	e=1	

3. a=1	8. a=4	13. a=4
b=2	b=3	b=3
c=3	c=2	c=2
d=4	d=1	d=1

4. a=1	9. a=4
b=2	b=3
c=3	c=2
d=4	d=1

5. a=1	10. a=4
b=2	b=3
c=3	c=2
d=4	d=1

Score totals can range from 13 to 55. Scores of 22 and less indicate evening types; scores of 23–43 indicate intermediate types; and scores of 44 and above indicate morning types. If you don't already do this, you should adjust your activities so your most important and challenging activities are undertaken when your cycle is high.

Chapter 10: How Power Oriented Are You?

This test is designed to compute your Machiavellian (Mach) score. To obtain your score, add the number you have checked on questions 1, 3, 4, 5, 9, and 10. For the other four questions, reverse the numbers you have checked: 5 becomes 1, 4 is 2, 2 is 4, 1 is 5. Total your ten numbers to find your score. The National Opinion Research Center, which used this short form of the scale in a random sample of American adults, found that the national average was 25.

The results of research using the Mach test found that men are generally more Machiavellian than women; older adults tend to have lower Mach scores than younger adults; and high-Machs tend to be in professions that emphasize the control and manipulation of individuals—for example, managers, lawyers, psychiatrists, and behavioral scientists.

Chapter 11: Is an Enriched Job for You?

This exercise is designed to assess the degree to which you desire complex, challenging work. A high need for growth suggests that you are more likely to experience the desired psychological states in the job characteristics model when you have an enriched job.

This twelve-item questionnaire taps the degree to which you have a strong versus weak desire to obtain growth satisfaction from your work.

Each item on the questionnaire yields a score from 1 to 7 (that is, "Strongly prefer A" is scored 1; "Neutral" is scored 4; and "Strongly prefer B" is scored 7). To obtain your individual growth need strength score, average the twelve items as follows:

#1, #2, #7, #8, #11, #12 (direct scoring)
#3, #4, #5, #6, #9, #10 (reverse scoring)

Average scores for typical respondents are close to the midpoint of 4.0. Research indicates that if you score high on this measure, you will respond positively to an enriched job. Conversely, if you score low, you will tend *not* to find enriched jobs satisfying or motivating.

Chapter 12: How Do You Define Life Success?

This questionnaire taps six dimensions of life success. These are the achievement of status and wealth; contribution to society; good family relationships; personal fulfillment; professional fulfillment; and security.

Calculate your scores as follows:

The STATUS/WEALTH SCORE is found by adding responses to items:

| _____ | _____ | _____ | _____ | _____ | _____ | _____ | _____ | _____ /8= _____ |
| 1 | 7 | 12 | 16 | 24 | 26 | 34 | 36 | Total |

The CONTRIBUTION TO SOCIETY SCORE is found by adding responses to items:

| _____ | _____ | _____ | _____ | _____ | _____ | _____ | _____ | _____ /8= _____ |
| 6 | 15 | 18 | 22 | 33 | 35 | 39 | 42 | Total |

The FAMILY RELATIONSHIPS SCORE is found by adding responses to items:

| _____ | _____ | _____ | _____ | _____ | _____ | _____ | _____ | _____ /8= _____ |
| 3 | 8 | 10 | 11 | 20 | 25 | 31 | 41 | Total |

The PERSONAL FULFILLMENT SCORE is found by adding responses to items:

| _____ | _____ | _____ | _____ | _____ | _____ | _____ | _____ | _____ /8= _____ |
| 2 | 14 | 17 | 23 | 27 | 29 | 38 | 40 | Total |

The PROFESSIONAL FULFILLMENT SCORE is found by adding responses to items:

| _____ | _____ | _____ | _____ | _____ | _____ /5=_____ |
| 5 | 13 | 21 | 32 | 37 | Total |

The SECURITY SCORE is found by adding responses to items:

| _____ | _____ | _____ | _____ | _____ | _____ /5=_____ |
| 4 | 9 | 19 | 28 | 30 | Total |

You can compare your scores with the following norms based on surveys of managers:

	Females (n = 439)	Males (n = 317)
Status/Wealth	3.48	3.65
Social Contribution	4.04	4.07
Family Relationships	4.44	4.28
Personal Fulfillment	4.60	4.43
Professional Fulfillment	4.21	4.15
Security	4.30	4.21

Chapter 13: How Ready Are You for Managing in a Turbulent World?

Score four points for each A, three for each B, two for each C, one for each D, and zero for each E. Compute the total, divide by 24, and round to one decimal place.

While the results are not intended to be more than suggestive, the higher your score, the more comfortable you seem to be with change. The test's author suggests analyzing scores as if they were grade point averages. In this way, a 4.0 average is an A, a 2.0 is a C, and scores below 1.0 flunk.

Using replies from nearly 500 MBA students and young managers, the range of scores was found to be narrow—between 1.0 and 2.2. The average score was between 1.5 and 1.6—a D+/C− sort of grade!

Chapter 14: Who Controls Your Life?

This exercise is designed to measure your locus of control. Give yourself 1 point for each of the following selections: 1B, 2A, 3A, 4B, 5B, 6A, 7A, 8A, 9B, and 10A. Scores can be interpreted as follows:

8–10 = High internal locus of control

6–7 = Moderate internal locus of control

5 = Mixed

3–4 = Moderate external locus of control

1–2 = High external locus of control

The higher your internal score, the more you believe that you control your own destiny. The higher your external score, the more you believe that what happens to you in your life is due to luck or chance.

Chapter 15: How Trustworthy Are You?

Add up your total score. It will be somewhere between 8 and 80.
What does your score mean?

65–80 = High trustworthiness

24–64 = Moderate trustworthiness

8–23 = Low trustworthiness

Chapter 16: What Needs Are Most Important to You?

Places the values you gave A, B, C, D, and E for each question in the spaces provided in the scoring key. Notice that the letters are not always in the same place for each question. Then, add up each column and obtain a total score for each of the motivation levels.

Scoring Key						
	Question 1	A	C	B	E	D
	Question 2	A	B	D	C	E
	Question 3	B	C	E	D	A
	Question 4	E	A	C	B	D
	Question 5	C	B	D	A	E
	Question 6	B	C	A	E	D
	Question 7	E	A	D	C	B
	Question 8	B	C	A	E	D
	Question 9	B	C	E	D	A
	Question 10	B	D	C	E	A
	TOTAL SCORE					
		I	II	III	IV	V
			MOTIVATION LEVELS			

The five motivation levels are as follows:

Level I   Physiological needs
Level II   Safety needs
Level III   Social needs
Level IV   Esteem needs
Level V   Self-actualization needs

Those levels that received the highest scores are the most important needs identified by you in your work. The lowest show those needs that have been relatively well satisfied or de-emphasized by you at this time.

Chapter 17: What Kind of Leader Are You?

To find your leadership style,

1. Circle the item numbers for items 8, 12, 17, 18, 19, 30, 34, and 35.
2. Write a "1" in front of the *circled items* to which you responded S (seldom) or N (never).
3. Write a "1" in front of *items not circled* to which you responded A (always) or F (frequently).
4. Circle the "1's" which you have written in front of the following items: 3, 5, 8, 10, 15, 18, 19, 22, 24, 26, 28, 30, 32, 34, and 35.
5. Count the circled "1's." This is your score for concern for people. Record the score.
6. Count the uncircled "1's." This is your score for concern for task. Record this number.
7. Now refer to the diagram. Find your score on the *concern for task* dimension on the left-hand arrow. Next, move to the right-hand arrow and find your score on the *concern for people* dimension. Draw a straight line that intersects the two scores. The point at which that line crosses the *shared leadership* arrow indicates your score on that dimension.

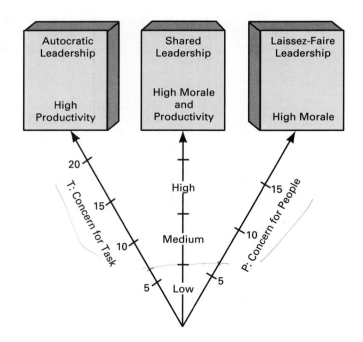

Chapter 18: What's Your Communication Style?

This questionnaire taps nine dimensions of communication style:

Dominant: The dominant communicator tends to take charge of social interactions.

Dramatic: The dramatic communicator manipulates and exaggerates stories, metaphors, rhythms, voice, and other stylistic devices to highlight or understate content.

Contentious: The contentious communicator is argumentative.

Animated: An animated communicator provides frequent and sustained eye contact, uses many facial expressions, and gestures often.

Impression leaving: The concept centers around whether the person is remembered because of the communicative stimuli that are projected.

Relaxed: This construct refers to whether the communicator is relaxed, tense, or anxious.

Attentive: In general, the attentive communicator makes sure that the other person knows that he is being listened to.

Open: Behavior associated with openness include activity that is characterized by being conversational, expansive, affable, convivial, gregarious, unreserved, somewhat frank, definitely extroverted, and obviously approachable.

Friendly: Friendly ranges from simply being unhostile to deep intimacy.

To get your score for each item, give yourself +2 for strong agreement, +1 for agreement, −1 for disagreement, and −2 for strong disagreement. The only exception are items with an asterisk (*), which should be reversed. Total your scores for each dimension and divide by the number of items.

Dominant = Items 25, 28, 31, 35, 41, 43
Dramatic = Items 18, 22, 32, 33, 48
Contentious = Items 10, 27, 30, 36, 37, 40, 42
Animated = Items 17 23, 44, 47
Impression leaving = Items 4, 5, 12, 14, 45
Relaxed = Items 1, 8*, 9, 15*, 16
Attentive = Items 3, 11, 20, 39, 49
Open = Items 21*, 24, 34, 50
Friendly = Items 2, 6, 38, 46

The remaining items tap your total communication image. They are used for research purposes only and are not included in our discussion.

The higher your score for any dimension, the more that dimension characterizes your communication style.

Chapter 19: How Willing Are You to Give Up Control?

Add up your total score for the eighteen items. Your score can be interpreted a follows:

72–90 points = Ineffective delegation
54–71 points = Delegation habits need substantial improvement
36–53 points = You still have room to improve
18–35 = Superior delegation

Chapter 20: Are You Computer Literate?

The correct answers are as follows:

1. B	11. E	21. A
2. A	12. A	22. E
3. E	13. D	23. D
4. B	14. A	24. A
5. C	15. B	25. A
6. D	16. E	26. B
7. A	17. A	27. E
8. B	18. D	28. A
9. D	19. E	29. B
10. D	20. C	30. D

Arbitrary cutoffs suggest:

25–30 = High literacy
20–24 = Considerable computer knowledge
15–19 = Some computer knowledge
10–14 = Modest computer knowledge
 0–9 = Very little knowledge of computers

Chapter 21: How's Your Knowledge of Japanese Manufacturing?

The correct answers are:

1. d	6. a
2. e	7. e
3. b	8. e
4. a	9. b
5. d	10. c

Scores of 9 or 10 correct indicate considerable knowledge of Japanese manufacturing and business practices. Scores of 6 or below suggest that you might benefit considerably by reading on Japanese practices.

ENDNOTES

Chapter 1

1. John Paul Newport, "Mission + Margin: The Nun as C.E.O.," *New York Times Magazine*, June 9, 1991, pp. 27–30.
2. U.S. Department of Labor, Bureau of Labor Statistics, *Employment and Earnings*, October 1989, Table A–22, 29.
3. Henri Fayol, *Industrial and General Administration* (Paris: Dunod, 1916).
4. Harold Koontz and Cyril O'Donnell, *Principles of Management: An Analysis of Managerial Functions* (New York: McGraw-Hill, 1955).
5. For a comprehensive review of this question, see Colin P. Hales, "What Do Managers Do? A Critical Review of the Evidence," *Journal of Management Studies*, January 1986, pp. 88–115.
6. This box is based on Nancy J. Perry, "The Arms Makers' Next Battle," *Fortune*, August 27, 1991, pp. 84–88.
7. Henry Mintzberg, *The Nature of Managerial Work* (New York: Harper & Row, 1973).
8. See, for example, Larry D. Alexander, "The Effect Level in the Hierarchy and Functional Area Have on the Extent Mintzberg's Roles Are Required by Managerial Jobs," *Academy of Management Proceedings* (San Francisco, 1979), pp. 186–89; Alan W. Lau and Cynthia M. Pavett, "The Nature of Managerial Work: A Comparison of Public and Private Sector Managers," *Group and Organization Studies*, December 1980, pp. 453–66; Morgan W. McCall, Jr., and C. A. Segrist, *In Pursuit of the Manager's Job: Building on Mintzberg*, Technical Report No. 14 (Greensboro, N.C.: Center for Creative Leadership, 1980); Cynthia M. Pavett and Alan W. Lau, "Managerial Work: The Influence of Hierarchical Level and Functional Specialty," *Academy of Management Journal*, March 1983, pp. 170–77; Hales, "What Do Managers Do? A Critical Review of the Evidence;" Allen I. Kraut, Patricia R. Pedigo, D. Douglas McKenna, and Marvin D. Dunnette, "The Role of the Manager: What's Really Important in Different Management Jobs," *Academy of Management Executive*, November 1989, pp. 286–93; and Mark J. Martinko and William L. Gardner, "Structured Observation of Managerial Work: A Replication and Synthesis," *Journal of Management Studies*, May 1990, pp. 330–57.
9. Pavett and Lau, "Managerial Work: The Influence of Hierarchical Level and Functional Specialty."
10. Stephen J. Carroll and Dennis A. Gillen, "Are the Classical Management Functions Useful in Describing Managerial Work?," *Academy of Management Review*, January 1987, p. 48.
11. See, for example, Harold Koontz, "Commentary on the Management Theory Jungle—Nearly Two Decades Later," in Harold Koontz, Cyril O'Donnell, and Heintz Weihrich (eds.), *Management: A Book of Readings*, 6th ed. (New York: McGraw-Hill, 1984), pp. 10–14; and Stephen J. Carroll and Dennis A. Gillen, "Are the Classical Management Functions Useful in Describing Managerial Work?," pp. 38–51.
12. Ibid.; and Peter Allan, "Managers at Work: A Large-Scale Study of the Managerial Job in New York City Government," *Academy of Management Journal*, September 1981, pp. 613–19.
13. Fred Luthans, Stuart A. Rosenkrantz, and Harry W. Hennessey, "What Do Successful Managers Really Do? An Observation Study of Managerial Activities," *The Journal of Applied Behavioral Science*, Vol. 21, No. 3, 1985, pp. 255–70; Fred Luthans, "Successful Vs. Effective Real Managers," *Academy of Management Executive*, May 1988, pp. 127–32; Fred Luthans, Richard M. Hodgetts, and Stuart A. Rosenkrantz, *Real Managers* (Cambridge, Mass.: Ballinger Publishing, 1988); and Fred Luthans, Dianne H. B. Welsh, and Lewis A. Taylor III, "A Descriptive Model of Managerial Effectiveness," *Group & Organization Studies*, June 1988, pp. 148–62.
14. See, for example, James W. Driscoll, Gary Cowger, and Robert Egan, "Private Managers and Public Myths—Public Managers and Private Myths," *Sloan Management Review*, Fall 1979, pp. 53–57; David Rogers, "Managing in the Public and Private Sectors; Similarities and Differences," *Management Review*, May 1981, pp. 48–54; Graham Allison, "Public and Private Management: Are They Fundamentally Alike in All Unimportant Respects?," in F. S. Lane (ed.), *Current Issues in Public Administration*, 2nd ed. (New York: St. Martin's Press, 1982); Douglas Yates, Jr., *The Politics of Management* (San Francisco: Jossey-Bass, 1985), pp. 12–39; J. Norman Baldwin, "Public vs. Private: Not That Different, Not That Consequential," *Public Personnel Management*, Summer 1987, pp. 181–91; and Hal G. Rainey, "Public Management: Recent Research on the Political Context and Managerial Roles, Structures, and Behaviors," *Journal of Management*, June 1989, pp. 229–50.
15. See, for example, William A. Nowlin, "Factors That Motivate Public and Private Sector Managers: A Comparison," *Public Personnel Management Journal*, Fall 1982, pp. 224–27.
16. U.S. Small Business Administration, *The State of Small Business: A Report of the President* (Washington, D.C.: GPO, 1986), p. x; "As Exports Rise, Big Companies Rev Up Hiring," *Business Week*, April 11, 1988, p. 91; "The 1990 Guide to Small Business," *U.S. News & World Report*, October 23, 1989; and T. Pouschine and M. Kripalani, "I Got Tired of Forcing Myself to Go to the Office," *Forbes*, May 25, 1992, pp. 104–14.
17. Joseph G. P. Paolillo, "The Manager's Self-Assessments of Managerial Roles: Small vs. Large Firms," *American Journal of Small Business*, January–March 1984, pp. 58–64.
18. See, for example, Gérald d'Amboise and Marie Muldowney, "Management Theory for Small Business: Attempts and Requirements," *Academy of Management Review*, April 1988, pp. 226–40.
19. Susan Chin, "Executive Sweets," *Forbes*, May 13, 1991, p. 48.
20. Cited in *Forbes*, May 27, 1991, p. 216.
21. This box is based on Joseph B. White, "How Detroit Diesel, Out From Under GM, Turned Around Fast," *Wall Street Journal*, August 16, 1991, p. A1.

Chapter 2

1. Based on Daniel Machalaba, "United Parcel Service Gets Deliveries Done by Driving Its Workers," *Wall Street Journal*, April 22, 1986, pp. 1, 26; and Michael Skratulia, "Scientific Management: A Case Study of the United Parcel Service," a research paper prepared under the supervision of Professor Stephen P. Robbins, San Diego State University, 1990.
2. Claude S. George, Jr., *The History of Management Thought*, 2nd ed. (Englewood Cliffs, N.J.: Prentice-Hall, 1972), p. 4.
3. Exodus 18:17–23.
4. Frederick W. Taylor, *Principles of Scientific Management* (New York: Harper and Brothers, 1911), p. 44.
5. See, for example, Frank B. Gilbreth, *Motion Study* (New York: D. Van Nostrand, 1911); and Frank B. Gilbreth and Lillian M. Gilbreth, *Fatigue Study* (New York: Sturgis and Walton Co., 1916).
6. Henri Fayol, *Industrial and General Administration* (Paris: Dunod, 1916).
7. Max Weber, *The Theory of Social and Economic Organizations*, ed. Talcott Parsons, trans. A. M. Henderson and Talcott Parsons (New York: Free Press, 1947).
8. W. Jack Duncan, *Great Ideas in Management* (San Francisco: Jossey-Bass, 1989), p. 137.
9. Robert A. Owen, *A New View of Society* (New York: E. Bliss and White, 1825).

10. Mary Parker Follett, *The New State: Group Organization the Solution of Popular Government* (London: Longmans, Green and Co., 1918).

11. Chester Barnard, *The Functions of the Executive* (Cambridge, Mass.: Harvard University Press, 1938).

12. Elton Mayo, *The Human Problems of an Industrial Civilization* (New York: Macmillan, 1933); and Fritz J. Roethlisberger and William J. Dickson, *Management and the Worker* (Cambridge, Mass.: Harvard University Press, 1939).

13. See, for example, Alex Carey, "The Hawthorne Studies: A Radical Criticism," *American Sociological Review*, June 1967, pp. 403–16; Richard H. Franke and James Kaul, "The Hawthorne Experiments: First Statistical Interpretations," *American Sociological Review*, October 1978, pp. 623–43; Berkeley Rice, "The Hawthorne Defect: Persistence of a Flawed Theory," *Psychology Today*, February 1982, pp. 70–74; Jeffrey A. Sonnenfeld, "Shedding Light on the Hawthorne Studies," *Journal of Occupational Behavior*, April 1985, pp. 111–30; and Stephen R. G. Jones, "Worker Interdependence and Output: The Hawthorne Studies Reevaluated," *American Sociological Review*, April 1990, pp. 176–90.

14. Dale Carnegie, *How to Win Friends and Influence People* (New York: Simon & Schuster, 1936).

15. Daniel A. Wren, *The Evolution of Management Thought*, 3rd ed. (New York: John Wiley & Sons, 1987), p. 422.

16. Abraham Maslow, *Motivation and Personality* (New York: Harper & Row, 1954).

17. Douglas McGregor, *The Human Side of Enterprise* (New York: McGraw-Hill, 1960).

18. Daniel A. Wren, *The Evolution of Management Thought*, p. 127.

19. Daniel Machalaba, "United Parcel Service Gets Deliveries Done by Driving Its Workers," p. 26.

20. Lyndall Urwick, *The Elements of Administration* (New York: Harper & Row, 1944).

21. Harold Koontz, "The Management Theory Jungle," *Journal of the Academy of Management*, December 1961, pp. 174–88.

22. Harold Koontz, ed., *Toward a Unified Theory of Management* (New York: McGraw-Hill, 1964).

23. Kenyon B. DeGreene, *Sociotechnical Systems: Factors in Analysis, Design and Management* (Englewood Cliffs, N.J.: Prentice-Hall, 1973), p. 13.

24. See, for example, Louis W. Fry and Deborah A. Smith, "Congruence, Contingency, and Theory Building," *Academy of Management Review*, January 1987, pp. 117–32.

25. See, for instance, R. R. Thomas, Jr., "From Affirmative Action to Affirming Diversity," *Harvard Business Review*, March–April 1990, pp. 107–17; B. Mandrell and S. Kohler-Gray, "Management Development That Values Diversity," *Personnel*, March 1990, pp. 41–47; and Joel Dreyfuss, "Get Ready for the New Work Force," *Fortune*, April 23, 1990, pp. 165–81.

26. Gary W. Loveman and John J. Gabarro, "The Managerial Implications of Changing Work Force Demographics: A Scoping Study," *Human Resource Management*, Spring 1991, pp. 7–29.

27. Joel Dreyfuss, "Get Ready for the New Workforce," p. 176.

28. B.R. Bergmann and W.R. Krause, "Evaluating and Forecasting Progress in Racial Integration of Employment," *Industrial and Labor Relations Review*, April 1968, pp. 399–409.

29. F. Schwartz, "Management Women and the New Facts of Life," *Harvard Business Review*, January–February 1989, pp. 65–76.

30. Rick Tetzeli, "Business Students Cheat Most," *Fortune*, July 1, 1991, p. 14.

31. See, for example, Bob Krone, "Total Quality Management: An American Odyssey," *The Bureaucrat*, Fall 1990, pp. 35–38; Andrea Gabor, *The Man Who Discovered Quality* (New York: Random House, 1990); Jim Clemmer, "How Total Is Your Quality Management?," *Canadian Business Review*, Spring 1991, pp. 38–41; and Marshall Sashkin and Kenneth J. Kiser, *Total Quality Management* (Seabrook, MD: Ducochon Press, 1991).

32. Albert C. Hyde, "Rescuing Quality Management from TQM," *The Bureaucrat*, Winter 1990–91, p. 16.

33. See Kenneth W. Thomas and Betty A. Velthouse, "Cognitive Elements of Empowerment: An 'Interpretive' Model of Intrinsic Task Motivation," *Academy of Management Review*, October 1990, pp. 666–81.

34. See S. Dentzer, "The Vanishing Dream," *U.S. News & World Report*, April 22, 1991, pp. 39–43; and Aaron Bernstein, "The Global Economy: Who Gets Hurt," *Business Week*, August 10, 1992, pp. 48–53.

Chapter 3

1. "J & J Will Pay Dearly to Cure Tylenol," *Business Week*, November 29, 1982; and "A Hard Decision to Swallow," *Time*, March 3, 1986, p. 59.

2. For insights into the symbolic view, see Jeffrey Pfeffer, "Management as Symbolic Action: The Creation and Maintenance of Organizational Paradigms," in L. L. Cummings and B. M. Staw (eds.), *Research in Organizational Behavior*, Vol. 3 (Greenwich, Conn.: JAI Press, 1981), pp. 1–52; Donald C. Hambrick and Sidney Finkelstein, "Managerial Discretion: A Bridge Between Polar Views of Organizational Outcomes," in L. L. Cummings and B. M. Staw (eds.), *Research in Organizational Behavior*, Vol. 9 (Greenwich, Conn.: JAI Press, 1987), pp. 369–406; John A. Byrne, "The Limits of Power," *Business Week*, October 23, 1987, pp. 33–35; James R. Meindl and Sanford B. Ehrlich, "The Romance of Leadership and the Evaluation of Organizational Performance," *Academy of Management Journal*, March 1987, pp. 91–109; Charles R. Schwenk, "Illusions of Management Control? Effects of Self-Serving Attributions on Resource Commitments and Confidence in Management," *Human Relations*, April 1990, pp. 333–47; and Sheila M. Puffer and Joseph B. Weintrop, "Corporate Performance and CEO Turnover: The Role of Performance Expectations," *Administrative Science Quarterly*, March 1991, pp. 1–19.

3. Leah Nathans Spiro, "George Ball Finally Falls Off the Rock," *Business Week*, February 25, 1991, p. 42.

4. See, for instance, John B. Judis, "Myth vs. Manager," *Business Month*, July 1990, pp. 24–33; and Paul Ingrassia and Bradley A. Stertz,"With Chrysler Ailing, Lee Iacocca Concedes Mistakes in Managing," *Wall Street Journal*, September 17, 1990, p. A1.

5. John B. Judis, "Myth vs. Manager."

6. Jeffrey Pfeffer, "Management as Symbolic Action: The Creation and Maintenance of Organizational Paradigms."

7. Linda Smircich, "Concepts of Culture and Organizational Analysis," *Administrative Science Quarterly*, September 1983, p. 339.

8. Alice M. Sapienza, "Believing Is Seeing: How Culture Influences the Decisions Top Managers Make," in Ralph H. Kilmann et al. (eds.), *Gaining Control of the Corporate Culture* (San Francisco: Jossey-Bass, 1985), p. 68.

9. Based on Geert Hofstede, B. Neuijen, D. D. Ohayv, and G. Sanders, "Measuring Organizational Culture: A Qualitative and Quantitative Study Across Twenty Cases," *Administrative Science Quarterly*, June 1990, pp. 286–316; and Charles A. O'Reilly III, J. Chatman, and D. F. Caldwell, "People and Organizational Culture: A Profile Comparison Approach to Assessing Person-Organization Fit," *Academy of Management Journal*, September 1991, pp. 487–516.

10. Donald C. Hambrick and Sidney Finkelstein, "Managerial Discretion: A Bridge Between Polar Views of Organizational Outcomes," pp. 384–85.

11. Edgar H. Schein, *Organizational Culture and Leadership* (San Francisco: Jossey-Bass, 1985), pp. 314–15.

12. See Edgar H. Schein, "The Role of the Founder in Creating Organizational Culture," *Organizational Dynamics*, Summer 1983, pp. 13–28; and Harrison M. Trice and Janice M. Beyer, "Cultural Leadership in Organizations," *Organization Science*, May 1991, pp. 149–69.

13. Robert H. Miles, *Macro Organizational Behavior* (Santa Monica, Calif.: Goodyear Publishing, 1980), p. 195.

14. John Markoff, "IBM Spins Off PC Business Into New Company," *New York Times*, September 3, 1992, p. C3.

15. Timothy S. Mescon and George S. Vozikis, "Federal Regulation—What Are the Costs?," *Business*, January–March 1982, pp.33–39.

16. See, for instance, Arthur S. Hayes, "Layoffs Take Careful Planning to Avoid Losing the Suits That Are Apt to Follow," *Wall Street Journal*, November 2, 1990, p. B1.
17. "Business Week/Harris Executive Poll," *Business Week*, October 23, 1987, p. 28.

Chapter 4

1. Based on Jonathan B. Levine, "GE Carves Out a Road East," *Business Week*, July 30, 1990, pp. 32–33; Shawn Tully, "GE in Hungary: Let There Be Light," *Fortune*, October 22, 1990, pp. 137–42; and John S. McClenahen, "Light in the East," *Industry Week*, March 2, 1992, pp. 14–19.
2. (1) France (Pechiney); (2) Japan (Sony); (3) U.S.; (4) Germany (Allianz); (5) Japan (Bridgestone); (6) U.S. (Ford); (7) Germany (Bayer AG): (8) United Kingdom (Grand Metropolitan); (9) Canada (Seagram Ltd.); and (10) United Kingdom (RTZ Plc).
3. Nancy Adler, *International Dimensions of Organizational Behavior*, 2nd ed. (Boston: PWS-Kent, 1991), p. 11.
4. See D. A. Ricks, M. Y. C. Fu, and J. S. Arpas, *International Business Blunders* (Columbus, Ohio: Grid, 1974); Amanda Bennett, "American Culture Is Often a Puzzle for Foreign Managers in the U.S.," *Wall Street Journal*, February 12, 1986, p. 29; and Charles F. Valentine, "Blunders Abroad," *Nation's Business*, March 1989, p. 54.
5. Bill Powell, "Japan's Bosses in America," *Business Month*, August 1990, pp. 34–36.
6. John Urquhart, "Canadian Firms, Fleeing the High Costs at Home, Relocate South of the Border," *Wall Street Journal*, February 7, 1991, p. A2.
7. See, for instance, Mark Maremont and Richard A. Melcher, "Tearing Down Even More Fences in Europe," *Business Week*, November 4, 1991, pp. 50–52; Sara Hammes, "Europe's Growing Market," *Fortune*, December 2, 1991, pp. 144–45; and Mark M. Nelson, "EC is Swamped by Would-Be Members," *Wall Street Journal*, May 13, 1992, p. A12.
8. See, for instance, "The Magnet of Growth in Mexico's North," *Business Week*, June 6, 1988, pp. 48–50; and Juanita Darling, "Mexico Is Learning a New Word for Wealth," *Los Angeles Times*, May 1, 1990, p. H4.
9. James P. Miller, "Zenith is Shifting Taiwan Jobs to Mexico, Signaling Trend in Other Manufacturers," *Wall Street Journal*, November 12, 1991, p. A6.
10. "The Rise of Gringo Capitalism," *Newsweek*, January 5, 1987, p. 40.
11. This box is based on "The Rise of Gringo Capitalism," *Newsweek*, January 5, 1987, pp. 40–41; and M. Satchell, "Poisoning the Border," *U.S. News and World Report*, May 6, 1991, pp. 33–41.
12. William J. Holstein, David Woodruff, and Amy Borrus, "Is Free Trade With Mexico Good or Bad for the U.S.?," *Business Week*, November 12, 1990, pp. 112–13; Ann Reilly Dowd, "Viva Free Trade With Mexico!," *Fortune*, June 17, 1991, pp. 97–100; and "Bush Bulls Ahead on Free Trade With Mexico," *Business Week*, February 24, 1992, pp. 46–47.
13. Ibid.
14. S. C. Gwynne, "From Yukon to Yucatán," *Time*, June 3, 1991, pp. 20–24.
15. Bernard Wysocki Jr., "Blocking Trade," *Wall Street Journal*, September 21, 1990, p. R31.
16. See, for example, Geert Hofstede, *Culture's Consequences: International Differences in Work-Related Values* (Beverly Hills, Calif.: Sage Publications, 1980), pp. 25–26.
17. See Nancy J. Adler, *International Dimensions of Organizational Behavior*, p. 58.
18. Geert Hofstede, *Culture's Consequences: International Differences in Work-Related Values*; and Geert Hofstede, "The Cultural Relativity of Organizational Practices and Theories," *Journal of International Business Studies*, Fall 1983, pp. 75–89.
19. Hofstede called this last dimension masculinity–femininity but we've changed it because of the strong sexist connotation in his choice of terms.

Chapter 5

1. Based on Tim Smart, "This Man Sounded the Silicone Alarm—in 1976," *Business Week*, January 27, 1992, p. 34; Bruce Ingersoll, "Criminal Inquiry of Dow Corning To Be Sought," *Wall Street Journal*, February 13, 1992, p. A3; Steven Fink, "Dow Corning's Moral Evasions," *New York Times*, February 16, 1992, p. F13; Philip J. Hilts, "Top Manufacturer of Breast Implant Replaces Chief," *New York Times*, February 11, 1992, p. A1; and Tatiana Pouschine, "The Survivors," *Forbes*, December 7, 1992, p. 148.
2. See "Ethics Are Lacking in Business," *Wall Street Journal*, August 20, 1990, p. 1; Milton R. Moskowitz, "Company Performance Roundup," *Business & Society Review*, Spring 1991, p. 76; Rick Tetzeli, "Business Students Cheat Most," *Fortune*, July 1, 1991, p. 14; and Gary L. Richard, "Bosses Pressure Corporate Financial Executives to Compromise Ethics," *Program Manager*, July–August 1991, pp. 34–41.
3. Archie B. Carroll, "A Three-Dimensional Conceptual Model of Corporate Performance," *Academy of Management Review*, October 1979, p. 499.
4. Milton Friedman, *Capitalism and Freedom* (Chicago: University of Chicago Press, 1962); and "The Social Responsibility of Business Is to Increase Its Profits," *New York Times Magazine*, September 13, 1970, p. 33.
5. Saul W. Gellerman, "Why 'Good' Managers Make Bad Ethical Choices," *Harvard Business Review*, July–August 1986, p. 89.
6. Ibid., p. 86.
7. Michele Galen, "Back in Jeopardy at Manville," *Business Week*, June 25, 1990, pp. 28–29.
8. Steven L. Wartick and Philip L. Cochran, "The Evolution of the Corporate Social Performance Model," *Academy of Management Review*, October 1985, p. 760.
9. This section is based on R. Joseph Monsen, Jr., "The Social Attitudes of Management," in Joseph M. McGuire (ed.), *Contemporary Management: Issues and Views* (Englewood Cliffs, N.J.: Prentice-Hall, 1974), p. 616; and Keith Davis and William C. Frederick, *Business and Society: Management, Public Policy, Ethics*, 5th ed. (New York: McGraw-Hill, 1984), pp. 28–41.
10. See, for example, Rogene A. Buchholz, *Essentials of Public Policy for Management*, 2nd ed. (Englewood Cliffs, N.J.: Prentice Hall, 1990).
11. See S. Prakash Sethi, "A Conceptual Framework for Environmental Analysis of Social Issues and Evaluation of Business Response Patterns," *Academy of Management Review*, January 1979, pp. 68–74.
12. See, for example, Donna J. Wood, "Corporate Social Performance Revisited," *Academy of Management Review*, October 1991, pp. 703–08.
13. Steven L. Wartick and Philip L. Cochran, "The Evolution of the Corporate Social Performance Model," p. 763.
14. Ibid., p. 762.
15. See, for instance, Philip Cochran and Robert A. Wood, "Corporate Social Responsibility and Financial Performance," *Academy of Management Journal*, March 1984, pp. 42–56; Kenneth Aupperle, Archie B. Carroll, and John D. Hatfield, "An Empirical Examination of the Relationship Between Corporate Social Responsibility and Profitability," *Academy of Management Journal*, June 1985, pp. 446–63; Jean B. McGuire, Alison Sundgren, and Thomas Schneeweis, "Corporate Social Responsibility and Firm Financial Performance," *Academy of Management Journal*, December 1988, pp. 854–72; and David M. Georgoff and Joel Ross, "Corporate Social Responsibility and Management Performance," paper presented at the National Academy of Management Conference; Miami; August 1991.
16. See Arieh A. Ullmann, "Data in Search of a Theory: A Critical Examination of the Relationships Among Social Performance, Social Disclosure, and Economic Performance of U.S. Firms," *Academy of Management Review*, July 1985, pp. 540–57; and Richard E. Wokutch

and Barbara A. Spencer, "Corporate Saints and Sinners: The Effects of Philanthropic and Illegal Activity on Organizational Performance," *California Management Review*, Winter 1987, pp. 62–77.

17. Joseph Weber, "Meet Du Pont's 'In-House Conscience,'" *Business Week*, June 24, 1991, pp. 62–65.

18. Jean B. McGuire, Alison Sungren, and Thomas Schneeweis, "Corporate Social Responsibility and Firm Financial Performance."

19. Philip Cochran and Robert A. Wood, "Corporate Social Responsibility and Financial Performance."

20. David M. Georgoff and Joel Ross, "Corporate Social Responsibility and Management Performance."

21. See Joanne Rockness and Paul F. Williams, "A Descriptive Study of Social Responsibility Mutual Funds," *Accounting, Organizations and Society*, Spring 1988, pp. 397–411.

22. See "Marketing: Cause-Related Marketing," *Wall Street Journal*, February 19, 1987; and "Cause-Related Marketing," *INC.*, July 1991, p. 72.

23. Kathleen K. Wiegner, "A Cause on Every Carton," *Forbes*, November 18, 1985, pp. 248–49; Monci Jo Williams, "How to Cash in on Do-Good Pitches," *Fortune*, June 9, 1986, pp. 71–80; and Zachary Schiller, "Doing Well by Doing Good," *Business Week*, December 5, 1988, pp. 53–57.

24. Kathleen K. Wiegner, "A Cause on Every Carton," p. 248.

25. "Cause-Related Marketing," *INC*, July 1991, p. 72.

26. Louis W. Fry, Gerald D. Keim, and Roger E. Meiners, "Corporate Contributions: Altruistic or For-Profit?" *Academy of Management Journal*, March 1982, pp. 94–106; and Timothy S. Mescon and Donn J. Tilson, "Corporate Philanthropy: A Strategic Approach to the Bottom-Line," *California Management Review*, Winter 1987, pp. 49–61.

27. Zachary Schiller, "Doing Well by Doing Good," p. 57.

28. See, for example, Archie B. Carroll, "The Pyramid of Corporate Social Responsibility: Toward the Moral Management of Organizational Stakeholders," *Business Horizons*, July–August 1991, pp. 39–48.

29. This section has been influenced by Kimberly B. Boal and Newman Peery, "The Cognitive Structure of Corporate Social Responsibility," *Journal of Management*, Fall–Winter 1985, pp. 71–82.

30. Archie B. Carroll, *Social Responsibility of Management* (Chicago: Science Research Associates, 1984), p. 13.

31. Keith Davis and William C. Frederick, *Business and Society*, p. 76.

32. Frederick D. Sturdivant, *Business and Society: A Managerial Approach*, 3rd ed. (Homewood, Ill.: Richard D. Irwin, 1985), p. 128.

33. Gerald F. Cavanagh, Dennis J. Moberg, and Manuel Valasquez, "The Ethics of Organizational Politics," *Academy of Management Journal*, June 1981, pp. 363–74. See F. Neil Brady, "Rules for Making Exceptions to Rules," *Academy of Management Review*, July 1987, pp. 436–44 for an argument that the theory of justice is redundant with the prior two theories.

34. David J. Fritzsche and Helmut Becker, "Linking Management Behavior to Ethical Philosophy—An Empirical Investigation," *Academy of Management Journal*, March 1984, pp. 166–75.

35. Brian Dumaine, "Exporting Jobs and Ethics," *Fortune*, October 5, 1992, p. 10.

36. This section is largely based on Linda Klebe Trevino, "Ethical Decision Making in Organizations: A Person-Situation Interactionist Model," *Academy of Management Review*, July 1986, pp. 601–17; and Thomas M. Jones, "Ethical Decision Making By Individuals in Organizations: An Issue-Contingent Model," *Academy of Management Review*, April 1991, pp. 366–95.

37. Lawrence Kohlberg, *Essays in Moral Development: The Philosophy of Moral Development*, Vol. 1 (New York: Harper & Row, 1981); and Lawrence Kohlberg, *Essays in Moral Development: The Psychology of Moral Development*, Vol. 2 (New York: Harper & Row, 1984).

38. See, for example, James Weber, "Managers' Moral Reasoning: Assessing Their Responses to Three Moral Dilemmas," *Human Relations*, July 1990, pp. 687–702.

39. John H. Barnett and Marvin J. Karson, "Personal Values and Business Decisions: An Exploratory Investigation," *Journal of Business Ethics*,

July 1987, pp. 371–82; and William C. Frederick and James Weber, "The Value of Corporate Managers and Their Critics: An Empirical Description and Normative Implications," in William C. Frederick and Lee E. Preston, eds., *Business Ethics: Research Issues and Empirical Studies* (Greenwich, Conn.: JAI Press, 1990), pp. 123–44.

40. Linda Klebe Trevino and Stuart A. Youngblood, "Bad Apples in Bad Barrels: A Causal Analysis of Ethical Decision-Making Behavior," *Journal of Applied Psychology*, August 1990, pp. 378–85.

41. Barry Z. Posner and William H. Schmidt, "Values and the American Manager: An Update," *California Management Review*, Spring 1984, pp. 202–16.

42. Bart Victor and John B. Cullen, "The Organizational Bases of Ethical Work Climates," *Administrative Science Quarterly*, March 1988, pp. 101–25; John B. Cullen, Bart Victor, and Carroll Stephens, "An Ethical Weather Report: Assessing the Organization's Ethical Climate," *Organizational Dynamics*, Autumn 1989, pp. 50–62; Bart Victor and John B. Cullen, "A Theory and Measure of Ethical Climate in Organizations," in William C. Frederick and Lee E. Preston, eds., *Business Ethics: Research Issues and Empirical Studies* (Greenwich Conn.: JAI Press, 1990), pp. 77–97; and Ronald R. Sims, "The Challenge of Ethical Behavior in Organizations," *Journal of Business Ethics*, July 1992, pp. 505–13.

43. Thomas M. Jones, "Ethical Decision Making By Individuals in Organizations: An Issue-Contingent Model," *Academy of Management Review*, April 1991, pp. 366–95.

44. Ibid., pp. 374–78.

45. John A. Byrne, "The Best-Laid Ethics Programs . . . ," *Business Week*, March 9, 1992, pp. 67–68.

46. Linda Klebe Trevino and Stuart A. Youngblood, "Bad Apples in Bad Barrels," p. 384.

47. See, for example, M. Cash Mathews, "Codes of Ethics: Organizational Behavior and Misbehavior," in William C. Frederick and Lee E. Preston, eds., *Business Ethics*, pp. 99–122.

48. Cited in Catherine Fredman, "Nationwide Examination of Corporate Consciences," *Working Women*, December 1991, p. 39.

49. Paul Richter, "Big Business Puts Ethics in Spotlight," *Los Angeles Times*, June 19, 1986, p. 29.

50. Fred R. David, "An Empirical Study of Codes of Business Ethics: A Strategic Perspective," paper presented at the 48th Annual Academy of Management Conference; Anaheim, California, August 1988.

51. Rick Wartzman, "Nature or Nurture? Study Blames Ethical Lapses on Corporate Goals," *Wall Street Journal*, October 9, 1987, p. 27.

52. Ibid.

53. D. R. Cressey and C. A. Moore, "Managerial Values and Corporate Codes of Ethics," *California Management Review*, Summer 1983, p. 71.

54. Laura Nash, "Ethics Without the Sermon," *Harvard Business Review*, November–December 1981, p. 81.

55. Cited in Susan J. Harrington, "What Corporate America is Teaching About Ethics," *Academy of Management Executive*, February 1991, p. 22.

56. Thomas A. Gavin, "Ethics Education," *Internal Auditor*, April 1989, pp. 54–57.

57. Ibid.

58. Ibid.

59. William Penn and Boyd D. Collier, "Current Research in Moral Development as a Decision Support System," *Journal of Business Ethics*, January 1985, pp. 131–36.

60. James Weber, "Measuring the Impact of Teaching Ethics to Future Managers: A Review, Assessment, and Recommendations," *Journal of Business Ethics*, April 1990, pp. 182–90.

61. "Ethics: Part of the Game at Citicorp," *Fortune*, October 26, 1987, p. 12.

62. See, for instance, Susan J. Harrington, "What Corporate America is Teaching About Ethics;" and Peter F. Miller and William T. Coady, "Teaching Work Ethics," *Education Digest*, February 1990, pp. 54–55.

63. Richard Ricklets, "Executives and General Public Say Ethical Behavior is Declining in U.S.," *Wall Street Journal*, October 31, 1983, p. 33.

64. See, for example, Archie B. Carroll, *Social Responsibility of Management*, p. 14.

Chapter 6

1. Based on John H. Taylor, "Risk Taker," *Forbes*, November 14, 1988, p. 108; Subrata N. Chakravarty, "Hit 'em Hardest With the Mostest," *Forbes*, September 16, 1991, pp. 48–51; Edward O. Welles, "Captain Marvel," *INC.*, January 1992, pp. 44–47; and Bridget O'Brian, "Southwest Airlines Is a Rare Carrier: It Still Makes Money," *Wall Street Journal*, October 26, 1992, p. A1.
2. William Pounds, "The Process of Problem Finding," *Industrial Management Review*, Fall 1969, pp. 1–19.
3. Roger J. Volkema, "Problem Formulation: Its Portrayal in the Texts," *Organizational Behavior Teaching Review*, Vol. 11, No. 3, 1986–87, pp. 113–26.
4. Morgan W. McCall, Jr., and Robert E. Kaplan, *Whatever It Takes: Decision Makers at Work* (Englewood Cliffs, N.J.: Prentice Hall, 1985), pp. 36–38.
5. This box is based on John McCormick, "Making Women's Issues Front-Page News," *Working Woman*, October 1991, pp. 78–81 and 106–08.
6. Herbert A. Simon, *The New Science of Management Decision* (New York: Harper & Row, 1960), p. 1.
7. See Herbert A. Simon, "Rationality in Psychology and Economics," *The Journal of Business*, October 1986, pp. 209–24; and Ann Langley, "In Search of Rationality: The Purposes Behind the Use of Formal Analysis in Organizations," *Administrative Science Quarterly*, December 1989, pp. 598–631.
8. See, for example, Milton Moskowitz, "Uprooting the Corporation," *Los Angeles Times*, October 1, 1989, p. IV-3.
9. Fremont A. Shull, Jr., André L. Delbecq, and Larry L. Cummings, *Organizational Decision Making* (New York: McGraw-Hill, 1970), p. 151.
10. A few of the more enlightening of these would include: Michael D. Cohen, James G. March, and Johan P. Olsen, "A Garbage Can Model of Organizational Choice," *Administrative Science Quarterly*, March 1972, pp. 1–25; Henry Mintzberg, Duru Raisinghani, and André Théorêt, "The Structure of 'Unstructured' Decision Processes," *Administrative Science Quarterly*, June 1976, pp. 246–75; Karl E. Weick, *The Social Psychology of Organizing*, rev. ed. (Reading, Mass.: Addison-Wesley, 1979); Anna Grandori, "A Prescriptive Contingency View of Organizational Decision Making," *Administrative Science Quarterly*, June 1984, pp. 192–209; and Paul C. Nutt, "Types of Organizational Decision Processes," *Administrative Science Quarterly*, September 1984, pp. 414–50.
11. Herbert A. Simon, "Information-Processing Models of Cognition," in M. R. Rosenzweig and L. W. Porter, eds,. *Annual Review of Psychology*, Vol. 30 (Palo Alto, Calif.: Annual Reviews, 1979), pp. 363–96.
12. Paul A. Anderson, "Decision Making by Objection and the Cuban Missile Crisis, *Administrative Science Quarterly*, June 1983, p. 217.
13. See Stephen P. Robbins, *Organizational Behavior: Concepts, Controversies, and Applications*, 6th ed. (Englewood Cliffs, N.J.: Prentice-Hall, 1993), pp. 140–143.
14. Leonard R. Sayles in McCall and Kaplan, *Whatever It Takes: Decision Makers at Work*, p. x.
15. McCall and Kaplan, p. 27.
16. Charles A. O'Reilly, III, "Variations in Decision Makers' Use of Information Source: The Impact of Quality and Accessibility of Information," *Academy of Management Journal*, December 1982, pp. 756–71.
17. Paul C. Nutt, "Types of Organizational Decision Processes."
18. Glen White, "Escalating Commitment to a Course of Action: A Reinterpretation," *Academy of Management Review*, April 1986, pp. 311–21.
19. Graham T. Allison, *Essence of Decision: Explaining the Cuban Missile Crisis*, (Boston: Little, Brown, 1971), p. 79.
20. Ibid., p. 175.
21. Ibid., p. 176.
22. Jeffrey Pfeffer, *Power in Organizations* (Marshfield, Mass.: Pitman Publishing, 1981).
23. Daniel Katz and Robert L. Kahn, *The Social Psychology of Organizations*, 2nd ed. (New York: John Wiley, 1978), p. 501.
24. Charles E. Lindholm, "The Science of 'Muddling Through,'" *Public Administration Review*, Spring 1959, pp. 79–88.
25. See, for example, James G. March, "Footnotes to Organizational Change," *Administrative Science Quarterly*, December 1981, pp. 563–77.
26. James G. March, "Decision-Making Perspective: Decisions in Organizations and Theories of Choice," in Andrew H. Van de Ven and William F. Joyce (eds.), *Perspectives on Organization Design and Behavior* (New York: Wiley-Interscience, 1981), pp. 232–33.
27. See Neil McK. Agnew and John L. Brown, "Bounded Rationality: Fallible Decisions in Unbounded Decision Space," *Behavioral Science*, July 1986, pp. 148–61; Bruce E. Kaufman, "A New Theory of Satisficing," *The Journal of Behavioral Economics*, Spring 1990, pp. 35–51; and David R. A. Skidd, "Revisiting Bounded Rationality," *Journal of Management Inquiry*, December 1992, pp. 343–47.
28. Bill Saporito, "How Quaker Oats Got Rolled," *Fortune*, October 8, 1990, pp. 129–38.
29. W. H. Agor, "The Logic of Intuition: How Top Executives Make Important Decisions," *Organizational Dynamics*, Winter 1986, p. 5; (W. H. Agor (ed.), *Intuition in Organizations* (Newbury Park, CA.: Sage Publications, 1989); and O. Behling and N. L. Eckel, "Making Sense Out of Intuition," *Academy of Management Executive*, February 1991, pp. 46–47.
30. W. H. Agor, "The Logic of Intuition," p. 9.
31. Ibid., pp. 12–13.
32. "This Meeting Will Come to Order," *Time*, December 6, 1985.
33. Irving L. Janis, *Victims of Groupthink* (Boston: Houghton Mifflin, 1972).
34. See, for example, Timothy W. Costello and Sheldon S. Zalkind, eds., *Psychology in Administration: A Research Orientation* (Englewood Cliffs, N.J.: Prentice-Hall, 1963), pp. 429–30; Robert A. Cooke and John A. Kernaghan, "Estimating the Difference Between Group Versus Individual Performance on Problem-Solving Tasks," *Group and Organization Studies*, September 1987, pp. 319–42; and Larry K. Michaelsen, Warren E. Watson, and Robert H. Black, "A Realistic Test of Individual Versus Group Consensus Decision Making," *Journal of Applied Psychology*, October 1989, pp. 834–39.
35. Andre L. Delbecq, Andrew H. Van de Ven, and David H. Gustafson, *Group Techniques for Program Planning* (Glenview, Ill.: Scott, Foresman, 1975).
36. Fremont A. Shull, André L. Delbecq, and Larry L. Cummings, *Organizational Decision Making*, p. 151.
37. This box is substantially based on Ellen F. Jackofsky, John W. Slocum, Jr., and Sara J. McQuaid, "Cultural Values and the CEO: Alluring Companions?," *Academy of Management Executive*, February 1988, pp. 39–49.
38. A. F. Osborn, *Applied Imagination: Principles and Procedures of Creative Thinking* (New York: Scribners, 1941).
39. The following discussion is based on André L. Delbecq, A. H. Van de Ven, and D. H. Gustafson, *Group Techniques for Program Planning: A Guide to Nominal and Delphi Processes* (Glenview, Ill.: Scott, Foresman, 1975).
40. See A. R. Dennis, J. F. George, L. M. Jessup, J. F. Nunamaker, Jr., and D. R. Vogel, "Information Technology to Support Group Work," *MIS Quarterly*, December 1988, pp. 591–619; D. W. Straub and R. A. Beauclair, "Current and Future Uses of Group Decision Support System Technology: Report on a Recent Empirical Study," *Journal of Management Information Systems*, Summer 1988, pp. 101–16; J. Bartimo, "At These Shouting Matches, No One Says a Word," *Business Week*, June 11, 1990, p. 78; and M.S. Poole, M. Holmes, and G. DeSanctis, "Conflict Management in a Computer-Supported Meeting Environment," *Management Science*, August 1991, pp. 926–53.
41. See William M. Bulkeley, " 'Computerizing' Dull Meetings Is Touted

As an Antidote to the Mouth That Bored," *Wall Street Journal*, January 28, 1992, p. B1.

Chapter 7

1. Based on "Coming from Japan," aired on ABC's "Frontline" on February 18, 1992.
2. See, for example, John A. Pearce II, K. Keith Robbins, and Richard B. Robinson, Jr., "The Impact of Grand Strategy and Planning Formality on Financial Performance," *Strategic Management Journal*, March–April 1987, pp. 125–34; Lawrence C. Rhyne, "Contrasting Planning Systems in High, Medium, and Low Performance Companies," *Journal of Management Studies*, July 1987, pp. 363–85; Richard Brahm and Charles B. Brahm, "Formal Planning and Organizational Performance: Assessing Emerging Empirical Research Trends," paper presented at the National Academy of Management Conference, New Orleans, August 1987; John A. Pearce II, Elizabeth B. Freeman, and Richard B. Robinson, Jr., "The Tenuous Link Between Formal Strategic Planning and Financial Performance," *Academy of Management Review*, October 1987, pp. 658–75; and Deepak K. Sinha, "The Contribution of Formal Planning to Decisions," *Strategic Management Journal*, October 1990, pp. 479–92.
3. Based on James E. Ellis, "Beyond Bunnies: Rewriting the Playboy Philosophy," *Business Week*, November 14, 1988, pp. 89–90; Joshua Levine, "The Rabbit Grows Up," *Forbes*, February 17, 1992, pp. 122–27; and John R. Dorfman, "Playboy's Major Lines Improve, Telling Some That Long-Awaited Turnaround is Working" *Wall Street Journal*, May 11, 1992, p. C2.
4. Russell Ackoff, "A Concept of Corporate Planning," *Long Range Planning*, September 1970, p. 3.
5. Michael B. McCaskey, "A Contingency Approach to Planning: Planning With Goals and Planning Without Goals," *Academy of Management Journal*, June 1974, pp. 281–91.
6. Several of these factors were suggested by J. Scott Armstrong, "The Value of Formal Planning for Strategic Decisions: Review of Empirical Research," *Strategic Management Journal*, July–September 1982, pp. 197–211; and Rudi K. Bresser and Ronald C. Bishop, "Dysfunctional Effects of Formal Planning: Two Theoretical Explanations," *Academy of Management Review*, October 1983, pp. 588–99.
7. Richard F. Vancil, "The Accuracy of Long-Range Planning," *Harvard Business Review*, September–October 1970, p. 99.
8. Based on Ronald Henkoff, "How to Plan for 1995," *Fortune*, December 31, 1990, pp. 70–77.
9. Rick Molz, "How Leaders Use Goals," *Long Range Planning*, October 1987, p. 91.
10. Y. K. Shetty, "New Look at Corporate Goals," *California Management Review*, Winter 1979, pp. 71–79.
11. "Icahn Threatens to Dismantle TWA," *San Diego Union*, March 3, 1986, p. A1.
12. From Sears' 1988 *Annual Report*, p. 12.
13. From Bell Atlantic's 1989 *Annual Report*, p. 3.
14. From Southern Illinois University at Edwardsville's 1992 college catalog, p. 4.
15. See, for instance, Charles K. Warriner, "The Problem of Organizational Purpose," *Sociological Quarterly*, Spring 1965, pp. 139–46; and Jeffrey Pfeffer, *Organizational Design* (Arlington Heights, IL.: AHM Publishing, 1978), pp. 5–12.
16. Ibid.
17. Ibid.
18. Francis D. Tuggle, *Organizational Processes* (Arlington Heights, Ill.: AHM Publishing, 1978), p. 108.
19. Pam Carroll, "Freedom," *Success*, June 1990, pp. 44–45.
20. The concept is generally attributed to Peter F. Drucker, *The Practice of Management* (New York: Harper & Row, 1954).
21. See, for example, Edwin A. Locke, "Toward a Theory of Task Motivation and Incentives," *Organizational Behavior and Human Performance*, May 1968, pp. 157–89; Edwin A. Locke, Karyl N. Shaw, Lise M. Saari, and Gary P. Latham, "Goal Setting and Task Performance: 1969–1980," *Psychological Bulletin*, July 1981, pp. 125–52; Mark E. Tubbs, "Goal Setting: A Meta-Analytic Examination of the Empirical Evidence," *Journal of Applied Psychology*, August 1986, pp. 474–83; Anthony J. Mento, R. P. Steel, and R. J. Karren, "A Meta-Analytic Study of the Effects of Goal Setting on Task Performance: 1966–1984," *Organizational Behavior and Human Decision Processes*, February 1987, pp. 52–83; and Edwin A. Locke and Gary P. Latham, *A Theory of Goal Setting and Task Performance* (Englewood Cliffs, NJ: Prentice Hall, 1990).
22. See, for example, Gary P. Latham and Lise M. Saari, "The Effects of Holding Goal Difficulty Constant on Assigned and Participatively Set Goals," *Academy of Management Journal*, March 1979, pp. 163–68; Miriam Erez, P. Christopher Earley, and Charles L. Hulin, "The Impact of Participation on Goal Acceptance and Performance: A Two-Step Model," *Academy of Management Journal*, March 1985, pp. 50–66; and Gary P. Latham, Miriam Erez, and Edwin A. Locke, "Resolving Scientific Disputes by the Joint Design of Crucial Experiments by the Antagonists: Application to the Erez-Latham Dispute Regarding Participation in Goal Setting," *Journal of Applied Psychology*, November 1988, pp. 753–72.
23. Gary P. Latham, Terence R. Mitchell, and Dennis L. Dossett, "Importance of Participative Goal Setting and Anticipated Rewards on Goal Difficulty and Job Performance," *Journal of Applied Psychology*, April 1978, pp. 163–71.
24. Robert Rodgers and John E. Hunter, "Impact of Management by Objectives on Organizational Productivity," *Journal of Applied Psychology*, April 1991, pp. 322–36.

Chapter 8

1. Claire Poole, "Born to Hustle," *Forbes*, May 28, 1990, pp. 190–94.
2. See, for example, Larry J. Rosenberg and Charles D. Schewe, "Strategic Planning: Fulfilling the Promise," *Business Horizons*, July–August 1985, pp. 54–62; and Walter Kiechel III, "Corporate Strategy for the 1990s," *Fortune*, February 29, 1988, pp. 34–42.
3. "A Solid Strategy Helps Companies' Growth," *Nation's Business*, October 1990, p. 10.
4. "Colleges Undergo Reassessment," *Time*, April 14, 1992, pp. 81.
5. William K. Hall, "SBUs: Hot, New Topic in Management of Diversification," *Business Horizons*, February 1978, p. 17.
6. N. Venkatraman and John E. Prescott, "Environment-Strategy Co-alignment: An Empirical Test of Its Performance Implications," *Strategic Management Journal*, January 1990, pp. 1–23.
7. See Susan E. Jackson and Jane E. Dutton, "Discerning Threats and Opportunities," *Administrative Science Quarterly*, September 1988, pp. 370–87.
8. See, for example, Jay B. Barney, "Organizational Culture: Can It Be a Source of Sustained Competitive Advantage?," *Academy of Management Review*, July 1986, pp. 656–65; Christian Scholz, "Corporate Culture and Strategy—The Problem of Strategic Fit," *Long Range Planning*, August 1987, pp. 78–87; Sebastian Green, "Understanding Corporate Culture and Its Relation to Strategy," *International Studies of Management and Organization*, Summer 1988, pp. 6–28; Toyohiro Kono, "Corporate Culture and Long-Range Planning," *Long Range Planning*, August 1990, pp. 9–19; and C. Marlene Fiol, "Managing Culture as a Competitive Resource: An Identity-Based View of Sustainable Competitive Advantage," *Journal of Management*, March 1991, pp. 191–211.
9. Bernard Wysocki, Jr., "Cross-Border Alliances Become Favorite Way to Crack New Markets," *Wall Street Journal*, March 26, 1990, p. A1.
10. This box is based on Jerry Paul Sheppard, "When the Going Gets Tough, the Tough Go Bankrupt," *Journal of Management Inquiry*, September 1992, pp. 183–92.
11. See William F. Glueck, *Business Policy: Strategy Formulation and Management Action*, 2nd ed. (New York: McGraw-Hill, 1976), pp. 120–47; John A. Pearce II, "Selecting Among Alternative Grand Strategies," *California Management Review*, Spring 1982, pp. 23–31; and Theodore T. Herbert and Helen Deresky, "Generic Strategies: An Empirical Investigation of Typology Validity and Strategy Content," *Strategic Management Journal*, March–April 1987, pp. 135–47.
12. "How to Be Happy in One Act," *Fortune*, December 19, 1988, p. 119.
13. See, for example, Kathryn Rudie Harrigan, *Strategies for Declining*

Businesses (Lexington, Mass.: Lexington, 1980); Kim S. Cameron, Myung U. Kim, and David A. Whetten, "Organizational Effects of Decline and Turbulence," *Administrative Science Quarterly*, June 1987, pp. 222–40; "Downsizing Record Set By Firms in Year: 56% Report Job Cuts," *Wall Street Journal*, August 12, 1991, p. A2; and Kim S. Cameron, Sarah J. Freeman, and Aneil K. Mishra "Best Practices in White-Collar Downsizing: Managing Contradictions," *Academy of Management Executive*, August 1991, pp. 57–73.

14. Phillipe Haspeslagh, "Portfolio Planning: Uses and Limits," *Harvard Business Review*, January–February 1982, pp. 58–73.

15. *Perspective on Experience* (Boston: Boston Consulting Group, 1970).

16. Donald C. Hambrick, Ian C. Macmillan, and Diana L. Day, "Strategic Attributes and Performance in the BCG Matrix: A PIMS-Based Analysis of Industrial Product Businesses," *Academy of Management Journal*, September 1982, pp. 510–31; H. Kurt Christensen, Arnold C. Cooper, and Cornelis A. DeKluyver, "The Dog Business: A Re-Examination," *Business Horizons*, November–December 1982, pp. 12–18; William Baldwin, "The Market Share Myth," *Forbes*, March 14, 1983, pp. 109–15; Richard A. Bettis and William K. Hall, "The Business Portfolio Approach—Where It Falls Down in Practice," *Long Range Planning*, April 1983, pp. 95–104; and Jaclyn Fierman, "How to Make Money in Mature Markets," *Fortune*, November 25, 1985, pp. 47–53.

17. Reed E. Nelson, "Is There Strategy in Brazil?," *Business Horizons*, July–August 1990, pp. 15–23.

18. See Raymond E. Miles and Charles C. Snow, *Organizational Strategy, Structure, and Process* (New York: McGraw-Hill, 1978); Donald C. Hambrick, "Some Tests of the Effectiveness and Functional Attributes of Miles and Snow's Strategic Types," *Academy of Management Journal*, March 1983, pp. 5–26; and Shaker A. Zahra and John A. Pearce II, "Research Evidence on the Miles-Snow Typology," *Journal of Management*, December 1990, pp. 751–68.

19. See, for example, Michael E. Porter, *Competitive Strategy: Techniques for Analyzing Industries and Competitors* (New York: Free Press, 1980); Michael E. Porter, *Competitive Advantage: Creating and Sustaining Superior Performance* (New York: Free Press, 1985); Gregory G. Dess and Peter S. Davis, "Porter's (1980) Generic Strategies as Determinants of Strategic Group Membership and Organizational Performance," *Academy of Management Journal*, September 1984, pp. 467–88; Gregory G. Dess and Peter S. Davis, "Porter's (1980) Generic Strategies and Performance: An Empirical Examination with American Data—Part I: Testing Porter," *Organization Studies*, No. 1, 1986, pp. 37–55; Gregory G. Dess and Peter S. Davis, "Porter's (1980) Generic Strategies and Performance: An Empirical Examination with American Data—Part II: Performance Implications," *Organization Studies*, No. 3, 1986, pp. 255–61; Michael E. Porter, "From Competitive Advantage to Corporate Strategy," *Harvard Business Review*, May–June 1987, pp. 43–59; Alan I. Murray, "A Contingency View of Porter's 'Generic Strategies,'" *Academy of Management Review*, July 1988, pp. 390–400; Charles W. L. Hill, "Differentiation Versus Low Cost or Differentiation and Low Cost: A Contingency Framework," *Academy of Management Review*, July 1988, pp. 401–12; Ingolf Bamberger, "Developing Competitive Advantage in Small and Medium-Sized Firms," *Long Range Planning*, October 1989, pp. 80–88; and Michael E. Porter, "Know Your Place," *INC.*, September 1991, pp. 90–93.

20. Danny Miller and Jean-Marie Toulouse, "Strategy, Structure, CEO Personality and Performance in Small Firms," *American Journal of Small Business*, Winter 1986, pp. 47–62.

21. Dean M. Schroeder and Alan G. Robinson, "America's Most Successful Export to Japan: Continuous Improvement Programs," *Sloan Management Review*, Spring 1991, pp. 67–81; and Richard J. Schonenberger, "Is Strategy Strategic? Impact of Total Quality Management on Strategy," *Academy of Management Executive*, August 1992, pp. 80–87.

22. John Hillkirk, "Workers Are the Key, Top Firms Find," *USA Today*, October 1, 1991, p. B1.

23. "E. I. DuPont de Nemours & Co., Inc.," *Profiles in Quality* (Needham Heights, MA: Allyn and Bacon, 1991), pp. 25–27.

24. Liz McMillen, "To Boost Quality and Cut Costs, Oregon State University Adopts a Customer-Oriented Approach to Campus Services," *Chronicle of Higher Education*, February 6, 1991, p. A27.

25. Banning Kent Lary, "An 'Instinct' For Computer Success," *Nation's Business*, April 1991, pp. 46–48; Hal Lancaster and Michael Allen, "Dell Computer Battles Its Rivals With a Lean Machine," *Wall Street Journal*, March 30, 1992, p. B3; Peter H. Lewis, "Michael Dell Says He's More Than Ready for a Good Fight," *New York Times*, July 5, 1992, p. F12 and Julie Pitta, "Why Dell Is a Survivor," *Forbes*, October 12, 1992, pp. 82–91.

26. See, for example, J. Barton Cunningham and Joe Lischeron, "Defining Entrepreneurship," *Journal of Small Business Management*, January 1991, pp. 45–61.

27. Adapted from Howard H. Stevenson, M. J. Roberts and H. I. Grousbeck, *New Business Ventures and the Entrepreneur* (Homewood, Il.: Irwin, 1989).

28. See, for instance, Thomas M. Begley and David P. Boyd, "A Comparison of Entrepreneurs and Managers of Small Business Firms," *Journal of Management*, Spring 1987, pp. 99–108.

29. Peter F. Drucker, *Innovation and Entrepreneurship* (New York: Harper & Row, 1985).

30. Gifford Pinchot III, *Intrapreneuring: Or, Why You Don't Have to Leave the Corporation to Become an Entrepreneur* (New York: Harper & Row, 1985).

31. Karl H. Vesper, *New Venture Strategies* (Englewood Cliffs, N.J.: Prentice-Hall, 1980), p. 14.

32. John A. Hornaday, "Research About Living Entrepreneurs," in Calvin A. Kent, Donald L. Sexton, and Karl H. Vesper (eds.), *Encyclopedia of Entrepreneurship* (Englewood Cliffs, N.J.: Prentice-Hall, 1982), p. 28.

33. Robert H. Brockhaus, Sr., "The Psychology of the Entrepreneur," in Calvin A. Kent, Donald L. Sexton, and Karl H. Vesper (eds.), *Encyclopedia of Entrepreneurship*, pp. 41–49.

34. This section is based on Robert D. Hisrich, "Entrepreneurship/ Intrapreneurship," *American Psychologist*, February 1990, pp. 209–22.

35. Based on Erik Calonius, "Meet the King of Video, *Fortune*, June 4, 1990, p. 208.

36. Howard H. Stevenson and David E. Gumpert, "The Heart of Entrepreneurship," *Harvard Business Review*, March–April 1985, pp. 85–94.

37. Executive Office of the President, *The State of Small Business* (Washington, D.C.: GPO, 1983), p. 70–71.

Chapter 9

1. Harry G. Summers, Jr., "Military Support Services Proved Their Worth in Supplying Victory," *Los Angeles Times*, March 1, 1991, p. A7; Russell Mitchell, "Half Audie Murphy, Half Jack Welch," *Business Week*, March 4, 1991, pp. 42–43; and William G. Pagonis and Jeffrey L. Cruikshank, *Moving Mountains: Lessons in Leadership and Logistics From the Gulf War* (Boston: HBS Press, 1992).

2. Mark Robichaux, "'Competitor Intelligence': A Grapevine to Rivals' Secrets," *Wall Street Journal*, April 12, 1989, p. B2.

3. John Diffenbach, "Corporate Environmental Analysis In Large U.S. Corporations," *Long Range Planning*, June 1983, pp. 107–16; Subhash C. Jain, "Environmental Scanning in U.S. Corporations," *Long Range Planning*, April 1984, pp. 117–28; Leonard M. Fuld, *Monitoring the Competition* (New York: John Wiley & Sons, 1988); and Elmer H. Burack and Nicholas J. Mathys, "Environmental Scanning Improves Strategic Planning," *Personnel Administrator*, April 1989, pp. 82–87.

4. William L. Renfro and James L. Morrison, "Detecting Signals of Change," *The Futurist*, August 1984, p. 49.

5. Benjamin Gilad, "The Role of Organized Competitive Intelligence in Corporate Strategy," *Columbia Journal of World Business*, Winter 1989, pp. 29–35; Betsy D. Gelb, Mary Jane Saxton, George M. Zinkhan, and Nancy D. Albers, "Competitive Intelligence: Insights From Executives," *Business Horizons*, January–February 1991, pp. 43–47; Leonard Fuld, "A Recipe For Business Intelligence," *Journal of Business Strategy*, January–February 1991, pp. 12–17; Gary B. Roush, "A Program For Sharing Corporate Intelligence," *Journal of Business Strategy*, January–February 1991, pp. 4–7; and Richard S.

Teitelbaum, "The New Role for Intelligence," *Fortune*, November 2, 1992, pp. 104–07.

6. Mark Robichaux, "'Competitor Intelligence': A Grapevine to Rivals' Secrets."

7. Manuel Werner, "Planning for Uncertain Futures: Building Commitment Through Scenario Planning," *Business Horizons*, May–June 1990, pp. 55–58.

8. This box is based on William H. Davidson, "The Role of Global Scanning in Business Planning," *Organizational Dynamics*, Winter 1991, pp. 5–16.

9. See James K. Glassman, "The Year of Gazing Dangerously," *Business Month*, March 1990, pp. 13–14; Anne B. Fisher, "Is Long-Range Planning Worth It?" *Fortune*, April 23, 1990, pp. 281–84; Jill Andresky Fraser, "On Target," *INC.*, April 1991, pp. 113–14; and Peter Schwartz, *The Art of the Long View* (New York: Doubleday/Currency, 1991).

10. P. Narayan Pant and William H. Starbuck, "Innocents in the Forest: Forecasting and Research Methods," *Journal of Management*, June 1990, pp. 433–60.

11. This section is based on Bruce Brocka and M. Suzanne Brocka, *Quality Management* (Homewood, Ill.: Business One Irwin, 1992), pp. 231–36; George A. Weimer, "Benchmarking Maps the Route to Quality," *Industry Week*, July 20, 1992, pp. 54–55; Jeremy Main, "How to Steal the Best Ideas Around," *Fortune*, October 19, 1992, pp. 102–106; and Howard Rothman, "You Need Not Be Big to Benchmark," *Nation's Business*, December 1992, pp. 64–65.

12. Patrice Duggan and Gale Eisenstodt, "The New Face of Japanese Espionage," *Forbes*, November 12, 1990, p. 96; and Michele Galen, "These Guys Aren't Spooks. They're 'Competitive Analysts'," *Business Week*, October 14, 1991, p. 97.

13. Thomas A. Stewart, "Why Budgets Are Bad for Business," *Fortune*, June 4, 1990, pp. 179–90.

14. Linda J. Shinn and M. Sue Sturgeon, "Budgeting from Ground Zero," *Association Management*, September 1990, pp. 45–58.

15. R. D. Behn, *Policy Termination: A Survey of the Current Literature and an Agenda for Future Research* (Washington, D.C.: Ford Foundation, 1977).

16. Peter A. Pyhrr, "Zero-Base Budgeting," *Harvard Business Review*, November–December 1970, pp. 111–18.

17. Virendra S. Sherlekar and Burton V. Dean, "An Evaluation of the Initial Year of Zero-Base Budgeting in the Federal Government," *Management Science*, August 1980, pp. 750–72.

18. John V. Pearson and Ray J. Michael, "Zero-Base Budgeting: A Technique for Planned Organizational Decline," *Long Range Planning*, June 1981, pp. 68–76.

19. See Harold E. Fearon, William A. Ruch, Vincent G. Reuter, C. David Wieters, and Ross R. Reck, *Fundamentals of Production/Operations Management*, 3rd ed. (St. Paul, Minn.: West Publishing, 1986), p. 97.

20. For a discussion of software and application to a project for restructuring a large retail chain, see Paul A. Strassmann, "The Best-Laid Plans," *INC.*, October 1988, pp. 135–88.

21. See, for example, Sarah Stiansen, "Breaking Even," *Success*, November 1988, p. 16.

22. Stephen E. Barndt and Davis W. Carvey, *Essentials of Operations Management* (Englewood Cliffs, N.J.: Prentice-Hall, 1982), p. 134.

23. Dori Jones Yang, "Boeing Knocks Down the Wall Between the Dreamers and the Doers," *Business Week*, October 28, 1991, pp. 120–21.

24. David A. Whetten and Kim S. Cameron, *Developing Management Skills*, (New York: HarperCollins, 1984), p. 106.

25. "Willa Martin: The Image to Survive," *Industry Week*, March 2, 1992, pp. 40–41.

26. Peter F. Drucker, *The Effective Executive* (New York: Harper & Row, 1967), pp. 47–51.

27. Ross A. Webber, *To Be a Manager* (Homewood, Ill.: Richard D. Irwin, 1981), p. 373.

28. For a more detailed discussion of these time-management suggestions, see R. A. Mackenzie, *The Time Trap* (New York: McGraw-Hill, 1975); R. A. Webber, *Time Is Money* (New York: Free Press, 1980);

M. E. Haynes, *Practical Time Management: How to Make the Most of Your Most Perishable Resource* (Tulsa, Okla.: Penn Well Books, 1985); and Alan Deutschman, "The CEO's Secret of Managing Time," *Fortune*, June 1, 1992, pp. 135–46.

Chapter 10

1. Tom Richman, "Reorganizing for Growth," *INC.*, January 1991, pp. 110–11.

2. Stephen P. Robbins, *Organization Theory: Structure, Design, and Applications*, 3rd ed. (Englewood Cliffs, N.J.: Prentice-Hall, 1990), Chapter 4.

3. See, for instance, Brian S. Moskal, "Supervisors, Begone!," *Industry Week*, June 20, 1988, p. 32; and Gregory A. Patterson, "Auto Assembly Lines Enter a New Era," *Wall Street Journal*, December 28, 1988, p. A2.

4. The matrix organization is an obvious example of an organization design that breaks the unity of command. See, for instance, David I. Cleland, ed., *Matrix Management Systems Handbook* (New York: Van Nostrand Reinhold, 1984); and Erik W. Larson and David H. Gobeli, "Matrix Management: Contradictions and Insights," *California Management Review*, Summer 1987, pp. 126–38.

5. See, for instance, David Kipnis, *The Powerholders* (Chicago: University of Chicago Press, 1976); Jeffrey Pfeffer, *Power in Organizations* (Marshfield, Mass.: Pitman Publishing, 1981); Henry Mintzberg, *Power In and Around Organizations* (Englewood Cliffs, N.J.: Prentice-Hall, 1983); and David W. Ewing, *"Do It My Way or You're Fired": Employee Rights and the Changing Role of Management Prerogatives* (New York: John Wiley, 1983).

6. See John R. P. French, Jr. and Bertram Raven, "The Bases of Social Power," in Dorwin Cartwright and A. F. Zander (eds.), *Group Dynamics: Research and Theory* (New York: Harper & Row, Pub., 1960), pp. 607–23; Philip M. Podsakoff and Chester A. Schreisheim, "Field Studies of French and Raven's Bases of Power: Critique, Reanalysis, and Suggestions for Future Research," *Psychological Bulletin*, May 1985, pp. 387–411; Ramesh K. Shukla, "Influence of Power Bases in Organizational Decision Making: A Contingency Model," *Decision Sciences*, July 1982, pp. 450–70; Dean E. Frost and Anthony J. Stahelski, "The Systematic Measurement of French and Raven's Bases of Social Power in Workgroups," *Journal of Applied Social Psychology*, April 1988, pp. 375–89; and Timothy R. Hinkin and Chester A. Schriesheim, "Development and Application of New Scales to Measure the French and Raven (1959) Bases of Social Power," *Journal of Applied Psychology*, August 1989, pp. 561–67.

7. Steven N. Brenner and Earl A. Molander, "Is the Ethics of Business Changing?," *Harvard Business Review*, January–February 1977, pp. 57–71.

8. Herbert C. Kelman and Lee H. Lawrence, "American Response to the Trial of Lt. William L. Calley," *Psychology Today*, June 1972, pp. 41–45; 78–81.

9. Lyndall Urwick, *The Elements of Administration* (New York: Harper & Row, 1944), pp. 52–53.

10. Quoted in Jim Braham, "Money Talks," *Industry Week*, April 17, 1989, p. 23.

11. John S. McClenahen, "Managing More People in the '90s" *Industry Week*, March 20, 1989, p. 30.

12. David Van Fleet, "Span of Management Research and Issues," *Academy of Management Journal*, September 1983, pp. 546–52.

13. John H. Sheridan, "Sizing Up Corporate Staffs," *Industry Week*, November 21, 1988, p. 47.

14. Tom Burns and G. M. Stalker, *The Management of Innovation* (London: Taristock, 1961).

15. Based on Barbara Buell and Robert D. Hof, "Hewlett-Packard Rethinks Itself," *Business Week*, April 1, 1991, pp. 76–79; Robert D. Hof, "Suddenly, Hewlett-Packard is Doing Everything Right," *Business Week*, March 23, 1992; and Stephen Kreider Yode, "Hewlett-Packard Is Too Busy to Notice Industry Slump," *Wall Street Journal*, May 11, 1992, p. B3.

16. Alfred D. Chandler, Jr., *Strategy and Structure: Chapters in the History of the Industrial Enterprise* (Cambridge, Mass.: MIT Press, 1962).

17. See, for instance, Raymond E. Miles and Charles C. Snow, *Organizational Strategy, Structure, and Process* (New York: McGraw-Hill, 1978); and Herman L. Boschken, "Strategy and Structure: Reconceiving the Relationship," *Journal of Management*, March 1990, pp. 135–50.

18. See, for instance, Peter M. Blau and Richard A. Schoenherr, *The Structure of Organizations* (New York: Basic Books, 1971); D. S. Pugh, "The Aston Program of Research: Retrospect and Prospect," in A. H. Van de Ven and W. F. Joyce (eds.), *Perspectives on Organization Design and Behavior* (New York: John Wiley, 1981), pp. 135–66; and R. Z. Gooding and J. A. Wagner III, "A Meta-Analytic Review of the Relationship Between Size and Performance: The Productivity and Efficiency of Organizations and Their Subunits," *Administrative Science Quarterly*, December 1985, pp. 462–81.

19. This box is based on Richard Preston, "Lean, Mean and American," *New York Times*, January 14, 1992, p. A15; Thomas A. Stewart, "The Search for the Organization of Tomorrow," *Fortune*, May 18, 1992, pp. 92–98; John A. Byrne, "Is Your Company Too Big?," *Business Week*, March 27, 1989, pp. 84–94; and Brian Dumaine, "Is Big Still Good?," *Fortune*, April 20, 1992, pp. 50–60.

20. C. Chet Miller, William H. Glick, Yau-De Wang, and George Huber, "Understanding Technology-Structure Relationships: Theory Development and Meta-Analytic Theory Testing," *Academy of Management Journal*, June 1991, pp. 370–99.

21. Joan Woodward, *Industrial Organization: Theory and Practice* (London: Oxford University Press, 1965).

22. Charles Perrow, *Organizational Analysis: A Sociological Perspective* (Belmont, Calif.: Wadsworth, 1970).

23. Donald Gerwin, "Relationships Between Structure and Technology," in P. C. Nystrom and W. H. Starbuck (eds.), *Handbook of Organizational Design*, Vol. 2 (New York: Oxford University Press, 1981), pp. 3–38; and Denise M. Rousseau and R. A. Cooke, "Technology and Structure: The Concrete, Abstract, and Activity Systems of Organizations," *Journal of Management*, Fall–Winter 1984, pp. 345–61.

24. See Stephen P. Robbins, *Organization Theory: Structure, Design, and Applications*, pp. 210–32.

25. Geert Hofstede, "Motivation, Leadership, and Organization: Do American Theories Apply Abroad?," *Organizational Dynamics*, Summer 1980, p. 60.

26. Ilan Vertinsky, David K. Tse, Donald A. Wehrung, and Kam-hon Lee, "Organizational Design and Management Norms: A Comparative Study of Managers' Perceptions in the People's Republic of China, Hong Kong, and Canada," *Journal of Management*, December 1990, pp. 853–67.

Chapter 11

1. Based on Carla Rapoport, "A Tough Swede Invades the U.S.," *Fortune*, June 29, 1992, pp. 76–79.

2. U.S. Department of Labor, Bureau of Labor Statistics, *Employment and Wages*, Springfield, Va.: National Technical Information Service 1986.

3. Tom Richman, "Out of the Lab: A Bite-Size Company," *Business Month*, September 1990, pp. 96–97; and Jennifer Reese, "How to Grow Big By Staying Small," *Fortune*, December 28, 1992, pp. 50–54.

4. Henry Mintzberg, *Structure in Fives: Designing Effective Organizations* (Englewood Cliffs, N.J.: Prentice-Hall, 1983), p. 157.

5. See, for instance, Jay Galbraith, "Matrix Organization Designs: How to Combine Functional and Project Forms," *Business Horizons*, February 1971, pp. 29–40; and Lawton R. Burns, "Matrix Management in Hospitals: Testing Theories of Structure and Development," *Administrative Science Quarterly*, September 1989, pp. 349–68.

6. See, for example, Neal E. Boudette, "Networks to Dismantle Old Structures," *Industry Week*, January 16, 1989, pp. 27–31; Walter W. Powell, "Neither Market Nor Hierarchy: Network Forms of Organization," in B. M. Staw and L. L. Cummings (eds.), *Research in Organizational Behavior*, Vol. 12 (Greenwich, Conn.: JAI Press, 1990), pp. 295–336; and Michael Selz, "Small Companies Thrive by Taking Over Some Specialized Tasks for Big Concerns," *Wall Street Journal*, September 11, 1991, p. B1.

7. Sumantra Ghoshal, "Global Strategy: An Organizing Framework," *Strategic Management Journal*, September–October, 1987, pp. 425–40.

8. William J. Altier, "Task Forces: An Effective Management Tool," *Sloan Management Review*, Spring 1986, pp. 69–76.

9. Henry Mintzberg, *Structure in Fives: Designing Effective Organizations*, p. 159.

10. See, for example, Ricky W. Griffin, "Toward an Integrated Theory of Task Design," in L. L. Cummings and Barry M. Staw (eds.), *Research in Organizational Behavior*, Vol. 9, (Greenwich, Conn.: JAI Press, 1987), pp. 79–120; and Michael Campion, "Interdisciplinary Approaches to Job Design: A Constructive Replication with Extensions," *Journal of Applied Psychology*, August 1988, pp. 467–81.

11. Martin J. Gannon, Brian A. Poole, and Robert E. Prangley, "Involuntary Job Rotation and Work Behavior," *Personnel Journal*, June 1972, pp. 446–48.

12. Stephen Phillips and Amy Dunkin, "King Customer," *Business Week*, March 12, 1990, p. 91.

13. R. W. Walters, "The Citibank Project: Improving Productivity Through Work Design," in *How to Manage Change Effectively*, ed. Donald L. Kirkpatrick (San Francisco: Jossey-Bass, 1985), pp. 195–208.

14. See, for example, J. R. Hackman and G. R. Oldham, *Work Redesign* (Reading, Mass.: Addison-Wesley, 1980); and John B. Miner, *Theories of Organizational Behavior* (Hinsdale, Ill: Dryden Press, 1980), pp. 231–66.

15. Toby D. Wall, Nigel J. Kemp, Paul L. R. Jackson, and Chris W. Clegg, "Outcomes of Autonomous Workgroups: A Long-Term Field Experiment," *Academy of Management Journal*, June 1986, pp. 280–304.

16. Barbara Presley Noble, "An Approach With Staying Power: Self-Managed Teams Helped an AT&T Plant Survive," *New York Times*, March 8, 1992, p. F23.

17. J. Richard Hackman and Greg R. Oldham, "Development of the Job Diagnostic Survey," *Journal of Applied Psychology*, April 1975, pp. 159–170.

18. J. Richard Hackman, "Work Design," in J. Richard Hackman and J. Lloyd Suttle (eds.), *Improving Life at Work* (Glenview, Ill.: Scott, Foresman, 1977), p. 129.

19. General support for the JCM is reported in Yitzhak Fried and Gerald R. Ferris, "The Validity of the Job Characteristics Model: A Review and Meta-Analysis," *Personnel Psychology*, Summer 1987, pp. 287–322.

20. J. Richard Hackman, "Work Design," pp. 136–40.

21. See, for instance, Randall B. Dunham, Jon L. Pierce, and Maria B. Castañeda, "Alternative Work Schedules: Two Field Quasi-Experiments," *Personnel Psychology*, Summer 1987, pp. 215–42.

22. Dan Olson and Arthur P. Brief, "The Impact of Alternative Workweeks," *Personnel*, January–February 1978, p. 73.

23. John M. Ivancevich and Herbert L. Lyon, "The Shortened Workweek: A Field Experiment," *Journal of Applied Psychology*, February 1977, pp. 34–37.

24. Cathy Trost, "To Cut Costs and Keep the Best People, More Concerns Offer Flexible Work Plans," *Wall Street Journal*, February 18, 1992, p. B1.

25. See, for example, Jay S. Kim and A. F. Campagna, "Effects of Flextime on Employee Attendance and Performance: A Field Experiment," *Academy of Management Journal*, December 1981, pp. 729–41; and David R. Ralston, William P. Anthony, and David J. Gustafson, "Employees May Love Flextime, But What Does It Do to the Organization's Productivity?," *Journal of Applied Psychology*, May 1985, pp. 272–79.

26. "Flextime Pros and Cons," *Boardroom Reports*, March 1, 1989, p. 15.

27. For a review of misconceptions surrounding flextime, see M. Ronald

Buckley, Diane C. Kicza, and Nancy Crane, "A Note on the Effectiveness of Flextime as an Organizational Intervention," *Public Personnel Management*, Fall 1987, pp. 259–67. See also Carol Hymowitz, "As Aetna Adds Flextime, Bosses Learn to Cope," *Wall Street Journal*, June 18, 1990, p. B1.

28. Patricia Amend, "Workers Get a Share of the Action: Job Sharing Splits Hours," *USA Today*, April 27, 1989, p. 9B.

29. Ellen Graham, "Flexible Formulas," *Wall Street Journal*, June 4, 1990, p. R34.

30. Ibid.

31. See, for example, "The 'Just In Time' Worker," *U.S. News & World Report*, November 23, 1987, pp. 45–46; Jack L. Simonetti, Nich Nykodym, and Louella M. Sell, "Temporary Employees: A Permanent Boon?" *Personnel*, August 1988, pp. 50–56; Michael A. Verespej, "Part-Time Workers: No Temporary Phenomenon," *Industry Week*, April 3, 1989, pp. 13–18; "Contingent Work Force is Growing Rapidly," *Wall Street Journal*, May 2, 1989, p. B1; and "Taking Stock of the Flexible Work Force," *Business Week*, July 24, 1989, p. 12.

32. Cited in Brian Dumaine, "How to Manage in a Recession," *Fortune*, November 5, 1990, p. 68.

33. David Kirkpatrick, "Smart New Ways to Use Temps," *Fortune*, February 15, 1988, p. 110.

34. "The Disposable Employee Is Becoming a Fact of Corporate Life," *Business Week*, December 15, 1986, pp. 52–56.

35. "Contingent Work Force Is Growing Rapidly."

36. "The Disposable Employee Is Becoming a Fact of Corporate Life," p. 52.

37. Ibid.

38. See, for example, Steve Shirley, "A Company Without Offices," *Harvard Business Review*, January–February 1986, pp. 127–36; C. A. Hamilton, "Telecommuting," *Personnel Journal*, April 1987, pp. 91–101; Donald C. Bacon, "Look Who's Working at Home," *Nation's Business*, October 1989, pp. 20–31; Michael Alexander, "Travel-Free Commuting," *Nation's Business*, December 1990, pp. 33–37; Leah Beth Ward, "The Mixed Blessings of Telecommuting," *New York Times*, September 20, 1992, p. F23; and David C. Churbuck and Jeffrey S. Young, "The Virtual Workplace," *Forbes*, November 23, 1992, pp. 184–90.

39. "Employers Set Rules for Doing Homework," *Wall Street Journal*, August 16, 1991, p. B1.

40. Ronald Henkoff, "Make Your Office More Productive," *Fortune*, February 25, 1991, p. 84.

41. Ibid.

Chapter 12

1. Kathy Rebello, "Microsoft: Bill Gates's Baby is on Top of the World. Can It Stay There?," *Business Week*, February 24, 1992, pp. 60–65; and Carrie Tibbetts, "Using Friendly Persuasion," *Working Woman*, August 1992, pp. 27–28.

2. See, for example, Steve Weiner, "Sears' Costly Win in a Hiring Suit," *Wall Street Journal*, March 18, 1986, p. 21.

3. Elmer H. Burack, "Corporate Business and Human Resource Planning Practices: Strategic Issues and Concerns," *Organizational Dynamics*, Summer 1986, pp. 73–87.

4. Thomas J. Bergmann and M. S. Taylor, "College Recruitment: What Attracts Students to Organizations?," *Personnel*, May–June 1984, pp. 34–46.

5. Judith R. Gordon, *Human Resource Management: A Practical Approach* (Boston: Allyn and Bacon, 1986), p. 170.

6. See, for example, Jean Powell Kirnan, John A. Farley, and Kurt F. Geisinger, "The Relationship Between Recruiting Source, Applicant Quality, and Hire Performance: An Analysis by Sex, Ethnicity, and Age," *Personnel Psychology*, Summer 1989, pp. 293–308.

7. See, for example, Leonard Greenhalgh, Anne T. Lawrence, and Robert I. Sutton, "Determinants of Work Force Reduction Strategies in Declining Organizations," *Academy of Management Review*, April 1988, pp. 241–54.

8. This story was directly influenced by a similar example in Arthur

9. "Creating Change by Committee," *Working Woman*, April 1992, pp. 29–30; and Julia Flynn, "Julia Stasch Raises the Roof for Feminism," *Business Week*, January 25, 1993, p. 102.

10. James J. Asher, "The Biographical Item: Can It Be Improved?," *Personnel Psychology*, Summer 1972, p. 266.

11. George W. England, *Development and Use of Weighted Application Blanks*, rev. ed. (Minneapolis: Industrial Relations Center, University of Minnesota, 1971).

12. John Aberth, "Pre-Employment Testing Is Losing Favor," *Personnel Journal*, September 1986, pp. 96–104.

13. Chris Lee, "Testing Makes a Comeback," *Training*, December 1988, pp. 49–59.

14. Ibid., p. 50.

15. Edwin E. Ghiselli, "The Validity of Aptitude Tests in Personnel Selection," *Personnel Psychology*, Winter 1973, p. 475.

16. G. Grimsley and H. F. Jarrett, "The Relation of Managerial Achievement to Test Measures Obtained in the Employment Situation: Methodology and Results," *Personnel Psychology*, Spring 1973, pp. 31–48; and Abraham K. Korman, "The Prediction of Managerial Performance: A Review," *Personnel Psychology*, Summer 1968, pp. 295–322.

17. I. T. Robertson and R. S. Kandola, "Work Sample Tests: Validity, Adverse Impact, and Applicant Reaction," *Journal of Occupational Psychology*, Vol. 55, No. 3, 1982, p. 171–83.

18. See, for example, B. B. Gaugler, D. B. Rosenthal, G. C. Thornton, III, and C. Bentson, "Meta-Analysis of Assessment Center Validity," *Journal of Applied Psychology*, August 1987, pp. 493–511; Richard Klimoski and Mary Brickner, "Why Do Assessment Centers Work? The Puzzle of Assessment Center Validity," *Personnel Psychology*, Summer 1987, pp. 243–60; Glenn M. McEvoy and Richard W. Beatty, "Assessment Centers and Subordinate Appraisals of Managers: A Seven-Year Examination of Predictive Validity," *Personnel Psychology*, Spring 1989, pp. 37–52; Michael J. Papa, "A Comparison of Two Methods of Managerial Selection," *Management Communication Quarterly*, November 1989, pp. 191–218; and Craig J. Russell and Karl W. Kuhnert, "New Frontiers in Management Selection Systems: Where Measurement Technologies and Theory Collide," *Leadership Quarterly*, Summer 1992, pp. 109–35.

19. Robert L. Dipboye, *Selection Interviews: Process Perspectives* (Cincinnati, Ohio: South-Western Publishing, 1992), p. 6.

20. See, for instance, Richard D. Arvey and James E. Campion, "The Employment Interview: A Summary and Review of Recent Research," *Personnel Psychology*, Summer 1982, pp. 281–322; and Michael M. Harris, "Reconsidering the Employment Interview: A Review of Recent Literature and Suggestions for Future Research," *Personnel Psychology*, Winter 1989, pp. 691–726.

21. Robert L. Dipboye, *Selection Interviews*, p. 180.

22. See, for instance, Eugene C. Mayfield in Neal Schmitt, "Social and Situational Determinants of Interview Decisions: Implications for Employment Interview," *Personnel Psychology*, Spring 1976, p. 81; Richard D. Arvey and James E. Campion, "The Employment Interview: A Summary and Review of Recent Research"; Milton D. Hakel, "Employment Interview," in K. M. Rowland and G. R. Ferris (eds.), *Personnel Management: New Perspectives* (Boston: Allyn and Bacon, 1982), p. 129–55; Edward C. Webster, *The Employment Interview: A Social Judgment Process* (Schomberg, Ontario: S.I.P. Publications, 1982), Michael M. Harris, "Reconsidering the Employment Interview"; and Amanda Peek Phillips and Robert L. Dipboye, "Correlational Tests of Predictions From a Process Model of the Interview," *Journal of Applied Psychology*, February 1989, pp. 41–52.

23. David A. DeCenzo and Stephen P. Robbins, *Human Resource Management*, 4th ed. (New York: John Wiley and Sons, 1994), pp. 208–209.

24. See Irwin L. Goldstein, "The Application Blank: How Honest Are the Responses?" *Journal of Applied Psychology*, October 1971, pp. 491–92; and Winifred Yu, "Firms Tighten Résumé Checks of Applicants," *Wall Street Journal*, August 20, 1985, p. 27.

25. Paul M. Muchinsky, "The Use of Reference Reports in Personnel Selection: A Review and Evaluation, *Journal of Occupational Psy-*

chology, April 1979, pp. 287–97; and R. R. Reilly and G. T. Chao, "Validity and Fairness of Some Alternative Employee Selection Procedures," *Personnel Psychology*, Spring 1982, pp. 1–62.

26. Cited in "If You Can't Say Something Nice . . . ," *Wall Street Journal*, March 4, 1988, p. 25.

27. Eugene C. Mayfield in Neal Schmitt, "Social and Situational Determinants of Interview Decisions: Implications for Employment Interview."

28. See "Resumé Falsehoods," *Boardroom Reports*, May 1, 1989, p. 15; and Joan E. Rigdon, "Deceptive Resumes Can Be Door-Openers But Can Become an Employee's Undoing," *Wall Street Journal*, June 17, 1992, p. B1.

29. Cited in "The Five Factors That Make for Airline Accidents," *Fortune*, May 22, 1989, p. 80.

30. Susan Dentzer, "How to Train Workers For the 21st Century," *U.S. News & World Report*, September 25, 1992, p. 73.

31. See, for example, Joan C. Szabo, "Boosting Workers' Basic Skills," *Nation's Business*, January 1992, pp. 38–40.

32. See, for example, David A. DeCenzo and Stephen P. Robbins, *Human Resource Management*, pp. 385–393.

33. BARS have not been without critics. See, for example, Luis R. Gomez-Mejia, "Evaluating Employee Performance: Does the Appraisal Instrument Make a Difference?," *Journal of Organizational Behavior Management*, Winter 1988, pp. 155–71.

34. Robert D. Bretz, Jr., George T. Milkovich, and Walter Read, "The Current State of Performance Appraisal Research and Practice: Concerns, Directions, and Implications," *Journal of Management*, June 1992, p. 331.

35. Ronald J. Burke, "Why Performance Appraisal Systems Fail," *Personnel Administration*, June 1972, pp. 32–40.

36. Donald E. Super and Douglas T. Hall, "Career Development: Exploration and Planning," in Mark R. Rosenzweig and Lyman W. Porter (eds.), *Annual Review of Psychology*, Vol. 29 (Palo Alto, Calif.: Annual Reviews, 1978), p. 334.

37. See, for instance, Elmer H. Burack, "The Sphinx's Riddle: Life and Career Cycles," *Training and Development Journal*, April 1984, pp. 53–61; and Douglas T. Hall and Associates, *Career Development in Organizations* (San Francisco: Jossey-Bass, 1986).

38. Douglas T. Hall and Judith Richter, "Career Gridlock: Baby Boomers Hit the Wall," *Academy of Management Executive*, August 1990, pp. 7–22.

39. James A. Breaugh, "Realistic Job Previews: A Critical Appraisal and Future Research Directions," *Academy of Management Review*, October 1983, pp. 612–19; and Steven L. Premack and John P. Wanous, "A Meta-Analysis of Realistic Job Preview Experiments," *Journal of Applied Psychology*, November 1985, pp. 706–19.

40. Alan N. Schoonmaker, *Executive Career Strategy* (New York: American Management Association, 1971); Andrew J. DuBrin, *Fundamentals of Organizational Behavior: An Applied Perspective*, 2nd ed. (Elmsford, N.Y.: Pergamon Press, 1978), Chapter 5; and Eugene E. Jennings, "Success Chess," *Management of Personnel Quarterly*, Fall 1980, pp. 2–8.

41. John E. Sheridan, John W. Slocum, Jr., Richard Buda, and Richard C. Thompson, "Effects of Corporate Sponsorship and Departmental Power on Career Tournaments," *Academy of Management Journal*, September 1990, pp. 578–602.

42. Charles Perrow, *Complex Organizations: A Critical Essay* (Glenview, Ill.: Scott, Foresman, 1972), p. 43.

43. John E. Sheridan, et al., "Effects of Corporate Sponsorship and Departmental Power on Career Tournaments."

44. Stephen C. Bushardt, Roy N. Moore, and Sukumar C. Debnath, "Picking the Right Person for Your Mentor," *S.A.M. Advanced Management Journal*, Summer 1982, pp. 46–51; Ellen A. Fagenson, "The Power of a Mentor," *Group and Organization Studies*, June 1988, pp. 182–94; and George F. Dreher and Ronald A. Ash, "A Comparative Study of Mentoring Among Men and Women in Managerial, Professional, and Technical Positions," *Journal of Applied Psychology*, October 1990, pp. 539–46.

45. See, for example, David Kirkpatrick, "Is Your Career on Track?" *Fortune*, July 2, 1990, pp. 38–48; Amy Saltzman, "Sidestepping Your

Way to the Top," *U.S. News & World Report*, September 17, 1990, pp. 60–61; and Bruce Nussbaum, "I'm Worried About My Job!," *Business Week*, October 7, 1991, pp. 94–97.

46. Susan Moffat, "Should You Work for the Japanese?," *Fortune*, December 3, 1990, p. 116.

47. Cynthia D. Fisher, "Current and Recurrent Challenges in HRM," *Journal of Management*, June 1989, p. 161.

48. Mark E. Mendenhall, E. Dunbar, and Gary R. Oddou, "Expatriate Selection, Training, and Career-Pathing: A Review and Critique," *Human Resource Management*, Spring 1987, pp. 331–45.

49. Vladimir Pucik and J. H. Katz, "Information, Control, and Human Resource Management in Multinational Firms," *Human Resource Management*, Spring 1986, pp. 121–32.

50. Cited in "More Picket Lines, Fewer Rank-and-Filers," *Business Week*, May 7, 1990, p. 24.

51. Aaron Bernstein, "Been Down So Long . . . ," *Business Week*, January 14, 1991, pp. 30–31.

52. Ibid.

53. Ibid.

54. Ibid.

55. See, for example, Michael A. Verespej, "Partnership in the Trenches," *Industry Week*, October 17, 1988, pp. 56–64; and "Unions and Management Are in a Family Way," *U.S. News & World Report*, June 12, 1989, p. 24.

56. See James E. Ellis, "Monsanto's New Challenges: Keeping Minority Workers," *Business Week*, July 8, 1991, p.61; and Taylor Cox, Jr. and Stacy Blake, "Managing Cultural Diversity: Implications for Organizational Competitiveness," *The Academy of Management Executive*, August 1991, pp. 45–56.

57. Kenneth E. Newgren, C. E. Kellogg, and William Gardner, "Corporate Responses to Dual-Career Couples: A Decade of Transformation," *Akron Business and Economic Review*, Summer 1988, p. 85.

58. Ibid., pp. 85–96.

59. Ibid., p. 89.

60. Ibid., p. 94.

61. Ibid., p. 92.

62. See, for example, Michele Galen, "Out of the Shadows," *Business Week*, October 28, 1991, pp. 30–31; and Joann S. Lublin, "Sexual Harassment is Topping Agenda in Many Executive Education Programs," *Wall Street Journal*, December 2, 1991, p. B1.

63. See David E. Terpstra and Douglas D. Baker, "Outcomes of Federal Court Decisions on Sexual Harassment," *Academy of Management Journal*, March 1992, pp. 181–90.

64. See Alan Deutschman, "Dealing With Sexual Harassment," *Fortune*, November 4, 1991, pp. 145–48; Robert T. Gray, "How to Deal With Sexual Harassment," *Nation's Business*, December 1991, pp. 28–31; and Troy Segal, "Getting Serious About Sexual Harassment," *Business Week*, November 9, 1992, pp. 78–82.

Chapter 13

1. Leah Nathans Spiro, "Less-Than-Fantastic Plastic," *Business Week*, November 9, 1992, pp. 58–59.

2. The idea for these metaphors came from Peter B. Vaill, *Managing as a Performing Art: New Ideas for a World of Chaotic Change* (San Francisco: Jossey-Bass, 1989).

3. See, for instance, Rosabeth Moss Kanter, "Transcending Business Boundaries: 12,000 World Managers View Change," *Harvard Business Review*, May–June 1991, pp. 151–64.

4. Kurt Lewin, *Field Theory in Social Science* (New York: Harper & Row, 1951).

5. See, for instance, Tom Peters, *Thriving on Chaos* (New York: Alfred A. Knopf, 1987).

6. Daniel M. Kehrer, "The Miracle of Theory Q," *Business Month*, September 1989, pp. 45–49.

7. Tom Peters, *Thriving on Chaos*, p. 3.

8. Ibid.

9. This box is based on John Huey, "Nothing is Impossible," *Fortune*, September 23, 1991, pp. 134–40.

10. See, for example, Barry M. Staw, "Counterforces to Change," in Paul S. Goodman, and Associates, (eds)., *Change in Organizations* (San Francisco, Calif.: Jossey-Bass Publishers, 1982), p. 87–121.

11. John P. Kotter and Leonard A. Schlesinger, "Choosing Strategies for Change," *Harvard Business Review*, March–April 1979, pp. 107–109.

12. Ibid., pp. 106–14.

13. See, for example, Wendell L. French and Cecil H. Bell, Jr., *Organization Development: Behavioral Science Interventions for Organization Improvement*, 4th ed. (Englewood Cliffs, N.J.: Prentice-Hall, 1990).

14. P. B. Smith, "Controlled Studies of the Outcome of Sensitivity Training," *Psychological Bulletin*, July 1975, pp. 597–622.

15. John P. Campbell and Marvin D. Dunnette, "Effectiveness of T-Group Experience in Managerial Training and Development," *Psychological Bulletin*, August 1968, pp. 73–104.

16. Morton A. Lieberman, Irvin D. Yalom, and Matthew B. Miles, *Encounter Groups: First Facts* (New York: Basic Books, 1973); and Carl A. Bramlette and Jeffrey H. Tucker, "Encounter Groups: Positive Change or Deterioration? More Data and a Partial Replication," *Human Relations*, April 1981, pp. 303–14.

17. Edgar H. Schein, *Process Consultation: Its Role in Organizational Development* (Reading, Mass.: Addison-Wesley, 1969), p. 9.

18. See Thomas H. Fitzgerald, "Can Change in Organizational Culture Really Be Managed?," *Organizational Dynamics*, Autumn 1988, pp. 5–15; Brian Dumaine, "Creating A New Company Culture," *Fortune*, January 15, 1990, pp. 127–31; and Peter F. Drucker, "Don't Change Corporate Culture—Use It!," *Wall Street Journal*, March 28, 1991, p. A14.

19. See, for example, Ralph H. Kilmann, Mary J. Saxton, and Roy Serpa, eds., *Gaining Control of the Corporate Culture* (San Francisco: Jossey-Bass, 1985); and Donald C. Hambrick and Sidney Finkelstein, "Managerial Discretion: A Bridge Between Polar Views of Organizational Outcomes," in L. L. Cummings and B. M. Staw (eds.), *Research in Organizational Behavior*, Vol. 9 (Greenwich, Conn.: JAI Press, 1987), p. 384.

20. Michael Albert, "Assessing Cultural Change Needs," *Training and Development Journal*, May 1985, pp. 94–98.

21. John P. Kotter and James L. Heskett, *Corporate Culture and Performance* (New York: Free Press, 1992).

22. Based on William Echikson, "How Hard It Is to Change Culture," *Fortune*, October 19, 1992, p. 114.

23. Dan Ciampa, *Total Quality: A User's Guide for Implementation* (Reading, MA.: Addison-Wesley, 1992), pp. 100–04.

24. Keith H. Hammonds, "Where Did We Go Wrong?," *Business Week*, Quality 1991 Special Issue, p. 38.

25. Dan Ciampa, *Total Quality*, pp. 113–52.

26. Keith H. Hammonds, "Where Did We Go Wrong?," p. 34.

27. Ibid., p. 35; and Dean M. Schroeder and Alan G. Robinson, "America's Most Successful Export to Japan: Continuous Improvement Programs," *Sloan Management Review*, Spring 1991, pp. 67–81.

28. Ibid., p. 38.

29. "Workplace Stress is Rampant, Especially With the Recession," *Wall Street Journal*, May 5, 1992, p. A1.

30. Adapted from Randall S. Schuler, "Definition and Conceptualization of Stress in Organizations," *Organizational Behavior and Human Performance*, April 1980, p. 189.

31. Ibid., p. 191.

32. "Stress and Boredom," *Behavior Today*, August 1975, pp. 22–25.

33. Robert L. Kahn, B. N. Wolfe, R. P. Quinn, and J. D. Snock, *Organizational Stress: Studies in Role Conflict and Ambiguity* (New York: John Wiley, 1964).

34. Thomas H. Holmes and Minoru Masuda, "Life Change and Illness Susceptibility," in J. P. Scott and E. C. Senay, (eds.), *Separation and Depression*, Publication No. 94 (Washington, D.C.: American Association for the Advancement of Science, 1973), pp. 176–79.

35. Arthur P. Brief, Randall S. Schuler, and Mary Van Sell, *Managing Job Stress* (Boston: Little, Brown, 1981), pp. 94–98.

36. See, for instance, Meyer Friedman and Ray H. Rosenman, *Type A Behavior and Your Heart* (New York: Knopf, 1974); and Muhammad Jamal, "Type A Behavior and Job Performance: Some Suggestive Findings," *Journal of Human Stress*, Summer 1985, pp. 60–68.

37. Randall S. Schuler, "Definition and Conceptualization of Stress in Organizations," pp. 200–205.

38. Terry A. Beehr and John E. Newman, "Job Stress, Employee Health, and Organizational Effectiveness: A Facet Analysis, Model, and Literature Review," *Personnel Psychology*, Winter 1978, pp. 665–99.

39. Ibid., p. 687.

40. Susan E. Jackson, "Participation in Decision Making as a Strategy for Reducing Job-Related Strain," *Journal of Applied Psychology*, February 1983, pp. 3–19.

41. See Randall S. Schuler, "Time Management: A Stress Management Technique," *Personnel Journal*, December 1979, pp. 851–55; and M. E. Haynes, *Practical Time Management: How to Make the Most of Your Most Perishable Resource* (Tulsa, Okla.: Penn Well Books, 1985).

42. Nealia S. Bruning and David R. Frew, "Effects of Exercise, Relaxation, and Management Skills Training on Physiological Stress Indicators; A Field Experiment," *Journal of Applied Psychology*, November 1987, pp. 515–21.

43. See, for example, K. Kelly, "3M Run Scared? Forget About It," *Business Week*, September 16, 1991, pp. 59–62; and R. Mitchell, "Masters of Innovation," *Business Week*, April 10, 1989, p. 58.

44. These definitions are based on Teresa M. Amabile, "A Model of Creativity and Innovation in Organizations," in B. M. Staw and L. L. Cummings (eds.), *Research in Organizational Behavior*, Vol. 10 (Greenwich, Conn.: JAI Press, 1988), p. 126.

45. This dilemma is based on Kevin Kelly, "When a Rival's Trade Secret Crosses Your Desk . . . ," *Business Week*, May 20, 1991, p. 48.

46. Fariborz Damanpour, "Organizational Innovation: A Meta-Analysis of Effects of Determinants and Moderators," *Academy of Management Journal*, September 1991, pp. 555–90.

47. Peter R. Monge, Michael D. Cozzens, and Noshir S. Contractor, "Communication and Motivational Predictors of the Dynamics of Organizational Innovation," *Organization Science*, May 1992, pp. 250–74.

48. See, for instance, Teresa M. Amabile, "A Model of Creativity and Innovation in Organizations," p. 147; Michael Tushman and David Nadler, "Organizing for Innovation," *California Management Review*, Spring 1986, pp. 74–92; Rosabeth Moss Kanter, "When a Thousand Flowers Bloom: Structural, Collective, and Social Conditions for Innovation in Organization," in B. M. Staw and L. L. Cummings (eds.), *Research in Organizational Behavior*, Vol. 10, pp. 169–211; and Gareth Morgan, "Endangered Species: New Ideas," *Business Month*, April 1989, pp. 75–77.

49. J. M. Howell and C. A. Higgins, "Champions of Change," *Business Quarterly*, Spring 1990, pp. 31–32.

Chapter 14

1. Based on Myrna Hellerman, "Giving Executives a Field Day," *Working Woman*, March 1992, pp. 37–40.

2. S. J. Breckler, "Empirical Validation of Affect, Behavior, and Cognition as Distinct Components of Attitude," *Journal of Personality and Social Psychology*, May 1984, pp. 1191–1205.

3. Paul P. Brooke, Jr., Daniel W. Russell, and James L. Price, "Discriminant Validation of Measures of Job Satisfaction, Job Involvement, and Organizational Commitment," *Journal of Applied Psychology*, May 1988, pp. 139–45.

4. Icek Ajzen and Martin Fishbein, *Understanding Attitudes and Predicting Behavior* (Englewood Cliffs, NJ: Prentice Hall, 1980).

5. Leon Festinger, *A Theory of Cognitive Dissonance* (Stanford, CA: Stanford University Press, 1957).

6. Victor H. Vroom, *Work and Motivation* (New York: John Wiley, 1964); and M. T. Iaffaldano and P. M. Muchinsky, "Job Satisfaction and Job Performance: A Meta-Analysis," *Psychological Bulletin*, March 1985, pp. 251–73.

7. See, for example, Jean B. Herman, "Are Situational Contingencies Limiting Job Attitude–Job Performance Relationship?," *Organizational Behavior and Human Performance*, October 1973, pp. 208–24; and M. M. Petty, Gail W. McGee, and Jerry W. Cavender, "A

Meta-Analysis of the Relationships Between Individual Job Satisfaction and Individual Performance," *Academy of Management Review*, October 1984, pp. 712–21.

8. Charles N. Greene, "The Satisfaction–Performance Controversy," *Business Horizons*, February 1972, pp. 31–41; Edward E. Lawler III, *Motivation and Organizations* (Monterey, Ca.: Brooks/Cole, 1973); and Petty, McGee, and Cavender, "A Meta-Analysis of the Relationships Between Individual Job Satisfaction and Individual Performance."

9. Based on Teri Lammers, "The Essential Employee Survey," *INC.*, December 1992, pp. 159–61.

10. See, for example, Edwin A. Locke, "The Nature and Causes of Job Satisfaction," in Marvin D. Dunnette (ed.), *Handbook of Industrial and Organizational Psychology*, pp. 1297–1350; and Peter W. Hom, Ralph Katerberg, Jr., and Charles L. Hulin, "Comparative Examination of Three Approaches to the Prediction of Turnover," *Journal of Applied Psychology*, June 1979, pp. 280–90.

11. Julian B. Rotter, "Generalized Expectancies for Internal Versus External Control of Reinforcement," *Psychological Monographs*, Vol. 80, No. 609 (1966).

12. See, for instance, Dennis W. Organ and Charles N. Greene, "Role Ambiguity, Locus of Control, and Work Satisfaction," *Journal of Applied Psychology*, February 1974, pp. 101–02; and Terence R. Mitchell, Charles M. Smyser, and Stan E. Weed, "Locus of Control: Supervision and Work Satisfaction," *Academy of Management Journal*, September 1975, pp. 623–31.

13. T. Adorno et al., *The Authoritarian Personality* (New York: Harper & Brothers, 1950).

14. Harrison Gough, "Personality and Personality Assessment," in Marvin D. Dunnette (ed.), *Handbook of Industrial and Organizational Psychology* (Skokie, Ill.: Rand McNally, 1976), p. 579.

15. R. G. Vleeming, "Machiavellianism: A Preliminary Review," *Psychological Reports*, February 1979, pp. 295–310.

16. Based on Joel Brockner, *Self-Esteem at Work* (Lexington, MA: Lexington Books, 1988), Chapters 1–4.

17. See M. Snyder, *Public Appearances/Private Realities: The Psychology of Self-Monitoring* (New York: W. H. Freeman, 1987).

18. Ibid.

19. R. N. Taylor and M. D. Dunnette, "Influence of Dogmatism, Risk-Taking Propensity, and Intelligence on Decision-Making Strategies for a Sample of Industrial Managers," *Journal of Applied Psychology*, August 1974, pp. 420–23.

20. Irving L. Janis and Leon Mann, *Decision Making: A Psychological Analysis of Conflict, Choice, and Commitment* (New York: Free Press, 1977).

21. N. Kogan and M. A. Wallach, "Group Risk Taking as a Function of Members' Anxiety and Defensiveness," *Journal of Personality*, March 1967, pp. 50–63.

22. John L. Holland, *Making Vocational Choices: A Theory of Vocational Personalities and Work Environments*, 2nd ed. (Englewood Cliffs, NJ: Prentice Hall, 1985).

23. See, for example, A. R. Spokane, "A Review of Research on Person–Environment Congruence in Holland's Theory of Careers," *Journal of Vocational Behavior*, June 1985, pp. 306–43; and D. Brown, "The Status of Holland's Theory of Career Choice," *Career Development Journal*, September 1987, pp. 13–23.

24. H. H. Kelley, "Attribution in Social Interaction," in E. Jones et al. (eds.), *Attribution: Perceiving the Causes of Behavior* (Morristown, NJ: General Learning Press, 1972).

25. See A. G. Miller and T. Lawson, "The Effect of an Informational Option on the Fundamental Attribution Error," *Personality and Social Psychology Bulletin*, June 1989, pp. 194–204.

26. B. F. Skinner, *Contingencies of Reinforcement* (East Norwalk, CT: Appleton-Century-Crofts, 1971).

Chapter 15

1. Myron Magnet, "The Truth About the American Worker," *Fortune*, May 4, 1992, pp. 64–65.

2. Bruce W. Tuckman and Mary Ann C. Jensen, "Stages of Small-Group Development Revisited," *Group and Organizational Studies*, Vol 2, No. 3, 1977, pp. 419–27.

3. Linda N. Jewell and H. J. Reitz, *Group Effectiveness in Organizations* (Glenview, Ill: Scott, Foresman, 1981).

4. Solomon E. Asch, "Effects of Group Pressure upon the Modification and Distortion of Judgments," in *Groups, Leadership and Men*, ed., Harold Guetzkow (Pittsburgh: Carnegie Press, 1951), pp. 177–90.

5. See, for instance, E. J. Thomas and C. F. Fink, "Effects of Group Size," *Psychological Bulletin*, July 1963, pp. 371–84; and Marvin E. Shaw, *Group Dynamics: The Psychology of Small Group Behavior*, 3rd ed. (New York: McGraw-Hill, 1981).

6. See Robert Albanese and David D. Van Fleet, "Rational Behavior in Groups: The Free-Riding Tendency," *Academy of Management Review*, April 1985, pp. 244–55.

7. See, for example, L. Berkowitz, "Group Standards, Cohesiveness, and Productivity," *Human Relations*, November 1954, pp. 509–19.

8. Stanley E. Seashore, *Group Cohesiveness in the Industrial Work Group* (Ann Arbor: University of Michigan, Survey Research Center, 1954).

9. This model is substantially based on the work of Paul S. Goodman, E. Ravlin, and M. Schminke, "Understanding Groups in Organizations," in L. L. Cummings and B. M. Staw (eds.), *Research in Organizational Behavior*, Vol. 9 (Greenwich, Conn.: JAI Press, 1987), pp. 124–28; and J. Richard Hackman, "The Design of Work Teams," in J. W. Lorsch (ed.), *Handbook of Organizational Behavior* (Englewood Cliffs, N.J.: Prentice-Hall, 1987), pp. 315–42.

10. Fred Friedlander, "The Ecology of Work Groups," in J. W. Lorsch (ed.), *Handbook of Organizational Behavior*, pp. 301–14.

11. Marvin E. Shaw, *Contemporary Topics in Social Psychology* (Morristown, N.J.: General Learning Press, 1976), pp. 350–51.

12. See, for example, J. Richard Hackman and C. G. Morris, "Group Tasks, Group Interaction Process and Group Performance Effectiveness: A Review and Proposed Integration," in L. Berkowitz (ed.), *Advances in Experimental Social Psychology* (New York: Academic Press, 1975), pp. 45–99.

13. Cited in "Work Team Trivia," *The Competitive Edge*, March/April 1992, p. 12.

14. Based on Eric Sundstrom, Kenneth P. DeMeuse, and David Futrell, "Work Teams," *American Psychologist*, February 1990, p. 120; and Carl E. Larson and Frank M. J. LaFasto, *TeamWork* (Newbury Park, CA: Sage Publications).

15. This box is based on "American Auto Makers Need Major Overhaul to Match the Japanese," *Wall Street Journal*, January 10, 1992, p. A1.

16. See, for instance, John Hillkirk, "New Award Cites Teams with Dreams," *USA Today*, April 10–12, 1992, p. 2A.

17. See Sundstrom, DeMeuse, and Futrell, "Work Teams;" Larson and LaFasto, *TeamWork*; J. Richard Hackman (ed.), *Groups That Work (and Those That Don't)* (San Francisco, Jossey-Bass, 1990); and Dean W. Tjosvold and Mary M. Tjosvold, *Leading the Team Organization* (New York: Lexington Books, 1991).

18. Larson and LaFasto, *TeamWork*, p. 75.

19. This section is based on Roger Cohen, "Suzuki in Hungary: Team Spirit Sags," *New York Times*, May 16, 1992, p. 17.

20. Bob Krone, "Total Quality Management: An American Odyssey," *The Bureaucrat*, Fall 1990, p. 37.

21. *Profiles in Quality: Blueprints for Action from 50 Leading Companies* (Boston: Allyn and Bacon, 1991), pp. 71–72 and 76–77.

Chapter 16

1. See Kenneth A. Kovach, "What Motivates Employees? Workers and Supervisors Give Different Answers," *Business Horizons*, September–October 1987, pp. 58–65.

2. Ralph Katerberg and Gary J. Blau, "An Examination of Level and Direction of Effort and Job Performance," *Academy of Management Journal*, June 1983, pp. 249–57.

3. Abraham Maslow, *Motivation and Personality* (New York: Harper & Row, 1954).

4. See, for example, Edward E. Lawler, III, and J. Lloyd Suttle, "A Causal Correlational Test of the Need Hierarchy Concept," *Organizational*

Behavior and Human Performance, April 1972, pp. 265–87; and Douglas T. Hall and Khalil E. Nongaim, "An Examination of Maslow's Need Hierarchy in an Organizational Setting," *Organizational Behavior and Human Performance*, February 1968, pp. 12–35.

5. Douglas McGregor, *The Human Side of Enterprise* (New York: McGraw-Hill, 1960).

6. Frederick Herzberg, Bernard Mausner, and Barbara Snyderman, *The Motivation to Work* (New York: John Wiley, 1959); and Frederick Herzberg, *The Managerial Choice: To Be Effective or to Be Human*, rev. ed. (Salt Lake City: Olympus, 1982).

7. See, for instance, Michael E. Gordon, Norman M. Pryor, and Bob V. Harris, "An Examination of Scaling Bias in Herzberg's Theory of Job Satisfaction," *Organizational Behavior and Human Performance*, February 1974, pp. 106–21; Edwin A. Locke and Roman J. Whiting, "Sources of Satisfaction and Dissatisfaction Among Solid Waste Management Employees," *Journal of Applied Psychology*, April 1974, pp. 145–56; and John B. Miner, *Theories of Organizational Behavior* (Hinsdale, Ill.: Dryden Press, 1980), pp. 76–105.

8. David C. McClelland, *The Achieving Society* (New York: Van Nostrand Reinhold, 1961); John W. Atkinson and Joel O. Raynor, *Motivation and Achievement* (Washington, D.C.: Winston, 1974); and David C. McClelland, *Power: The Inner Experience* (New York: Irvington, 1975).

9. David C. McClelland, *The Achieving Society*.

10. David C. McClelland and David G. Winter, *Motivating Economic Achievement* (New York: Free Press, 1969).

11. David C. McClelland, *Power: The Inner Experience*; David C. McClelland and David H. Burnham, "Power Is the Great Motivator," *Harvard Business Review*, March–April 1976, pp. 100–10.

12. "McClelland: An Advocate of Power," *International Management*, July 1975, pp. 27–29.

13. David Miron and David C. McClelland, "The Impact of Achievement Motivation Training on Small Businesses," *California Management Review*, Summer 1979, pp. 13–28.

14. James C. Naylor and Daniel R. Ilgen, "Goal Setting: A Theoretical Analysis of a Motivational Technique," in B. M. Staw and L. L. Cummings (eds.), *Research in Organizational Behavior*, Vol. 6 (Greenwich, Conn.: JAI Press, 1984), pp. 95–140.

15. John B. Miner, *Theories of Organizational Behavior*, p. 65.

16. Cited in J. Greenwald, "Workers: Risks and Rewards," *Time*, April 15, 1991, p. 42.

17. Cited in Joann S. Lublin, "A New Track," *Wall Street Journal*, April 22, 1992, p. R5.

18. Brian Dumaine, "Unleash Workers and Cut Costs," *Fortune*, April 22, 1992, p. 88.

19. Greenwald, "Workers: Risks and Rewards," pp. 42–43.

20. B. F. Skinner, *Science and Human Behavior* (New York: Free Press, 1953); and B. F. Skinner, *Beyond Freedom and Dignity* (New York: Knopf, 1972).

21. The same data, for instance, can be interpreted in either goal-setting or reinforcement terms, as shown in Edwin A. Locke, "Latham vs. Komaki: A Tale of Two Paradigms," *Journal of Applied Psychology*, February 1980, pp. 16–23.

22. J. Stacey Adams, "Inequity in Social Exchanges," in Leonard Berkowitz (ed.), *Advances in Experimental Social Psychology*, Vol. 2 (New York: Academic Press, 1965), pp. 267–300.

23. Paul S. Goodman, "An Examination of Referents Used in the Evaluation of Pay," *Organizational Behavior and Human Performance*, October 1974, pp. 170–95; Simcha Ronen, "Equity Perception in Multiple Comparisons: A Field Study," *Human Relations*, April 1986, pp. 333–46; R. W. Scholl, E. A. Cooper, and J. F. McKenna, "Referent Selection in Determining Equity Perception: Differential Effects on Behavioral and Attitudinal Outcomes," *Personnel Psychology*, Spring 1987, pp. 113–27; and Carol T. Kulik and Maureen L. Ambrose, "Personal and Situational Determinants of Referent Choice," *Academy of Management Review*, April 1992, pp. 212–37.

24. Paul S. Goodman and A. Friedman, "An Examination of Adams' Theory of Inequity," *Administrative Science Quarterly*, September 1971, pp. 271–88.

25. See, for example, Michael R. Carrell, "A Longitudinal Field Assessment of Employee Perceptions of Equitable Treatment," *Organiza-*

tional Behavior and Human Performance, February 1978, pp. 108–18; Robert G. Lord and Jeffrey A. Hohenfeld, "Longitudinal Field Assessment of Equity Effects on the Performance of Major League Baseball Players," *Journal of Applied Psychology*, February 1979, pp. 19–26; and John E. Dittrich and Michael R. Carrell, "Organizational Equity Perceptions, Employee Job Satisfaction, and Departmental Absence and Turnover Rates," *Organizational Behavior and Human Performance*, August 1979, pp. 29–40.

26. Paul S. Goodman, "Social Comparison Process in Organizations," in B. M. Staw and G. R. Salancik (eds.), *New Directions in Organizational Behavior* (Chicago: St. Clair, 1977), pp. 97–132.

27. This box is based on J. Castro, "How's Your Pay?," *Time*, April 15, 1991, pp. 40–41; J. A. Byrne, "The Flap Over Executive Pay," *Business Week*, May 6, 1991, pp. 90–96; and T. McCarroll, "Motown's Fat Cats," *Time*, January 20, 1992, pp. 34–35.

28. Victor H. Vroom, *Work and Motivation* (New York: John Wiley, 1964).

29. See, for example, Herbert G. Heneman, III, and Donald P. Schwab, "Evaluation of Research on Expectancy Theory Prediction of Employee Performance," *Psychological Bulletin*, July 1972, pp. 1–9; and Leon Reinharth and Mahmoud Wahba, "Expectancy Theory as a Predictor of Work Motivation, Effort Expenditure, and Job Performance," *Academy of Management Journal*, September 1975, pp. 502–37.

30. See, for example, Victor H. Vroom, "Organizational Choice: A Study of Pre-and-Postdecision Processes," *Organizational Behavior and Human Performance*, April 1966, pp. 212–25; and Lyman W. Porter and Edward E. Lawler, III, *Managerial Attitudes and Performance* (Homewood, Ill.: Richard D. Irwin, 1968).

31. Among academicians these three variables are typically referred to as *valence, instrumentality*, and *expectancy*, respectively.

32. This four-step discussion was adapted from K. F. Taylor, "A Valence-Expectancy Approach to Work Motivation," *Personnel Practice Bulletin*, June 1974, pp. 142–48.

33. Geert Hofestede, "Motivation, Leadership, and Organizations: Do American Theories Apply Abroad?," *Organizational Dynamics*, Summer 1980, p. 55.

34. Adi Ignatius, "Now if Ms. Wong Insults a Customer, She Gets an Award," *Wall Street Journal*, January 24, 1989, p. 1.

35. See, for instance, Marc Siegall, "The Simplistic Five: An Integrative Framework For Teaching Motivation," *The Organizational Behavior Teaching Review*, Vol. 12, No. 4 (1987–88), pp. 141–43.

36. Itzhak Harpaz, "The Importance of Work Goals: An International Perspective," *Journal of International Business Studies*, First Quarter 1990, pp. 75–93.

37. This box is based on "F. Suzanne Jenniches," *Industry Week*, March 2, 1992, pp. 32–36.

38. Laurie A. Broedling, "Relationship of Internal–External Control to Work Motivation and Performance in an Expectancy Model," *Journal of Applied Psychology*, February 1975, pp. 65–70; and Terry L. Lied and Robert D. Pritchard, "Relationships Between Personality Variables and Components of the Expectancy-Valence Model," *Journal of Applied Psychology*, August 1976, pp. 463–67.

39. David W. Belcher and Thomas J. Atchison, "Equity Theory and Compensation Policy," *Personnel Administration*, Vol. 33, No. 3 (1970), pp. 22–33; and Thomas J. Atchison and David W. Belcher, "Equity Rewards and Compensation Administration," *Personnel Administration*, Vol. 34, No. 2 (1971), pp. 32–36.

40. Edwin A. Locke, D. B. Feren, V. M. McCaleb, K. N. Shaw, and A. T. Denny, "The Relative Effectiveness of Four Methods of Motivating Employee Performance," in *Changes in Working Life*, eds., K. D. Duncan, M. M. Gruneberg, and D. Wallis (London: John Wiley, 1980), pp. 363–83.

Chapter 17

1. See "A Renegade for All Seasons," *Success*, February 1991, p. 28; Priscilla Painton, "The Taming of Ted Turner," *Time*, January 6, 1992, pp. 34–39; and Subrata N. Chakravarty, "What New Worlds to Conquer?" *Forbes*, January 4, 1993, pp. 82–87.

2. See Shelly A. Kirkpatrick and Edwin A. Locke, "Leadership: Do Traits Matter?" *Academy of Management Executive*, May 1991, pp. 48–60.

3. Ralph M. Stogdill and Alvin E. Coons, eds., *Leader Behavior: Its Description and Measurement*, Research Monograph No. 88 (Columbus: Ohio State University, Bureau of Business Research, 1951). For an updated literature review of the Ohio State research, see Steven Kerr, Chester A. Schriesheim, Charles J. Murphy, and Ralph M. Stogdill, "Toward a Contingency Theory of Leadership Based upon the Consideration and Initiating Structure Literature," *Organizational Behavior and Human Performance*, August 1974, pp. 62–82; and Bruce M. Fisher, "Consideration and Initiating Structure and Their Relationships with Leader Effectiveness: A Meta-Analysis," in F. Hoy (ed.), *Proceedings of the 48th Annual Academy of Management Conference*, Anaheim, Calif., 1988, pp. 201–05.

4. Kevin D. Thompson, "Blazing New Trails," *Black Enterprise*, January 1991, pp. 55–57.

5. R. Kahn and D. Katz, "Leadership Practices in Relation to Productivity and Morale," in D. Cartwright and A. Zander (eds.), *Group Dynamics: Research and Theory*, 2nd ed. (Elmsford, N.Y.: Row, Paterson, 1960).

6. Robert R. Blake and Jane S. Mouton, *The Managerial Grid III* (Houston: Gulf Publishing, 1984).

7. L. L. Larson, J. G. Hunt, and R. N. Osborn, "The Great Hi-Hi Leader Behavior Myth: A Lesson from Occam's Razor," *Academy of Management Journal*, December 1976, pp. 628–41; and Paul C. Nystrom, "Managers and the Hi-Hi Leader Myth," *Academy of Management Journal*, June 1978, pp. 325–31.

8. See, for example, the three styles—autocratic, participative, and laissez-faire—proposed by Kurt Lewin and Ronald Lippitt, "An Experimental Approach to the Study of Autocracy and Democracy: A Preliminary Note," *Sociometry*, No. 1, (1938), 292–380; or the 3-D theory proposed by William J. Reddin, *Managerial Effectiveness* (New York: McGraw-Hill, 1970).

9. Jeffrey C. Barrow, "The Variables of Leadership: A Review and Conceptual Framework," *Academy of Management Review*, April 1977, pp. 231–51.

10. Fred E. Fiedler, *A Theory of Leadership Effectiveness* (New York: McGraw-Hill, 1967).

11. Lawrence H. Peters, D. D. Hartke, and J. T. Pholmann, "Fiedler's Contingency Theory of Leadership: An Application of the Meta-Analysis Procedures of Schmidt and Hunter," *Psychological Bulletin*, March 1985, pp. 274–85.

12. See, for instance, Robert W. Rice, "Psychometric Properties of the Esteem for the Least Preferred Co-worker (LPC) Scale," *Academy of Management Review*, January 1978, pp. 106–18; and Chester A. Schriesheim, B. D. Bannister, and W. H. Money, "Psychometric Properties of the LPC Scale: An Extension of Rice's Review," *Academy of Management Review*, April 1979, pp. 287–90.

13. See Edgar H. Schein, *Organizational Psychology*, 3rd ed. (Englewood Cliffs, N.J.: Prentice-Hall, 1980), pp. 116–17; and Boris Kabanoff, "A Critique of Leader Match and Its Implications for Leadership Research," *Personnel Psychology*, Winter 1981, pp. 749–64.

14. Paul Hersey and Kenneth H. Blanchard, "So You Want to Know Your Leadership Style?," *Training and Development Journal*, February 1974, pp. 1–15; and Paul Hersey and Kenneth H. Blanchard, *Management of Organizational Behavior: Utilizing Human Resources*, 4th ed. (Englewood Cliffs, N.J.: Prentice-Hall, 1982), pp. 150–61.

15. Paul Hersey and Kenneth H. Blanchard, *Management of Organizational Behavior: Utilizing Human Resources*, p. 171.

16. Paul Hersey and Kenneth H. Blanchard, "Grid Principles and Situationalism: Both! A Response to Blake and Mouton," *Group and Organization Studies*, June 1982, pp. 207–10.

17. R. K. Hambleton and R. Gumpert, "The Validity of Hersey and Blanchard's Theory of Leader Effectiveness," *Group & Organization Studies*, June 1982, pp. 225–42; Claude L. Graeff, "The Situational Leadership Theory: A Critical View," *Academy of Management Review*, April 1983, pp. 285–91; Robert P. Vecchio, "Situational Leadership Theory: An Examination of a Prescriptive Theory," *Journal of Applied Psychology*, August 1987, pp. 444–51; Jane R. Goodson, Gail W. McGee, and James F. Cashman, "Situational Leadership Theory: A Test of Leadership Prescriptions," *Group & Organization Studies*, December 1989, pp. 446–61; and Warren Blank, John R. Weitzel, and Stephen G. Green, "A Test of the Situational Leadership Theory," *Personnel Psychology*, Autumn 1990, pp. 579–97.

18. Robert P. Vecchio, "Situational Leadership Theory: An Examination of a Prescriptive Theory."

19. Warren Blank, John R. Weitzel, and Stephen G. Green, "A Test of the Situational Leadership Theory."

20. Robert J. House, "A Path-Goal Theory of Leader Effectiveness," *Administrative Science Quarterly*, September 1971, pp. 321–38; Robert J. House and Terence R. Mitchell, "Path-Goal Theory of Leadership," *Journal of Contemporary Business*, Autumn 1974, p. 86; and Robert J. House, "Retrospective Comment," in Louis E. Boone and Donald D. Bowen (eds.), *The Great Writings in Management and Organizational Behavior*, 2nd ed. (New York: Random House, 1987), pp. 354–64.

21. Julie Indrik, "Path-Goal Theory of Leadership: A Meta-Analysis," paper presented at the National Academy of Management Conference, Chicago, August 1986; and Robert T. Keller, "A Test of the Path-Goal Theory of Leadership With Need for Clarity as a Moderator in Research and Development Organizations," *Journal of Applied Psychology*, April 1989, pp. 208–12.

22. Victor H. Vroom and Phillip W. Yetton, *Leadership and Decision-Making* (Pittsburgh: University of Pittsburgh Press, 1973).

23. Victor H. Vroom and Arthur G. Jago, *The New Leadership: Managing Participation in Organizations* (Englewood Cliffs: Prentice Hall, 1988). See especially Chapter 8.

24. See, for example, R. H. George Field, "A Test of the Vroom-Yetton Normative Model of Leadership," *Journal of Applied Psychology*, October 1982, pp. 523–32; Carrie R. Leana, "Power Relinquishment Versus Power Sharing: Theoretical Clarification and Empirical Comparison of Delegation and Participation," *Journal of Applied Psychology*, May 1987, pp. 228–33; Jennifer T. Ettling and Arthur G. Jago, "Participation Under Conditions of Conflict: More on the Validity of the Vroom-Yetton Model," *Journal of Management Studies*, January 1988, pp. 73–83; and R. H. George Field and Robert J. House, "A Test of the Vroom-Yetton Model Using Manager and Subordinate Reports," *Journal of Applied Psychology*, June 1990, pp. 362–66.

25. Steven Kerr and John M. Jermier, "Substitutes for Leadership: Their Meaning and Measurement," *Organizational Behavior and Human Performance*, December 1978, pp. 375–403; Jon P. Howell and Peter W. Dorfman, "Substitutes for Leadership: Test of a Construct," *Academy of Management Journal*, December 1981, pp. 714–28; Peter W. Howard and William F. Joyce, "Substitutes for Leadership: A Statistical Refinement," paper presented at the 42nd Annual Academy of Management Conference; New York, August 1982; Jon P. Howell, Peter W. Dorfman, and Steven Kerr, "Leadership and Substitutes for Leadership," *Journal of Applied Behavioral Science*, vol. 22, no. 1, 1986, pp. 29–46; and Jon P. Howell, D. E. Bowen, Peter W. Dorfman, Steven Kerr, and Philip M. Podsakoff, "Substitutes for Leadership: Effective Alternatives to Ineffective Leadership," *Organizational Dynamics*, Summer 1990, pp. 21–38.

26. Geert Hofstede, "Motivation, Leadership, and Organization: Do American Theories Apply Abroad?" *Organizational Dynamics*, Summer 1980, p. 57.

27. See, for instance, James C. McElroy, "A Typology of Attribution Leadership Research," *Academy of Management Review*, July 1982, pp. 413–17; James R. Meindl and Sanford B. Ehrlich, "The Romance of Leadership and the Evaluation of Organizational Performance," *Academy of Management Journal*, March 1987, pp. 91–109; James C. McElroy and J. David Hunger, "Leadership Theory as Causal Attribution of Performance," in James G. Hunt, B. Ran Baliga, H. P. Dachler, and Chester A. Schriesheim, eds., *Emerging Leadership Vistas* (Lexington, Mass.: Lexington Books, 1988); and Boas Shami, "Attribution of Influence and Charisma to the Leader: The Romance of Leadership Revisited," *Journal of Applied Social Psychology*, March 1992, pp. 1–15.

28. Robert G. Lord, C. L. DeVader and G. M. Alliger, "A Meta-Analysis of the Relation Between Personality Traits and Leadership Perceptions: An Application of Validity Generalization Procedures," *Journal of Applied Psychology*, August 1986, pp. 402–10.

29. Gary N. Powell and D. Anthony Butterfield, "The 'High-High' Leader Rides Again!," *Group and Organization Studies*, December 1984, pp. 437–50.
30. James R. Meindl, Sanford B. Ehrlich, and Janet M. Dukerich, "The Romance of Leadership," *Administrative Science Quarterly*, March 1985, pp. 78–102.
31. Barry M. Staw and Jerry Ross, "Commitment in an Experimenting Society: A Study of the Attribution of Leadership from Administrative Scenarios," *Journal of Applied Psychology*, June 1980, pp. 249–60.
32. Jay C. Conger and R. N. Kanungo, "Behavioral Dimensions of Charismatic Leadership," in J. A. Conger, R. N. Kanungo and Associates, *Charismatic Leadership* (San Francisco: Jossey-Bass, 1988), p. 79.
33. Robert J. House, "A 1976 Theory of Charismatic Leadership," in J. G. Hunt and L. L. Larson (eds.), *Leadership: The Cutting Edge* (Carbondale: Southern Illinois University Press, 1977), pp. 189–207.
34. Warren Bennis, "The 4 Competencies of Leadership," *Training and Development Journal*, August 1984, pp. 15–19.
35. Jay A. Conger and R. N. Kanungo, "Behavioral Dimensions of Charismatic Leadership," pp. 78–97.
36. Robert J. House, J. Woycke, and E. M. Fodor, "Charismatic and Noncharismatic Leaders: Differences in Behavior and Effectiveness," in J. A. Conger and R. N. Kanungo, *Charismatic Leadership*, pp. 103–04.
37. Jay C. Conger and R. N. Kanungo, "Training Charismatic Leadership: A Risky and Critical Task," in J. A. Conger and R. N. Kanungo, *Charismatic Leadership*, pp. 309–23.
38. Jane M. Howell and Peter J. Frost, "A Laboratory Study of Charismatic Leadership," *Organizational Behavior and Human Decision Processes*, April 1989, pp. 243–69.
39. Robert J. House, "A 1976 Theory of Charismatic Leadership."
40. D. Machan, "The Charisma Merchants," *Forbes*, January 23, 1989, pp. 100–01.
41. See James M. Burns, *Leadership* (New York: Harper & Row, 1978); B. M. Bass, *Leadership and Performance Beyond Expectations* (New York: Free Press, 1985); and B. M. Bass, "From Transactional to Transformational Leadership: Learning to Share the Vision," *Organizational Dynamics*, Winter 1990, pp. 19–31.
42. B. M. Bass, "Leadership: Good, Better, Best," *Organizational Dynamics*, Winter 1985, pp. 26–40; and J. Seltzer and B. M. Bass, "Transformational Leadership: Beyond Initiation and Consideration," *Journal of Management*, December 1990, pp. 693–703.
43. B. J. Avolio and B. M. Bass, "Transformational Leadership, Charisma and Beyond." Working paper, School of Management, State University of New York, Binghamton, 1985, p. 14.
44. Cited in B. M. Bass and B. J. Avolio, "Developing Transformational Leadership: 1992 and Beyond," *Journal of European Industrial Training*, January 1990, p. 23.
45. J. J. Hater and B. M. Bass, "Supervisors' Evaluation and Subordinates' Perceptions of Transformational and Transactional Leadership," *Journal of Applied Psychology*, November 1988, pp. 695–702.
46. B. M. Bass and B. J. Avolio, "Developing Transformational Leadership."
47. See, for instance, Mary Billard, "Do Women Make Better Managers?" *Working Woman*, March 1992, pp. 68–71, 106–07.
48. See J. Grant, "Women as Managers; What They Can Offer to Organizations," *Organizational Dynamics*, Winter 1988, pp. 56–63; Sally Helgesen, *The Female Advantage: Women's Ways of Leadership* (New York: Doubleday, 1990); Alice H. Eagly and Blair T. Johnson, "Gender and Leadership Style: A Meta-Analysis," *Psychological Bulletin*, September 1990, pp. 233–56; Judith B. Rosener, "Ways Women Lead," *Harvard Business Review*, November–December 1990, pp. 119–25; "Debate: Ways Men and Women Lead," *Harvard Business Review*, January–February 1991, pp. 150–60; and Alice H. Eagly, Steven J. Karau, and Blair T. Johnson, "Gender and Leadership Style Among School Principals: A Meta-Analysis," *Educational Administration Quarterly*, February 1992, pp. 76–102.
49. Ibid.
50. Ibid.
51. Sally Helgesen, *The Female Advantage*.
52. Gregory H. Dobbins, William S. Long, Esther J. Dedrick, and Tanya Cheer Clemons, "The Role of Self-Monitoring and Gender on Leader Emergence: A Laboratory and Field Study," *Journal of Management*, September 1990, pp. 609–18.
53. Amanda Bennett, *The Death of the Organization Man* (New York: William Morrow, 1990), p. 205.

Chapter 18

1. See, for instance, J. C. McCrosky, "Oral Communication Apprehension: A Reconceptualization," in M. Burgoon, ed., *Communication Yearbook 6* (Newbury Park, CA: Sage, 1982), pp. 136–70.
2. Larry E. Penley, Elmore R. Alexander, I. Edward Jernigan, and Catherine I. Henwood, "Communication Abilities of Managers: The Relationship to Performance," *Journal of Management*, March 1991, pp. 57–76.
3. Charlotte Olmstead Kursh, "The Benefits of Poor Communication," *Psychoanalytic Review*, Summer–Fall 1971, pp. 189–208.
4. David K. Berlo, *The Process of Communication* (New York: Holt, Rinehart, & Winston, 1960), pp. 30–32.
5. Ibid., p. 54.
6. Ibid., p. 103.
7. Albert Mehrabian, "Communication Without Words," *Psychology Today*, September 1968, pp. 53–55.
8. Based on Shoukry D. Saleh, "Relational Orientation and Organizational Functioning: A Cross-Cultural Perspective," *Canadian Journal of Administrative Sciences*, September 1987, p. 276–93.
9. Jesus Sanchez, "The Art of Deal Making," *Los Angeles Times*, February 15, 1988, Part IV, p. 3.
10. Abraham K. Korman, "A Cause of Communication Failure," *Personnel Administration*, September 1960, pp 17–21; and C. H. Weaver, "The Quantification of the Frame of Reference in Labor Management Communication," *Journal of Applied Psychology*, February 1958, pp. 1–19.
11. T. D. Lewis and G. H. Graham, "Six Ways to Improve Your Communication Skills," *Internal Auditor*, May 1988, p. 25.
12. Robert J. Graham, "Understanding the Benefits of Poor Communication," *Interfaces*, June 1981, pp. 80–82.
13. See, for instance, John D. Pettit, Jr., Bobby C. Vaught, and Robert L. Trewatha, "Interpersonal Skill Training: A Prerequisite for Success," *Business*, April–June 1990, pp. 8–14; and Dana Milbank, "Managers Are Sent to 'Charm Schools' to Discover How to Polish Up Their Acts," *Wall Street Journal*, December 14, 1990, p. B1.
14. C. Hymowitz, "Five Main Reasons Why Managers Fail," *Wall Street Journal*, May 2, 1988, p. 25.
15. D. Milbank, "Managers Are Sent to 'Charm Schools' to Discover How to Polish Up Their Acts."
16. Lyman W. Porter and Lawrence E. McKibbin, *Future of Management Education and Development: Drift or Thrust into the 21st Century?* (New York: McGraw-Hill, 1988).
17. See, for instance, Stephen P. Robbins, *Training in InterPersonal Skills: TIPS for Managing People at Work* (Englewood Cliffs, NJ; Prentice-Hall, 1989); Chad T. Lewis, Joseph E. Garcia, and Sarah M. Jobs, *Managerial Skills in Organizations* (Boston: Allyn and Bacon, 1990); and David A. Whetten and Kim Cameron, *Developing Managerial Skills*, 2nd ed. (New York: HarperCollins, 1992).
18. Carl R. Rogers and Richard E. Farson, *Active Listening* (Chicago: Industrial Relations Center of the University of Chicago, 1976).
19. Stephen P. Robbins, *Training in InterPersonal Skills: TIPS for Managing People at Work*, pp. 31–34.
20. Phillip L. Hunsaker and Anthony J. Alessandra, *The Art of Managing People* (Englewood Cliffs, N.J.: Prentice-Hall, 1980), p. 123.
21. Cynthia Fisher, "Transmission of Positive and Negative Feedback to Subordinates: A Laboratory Investigation," *Journal of Applied Psychology*, October 1979, pp. 533–40.
22. Daniel Ilgen, Cynthia D. Fisher, and M. Susan Taylor, "Consequences of Individual Feedback on Behavior in Organizations," *Journal of Applied Psychology*, August 1979, pp. 349–71.
23. Fernando Bartolome, "Teaching About Whether to Give Negative Feedback," *The Organizational Behavior Teaching Review*, Vol. 9, No. 2, 1986–87, pp. 95–104.

24. Keith Halperin, C. R. Snyder, Randee J. Shenkel, and B. Kent Houston, "Effect of Source Status and Message Favorability on Acceptance of Personality Feedback," *Journal of Applied Psychology*, February 1976, pp. 85–88.

25. Cyril R. Mill, "Feedback: The Art of Giving and Receiving Help," in Larry Porter and Cyril R. Mill (eds.), *The Reading Book for Human Relations Training* (Bethel, Maine: NTL Institute for Applied Behavioral Science, 1976), pp. 18–19.

26. Ibid.

27. Ibid.

28. Ibid.

29. Kathleen S. Verderber and Rudolph F. Verderber, *Inter-Act: Using Interpersonal Communication Skills*, 4th ed. (Belmont, Calif.: Wadsworth, 1986).

30. Lyle E. Bourne, Jr. and C. Victor Bunderson, "Effects Delay of Information Feedback and Length of Post-Feedback Interval on Concept Identification," *Journal of Experimental Psychology*, January 1963, pp. 1–5.

31. Cyril R. Mill, "Feedback: The Art of Giving and Receiving Help," pp. 18–19.

32. Kathleen S. Verderber and Rudolph F. Verderber, *Inter-Act: Using Interpersonal Communication Skills*.

33. B. Katerina Hackman and Dexter C. Dunphy, "Managerial Delegation," in Cary L. Cooper and Ivan T. Robertson, eds., *International Review of Industrial and Organizational Psychology*, Vol. 5 (Chichester, England: John Wiley & Sons, 1990), pp. 35–57.

34. Carrie R. Leana, "Predictors and Consequences of Delegation," *Academy of Management Journal*, December 1986, pp. 754–74.

35. Lawrence L. Steinmetz, *The Art and Skill of Delegation* (Reading, Mass.: Addison-Wesley, 1976).

36. Charles D. Pringle, "Seven Reasons Why Managers Don't Delegate," *Management Solutions*, November 1986, pp. 26–30.

37. Stephen P. Robbins, *Training in InterPersonal Skills: TIPS for Managing People at Work*, pp. 133–35.

38. This box is based on Alan Prendergast, "Learning to Let Go," *Working Woman*, January 1992, pp. 42–45.

39. Richard D. Arvey and Allen P. Jones, "The Use of Discipline in Organizational Settings," in L. L. Cummings and Barry M. Staw (eds.), *Research in Organizational Behavior*, Vol. 7 (Greenwich, Conn.: JAI Press, 1985), pp. 367–408.

40. Douglas McGregor, "Hot Stove Rules of Discipline," in George Strauss and Leonard Sayles (eds.), *Personnel: The Human Problems of Management* (Englewood Cliffs, N.J.: Prentice-Hall, 1967).

41. Stephen P. Robbins, *Training in InterPersonal Skills: TIPS for Managing People at Work*, pp. 111–14.

42. Joseph Seltzer, "Discipline with a Clear Sense of Purpose," *Management Solutions*, February 1987, pp. 32–37.

43. Kenneth W. Thomas and Warren H. Schmidt, "A Survey of Managerial Interests With Respect to Conflict," *Academy of Management Journal*, June 1976, pp. 315–18.

44. Ibid.

45. J. Graves, "Successful Management and Organizational Mugging," in J. Papp (ed.), *New Directions in Human Resource Management* (Englewood Cliffs, N.J.: Prentice-Hall, 1978).

46. This section is adapted from Stephen P. Robbins, *Managing Organizational Conflict: A Nontraditional Approach* (Englewood Cliffs, N.J.: Prentice-Hall, 1974), pp. 11–14.

47. Ralph H. Kilmann and Kenneth W. Thomas, "Developing a Forced-Choice Measure of Conflict Handling Behavior: The MODE Instrument," *Educational and Psychological Measurement*, Summer 1977, pp. 309–25.

48. Leonard Greenhalgh, "Managing Conflict," *Sloan Management Review*, Summer 1986, pp. 45–51.

49. Stephen P. Robbins, *Managing Organizational Conflict: A Nontraditional Approach*, pp. 31–55.

50. Charlotte O. Kursh, "The Benefits of Poor Communication," *The Psychoanalytic Review*, Summer–Fall 1971, pp. 189–208.

51. Kenneth W. Thomas, "Conflict and Conflict Management," in Marvin Dunnette (ed.), *Handbook of Industrial and Organizational Psychology* (Chicago: Rand McNally, 1976), pp. 889–935.

52. See, for instance, Dean Tjosvold and David W. Johnson, *Productive Conflict Management Perspectives for Organizations* (New York: Irvington Publishers, 1983).

53. Stephen P. Robbins, *Managing Organizational Conflict: A Nontraditional Approach*, pp. 78–89.

54. James A. Wall, Jr., *Negotiation: Theory and Practice* (Glenview, Il.: Scott, Foresman, 1985).

55. Richard E. Walton and R. B. McKersie, *A Behavioral Theory of Labor Negotiations: An Analysis of a Social Interaction System* (New York: McGraw-Hill, 1965).

56. Kenneth W. Thomas, "Conflict and Negotiation Processes in Organizations," in Marvin D. Dunnette and L. M. Hough (eds.), *Handbook of Industrial and Organizational Psychology*, 2nd ed., Vol. 3 (Palo Alto, CA: Consulting Psychologists Press, 1992, pp. 651–717).

57. Max H. Bazerman and Margaret A. Neale, *Negotiating Rationally* (New York: Free Press, 1992).

58. Based on Roger Fisher and William Ury, *Getting to Yes: Negotiating Agreement Without Giving In* (Boston: Houghton Mifflin, 1981); James A. Wall, Jr. and Michael W. Blum, "Negotiations," *Journal of Management*, June 1991, pp. 295–96; and Max H. Bazerman and Margaret A. Neale, *Negotiating Rationally*.

Chapter 19

1. Warren E. Leary, "Failure to Find Telescope Flaws is Tied to Faulty Management," *New York Times*, November 28, 1990, p. C3; and David Bjerklie, "Roots of the Hubble's Troubles," *Time*, December 10, 1990, p. 78.

2. Kenneth A. Merchant, "The Control Function of Management," *Sloan Management Review*, Summer 1982, pp. 43–55.

3. Eric Flamholtz, "Organizational Control Systems as a Managerial Tool," *California Management Review*, Winter 1979, p. 55.

4. Steven Kerr, "On the Folly of Rewarding *A*, While Hoping for *B*," *Academy of Management Journal*, December 1975, pp. 769–83.

5. Harold Koontz and Robert W. Bradspies, "Managing Through Feedforward Control," *Business Horizons*, June 1972, pp. 25–36.

6. William H. Newman, *Constructive Control: Design and Use of Control Systems* (Englewood Cliffs, N.J.: Prentice-Hall, 1975), p. 33.

7. This is based on Zachary Schiller and Walecia Konrad, "If You Light Up on Sunday, Don't Come In on Monday," *Business Week*, August 26, 1991, pp. 68–72; and G. Bylinsky, "How Companies Spy on Employees," *Fortune*, November 4, 1991, p. 131–40.

8. John P. Campbell, "On the Nature of Organizational Effectiveness," in Paul S. Goodman, J. M. Pennings, and Associates (eds.), *New Perspectives on Organizational Effectiveness* (San Francisco: Jossey-Bass, 1977), pp. 36–41.

9. Arie Y. Lewin and John W. Minton, "Determining Organizational Effectiveness: Another Look, and an Agenda for Research," *Management Science*, May 1986, pp. 514–38.

10. Stephen Strasser, J. D. Eveland, Gaylord Cummins, O. Lynn Deniston, and John H. Romani, "Conceptualizing the Goal and System Models of Organizational Effectiveness—Implications for Comparative Evaluation Research," *Journal of Management Studies*, July 1981, pp. 321–40.

11. Ibid.

12. Jeffrey Pfeffer and Gerald Salancik, *The External Control of Organizations* (New York: Harper & Row, 1978).

13. Based on "Preston Smith: The High-Tech Way to Success on the Slopes," *Business Week*, December 5, 1988, p. 64; and David H. Freedman, "An Unusual Way to Run a Ski Business," *Forbes ASAP*, October 1992, pp. 27–32.

14. See, for instance, William H. Newman, *Constructive Control: Design and Use of Control Systems*.

15. Based on a tape recording made by the Dallas Fire Department and made available under the Texas Open Records Act.

16. Cited in Archie B. Carroll, "In Search of the Moral Manager," *Business Horizons*, March–April 1987, p. 7.

17. See, for instance, Bernard J. Jaworski and S. Mark Young, "Dysfunctional Behavior and Management Control: An Empirical Study of Marketing Managers," *Accounting, Organizations and Society*, January 1992, pp. 17–35.

18. Edward E. Lawler III and John Grant Rhode, *Information and Control in Organizations* (Santa Monica, Calif.: Goodyear, 1976), p. 108.
19. James D. Thompson, *Organizations in Action* (New York: McGraw-Hill, 1967), p. 124.

Chapter 20

1. Jeffrey Rothfeder and Jim Bartimo, "How Software Is Making Food Sales a Piece of Cake," *Business Week*, July 2, 1990, pp. 54–55.
2. John T. Small and William B. Lee, "In Search of an MIS," *MSU Business Topics*, Autumn 1975, pp. 47–55.
3. Herbert A. Simon, *Administrative Behavior*, 3rd ed. (New York: Free Press, 1976), p. 294.
4. John C. Carter and Fred N. Silverman, "Establishing an MIS," *Journal of Systems Management*, January 1980, p. 15.
5. See, for instance, Everett M. Rogers, "Information Technologies: How Organizations Are Changing," in Gerald M. Goldhaber and George A. Barnett, eds., *Handbook of Organizational Communication* (Norwood, N.J.: Ablex Publishing, 1988), pp. 437–44.
6. Keith Davis, "Management Communication and the Grapevine," *Harvard Business Review*, September–October 1953, pp. 43–49; and Harold Sutton and Lyman W. Porter, "A Study of the Grapevine in a Governmental Organization," *Personnel Psychology*, Summer 1968, pp. 223–30.
7. See W. David Gardner and Joseph Kelly, "Technology: A Price/Performance Game," *Dun's Review*, August 1981, pp. 66–68; "Computers: The New Look," *Business Week*, November 30, 1987, pp. 112–23; and William M. Bulkeley, "PC Networks Begin to Oust Mainframes in Some Companies," *Wall Street Journal*, May 23, 1990, p. A1, A13.
8. John T. Small and William B. Lee, "In Search of an MIS."
9. Based on W. R. Swinyard, H. Rinne, and A. Keng Kau, "The Morality of Software Piracy: A Cross-Cultural Analysis," *Journal of Business Ethics*, August 1990, pp. 655–64; Faye Rice, "How Copycats Steal Billions," *Fortune*, April 22, 1991, pp. 157–58; and Neil Holmes, "Ethics: Software Piracy," *Management Accounting*, January 1992, p. 60.
10. See Steven A. Stanton, "End-User Computing: Power to the People," *Journal of Information Systems Management*, Summer 1988, pp. 79–81; and Glen L. Boyer and Dale McKinnon, "End-User Computing Is Here to Stay," *Supervisory Management*, October 1989, pp. 17–22.
11. See George F. Kimmerling, "Gaining Firm Ground," *Training and Development Journal*, March 1986, pp. 22–25 and Jeffrey Rothfeder, "CIO is Starting to Stand For 'Career Is Over,'" *Business Week*, February 26, 1990, pp. 78–80.
12. See, for example, David Kirkpatrick, "Here Comes the Payoff From PCs," *Fortune*, March 23, 1992, pp. 93–102.
13. "Networking the Nation," *Time*, June 16, 1986, p. 38.
14. "How the Leader in Networking Practices What It Preaches," *Business Week*, May 16, 1988, p. 96.
15. "Electronic Mail: Neither Rain, Nor Sleet, Nor Software . . . ," *Business Week*, February 20, 1989, p. 36; and "Neither Rain, Nor Sleet, Nor Computer Glitches . . . ," *Business Week*, May 8, 1989, pp. 135–37.
16. See, for example, "An Electronic Pipeline That's Changing the Way America Does Business," *Business Week*, August 3, 1987, pp. 80–82; and Therese R. Walter, "Network Interference," *Industry Week*, May 2, 1988, pp. 43–45.
17. See, for example, Hugh J. Watson and Robert I. Mann, "Expert Systems: Past, Present, and Future," *Journal of Information Systems Management*, Fall 1988, pp. 39–46; Eugene Linden, "Putting Knowledge to Work," *Time*, March 28, 1988, pp. 60–63; and Evan I. Schwartz, "Smart Programs Go To Work," *Business Week*, March 2, 1992, pp. 97–105.
18. See, for example, Fred L. Luconi, Thomas W. Malone, and Michael S. Scott Morton, "Expert Systems: The Next Challenge for Managers," *Sloan Management Review*, Summer 1986, pp. 3–14; and Beth Enslow, "The Payoff From Expert Systems," *Across The Board*, January–February 1989, pp. 54–58.
19. Fred L. Luconi, Thomas W. Malone, and Michael S. Scott Morton, "Expert Systems: The Next Challenge for Managers," p. 4.
20. Cited in Thomas A. Stewart, "Brainpower," *Fortune*, June 3, 1991, p. 44.
21. Laurence Hooper, "Future Shock," *Wall Street Journal*, June 4, 1990, p. R19.
22. "Technology and Managing People," 1988 *INC. Office Guide*, pp. 48–49.
23. Charles A. O'Reilly, III, "Individuals and Information Overload in Organizations: Is More Necessarily Better?" *Academy of Management Journal*, December 1980, pp. 684–96.
24. Robert W. Zmud, "An Empirical Investigation of the Dimensionality of the Concept of Information," *Decision Sciences*, April 1978, pp. 187–95.
25. See, for example, G. W. Dickson and John K. Simmons, "The Behavioral Side of MIS," *Business Horizons*, August 1970, pp. 59–71; Craig Brod, "Managing Technostress: Optimizing the Use of Computer Technology," *Personnel Journal*, October 1982, p. 754; and Sara Kiesler, Jane Siegel, and Timothy W. McGuire, "Social Psychological Aspects of Computer-Mediated Communication," *American Psychologist*, January 1985, pp. 14–19.
26. Blake Ives and Margrethe H. Olson, "User Involvement and MIS Success: A Review of Research," *Management Science*, May 1984, pp. 586–603.
27. See, for instance, John C. Henderson and Michael E. Treacy, "Managing End-User Computing for Competitive Advantage," *Sloan Management Review*, Winter 1986, pp. 2–14; Peter Coy, "The New Realism in Office Systems," *Business Week*, June 15, 1992, p. 128–33; and Myron Magnet, "Who's Winning the Information Revolution," *Fortune*, November 30, 1992, pp. 110–17.
28. Thomas McCarroll, "Big Eagles and Sitting Ducks," *Time*, May 15, 1989, p. 54.
29. Stephen D. Solomon, "Use Technology to Manage People," *INC.*, May 1990, pp. 124–26.
30. "Cutting Out the Middleman," *Forbes*, January 6, 1992, p. 169.
31. This box is based on Gary Robins, "System Helps Execs Keep Pace," *Stores*, April 1992, pp. 32–34.
32. See, for instance, Gene Bylinsky, "Saving Time With New Technology," *Fortune*, December 30, 1991, pp. 98–104.
33. See, for instance, Stephen W. Quickel, "Management Joins the Computer Age," *Business Month*, May 1989, pp. 42–46; and George P. Huber, "A Theory of the Effects of Advanced Information Technology on Organizational Design, Intelligence, and Decision Making," *Academy of Management Review*, January 1990, pp. 47–71.
34. Lynda M. Applegate, James I. Cash, Jr., and D. Quinn Mills, "Information Technology and Tomorrow's Manager," *Harvard Business Review*, November–December 1988, pp. 128–36.
35. Joseph H. Boyett and Henry P. Conn, *Workplace 2000* (New York: Dutton, 1991), p. 25.
36. Ibid.
37. Stephen P. Robbins, *Organization Theory: Structure, Design, and Applications*, 3rd ed. (Englewood Cliffs, NJ: Prentice Hall, 1990), pp. 267–68.
38. Jeffrey Pfeffer, *Managing With Power* (Boston: Harvard Business School Press, 1992), pp. 247–65.
39. Michael Newman and David Rosenberg, "Systems Analysts and the Politics of Organizational Control," *Omega*, Vol. 13, No. 5 (1985), pp. 393–406.
40. This section is based on Richard C. Huseman and Edward W. Miles, "Organizational Communication in the Information Age: Implications of Computer-Based Systems," *Journal of Management*, Summer 1988, pp. 181–204.

Chapter 21

1. Based on Lois Therrien, "The Rival Japan Respects," *Business Week*, November 13, 1989, pp. 108–18; Mark Stuart Gill, "Stalking Six Sigma," *Business Month*, January 1990, pp. 42–46; and Lois Therrien, "Spreading the Message," *Business Week*, Quality 1991 Special Issue, pp. 60–61.

GLOSSARY

The number in parentheses following each term indicates the chapter in which the term is defined.

ABC system (21) A priority system for monitoring inventory items.

acceptance sampling (21) A quality control procedure in which a sample is taken and a decision to accept or reject a whole lot is based on a calculation of sample risk error.

acceptance view of authority (2) The theory that authority comes from the willingness of subordinates to accept it.

accommodation (18) Resolving conflicts by placing another's needs and concerns above one's own.

active listening (18) Listening for full meaning without making premature judgments or interpretations.

activities (9) The time or resources needed to progress from one event to another in a PERT network.

adjourning (15) The final stage in group development for temporary groups, characterized by concern with wrapping up activities rather than task performance.

affective component of an attitude (14) The emotional or feeling segment of an attitude.

affirmative action programs (12) Programs that enhance the organizational status of members of protected groups.

aggregate planning (21) Planning overall production activities and their associated operating resources.

analyzer (8) A business-level strategy that seeks to minimize risk by following competitors' innovations but only after they have proven successful.

assessment centers (12) Places in which job candidates undergo performance simulation tests that evaluate managerial potential.

assumed similarity (14) The belief that others are like oneself.

attitude surveys (14) Eliciting responses from employees through questionnaires about how they feel about their jobs, work groups, supervisors, and/or the organization.

attitudes (14) Evaluative statements concerning objects, people, or events.

attribute sampling (21) A quality control technique that classifies items as acceptable or unacceptable on the basis of a comparison to a standard.

attribution theory (14) A theory used to develop explanations of how we judge people differently depending on the meaning we attribute to a given behavior.

attribution theory of leadership (17) Proposes that leadership is merely an attribution that people make about other individuals.

authoritarianism (14) A measure of a person's belief that there should be status and power differences among people in organizations.

authority (10) The rights inherent in a managerial position to give orders and expect them to be obeyed.

autonomy (11) The degree to which a job provides substantial freedom, independence, and discretion to an individual in scheduling and carrying out his or her work.

avoidance (18) Withdrawal from or suppression of conflict.

basic corrective action (19) Determining how and why performance has deviated and correcting the source of deviations.

batch processing (20) Storing data and processing them all at the same time.

BCG matrix (8) Strategy tool to guide resource allocation decisions based on market share and growth of SBUs.

behavior (14) The actions of people.

behavioral component of an attitude (14) An intention to behave in a certain way toward someone or something.

behavioral science theorists (2) Psychologists and sociologists who relied on the scientific method for the study of organizational behavior.

behavioral theories (17) Theories identifying behaviors that differentiate effective from ineffective leaders.

behaviorally anchored rating scales (BARS) (12) A performance appraisal technique in which an evaluator rates employees on specific job behaviors derived from performance dimensions.

benchmarking (9) The search for the best practices among competitors or noncompetitors that lead to their superior performance.

bi-modal work force (2) Employees tend to perform either low-skilled service jobs for near-minimum wage or high-skilled, well-paying jobs.

body language (18) Gestures, facial configurations, and other movements of the body that convey meaning.

bona fide occupational qualifications (BFOQ) (12) A criterion such as sex, age, or national origin may be used as a basis for hiring if it can be clearly demonstrated to be job related.

bounded rationality (6) Behavior that is rational within the parameters of a simplified model that captures the essential features of a problem.

brainstorming (6) An idea-generating process that encourages alternatives while withholding criticism.

break-even analysis (9) A technique for identifying the point at which total revenue is just sufficient to cover total costs.

budget (9) A numerical plan for allocating resources to specific activities.

bureaucracy (2) A form of organization marked by division of labor, hierarchy, rules and regulations, and impersonal relationships.

business-level strategy (8) Seeks to determine how a corporation should compete in each of its businesses.

capacity planning (21) Assessing an operating system's ability to produce a desired number of output units for each type of product during a given time period.

capital expenditure budget (9) A budget that forecasts investments in property, buildings, and major equipment.

career (12) The sequence of positions occupied by a person during the course of a lifetime.

cash budget (9) A budget that forecasts how much cash an organization will have on hand and how much it will need to meet expenses.

cash cows (8) Products that demonstrate low growth but have a high market share.

cause-related marketing (5) Performing social actions that are motivated directly by profits.

centralization (10) The concentration of decision-making authority in upper management.

certainty (6) A situation in which a manager can make accurate decisions because the outcome of every alternative is known.

chain of command (10) The flow of authority from the top to the bottom of an organization.

change (13) An alteration in people, structure, or technology.

change agents (13) People who act as catalysts and manage the change process.

channel (18) The medium by which a message travels.

charismatic leadership (17) Followers make attributions of heroic or extraordinary leadership abilities when they observe certain behaviors.

classical theorists (2) The term used to describe the scientific management theorists and general administrative theorists.

classical view (5) The view that management's only social responsibility is to maximize profits.

closed systems (2) Systems that neither are influenced by nor interact with their environment.

code of ethics (5) A formal statement of an organization's primary values and the ethical rules it expects its employees to follow.

coercive power (10) Power that is dependent on fear.

cognitive component of an attitude (14) The beliefs, opinions, knowledge, or information held by a person.

cognitive dissonance (14) Any incompatibility between two or more attitudes or between behavior and attitudes.

collaboration (18) Resolving conflict by seeking a solution advantageous to all parties.

collective bargaining (12) A process for negotiating a union contract and for administering the contract after it has been negotiated.

collectivism (4) A cultural dimension in which people expect others in their group to look after them and protect them when they are in trouble.

combination strategy (8) A corporate-level strategy that pursues two or more of the following strategies—stability, growth, or retrenchment—simultaneously.

commitment concept (7) Plans should extend far enough to see through current commitments.

committee structure (11) A structure that brings together a range of individuals from across functional lines to deal with problems.

communication (18) The transferring and understanding of meaning.

communication networks (20) Vertical and horizontal communication patterns.

communication process (18) The seven stages in which meaning is transmitted and understood.

competitor intelligence (9) Environmental scanning activity that seeks to identify who competitors are, what they're doing, and how their actions will affect the focus organization.

complexity (10) The amount of differentiation in an organization.

compressed workweek (11) A workweek comprised of four ten-hour days.

compromise (18) A solution to conflict in which each party gives up something of value.

computer-integrated manufacturing (CIM) (21) Combines the organization's strategic business plan and manufacturing plan with state-of-the-art computer applications.

concurrent control (19) Control that occurs while an activity is in progress.

conditional maintenance (21) Maintenance that calls for an overhaul or repair in response to an inspection.

conflict (18) Perceived incompatible differences that result in interference or opposition.

consideration (17) The extent to which a person has job relationships characterized by mutual trust, respect for subordinates' ideas, and regard for their feelings.

contingency approach (2) Recognizing and responding to situational variables as they arise.

contingent workers (11) Temporary and part-time workers who supplement an organization's permanent work force.

control (19) The process of monitoring activities to ensure they are being accomplished as planned and of correcting any significant deviations.

control process (19) The process of measuring actual performance, comparing it against a standard, and taking managerial action to correct deviations or inadequate standards.

controlling (1) Monitoring activities to ensure that they are being accomplished as planned and correcting any significant deviations.

corporate-level strategy (8) Seeks to determine what businesses a corporation should be in.

cost center (21) A unit in which managers are held responsible for all associated costs.

cost-leadership strategy (8) The strategy an organization follows when it wants to be the lowest-cost producer in its industry.

creativity (13) The ability to combine ideas in a unique way or to make unusual associations between ideas.

critical incidents (12) A performance appraisal technique in which an evaluator lists key behaviors that separate effective from ineffective job performance.

critical path (9) The longest sequence of activities in a PERT network.

cumulative learning curve (8) Assumes that when a business increases the amount of product manufactured, the per-unit cost of the product will decrease.

customer departmentalization (10) Grouping activities on the basis of common customers.

data (20) Raw, unanalyzed facts.

data base management (20) A computerized system that allows the user to organize, get at easily, and select and review a precise set of data from a larger base of data.

decentralization (10) The handing down of decision-making authority to lower levels in an organization.

decision criteria (6) Criteria that define what is relevant in a decision.

decision-making process (6) A set of eight steps that include identifying a problem, selecting an alternative, and evaluating the decision's effectiveness.

decisional roles (1) Roles that include those of entrepreneur, disturbance handler, resource allocator, and negotiator.

decoding (18) Retranslating a sender's message.

decruitment (12) Techniques for reducing the labor supply within an organization.

defender (8) A business-level strategy that seeks stability by producing only a limited set of products directed at a narrow segment of the total potential market.

deindustrialization (21) The conversion of an economy from dominance by manufacturing to dominance by service-oriented businesses.

delegation (18) The assignment of authority and responsibility to another person to carry out specific activities.

Delphi technique (6) A group decision-making technique in which members never meet face to face.

devil's advocate (18) A person who purposely presents arguments that run counter to those proposed by the majority.

diagonal communication (20) Communication that cuts across functions and levels in an organization.

differentiation strategy (8) The strategy a firm follows when it wants to be unique in its industry along dimensions widely valued by buyers.

direct costs (21) Costs incurred in proportion to the output of a particular good or service.

directional plans (7) Flexible plans that set out general guidelines.

discipline (18) Actions taken by a manager to enforce the organization's standards and regulations.

discretionary time (9) The part of a manager's time that is controllable.

distinctive competence (8) The unique skills and resources that determine the organization's competitive weapons.

distributive bargaining (18) Negotiations that seek to divide up a fixed amount of resources: a win–lose situation.

division of labor (2) The breakdown of jobs into narrow, repetitive tasks.

divisional structure (11) An organization structure made up of autonomous, self-contained units.

dogs (8) Products that demonstrate low growth and low market share.

downward communication (20) Communication that flows from a manager down the authority hierarchy.

dual-career couples (12) Couples in which both partners have a professional, managerial, or administrative occupation.

dysfunctional conflicts (18) Conflicts that prevent an organization from achieving its goals.

economic order quantity model (EOQ) (21) A technique for balancing purchase, ordering, carrying, and stockout costs to derive the optimum quantity for a purchase order.

effectiveness (1) Goal attainment.

efficiency (1) The relationship between inputs and outputs; seeks to minimize resource costs.

ego strength (5) A personality characteristic that measures the strength of a person's convictions.

electronic mail (18) Instantaneous transmission of written messages on computers that are linked together.

electronic meetings (6) Decision-making groups that interact by way of linked computers.

empowerment (2) Increasing the decision-making discretion of workers.

encoding (18) Converting a message into symbols.

end-user (20) The person who uses information and assumes responsibility for its control.

entrepreneurship (8) A process by which individuals pursue opportunities, fulfilling needs and wants through innovation, without regard to the resources they currently control.

environment (3) Outside institutions or forces that potentially affect an organization's performance.

environmental complexity (3) The number of components in an organization's environment and the extent of an organization's knowledge about its environmental components.

environmental scanning (9) The screening of much information to detect emerging trends and create scenarios.

environmental uncertainty (3) The degree of change and complexity in an organization's environment.

equity theory (16) The theory that an employee compares his or her job's inputs–outcomes ratio to that of relevant others and then corrects any inequity.

escalation of commitment (6) An increased commitment to a previous decision despite evidence that it may have been wrong.

esteem needs (16) Internal factors such as self-respect, autonomy, and achievement; and external factors such as status, recognition, and attention.

ethics (5) Rules and principles that define right and wrong conduct.

European Community (4) Currently the 330 million people living in the following 12 full-member countries: Belgium, Denmark, France, Greece, Ireland, Italy, Luxembourg, Netherlands, Portugal, Spain, the United Kingdom, and Germany.

events (9) End points that represent the completion of major activities in a PERT network.

expectancy theory (16) The theory that an individual tends to act in a certain way based on the expectation that the act will be followed by a given outcome and on the attractiveness of that outcome to the individual.

expense budget (9) A budget that lists the primary activities undertaken by a unit and allocates a dollar amount to each.

expert power (10) Power based on one's expertise, special skill, or knowledge.

expert systems (20) Software programs that encode the relevant experience of a human expert.

facilities layout planning (21) Assessing and selecting among alternative layout options for equipment and work stations.

facilities location planning (21) The design and location of an operations facility.

feedback (11) The degree to which carrying out the work activities required by a job results in an individual's obtaining direct and clear information about the effectiveness of his or her performance.

feedback control (19) Control imposed after an action has occurred.

feedforward control (19) Control that prevents anticipated problems.

Fiedler contingency model (17) The theory that effective groups depend on a proper match between a leader's style of interacting with subordinates and the degree to which the situation gives control and influence to the leader.

filtering (18) The deliberate manipulation of information to make it appear more favorable to the receiver.

first-line managers (1) Supervisors; the lowest level of management.

fixed budget (9) A budget that assumes a fixed level of sales or production.

fixed-interval reordering system (21) A system that uses time as the determining factor for reviewing and reordering inventory items.

fixed-point reordering system (21) A system that "flags" the fact that inventory needs to be replenished when it reaches a certain level.

fixed-position layout (21) A manufacturing layout in which the product stays in place while tools, equipment, and human skills are brought to it.

flexible manufacturing systems (21) Systems in which custom-made products can be mass produced by means of computer-aided design, engineering, and manufacturing.

flexible work hours (flextime) (11) A scheduling system in which employees are required to work a number of hours a week, but are free, within limits, to vary the hours of work.

focus strategy (8) The strategy a company follows when it pursues a cost or differentiation advantage in a narrow industry segment.

forcing (18) Satisfying one's own needs at the expense of another's.

forecasts (9) Predictions of future outcomes.

formal communication (20) Communication that follows the authority chain of command or that is necessary to do a job.

formalization (10) The degree to which an organization relies on rules and procedures to direct the behavior of employees.

forming (15) The first stage in group development, characterized by much uncertainty.

functional conflicts (18) Conflicts that support an organization's goals.

functional departmentalization (10) Grouping activities by functions performed.

functional structure (11) A design that groups similar or related occupational specialties together.

functional-level strategy (8) Seeks to determine how to support the business-level strategy.

fundamental attribution error (14) The tendency to underestimate the influence of external factors and overestimate the influence of internal factors when making judgments about the behavior of others.

Gantt chart (2) A graphic bar chart that shows the relationship between work planned and completed on one axis and time elapsed on the other.

general administrative theorists (2) Writers who developed general theories of what managers do and what constitutes good management practice.

general environment (3) Everything outside the organization.

geographic departmentalization (10) Grouping activities on the basis of territory.

goal-setting theory (16) Specific goals increase performance and difficult goals, when accepted, result in higher performance than easy goals.

grapevine (20) The informal communication network.

graphic rating scales (12) A performance appraisal technique in which an evaluator rates a set of performance factors on an incremental scale.

group (15) Two or more interacting and interdependent individuals who come together to achieve particular objectives.

group cohesiveness (15) The degree to which members are attracted to one another and share the group's goals.

group order ranking (12) A performance appraisal approach that groups employees into ordered classifications.

groupthink (6) The withholding by group members of different views in order to appear in agreement.

growth strategy (8) A corporate-level strategy that seeks to increase the level of the organization's operations. This typically includes increasing revenues, employees, and/or market share.

halo effect (14) The general impression of an individual based on a single characteristic.

Hawthorne studies (2) A series of studies during the 1920s and 1930s that provided new insights into group norms and behavior.

hierarchy of needs theory (16) Maslow's theory that there is a hierarchy of five human needs: physiological, safety, social, esteem, and self-actualization. As each need is substantially satisfied, the next becomes dominant.

high–high leader (17) A leader high in both initiating structure and consideration.

"hot stove" rule (18) Discipline should immediately follow an infraction, provide ample warning, be consistent, and be impersonal.

human relations movement (2) The belief, for the most part unsubstantiated by research, that a satisfied worker will be productive.

human relations view of conflict (18) The view that conflict is a natural and inevitable outcome in any organization.

human resource management process (12) Activities necessary for staffing the organization and sustaining high employee performance.

human resource planning (12) The process by which management ensures that it has the right personnel, who are capable of completing those tasks that help the organization reach its objectives.

human resources approach (2) The study of management that focuses on human behavior.

hygiene factors (16) Factors that eliminate dissatisfaction.

ill-structured problems (6) New problems in which information is ambiguous or incomplete.

immediate corrective action (19) Correcting an activity at once in order to get performance back on track.

implementation (6) Conveying a decision to those affected and getting their commitment to it.

incremental budget (9) A budget that allocates funds to departments according to allocations in the previous period.

indirect costs (21) Costs that are largely unaffected by changes in output.

individual ranking (12) A performance appraisal approach that ranks employees in order from highest to lowest.

individualism (4) A cultural dimension in which people are supposed to look after their own interests and those of their immediate family.

Industrial Revolution (2) The advent of machine power, mass production, and efficient transportation.

informal communication (20) Communication that is not approved by management and not defined by the structural hierarchy.

information (20) Analyzed and processed data.

informational roles (1) Roles that include monitoring, disseminating, and spokesperson activities.

initiating structure (17) The extent to which a leader defines and structures his or her role and those of subordinates to attain goals.

innovation (13) The process of taking a creative idea and turning it into a useful product, service, or method of operation.

integrated work team (11) A group that accomplishes many tasks by making specific assignments to members and rotating jobs among members as the tasks require.

integrative bargaining (18) Negotiation that seeks one or more settlements that can create a win–win solution.

interactionist view of conflict (18) The view that some conflict is necessary for an organization to perform effectively.

intergroup development (13) Changing the attitudes, stereotypes, and perceptions that work groups have of each other.

interpersonal communication (18) Communication between two or more people in which the parties are treated as individuals rather than objects.

interpersonal roles (1) Roles that include figurehead, leadership, and liaison activities.

intrapreneurship (8) Creating the entrepreneurial spirit in a large organization.

job analysis (12) An assessment that defines jobs and the behaviors necessary to perform them.

job characteristics model (11) A framework for analyzing and designing jobs; identifies five primary job characteristics, their interrelationships, and impact on outcome variables.

job depth (11) The degree of control employees have over their work.

job description (12) A written statement of what a jobholder does, how it is done, and why it is done.

job design (11) The way in which tasks are combined to form complete jobs.

job enlargement (11) The horizontal expansion of a job; an increase in job scope.

job enrichment (11) Vertical expansion of a job by adding planning and evaluating responsibilities.

job involvement (14) The degree to which an employee identifies with his or her job, actively participates in it, and considers his or her job performance important to his or her self-worth.

job rotation (11) Periodic lateral transfers of workers among jobs involving different tasks.

job satisfaction (14) A person's general attitude toward his or her job.

job scope (11) The number of different tasks required in a job and the frequency with which the job cycle is repeated.

job sharing (11) The practice of having two or more people split a forty-hour-a-week job.

job specification (12) A statement of the minimum acceptable qualifications that an incumbent must possess to perform a given job successfully.

just-in-time (JIT) inventory system (21) A system in which inventory items arrive when they are needed in the production process instead of being stored in stock.

kanban (21) The Japanese name for a just-in-time inventory process.

labor–management relations (12) The formal interactions between unions and an organization's management.

labor union (12) An organization that represents workers and seeks to protect their interests through collective bargaining.

lateral communication (20) Communication among any horizontally equivalent personnel.

leader–member relations (17) The degree of confidence, trust, and respect subordinates have in their leader.

leaders (17) Those who are able to influence others and who possess managerial authority.

leader-participation model (17) A leadership theory that provides a set of rules to determine the form and amount of participative decision making in different situations.

leading (1) Includes motivating subordinates, directing others, selecting the most effective communication channels, and resolving conflicts.

learning (14) Any relatively permanent change in behavior that occurs as a result of opinions.

least-preferred co-worker (LPC) questionnaire (17) A questionnaire that measures whether a person is task or relationship oriented.

legitimate power (10) Power based on one's position in the formal hierarchy.

life cycle of the organization (7) Four stages that organizations go through: formation, growth, maturity, and decline.

line authority (10) The authority that entitles a manager to direct the work of a subordinate.

linear programming (9) A mathematical technique that solves resource allocation problems.

load chart (9) A modified Gantt chart that schedules capacity by work stations.

locus of control (5) A personality attribute that measures the degree to which people believe they are masters of their own fate.

long-term plans (7) Plans that extend beyond five years.

Machiavellianism (14) A measure of the degree to which people are pragmatic, maintain emotional distance, and believe that ends justify means.

management (1) The process of getting activities completed efficiently with and through other people.

management by objectives (MBO) (7) A system in which specific performance objectives are jointly determined by subordinates and their superiors, progress toward objectives is periodically reviewed, and rewards are allocated on the basis of this progress.

management functions (1) Planning, organizing, leading, and controlling.

management information system (MIS) (20) A system that provides management with needed information on a regular basis.

management roles (1) Specific categories of managerial behavior.

managerial grid (17) A two-dimensional portrayal of leadership based on concerns for people and for production.

managers (1) Individuals in an organization who direct the activities of others.

manufacturing organizations (21) Organizations that produce physical goods such as steel, automobiles, textiles, and farm machinery.

maquiladoras (4) Domestic Mexican firms that manufacture or assemble products for a foreign company. The products are then sent back to the foreign company for sale and distribution.

marginal analysis (9) A planning technique that assesses the incremental costs or revenues in a decision.

mass production (10) Large-batch manufacturing.

master schedule (21) A schedule that specifies quantity and type of items to be produced: how, when, and where they should be produced; labor force levels; and inventory.

material requirements planning (MRP) (21) A system that dissects products into the materials and parts necessary for purchasing, inventorying, and priority-planning purposes.

matrix structure (11) A structural design that assigns specialists from functional departments to work on one or more projects that are led by a project manager.

maturity (17) The ability and willingness of people to take responsibility for directing their own behavior.

mechanistic organization (bureaucracy) (10) A structure that is high in complexity, formalization, and centralization.

mentor (12) A person who sponsors or supports another employee who is lower in the organization.

message (18) A purpose to be conveyed.

mission (8) The purpose of an organization.

motivation (16) The willingness to exert high levels of effort to reach organizational goals, conditioned by the effort's ability to satisfy some individual need.

motivation-hygiene theory (16) The theory that intrinsic factors are related to job satisfaction, while extrinsic factors are associated with dissatisfaction.

motivators (16) Factors that increase job satisfaction.

multinational corporations (MNCs) (4) Companies that maintain significant operations in more than one country simultaneously but manage them all from one base in a home country.

multiperson comparison (12) A performance appraisal technique in which individuals are compared to one another.

national culture (4) The attitudes and perspectives shared by individuals from a specific country that shape their behavior and the way they see the world.

need (16) An internal state that makes certain outcomes appear attractive.

need for achievement (16) The drive to excel, to achieve in relation to a set of standards, to strive to succeed.

need for affiliation (16) The desire for friendly and close interpersonal relationships.

need for power (16) The need to make others behave in a way that they would not have behaved otherwise.

negotiation (18) A process in which two or more parties exchange goods or services and attempt to agree upon the exchange rate for them.

network structure (11) A small centralized organization that relies on other organizations to perform its basic business functions on a contract basis.

networking (20) Linking computers so that they can communicate with each other.

noise (18) Disturbances that interfere with the transmission of a message.

nominal group technique (6) A decision-making technique in which group members are physically present but operate independently.

nonprogrammed decisions (6) Unique decisions that require a custom-made solution.

nonverbal communication (18) Communication transmitted without words.

norming (15) The third stage of group development, characterized by close relationships and cohesiveness.

norms (15) Acceptable standards shared by a group's members.

objectives (7) Desired outcomes for individuals, groups, or entire organizations.

omnipotent view (3) The view that managers are directly responsible for the success or failure of an organization.

open systems (2) Dynamic systems that interact with and respond to their environment.

operant conditioning (14) A type of conditioning in which desired voluntary behavior leads to a reward or prevents a punishment.

operational plans (7) Plans that specify details on how overall objectives are to be achieved.

operations management (21) The design, operation, and control of the transformation process that converts resources into finished goods and services.

operatives (1) People who work directly on a job or task and have no responsibility for overseeing the work of others.

organic organization (adhocracy) (10) A structure that is low in complexity, formalization, and centralization.

organization (1) A systematic arrangement of people to accomplish some specific purpose.

organization design (10) The construction or changing of an organization's structure.

organizational development (OD) (13) Techniques to change people and the quality of interpersonal work relationships.

organization structure (10) An organization's framework as expressed by its degree of complexity, formalization, and centralization.

organizational behavior (14) The study of the actions of people at work.

organizational commitment (14) An employee's orientation toward the organization in terms of his or her loyalty to, identification with, and involvement in the organization.

organizational culture (3) A system of shared meaning within an organization that determines, in large degree, how employees act.

organizational goals approach (19) Appraising an organization's effectiveness according to whether it accomplishes its goals.

organizing (1) Determining what tasks are to be done, who is to do them, how the tasks are to be grouped, who reports to whom, and where decisions are to be made.

orientation (12) The introduction of a new employee into his or her job and the organization.

paired comparison (12) A performance appraisal approach in which each employee is compared to every other employee and rated as either the superior or weaker member of the pair.

paraphrasing (18) Restating what a speaker has said but in your own words.

parochialism (4) A selfish, narrow view of the world; an inability to recognize differences between people.

path-goal theory (17) The theory that a leader's behavior is acceptable to subordinates insofar as they view it as a source of either immediate or future satisfaction.

perception (14) The process of organizing and interpreting sensory impressions in order to give meaning to the environment.

performance appraisal (12) The evaluation of an individual's work performance in order to arrive at objective personnel decisions.

performing (15) The fourth stage of group development, when the group is fully functional.

personality (14) A combination of psychological traits that classifies a person.

PERT network (9) A flowchartlike diagram showing the sequence of activities needed to complete a project and the time or cost associated with each.

physiological needs (16) Basic food, drink, shelter, and sexual needs.

planning (1) Includes defining goals, establishing strategy, and developing plans to coordinate activities.

policy (6) A guide that establishes parameters for making decisions.

position power (17) The degree of influence a leader has over power variables such as hiring, firing, discipline, promotions, and salary increases.

power (10) The capacity to influence decisions.

power distance (4) A cultural measure of the extent to which a society accepts the unequal distribution of power in institutions and organizations.

preventive maintenance (21) Maintenance performed before a breakdown occurs.

principles of management (2) Universal truths of management that can be taught in school.

probability theory (9) The use of statistics to analyze past predictable patterns and to reduce risk in future plans.

problem (6) A discrepancy between an existing and a desired state of affairs.

problem analyzability (10) The type of search procedures employees follow in responding to exceptions.

procedure (6) A series of interrelated sequential steps that can be used to respond to a structured problem.

process approach (2) Management performs the functions of planning, organizing, leading, and controlling.

process consultation (13) Help given by an outside consultant to a manager in perceiving, understanding, and acting upon process events.

process control (21) A quality control procedure in which sampling is done during the transformation process to determine whether the process itself is under control.

process departmentalization (10) Grouping activities on the basis of product or customer flow.

process layout (21) Arranging manufacturing components together according to similarity of function.

process planning (21) Determining how a product or service will be produced.

process production (10) Continuous-process production.

product departmentalization (10) Grouping activities by product line.

product layout (21) Arranging manufacturing components according to the progressive steps by which a product is made.

productivity (21) The overall output of goods and services produced, divided by the inputs needed to generate that output.

profit budget (9) A budget used by separate units of an organization that combines revenue and expense budgets to determine the unit's profit contribution.

Program Evaluation and Review Technique (PERT) (9) A technique for scheduling complicated projects comprising many activities, some of which are interdependent.

programmed decision (6) A repetitive decision that can be handled by a routine approach.

prospector (8) A business-level strategy that seeks innovation by finding and exploiting new product and market opportunities.

qualitative forecasting (9) Uses the judgment and opinions of knowledgeable individuals to predict future outcomes.

quality circles (15) Work groups that meet regularly to discuss, investigate, and correct quality problems.

quality of life (4) A national culture attribute that reflects the emphasis placed upon relationships and concern for others.

quantitative approach (2) The use of quantitative techniques to improve decision making.

quantitative forecasting (9) Applies a set of mathematical rules to a series of past data to predict future outcomes.

quantity of life (4) A national culture attribute describing the extent to which societal values are characterized by assertiveness and materialism.

question marks (8) Products that demonstrate high growth but low market share.

queuing theory (9) A technique that balances the cost of having a waiting line against the cost of service to maintain that line.

range of variation (19) The acceptable parameters of variance between actual performance and the standard.

rational (6) Describes choices that are consistent and value-maximizing within specified constraints.

reactor (8) A business-level strategy that characterizes inconsistent and unstable decision patterns.

real objectives (7) Objectives that an organization actually pursues, as defined by the actions of its members.

real-time processing (20) The continuous updating of data as transactions occur.

realistic job preview (12) Exposing job candidates to both negative and positive information about a job and an organization.

recruitment (12) The process of locating, identifying, and attracting capable applicants.

referent power (10) Power based on identification with a person who has desirable resources or personal traits.

referents (16) The persons, systems, or selves against which individuals compare themselves to assess equity.

reinforcement theory (16) Behavior is a function of its consequences.

reinforcer (16) Any consequences immediately following a response that increases the probability that the behavior will be repeated.

reliability (12) The ability of a selection device to measure the same thing consistently.

remedial maintenance (21) Maintenance that calls for the overhaul, replacement, or repair of equipment when it breaks down.

response time (9) Uncontrollable time spent responding to requests, demands, and problems initiated by others.

responsibility (10) An obligation to perform assigned activities.

retrenchment strategy (8) A corporate-level strategy that seeks to reduce the size or diversity of an organization's operations.

revenue budget (9) A budget that projects future sales.

revenue forecasting (9) Predicting future revenues.

reward power (10) Power based on the ability to distribute anything that others may value.

rights view of ethics (5) Decisions are concerned with respecting and protecting basic rights of individuals.

risk (6) Those conditions in which the decision maker has to estimate the likelihood of certain outcomes.

role (15) A set of behavior patterns expected of someone occupying a given position in a social unit.

rule (6) An explicit statement that tells managers what they ought or ought not to do.

safety needs (16) A person's needs for security and protection from physical and emotional harm.

satisficing (6) Acceptance of solutions that are "good enough."

scenario (9) A consistent view of what the future is likely to be.

scheduling (9) A listing of necessary activities, their order of accomplishment, who is to do each, and time needed to complete them.

scientific management (2) The use of the scientific method to define the "one best way" for a job to be done.

selection process (12) The process of screening job applicants to ensure that the most appropriate candidates are hired.

selectivity (14) The process by which people assimilate certain bits and pieces of what they observe, depending on their interests, background, and attitudes.

self-actualization needs (16) A person's drive to become what he or she is capable of becoming.

self-esteem (14) An individual's degree of like or dislike for him or herself.

self-managed work team (1) A vertically integrated team that is given almost complete autonomy in determining how a task will be done.

self-monitoring (14) A personality trait that measures an individual's ability to adjust his or her behavior to external situational factors.

self-serving bias (14) The tendency for individuals to attribute their own successes to internal factors while putting the blame for failures on external factors.

sensitivity training (13) A method of changing behavior through unstructured group interaction.

service organizations (21) Organizations that produce nonphysical outputs such as educational, medical, and transportation services that are intangible, can't be stored in inventory, and incorporate the customer or client in the actual production process.

sexual harassment (12) Behavior marked by sexually suggestive remarks, unwanted touching and sexual advances, requests for sexual favors, or other verbal or physical conduct of a sexual nature.

shaping behavior (14) Systematically reinforcing each successive step that moves an individual closer to the desired response.

short-term plans (7) Plans that cover less than one year.

simple structure (11) An organization that is low in complexity and formalization but high in centralization.

simulation (9) A model of a real-word phenomenon that contains one or more variables that can be manipulated in order to assess their impact.

situational leadership theory (17) A contingency theory that focuses on followers' maturity.

skill variety (11) The degree to which a job includes a variety of activities that call for a number of different skills and talents.

small business (1) An independently owned and operated

profit-seeking enterprise having fewer than five hundred employees.

social learning theory (14) People can learn through observation and direct experience.

social needs (16) A person's need for affection, belongingness, acceptance, and friendship.

social obligation (5) The obligation of a business to meet its economic and legal responsibilities.

social responsibility (5) An obligation, beyond that required by the law and economics, for a firm to pursue long-term goals that are good for society.

social responsiveness (5) The capacity of a firm to adapt to changing societal conditions.

socioeconomic view (5) The view that management's social responsibility goes well beyond the making of profits to include protecting and improving society's welfare.

span of control (10) The number of subordinates a manager can direct efficiently and effectively.

specific environment (3) The part of the environment that is directly relevant to the achievement of an organization's goals.

specific plans (7) Plans that are clearly defined and leave no room for interpretation.

spreadsheets (20) Software packages that allow users to turn a computer's memory into a large worksheet in which data and formulas can be entered to perform a variety of calculations.

stability strategy (8) A corporate-level strategy characterized by an absence of significant change.

staff authority (10) Authority that supports, assists, and advises holders of line authority.

stakeholders (5) Any constituency in the environment that is affected by an organization's decisions and policies.

stars (8) Products that demonstrate high growth and high market share.

stated objectives (7) Official statements of what an organization says—and what it wants various publics to believe—are its objectives.

status (15) A prestige grading, position, or rank within a group.

stereotyping (14) Judging a person on the basis of one's perception of a group to which he or she belongs.

storming (15) The second stage of group development, characterized by intragroup conflict.

strategic business unit (SBU) (8) A single business or collection of businesses that is independent and formulates its own strategy.

strategic constituencies approach (19) Appraising an organization's effectiveness according to how well the organization satisfies the demands of its key constituencies.

strategic management process (8) A nine-step process encompassing strategic planning, implementation, and evaluation.

strategic plans (7) Plans that are organizationwide, establish overall objectives, and position an organization in terms of its environment.

stress (13) A dynamic condition in which an individual is confronted with an opportunity, constraint, or demand related to what he or she desires for which the outcome is perceived to be both uncertain and important.

strong cultures (3) Organizations in which the key values are intensely held and widely shared.

stuck in the middle (8) Descriptive of organizations that cannot compete through cost-leadership, differentiation, or focus strategies.

survey feedback (13) A technique for assessing attitudes, identifying discrepancies in them, and resolving the differences by using survey information in feedback groups.

SWOT analysis (8) Analysis of an organization's strengths and weaknesses, and its environmental opportunities and threats.

symbolic view (3) The view that management has only a limited effect on substantive organizational outcomes because of the large number of factors outside of management's control.

systems approach (2) A theory that sees an organization as a set of interrelated and interdependent parts.

systems approach to organizational effectiveness (19) Appraising an organization's effectiveness in terms of both means and ends.

task force structure (11) A temporary structure created to accomplish a specific, well-defined, complex task that requires the involvement of personnel from other organizational subunits.

task identity (11) The degree to which a job requires completion of a whole and identifiable piece of work.

task significance (11) The degree to which a job has a substantial impact on the lives or work of other people.

task structure (17) The degree to which the job assignments are procedurized.

task variability (10) The number of exceptions individuals encounter in their work.

team building (13) Interaction among members of work teams to learn how each member thinks and works.

technological forecasting (9) Predicting changes in technology and when new technologies are likely to be economically feasible.

telecommuting (11) The linking by computer and modem of workers at home with co-workers and management at an office.

theory of justice view of ethics (5) Decision makers seek to impose and enforce rules fairly and impartially.

Theory X (16) The assumption that employees dislike work, are lazy, seek to avoid responsibility, and must be coerced to perform.

Theory Y (16) The assumption that employees are creative, seek responsibility, and can exercise self-direction.

therbligs (2) A classification scheme for labeling seventeen basic hand motions.

three-needs theory (16) The needs for achievement, power, and affiliation are major motives in work.

time management (9) A personal form of scheduling time effectively.

total quality management (TQM) (2) A philosophy of management that is driven by customer needs and expectations.

traditional objective setting (7) Objectives are set at the top and then broken down into subgoals for each level in an organization. The top imposes its standards on everyone below.

traditional view of authority (2) The view that authority comes from above.

traditional view of conflict (18) The view that all conflict is bad and must be avoided.

trait theories (17) Theories isolating characteristics that differentiate leaders from nonleaders.

transactional leaders (17) Leaders who guide or motivate their followers in the direction of established goals by clarifying role and task requirements.

transformational leaders (17) Leaders who provide individualized consideration, intellectual stimulation, and possess charisma.

transnational corporations (TNCs) (4) Companies that maintain significant operations in more than one country simultaneously and decentralized decision making in each operation to the local country.

Type A behavior (13) Behavior marked by a chronic sense of time urgency and an excessive competitive drive.

Type B behavior (13) Behavior that is relaxed, easygoing, and noncompetitive.

uncertainty (6) A situation in which a decision maker has neither certainty nor reasonable probability estimates available.

uncertainty avoidance (4) A cultural measure of the degree to which people tolerate risk and unconventional behavior.

unit production (10) The production of items in units or small batches.

unity of command (10) The principle that a subordinate should have one and only one superior to whom he or she is directly responsible.

upward communication (20) Communication that flows from subordinates to higher-level managers.

utilitarian view of ethics (5) Decisions are made solely on the basis of their outcomes or consequences.

validity (12) The proven relationship that exists between a selection device and some relevant criterion.

values (5) Basic convictions about what is right and wrong.

variable budget (9) A budget that takes into account those costs that vary with volume.

variable sampling (21) A quality control technique in which a measurement is taken to determine how much an item varies from the standard.

verbal intonation (18) An emphasis given to words or phrases that conveys meaning.

vestibule training (12) Training in which employees learn on the same equipment they will be using but in a simulated work environment.

well-structured problems (6) Straightforward, familiar, easily defined problems.

whistleblowing (3) Reporting unethical practices by your employer to outsiders such as the press, government agencies, or public interest groups.

word processing (20) Software packages that allow users to write, change, edit, revise, delete, or print letters, reports, and manuscripts.

work force diversity (2) Employees in organizations are heterogeneous in terms of gender, race, ethnicity, or other characteristics.

work sampling (12) A personnel selection device in which job applicants are presented with a miniature replica of a job and are asked to perform tasks central to that job.

work teams (11) Groups of individuals that cooperate in completing a set of tasks.

written essay (12) A performance appraisal technique in which an evaluator writes out a description of an employee's strengths, weaknesses, past performance, and potential and then makes suggestions for improvement.

zero-base budgeting (ZBB) (9) A system in which budget requests start from scratch, regardless of previous appropriations.

ACKNOWLEDGMENT OF ILLUSTRATIONS

282 Courtesy Cessna Aircraft Company   **284** Courtesy Johnson & Johnson and Dana Duke   **288** Courtesy Time Warner, Inc.   **291** WESTLIGHT   **295** Hewlett Packard   **296** Michael L. Abramson

Chapter 11:

307 Kevin Cuddy, Ocean, 1990. Acrylic and pastel on paper. © Kevin Cuddy, 1993   **308** Tomas Sodergren   **312** Photo by Julie Hoak, Courtesy Thermo Electron Corporation   **313** Peter Menzel/Stock Boston   **319** Reinstein/ Uniphoto   **322** J. P. Morgan   **322** Laima Druskis   **322** Shirley Zeiberg   **322** J. P. Morgan   **322** Shirley Zeiberg   **322** Shirley Zeiberg   **322** Eaton Corporation   **324** Ed Kashi   **326** Courtesy Picker International, Inc. Photo by Don Snyder   **329** Blair Seitz/Photo Researchers   **330** Peter Gregoire   **332** Ed Bock/The Stock Market

Chapter 12:

339 Kevin Cuddy, Ocean, 1990. Acrylic and pastel on paper. © Kevin Cuddy, 1993   **340** Peter Sibbard   **344** Najlah Feanney/SABA   **349** Courtesy Stein & Company   **350** Kevin Horan   **351** Courtesy Auto Alliance International   **355** Shaun van Steyn/Uniphoto   **356** Scott Goldsmith   **361** William Campbell/Time Magazine   **364** Courtesy Paramount Communications, Inc.   **366** D. E. Cox/Tony Stone Worldwide/Chicago   **370** Michael Keller/ Uniphoto

Chapter 13:

379 Kevin Cuddy, Ocean, 1990. Acrylic and pastel on paper. © Kevin Cuddy, 1993   **380** John S. Abbott   **382** Katherine Lambert   **387** Bob Daemmrich/Stock Boston   **391** Bob Daemmrich/Uniphoto   **394** Andy Freeberg   **395** Daniel Giry/REA/SABA   **396** Gary Moss Photography   **397** Jeffrey Lowe/Onyx   **401** Courtesy Intel

Chapter 14:

413 Diana Ong/Superstock   **414** Gwendolin Cates   **420** Courtesy Multiplex Company, Inc.   **421** Brian Smith/ Stock Boston   **423** Les Stone/Sygma   **423** Barbara Filet/ Tony Stone Worldwide/Chicago   **430** Courtesy Mary Kay Cosmetics, Inc.   **430** Sepp Seitz/Woodfin Camp & Associates

Chapter 15:

439 Diana Ong/Superstock   **440** Courtesy Nucor Steel   **442** Blake Little/Onyx   **445** David M. Grossman/Photo Researchers   **447** Steven Rubin/JB Pictures   **452** Peter Yates/SABA   **453** Bruce Zake   **454** Kevin Horan   **456** Michael L. Abramson

Chapter 16:

463 Diana Ong/Superstock   **464** Robert E. Daemmrich/ Tony Stone Worldwide/Chicago   **467** Ron Haviv/SABA   **470** John S. Abbott   **471** Ken Karp   **472** Ron Haviv/ SABA   **475** John S. Abbott   **478** Courtesy The Lincoln Electric Company   **482** Rob Kinmonth   **483** Courtesy Westinghouse Electric Systems   **485** Courtesy Whirlpool Corporation

Chapter 17:

493 Diana Ong/Superstock   **494** Reuters/Bettmann   **496** Jacques Chenet/Woodfin Camp & Associates   **498** Courtesy Corning, Inc.   **499** Courtesy Miami Herald   **504** Larry Downing/Woodfin Camp & Associates   **508** Kurt Stier   **514** D. Kirkland/Sygma   **516** P. G. Bentley

Chapter 18:

525 Diana Ong/Superstock   **526** Richard Pasley/Stock Boston   **530** David Burnett/Contact Press Images   **534** Dennis E. Cox   **536** John Hillery/Black Star   **542** Michael L. Abramson/Woodfin Camp & Associates   **543** Joyce Ravid/Onyx   **545** AP/Wide World Photos   **548** Bryce Flynn/Picture Group   **554** Will & Deni McIntyre/Photo Researchers

Chapter 19:

569 Kevin Cuddy, Puppeteer, 1990–91. Mixed media on paper. © Kevin Cuddy, 1993   **570** NASA   **572** Steve Woit   **575** Richard Pasley/Stock Boston   **581** John Swart/AP/Wide World Photos   **584** Courtesy Goodyear Tire   **585** Courtesy Preston Smith   **586** NASA   **589** Rhoda Sidney/Stock Boston

Chapter 20:

595 Kevin Cuddy, Puppeteer, 1990–91. Mixed media on paper. © Kevin Cuddy, 1993   **596** Reid Horn   **598** John Rae   **599** John S. Abbott   **603** IBM   **605** Sygma   **607** Phil Schofield   **613** Courtesy EDS Information Center   **615** STORES Magazine   **616** Paul Meredith

Chapter 21:

625 Kevin Cuddy, Puppeteer, 1990–91. Mixed media on paper. © Kevin Cuddy, 1993   **626** Ten Morrison/Still Life Stock   **628** Ford Motor Company   **630** Courtesy Reynolds Aluminum   **631** Quality International   **635** Courtesy Reynolds Metals Company   **644** Courtesy Levi Strauss and Company   **647** IBM   **649** T. Michael Keza   **651** Louis Psihoyos/Matrix

NAME INDEX

Note: Page numbers with an "S-" prefix locate entries in the main text; numbers with an "E-" prefix locate entries in the Endnotes section.

Aberth, John, E-10
Ackoff, Russell, E-6
Adam, Everett E., Jr., S-273, S-637, E-19
Adams, J. Stacey, S-474, E-14
Adler, Nancy J., E-3
Adorno, T., E-13
Agnew, Neil McK., E-5
Agor, Weston H., S-176, E-5
Ajzen, Icek, E-12
Akin, Joe, S-594
Albanese, Robert, E-13
Albers, Nancy D., E-7
Albert, Michael, E-12
Alessandra, Anthony J., E-16
Alexander, Elmore R., E-16
Alexander, Larry D., E-1
Alexander, Michael, E-10
Allan, Peter, E-1
Allen, Michael, E-7
Allen, Robert, S-392–93
Alliger, G.M., E-15
Allison, Graham T., E-1, E-5
Altier, William J., E-9
Amabile, Teresa M., E-12
Ambrose, Maureen L., E-14
Amend, Patricia, E-10
Amram, Yosi, S-598
Anderson, Paul A., E-5
Anthony, William P., E-9
Applegate, Lynda M., E-18
Aquilano, Nicholas J., E-19
Armstrong, J. Scott, E-6
Armstrong, Larry, E-19
Arpas, J.S., E-3
Arvey, Richard D., E-10, E-17
Asch, Solomon E., S-446, S-448, E-13
Ash, Mary Kay, S-75
Ash, Ronald A., E-11
Asher, James J., E-10
Atchison, Thomas J., E-14
Atkinson, John W., E-14
Aupperle, Kenneth, E-3
Austin, Nancy K., S-461
Avolio, B.J., E-16
Azcarraga, Emilo, S-237–38

Bacon, Donald C., E-10
Bailey, Chuck, S-376
Baker, Douglas D., E-11
Baldwin, J. Norman, E-1
Baldwin, William, E-7
Bamberger, Ingolf, E-7
Bannister, B.D., E-15
Barnard, Chester, S-39–40, S-46, E-2
Barndt, Stephen E., E-8, E-19

Barnett, John H., E-4
Barnevik, Percy, S-308
Barney, Jay B., E-6
Barrett, Dermot, S-601
Barrington, Jeff, S-127
Barrow, Jeffrey C., E-15
Bartimo, Jim, E-5, E-18
Bartolomé, Fernando, S-454, E-16
Bass, B.M., E-16
Bavelas, Alex, S-601
Bazerman, Max H., E-17
Beatty, Richard W., E-10
Beauclair, R.A., E-5
Becker, Helmut, E-4
Bedeian, Arthur G., S-276
Beeby, Robert, S-596
Beehr, Terry A., E-12
Begley, Thomas M., E-7
Behling, O., E-5
Behn, R.D., E-8
Belcher, David W., E-14
Bell, Cecil H., Jr., E-12
Bennett, Amanda, S-108, E-3, E-16
Bennis, Warren, S-512, E-16
Bentson, C., E-10
Bergmann, B.R., E-2
Bergmann, Thomas J., E-10
Berkowitz, L., E-13
Berlo, David K., E-16
Bernstein, Aaron, E-2, E-11
Berrios, William, S-267
Bettis, Richard A., E-7
Betts, Kathleen, S-306
Beyer, Janice M., E-2
Billard, Mary, E-16
Bishop, Ronald C., E-6
Bishop, Steven, S-562
Bjerklie, David, E-17
Blake, Robert R., S-499–500, E-5, E-15
Blake, Stacy, E-11
Blanchard, Kenneth H., S-504–5, E-15
Blank, Warren, E-15
Blau, Gary J., E-13
Blau, Peter M., E-9
Blum, Michael W., E-17
Boal, Kimberly B., E-4
Boff, Larry, S-587
Borrus, Amy, E-3
Boschken, Herman L., E-9
Boudette, Neal E., E-9
Bourne, Lyle E., Jr., E-17
Bowen, D.E., E-15
Boyd, David P., E-7
Boyer, Glen L., E-18
Boyett, Joseph H., E-18, E-19
Braccini, Steve, S-59

Bradspies, Robert W., E-17
Brady, F. Neil, E-4
Braham, Jim, E-8
Brahm, Charles B., E-6
Brahm, Richard, E-6
Bramlette, Carl A., E-12
Branson, Richard, S-524
Breaugh, James A., E-11
Breckler, S.J., E-12
Brennan, Edward A., S-581
Brenner, Steven N., E-8
Bresser, Rudi K., E-6
Bretz, Robert D., Jr., E-11
Brickner, Mary, E-10
Brief, Arthur P., E-9, E-12
Brock, Floyd, S-621
Brocka, Bruce, E-8
Brocka, M. Suzanne, E-8
Brockhaus, Robert H., Sr., E-7
Brockner, J., E-13
Brod, Craig, E-18
Broedling, Laurie A., E-14
Brooke, Paul P., Jr., E-12
Brown, D., E-13
Brown, John L., E-5
Bruning, Nealia S., E-12
Buchholz, Rogene A., E-3
Buckley, M. Ronald, E-9-10
Buckley, William F., Jr., S-533
Buda, Richard, E-11
Buell, Barbara, E-8
Bulkeley, William M., S-407, E-5–6, E-18
Bunderson, C. Victor, E-17
Burack, Elmer H., E-7, E-10, E-11
Burke, Ronald J., E-11
Burnham, David H., E-14
Burnham, Duane L., S-475
Burns, James M., E-16
Burns, Lawton R., E-9
Burns, Tom, E-8
Bushardt, Stephen C., E-11
Butterfield, D. Anthony, E-16
Bylinsky, Gene, E-17, E-18
Byrne, John A., E-2, E-4, E-9, E-14

Caldwell, D.F., E-2
Calloway, D. Wayne, S-394
Calonius, Erik, E-7
Cameron, Kim S., E-7, E-8, E-16
Campagna, A.F., E-9
Campbell, John P., E-12, E-17
Campion, James E., E-10
Campion, Michael, E-9
Carey, Alex, E-2
Carnegie, Andrew, S-32

ORGANIZATION INDEX

SUBJECT INDEX